CLYMER®

# SUZUKI

## LS650 SAVAGE SINGLE • 1986-1988

*The world's finest publisher of mechanical how-to manuals*

INTERTEC PUBLISHING
P.O. Box 12901, Overland Park, Kansas 66282-2901

FIRST EDITION
First Printing September, 1990
Second Printing November, 1994
Third Printing November, 1997
Fourth Printing March, 2001

Printed in U.S.A.

CLYMER and colophon are registered trademarks of Intertec Publishing.

ISBN: 0-89287-517-8

Library of Congress: 90-55660

*Technical photography by Ed Scott.*

*Technical and photographic assistance by David Morgan, Los Angeles, California.*

*Motorcycle courtesy of Marina Suzuki, Los Angeles, California.*

*Technical illustrations by Mitzi McCarthy.*

*COVER: Photographed by Mark Clifford, Mark Clifford Photography, Los Angeles, California.*

# CLYMER PUBLICATIONS

## Intertec Directory & Book Division

# CONTENTS

# QUICK REFERENCE DATA

## TIRE INFLATION PRESSURE (COLD)*

| | Tire pressure | | | |
|---|---|---|---|---|
| | Front | | Rear | |
| Load | psi | kPa | psi | kPa |
| Solo riding | 28 | 200 | 28 | 200 |
| Dual riding | 32 | 225 | 36 | 250 |

* Tire inflation pressure for factory equipped tires. Aftermarket tires may require different inflation pressure.

## ENGINE OIL CAPACITY

| Oil change | | Oil and filter change | | Overhaul | |
|---|---|---|---|---|---|
| Liters | U.S. qt. | Liters | U.S. qt. | Liters | U.S. qt. |
| 1.8 | 1.9 | 2.4 | 2.5 | 2.4 | 2.5 |

## MAINTENANCE AND TUNE UP TORQUE SPECIFICATIONS

| Item | N·m | ft.-lb. |
|---|---|---|
| Oil drain plug | 12-18 | 8.5-13 |
| Fork cap bolt | 35-55 | 25.5-40 |
| Rear axle nut | 55-88 | 40-63 |
| Front brake caliper mounting bolts | 25-40 | 18-29 |
| Cylinder head nuts (9 mm) | 29-33 | 21-24 |
| Cylinder head-to-cylinder nuts (8 mm) | 23-27 | 16-19 |
| Cylinder-to-crankcase nuts | 8-12 | 6-8.5 |
| Rocker arm shaft (exhaust) set bolt | 8-10 | 6-7 |

## TUNE-UP SPECIFICATIONS

| | |
|---|---|
| Valve clearance | |
| Intake and exhaust | 0.08-0.13 mm (0.003-0.005 in.) |
| Automatic decompression cable free play | 3-5 mm (0.12-0.20 in.) |
| Cylinder compression | |
| Standard | 1,000-1,400 kPa (145-203 psi) |
| Service limit | 800 kPa (116 psi) |
| Spark plug type | |
| Standard heat range | NGK DP8EA-9, ND X24EP-U9 |
| Hotter heat range | NGK DP7EA-9, ND X22EP-U9 |
| Spark plug gap | 0.8-0.9 mm (0.031-0.035 in.) |
| Idle speed | 1,000-1,200 rpm |

## DRIVE BELT SPECIFICATIONS

| | |
|---|---|
| Drive belt | |
| Type | Bando 133U-14M 40.0 |
| Number of teeth | 133 |

## REPLACEMENT BULBS

| Item | Voltage/wattage |
|---|---|
| Headlight | 12V 55/60W |
| Taillight/brake light | 12V 8/23W |
| License plate light | 12V 8W |
| Turn signal light | 12V 23W |
| Front position light | 12V 8W |
| Speedometer | |
| Illumination light | 12V 3W |
| Indicator light | |
| Sidestand check light, turn signal, neutral | 12V 3W |
| High beam | 12V 1.7W |

# *INTRODUCTION*

This detailed, comprehensive manual covers the Suzuki LS650 Savage single from 1986-1988.

The expert text gives complete information on maintenance, tune-up, repair and overhaul. Hundreds of photos and drawings guide you through every step. This book includes all you will need to know to keep your Suzuki running right. Throughout this book, where differences occur among the models, they are clearly identified.

A shop manual is a reference. You want to be able to find information fast. As in all Clymer books, this one is designed with you in mind. All chapters are thumb tabbed. Important items are extensively indexed at the rear of the book. All procedures, tables, photos, etc., in this manual are for the reader who may be working on the bike for the first time or using this manual for the first time. All the most frequently used specifications and capacities are summarized in the *Quick Reference Data* pages at the front of the book.

Keep the book handy in your tool box. It will help you better understand how your bike runs, lower repair costs and generally improve your satisfaction with the bike.

## CHAPTER ONE

# GENERAL INFORMATION

### MANUAL ORGANIZATION

All dimensions and capacities are expressed in English units familiar to U.S. mechanics as well as in metric units. Refer to **Table 1** for decimal and metric equivalents.

This chapter provides general information and discusses equipment and tools useful both for preventive maintenance and troubleshooting.

Chapter Two provides methods and suggestions for quick and accurate diagnosis and repair of problems. Troubleshooting procedures discuss typical symptoms and logical methods to pinpoint the trouble.

Chapter Three explains all periodic lubrication and routine maintenance necessary to keep the Suzuki running well. Chapter Three also includes recommended tune-up procedures, eliminating the need to constantly consult chapters on the various assemblies.

Subsequent chapters describe specific systems such as the engine, clutch, transmission, fuel, exhaust, suspension and brakes. Each chapter provides disassembly, repair and assembly procedures in simple step-by-step form.

If a repair is impractical for a home mechanic, it is so indicated. It is usually faster and less expensive to take such repairs to a dealer or competent repair shop. Specifications concerning a particular system are included at the end of the appropriate chapter.

Some of the procedures in this manual specify special tools. In most cases, the tool is illustrated either in actual use or alone. Well equipped mechanics may find they can substitute similar tools already on hand or can fabricate their own.

**Tables 1-4** are at the end of this chapter.

### NOTES, CAUTIONS AND WARNINGS

The terms *NOTE, CAUTION* and *WARNING* have specific meanings in this manual. A *NOTE* provides additional information to make a step or procedure easier or clearer. Disregarding a *NOTE* could cause inconvenience, but would not cause equipment damage or personal injury.

A *CAUTION* emphasizes areas where equipment damage could result. Disregarding a *CAUTION* could cause permanent mechanical damage; however, personal injury is unlikely.

A *WARNING* emphasizes areas where personal injury or even death could result from negligence.

Mechanical damage may also occur. *WARNINGS* are to be taken *seriously.* In some cases, serious injury or death has resulted from disregarding similar warnings.

Throughout this manual keep in mind 2 conventions. "Front" refers to the front of the bike. The front of any component, such as the engine, is the end which faces toward the front of the bike. The "left-" and "right-hand" sides refer to the position of the parts as viewed by a rider sitting on the seat facing forward. For example, the throttle control is on the right-hand side and the clutch lever is on the left-hand side. These rules are simple, but even experienced mechanics occasionally become disoriented.

## SAFETY FIRST

Professional mechanics can work for years and never sustain a serious injury. If you observe a few rules of common sense and safety, you can enjoy many hours servicing your own machine. If you ignore these rules, you can hurt yourself or damage the bike.

1. *Never* use gasoline as a cleaning solvent.
2. Never smoke or use a torch in the vicinity of flammable liquids such as cleaning solvent in open containers.
3. If welding or brazing is required on the machine, remove the fuel tank to a safe distance, at least 50 feet away.
4. Use the proper sized wrenches to avoid damage to nuts and injury to yourself.
5. When loosening a tight or stuck nut, think about what would happen if the wrench should slip. Be careful; protect yourself accordingly.
6. Keep your work area clean and uncluttered.
7. Wear safety goggles during all operations involving drilling, grinding or the use of a cold chisel.
8. Never use worn tools.
9. Keep a fire extinguisher handy and be sure it is rated for gasoline and electrical fires.

## SERVICE HINTS

Most of the service procedures covered are straightforward and can be performed by anyone reasonably handy with tools. It is suggested, however, that you consider your own capabilities carefully before attempting any operation involving major disassembly of the engine.

Take your time and do the job right. Do not forget that a newly rebuilt engine must be broken in the same as a new one. Keep the rpm within the limits given in your owner's manual when you get back on the road.

1. There are many items available that can be used on your hands before and after working on your bike. A little preparation before getting "all greased up" will help when cleaning up later. Before starting out, work Vaseline, soap or a product such as Invisible Glove (**Figure 1**) onto your forearms, into your hands and under your fingernails and cuticles. This will make cleanup a lot easier. For cleanup, use a waterless hand soap such as Sta-Lube and then finish up with powdered Boraxo and a fingernail brush (**Figure 2**).

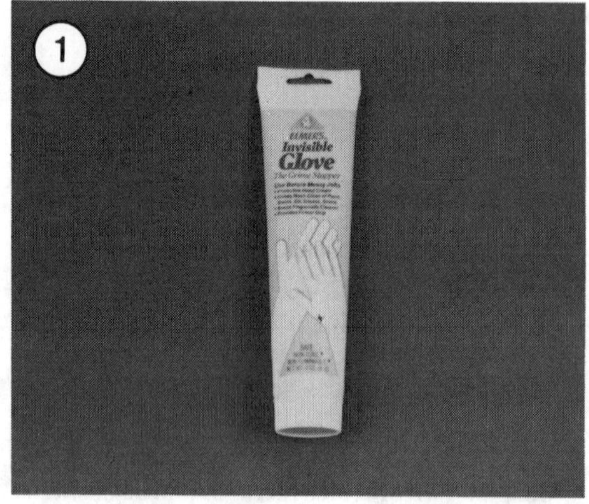


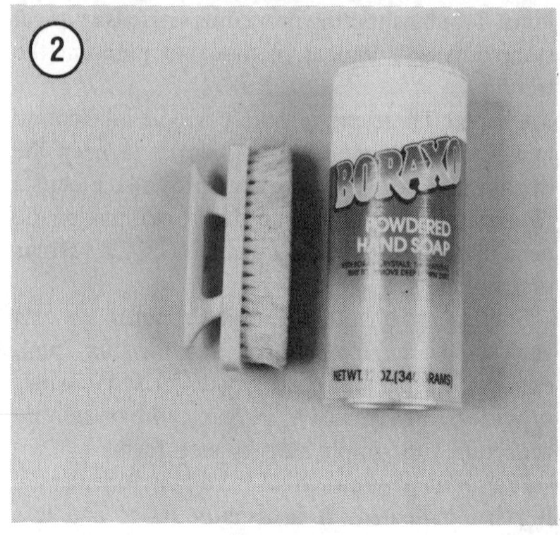

2. Repairs go much faster and easier if the bike is clean before you begin work. There are special cleaners, such as Gunk or Bel-Ray Degreaser for washing the engine and related parts. Just spray or brush on the cleaning solution, let it stand, then rinse it away with a garden hose. Clean all oily or greasy parts with cleaning solvent as you remove them.

*WARNING*

***Never** use gasoline as a cleaning agent. It presents an extreme fire hazard. Be sure to work in a well-ventilated area when using cleaning solvent. Keep a fire extinguisher, rated for gasoline fires, handy in any case.*

3. Special tools are required for some repair procedures. These may be purchased from a Suzuki dealer or motorcycle shop, rented from a tool rental dealer or fabricated by a mechanic or machinist (often at a considerable savings).
4. Much of the labor charged by mechanics is to remove and disassemble other parts to reach the defective unit. It is usually possible to perform the preliminary operations yourself and then take the defective unit in to the dealer for repair.
5. Once you have decided to tackle the job yourself, read the entire section *completely* while looking at the actual parts before starting the job. Making sure you have identified the proper one. Study the illustrations and text until you have a good idea of what is involved in completing the job satisfactorily. If special tools or replacement parts are required, make arrangements to get them before you start. It is frustrating and time-consuming to get partly into a job and then be unable to complete it.

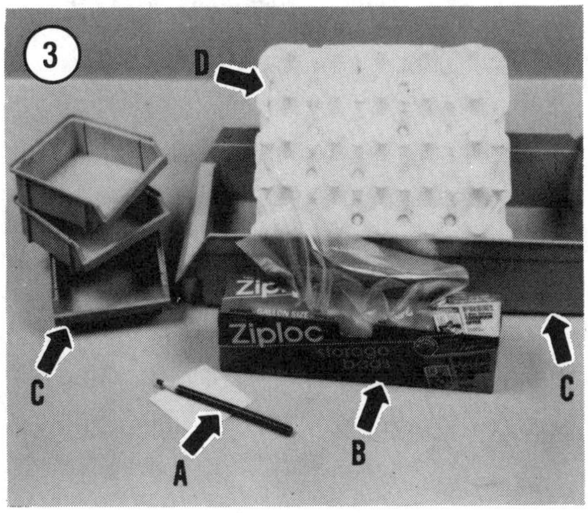


6. Simple wiring checks can be easily made at home, but knowledge of electronics is almost a necessity for performing tests with complicated electronic testing gear.
7. Whenever servicing the engine or transmission, or when removing a suspension component, the bike should be secured in a safe manner. If the bike is to be parked on the sidestand or center stand, check the stand to make sure it is secure and not damaged. Block the front and rear wheels if they remain on the ground. A small hydraulic jack and a block of wood can be used to raise the chassis. If the transmission is not going to be worked on and the drive chain is connected to the rear wheel, shift the transmission into first gear.
8. Disconnect the negative battery cable when working on or near the electrical, clutch or starter systems and before disconnecting any electrical wires. On most batteries, the negative terminal will be marked with a minus (–) sign and the positive terminal with a plus (+) sign.
9. During disassembly of parts, keep a few general cautions in mind. Force is rarely needed to get things apart. If parts are a tight fit, such as a bearing in a case, there is usually a tool designed to separate them. Never use a screwdriver to pry parts with machined surfaces such as crankcase halves. You will mar the surfaces and end up with leaks.
10. Make diagrams (or take a Polaroid picture) wherever similar-appearing parts are found. For instance, crankcase bolts are often not the same length. You may think you can remember where everything came from, but mistakes are costly. There is also the possibility you may be sidetracked and not return to work for days or even weeks, in which interval carefully laid out parts may have become disturbed.
11. Tag all similar internal parts for location and mark all mating parts for position (A, **Figure 3**). Record number and thickness of any shims as they are removed. Small parts such as bolts can be identified by placing them in plastic sandwich bags (B, **Figure 3**). Seal and label them with masking tape.
12. Place parts from a specific area of the engine (e.g. cylinder head, cylinder, clutch, shift mecha-

nism, etc.) into plastic boxes (C, **Figure 3**) to keep them separated.

13. When disassembling transmission shaft assemblies, use an egg flat (the type that restaurants get their eggs in) (D, **Figure 3**) and set the parts from the shaft in one of the depressions in the same position from which it was removed.

14. Wiring should be tagged with masking tape and marked as each wire is removed. Again, do not rely on memory alone.

15. Protect finished surfaces from physical damage or corrosion. Keep gasoline and hydraulic brake fluid off plastic parts and painted and plated surfaces.

16. Frozen or very tight bolts and screws can often be loosened by soaking with penetrating oil, such as WD-40 or Liquid Wrench, then sharply striking the bolt head a few times with a hammer and punch (or screwdriver for screws). Avoid heat unless absolutely necessary, since it may melt, warp or remove the temper from many parts.

17. No parts, except those assembled with a press fit, require unusual force during assembly. If a part is hard to remove or install, find out why before proceeding.

18. Cover all openings after removing parts to keep dirt, small tools, etc., from falling in.

19. Wiring connections and brake components should be kept clean and free of grease and oil.

20. When assembling 2 parts, start all fasteners, then tighten evenly.

21. When assembling parts, be sure all shims and washers are installed exactly as they came out.

22. Whenever a rotating part butts against a stationary part, look for a shim or washer.

23. Use new gaskets if there is any doubt about the condition of the old ones. A thin coat of oil on gaskets may help them seal effectively.

24. Heavy grease can be used to hold small parts in place if they tend to fall out during assembly. However, keep grease and oil away from electrical and brake components.

25. High spots may be sanded off a piston with sandpaper, but fine emery cloth and oil will do a much more professional job.

26. Carbon can be removed from the head, the piston crown and the exhaust port with a dull screwdriver. Do *not* scratch machined surfaces. Wipe off the surface with a clean cloth when finished.

27. The carburetors are best cleaned by disassembling them and soaking the parts in a commercial carburetor cleaner. Never soak gaskets and rubber parts in these cleaners. Never use wire to clean out jets and air passages; they are easily damaged. Use compressed air to blow out the carburetor *after* the float has been removed.

28. A baby bottle makes a good measuring device for adding oil to the front forks. Get one that is graduated in fluid ounces and cubic centimeters. After it has been used for this purpose, do *not* let a small child drink out of it as there will always be an oil residue in it.

29. Some operations require special equipment, for example, use of a press. It would be wiser to have these performed by a shop equipped for such work, rather than trying to do the job yourself with makeshift equipment. Other procedures require precise measurements. Unless you have the skills and equipment required, it would be better to have a qualified repair shop make the measurements for you.

## SPECIAL TIPS

Because of the extreme demands placed on a bike, several points should be kept in mind when performing service and repair. The following items are general suggestions that may improve the overall life of the machine and help avoid costly failures.

*CAUTION*

*When applying Loctite Threadlocker, or similar locking compound, to fastener (screw or bolt) threads, it will make it much harder to remove the*

*screw during removal. If blue Loctite Threadlocker (No. 242) is used, the torque required to loosen the fastener is 110-120% greater than the applied torque used to tighten the fastener. If red Loctite Threadlocker (No. 271) is used, the torque required to loosen the fastener is 200-250% greater than the applied torque used to tighten the fastener. Because of this factor, use Loctite, or equivalent, sparingly as it will make fastener removal very difficult if too much locking compound is applied.*

1. Use a locking compound such as Loctite Threadlocker No. 242 (**Figure 4**) on all bolts and nuts, even if they are secured with lockwashers. This type of Loctite does not harden completely and allows easy removal of the bolt or nut. A screw or bolt lost from an engine cover or bearing retainer could easily cause serious and expensive damage before its loss is noticed. Make sure the threads are clean and free of grease and oil. Clean with contact cleaner before applying the Loctite.

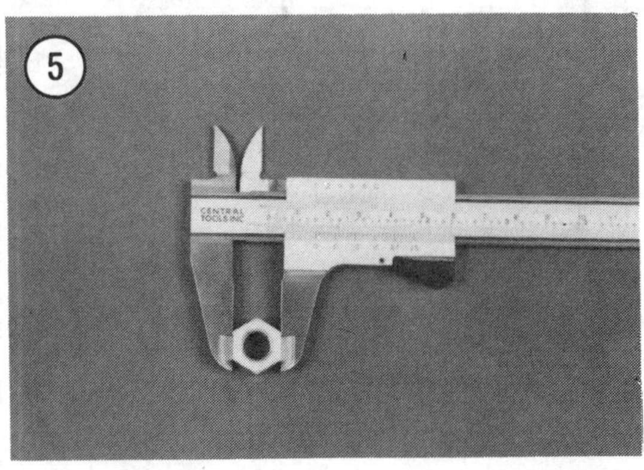


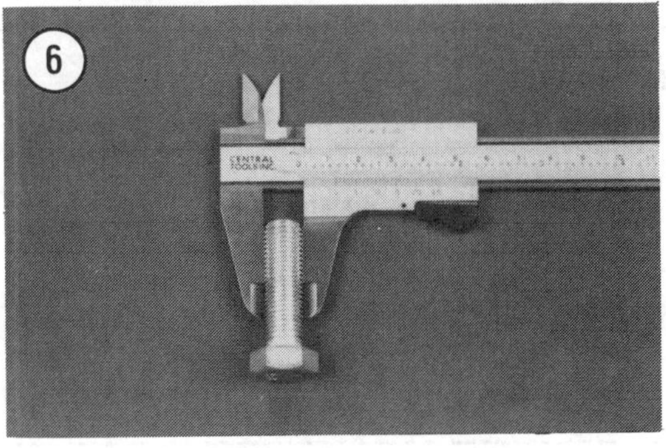


When applying Loctite, use a *small* amount. If too much is used, it can work its way down the threads and stick parts together not meant to be stuck. Keep a tube of both blue (No. 242) and red (No. 271) Loctite Threadlocker in your tool box. When used properly, it is cheap insurance.

2. Use a hammer-driven impact tool to remove and install all bolts, particularly engine cover screws. These tools help prevent the rounding off of bolt heads and ensure a tight installation.
3. When replacing missing or broken fasteners (bolts, nuts and screws), especially on the engine or frame components, always use Suzuki replacement parts. They are specially hardened for each application. The wrong 50-cent bolt could easily cause serious and expensive damage, not to mention rider injury.
4. When installing gaskets in the engine, always use Suzuki replacement gaskets *without* sealer, unless designated. These gaskets are designed to swell when they come in contact with oil. Gasket sealer will prevent the gaskets from swelling as intended, which can result in oil leaks. These Suzuki gaskets are cut from material of the precise thickness needed. Installation of a too thick or too thin gasket in a critical area could cause engine damage.

## TORQUE SPECIFICATIONS

Torque specifications throughout this manual are given in Newton meters (N•m) and foot-pounds (ft.-lb.). Newton meters have been adopted in place of meter kilograms (mkg) in accordance with the International Modernized Metric System. Tool manufacturers offer torque wrenches calibrated in both Newton meters and foot-pounds.

Existing torque wrenches calibrated in meter kilograms can be used by performing a simple conversion. All you have to do is move the decimal point one place to the right; for example, 4.7 mkg = 47 N•m. This conversion is accurate enough for mechanical work even though the exact mathematical conversion is 3.5 mkg = 34.3 N•m.

Refer to **Table 2** for standard torque specifications for various size screws, bolts and nuts that may not be listed in the respective chapters. To use the table, first determine the size of the bolt or nut. Use a vernier caliper and measure across the flats of the nut (**Figure 5**) and across the threads for a bolt (**Figure 6**).

## FASTENERS

The materials and designs of the various fasteners used on your Suzuki are not arrived at by chance or accident. Fastener design determines the type of tool required to work the fastener. Fastener material is carefully selected to decrease the possibility of physical failure.

### Threads

Nuts, bolts and screws are manufactured in a wide range of thread patterns. To join a nut and bolt, the diameter of the bolt and the diameter of the hole in the nut must be the same. It is just as important that the threads on both be properly matched.

The best way to tell if the threads on 2 fasteners are matched is to turn the nut on the bolt (or the bolt into the threaded hole in the piece of equipment), with your fingers only. Be sure both pieces are clean. If much force is required, check the thread condition on each fastener. If the thread condition is good, but the fastener jams, the threads are not compatible. A thread pitch gauge (**Figure 7**) can also be used to determine pitch. Suzuki motorcycles are manufactured with metric standard fasteners. The threads are cut differently than those of American fasteners (**Figure 8**).

Most threads are cut so that the fastener must be turned *clockwise* to tighten it. These are called right-hand threads. Some fasteners have left-hand threads; they must be turned *counterclockwise* to be tightened. Left-hand threads are used in locations where normal rotation of the equipment would tend to loosen a right-hand threaded fastener. When left-hand threads are used in this manual they are identified in the text.

### Machine Screws

There are many different types of machine screws. **Figure 9** shows a number of screw heads requiring different types of turning tools. Heads are also designed to protrude above the metal (round or hex) or to be slightly recessed in the metal (flat). See **Figure 10**.

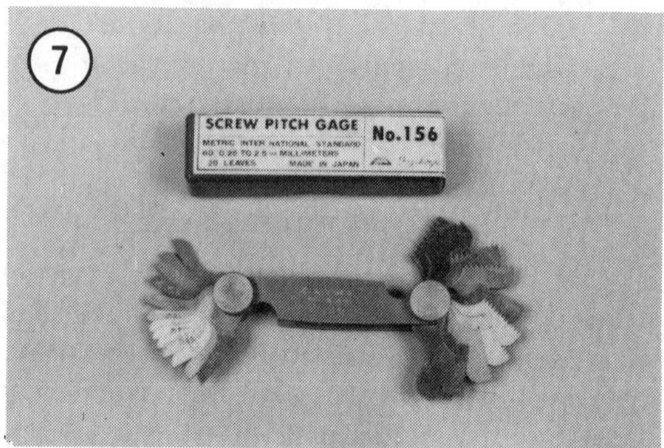


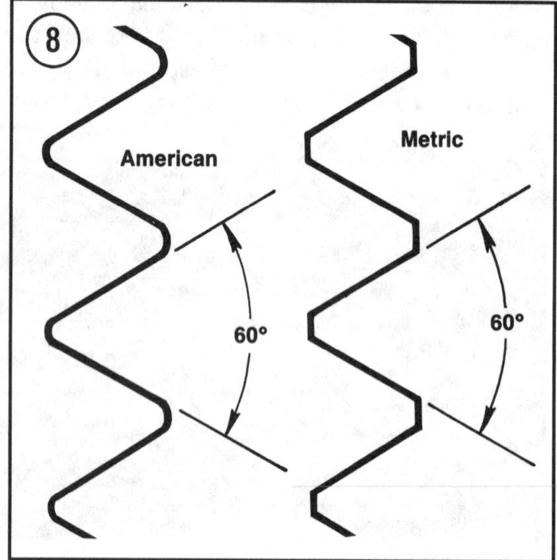


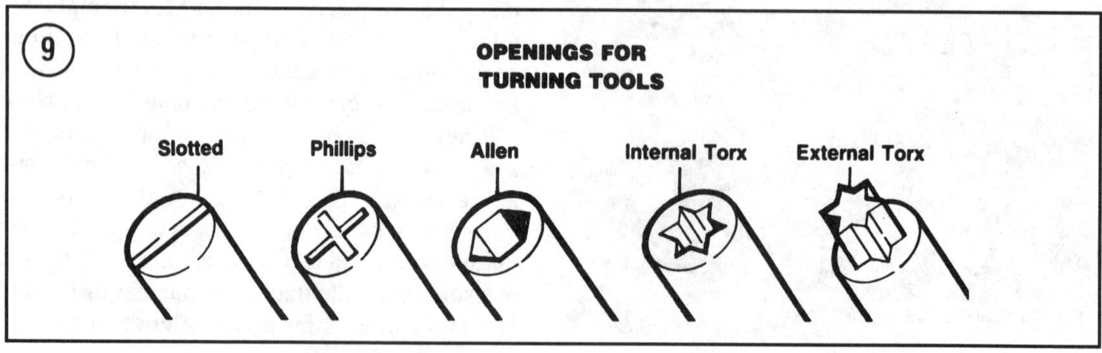

## Bolts

Commonly called bolts, the technical name for these fasteners is cap screws. Metric bolts are described by the diameter and pitch (the distance between each thread). For example, an M8 × 1.25 bolt is one that has a diameter of 8 millimeters and a distance of 1.25 millimeters between each thread. The measurement across 2 flats on the head of the bolt indicates the proper wrench size to be used. Use a vernier caliper and measure across the threads (**Figure 6**) to determine the bolt diameter.

## Nuts

Nuts are manufactured in a variety of types and sizes. Most are hexagonal (6-sided) and fit on bolts, screws and studs with the same diameter and pitch.

**Figure 11** shows several types of nuts. The common nut is generally used with a lockwasher. Self-locking nuts have a nylon insert which prevents the nut from loosening; no lockwasher is required. Wing nuts are designed for fast removal by hand. Wing nuts are used for convenience in non-critical locations.

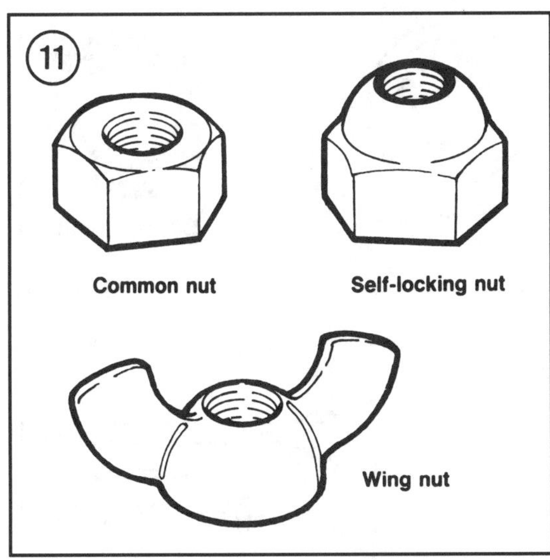


To indicate the size of a nut, manufacturer's specify the diameter of the opening and the threads per inch. This is similar to bolt specifications, but without the length dimension. The measurement across 2 flats on the nut indicate the proper wrench size to be used. **Figure 5** shows how to determine nut size.

## Self-Locking Fasteners

Several types of bolts, screws and nuts incorporate a system that develops interference between the bolt, screw nut or tapped hole threads. Interference is achieved in various ways: by distorting threads, coating threads with dry adhesive or nylon, distorting the top of an all-metal nut, using a nylon insert in the center or at the top of a nut, etc.

Self-locking fasteners offer greater holding strength and better vibration resistance. Some self-locking fasteners can be reused if in good condition. Others, like the nylon insert nut, form an initial locking condition when the nut is first installed; the nylon forms closely to the bolt thread pattern, thus reducing any tendency for the nut to loosen. When the nut is removed, its locking efficiency is greatly reduced. For greatest safety it is recommended that new self-locking fasteners be installed whenever they are removed.

## Washers

There are 2 basic types of washers: flat washers and lockwashers. Flat washers are simple discs with a hole to fit a screw or bolt. Lockwashers are

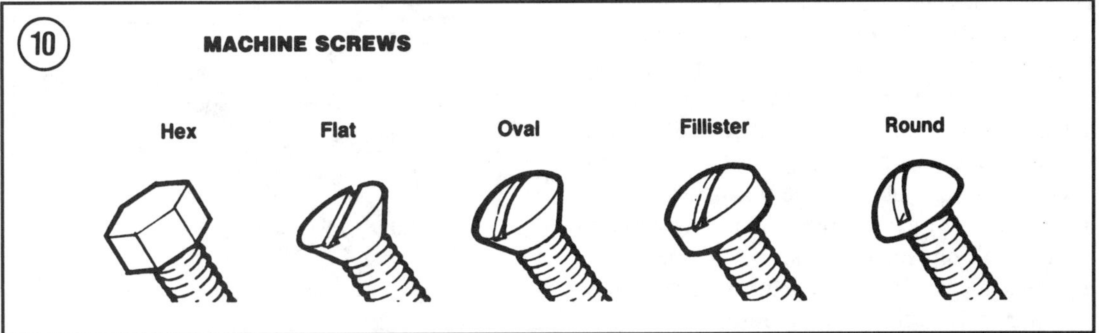

designed to prevent a fastener from working loose due to vibration, expansion and contraction. **Figure 12** shows several types of washers. Washers are also used in the following functions:

a. As spacers.
b. To prevent galling or damage of the equipment by the fastener.
c. To help distribute fastener load during torquing.
d. As fluid seals (copper or laminated washers).

Note that flat washers are often used between a fastener to provide a smooth bearing surface. This allows the fastener to be turned easily with a tool.

### Cotter Pins

Cotter pins (**Figure 13**) are used to secure special kinds of fasteners. The threaded stud must have a hole in it; the nut or nut lock piece has castellations around which the cotter pin end wraps. Cotter pins should not be reused after removal as the ends may break and the cotter pin could then fall out.

### Circlips

Circlips (or snap rings) can be internal or external design. They are used to retain items on shafts (external type) or within tubes (internal type). In some applications, circlips of varying thickness are used to control the end play of parts assemblies. These are often called selective circlips. Circlips should be replaced during installation, as removal weakens and deforms them.

Two basic types of circlips are available: machined and stamped circlips. Machined circlips (**Figure 14**) can be installed in either direction (shaft or housing) because both faces are machined, thus creating two sharp edges. Stamped circlips (**Figure 15**) are manufactured with one sharp edge and one rounded edge. When installing stamped circlips in a thrust situation (transmission shafts, fork tubes, etc.), the sharp edge must face away from the part producing the thrust. When installing circlips, observe the following:

a. Compress or expand the circlip only enough to install or remove them.
b. After the circlip is installed, make sure it is completely seated in its groove.

## LUBRICANTS

Periodic lubrication assures long life for any type of equipment. The *type* of lubricant used is just as important as the lubrication service itself, although in an emergency the wrong type of lubricant is better than none at all. The following paragraphs describe the types of lubricants most often used on motorcycle equipment. Be sure to follow the motorcycle manufacturer's recommendations for lubricant types.

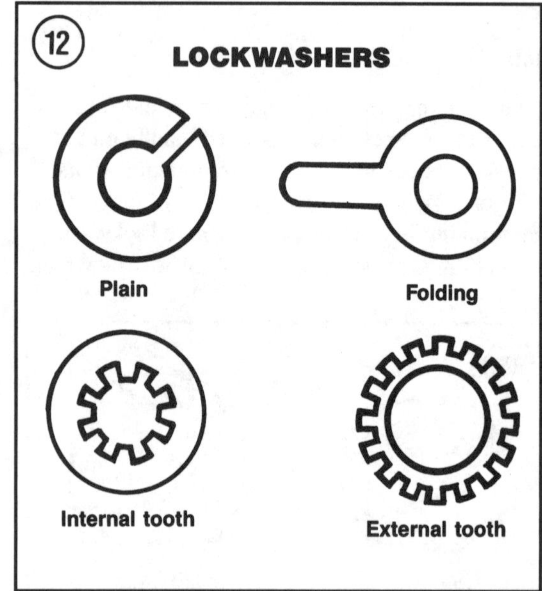


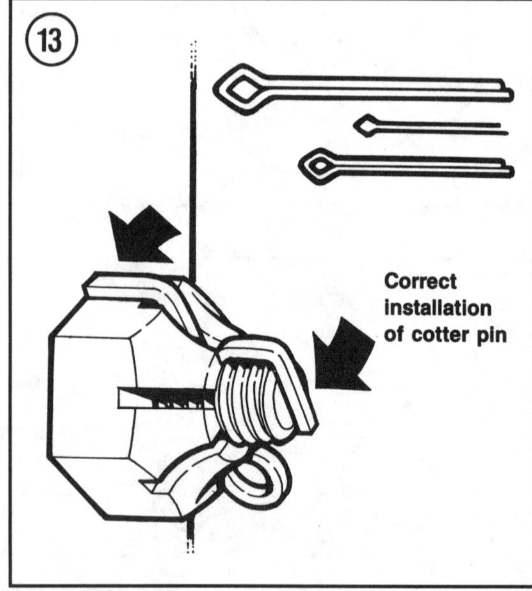

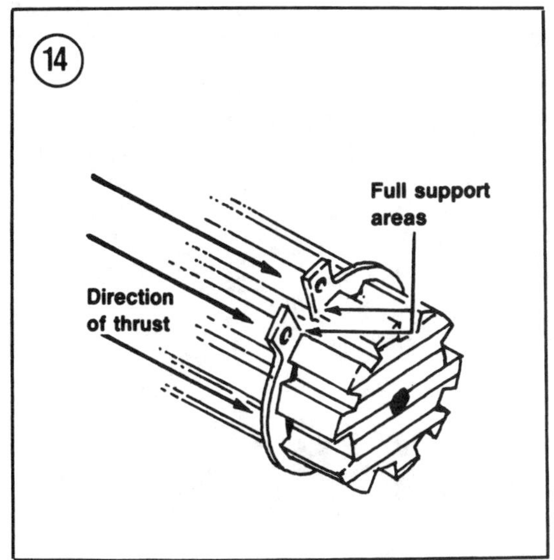


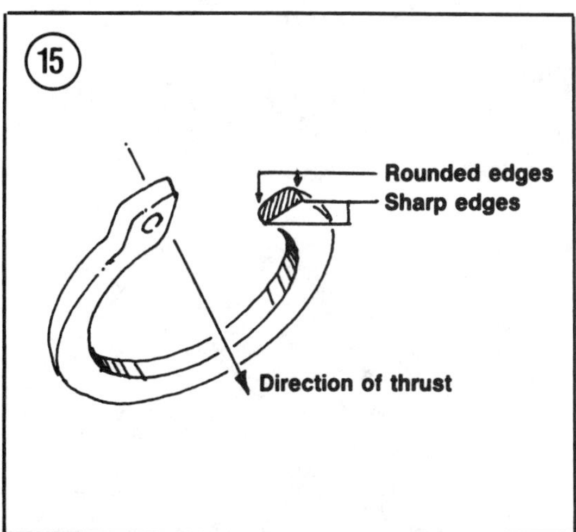


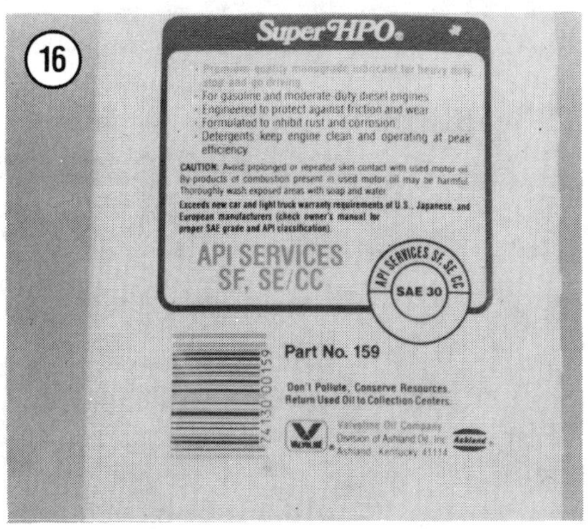


Generally, all liquid lubricants are called "oil." They may be mineral-based (including petroleum bases), natural based (vegetable and animal bases), synthetic-based or emulsions (mixtures). "Grease" is an oil to which a thickening base has been added so that the end product is semi-solid. Grease is often classified by the type of thickener added; lithium soap is commonly used.

## Engine Oil

Oil for motorcycle and automotive engines is classified by the American Petroleum Institute (API) and the Society of Automotive Engineers (SAE) in several categories. Oil containers display these classifications on the top of the can or on the bottle label (**Figure 16**).

API oil classification is indicated by letters; oils for gasoline engines are identified by an "S." The engines covered in this manual require SE or SF classified oil.

Viscosity is an indication of the oil's thickness. The SAE uses numbers to indicate viscosity; thin oils have low numbers while thick oils have high numbers. A "W" after the number indicates that the viscosity testing was done at low temperature to simulate cold-weather operation. Engine oils fall into the 5W-30 and 20W-50 range.

Multi-grade oils (for example 10W-40) maintain the same viscosity at low temperatures and at high temperatures. This allows the oil to perform efficiently across a wide range of engine operating conditions. The lower the number, the better the engine will start in cold climates. Higher numbers are usually recommended for engines running in hot weather conditions.

## Grease

Greases are graded by the National Lubricating Grease Institute (NLGI). Greases are graded by number according to the consistency of the grease; these range from No. 000 to No. 6, with No. 6 being the most solid. A typical multipurpose grease is NLGI No. 2. For specific applications, equipment manufacturers may require grease with an additive such as molybdenum disulfide (MOS2).

## EXPENDABLE SUPPLIES

Certain expendable supplies are required during maintenance and repair work. These include grease, oil, gasket cement, wiping rags and cleaning solvent. Ask your dealer for the special locking compounds, silicone lubricants and other products (**Figure 17**) which make vehicle maintenance simpler and easier. Cleaning solvent or kerosene is available at some service stations or hardware stores.

## PARTS REPLACEMENT

Suzuki makes frequent changes during a model year—some minor, some relatively major. When you order parts from the dealer or other parts distributor, always order by engine and frame number. Write the numbers down and carry them with you. Compare new parts to old before purchasing them. If they are not alike, have the parts manager explain the difference to you.

## SERIAL NUMBERS

You must know the model serial number and VIN number for registration purposes and when ordering replacement parts.

The frame serial number is stamped on the right-hand side of the steering head (**Figure 18**). The vehicle identification number (VIN) is on the left-hand side of the frame (**Figure 19**). The engine serial number is located on the top right-hand surface of the crankcase (**Figure 20**). The carburetor identification number is located on the left-hand side of the carburetor body (**Figure 21**). On California models, the vacuum hose label is located on the frame down-tube (**Figure 22**).

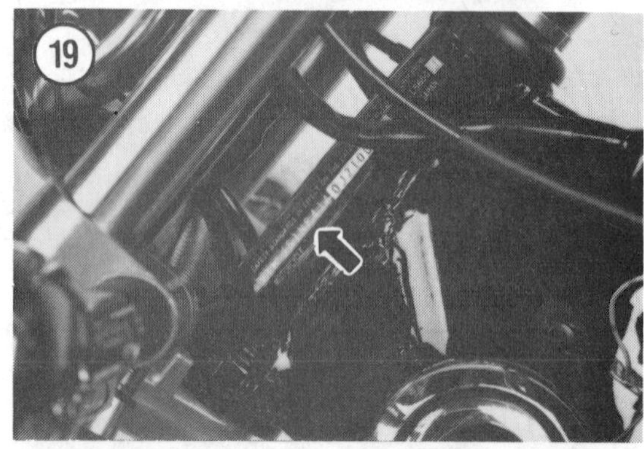


## BASIC HAND TOOLS

A number of tools are required to maintain a bike in top riding condition. You may already have some of these tools for home or car repairs. There are also tools made especially for bike repairs; these you will have to purchase. In any case, a wide variety of quality tools will make bike repairs easier and more effective.

Top quality tools are essential; they are also more economical in the long run. If you are now starting to build your tool collection, stay away from the "advertised specials" featured at some parts

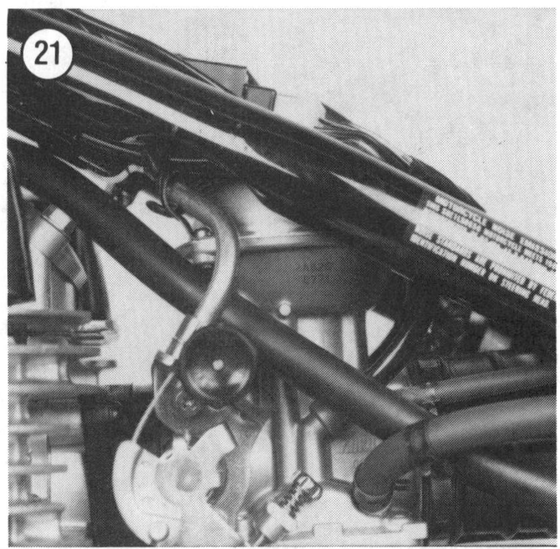

21

22

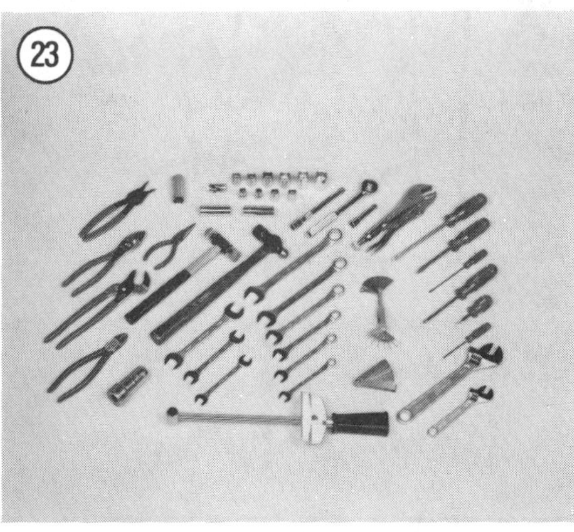

23

houses, discount stores and chain drug stores. These are usually a poor grade tool that can be sold cheaply and that is exactly what they are—*cheap*. They are usually made of inferior material and are thick, heavy and clumsy. Their rough finish makes them difficult to clean and they usually don't last very long. The Stanley line, available from most hardware stores is a good all-around line of tools and will last you a lifetime if you take care of them. Also, be careful when lending tools—make sure they are returned promptly; if not, your collection will soon disappear.

Quality tools are made of alloy steel and are heat treated for greater strength. They are lighter and better balanced than cheap ones. Their surface is smooth, making them a pleasure to work with and easy to clean. The initial cost of good-quality tools may be more, but it is cheaper in the long run. Don't try to buy everything in all sizes in the beginning; do it a little at a time until you have the necessary tools.

Keep your tools clean and in a tool box. Keep them organized with the sockets and related drives together and the open end and box wrenches together, etc. After using a tool, wipe off dirt and grease with a clean cloth and place the tool in its correct place. Doing this will save a lot of time you would have spent trying to find a socket buried in a bunch of clutch parts.

The following tools are required to perform virtually any repair job on a bike. Each tool is described and the recommended size given for starting a tool collection. **Table 3** includes the tools that should be on hand for simple home repairs and/or major overhaul as shown in **Figure 23**, additional tools and some duplicates may be added as you become more familiar with the bike. Almost all motorcycles and bikes (with the exception of the U.S. built Harley and some English bikes) use metric size bolts and nuts. If you are starting your collection now, buy metric sizes.

### Screwdrivers

The screwdriver is a very basic tool, but if used improperly it will do more damage than good. The slot on a screw has a definite dimension and shape. A screwdriver must be selected to conform with that shape. Use a small screwdriver for small screws and a large one for large screws or the screw head will be damaged.

Two basic types of screwdrivers are required to repair the bike—a common (flat blade) screwdrivers (**Figure 24**) and the Phillips screwdrivers (**Figure 25**).

Screwdrivers are available in sets which often include an assortment of common and Phillips blades. If you buy them individually, buy at least the following:

a. Common screwdriver—5/16 × 6 in. blade.
b. Common screwdriver—3/8 × 12 in. blade.
c. Phillips screwdriver—size 2 tip, 6 in. blade.

Use screwdrivers only for driving screws. Never use a screwdriver for prying or chiseling. Do not try to remove a Phillips or Allen head screw with a common screwdriver; you can damage the head so that the proper tool will be unable to remove it.

Keep screwdrivers in the proper condition and they will last longer and perform better. Always keep the tip of a common screwdriver in good condition. **Figure 26** shows how to grind the tip to the proper shape if it becomes damaged. Note the parallel sides of the tip.

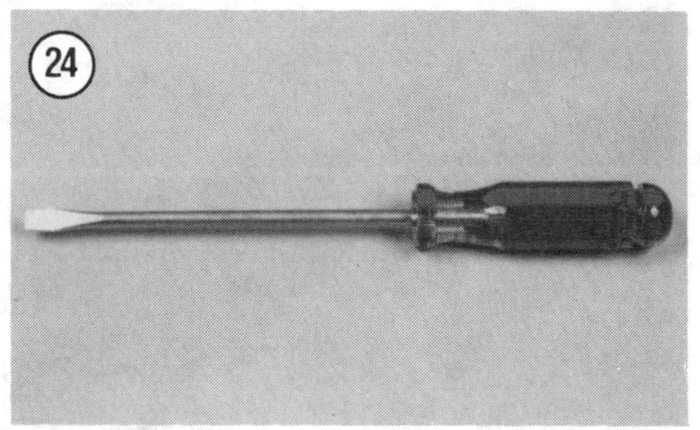
24

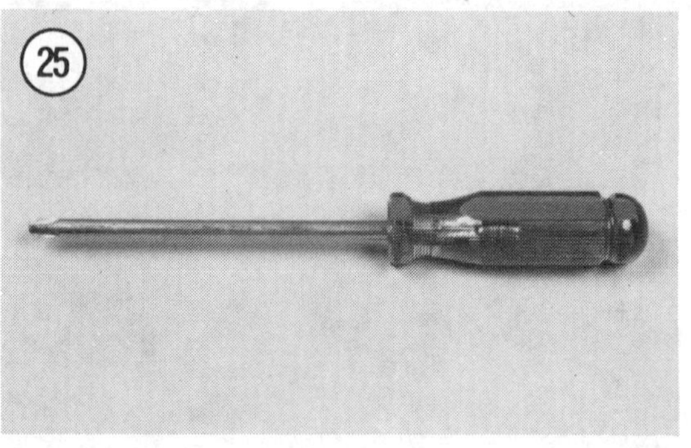
25

26

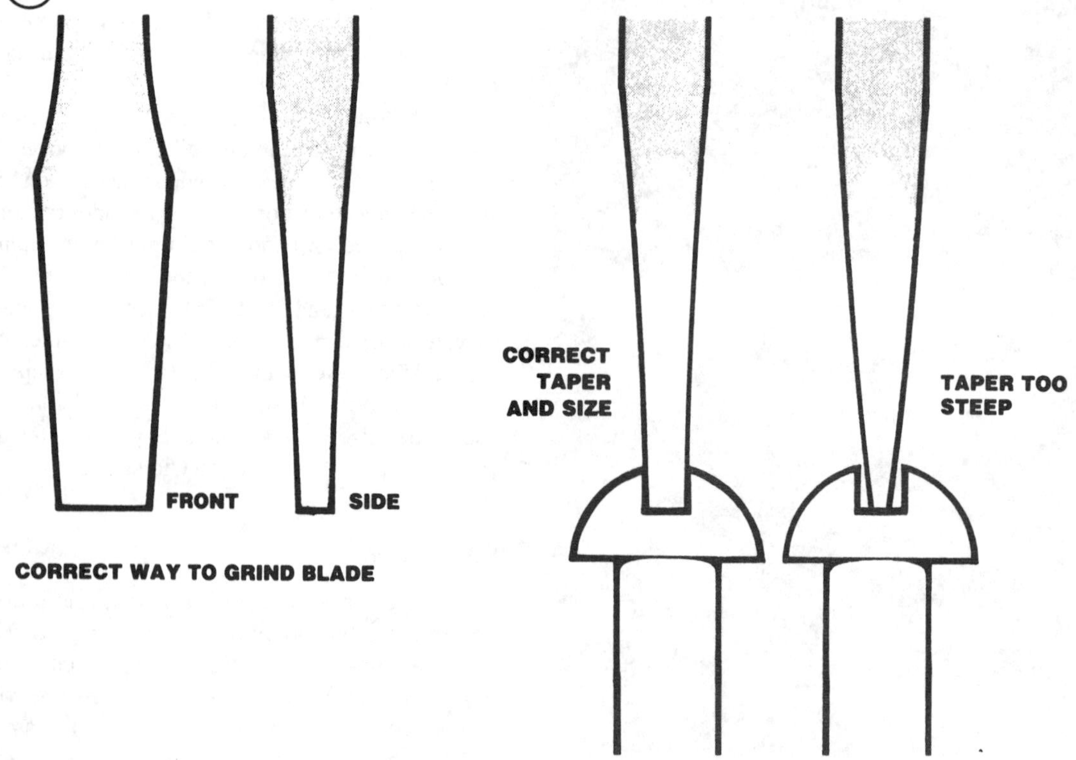

FRONT
SIDE
CORRECT WAY TO GRIND BLADE
CORRECT TAPER AND SIZE
TAPER TOO STEEP

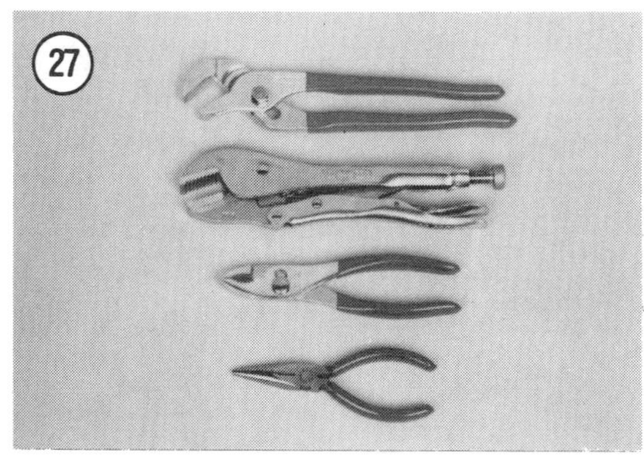
27

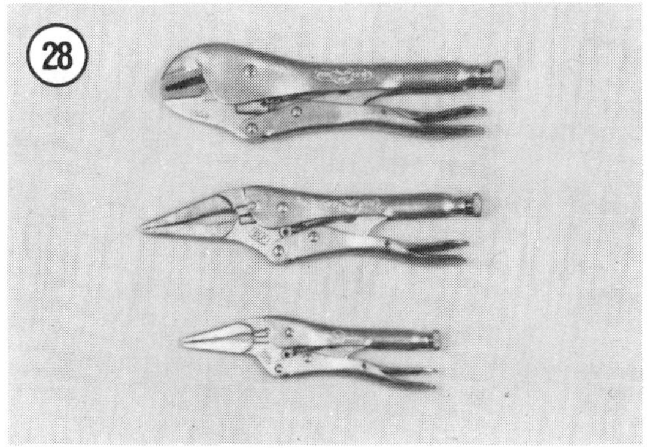
28

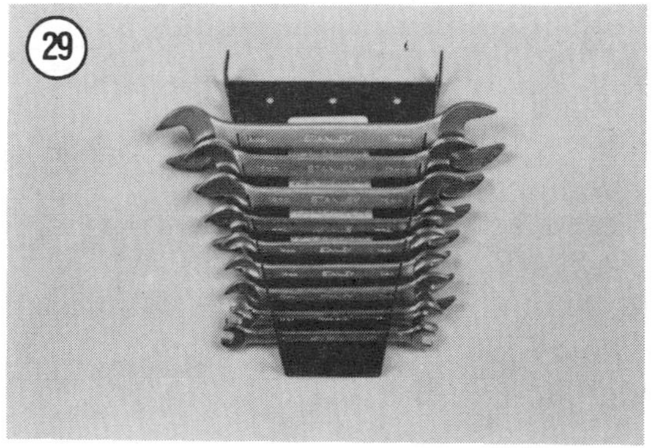
29

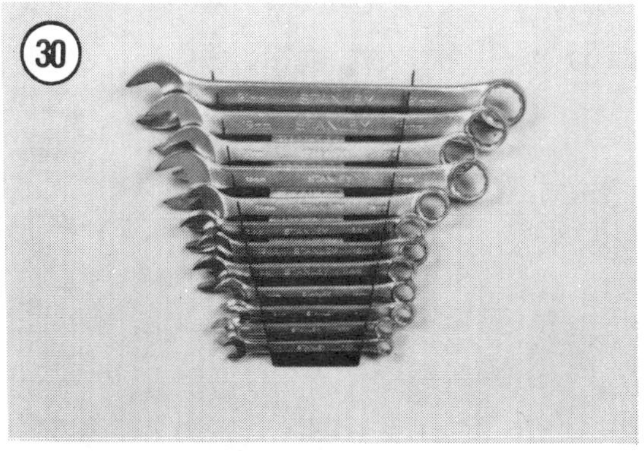
30

### Pliers

Pliers come in a wide range of types and sizes. Pliers are useful for cutting, bending and crimping. They should never be used to cut hardened objects or to turn bolts or nuts. **Figure 27** shows several pliers useful in bike repairs.

Each type of pliers has a specialized function. Gas pliers are general purpose pliers and are used mainly for holding things and for bending. Vise Grips are used as pliers or to hold objects very tight like a vise (**Figure 28**). Needlenose pliers are used to hold or bend small objects. Channel lock pliers can be adjusted to hold various sizes of objects; the jaws remain parallel to grip around objects such as pipe or tubing. There are many more types of pliers. The ones described here are most suitable for bike repairs.

### Box and Open-end Wrenches

Box and open-end wrenches are available in sets or separately in a variety of sizes. The size number stamped near the end refers to the distance between 2 parallel flats on the hex head bolt or nut.

Box wrenches are usually superior to open-end wrenches. Open-end wrenches (**Figure 29**) grip the nut on only 2 flats. Unless it fits well, it may slip and round off the points on the nut. The box wrench grips all 6 flats. Both 6-point and 12-point openings on box wrenches are available. The 6-point gives superior holding power; the 12-point allows a shorter swing.

Combination wrenches (**Figure 30**) which are open on one side and boxed on the other are also available. Both ends are the same size.

### Adjustable (Crescent) Wrenches

An adjustable wrench (also called crescent wrench) can be adjusted to fit nearly any nut or bolt head. See **Figure 31**. However, it can loosen and slip, causing damage to the nut and injury to your knuckles. Use an adjustable wrench only when other wrenches are not available.

Adjustable wrenches come in sizes ranging from 4-18 in. overall. A 6 or 8 in. wrench is recommended as an all-purpose wrench.

### Socket Wrenches

This type is undoubtedly the fastest, safest and most convenient to use. See **Figure 32**. Sockets which attach to a ratchet handle are available with 6-point or 12-point openings and 1/4, 3/8, 1/2 and 3/4 inch drives. The drive size indicates the size of the square hole which mates with the ratchet handle.

### Allen Wrenches

Allen wrenches (**Figure 33**) are available in sets or separately in a variety of sizes. These sets come in SAE and metric size, so be sure to buy a metric set. Suzuki uses a lot of Allen bolts (sometimes called socket bolts) on the engine and on the front fairing.

### Torque Wrench

A torque wrench is used with a socket to measure how tightly a nut or bolt is installed. They come in a wide price range and with either 3/8 or 1/2 in. square drive (**Figure 34**). The drive size indicates the size of the square drive which mates with the socket. Purchase one that measures 0-280 N•m (0-200 ft.-lb.).

### Impact Driver

This tool might have been designed with the bike in mind. See **Figure 35**. It makes removal of engine and clutch parts easy and eliminates damage to bolts and screw slots. Impact drivers are available at most large hardware, motorcycle or auto parts stores.

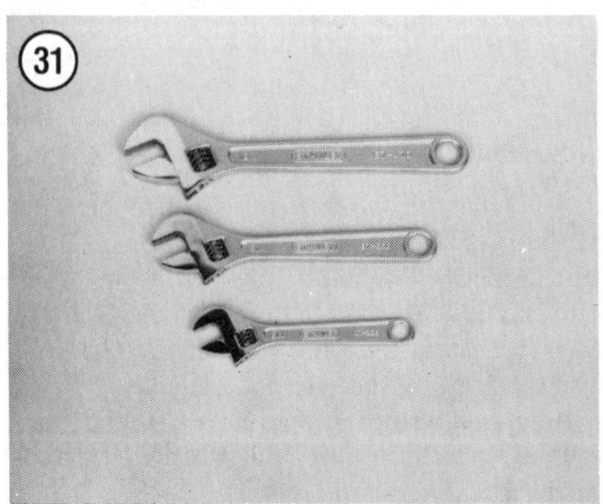


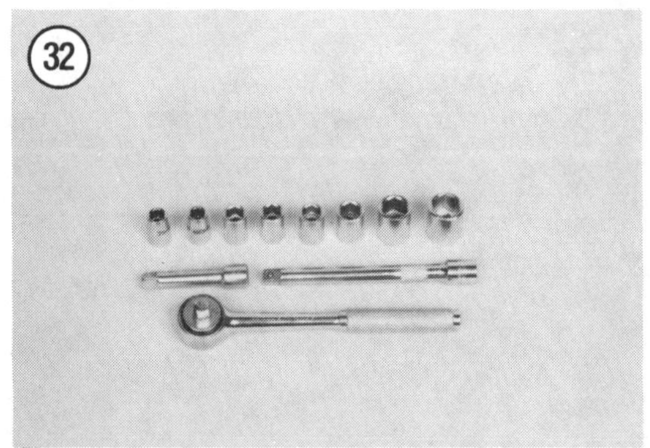


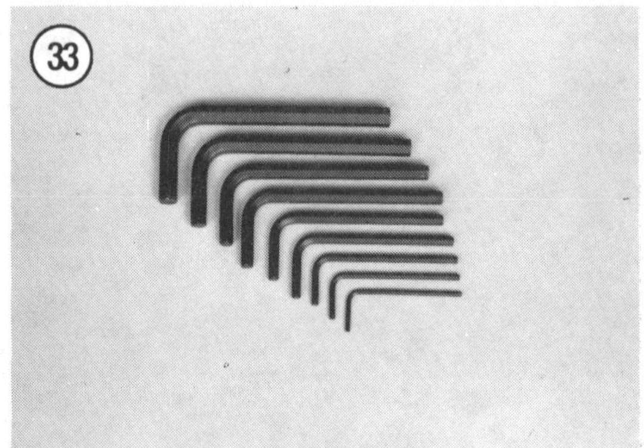


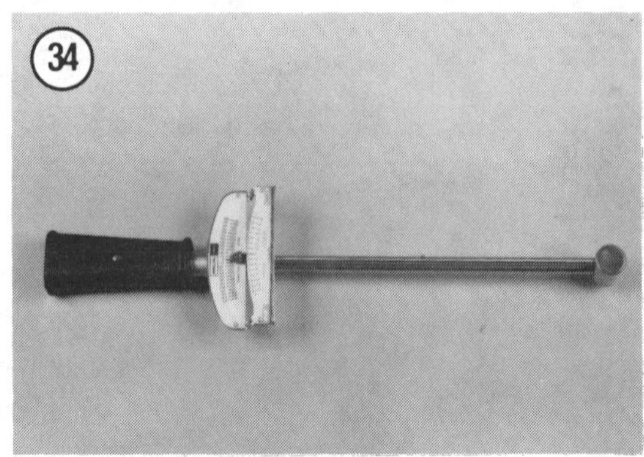


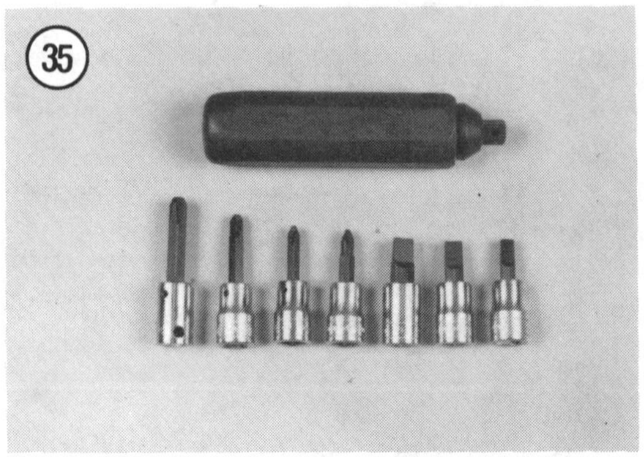

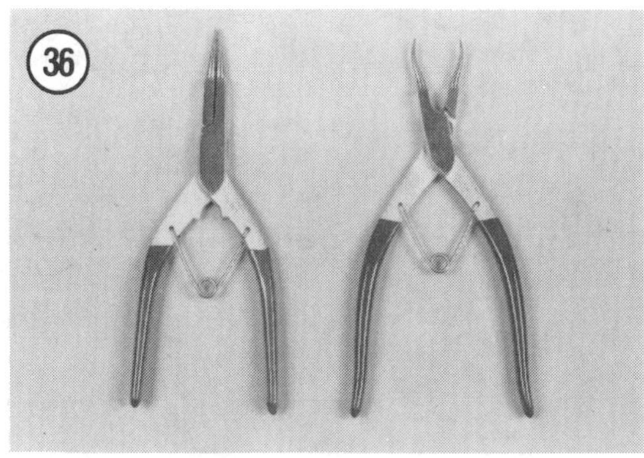
36

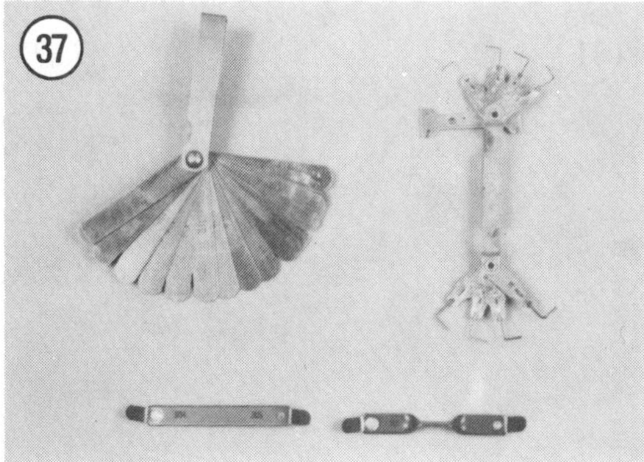
37

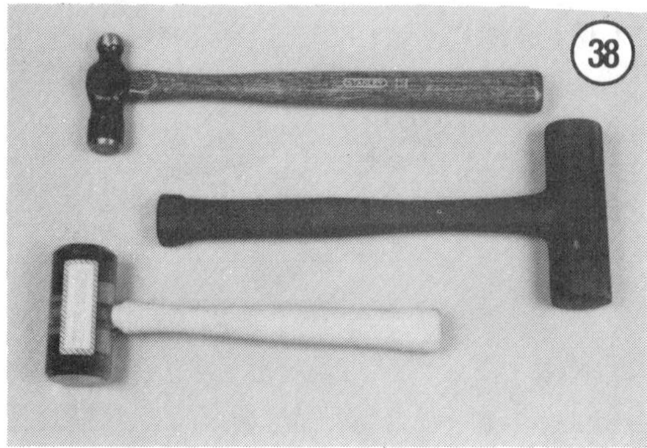
38

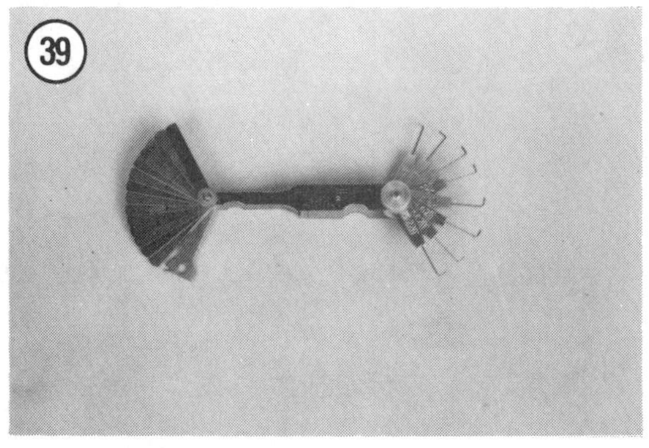
39

## Circlip Pliers

Circlip pliers (sometimes referred to as snap-ring pliers) are necessary to remove the circlips used on the transmission shaft assemblies and the transmission assemblies. See **Figure 36**.

## Hammers

The correct hammer is necessary for bike repairs. Use only a hammer with a face (or head) of rubber or plastic or the soft-faced type that is filled with buck shot. See **Figure 37**. These are sometimes necessary in engine tear-downs. *Never* use a metal-faced hammer on the bike as severe damage will result in most cases. You can always produce the same amount of force with a soft-faced hammer.

## Ignition Gauge

This tool (**Figure 38**) has both flat and wire measuring gauges and is used to measure spark plug gap. It is also equipped with the special tool used to adjust the side electrode on the spark plug. This tool is available at most auto or motorcycle supply stores.

## Feeler Gauges

Feeler gauges come in assorted sets and types (**Figure 39**). Some are strictly flat, some are a combination of flat and wire. Others are used specifically for valve adjustment and are bent at a certain angle to make it easy to use them in the normally tight areas of a cylinder head.

## Tap and Die Set

A complete tap and die set (**Figure 40**) is a relatively expensive tool. But when you need a tap or die to clean up a damaged thread, there is virtually no substitute. Be sure to purchase one for *Metric* threads if your are working on Japanese bikes. British and Italian bikes use a unique thread of their own and the Harley-Davidson uses American standard (SAE).

### Other Special Tools

A few other special tools may be required for major service. These are described in the appropriate chapters and are available either from a Suzuki dealer or other manufacturers as indicated.

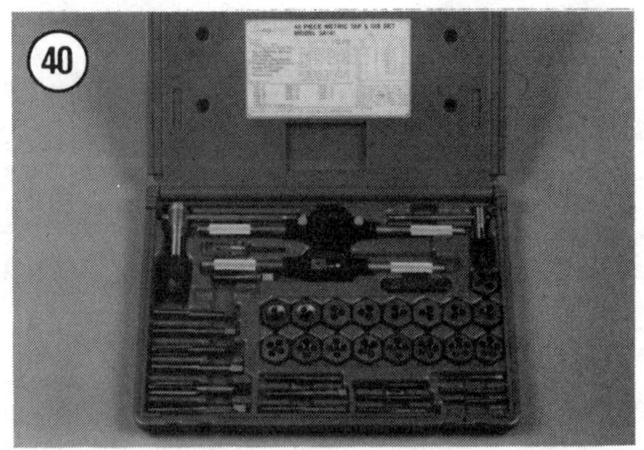
40

## TUNE-UP AND TROUBLESHOOTING TOOLS

### Multimeter or Volt-Ohm Meter

This instrument (**Figure 41**) is invaluable for electrical system troubleshooting and service. A few of its functions may be duplicated by homemade test equipment, but for the serious mechanic it is a must. Its uses are described in the applicable sections of the book.

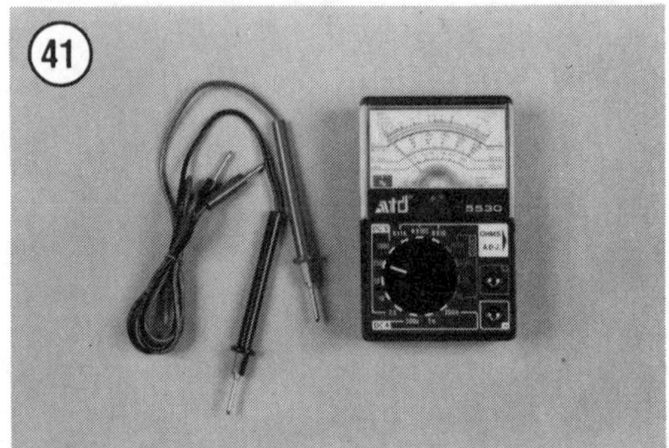
41

### Strobe Timing Light

This instrument is necessary for tuning. By flashing a light at the precise instant the spark plug fires, the position of the timing mark can be seen. Marks on the alternator flywheel line up with the stationary mark on the crankcase while the engine is running.

Suitable lights range from inexpensive neon bulb types to powerful xenon strobe lights (**Figure 42**). Neon timing lights are difficult to see and must be used in dimly lit areas. Xenon strobe timing lights can be used outside in bright sunlight. Both types work on the bike; use according to the manufacturer's instructions.

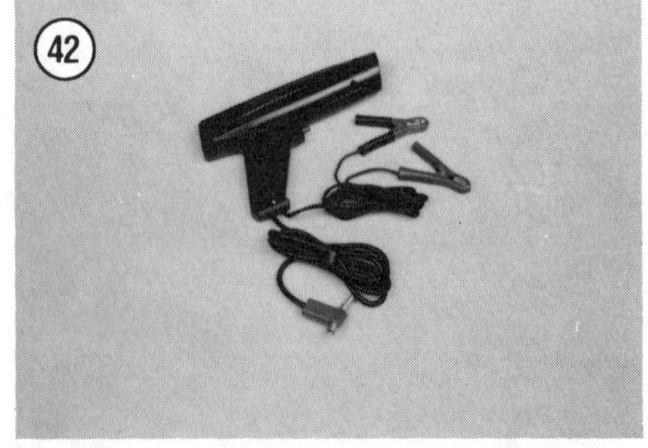
42

### Portable Tachometer

A portable tachometer is necessary for tuning (**Figure 43**). Ignition timing and carburetor adjustments must be performed at the specified engine speed. The best instrument for this purpose is one with a low range of 0-1,000 or 0-2,000 rpm and a high range of 0-4,000 rpm. Extended range (0-6,000 or 0-8,000 rpm) instruments lack accuracy at lower speeds. The instrument should be capable of detecting changes of 25 rpm on the low range.

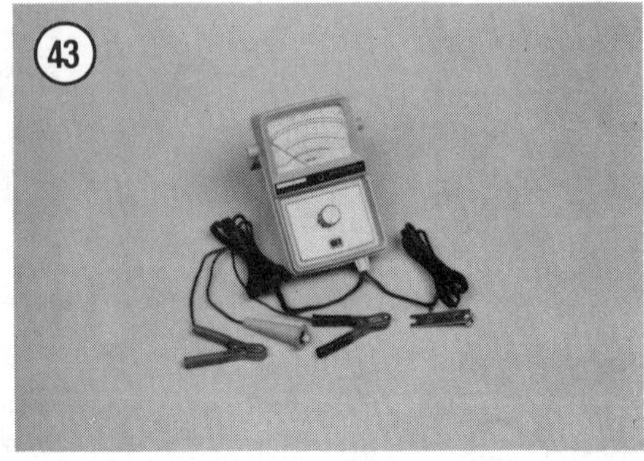
43

### Compression Gauge

A compression gauge (**Figure 44**) measures the engine compression. The results, when properly

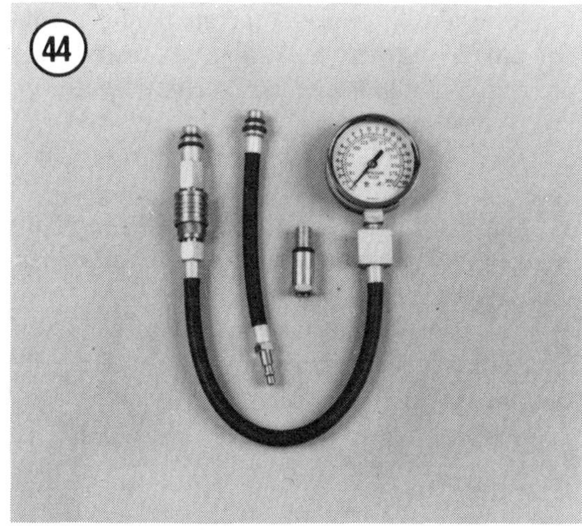
44

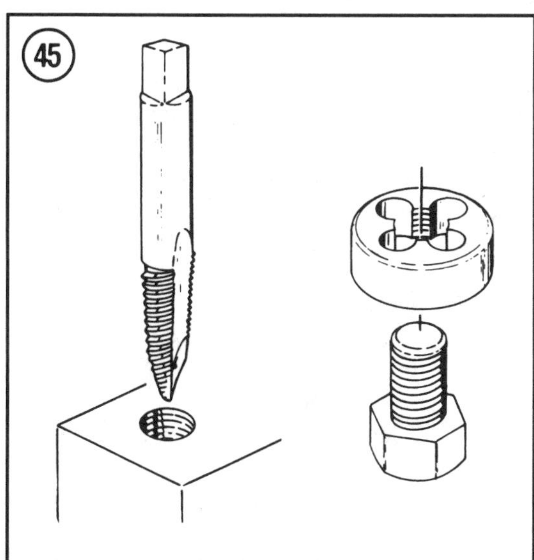
45

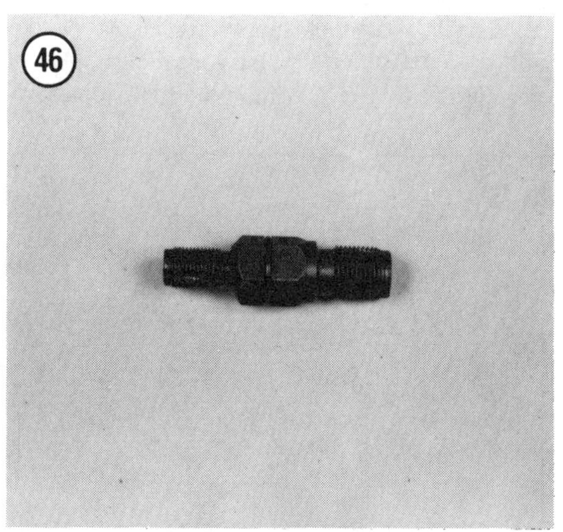
46

interpreted, can indicate general ring and valve condition. They are available from motorcycle or auto supply stores and mail order outlets.

## MECHANIC'S TIPS

### Removing Frozen Nuts and Screws

When a fastener rusts and cannot be removed, several methods may be used to loosen it. First, apply penetrating oil such as Liquid Wrench or WD-40 (available at any hardware or auto supply store). Apply it liberally and let it penetrate for 10-15 minutes. Rap the fastener several times with a small hammer; do not hit it hard enough to cause damage. Reapply the penetrating oil if necessary.

For frozen screws, apply penetrating oil as described, then insert a screwdriver in the slot and rap the top of the screwdriver with a hammer. This loosens the rust so the screw can be removed in the normal way. If the screw head is too chewed up to use a screwdriver, grip the head with Vise Grip pliers and twist the screw out.

### Remedying Stripped Threads

Occasionally, threads are stripped through carelessness or impact damage. Often the threads can be cleaned up by running a tap (for internal threads on nuts) or die (for external threads on bolts) through the threads (**Figure 45**). To clean or repair spark plug threads, a spark plug tap (**Figure 46**) can be used.

If the internal threads in a part are damaged beyond the use of a tap, the damaged threads can be replaced with a Heli-Coil, or equivalent, master thread repair pack (**Figure 47**). These kits have all the necessary items to repair a damaged internal thread.

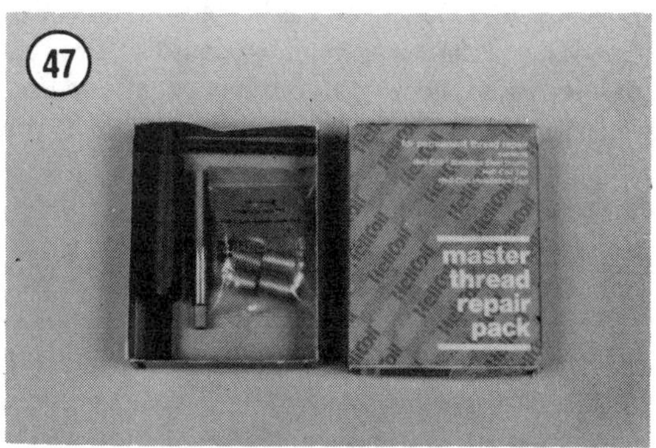

47

### Removing Broken Screws or Bolts

When the head breaks off a screw or bolt, several methods are available for removing the remaining portion.

If a large portion of the remainder projects out, try gripping it with Vise Grips. If the projecting portion is too small, file it to fit a wrench or cut a slot in it to fit a screwdriver. See **Figure 48**.

If the head breaks off flush, use a screw extractor. To do this, centerpunch the remaining portion of the screw or bolt. Drill a small hole in the screw and tap the extractor into the hole. Back the screw out with a wrench on the extractor. See **Figure 49**.

## RIDING SAFETY

### General Tips

1. Read your owner's manual and know your machine.
2. Check the throttle and brake controls before starting the engine.
3. Know how to make an emergency stop.
4. Never add fuel while anyone is smoking in the area or when the engine is running.
5. Never wear loose scarves, belts or boot laces that could catch on moving parts. Do *not* ride in tennis shoes as the laces may work loose and get caught on the footpeg (or other part of the bike). If the lace gets caught, you will not be able to place your foot on the ground when coming to a stop. Thus, the bike may fall over on top of you as you will not be able to balance the bike's weight.
6. Always wear eye and head protection and protective clothing to protect your *entire* body. Today's riding apparel is very stylish and you will be ready for action as well as being well protected.
7. Riding in the winter months requires a good set of clothes to keep your body dry and warm, otherwise your entire trip may be miserable. If you dress properly, moisture will evaporate from your body. If you become too hot and if your clothes trap the moisture, you will become cold. Even mild temperatures can be very uncomfortable and dangerous when combined with a strong wind or traveling at high speed. See **Table 4** for wind chill factors. Always dress according to what the wind chill factor is, not the ambient temperature.
8. Never allow anyone to operate the bike without proper instruction. This is for their bodily protection and to keep your machine from damage or destruction.
9. Use the "buddy system" for long trips, just in case you have a problem or run out of gas.
10. Never attempt to repair your machine with the engine running except when necessary for certain tune-up procedures.
11. Check all of the machine components and hardware frequently, especially the wheels and the steering.

### Operating Tips

1. Never operate the bike in crowded areas or steer toward people.
2. Avoid dangerous terrain.
3. Cross highways (where permitted) at a 90° angle after looking in both directions. Post traffic guards if crossing in groups.
4. Do not ride the bike on or near railroad tracks. The bike engine and exhaust noise can drown out the sound of an approaching train.
5. Keep the headlight, turn signal lights and taillight free of dirt.
6. Always steer with both hands.
7. Be aware of the terrain and avoid operating the bike at excessive speed.
8. Do not panic if the throttle sticks. Turn the engine stop switch to the OFF position.
9. Do not tailgate. Rear end collisions can cause injury and machine damage.
10. Do not mix alcoholic beverages or drugs with riding—*ride straight*.
11. Check your fuel supply regularly. Do not attempt to travel farther than your fuel supply will permit you to arrive at the next fuel stop.

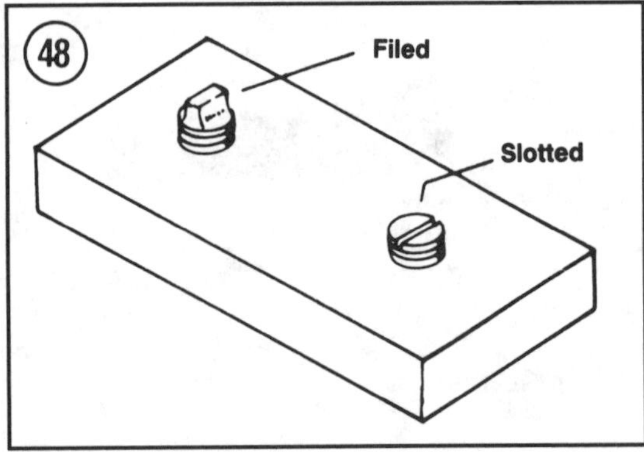

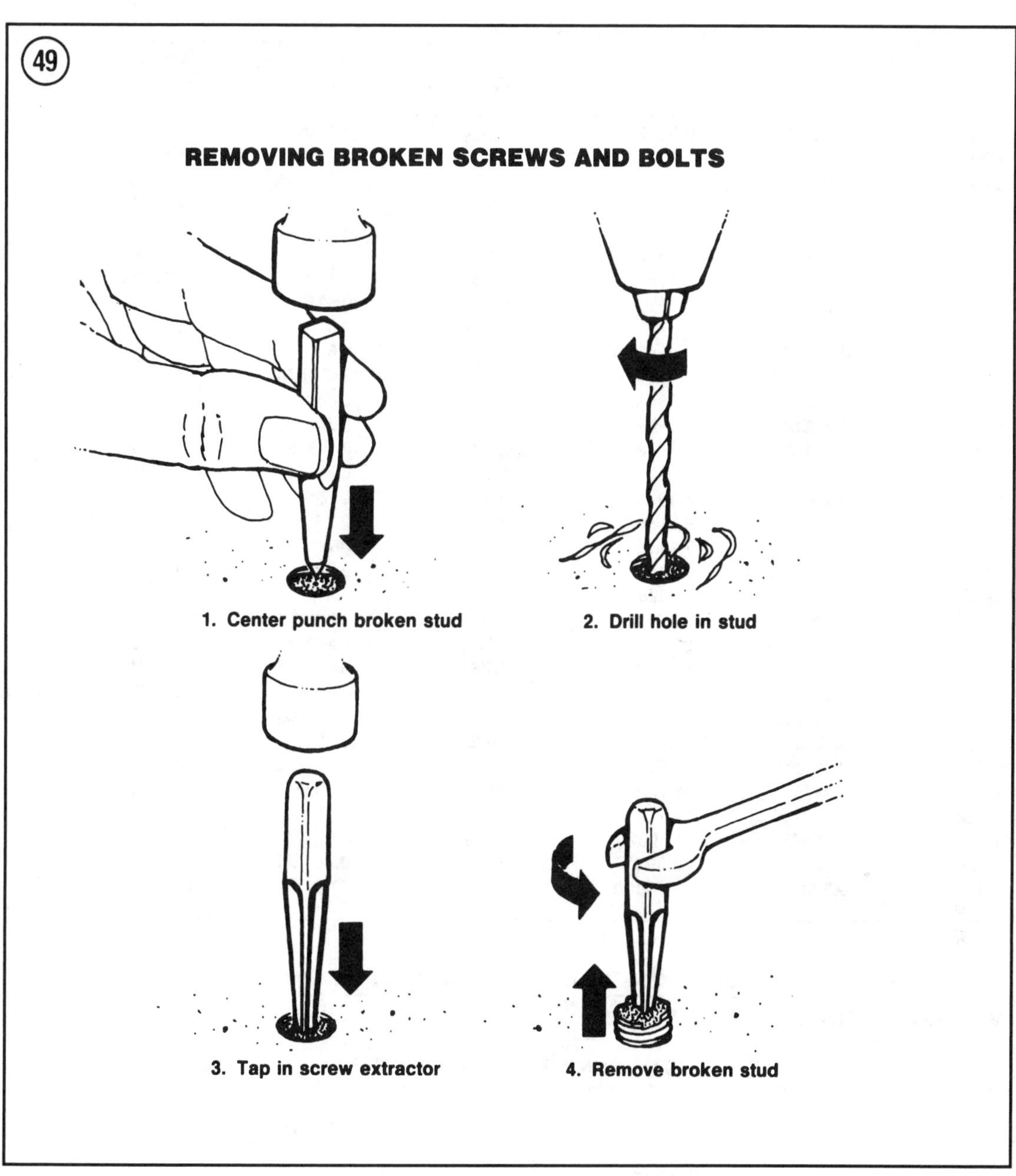


**Tables are on the following pages.**

**Table 1 DECIMAL AND METRIC EQUIVALENTS**

| Fractions | Decimal in. | Metric mm | Fractions | Decimal in. | Metric mm |
|---|---|---|---|---|---|
| 1/64 | 0.015625 | 0.39688 | 33/64 | 0.515625 | 13.09687 |
| 1/32 | 0.03125 | 0.79375 | 17/32 | 0.53125 | 13.49375 |
| 3/64 | 0.046875 | 1.19062 | 35/64 | 0.546875 | 13.89062 |
| 1/16 | 0.0625 | 1.58750 | 9/16 | 0.5625 | 14.28750 |
| 5/64 | 0.078125 | 1.98437 | 37/64 | 0.578125 | 14.68437 |
| 3/32 | 0.09375 | 2.38125 | 19/32 | 0.59375 | 15.08125 |
| 7/64 | 0.109375 | 2.77812 | 39/64 | 0.609375 | 15.47812 |
| 1/8 | 0.125 | 3.1750 | 5/8 | 0.625 | 15.87500 |
| 9/64 | 0.140625 | 3.57187 | 41/64 | 0.640625 | 16.27187 |
| 5/32 | 0.15625 | 3.96875 | 21/32 | 0.65625 | 16.66875 |
| 11/64 | 0.171875 | 4.36562 | 43/64 | 0.671875 | 17.06562 |
| 3/16 | 0.1875 | 4.76250 | 11/16 | 0.6875 | 17.46250 |
| 13/64 | 0.203125 | 5.15937 | 45/64 | 0.703125 | 17.85937 |
| 7/32 | 0.21875 | 5.55625 | 23/32 | 0.71875 | 18.25625 |
| 15/64 | 0.234375 | 5.95312 | 47/64 | 0.734375 | 18.65312 |
| 1/4 | 0.250 | 6.35000 | 3/4 | 0.750 | 19.05000 |
| 17/64 | 0.265625 | 6.74687 | 49/64 | 0.765625 | 19.44687 |
| 9/32 | 0.28125 | 7.14375 | 25/32 | 0.78125 | 19.84375 |
| 19/64 | 0.296875 | 7.54062 | 51/64 | 0.796875 | 20.24062 |
| 5/16 | 0.3125 | 7.93750 | 13/16 | 0.8125 | 20.63750 |
| 21/64 | 0.328125 | 8.33437 | 53/64 | 0.828125 | 21.03437 |
| 11/32 | 0.34375 | 8.73125 | 27/32 | 0.84375 | 21.43125 |
| 23/64 | 0.359375 | 9.12812 | 55/64 | 0.859375 | 21.82812 |
| 3/8 | 0.375 | 9.52500 | 7/8 | 0.875 | 22.22500 |
| 25/64 | 0.390625 | 9.92187 | 57/64 | 0.890625 | 22.62187 |
| 13/32 | 0.40625 | 10.31875 | 29/32 | 0.90625 | 23.01875 |
| 27/64 | 0.421875 | 10.71562 | 59/64 | 0.921875 | 23.41562 |
| 7/16 | 0.4375 | 11.11250 | 15/16 | 0.9375 | 23.81250 |
| 29/64 | 0.453125 | 11.50937 | 61/64 | 0.953125 | 24.20937 |
| 15/32 | 0.46875 | 11.90625 | 31/32 | 0.96875 | 24.60625 |
| 31/64 | 0.484375 | 12.30312 | 63/64 | 0.984375 | 25.00312 |
| 1/2 | 0.500 | 12.70000 | 1 | 1.00 | 25.40000 |

**Table 2 STANDARD TORQUE SPECIFICATIONS**

| Bolt diameter (mm) | N·m | ft.-lb. |
|---|---|---|
| | **Conventional or "4" Marked Bolt*** | |
| 4 | 1-2 | 0.7-1.5 |
| 5 | 2-4 | 1.5-3.0 |
| 6 | 4-7 | 3-5 |
| 8 | 10-16 | 7-11.5 |
| 10 | 22-35 | 16-25.5 |
| 12 | 35-55 | 25.5-40 |
| 14 | 50-80 | 36-58 |
| 16 | 80-130 | 58-94 |
| 18 | 130-190 | 94-137.5 |
| | **"7" Marked Bolt*** | |
| 4 | 1.5-3 | 1-2 |
| 5 | 3-6 | 2-4.5 |
| 6 | 8-12 | 6-8.5 |

(continued)

**Table 2 STANDARD TORQUE SPECIFICATIONS (continued)**

| Bolt diameter (mm) | N·m | ft.-lb. |
|---|---|---|
| | "7" Marked Bolt* (continued) | |
| 8 | 18-28 | 13-20 |
| 10 | 40-60 | 29-43.5 |
| 12 | 70-100 | 50.5-72.5 |
| 14 | 110-160 | 79.5-115.5 |
| 16 | 170-250 | 123-181 |
| 18 | 200-280 | 144-202 |

* Number is marked on top of Suzuki bolt head. These are Suzuki numbers and do not appear on after-market bolts.

**Table 3 WORKSHOP TOOLS**

| Tool | Size or specification |
|---|---|
| Screwdriver | |
| Common | 1/8 x 4 in. blade |
| Common | 5/16 x 8 in. blade |
| Common | 3/8 x 12 in. blade |
| Phillips | Size 2 tip, 6 in. overall |
| Pliers | |
| Slip joint | 6 in. overall |
| Vise Grips | 10 in. overall |
| Needlenose | 6 in. overall |
| Channelock | 12 in. overall |
| Snap ring | Assorted |
| Wrenches | |
| Box-end set | Assorted |
| Open-end set | Assorted |
| Cresent | 6 in. and 12 in. overall |
| Socket set | 1/2 in. drive ratchet with assorted metric sockets |
| Socket drive extensions | 1/2 in. drive, 2 in., 4 in. and 6 in. |
| Socket universal joint | 1/2 in. drive |
| Allen | Socket driven (long and short), T-handle driven and 90° |
| Hammers | |
| Soft faced | — |
| Plastic faced | — |
| Metal faced | — |
| Other special tools | |
| Impact driver | 1/2 in. drive with assorted bits |
| Torque wrench | 1/2 in. drive |
| Flat feeler gauge | Metric set |

**Table 4 WIND CHILL FACTOR**

| Estimated Wind Speed in MPH | Actual Thermometer Reading (°F) | | | | | | | | | | | |
|---|---|---|---|---|---|---|---|---|---|---|---|---|
| | 50 | 40 | 30 | 20 | 10 | 0 | −10 | −20 | −30 | −40 | −50 | −60 |
| | Equivalent Temperature (°F) | | | | | | | | | | | |
| Calm | 50 | 40 | 30 | 20 | 10 | 0 | −10 | −20 | −30 | −40 | −50 | −60 |
| 5 | 48 | 37 | 27 | 16 | 6 | −5 | −15 | −26 | −36 | −47 | −57 | −68 |
| 10 | 40 | 28 | 16 | 4 | −9 | −21 | −33 | −46 | −58 | −70 | −83 | −95 |
| 15 | 36 | 22 | 9 | −5 | −18 | −36 | −45 | −58 | −72 | −85 | −99 | −112 |
| 20 | 32 | 18 | 4 | −10 | −25 | −39 | −53 | −67 | −82 | −96 | −110 | −124 |
| 25 | 30 | 16 | 0 | −15 | −29 | −44 | −59 | −74 | −88 | −104 | −118 | −133 |
| 30 | 28 | 13 | −2 | −18 | −33 | −48 | −63 | −79 | −94 | −109 | −125 | −140 |
| 35 | 27 | 11 | −4 | −20 | −35 | −49 | −67 | −82 | −98 | −113 | −129 | −145 |
| 40 | 26 | 10 | −6 | −21 | −37 | −53 | −69 | −85 | −100 | −116 | −132 | −148 |
| * | | | | | | | | | | | | |
| | Little Danger (for properly clothed person) | | | | Increasing Danger | | | Great Danger | | | | |
| | | | | | *Danger from freezing of exposed flesh. | | | | | | | |

*Wind speeds greater than 40 mph have little additional effect.

# CHAPTER TWO



# TROUBLESHOOTING

Diagnosing mechanical problems is relatively simple if you use orderly procedures and keep a few basic principles in mind.

The troubleshooting procedures in this chapter analyze typical symptoms and show logical methods of isolating causes. These are not the only methods. There may be several ways to solve a problem, but only a systematic, methodical approach can guarantee success.

Never assume anything. Do not overlook the obvious. If you are riding along and the engine suddenly quits, check the easiest, most accessible problems first. Is there gasoline in the tank? Is the fuel shutoff valve in the ON position? Has a spark plug wire cap come loose? Check the ignition switch and key. Sometimes the weight of the key ring may suddenly turn the ignition off.

If nothing obvious turns up in a quick check, look a little further. Learning to recognize and describe symptoms will make repairs easier for you or a mechanic at the shop. Describe problems accurately and fully. Saying that "it won't run" isn't the same as saying "it quit at high speed and won't start" or that "it sat in my garage for 3 months and then wouldn't start."

Gather as many symptoms together as possible to aid in diagnosis. Note whether the engine lost power gradually or all at once. Remember that the more complicated a machine is, the easier it is to troubleshoot because symptoms point to specific problems.

After the symptoms are defined, areas which could cause the problems are tested and analyzed. Guessing at the cause of a problem may provide the solution, but it can easily lead to frustration, wasted time and a series of expensive, unnecessary parts replacements.

You do not need fancy equipment or complicated test gear to determine whether repairs can be attempted at home. A few simple checks could save a large repair bill and time lost while the bike sits in a dealer's service department. On the other hand, be realistic and don't attempt repairs beyond your abilities. Service departments tend to charge a lot for putting together a disassembled engine that may have been abused. Some dealers won't even take on such a job—so use common sense and don't get in over your head.

## OPERATING REQUIREMENTS

An engine needs 3 basics to run properly: correct fuel/air mixture, compression and a spark at the correct time. If one or more are missing, the engine just won't run. The electrical system is the weakest link of the 3 basics. More problems result from electrical breakdowns than from any other source. Keep that in mind before you begin tampering with carburetor adjustments and the like.

If the bike has been sitting for any length of time and refuses to start, check and clean the spark plug and then look to the gasoline delivery system. This includes the fuel tank, fuel shutoff valve and the fuel line to the carburetor and the vacuum line to the fuel shutoff valve. Gasoline deposits may have formed and gummed up the carburetor's jets and air passages. Gasoline tends to lose its potency after standing for long periods. Condensation may contaminate the fuel with water. Drain the old fuel and try starting with a fresh tankful.

## EMERGENCY TROUBLESHOOTING

When the bike is difficult to start or won't start at all, it does not help to wear down the battery with the starter. Check for obvious problems even before getting out your tools. Go down the following list step-by-step. Do each one; you may be embarrassed to find your engine stop switch is stuck in the OFF position, but that is better than wearing down the battery. If it still will not start, refer to the appropriate troubleshooting procedure which follows in this chapter.

*WARNING*

*Do not use an open flame near the fuel tank. A serious explosion could result.*

1. Is there fuel in the tank? Open the filler cap (**Figure 1**) and rock the bike. Listen for fuel sloshing around.
2. Is the fuel shutoff valve (**Figure 2**) in the ON position and is the vacuum line from the valve to the base of the carburetor (**Figure 3**) still connected?
3. Make sure the engine stop switch (**Figure 4**) is not in the OFF position.
4. Is the spark plug wire cap (**Figure 5**) on tight? Push it on and slightly rotate it to clean the electrical connection between the plug and the connector.
5. Is the choke in the correct position. The knob (**Figure 6**) should be pulled *out* for a cold engine and pushed *in* for a warm engine.
6. Is the automatic decompression cable (**Figure 7**) properly adjusted. If the cable is improperly adjusted it will result in difficult engine starting or even engine damage. Refer to Chapter Three.

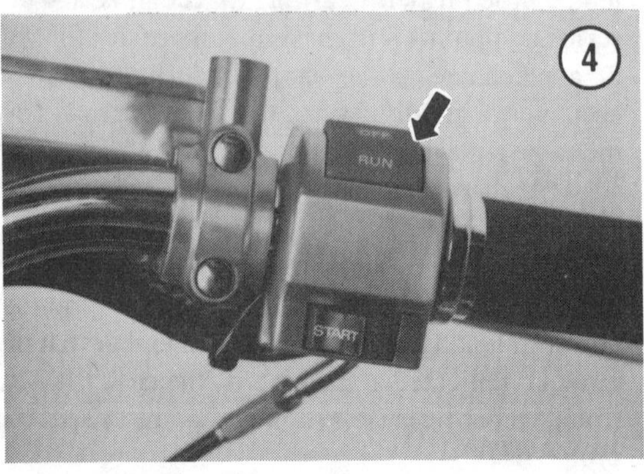

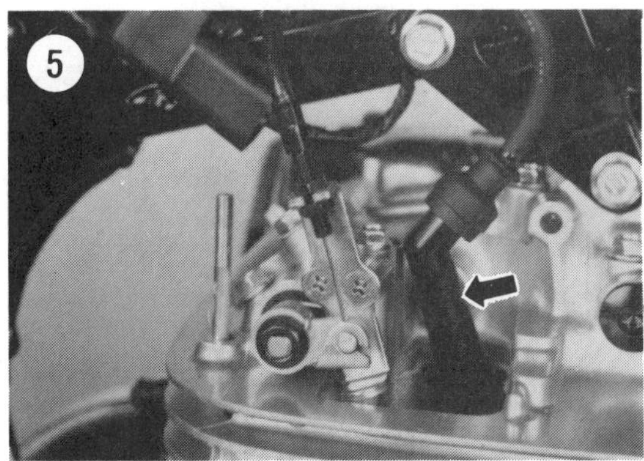


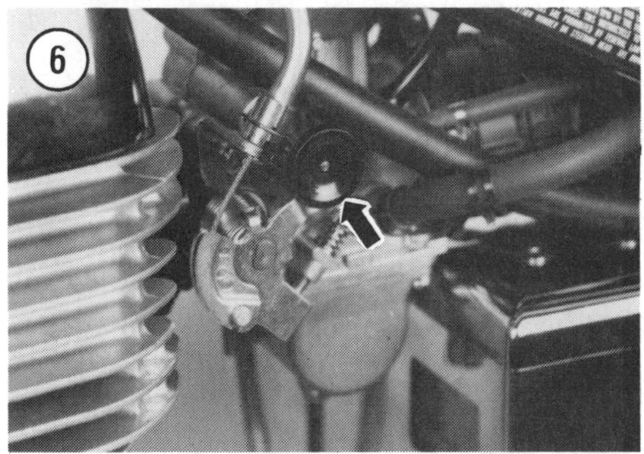


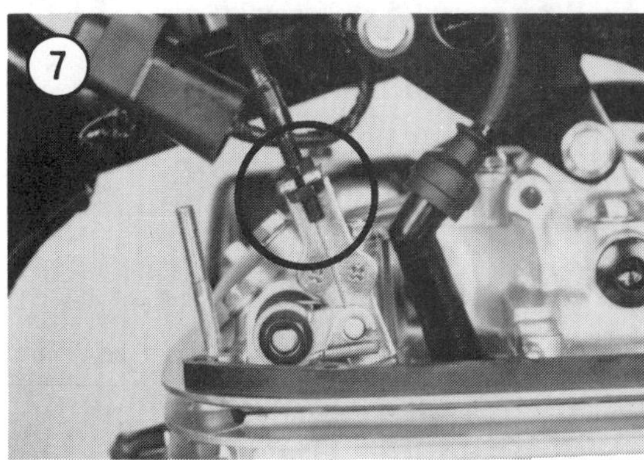

## ENGINE STARTING

An engine that refuses to start or is difficult to start is very frustrating. More often than not, the problem is very minor and can be found with a simple and logical troubleshooting approach.

The following items show a beginning point from which to isolate engine starting problems.

2

### Engine Fails to Start

Perform the following spark test to determine if the ignition system is operating properly.

1. Remove the spark plug from the cylinder as described under *Spark Plug Removal/Cleaning* in Chapter Three.
2. Connect the spark plug wire and connector to the spark plug and touch the spark plug's base to a good ground such as the engine cylinder head (**Figure 8**). Make sure the spark plug is against bare metal, not a painted surface. Position the spark plug so you can see the electrodes.
3. Crank the engine over with the starter. A fat blue spark should be evident across the plug's electrodes.

*WARNING*

*If it is necessary to hold the high voltage lead, do so with an insulated pair of pliers. The high voltage generated by the ignition signal generator and ignitor unit could produce serious or fatal shocks.*

4. If the spark is good, check for one or more of the following possible malfunctions:
   a. Obstructed fuel line.
   b. Low compression.
   c. Leaking head gasket.
   d. Choke not operating properly.
   e. Throttle not operating properly.
   f. Improperly adjusted automatic decompression cable.
5. If spark is not good, check for one or more of the following:
   a. Weak ignition coil.
   b. Weak ignition signal generator.
   c. Weak or faulty ignitor unit.
   d. Broken or shorted high tension lead to the spark plug.
   e. Loose electrical connections.
   f. Loose or broken ignition coil ground wire.

### Engine is Difficult to Start

Check for one or more of the following possible malfunctions:

a. Fouled spark plug.
b. Improperly adjusted choke.
c. Contaminated fuel system.
d. Improperly adjusted carburetor.
e. Weak ignition coil.
f. Weak ignition signal generator.
g. Weak or faulty igniter unit.
h. Incorrect type ignition coil.
i. Poor compression.
j. Improperly adjusted automatic decompression cable.

### Engine Will Not Crank

Check for one or more of the following possible malfunctions:

a. Discharged battery.
b. Broken starter gears.
c. Seized piston.
d. Seized crankshaft bearings.
e. Broken connecting rod.
f. Locked-up transmission or clutch assembly.

## ENGINE PERFORMANCE

In the following check list, it is assumed that the engine runs, but is not operating at peak performance. This will serve as a starting point from which to isolate a performance malfunction.

The possible causes for each malfunction are listed in a logical sequence and in order of probability.

### Engine Will Not Start or is Hard to Start

a. Fuel tank empty.
b. Obstructed fuel line or fuel shutoff valve.
c. Sticking float valve in carburetor.
d. Carburetor incorrectly adjusted.
e. Improper choke operation.
f. Fouled or improperly gapped spark plug.
g. Weak ignition signal generator.
h. Weak or faulty ignitor unit.
i. Ignition timing incorrect (faulty component in system).
j. Broken or shorted ignition coil.
k. Improper valve timing.
l. Clogged air filter element.
m. Contaminated fuel.
n. Improperly adjusted automatic decompression cable.

### Engine Will Not Idle or Idles Erratically

a. Carburetor incorrectly adjusted.
b. Fouled or improperly gapped spark plug.
c. Leaking head gasket or vacuum leak.
d. Weak ignition signal generator.
e. Weak or faulty ignitor unit.
f. Ignition timing incorrect (faulty component in system).
g. Improper valve timing.
h. Obstructed fuel line or fuel shutoff valve.

### Engine Misses at High Speed

a. Fouled or improperly gapped spark plug.
b. Improper ignition timing (faulty component in system).
c. Improper carburetor main jet selection.
d. Clogged jets in the carburetor(s).
e. Weak ignition coil.
f. Weak ignition signal generator.
g. Weak or faulty ignitor unit.
h. Improper valve timing.
i. Obstructed fuel line or fuel shutoff valve.

### Engine Continues to Run with Ignition Off

a. Excessive carbon buildup in engine.
b. Vacuum leak in intake system.
c. Contaminated or incorrect fuel octane rating.

### Engine Overheating

a. Obstructed cooling fins on the cylinder and cylinder head.
b. Improper ignition timing (faulty component in system).
c. Improper spark plug heat range.
d. Engine oil level low.

### Engine Misses at Idle

a. Fouled or improperly gapped spark plug.
b. Spark plug cap faulty.
c. Ignition cable insulation deteriorated (shorting out).

d. Dirty or clogged air filter element.
e. Carburetor incorrectly adjusted (too lean or too rich).
f. Choke valve stuck.
g. Clogged jet(s) in the carburetor.
h. Carburetor float height incorrect.

### Engine Backfires— Explosions in Mufflers

a. Fouled or improperly gapped spark plug.
b. Spark plug cap faulty.
c. Ignition cable insulation deteriorated (shorting out).
d. Ignition timing incorrect.
e. Improper valve timing.
f. Contaminated fuel.
g. Burned or damaged intake and/or exhaust valves.
h. Weak or broken intake and/or exhaust valve springs.

### Pre-ignition (Fuel Mixture Ignites Before Spark Plug Fires)

a. Hot spot in combustion chamber (piece of carbon).
b. Valve(s) stuck in guide.
c. Overheating engine.

### Smoky Exhaust and Engine Runs Roughly

a. Carburetor mixture too rich.
b. Choke not operating correctly.
c. Water or other contaminants in fuel.
d. Clogged fuel line.
e. Clogged air filter element.

### Engine Loses Power at Normal Riding Speed

a. Carburetor incorrectly adjusted.
b. Engine overheating.
c. Improper ignition timing (faulty component in system).
d. Weak ignition signal generator.
e. Weak or faulty ignitor unit.
f. Incorrectly gapped spark plug.
g. Weak ignition coil.
h. Obstructed mufflers.
i. Dragging brake(s).

### Engine Lacks Acceleration

a. Carburetor mixture too lean.
b. Clogged fuel line.
c. Improper ignition timing (faulty component in system).
d. Improper valve clearance.
e. Dragging brake(s).

## ENGINE NOISES

1. *Knocking or pinging during acceleration*—Caused by using a lower octane fuel than recommended. May also be caused by poor fuel. Pinging can also be caused by a spark plug of the wrong heat range. Refer to *Spark Plug Selection* in Chapter Three.
2. *Slapping or rattling noises at low speed or during acceleration*—May be caused by piston slap (excessive piston to cylinder wall clearance).
3. *Knocking or rapping while decelerating*—Usually caused by excessive rod bearing clearance.
4. *Persistent knocking and vibration*—Usually caused by excessive main bearing clearance.
5. *Rapid on-off squeal*—Compression leak around cylinder head gasket or spark plugs.

## EXCESSIVE VIBRATION

This can be difficult to find without disassembling the engine. Usually this is caused by loose engine mounting hardware or faulty balancer assembly.

## FRONT SUSPENSION AND STEERING

Poor handling may be caused by improper tire pressure, a damaged or bent frame or front steering components, a worn front fork assembly, worn wheel bearings or dragging brakes.

## BRAKE PROBLEMS

Sticking brake pads or shoes may be caused by a stuck piston in a caliper assembly or warped pad shim or disc or out-of-round drum.

# CHAPTER THREE

# LUBRICATION, MAINTENANCE AND TUNE-UP

A motorcycle, even in normal use, is subjected to tremendous heat, stress and vibration. When neglected, any bike becomes unreliable and actually dangerous to ride.

To gain the utmost in safety, performance and useful life from the Suzuki Savage, it is necessary to make periodic inspections and adjustments. Frequently minor problems are found during these inspections that are simple and inexpensive to correct at the time. If they are not found and corrected at this time, they could lead to major and more expensive problems later on.

Start out by doing simple tune-up, lubrication and maintenance. Tackle more involved jobs as you become more acquainted with the bike.

**Tables 1-6** are located at the end of this chapter.

## ROUTINE CHECKS

The following simple checks should be performed during each stop at a service station for gas.

### Engine Oil Level

Refer to *Periodic Lubrication* in this chapter.

### General Inspection

1. Quickly inspect the engine for signs of oil or fuel leakage.
2. Check the tires for embedded stones. Pry them out with a suitable tool such as a screwdriver from your tool kit.
3. Make sure all lights work.

*NOTE*

*At least check the brake light. It can burn out at any time. Motorists cannot stop as quickly as you and need all the warning you can give.*

### Tire Pressure

Tire pressure must be checked with the tires cold. Correct tire pressure varies with the load you are carrying or if you have a passenger. See **Table 1**.

### Battery

The electrolyte level must be between the upper and lower level marks on the case (**Figure 1**) as viewed through the opening in the battery case. For complete details see *Battery* in this chapter.

Check the level more frequently in hot weather; electrolyte will evaporate rapidly as heat increases.

### Crankcase Breather Hose

Inspect the hose (**Figure 2**) for cracks and deterioration and make sure that the hose clamps are tight.

### Evaporative Emission Control System (Calif. Models)

Inspect the hoses to make sure they are not kinked or bent and that they are securely connected to their respective parts. Refer to the vacuum hose routing label (**Figure 3**) on the frame down tube.

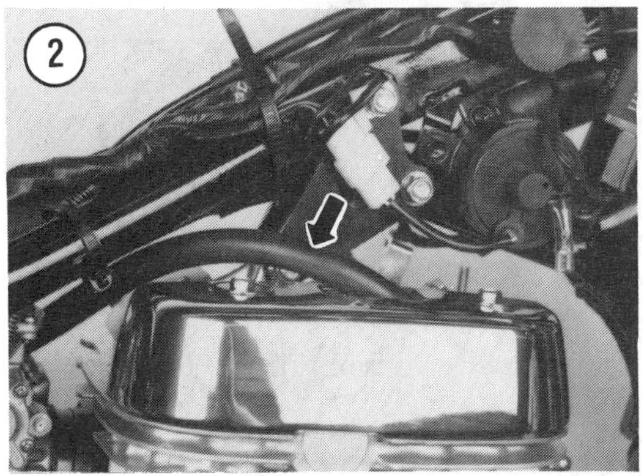

### Lights and Horn

With the engine running, check the following.

1. Pull the front brake lever on and check that the brake light comes on.
2. Push the rear brake pedal down and check that the brake light comes on soon after you have begun depressing the pedal.
3. Turn the ignition switch ON. Press the headlight dimmer switch to both the HI and LO positions and check to see that both headlight elements are working in BOTH headlights.
4. Turn the turn signal switch to the left and right positions and check that all 4 turn signals are working.
5. Push the horn button and make sure the horn blows loudly.
6. If during the test, the rear brake pedal traveled too far before the brake light came on, adjust the rear brake light switch as described in Chapter Eight.
7. If the horn or any of the lights failed to operate properly, refer to Chapter Eight.

## PRE-CHECKS

The following checks should be performed before the first ride of the day.

1. Inspect all fuel lines and fittings for wetness.
2. Make sure the fuel tank is full of fresh gasoline.
3. Make sure the engine oil level is correct.
4. Check the operation of the front brake. Add hydraulic fluid to the front brake master cylinder if necessary.
5. Check the operation of the clutch. If necessary, adjust the clutch free-play as described in this chapter.
6. Check the throttle and the rear brake pedal. Make sure they operate properly with no binding.
7. Inspect the front and rear suspension; make sure they have a good solid feel with no looseness.
8. Check tire pressure. Refer to **Table 1**.
9. Check the exhaust system for damage.
10. Check the tightness of all fasteners, especially engine mounting hardware.

## SERVICE INTERVALS

The services and intervals shown in **Table 2** are recommended by the factory. Strict adherence to these recommendations will ensure long service from the Suzuki. If the bike is run in an area of high humidity, the lubrication services must be done more frequently to prevent possible rust damage.

For convenience when maintaining your motorcycle, most of the services shown in these tables are described in this chapter. However, some procedures which require more than minor disassembly or adjustment are covered elsewhere in the appropriate chapter.

## TIRES AND WHEELS

### Tire Pressure

Tire pressure should be checked and adjusted to maintain the smoothness of the tire, good traction and handling and to get the maximum life out of the tire. A simple, accurate gauge (**Figure 4**) can be purchased for a few dollars and should be carried in your motorcycle tool kit. The appropriate tire pressures are shown in **Table 1**.

*NOTE*

*After checking and adjusting the air pressure, make sure to install the air valve cap (**Figure 5**). The cap prevents small pebbles and dirt from collecting in the valve stem; this could allow air leakage or result in incorrect tire pressure readings.*

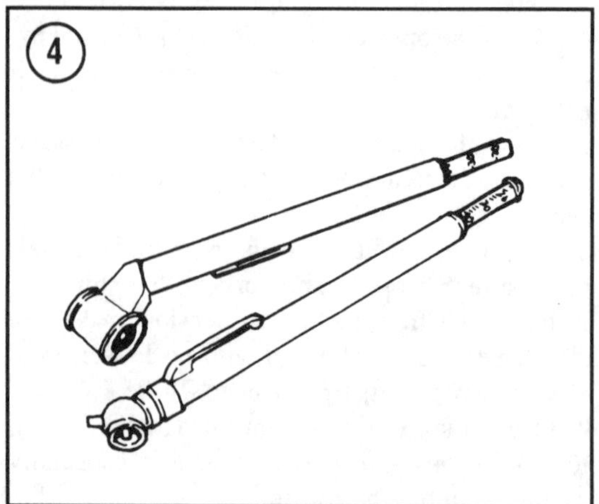

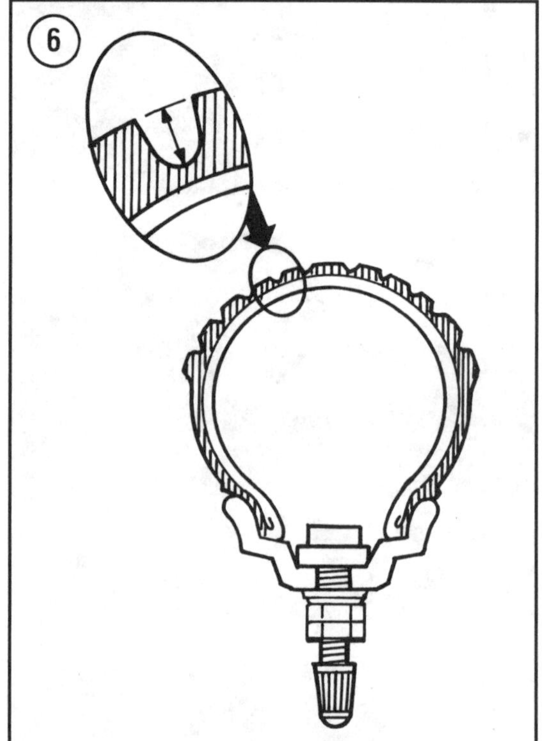


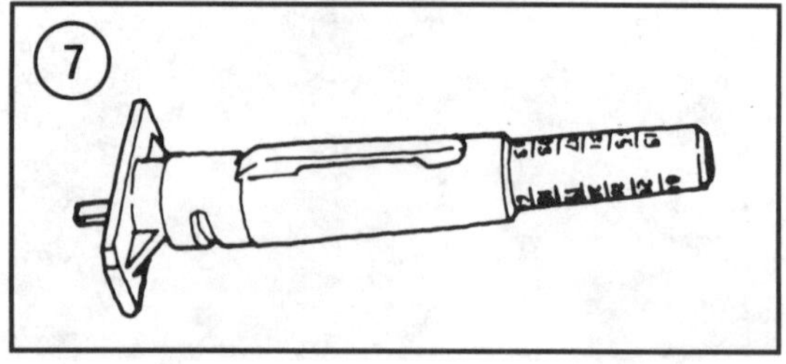

### Tire Inspection

The tires take a lot of punishment so inspect them periodically for excessive wear, cuts, abrasions, etc. If you find a nail or other object in the tire, mark its location with a light crayon before removing it. This will help locate the hole for repair. Refer to Chapter Nine for tire changing and repair information.



Check local traffic regulations concerning minimum tread depth. Measure the tread depth (**Figure 6**) of the tire tread using a tread depth gauge (**Figure 7**) or small ruler. Suzuki recommends that original equipment tires be replaced when the tread depth has worn to the following dimension or less:

a. Front tire: 1.6 mm (0.06 in.).
b. Rear tire: 2.0 mm (0.08 in.).

### Rim Inspection

Frequently inspect the wheel rims. If a rim has been damaged, it might have been enough to knock it out of alignment. Improper wheel alignment can cause severe vibration and result in an unsafe riding condition.

## BATTERY

### Removal, Installation and Electrolyte Level Check

The battery is the heart of the electrical system. Check and service the battery at the interval indicated in **Table 2**. The majority of electrical system troubles can be attributed to neglect of this vital component.

1. Remove the seat as described in Chapter Twelve.
2. Remove the screws securing the right-hand and left-hand frame covers (**Figure 8**).
3. First, disconnect the battery negative (–) lead (**Figure 9**).
4. Using the ignition key, unlock and remove the tool holder cover (**Figure 10**).
5. Remove the tool pouch from the tool holder.
6. Remove the screws (**Figure 11**) securing the tool holder and remove the tool holder (**Figure 12**).
7. Disconnect the breather tube (**Figure 13**) from the battery. Leave the breather tube routed through the frame.

8. Pull back the rubber boot (A, **Figure 14**) and disconnect the battery positive (+) lead (B, **Figure 14**).

9. Carefully slide the battery out of the battery case.

10. The electrolyte level should be maintained between the 2 marks on the battery case.

*WARNING*

*Protect your eyes, skin and clothing. If electrolyte gets into your eyes, flush your eyes thoroughly with clean water and get prompt medical attention.*

*CAUTION*

*Be careful not to spill battery electrolyte on plastic, painted or plated surfaces. The liquid is highly corrosive and will damage the finish. If it is spilled, wash it off immediately with soapy water and thoroughly rinse with clean water.*

11. Remove the cap from the battery cells and add distilled water to correct the level. *Never* add electrolyte (acid) to correct the level.

*NOTE*

*If distilled water has been added, reinstall the battery caps and gently shake the battery for several minutes to mix the existing electrolyte with the new water.*

*CAUTION*

*If distilled water is going to be added to a battery in freezing or near freezing weather; add it to the battery, dress warmly and then ride the bike for a minimum of 30 minutes. This will help mix the just added water into the electrolyte in the battery. Distilled water is lighter than electrolyte and will float on top of the electrolyte if it is not mixed in properly. If the water stays on the top, it may freeze and fracture the battery case.*

12. After the fluid level has been corrected and the battery allowed to stand for a few minutes, remove the battery caps and check the specific gravity of the electrolyte with a hydrometer (**Figure 15**). See *Testing* in this section.

13. After the battery has been refilled, recharged or replaced, install it by reversing these removal steps.

*CAUTION*

*If the breather tube was removed from the frame, be sure to route it so that residue will not drain onto any part of the bike's frame as shown in **Figure 16**. The tube must be free of bends or twists as any restrictions may pressurize the battery and damage it.*

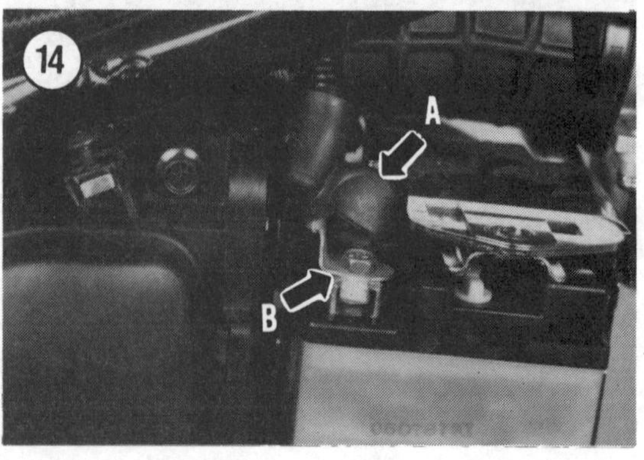

### Testing

Hydrometer testing is the best way to check battery condition. Use a hydrometer with numbered graduations from 1.100 to 1.300 rather than one with color-coded bands. To use the hydrometer, squeeze the rubber ball, insert the tip into the cell and release the pressure on the ball. Draw enough electrolyte to float the weighted float inside the hydrometer. Note the number in line with the surface of the electrolyte; this is the specific gravity for this cell. Squeeze the rubber ball again and return the electrolyte to the cell from which it came.

The specific gravity of the electrolyte in each battery cell is an excellent indication of that cell's condition. A fully charged cell will read from 1.260-1.280, while a cell in good condition reads from 1.230-1.250 and anything below 1.140 is discharged.

Specific gravity varies with temperature. For each 10° the electrolyte temperature exceeds 27° C (80° F), add 0.004 to readings indicated on the hydrometer. Subtract 0.004 for each 10° below 27° C (80° F).

If the cells test in the poor range, the battery requires recharging. The hydrometer is useful for checking the progress of the charging operation. **Table 3** shows approximate state of charge.

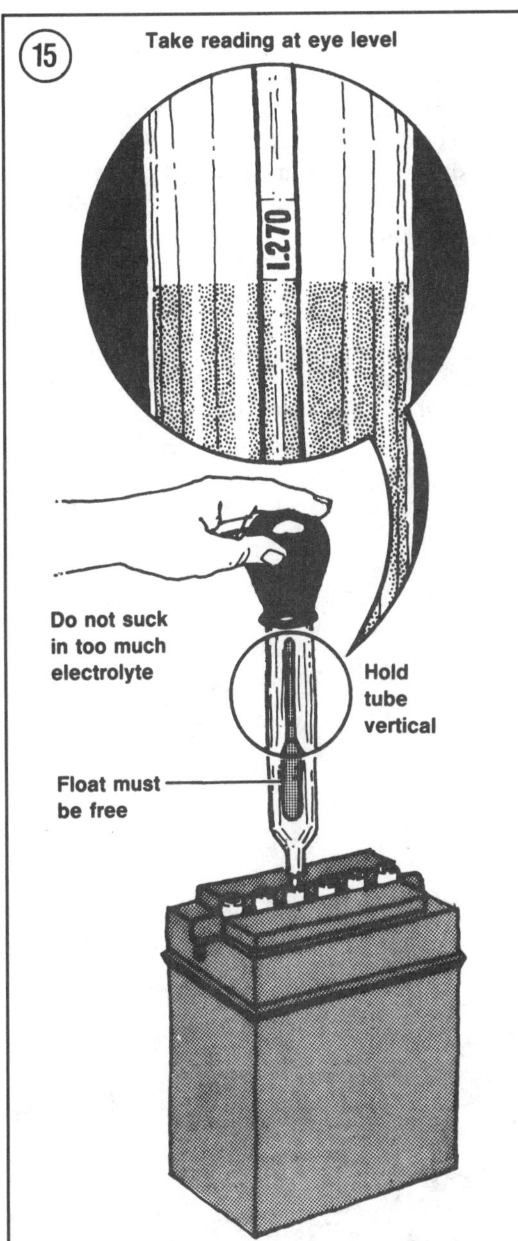


### Charging

*WARNING*

*During the charging process, highly explosive hydrogen gas is released from the battery. The battery should be charged only in a well-ventilated area away from any open flames (including pilot lights on home gas appliances). Do not allow any smoking in the area.*

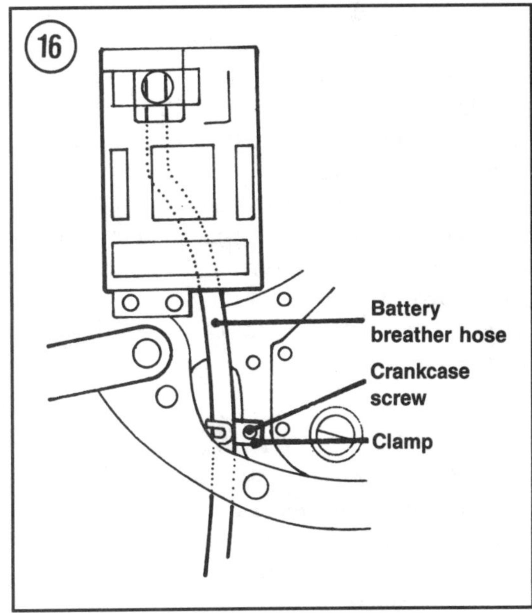

*Never check the charge by arcing (connecting pliers or other metal objects) across the terminals; the resulting spark can ignite the hydrogen gas.*

*CAUTION*
*Always remove the battery from the bike's frame before connecting the battery charger. Never recharge a battery in the bike's frame; the corrosive mist that is emitted during the charging process will corrode all surrounding surfaces.*

1. Connect the positive (+) charger lead to the positive (+) battery terminal and the negative (-) charger lead to the negative (-) battery terminal.
2. Remove all vent caps from the battery, set the charger to 12 volts and switch the charger ON. If the output of the charger is variable, it is best to select a low setting—1 1/2 to 2 amps.

*CAUTION*
*The electrolyte level must be maintained at the upper level during the charging cycle; check and refill as necessary.*

3. After the battery has been charged for about 8 hours, turn the charger OFF, disconnect the leads and check the specific gravity of each cell. It should be within the limits specified in **Table 3**. If it is, and remains stable for 1 hour, the battery is considered charged.
4. Clean the battery terminals, electrical cable connectors and surrounding case and reinstall the battery in the frame, reversing the removal steps. Coat the battery terminals with Vaseline or silicone spray to retard corrosion and decomposition of the terminals.

*CAUTION*
*Route the breather tube so that is does not drain onto any part of the frame. The tube must be free of bends or twists as any restriction may pressurize the battery and damage it.*

### New Battery Installation

When replacing the old battery with a new one, be sure to charge it completely (specific gravity 1.260-1.280) before installing it in the bike. Failure to do so or using the battery with a low electrolyte level will permanently damage the new battery.

## PERIODIC LUBRICATION

### Oil

Oil is graded according to its viscosity, which is an indication of how thick it is. The Society of Automotive Engineers (SAE) system distinguishes oil viscosity by numbers. Thick oils have higher viscosity numbers than thin oils. For example, an SAE 5 oil is a thin oil while an SAE 90 oil is relatively thick.

### Grease

A good-quality grease (preferably waterproof) should be used (**Figure 17**). Water does not wash grease off parts as easily as it washes oil off. In addition, grease maintains its lubricating qualities

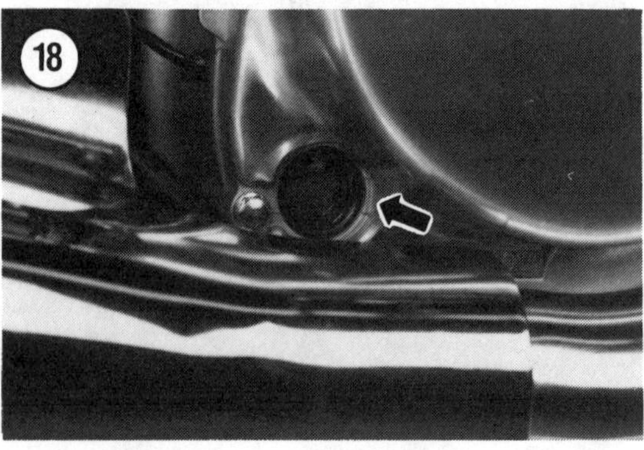

better than oil on long and strenuous rides. In a pinch, though, the wrong lubricant is better than none at all. Correct the situation as soon as possible.

### Engine Oil Level Check

Engine oil level is checked with the oil level inspection window, located at the right-hand side of the engine on the clutch cover.

1. Place the bike on level ground.
2. Start the engine and let it idle for 2-3 minutes.
3. Shut off the engine and let the oil settle for 1-2 minutes.
4. Have an assistant hold the bike in the true vertical position. A false reading will be given if the bike is tipped either to the right or left.
5. Look at the oil level inspection window. The oil level should be at the "F" mark (**Figure 18**). If the level is below the lower "F" line, add the recommended weight engine oil (**Figure 19**) to correct the level.

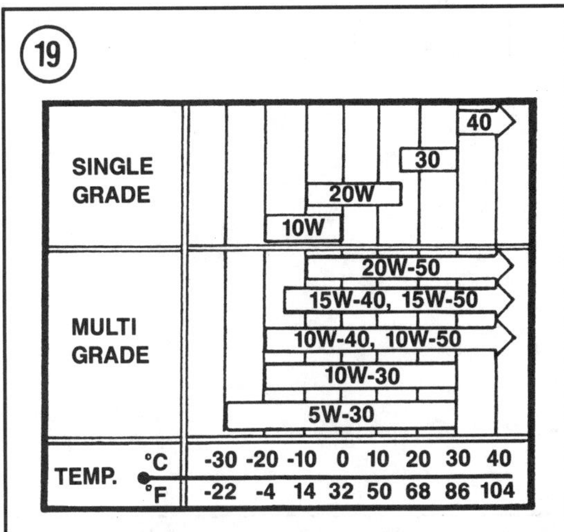


19

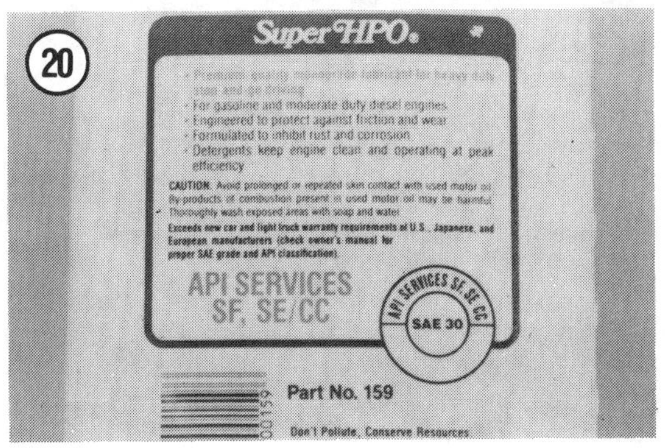


20

### Engine Oil and Oil Filter Change

Change the engine oil and the oil filter at the same time at the factory-recommended oil change interval indicated in **Table 2**. This assumes that the motorcycle is operated in moderate climates. In extreme climates, oil should be changed every 30 days. The time interval is more important than the mileage interval because acids formed by combustion blowby will contaminate the oil even if the motorcycle is not run for several months. If the motorcycle is operated under dusty conditions, the oil will get dirty more quickly and should be changed more frequently than recommended.

Use only a high-quality detergent motor oil with an API classification of SE or SF. The quality rating is stamped on top of the can or printed on the label on the plastic bottle (**Figure 20**). Try to use the same brand of oil at each change. Use of oil additives is not recommended as it may cause clutch slippage (wet-clutch models). Refer to **Figure 19** for correct oil viscosity to use under anticipated ambient temperatures (not engine oil temperature).

*CAUTION*

*Do not add any friction-reducing additives to the oil as they will cause clutch slippage. Do not use an engine oil with graphite added. The use of graphite oil will void any applicable Suzuki warranty. It is not established at this time if graphite will build up on the clutch friction plates and cause clutch problems. Until further testing is done by the oil and motorcycle industries, do not use this type of oil.*

To change the engine oil and filter (**Figure 21**) you will need the following:

a. Drain pan.
b. Funnel.
c. Can opener or pour spout (oil in cans).
d. 17 mm wrench (drain plug).
e. Oil filter wrench.
f. Oil (refer to **Table 4** for quantity).
g. New oil filter element.

There are a number of ways to discard the old oil safely. Some service stations and oil retailers will accept your used oil for recycling; some may

3

even give you money for it. Never drain the oil onto the ground nor place it in your household trash.

1. Start the engine and let it reach operating temperature; 15-20 minutes of stop-and-go riding is usually sufficient.

2. Turn the engine off and place the bike on level ground on the sidestand.

3. Place a drain pan under the left-hand side of the crankcase and remove the 17 mm drain plug (**Figure 22**). Remove the dipstick/oil filler cap (**Figure 23**); this will speed up the flow of oil.

4. Inspect the sealing washer on the crankcase drain plug. Replace it if its condition is in doubt.

5. Install the drain plug and sealing washer and tighten to the torque specification listed in **Table 5**.

6. Move the drain pan under the right-hand crankcase cover.

*WARNING*

*Protect your hands from the exhaust header pipe. The exhaust system will be **HOT** and is very close to the oil filter cover.*

(21)

**OIL FILTER ASSEMBLY**

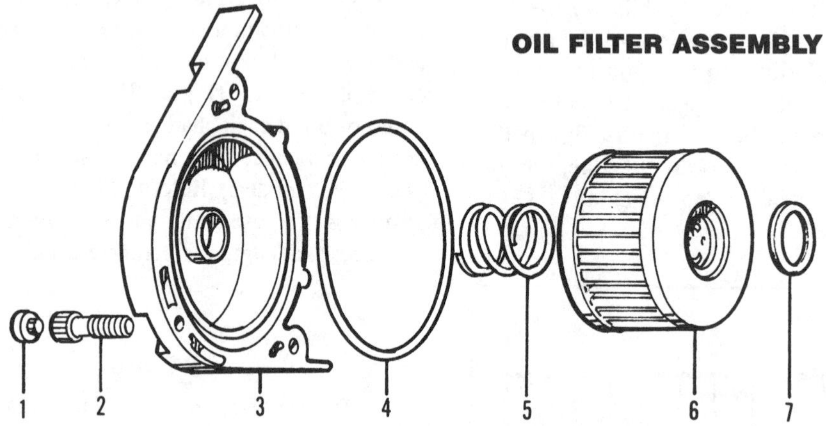

1 2 3 4 5 6 7

1. Trim cap
2. Allen bolt
3. Cover
4. O-ring seal
5. Spring
6. Oil filter
7. O-ring seal

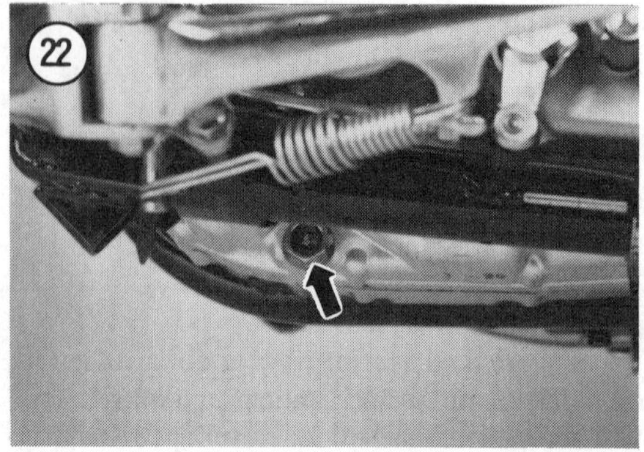

7. Remove the bolts (**Figure 24**) securing the oil filter cover on the right-hand crankcase cover.

*NOTE*

*Some residual oil will run out after the oil filter cover is removed. If possible, lean the bike over to the left. This will keep most of the oil within the oil filter recess in the right-hand crankcase cover and allow it to drain back into the engine.*

8. Remove the oil filter cover; don't lose the small spring (**Figure 25**) on the center inner surface of the cover. Don't lose the O-ring seal in the cover.
9. Remove the oil filter (**Figure 26**) and place it in a plastic bag to keep the oil from running out of it.
10. Clean out the oil filter recess in the right-hand crankcase cover (A, **Figure 27**) with a shop rag and cleaning solvent. Remove any oil sludge if necessary. Wipe it dry with a clean, lint-free cloth.
11. Inspect the O-ring seal (B, **Figure 27**) for deterioration; replace if necessary.
12. If removed, install a new O-ring seal (**Figure 28**) on oil filter mounting flange in right-hand crankcase cover.
13. Make sure the O-ring seal (**Figure 29**) is in place in the recess in the cover. Make sure it is correctly seated to prevent an oil leak.
14. Apply a light coat of clean engine oil to the O-ring seal in the oil filter cover and to the O-ring seal in the recess in the right-hand crankcase cover.
15. Install the new oil filter, with the open end going in first, into the recess in the right-hand crankcase cover.
16. Make sure the spring (**Figure 25**) is in the center of the oil filter cover and install the cover.

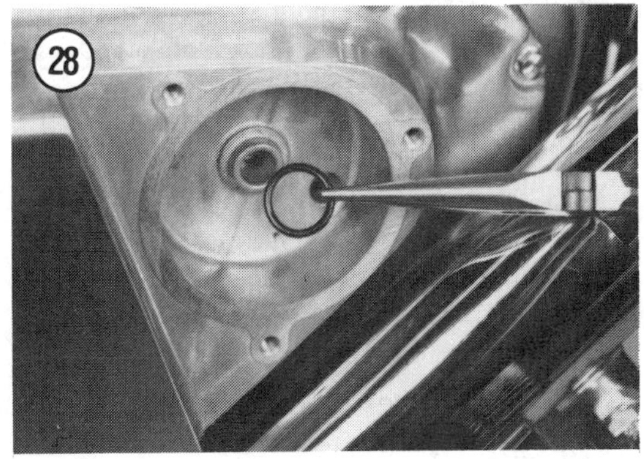


3

17. Install the bolts securing the cover and tighten in a crisscross pattern. Tighten the bolts securely.
18. During oil filter removal, some oil may have dripped onto the exhaust header pipe. Before starting the engine, wipe off any spilled oil with a shop cloth. If necessary, spray some electrical contact cleaner on the pipe to remove the oil residue. If the oil is not cleaned off, it will smoke once the exhaust pipe gets hot.
19. Insert a funnel into the oil fill hole and fill the engine with the correct viscosity and quantity of oil. Refer to **Table 4**.
20. Install the dipstick/oil filler cap.
21. Remove the oil drain pan from under the engine and discard the oil properly.
22. Start the engine, let it run at idle speed and check for leaks.
23. Turn the engine off and check for correct oil level; adjust as necessary.

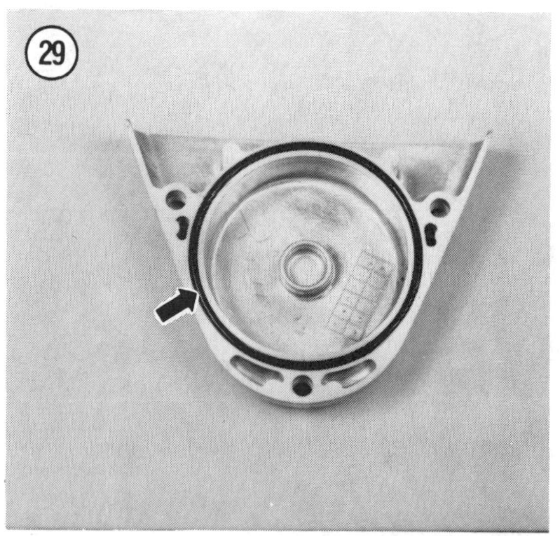


### Front Fork Oil Change

It is a good practice to change the fork oil at the interval listed in **Table 2** or once a year. If it becomes contaminated with dirt or water, change it immediately.

The front forks are not equipped with a drain screw. In order to change the fork oil, the forks must be removed from the bike.

1. Remove one of the front fork assemblies as described in Chapter Nine.
2. Remove the spacer and the spring seat (A, **Figure 30**).
3. Place a shop cloth around the top of the fork tube and withdraw the fork spring (B, **Figure 30**) from the fork tube.
4. Turn the fork assembly upside down in a drain pan and let the oil drain out. Let the oil drain for 10-15 minutes.
5. Stroke the fork assembly in and out several times (**Figure 31**) to expel as much of the old fork oil as possible.

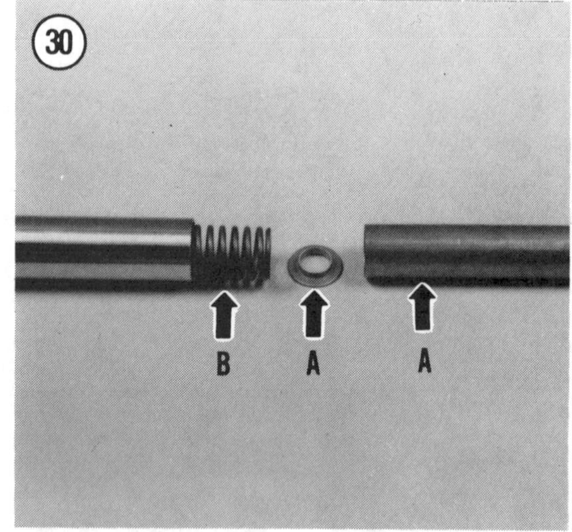


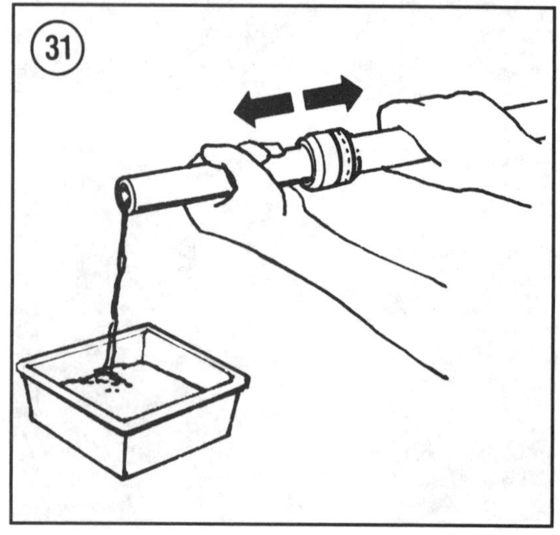


*NOTE*
*Suzuki recommends that the fork oil level be measured, if possible, to ensure a more accurate filling.*

*NOTE*
*To measure the correct amount of fluid, use a plastic baby bottle. These*

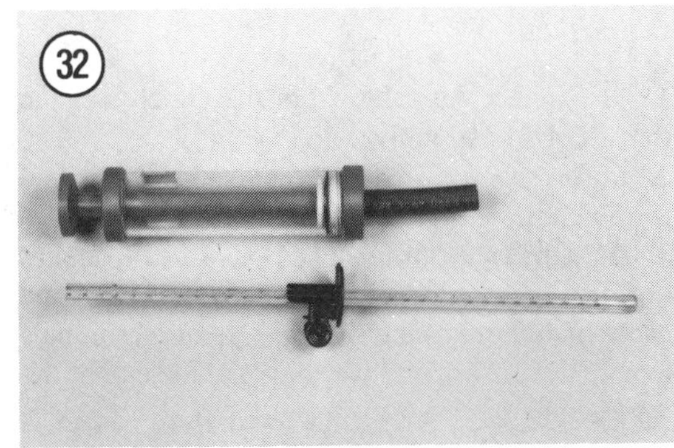


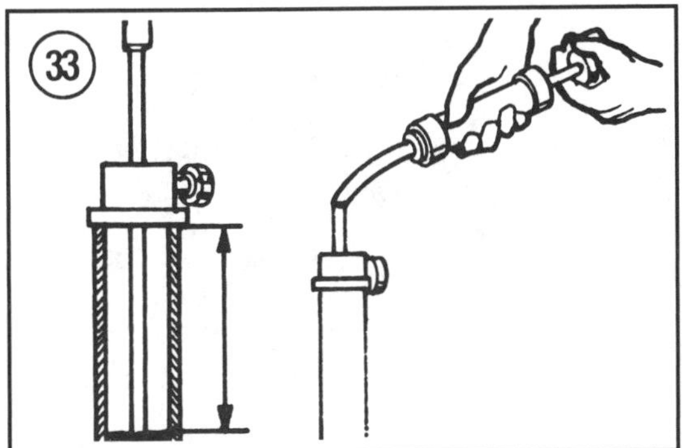


*bottles have measurements in fluid ounces (oz.) and cubic centimeters (cc) on the side.*

6. Compress the fork completely.
7. Add 441 cc (14.91 oz.) of SAE 15 fork oil to the fork assembly.
8. Hold the fork assembly as close to perfectly vertical as possible.
9. Use an accurate ruler or the Suzuki oil level gauge (part No. 09943-74111), or equivalent (**Figure 32**), to achieve the correct oil level of 75 mm (2.95 in.). Refer to **Figure 33**.

*NOTE*

*An oil level measuring devise can be made as shown in **Figure 34**. Position the lower edge of the hose clamp the specified oil level distance up from the small diameter hole. Fill the fork with a few cubic centimeters more than the required amount of oil. Position the hose clamp on the top edge of the fork tube and draw out the excess oil. Oil*

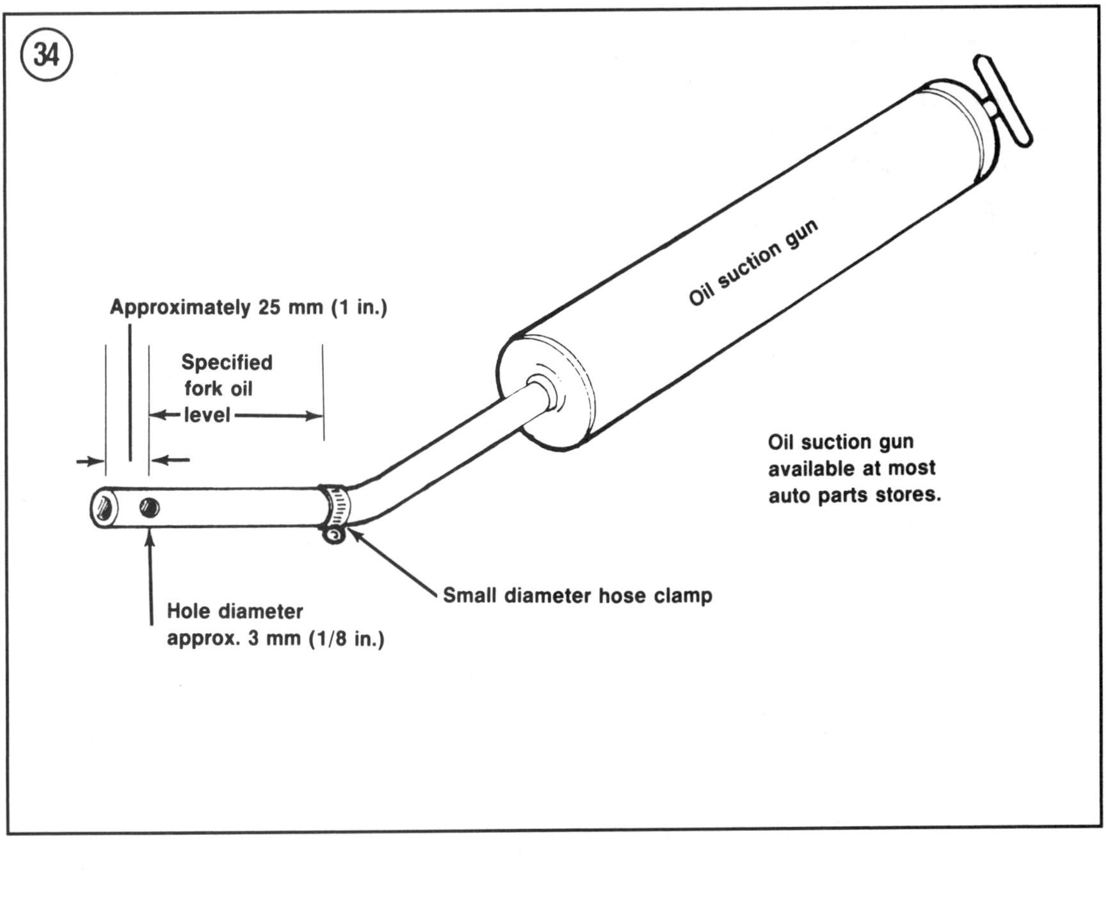

34

Oil suction gun

Approximately 25 mm (1 in.)

Specified fork oil level

Oil suction gun available at most auto parts stores.

Small diameter hose clamp

Hole diameter approx. 3 mm (1/8 in.)

*is sucked out until the level reaches the small diameter hole. A precise oil level can be achieved with this simple device.*

10. Allow the oil to settle completely and recheck the oil level measurement. Adjust the oil level if necessary.
11. Install the fork spring with the wide pitch coils (**Figure 35**) going in first.
12. Inspect the O-ring seal (**Figure 36**) on the fork cap bolt; replace if necessary.
13. Install the spring seat and spacer.
14. Install the front fork assembly as described in Chapter Nine.
15. After the fork assembly has been installed; tighten the fork cap bolt to the torque specification listed in **Table 5**.
16. Repeat Steps 1-15 for the other fork assembly.
17. Road test the bike and check for leaks.

## Control Cables

The control cables should be lubricated at the interval listed in **Table 2**. They should also be inspected at this time for fraying and the cable sheath checked for chafing. The cables are relatively inexpensive and should be replaced when found to be faulty.

The control cables can be lubricated either with oil or any popular cable lubricants and a cable lubricator. The first method requires more time and the complete lubrication of the entire cable is less certain.

On the throttle cable it is necessary to remove the screws securing the right-hand switch assembly together to gain access to the throttle cable end.

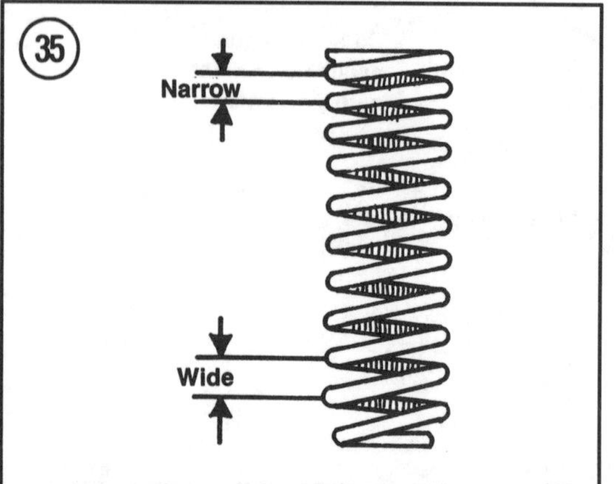


### *Oil method*

1. Disconnect the cable from the clutch and the throttle grip assembly.
2. Make a cone of stiff paper and tape it to the end of the cable sheath (**Figure 37**).
3. Hold the cable upright and pour a small amount of thin oil (SAE 10W-30) into the cone. Work the cable in and out of the sheath for several minutes to help the oil work its way down to the end of the cable.

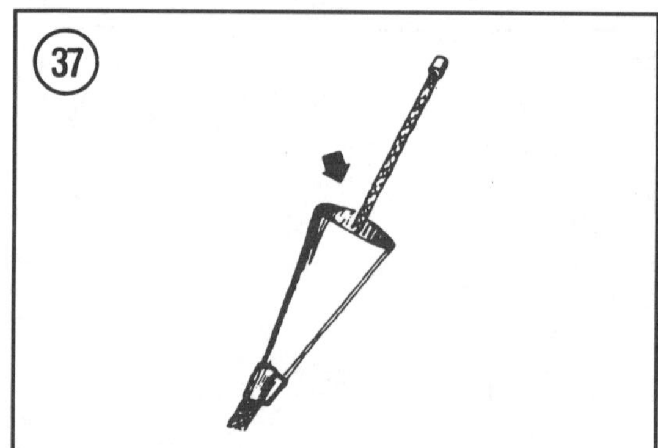


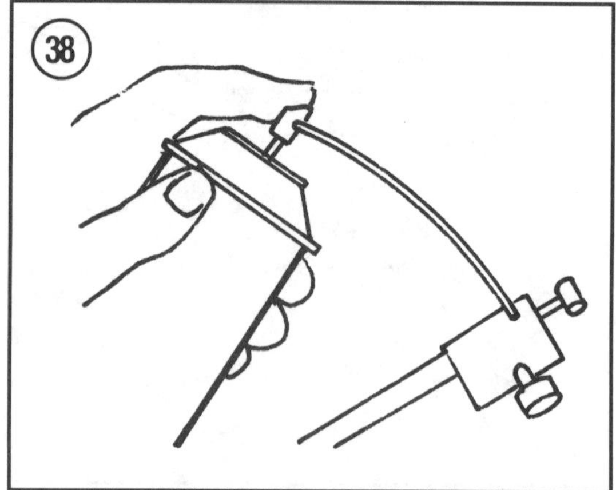

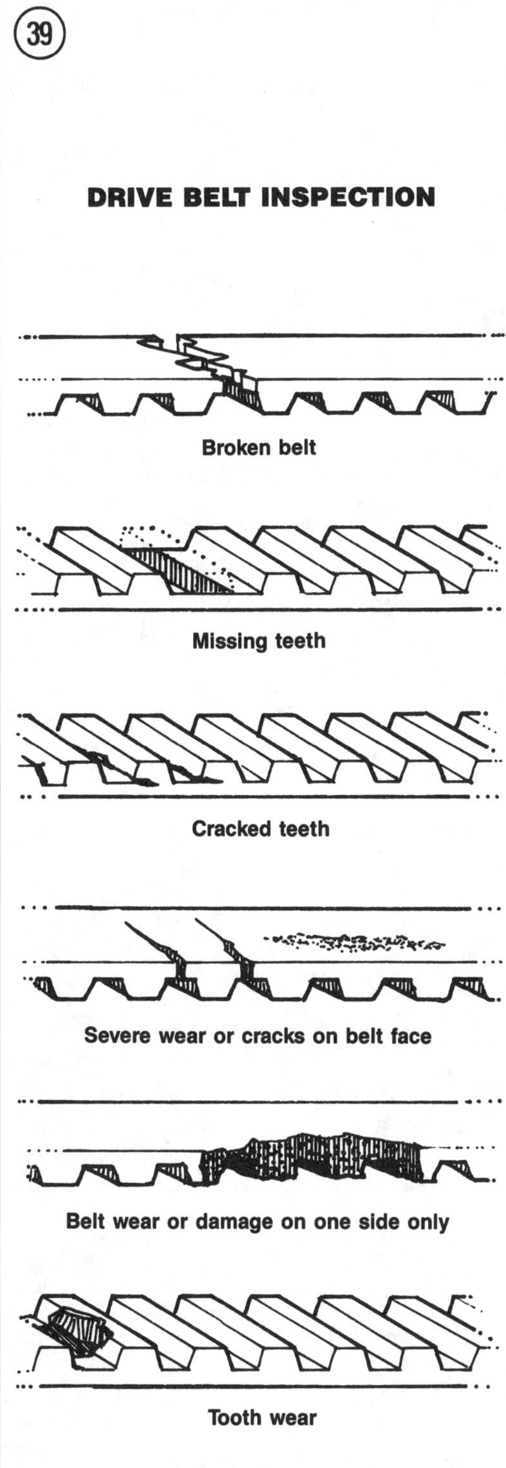


*NOTE*
*To avoid a mess, place a shop cloth at the end of the cable to catch the oil as it runs out.*

4. Remove the cone, reconnect the cable and adjust the cable(s) as described in this chapter.

*NOTE*
*While the throttle cable is removed and the switch assembly disassembled, apply a light coat of grease to the metal surfaces of the throttle grip assembly.*

### *Lubricator method*

1. Disconnect the cable from the clutch and the throttle grip assembly.
2. Attach a lubricator following the manufacturer's instructions (**Figure 38**).
3. Insert the nozzle of the lubricant can in the lubricator, press the button on the can and hold down until the lubricant begins to flow out of the other end of the cable.
4. Remove the lubricator, reconnect the cable(s) and adjust the cable as described in this chapter.

### Miscellaneous Lubrication Points

Lubricate the clutch lever, front brake lever, sidestand pivot point and the footpeg pivot points. Use SAE 10W-40 engine oil.

## PERIODIC MAINTENANCE

### Drive Belt Inspection

The drive belt should be inspected at the interval listed in **Table 2** or more often if ridden in wet or dusty conditions.

1. Place the transmission in NEUTRAL.
2. Place wood block(s) under the frame and engine until the rear wheel is off the ground. Support the bike securely.
3. Slowly rotate the rear wheel by hand and observe the drive belt as it passes by.
4. Check the inner (tooth side) and outer (smooth side) surfaces of the belt for wear or damage as shown in **Figure 39**.

5. If the drive belt exhibits any of these problems, replace the drive belt as described under *Drive Belt Removal/Installation* in Chapter Ten.
6. Remove the wood block(s) from under the engine.

## Drive Belt Adjustment

The drive belt tension should be checked and adjusted at the interval listed in **Table 2** or more often if ridden in wet or dusty conditions. The adjustment procedure must be performed with the Suzuki special tool (**Figure 40**) furnished in the factory tool kit.

1. Place the bike on the sidestand for the most accurate adjustment.
2. Place the transmission in NEUTRAL.
3. Place the drive belt tensioner adjuster as follows:
   a. Place the upper portion in the receptacle in the swing arm (**Figure 41**).
   b. Place the lower portion on one of the drive belt teeth (**Figure 42**).
4. The drive belt tension is correct if the centerline on the adjuster aligns with the end of the case (**Figure 43**). If the tension is not correct, proceed to Step 5.
5. Loosen the axle nut (**Figure 44**).
6. Loosen the adjuster bolt locknut (A, **Figure 45**) on each side.
7. Turn the adjuster bolt (B, **Figure 45**) in either direction, in equal amounts, to either increase or decrease drive belt tension. After adjustment is complete, make sure the mark on the drive belt adjusters are on the same scale mark (**Figure 46**) on the swing arm on both sides.
8. Tighten the adjuster bolt locknut (A, **Figure 45**) securely on each side.

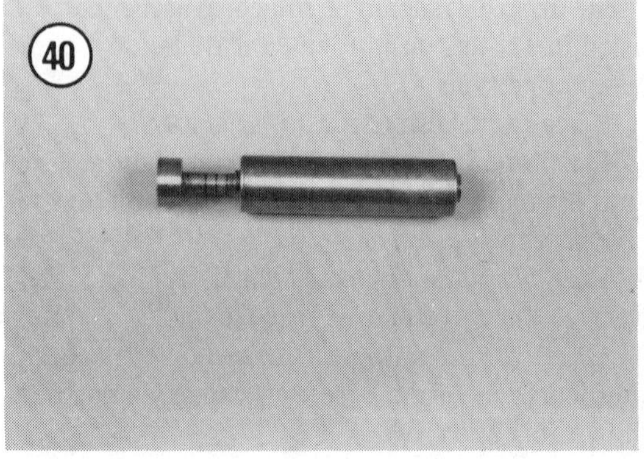
40

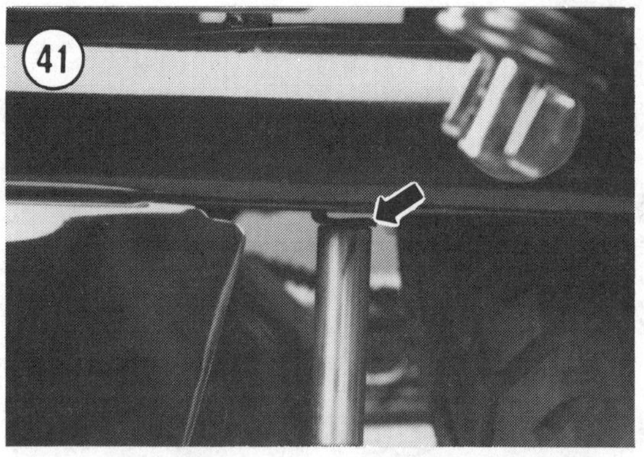
41

42

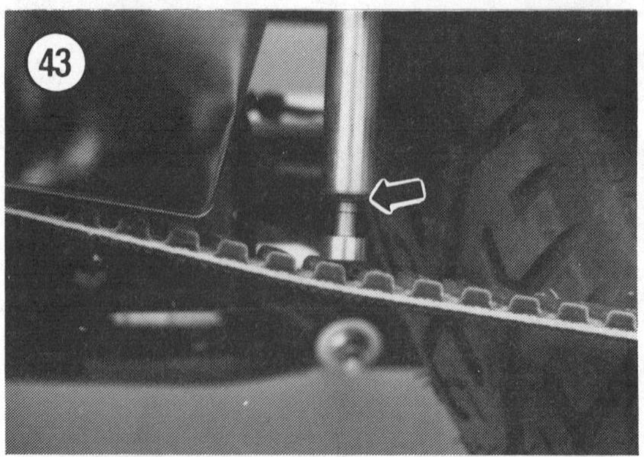
43

44

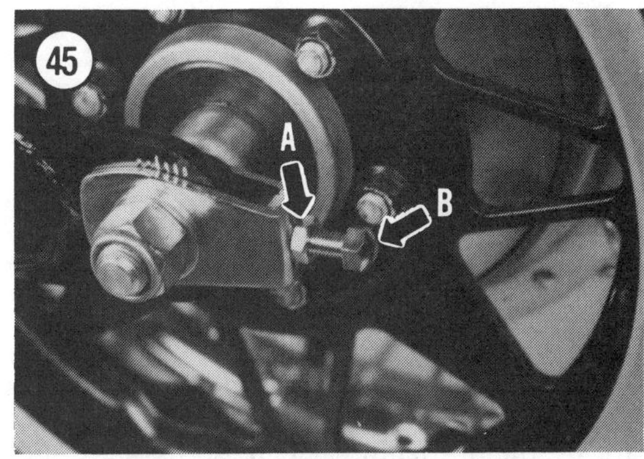

9. Roll the bike forward to rotate the rear wheel to move the belt to another position and recheck the free play; belts tend to wear or stretch more evenly than chains do, but the free play may not remain constant over the entire length.

*WARNING*

*Excessive free play can result in drive belt damage or shredding which could cause a serious accident.*

10. If the drive belt cannot be adjusted within the limits, it is excessively worn and stretched and should be replaced.
11. Tighten the rear axle nut to the torque specification listed in **Table 5**.
12. Make sure the adjuster bolt locknuts are tightened securely on each side.

## Disc Brake Fluid Level

The fluid level should be between the upper and lower marks within the reservoir. If the brake fluid level reaches the lower level mark, visible through the viewing port (**Figure 47**) on the master cylinder reservoir, the fluid level must be corrected by adding fresh brake fluid.

1. Place the bike on level ground and position the handlebars so the front master cylinder reservoir is *level*.
2. Clean any dirt from the area around the top cover before removing the cover.
3. Remove the screws securing the top cover. Remove the top cover (**Figure 48**) and the diaphragm.

*NOTE*

***Figure 49** is shown with the master cylinder removed and disassembled for clarity. It is not necessary to remove or disassemble the master cylinder to perform this procedure.*

4. Add brake fluid until the level is to the upper level line within the master cylinder reservoir (**Figure 49**).

*WARNING*

*Use only brake fluid from a sealed container and clearly marked DOT 3 or DOT 4 (specified for disc brakes).*

*Others may vaporize and cause brake failure. Do not intermix different brands or types of brake fluid as they may not be compatible. Do not intermix a silicone based (DOT 5) brake fluid as it can cause brake component damage leading to brake system failure.*

*CAUTION*

*Be careful when handling brake fluid. Do not spill it on painted or plated surfaces or plastic parts as it will destroy the surface. Wash the area immediately with soapy water and thoroughly rinse it off.*

5. Reinstall the diaphragm and the top cover. Tighten the screws securely.

### Disc Brake Lines

Check brake line between the master cylinder and the brake caliper. If there is any leakage, tighten the connections and bleed the brakes as described under *Bleeding the System* in Chapter Eleven. If this does not stop the leak or if a brake line is obviously damaged, cracked or chafed, replace the brake line and bleed the system.

### Disc Brake Pad Wear

Inspect the brake pads for excessive or uneven wear.

1. Remove the bolts, lockwashers and washers (**Figure 50**) securing the caliper to the front fork slider.
2. Carefully slide the caliper assembly off of the brake disc.
3. Look into the caliper assembly and check the wear grooves on the brake pads.
4. Replace both pads if the wear line on the pads reaches the brake disc. Replace the pads as described under *Front Brake Pad Replacement* in Chapter Eleven.
5. If the brake pads are okay; perform the following:
   a. Carefully reinstall the brake caliper assembly onto the brake disc. Do not damage the leading edge of the brake pads during installation.
   b. Install the caliper mounting bolts, lockwashers and washers.
   c. Tighten the caliper mounting bolts to the torque specification listed in **Table 5**.

### Disc Brake Fluid Change

Every time the reservoir cap is removed, a small amount of dirt and moisture enters the brake fluid. The same thing happens if a leak occurs or any part of the hydraulic system is loosened or

disconnected. Dirt can clog the system and cause unnecessary wear. Water in the brake fluid vaporizes at high temperature, impairing the hydraulic action and reducing the brake's stopping ability.

To maintain peak performance, change the brake fluid as indicated in **Table 2**. To change brake fluid, follow the *Bleeding the System* procedure in Chapter Eleven. Continue adding new fluid to the master cylinders and bleeding out at the calipers until the fluid leaving the caliper is clean and free of contaminants.

*WARNING*

*Use only brake fluid from a sealed container and clearly marked DOT 3 or DOT 4 (specified for disc brakes). Others may vaporize and cause brake failure. Do not intermix different brands or types of brake fluid as they may not be compatible. Do not intermix a silicone based (DOT 5) brake fluid as it can cause brake component damage leading to brake system failure.*

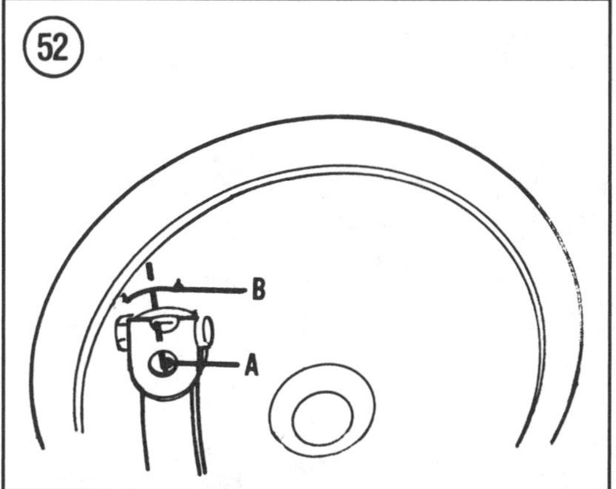


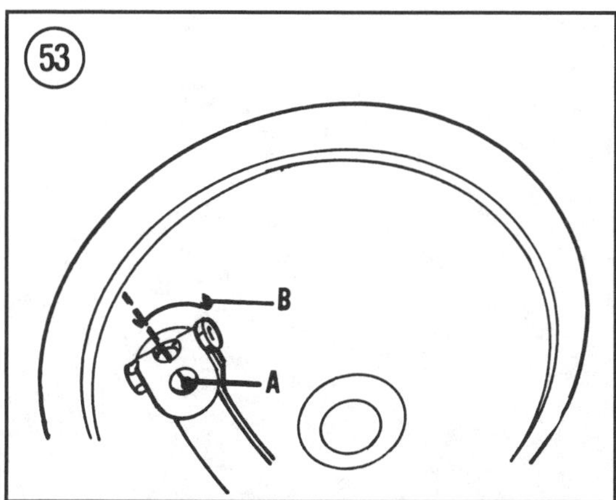


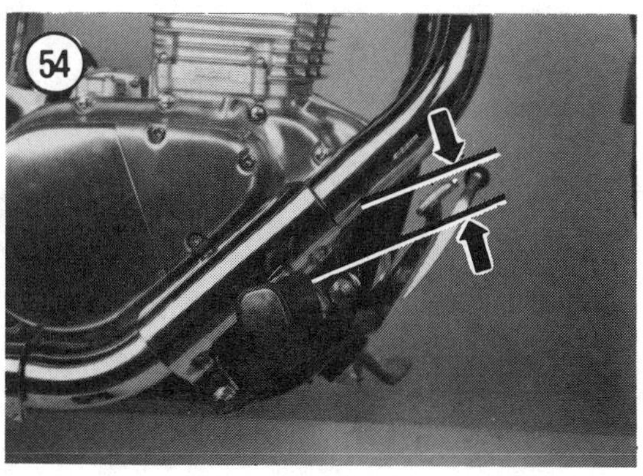


## Rear Brake Lining Wear Indicator

The rear brake is equipped with a brake lining wear indicator (**Figure 51**). This enables you to check the brake lining condition without removing the rear wheel and brake assembly for inspection purposes.

1. Apply the rear brake fully.
2. Observe where the line on the brake camshaft (A, **Figure 52**) falls within the embossed wear range (B, **Figure 52**) on the brake panel.
3. If the line falls within this range, the brake lining thickness is within specification and does not requirc any service.
4. If the line falls outside of this range (**Figure 53**), the brake lining is worn to the point that it requires replacement.
5. If necessary, replace the rear brake linings as described under *Rear Drum Brake* in Chapter Eleven.

## Rear Brake Pedal Height and Freeplay Adjustment

The rear brake pedal height and freeplay should be adjusted at the interval listed in **Table 2**. The pedal height will change with brake shoe wear. The top of the bráke pedal should be positioned 60 mm (2.4 in.) above the top *flat* surface of the footpeg (**Figure 54**). The brake pedal freeplay should be 20-30 mm (0.8-1.2 in.) (**Figure 55**).

1. Make sure the brake pedal is in the at-rest position.

*NOTE*

***Figure 56** is shown with the rear brake pedal assembly removed from the frame for clarity. The locknut and adjuster bolt can be reached from under the pedal assembly without removing the assembly.*

2. To change height position, loosen the locknut (A, **Figure 56**) and turn the adjuster bolt (B, **Figure 56**) until the correct height is achieved. Tighten the locknut (A) securely.
3. To change the freeplay adjustment, turn the adjust nut (**Figure 57**) at the end of the brake cable. Turn the adjust nut in either direction until the correct amount of freeplay is achieved.

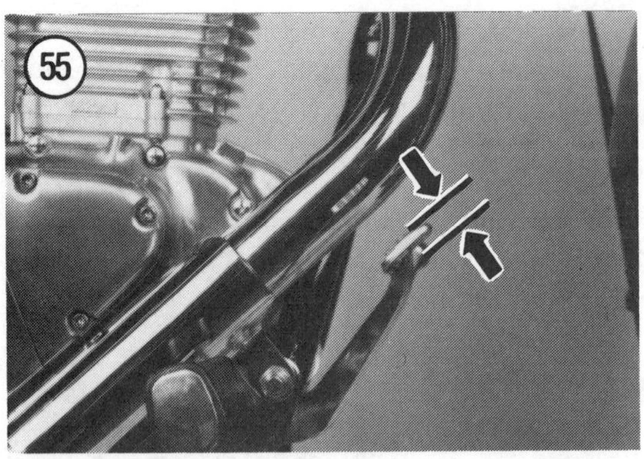

55

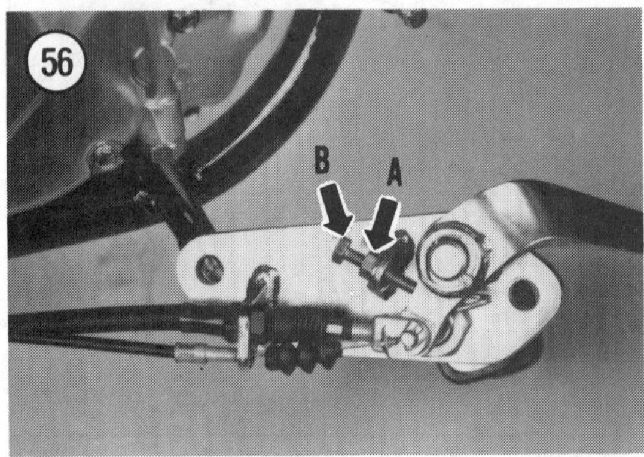


56

### Clutch Adjustment

Adjust the clutch at the interval indicated in **Table 2**. For the clutch to fully engage and disengage, there must be 3 mm (0.12 in.) of free play between the lever and the lever housing (**Figure 58**).

1. Minor adjustments can be made at the upper adjuster at the hand lever as follows:
   a. Slide the rubber boot (**Figure 59**) off the adjuster and locknut.
   b. Loosen the locknut (A, **Figure 60**) and turn the adjuster (B, **Figure 60**) in or out to obtain the correct amount of free play.

*NOTE*

*If the proper amount of free play cannot be achieved at the hand lever, additional adjustment can be made at the clutch actuating lever on the right-hand crankcase cover.*

2. Major adjustments are made at the clutch actuating lever as follows:
   a. At the clutch lever, loosen the locknut and turn the adjuster (B, **Figure 60**) in all the way toward the hand grip.
   b. At the right-hand crankcase cover, loosen the locknuts (A, **Figure 61**) and turn the adjuster (B, **Figure 61**) until the correct amount of free play can be achieved.
   c. Tighten the locknuts (A, **Figure 61**).
3. If necessary, do some final adjusting at the clutch lever as described in Step 1.

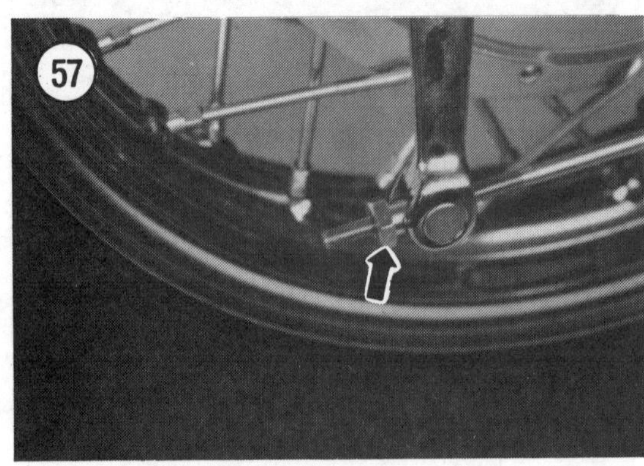

57

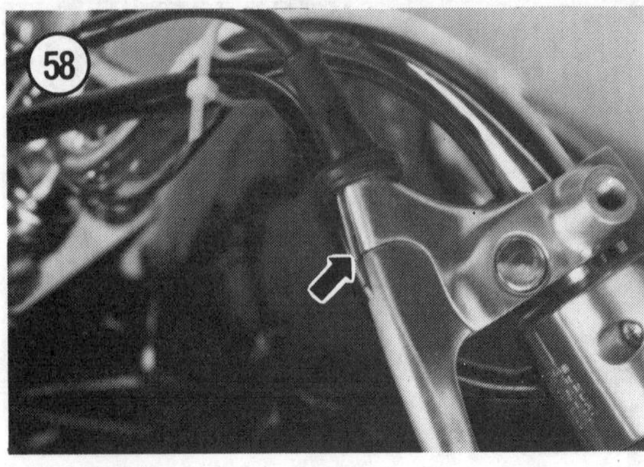

58

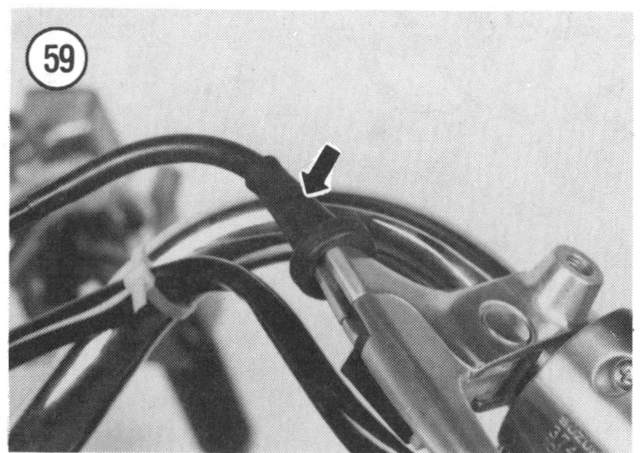


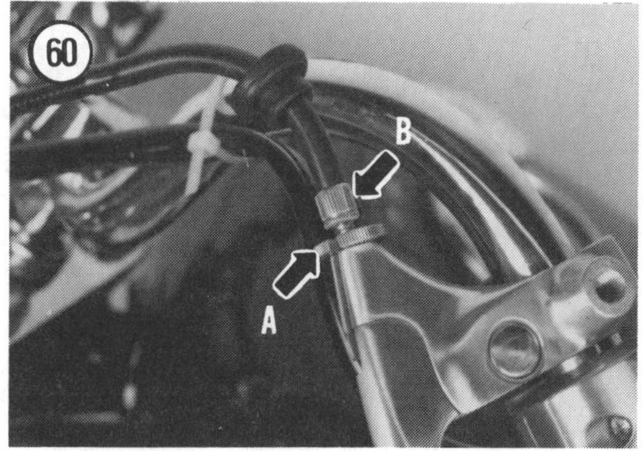


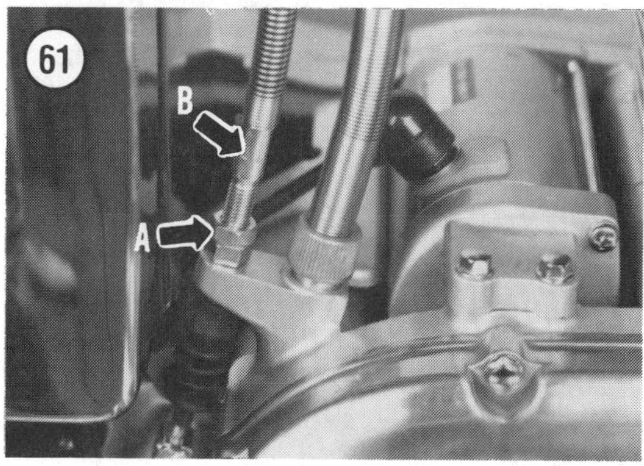


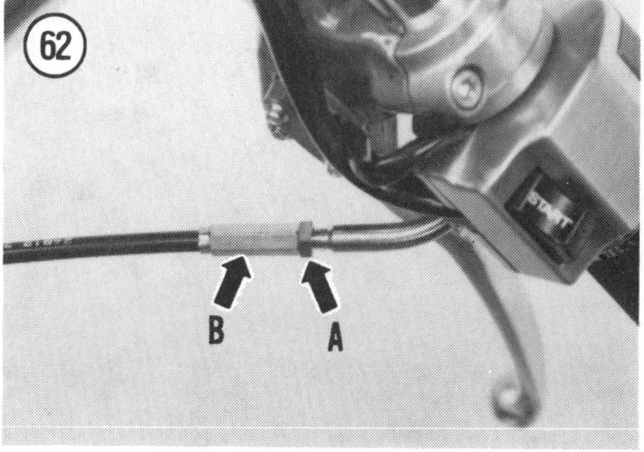


4. After adjustment is complete, check that the locknut(s) is tight at the clutch actuating lever on the crankcase cover and at the hand lever.
5. Road test the bike to make sure the clutch fully disengages when the lever is pulled in; if it does not, the bike will creep in gear when stopped. Make sure the clutch fully engages; if it does not, the clutch will slip, particularly when accelerating in high gear.
6. If the proper amount of adjustment cannot be achieved using this procedure, the cable has stretched to the point where it needs replacing. Refer to *Clutch Cable Replacement* in Chapter Five for complete procedure.

3

### Throttle Cable Adjustment

Adjust the throttle cable at the interval indicated in **Table 2**. The throttle cable should have 0.5-1.0 mm (0.02-0.04 in.) of free play. If adjustment is necessary, perform the following:
1. At the throttle lever end of the throttle cable, loosen the locknut (A, **Figure 62**) and turn the adjuster (B, **Figure 62**) in either direction until the correct amount of free play is achieved.
2. Tighten the locknut (A, **Figure 62**).
3. If the proper amount of adjustment cannot be achieved using this procedure, the cable has stretched to the point where it needs replacing. Refer to *Throttle Cable Replacement* in Chapter Seven.
4. Check the throttle cable from the throttle grip to the carburetor. Make sure it is not kinked or chafed. Replace as necessary.
5. Make sure the throttle grip rotates freely from a fully closed to fully open position. Check with the handlebar at center, at full right and at full left. If necessary, remove the throttle grip and apply a lithium base grease to the rotating surfaces.

*WARNING*

*With the engine idling, move the handlebar from side-to-side. If idle speed increases during this movement, the throttle cable may need adjusting or may be incorrectly routed through the frame. Correct this problem immediately. Do **not** ride the bike in this unsafe condition.*

## Automatic Decompression Cable Adjustment

Adjust the automatic decompression cable at the interval indicated in **Table 2**. If the engine is difficult to start, the automatic decompression cable probably needs adjusting.

1. Remove the seat as described under *Seat Removal/Installation* in Chapter Twelve.
2. Remove the fuel tank as described under *Fuel Tank Removal/Installation* in Chapter Seven.
3. Remove the bolt and cap nut securing the cylinder head left-hand cover (**Figure 63**). Remove the cover and rubber cushions.
4. Carefully disconnect the spark plug lead (**Figure 64**) from the spark plug.
5. Remove the spark plug from the cylinder head.

*NOTE*

*Either use a wide flat-tipped screwdriver or a special tool made by Honda. This special tool (**Figure 65**) (Honda part No. 07700-0010001) is made specifically for this purpose and if carefully used, will not mar or damage the surface on the inspection cover.*

6. Remove the valve timing inspection cover (**Figure 66**) on the left-hand crankcase cover.
7. Remove the bolts (**Figure 67**) securing both valve adjuster covers on cylinder head. Remove both covers.

*NOTE*

*A cylinder at TDC will have free play in **both** the intake and exhaust valve rocker arms indicating that both the intake and exhaust valves are closed.*

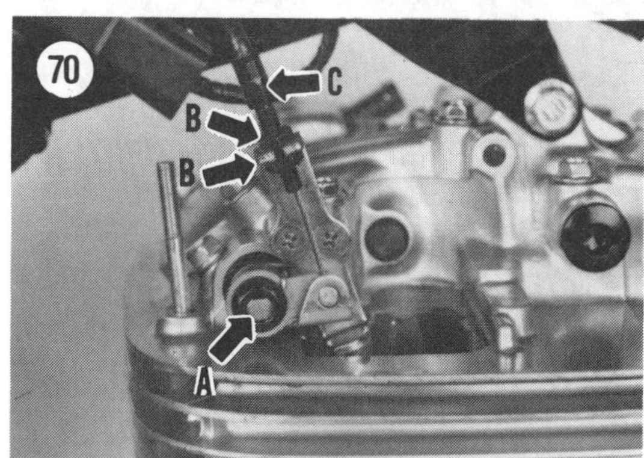


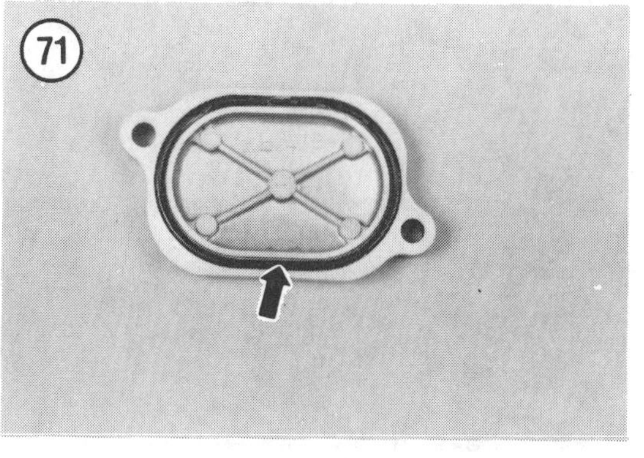


8. Use a 17 mm wrench (**Figure 68**) on the alternator rotor bolt. Rotate the engine *clockwise*, as viewed from the left-hand side, until the engine is at top dead center (TDC) on the compression stroke. Align the groove on the end of the alternator rotor with the notch in the alternator cover (**Figure 69**).

9. With the groove aligned with the notch, jiggle both rocker arms and make sure *both* have free play. If one rocker arm is still under tension, rotate the engine an additional 180° until both rocker arms have free play.

10. Recheck that the groove on the end of the alternator rotor is aligned with the notch in the alternator cover.

11. Pull up on the actuator lever assembly (A, **Figure 70**) and check the end length of the shaft. The actuator shaft should move out of the body 3-5 mm (0.12-0.20 in.). This amount of free play is necessary for the decompressor to operate correctly.

12. If the free play is not correct, perform the following:

a. Loosen the locknut (B, **Figure 70**) on each side of the cable bracket.
b. Move the cable adjuster (C, **Figure 70**) either up or down until the correct amount of free play is achieved.
c. Tighten both locknuts and recheck the free play. Readjust if necessary.

13. Inspect the seal (**Figure 71**) on the valve adjuster covers, replace if necessary. Install both covers and tighten the bolts securely.

14. Inspect the O-ring seal on valve timing inspection cover (**Figure 72**), replace if necessary. Install the cover on the left-hand crankcase cover and tighten securely.

3

15. Install the spark plug and reconnect the spark plug lead.
16. Make sure the rubber cushions (**Figure 73**) are in place on the cylinder head left-hand cover and install the cover.
17. Install the bolt and cap nut securing the cylinder head left-hand cover (**Figure 63**). Tighten the bolt and cap nut securely.
18. Install the fuel tank as described under *Fuel Tank Removal/Installation* in Chapter Seven.
19. Install the seat as described under *Seat Removal/Installation* in Chapter Twelve.

### Camshaft Chain Tensioner Adjustment

There is *no* provision for cam chain tensioner adjustment on this engine. Camshaft chain tension is maintained automatically.

### Air Filter Element

The air filter element should be removed and cleaned at the interval listed in **Table 2**. The air filter element should be replaced at the interval listed in **Table 2** or sooner if soiled, severely clogged or broken in any area.

The air filter removes dust and abrasive particles from the air before the air enters the carburetor and the engine. Without the air filter, very fine particles could enter into the engine and cause rapid wear of the piston rings, cylinder and bearings and might clog small passages in the carburetor. Never run the bike without the air filter element installed.

Proper air filter servicing can do more to ensure long service from your engine than almost any other single item.

### Air Filter Element Removal/Cleaning/Installation

1. Place the bike on the sidestand.
2. Remove the seat as described under *Seat Removal/Installation* in Chapter Twelve.
3. Remove the screws securing the frame right-hand side cover (**Figure 74**) and remove the cover.
4. Remove the screw (A, **Figure 75**) securing the air filter case cover (B, **Figure 75**) and remove the cover.
5. Remove the screw (A, **Figure 76**) securing the air filter element in the air box.
6. Withdraw the element assembly (B, **Figure 76**) from the air box.
7. Wipe out the interior of the air box with a shop rag dampened with cleaning solvent. Remove any foreign matter that may have passed through a broken element.
8. Gently tap the air filter element to loosen the dirt and dust.

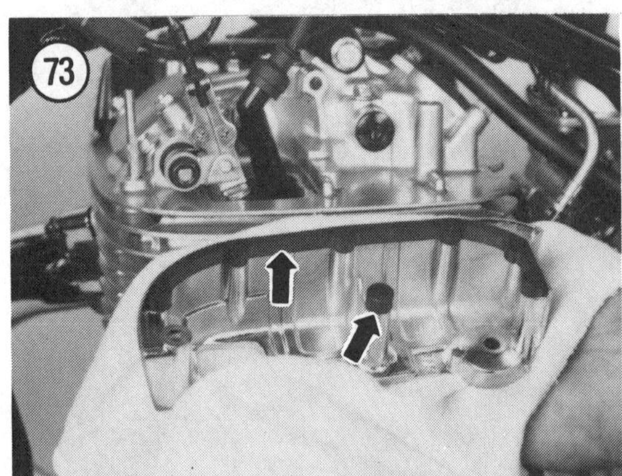
73

74

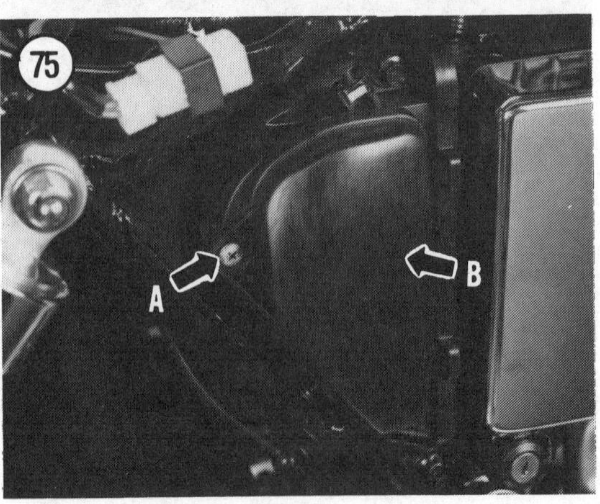

75

*CAUTION*
*In the next step, do not direct compressed air toward the outside (opposite the carburetor side) surface of the element. If air pressure is directed to the outside surface it will force the dirt and dust into the pores of the element thus restricting air flow.*

9. Apply compressed air toward the *inside surface* (**Figure 77**), or carburetor side, of the element to remove all loosened dirt and dust from the element.

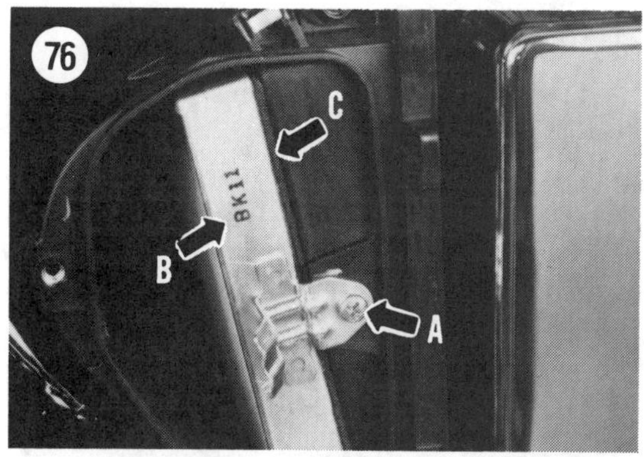

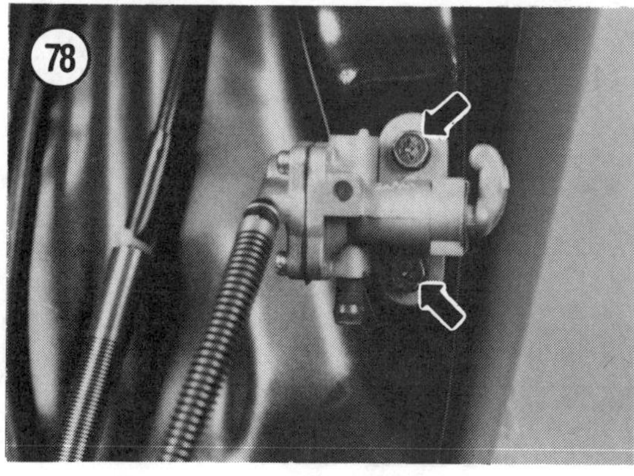


10. Inspect the element. If it is torn or damaged in any area, it must be replaced. Do *not* run the bike with a damaged element as it may allow dirt to enter the engine.
11. Make sure the element is correctly seated in the air box so the sealing surface is tight up against the air box surfaces (C, **Figure 76**). Make sure there is no air leak.
12. Install the screw securing the air filter element in the air box and tighten securely.
13. Install the air filter case cover and screw. Tighten the screw securely.
14. Install the frame right-hand side cover and screws. Tighten the screws securely.
15. Install the seat as described in Chapter Twelve.



### Fuel Shutoff Filter and Valve Removal/Installation

The fuel filter is built into the shutoff valve and removes particles which might otherwise enter into the carburetor and may cause the float needle to remain in the open position.

1. Remove the fuel tank as described in Chapter Seven.
2. If necessary, drain the fuel from the fuel tank into a clean sealable metal container. If the fuel is kept clean it can be reused.
3. Place an old blanket or several shop cloths on the workbench to protect the fuel tank's painted surface. Place the fuel tank upside down on these protective items.
4. Remove the screws and washers (**Figure 78**) securing the fuel shutoff valve to the fuel tank.
5. Remove the valve from the fuel tank. Don't lose the O-ring seal between the fuel tank and the valve.
6. After removing the valve from the fuel tank, insert a corner of a lint-free cloth into the opening in the tank to prevent the entry of foreign matter.
7. Clean the filter with a medium-soft toothbrush and blow out with compressed air. Replace the filter if it is broken in any area.
8. Install by reversing these removal steps. Note the following during installation.
9. Be sure to install the O-ring seal between the shutoff valve and the fuel tank. Tighten the screws securely.
10. Install the fuel tank as described in Chapter Seven.
11. Start the engine and check for fuel leaks.

## Fuel Line Inspection

Inspect the fuel line from the fuel shutoff valve to the carburetor (**Figure 79**). If it is cracked or starting to deteriorate, it must be replaced. Make sure the hose clamps are in place and holding securely.

*WARNING*
*A damaged or deteriorated fuel line presents a very dangerous fire hazard to both the rider and the vehicle if fuel should spill onto a hot engine or exhaust pipe.*

## Crankcase Breather (U.S. Only)

Inspect the breather hose (**Figure 80**) from the cylinder head breather cover to the air filter air case. If it is cracked or starting to deteriorate it must be replaced. Make sure the hose clamps are in place and holding securely.

## Evaporative Emission Control System (California Models Only)

Fuel vapor from the fuel tank is routed into a charcoal canister when the engine is stopped. When the engine is started, these vapors are drawn through the valve, then into the carburetor and on into the engine to be burned. Make sure all vacuum hoses are correctly routed and attached. Inspect the hoses and replace any if necessary.

Refer to Chapter Seven for detailed information on the evaporative emission control system and for vacuum hose routing.

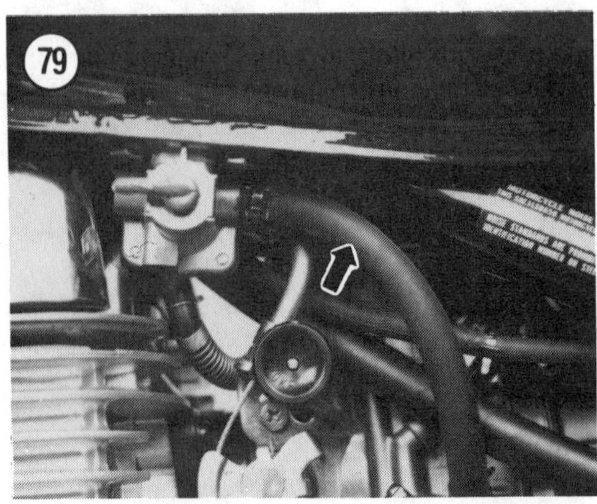


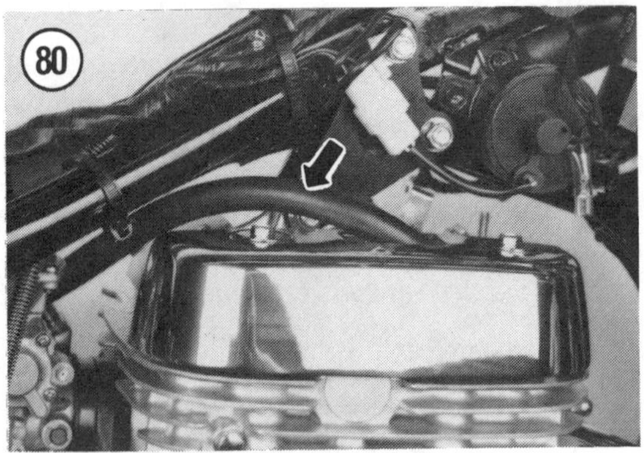


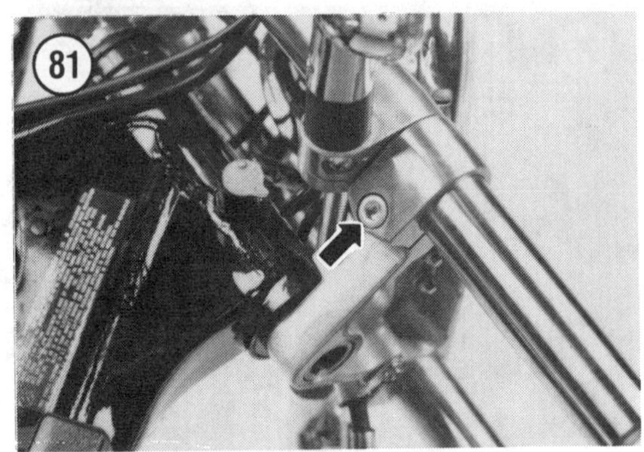

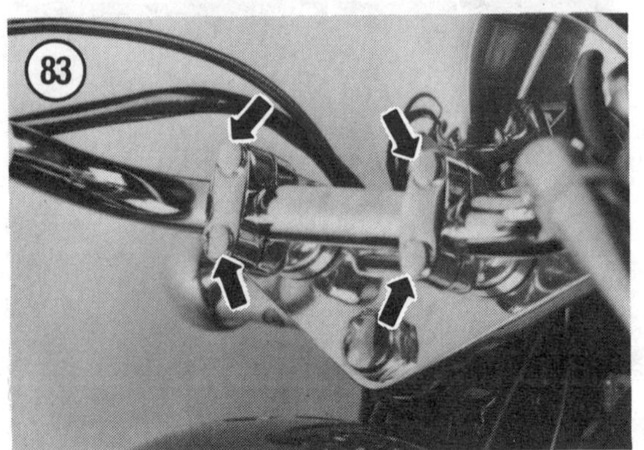

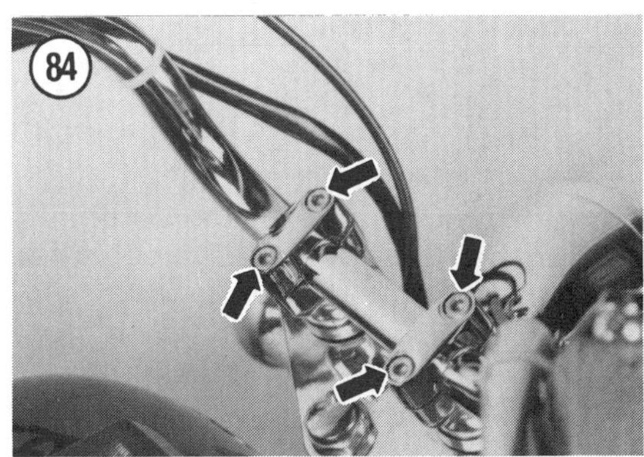

84

85

86

87

### Exhaust System

Check for leakage at all fittings. Tighten all bolts and nuts. Replace any gaskets if necessary. Refer to *Exhaust System* in Chapter Seven.



### Wheel Bearings

There is no factory-recommended mileage interval for cleaning and repacking the wheel bearings. They should be inspected and serviced, if necessary, every time the wheel is removed or whenever there is a likelihood of water contamination. The correct service procedures are covered in Chapter Nine and Chapter Ten.

### Front Suspension Check

1. Apply the front brake and pump the forks up and down as vigorously as possible. Check for smooth operation and check for any oil leaks.
2. Make sure the lower fork bridge bolt is tight (**Figure 81**) on each side.
3. Make sure the fork top cap bolt (**Figure 82**) is tight on each fork leg.
4. Remove the trim caps (**Figure 83**) and make sure the bolts (**Figure 84**) securing the handlebars are tight and that the handlebars are secure.
5. Make sure the front axle (**Figure 85**) and axle clamp bolt are tight (**Figure 86**).

*CAUTION*

*If any of the previously mentioned bolts and nuts are loose, refer to Chapter Nine for correct procedures and torque specifications.*

### Rear Suspension Check

1. Place a wood block(s) under each side of the frame to support it securely with the rear wheel off the ground.
2. Push hard on the rear wheel (sideways) to check for side play in the rear swing arm bearings. Remove the wood block(s).
3. Check the tightness of the upper and lower mounting nuts (**Figure 87**) on the shock absorber.

4. Remove the cap (**Figure 88**) and make sure the swing arm pivot bolt and nut (**Figure 89**) are tight.
5. Make sure the rear axle nut is tight (**Figure 90**).

*CAUTION*
*If any of the previously mentioned bolts and nuts are loose, refer to Chapter Ten for correct procedures and torque specifications.*

### Nuts, Bolts and Other Fasteners

Constant vibration can loosen many of the fasteners on the motorcycle. Check the tightness of all fasteners, especially those on:

a. Engine mounting hardware.
b. Engine crankcase covers.
c. Handlebar and front forks.
d. Gearshift lever.
e. Brake pedal and lever.
f. Sprocket bolts and nuts.
g. Exhaust system.
h. Lighting equipment.

### Steering Head Adjustment Check

Check the steering head bearings for looseness at the interval listed in **Table 2**.

Place a wood block(s) under each side of the frame to support it securely with the front wheel off the ground.

Hold onto the front fork tube and gently rock the fork assembly back and forth. If you feel looseness, refer to Chapter Nine.

## TUNE-UP

Perform a complete tune-up at the interval listed in **Table 2** for normal riding. More frequent tune-ups may be required if the bike is ridden in stop-and-go traffic. The purpose of the tune-up is to restore the performance lost due to normal wear and deterioration of parts.

The spark plug should be routinely replaced at every other tune-up or if the electrodes show signs of erosion. In addition, this is a good time to clean the air filter element. Have the new parts on hand before you begin.

Because the different systems in an engine interact, the procedures should be done in the following order:

a. Torque cylinder head nuts.
b. Adjust valve clearances.
c. Run a compression test.
d. Set the idle speed.
e. Replace the spark plug.

**Table 6** summarizes tune-up specifications.

To perform a tune-up on your Suzuki, you will need the following tools and equipment:

a. 17 mm spark plug wrench.
b. Socket wrench and assorted sockets.
c. Flat feeler gauge.

88

89

90

d. Compression gauge.
e. Spark plug wire feeler gauge and gapper tool.

### Cylinder Head and Cylinder Nuts and Bolt Tightening

The cylinder head is held in place with 4 nuts at the top under the cylinder head cover. There are also 2 cylinder head-to-cylinder nuts, one at the front and one at the rear.

There are 2 cylinder-to-crankcase nuts.

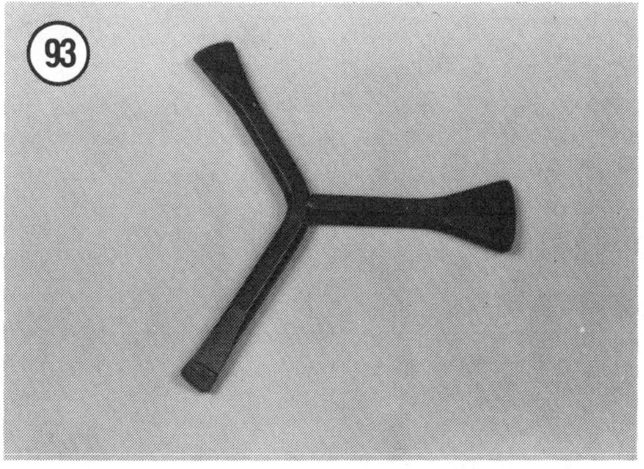

The nuts should be tightened after the first 600 miles (1,000 km) of the purchase of a new bike and at the same mileage after the cylinder head has been removed for service.

*NOTE*
*In **some** cases the cylinder head cover can be removed with the engine in the frame. This depends on the manufacturing tolerances of your specific frame. If the frame is a little on the "small" side from top to bottom, in the engine mounting area, or if one of the engine mounting bosses is a little off tolerance it will be impossible to remove the cylinder head cover, camshaft and the cylinder head with the engine in the frame. It is suggested that the engine be removed from the frame for this procedure.*

*CAUTION*
*If you choose to try to remove the cylinder head cover with the engine in the frame, **do so carefully**—do not try to force anything off if there isn't enough room between the engine and the top of the frame rail.*

*NOTE*
*This procedure must be performed with the engine cold (at room temperature). For best results, let the engine sit overnight and perform this procedure the first thing in the morning.*

1. Place the bike on the sidestand.
2. Remove the seat as described in Chapter Twelve.
3. Remove the fuel tank as described in Chapter Seven.
4. Remove the bolt and cap nut securing the cylinder head left-hand cover (**Figure 91**). Remove the cover and rubber cushions.
5. Carefully disconnect the spark plug lead (**Figure 92**) from the spark plug.
6. Remove the spark plug from the cylinder head.

*NOTE*
*Either use a wide flat-tipped screwdriver or a special tool made by Honda. This special tool (**Figure 93**)*

*(Honda part No. 07700-0010001) is made specifically for this purpose and if carefully used, will not mar or damage the surface on the inspection cover.*

7. Remove the valve timing inspection cover (**Figure 94**) on the left-hand crankcase cover.
8. Remove the bolts (**Figure 95**) securing both valve adjuster covers on cylinder head. Remove both covers.

*NOTE*
*A cylinder at TDC will have free play in **both** the intake and exhaust valve rocker arms indicating that both the intake and exhaust valves are closed.*

9. Use a 17 mm wrench (**Figure 96**) on the alternator rotor bolt. Rotate the engine *clockwise,* as viewed from the left-hand side, until the engine is at top dead center (TDC) on the compression stroke. Align the groove on the end of the alternator rotor with the notch in the alternator cover (**Figure 97**).
10. With the groove aligned with the notch, jiggle both rocker arms and make sure *both* have free play. If one rocker arm is still under tension, rotate the engine an additional 180 degrees until both rocker arms have free play.
11. Again check that the groove on the end of the alternator rotor is aligned with the notch in the alternator cover.

*NOTE*
*The following steps are shown with the engine removed from the frame and*

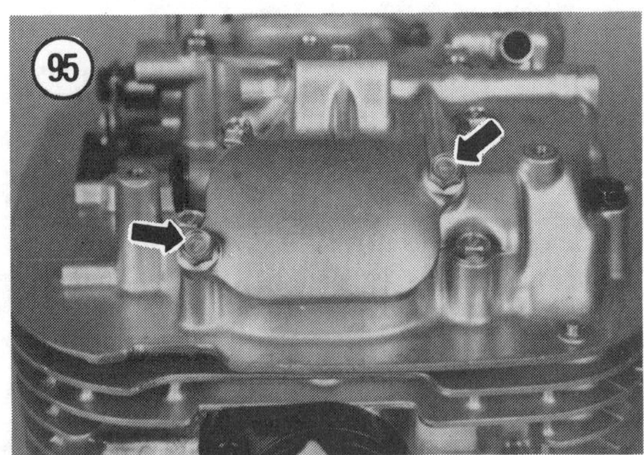

*partially disassembled for clarity. It is not necessary to remove the engine or remove the items shown to tighten the cylinder head and cylinder nuts and bolt.*

*CAUTION*

*In the following step, do **not** remove the bolt with a concave head and marked with an "A" (**Figure 98**). This bolt secures the exhaust valve rocker arm shaft in place and must be left in place at this time.*

12. Using a crisscross pattern, loosen and remove the bolts securing the cylinder head cover (**Figure 99**) to the cylinder head.
13. Remove the cylinder head cover. Don't lose the locating dowels.
14. Remove the head seal cap (**Figure 100**) from the cylinder head.
15. Using a crisscross pattern, loosen and remove all cylinder head nuts (**Figure 101**).
16. Apply engine oil to the nuts.
17. Tighten the cylinder head nuts in a crisscross pattern. Tighten to the torque specification listed in **Table 5**.
18. Tighten the cylinder head-to-cylinder nut at the front (**Figure 102**) and at the rear (**Figure 103**). Tighten these nuts to the torque specification listed in **Table 5**.
19. Install all items removed by reversing these removal steps. Note the following during installation.

3

20. Inspect the seal (**Figure 104**) on the valve adjuster covers, replace if necessary. Install both covers and tighten the bolts securely.
21. Inspect the O-ring seal on valve timing inspection cover (**Figure 105**), replace if necessary. Install the cover on the left-hand crankcase cover and tighten securely.
22. Make sure the rubber cushions (**Figure 106**) are in place on the cylinder head left-hand cover and install the cover.

### Valve Clearance Measurement and Adjustment

Valve clearance measurement and adjustment must be performed with the engine cool, at room temperature (below 35° C/95° F). The correct valve clearance is listed in **Table 6**. The exhaust valves are located at the front of the engine and the intake valves are located at the rear of the engine. There are two intake and two exhaust valves.

*NOTE*
*The automatic decompression cable must be adjusted prior to adjusting the valves.*

1. Adjust the automatic decompression cable as described in this chapter.
2. Remove the seat as described in Chapter Twelve.
3. Remove the fuel tank as described in Chapter Seven.
4. Remove the bolt and cap nut securing the cylinder head left-hand cover (**Figure 91**). Remove the cover and rubber cushions.
5. Carefully disconnect the spark plug lead (**Figure 92**) from the spark plug.
6. Remove the spark plug from the cylinder head.

*NOTE*
*Either use a wide flat-tipped screwdriver or a special tool made by Honda. This special tool (**Figure 93**) (Honda part No. 07700-0010001) is made specifically for this purpose and if carefully used, will not mar or damage the surface on the inspection cover.*

7. Remove the valve timing inspection cover (**Figure 94**) on the left-hand crankcase cover.
8. Remove the bolts (**Figure 95**) securing both valve adjuster covers on cylinder head. Remove both covers.

*NOTE*
*A cylinder at TDC will have free play in **both** the intake and exhaust valve rocker arms indicating that both the intake and exhaust valves are closed.*

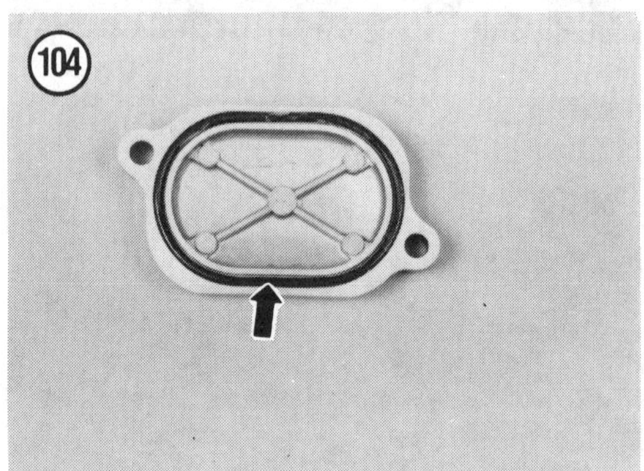
104

105

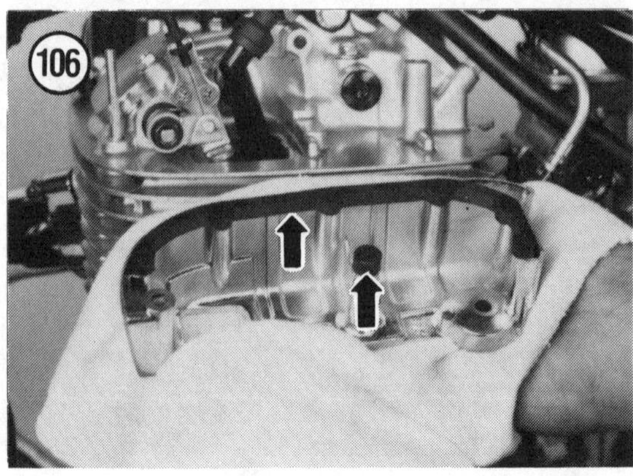
106

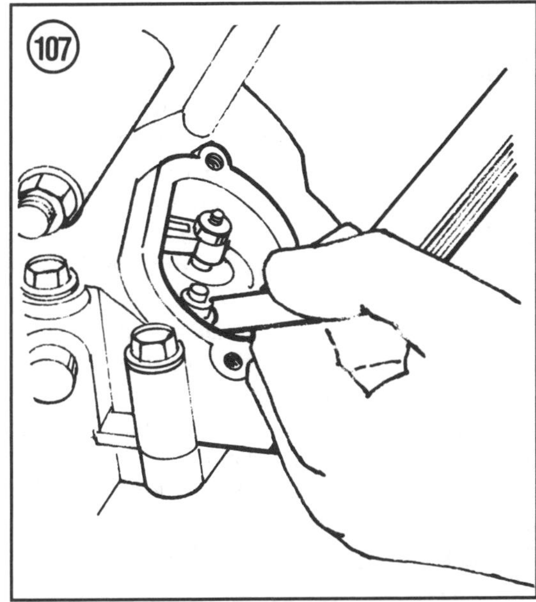

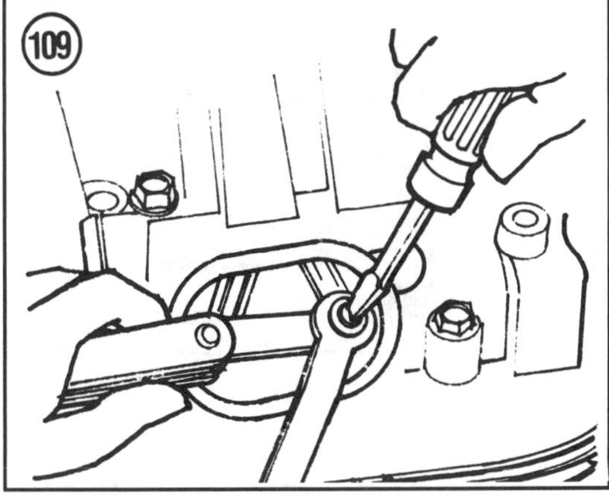


9. Use a 17 mm wrench (**Figure 96**) on the alternator rotor bolt. Rotate the engine *clockwise,* as viewed from the left-hand side, until the engine is at top dead center (TDC) on the compression stroke. Align the groove on the end of the alternator rotor with the notch in the alternator cover (**Figure 97**).

10. With the groove aligned with the notch, jiggle both rocker arms and make sure *both* have free play. If one rocker arm is still under tension, rotate the engine an additional 180° until both rocker arms have free play.

11. Again check that the groove on the end of the alternator rotor is aligned with the notch in the alternator cover.

*NOTE*

*The following steps are shown with the engine removed from the frame for clarity. It is not necessary to remove the engine to adjust the valves.*

12. With the engine in this position, check the clearance of the intake and exhaust valves.

13. Check the clearance by inserting a flat feeler gauge between the adjusting screw and each valve stem (**Figure 107**). When the clearance is correct, there will be a slight drag on the feeler gauge when it is inserted and withdrawn.

*CAUTION*

*Adjust both the right- and left-hand valve clearance as close to each other as possible.*

14. To correct the clearance, perform the following:
  a. Loosen the adjuster locknut (**Figure 108**) on one of the exhaust valve adjusters.
  b. Screw the adjuster in or out so there is a slight resistance felt on the feeler gauge (**Figure 109**).
  c. Hold the adjuster to prevent it from turning further and tighten the locknut to the torque specification listed in **Table 5**.
  d. Then, recheck the clearance to make sure the adjuster did not turn after the correct clearance was achieved. Readjust if necessary.
  e. Repeat for the adjuster of the other valve controlled by the same rocker arm.
  f. Repeat this step for the other exhaust valve.

3

15. Repeat Step 14 for the intake valves.
16. Rotate the engine several complete revolutions and recheck the valve clearances. Readjust if necessary.
17. After the valves are adjusted correctly, recheck and adjust if necessary the automatic decompression cable as described in this chapter.
18. Inspect the seal (**Figure 104**) on the valve adjuster covers, replace if necessary. Install both covers and tighten the bolts securely.
19. Inspect the O-ring seal on valve timing inspection cover (**Figure 105**), replace if necessary. Install the cover on the left-hand crankcase cover and tighten securely.
20. Install the spark plug and reconnect the spark plug lead.
21. Make sure the rubber cushions (**Figure 106**) are in place on the cylinder head left-hand cover and install the cover.
22. Install the bolt and cap nut securing the cylinder head left-hand cover (**Figure 91**). Tighten the bolt and cap nut securely.
23. Install the fuel tank as described in Chapter Seven.
24. Install the seat as described in Chapter Twelve.

### Compression Test

Check the cylinder compression at the interval indicated in **Table 2**. Record the results and compare them to the results at the next interval. A running record will show trends in deterioration so that corrective action can be taken before complete failure.

The results when properly interpreted, can indicate general cylinder, piston ring and valve condition.

1. Warm the engine to normal operating temperature, then shut it off. Make sure the choke valve and throttle valve are completely open.
2. Remove the seat as described in Chapter Twelve.
3. Remove the fuel tank as described in Chapter Seven.
4. Remove the bolt and cap nut securing the cylinder head left-hand cover (**Figure 91**). Remove the cover and rubber cushions.
5. Carefully disconnect the spark plug lead (**Figure 110**) from the spark plug.
6. Connect the compression tester to the cylinder following the manufacturer's instructions.
7. Crank the engine over until there is no further rise in pressure.
8. Remove the tester and record the reading. When interpreting the results, actual readings are not as

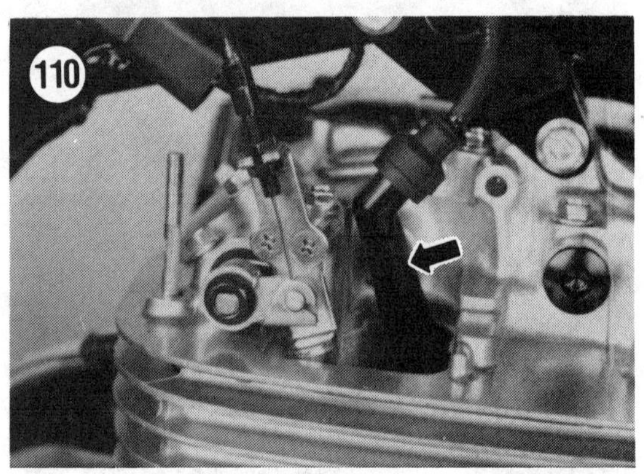


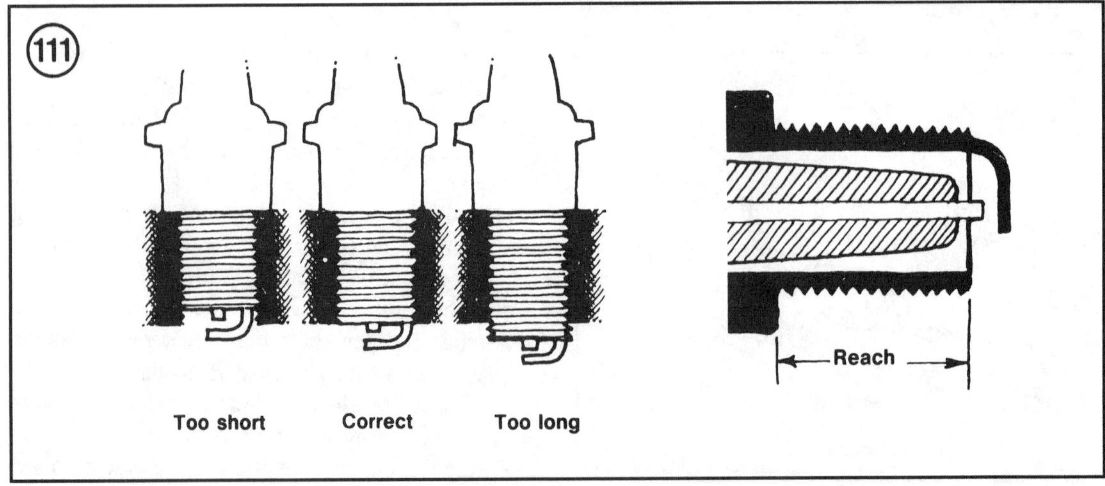

important as the difference between the readings. The recommended standard and service limit cylinder compression pressures are listed in **Table 6**. Greater differences than that listed in **Table 6** indicate broken rings, leaky or sticking valves, a blown head gasket or a combination of all.

If a low reading (10% or more) is obtained, it indicates valve or ring trouble. To determine which, pour about a teaspoon of engine oil through the spark plug hole onto the top of the piston. Turn the engine over once to distribute the oil, then take another compression test and record the reading. If the compression increases significantly, the valves are good but the rings are defective. If the compression does not increase, the valves require servicing. A valve(s) could be hanging open, but not burned, or a piece of carbon could be on a valve seat.

### Spark Plug Selection

Spark plugs are available in various heat ranges, hotter or colder than plugs originally installed at the factory.

Select a plug of the heat range designed for the loads and temperature conditions under which the bike will be run. The use of incorrect heat ranges can cause a seized piston, scored cylinder wall or damaged piston crown.

In general, use a hot plug for low speeds, low engine loads and low temperatures. Use a cold plug for high speeds, high engine loads and high temperatures. The plug should operate hot enough to burn off unwanted deposits, but not so hot that it is damaged or causes preignition. A spark plug of the correct heat range will show a light tan color on the portion of the insulator within the cylinder after the plug has been in service.

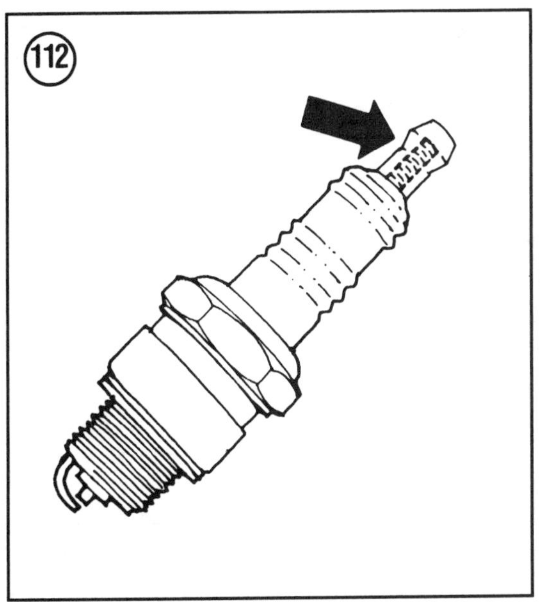


The reach (length) of a spark plug (**Figure 111**) is also important. A longer than normal plug could interfere with the valves and pistons, causing permanent and severe damage. The recommended spark plug heat ranges are listed in **Table 6**.

### Spark Plug Removal/Cleaning

1. Remove the fuel tank as described in Chapter Seven.
2. Remove the bolt and cap nut securing the cylinder head left-hand cover (**Figure 91**). Remove the cover and rubber cushions.

*CAUTION*

*If any dirt falls into the cylinder when the plug is removed, serious engine damage could occur.*

3. Use compressed air and blow away any dirt that may have passed by the rubber boot on the spark plug lead and accumulated in the spark plug well.
4. Remove the spark plug with an 17 mm spark plug wrench.

*NOTE*

*If plug is difficult to remove, apply penetrating oil around base of plug and let it soak in about 10-20 minutes.*

5. Inspect the spark plug carefully. Look for a broken center porcelain, excessively eroded electrodes and excessive carbon or oil fouling. Replace such a plug. If deposits are light, the plug may be cleaned in solvent with a wire brush or in a special spark plug sandblast cleaner. Regap the plug as explained in this chapter.

### Spark Plug Gapping and Installation

A new plug should be carefully gapped to ensure a reliable, consistent spark. You must use a special spark plug gapping tool with a wire feeler gauge.

1. Remove the new plug from the box. Do *not* screw on the small piece (**Figure 112**) that is sometimes loose in the box, it is not to be used.

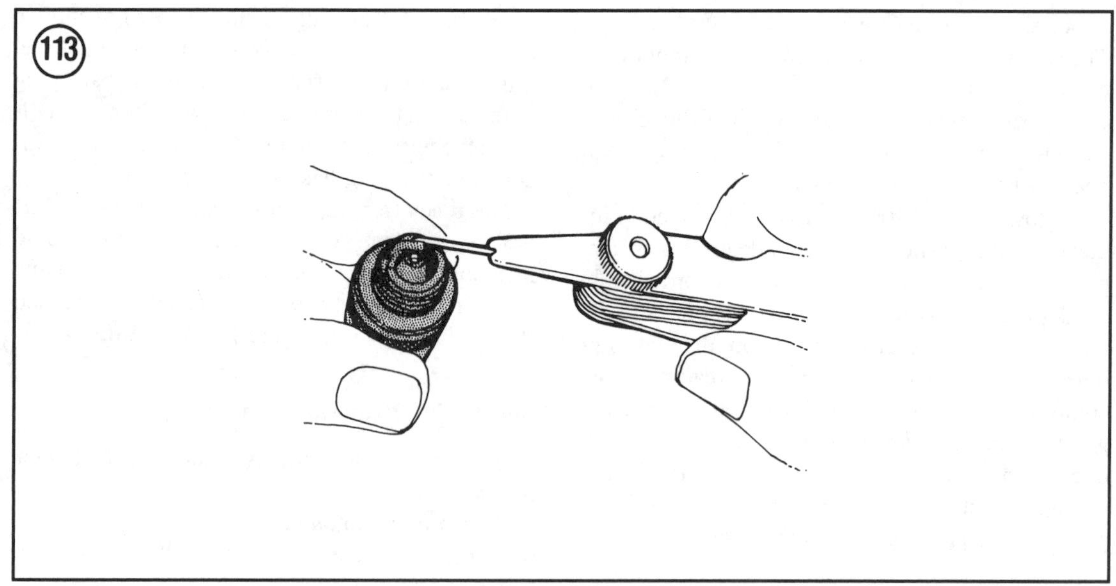

114

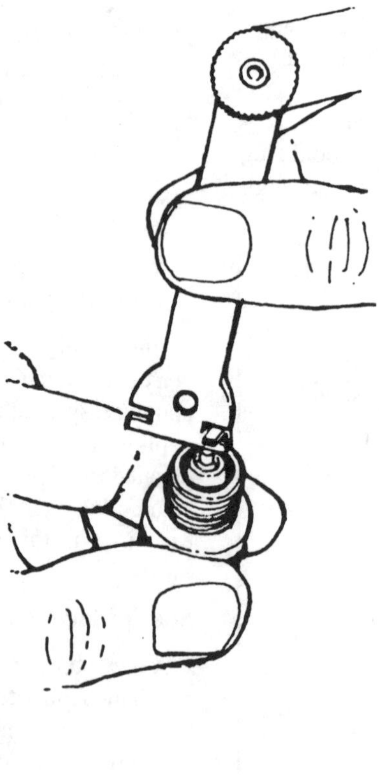

2. Insert a wire feeler gauge between the center and the side electrode of the plug (**Figure 113**). The correct gap is listed in **Table 6**.
3. If the gap is correct, you will feel a slight drag as you pull the wire through. If there is no drag or the gauge won't pass through, bend the side electrode *with the gapping tool* (**Figure 114**) to set the proper gap.
4. Put a *small* drop of oil or aluminum anti-seize compound on the threads of the spark plug.
5. Screw the spark plug in by hand until it seats. Very little effort is required. If force is necessary, you have the plug cross-threaded; unscrew it and try again.
6. Tighten the spark plug an additional 1/2 turn after the gasket has made contact with the head. If you are reinstalling old, regapped plug and are reusing the old gasket, only tighten an additional 1/4 turn.

*NOTE*

*Do not overtighten. This will only squash the gasket and destroy its sealing ability.*

7. Install the spark plug lead; make sure the lead is on tight.
8. Install the cylinder head left-hand cover and bolt and nut. Tighten the bolt and nut securely.
9. Install the fuel tank as described in Chapter Seven.

### Reading Spark Plugs

Much information about engine and spark plug performance can be determined by careful examination of the spark plug. This information is more valid after performing the following steps.

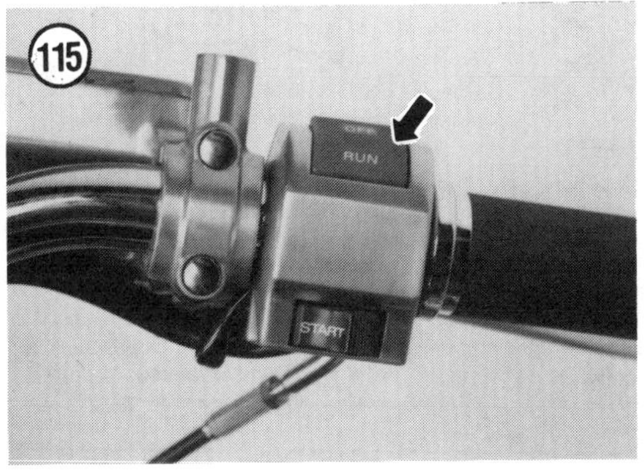


1. Ride the bike a short distance at full throttle in any gear.
2. Turn the engine stop switch (**Figure 115**) to the OFF position before closing the throttle and simultaneously pull in the clutch or shift to NEUTRAL; coast and brake to a stop.
3. Remove the spark plug and examine it. Compare it to **Figure 116**. If the insulator is white or burned, the plug is too hot and should be replaced with a colder one. If the plug has a light tan or gray colored deposit and no abnormal gap wear or electrode erosion is evident, the plug and the engine are running properly. A too-cold plug will have sooty or oily deposits ranging in color from dark brown to black. Replace with a hotter plug and check for too-rich carburetion or evidence of oil blowby at the piston rings. If the plug exhibits a black insulator tip, a damp and oily film over the firing end and a carbon layer over the entire nose, it is oil fouled. An oil fouled plug can be cleaned, but it is better to replace it.
4. If the existing spark plug is okay, reinstall it. If not, replace with a new one.

3

### Carburetor Idle Speed Adjustment

Before making this adjustment, the air filter element must be clean and the engine must have adequate compression. See *Compression Test* in this chapter. Otherwise this procedure cannot be done properly.

1. Start the engine and let reach normal operating temperature. Make sure the choke knob is in the open position.
2. Connect a portable tachometer following the manufacturer's instructions.
3. Turn the idle adjust screw (**Figure 117**) in or out to adjust idle speed.
4. The correct idle speed is listed in **Table 6**.
5. Open and close the throttle a couple of times. Check for variations in idle speed; readjust if necessary.

*WARNING*

*With the engine running at idle speed, move the handlebar from side-to-side. If the idle speed increases during this*

**116**

## SPARK PLUG CONDITION

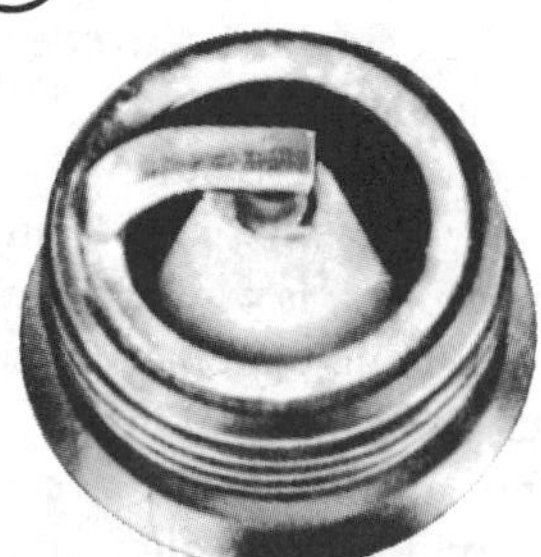

**NORMAL**

- Identified by light tan or gray deposits on the firing tip.
- Can be cleaned.

**GAP BRIDGED**

- Identified by deposit buildup closing gap between electrodes.
- Caused by oil or carbon fouling. If deposits are not excessive, the plug can be cleaned.

**OIL FOULED**

- Identified by wet black deposits on the insulator shell bore and electrodes.
- Caused by excessive oil entering combustion chamber through worn rings and pistons, excessive clearance between valve guides and stems, or worn or loose bearings. Can be cleaned. If engine is not repaired, use a hotter plug.

**CARBON FOULED**

- Identified by black, dry fluffy carbon deposits on insulator tips, exposed shell surfaces and electrodes.
- Caused by too cold a plug, weak ignition, dirty air cleaner, too rich a fuel mixture, or excessive idling. Can be cleaned.

**LEAD FOULED**

- Identified by dark gray, black, yellow, or tan deposits or a fused glazed coating on the insulator tip.
- Caused by highly leaded gasoline. Can be cleaned.

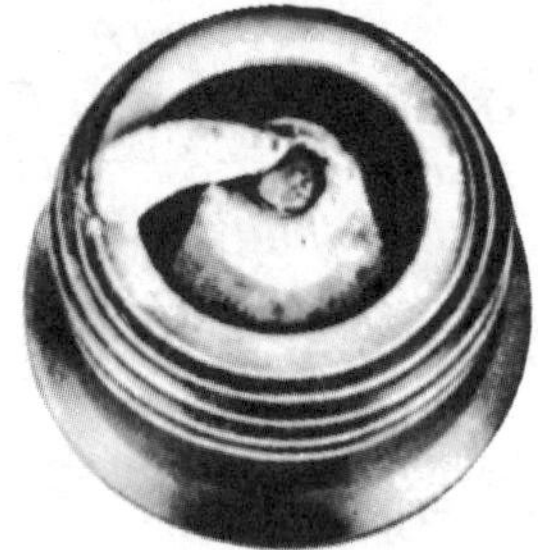

**WORN**

- Identified by severely eroded or worn electrodes.
- Caused by normal wear. Should be replaced.

**FUSED SPOT DEPOSIT**

- Identified by melted or spotty deposits resembling bubbles or blisters.
- Caused by sudden acceleration. Can be cleaned.

**OVERHEATING**

- Identified by a white or light gray insulator with small black or gray brown spots and with bluish-burnt appearance of electrodes.
- Caused by engine overheating, wrong type of fuel, loose spark plugs, too hot a plug, or incorrect ignition timing. Replace the plug.

**PREIGNITION**

- Identified by melted electrodes and possibly blistered insulator. Metallic deposits on insulator indicate engine damage.
- Caused by wrong type of fuel, incorrect ignition timing or advance, too hot a plug, burned valves, or engine overheating. Replace the plug.

*movement, the throttle cable may need adjusting or it may be incorrectly routed through the frame. Correct this problem immediately. Do **not** ride the bike in this unsafe condition.*

### Carburetor Idle Mixture

The idle mixture (pilot screw) is preset at the factory and *is not to be reset*. Do not adjust the pilot screw unless the carburetor has been overhauled. If so, refer to Chapter Seven for service procedures.

3

**Table 1 TIRE INFLATION PRESSURE (COLD)***

| | Tire pressure | | | |
|---|---|---|---|---|
| | Front | | Rear | |
| **Load** | **psi** | **kPa** | **psi** | **kPa** |
| Solo riding | 28 | 200 | 28 | 200 |
| Dual riding | 32 | 225 | 36 | 250 |

* Tire inflation pressure for factory equipped tires. Aftermarket tires may require different inflation pressure.

**Table 2 MAINTENANCE SCHEDULE***

| | |
|---|---|
| **Before each ride** | Inspect tires and rims and check inflation pressure<br>Check steering for smooth operation with no excessive play or restrictions<br>Check brake operation and for fluid leakage on front disc brake<br>Check fuel supply. Make sure there is enough fuel for the intended ride<br>Check for fuel leakage<br>Check all lights for proper operation<br>Check engine oil level<br>Check for smooth throttle operation<br>Check gearshift lever operation<br>Check clutch operation<br>Inspect drive belt for wear or damage<br>Check drive belt tension. Adjust if necessary |
| **Every 2,000 miles (3,000 km) or 6 months** | Clean the air filter element<br>Check and adjust automatic decompression cable free play, if necessary<br>Inspect drive belt. Adjust tension if necessary |
| **Every 4,000 miles (6,000 km) or 12 months** | Tighten exhaust pipe nuts<br>Inspect and adjust if necessary the valve clearance<br>Check and adjust idle speed<br>Clean and inspect spark plug<br>Replace engine oil and filter |

(continued)

**Table 2 MAINTENANCE SCHEDULE (continued)**

| | |
|---|---|
| **Every 4,000 miles (6,000 km) or 12 months** | Check and adjust clutch operation and free play<br>Inspect front brake hose for leakage<br>Check brake fluid level in the brake master cylinder<br>Inspect fuel line for damage or leakage<br>Inspect evaporation emission lines for damage or leakage (California models)<br>Check all brake system components<br>Inspect the brake pads and shoes for wear<br>Check and tighten the front axle and clamp bolt<br>Check and tighten the rear axle nut<br>Lubricate control cables<br>Inspect drive and driven pulleys for wear and mounting tightness |
| **Every 7,500 miles (12,000 km) or 24 months** | Replace the spark plug<br>Replace air filter element<br>Inspect steering head bearings<br>Check all suspension components for wear or damage |
| **Every 2 years** | Drain and replace hydraulic brake fluid |
| **Every 4 years** | Replace the brake hose<br>Replace the fuel lines<br>Replace evaporative emission lines (California models) |

* This Suzuki factory maintenance schedule should be considered as a guide to general maintenance and lubrication intervals. Harder than normal use and exposure to mud, water, sand, high humidity, etc. (or if used for racing) will naturally dictate more frequent attention to most maintenance items.

**Table 3 BATTERY STATE OF CHARGE**

| Specific Gravity | State of Charge |
|---|---|
| 1.110-1.130 | Discharged |
| 1.140-1.160 | Almost discharged |
| 1.170-1.190 | One-quarter charged |
| 1.200-1.220 | One-half charged |
| 1.230-1.250 | Three-quarters charged |
| 1.260-1.280 | Fully charged |

**Table 4 ENGINE OIL CAPACITY**

| Oil change | | Oil and filter change | | Overhaul | |
|---|---|---|---|---|---|
| Liters | U.S. qt. | Liters | U.S. qt. | Liters | U.S. qt. |
| 1.8 | 1.9 | 2.4 | 2.5 | 2.4 | 2.5 |

**Table 5 MAINTENANCE AND TUNE UP TORQUE SPECIFICATIONS**

| Item | N·m | ft.-lb. |
|---|---|---|
| Oil drain plug | 12-18 | 8.5-13 |
| Fork cap bolt | 35-55 | 25.5-40 |
| Rear axle nut | 55-88 | 40-63 |
| Front brake caliper mounting bolts | 25-40 | 18-29 |
| Cylinder head nuts (9 mm) | 29-33 | 21-24 |
| Cylinder head-to-cylinder nuts (8 mm) | 23-27 | 16-19 |
| Cylinder-to-crankcase nuts | 8-12 | 6-8.5 |
| Rocker arm shaft (exhaust) set bolt | 8-10 | 6-7 |

**Table 6 TUNE-UP SPECIFICATIONS**

| | |
|---|---|
| Valve clearance | |
| Intake and exhaust | 0.08-0.13 mm (0.003-0.005 in.) |
| Automatic decompression cable | |
| free play | 3-5 mm (0.12-0.20 in.) |
| Cylinder compression | |
| Standard | 1,000-1,400 kPa (145-203 psi) |
| Service limit | 800 kPa (116 psi) |
| Spark plug type | |
| Standard heat range | NGK DP8EA-9, ND X24EP-U9 |
| Hotter heat range | NGK DP7EA-9, ND X22EP-U9 |
| Spark plug gap | 0.8-0.9 mm (0.031-0.035 in.) |
| Idle speed | 1,000-1,200 rpm |

3

CHAPTER FOUR

# ENGINE

The Suzuki LS650 Savage is equipped with an air-cooled, 4-stroke, single cylinder engine with a single overhead camshaft. The cylinder head incorporates a pair of dual intake and dual exhaust valves with a single rocker arm operating each set of valves. Each valve has it own adjuster. The camshaft is chain-driven from the sprocket on the right-hand end of the crankshaft.

To make starting easier for the large displacement single, the exhaust valves are opened slightly during the beginning of the starting cycle via an automatic decompression system. This automatic system is integrated with the starting system and requires no rider input. The system does require routine adjustment to maintain the correct amount of freeplay and is covered in Chapter Three.

This chapter provides complete service and overhaul procedures including information for removal, disassembly, inspection, service and reassembly of the engine. Although the clutch, transmission and internal gearshift mechanisms are located within the engine, the clutch is covered in Chapter Five and the transmission and internal gearshift mechanism is covered in Chapter Six to simplify this material.

Refer to **Table 1** for complete engine specifications and to **Table 2** for torque specifications. **Table 1** and **Table 2** are located at the end of this chapter.

Before starting any work, re-read Chapter One of this book. You will do a better job with this information fresh in your mind.

Throughout the text there is frequent mention of the right-hand and left-hand side of the engine. This refers to the engine as it sits in the bike's frame, *not* as it sits on your workbench. The "right-" and "left-hand" side refers to a rider sitting on the seat facing forward.

Throughout the engine chapter there is reference made to one specific sealant—Three-Bond No. 1216. This is the only type of sealant specified by U.S. Suzuki and is available from most Suzuki dealers. It is a hardening type of sealant, but it retains its elasticity even when subjected to engine heat. Other types of sealant, even those manufactured by Three-Bond, will eventually become brittle and there will be an oil leak.

## ENGINE PRINCIPLES

**Figure 1** explains how the engine works. This will be helpful when troubleshooting or repairing the engine.

(1)

## 4-STROKE PRINCIPLES

Carburetor

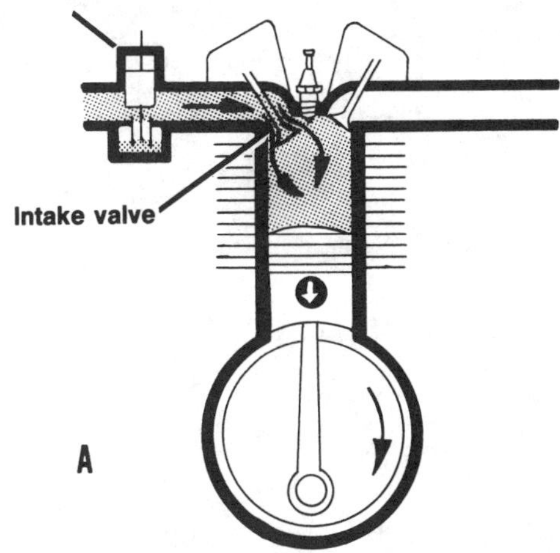


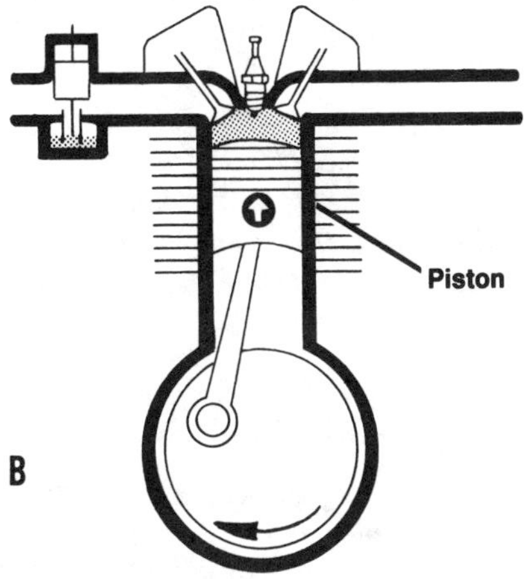


As the piston travels downward, the exhaust valve is closed and the intake valve opens, allowing the new air-fuel mixture from the carburetor to be drawn into the cylinder. When the piston reaches the bottom of its travel (BDC), the intake valve closes and remains closed for the next 1 1/2 revolutions of the crankshaft.

While the crankshaft continues to rotate, the piston moves upward, compressing the air-fuel mixture.

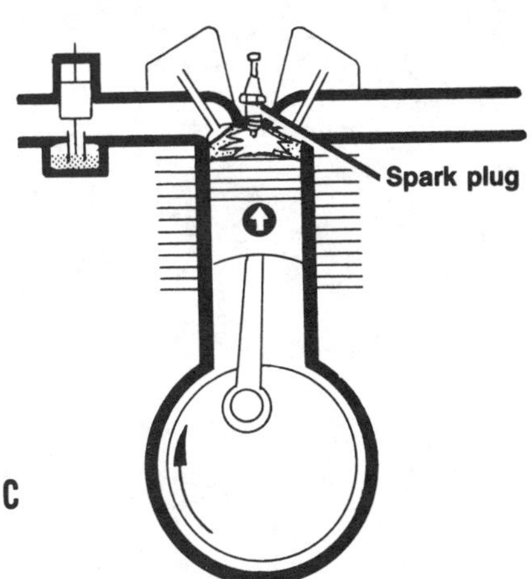


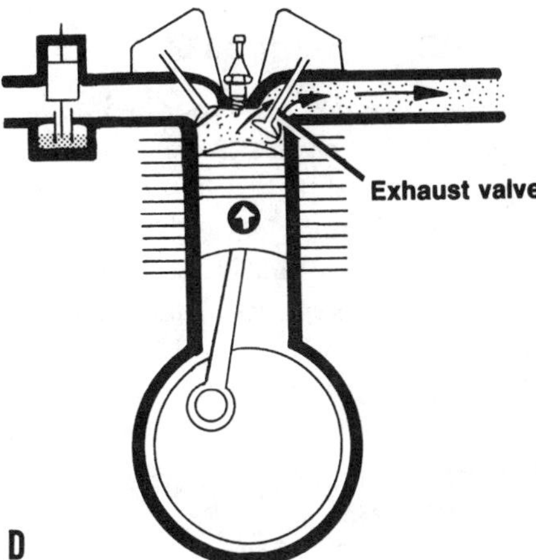


As the piston almost reaches the top of its travel, the spark plug fires, igniting the compressed air-fuel mixture. The piston continues to top dead center (TDC) and is pushed downward by the expanding gases.

When the piston almost reaches BDC, the exhaust valve opens and remains open until the piston is near TDC. The upward travel of the piston forces the exhaust gases out of the cylinder. After the piston has reached TDC, the exhaust valve closes and the cycle starts all over again.

## ENGINE COOLING

Cooling is provided by air passing over the cooling fins on the cylinder head and cylinder. It is important to keep these fins free from buildup of dirt, oil, grease and other foreign matter. Brush out the fins with a whisk broom or small stiff paint brush.

*CAUTION*

*Remember, these fins are thin in order to dissipate heat and may be damaged if struck too hard while cleaning them.*

## SERVICING ENGINE IN FRAME

The following components can be serviced while the engine is mounted in the frame (the bike's frame is a great holding fixture for breaking loose stubborn bolts and nuts):

a. Carburetor assembly.
b. Exhaust system.
c. Alternator and starter.
d. Clutch assembly.
e. External shift mechanism.

## ENGINE REMOVAL/INSTALLATION

1. Remove the seat as described under *Seat Removal/Installation* in Chapter Twelve.
2. Remove the fuel tank as described under *Fuel Tank Removal/Installation* in Chapter Seven.
3. Remove the battery and battery box as described under *Battery Box Removal/Installation* in Chapter Eight.
4. Disconnect the clutch cable as follows:

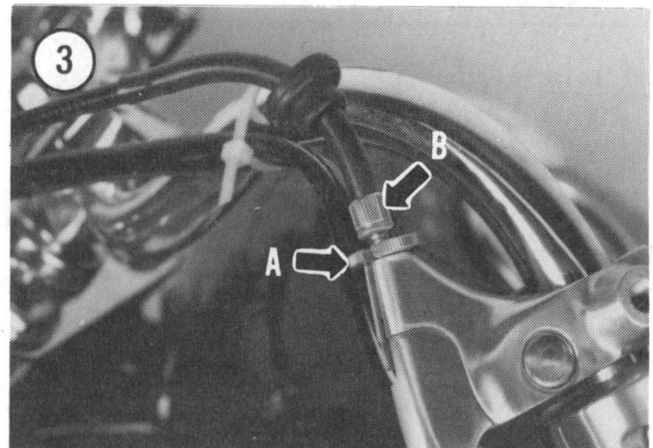


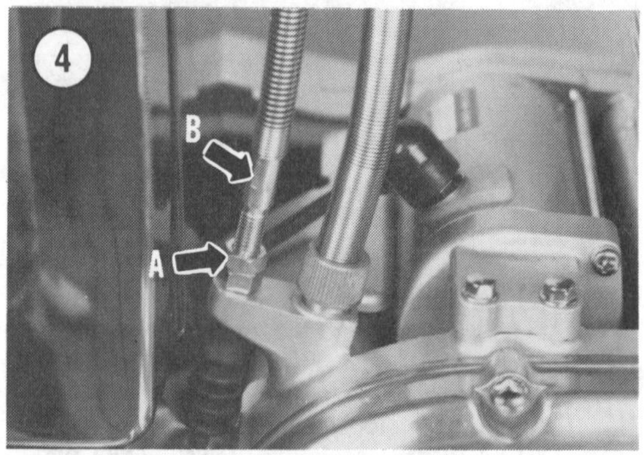

a. At the clutch lever, slide back the rubber boot (**Figure 2**).
b. Loosen the locknut (A, **Figure 3**) and turn the adjuster (B, **Figure 3**) in all the way toward the hand grip.
c. At the right-hand crankcase cover, loosen the locknuts (A, **Figure 4**) and turn the adjuster (B, **Figure 4**) until there is maximum slack in the cable.
d. Pry open the locking tab (**Figure 5**) on the release arm.
e. Place a 19 mm open end wrench (**Figure 6**) on the clutch release arm and carefully push down on the wrench. This will allow additional slack in the cable.
f. Disengage the clutch cable from the release arm (**Figure 7**) and the receptacle on the right-hand crankcase cover.

5. Remove the exhaust system as described under *Exhaust System Removal/Installation* in Chapter Seven.
6. Remove the right-hand (**Figure 8**) and the left-hand frame covers.
7. Disconnect the breather hose (**Figure 9**) from the cylinder head cover.
8. Remove the fasteners securing the cylinder head right-hand (**Figure 10**) top cover. Don't lose the washers under the rubber cushions (**Figure 11**).
9. Remove the fasteners securing the cylinder head left-hand (**Figure 12**) top cover. Don't lose the rubber cushions (**Figure 13**).
10. Disconnect the spark plug lead (**Figure 14**) and lift it up out of the way.

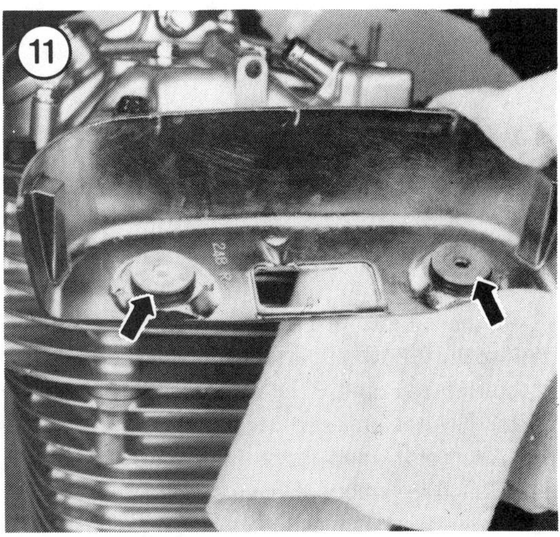

4

11. Remove the carburetor as described under *Carburetor Removal/Installation* in Chapter Seven.
12. Drain the engine oil as described under *Engine Oil and Filter Change* in Chapter Three.

*NOTE*
*Do not disconnect the decompression lever cable from the lever.*

13. Remove the screws (A, **Figure 15**) securing the automatic decompression cable mounting bracket. Unhook the cable end from the lever (B, **Figure 15**) and move the cable and mounting bracket out of the way.
14. Remove the gearshift linkage as described under *Gearshift Linkage Removal/Installation* in Chapter Six.
15. Remove the drive belt and drive belt pulley (A, **Figure 16**) as described under *Drive Pulley and Drive Belt Removal/Installation* in Chapter Ten.
16. Refer to the following figures and disconnect the following electrical connectors:
   a. **Figure 17**: alternator stator (3-pin electrical connector containing 3 yellow wires).
   b. **Figure 18**: neutral indicator (1-pin electrical connector containing 1 blue wire).
   c. **Figure 19**: signal generator (2-pin electrical connector containing 2 wires, 1 orange and 1 green wire) and the sidestand indicator (2-pin electrical connector containing 1 green/white and 1 black/white wire).

*NOTE*
*If you are just removing the engine and are not planning to disassemble it, do not perform Step 17.*

17. If the engine is going to be disassembled, remove the following parts while the engine is still in the frame. Remove the following as described in this chapter unless otherwise noted:
   a. Alternator and starter (Chapter Seven).
   b. Clutch assembly (Chapter Five).
   c. External shift mechanism (Chapter Six).

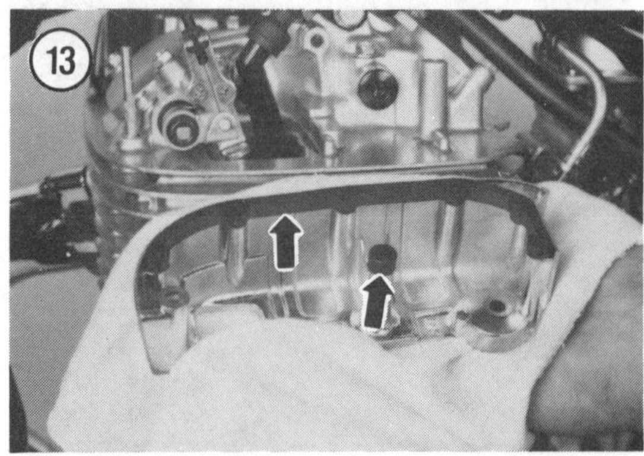

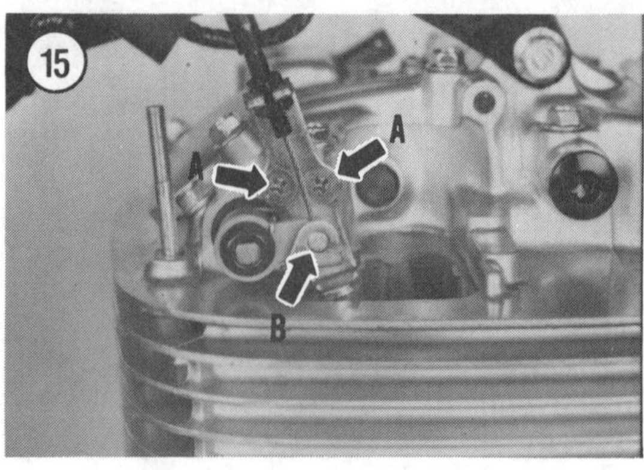

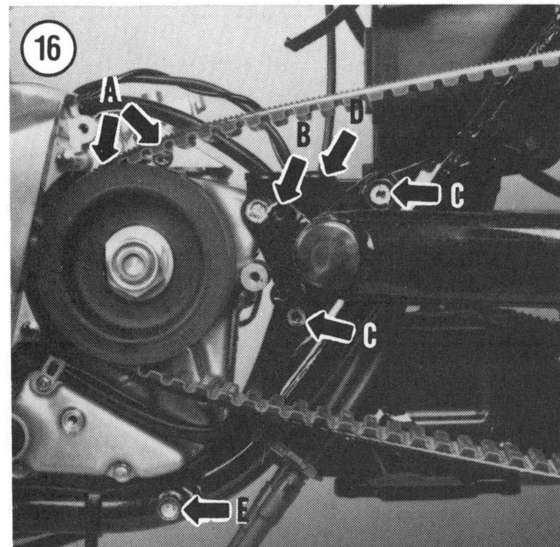


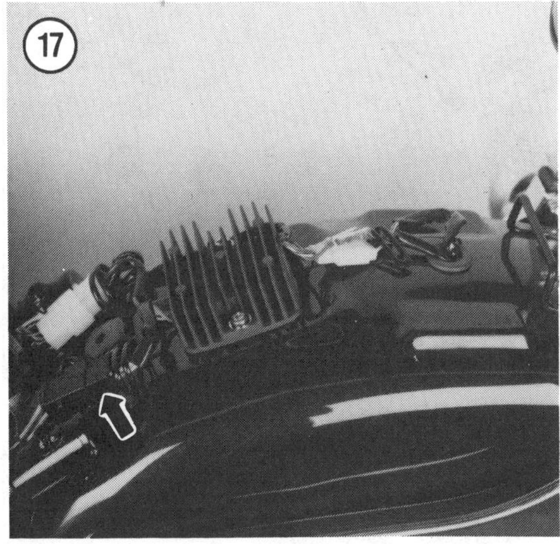

18. Take a final look all over the engine to make sure everything has been disconnected.
19. Place a suitable size jack, with a piece of wood to protect the crankcase, under the engine. Apply a small amount of jack pressure up on the engine.

*NOTE*
*There are many different bolt sizes and lengths, different combinations of washers, lockwashers and different holding plates. It is suggested that when **each set** of bolts, nuts, washers, spacers and holding plates are removed that you place them in a separate plastic bag or box to keep them separated. This will save a lot of time when installing the engine.*

*CAUTION*
*Continually adjust jack pressure during engine removal and installation to prevent damage to the mounting bolts threads and hardware.*

20. Refer to **Figure 20** and perform the following:
    a. Remove the cylinder head bolts, lockwashers, washers holding plates and nuts (**Figure 21**).
    b. Remove the rear upper through-bolt, washer and nut (B, **Figure 16**).
    c. Rear upper Allen bolts (C, **Figure 16**) and holding plate (D, **Figure 16** ) on each side.

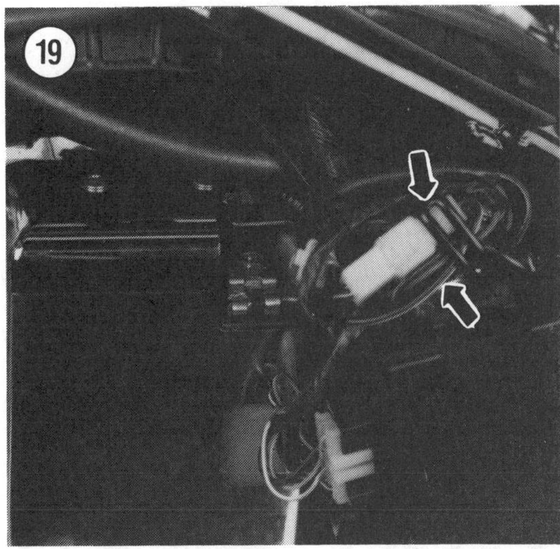

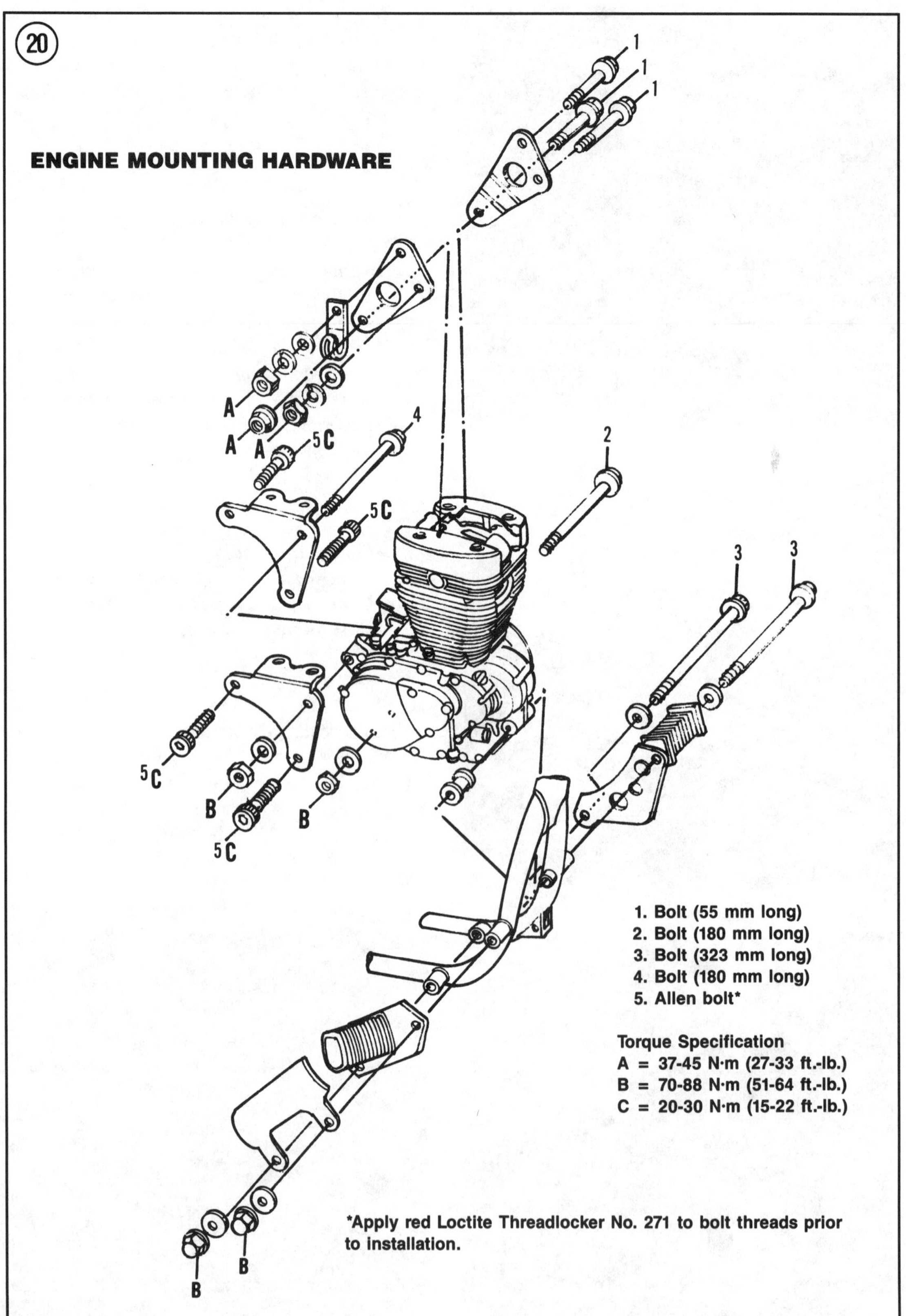
20
ENGINE MOUNTING HARDWARE
1
1
1
A
A
A
A
5C
4
5C
2
3
3
5C
B
B
5C
B
B
1. Bolt (55 mm long)
2. Bolt (180 mm long)
3. Bolt (323 mm long)
4. Bolt (180 mm long)
5. Allen bolt*
Torque Specification
A = 37-45 N·m (27-33 ft.-lb.)
B = 70-88 N·m (51-64 ft.-lb.)
C = 20-30 N·m (15-22 ft.-lb.)
*Apply red Loctite Threadlocker No. 271 to bolt threads prior to installation.

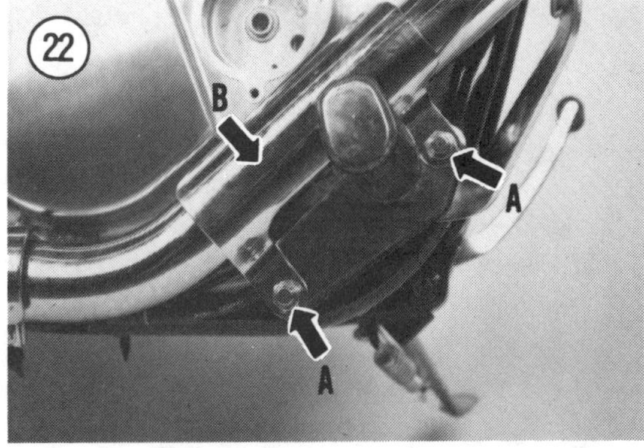

d. Remove the front cap nuts (A, **Figure 22**) and washer from the front through-bolts. Remove the exhaust pipe heat shield (B, **Figure 22**).
e. Tap the front through-bolt toward the left-hand side and remove the front footpeg and rear brake pedal assemblies (**Figure 23**) from the right-hand side. Move the assembly out of the way.
f. Withdraw the front through-bolts (**Figure 24**) and washers and remove the left-hand footpeg assembly. Don't lose the spacer on the right-hand side.
g. Remove the lower rear through-bolt (E, **Figure 16**), washer and nut.

*CAUTION*

*The following steps require the aid of a helper to safely remove the engine assembly from the frame. Due to the weight of the engine, it is suggested that one helper assist you in the removal of the engine.*

21. Gradually raise the engine assembly to clear the frame and pull the engine out through the right-hand side of the frame. Take the engine to a workbench for further disassembly.
22. Install by reversing these removal steps. Note the following during installation.
23. Refer to **Figure 20** and tighten the mounting bolts and nuts to the torque specifications in **Table 2**.
24. Fill the engine with the recommended type and quantity of oil; refer to Chapter Three.
25. Adjust the clutch as described under *Clutch Adjustment* in Chapter Three.
26. Adjust the drive belt as described under *Drive Chain Adjustment* in Chapter Three.
27. Check the freeplay on the automatic decompression release lever, adjust if necessary as described under *Automatic Decompression Cable Adjustment* in Chapter Three.
28. Start the engine and check for leaks.

## CYLINDER HEAD COVER, CAMSHAFT AND CYLINDER HEAD

Refer to **Figure 25** for the cylinder head cover and cylinder head and to **Figure 26** for the camshaft for this procedure.

(25)

**CYLINDER HEAD AND COVER**

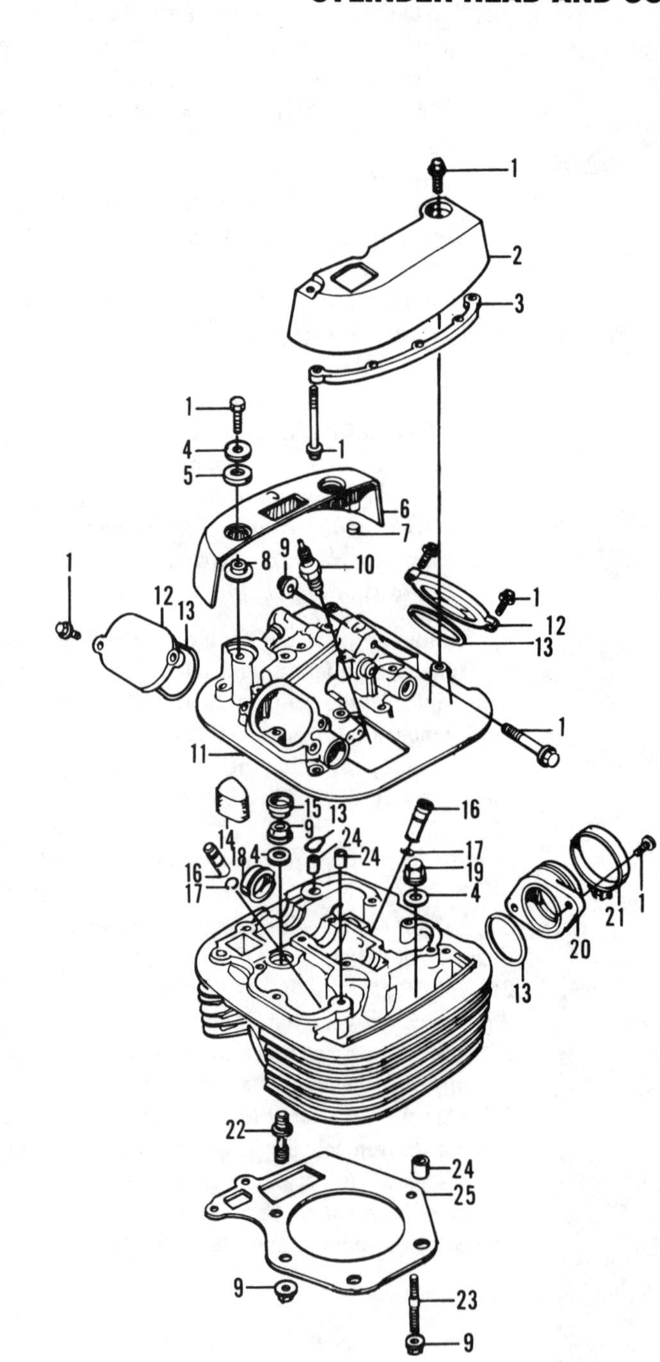

1. Bolt
2. Left-hand top cover
3. Rubber gasket
4. Washer
5. Rubber bushing
6. Right-hand top cover
7. Rubber stopper
8. Special washer
9. Cap nut
10. Spark plug
11. Cylinder head cover
12. Valve adjuster cover
13. Gasket
14. Wire mesh
15. Head seal cap
16. Valve guide
17. Ring
18. Plug
19. Cap nut
20. Intake tube
21. Clamp ring
22. Threaded stud
23. Threaded stud
24. Locating dowel
25. Head gasket

### Removal

*CAUTION*
*To prevent any warpage and damage, remove the cylinder head assembly only when the engine is at room temperature.*

*NOTE*
*Only in some cases can the cylinder head cover be removed with the engine in the frame. This depends on the manufacturing tolerances of your specific frame. If the frame is a little on the "small" side from top to bottom, in the engine mounting area, or if one of the engine mounting bosses is a little off tolerance it will be impossible to remove the cylinder head cover, camshaft and the cylinder head with the engine in the frame. It is suggested that the engine be removed from the frame for this procedure.*

*CAUTION*
*If you choose to try to remove the upper end with the engine in the frame, do so **carefully**—do not try to force anything off if there isn't enough room between the engine and the top of the frame rail.*



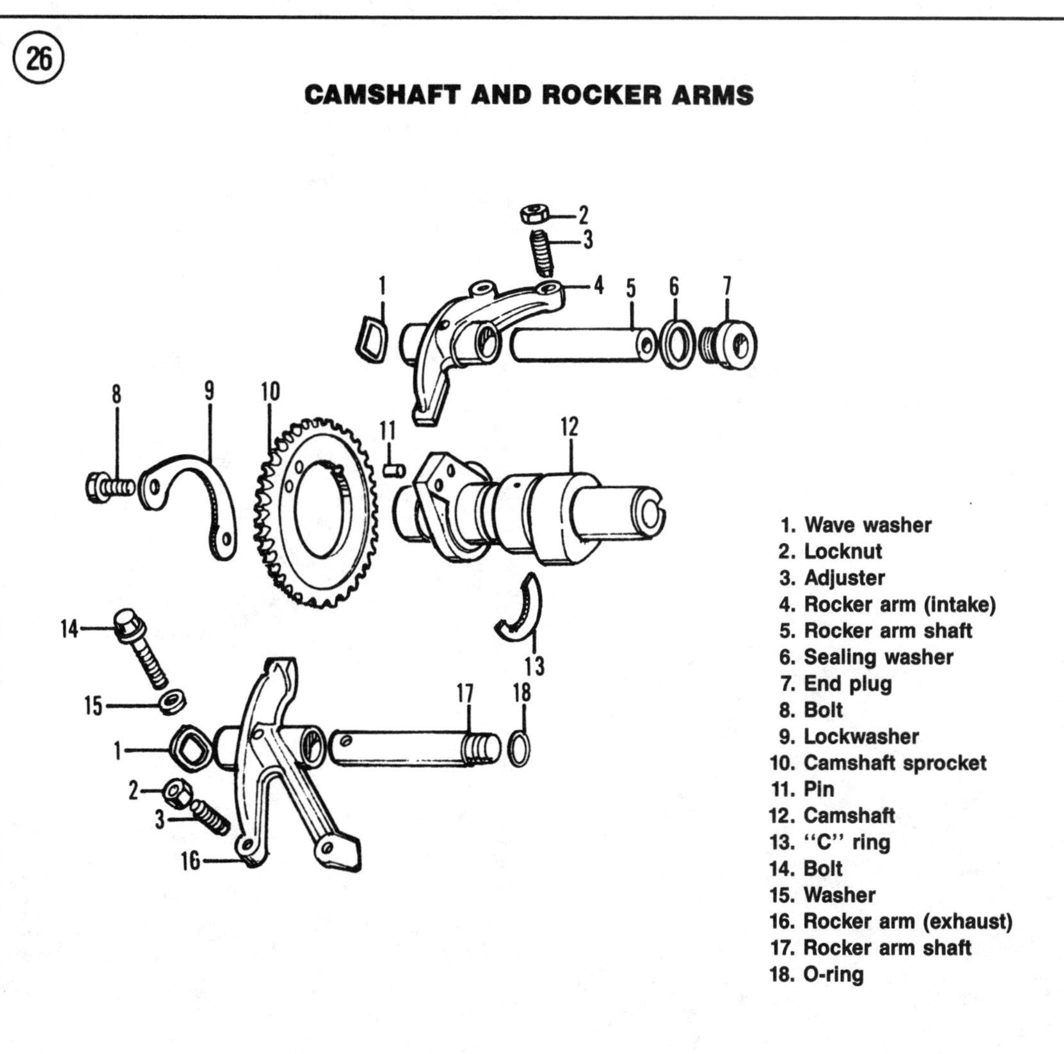

1. Remove the bolts (**Figure 27**) securing the valve adjuster cover and remove the covers. Don't lose the rubber gasket on each cover.

*NOTE*
*Steps 2-4 are necessary to relieve strain on the cylinder head cover by positioning the camshaft lobes down. With the lobes facing down there is no pressure on the rocker arms.*

*NOTE*
*Either use a wide, flat-tipped screwdriver or a special tool made by Honda (yes, Honda not Suzuki). This special tool (**Figure 28**) (Honda part No. 07700-0010001) is made specifically for this purpose and if carefully used, will not mar nor damage the surface on the inspection cover. If you use a screwdriver, do so carefully otherwise the cover can be damaged.*

2. Remove the valve timing inspection cover (**Figure 29**) on the left-hand crankcase cover.
3. Use a 17 mm wrench (**Figure 30**) on the alternator rotor bolt. Rotate the engine *clockwise,* as viewed from the left-hand side, until the engine is at top dead center (TDC). Align the groove on the end of the alternator rotor with the notch in the alternator cover (**Figure 31**).

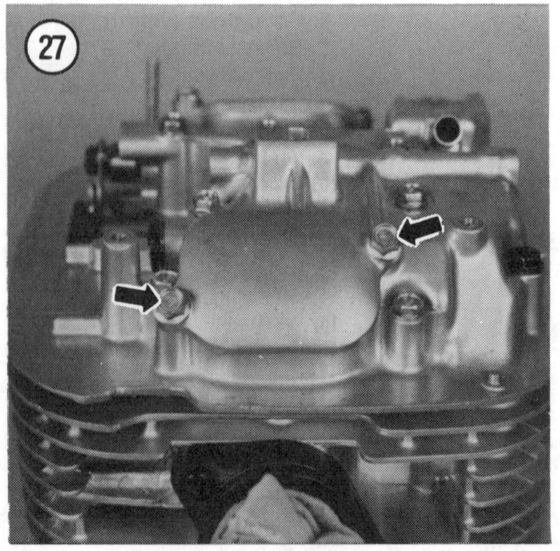


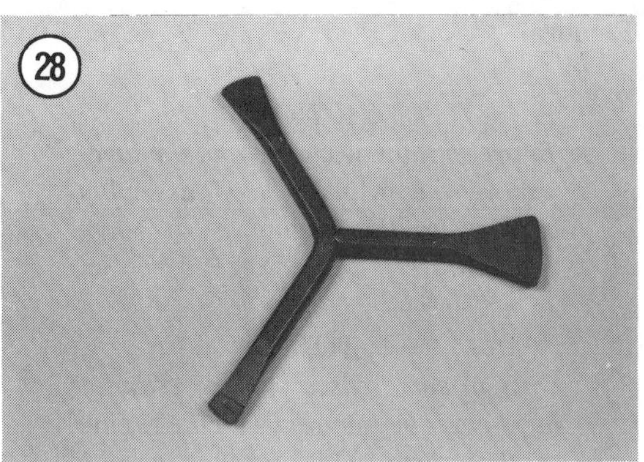


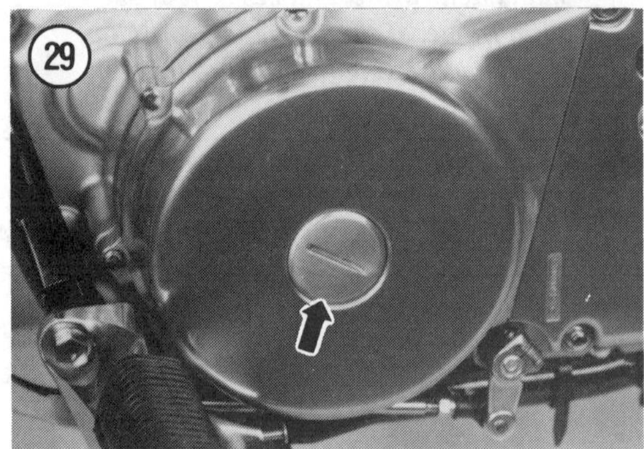

32

33

34

35

4. With the groove aligned with the notch, jiggle both rocker arms and make sure *both* have free play. If one rocker arm is still under tension, rotate the engine an additional 180° until both rocker arms have free play.
5. Remove the engine from the frame as described under *Engine Removal/Installation* in this chapter.
6. Remove the right-hand crankcase cover as described in this chapter.



*CAUTION*

*In the following step, do **not** remove the bolt with a concave head and marked with an "A" (**Figure 32**). This bolt secures the exhaust valve rocker arm shaft in place and must be left in place at this time.*

7. Using a crisscross pattern, loosen, then remove the bolts securing the cylinder head cover (**Figure 33**) to the cylinder head.
8. Remove the cylinder head cover. Don't lose the locating dowels.
9. Remove the loose bolt (**Figure 34**) used to hold the left-hand top cover in place.
10. Remove the cylinder head plug (**Figure 35**) from left-hand side of the cylinder head.
11. Remove the circlip (**Figure 36**) securing the camshaft chain tensioner adjuster to the threaded stud.

36

12. Place an open end wrench (A, **Figure 37**) on the backside of the camshaft chain tensioner adjuster.
13. Remove the bolt (B, **Figure 37**) securing the camshaft chain tensioner adjuster to the camshaft chain tensioner. Remove the tensioner adjuster assembly.
14. Straighten the locking tab on the lockwasher and loosen the camshaft sprocket bolt (**Figure 38**).
15. Use a 17 mm wrench on the alternator rotor bolt. Rotate the engine *clockwise,* as viewed from the left-hand side, until the other camshaft sprocket bolt is exposed.
16. Straighten the locking tab on the lockwasher and loosen the camshaft sprocket bolt (**Figure 39**). Remove this bolt.
17. Again rotate the engine *clockwise,* as viewed from the left-hand side, until the remaining camshaft sprocket bolt is exposed. Remove this bolt and the lockwasher.
18. Disengage the camshaft drive chain (**Figure 40**) from the camshaft sprocket.
19. Pull the camshaft toward the left-hand side and remove the camshaft sprocket from the cylinder head.
20. Tie a piece of wire to the drive chain and secure the other end to the exterior of the engine.
21. Remove the camshaft from the cylinder head. Don't lose the locating pin (**Figure 41**) from the end of the camshaft.
22. Remove the camshaft C-ring from the groove in the cylinder head.

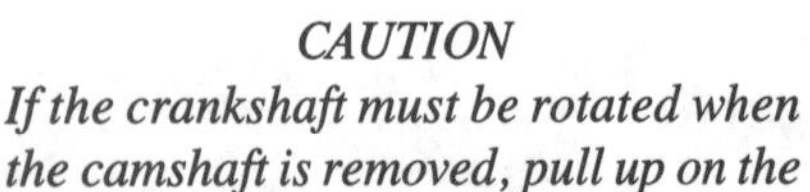
*CAUTION*
*If the crankshaft must be rotated when the camshaft is removed, pull up on the*

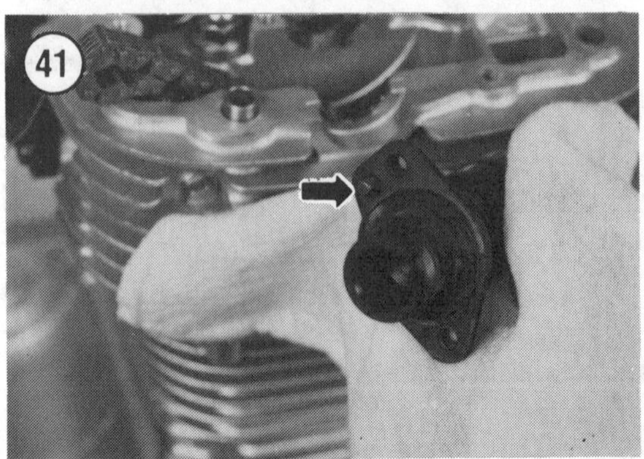

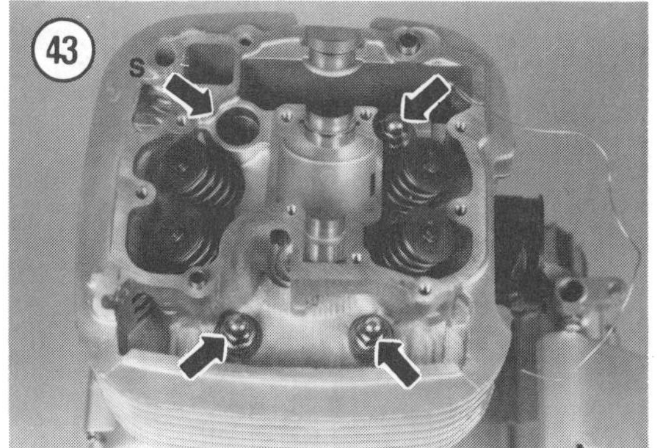

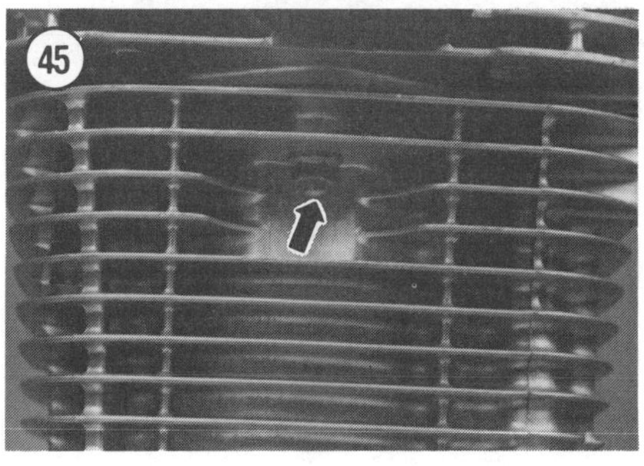


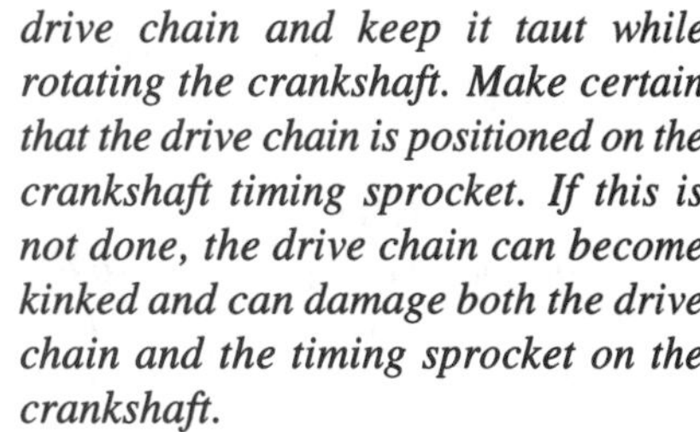
*drive chain and keep it taut while rotating the crankshaft. Make certain that the drive chain is positioned on the crankshaft timing sprocket. If this is not done, the drive chain can become kinked and can damage both the drive chain and the timing sprocket on the crankshaft.*

23. Remove the head seal cap (**Figure 42**) from the cylinder head.
24. Using a crisscross pattern, loosen the bolts (**Figure 43**) securing the cylinder head to the crankcase studs. Remove the nuts and copper washers.
25. Remove the nuts securing the front (**Figure 44**) and rear (**Figure 45**) of the cylinder head to the cylinder.
26. Remove the bolt and washer (**Figure 46**) securing the camshaft chain tensioner to the cylinder head.
27. Loosen the cylinder head (A, **Figure 47**) by tapping around the perimeter with a rubber or soft-

faced mallet. If necessary, *gently* pry the head loose with a broad-tipped screwdriver.

*CAUTION*
*Remember the cooling fins are fragile and may be damaged if tapped on or pried too hard. Never use a metal hammer.*

28. Lift the cylinder head straight up and off the cylinder and crankcase studs. Guide the camshaft chain through the opening in the cylinder head and retie the wire to the exterior of the engine. This will prevent the drive chain from falling down into the crankcase.
29. Remove the cylinder head gasket and discard it. Don't lose the locating dowels.
30. Inspect the cylinder head cover, the cylinder head and camshaft as described in this chapter.

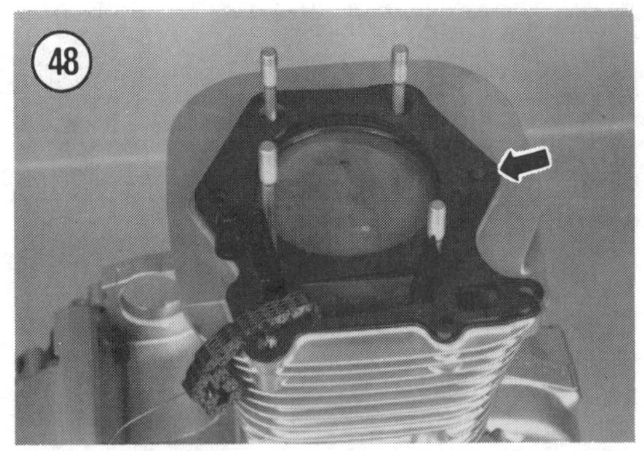


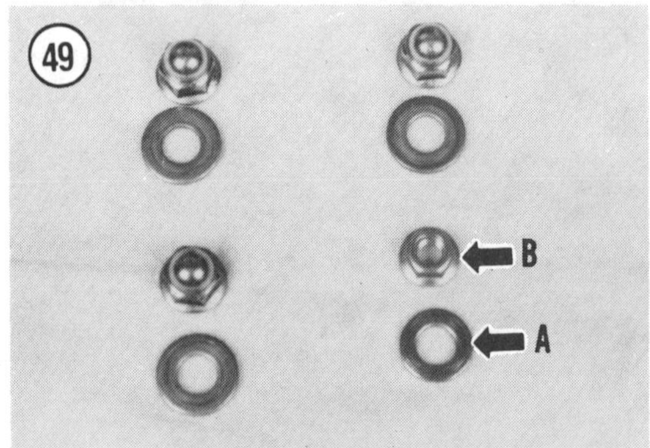


### Installation

1. If removed, install the locating dowel in the cylinder.
2. Install a new cylinder head gasket (**Figure 48**).
3. Carefully slide the cylinder head onto the cylinder. Feed the camshaft chain through the chain cavity in the cylinder head and secure the other end of the wire again (B, **Figure 47**).
4. Apply oil to the threads of the crankcase threaded studs.

*NOTE*
*There is one copper washer that is smaller in diameter than the remaining three. This smaller washer (A, **Figure 49**) goes with the standard nut (non-cap type) (B, **Figure 49**). The larger diameter copper washers go with the cap nuts.*

5. Install the smaller copper washer and standard type nut on the front right-hand crankcase stud (S, **Figure 43**).
6. Install the larger copper washers and cap nuts onto the remaining crankcase studs.
7. Tighten the nuts in the crisscross pattern to the torque specification listed in **Table 2**.

52

*CAUTION*
*In Step 8, be sure to apply the recommended sealant to the cap and* ***be sure to install the cap*** *in the cylinder head. If the cap is not sealed properly, is installed crookedly, or if it is not installed at all, there will be an oil leak of large proportions by the exhaust port. Not only will this lead to an oily mess, you may also lose enough oil to ruin the engine.*

53

8. Apply a coat of Three Bond No. 1216 in the groove (**Figure 50**) of the head seal cap and install the cap into the hole in the cylinder head (**Figure 42**). Make sure the cap is pushed in all the way until it bottoms out and is seated squarely in the hole.
9. Install the nuts securing the front (**Figure 44**) and rear (**Figure 45**) of the cylinder head to the cylinder. Tighten the nuts to the torque specification listed in **Table 2**.
10. Install the bolt and washer (**Figure 51**) securing the camshaft chain tensioner to the cylinder head. Tighten securely.
11. Remove the left-hand crankcase cover as described in this chapter.

54

*CAUTION*
*In Step 11, pull up on the drive chain and keep it taut while rotating the crankshaft. Make certain that the drive chain is positioned on the crankshaft timing sprocket. If this is not done, the drive chain may become kinked and may damage both the drive chain and the timing sprocket on the crankshaft.*

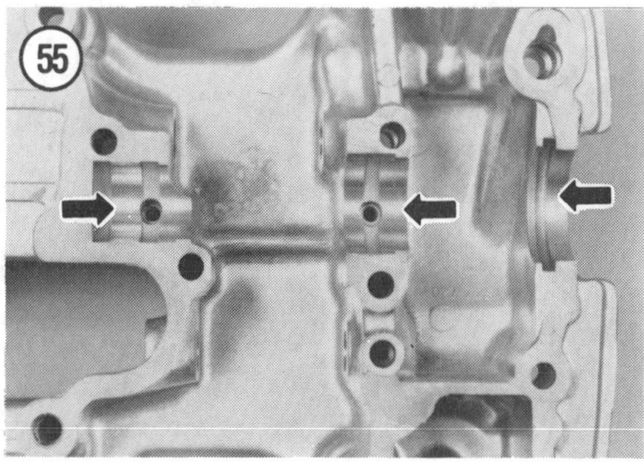
55

12. Use a 17 mm wrench on the alternator rotor bolt (**Figure 52**). Rotate the engine *clockwise,* as viewed from the left-hand side, until the "T" mark aligns with the index mark (**Figure 53**) on the crankcase.
13. Apply molybdenum disulfide grease to the camshaft bearing journal surfaces in the cylinder head (**Figure 54**) and cylinder head cover (**Figure 55**).

14. Apply molybdenum disulfide grease to the camshaft bearing journals.
15. Make sure the locating pin (**Figure 56**) is in place in the end of the camshaft.
16. Pull up on the camshaft drive chain and insert the camshaft through the chain and into the cylinder head (**Figure 57**).
17. Rotate the camshaft so the lobes are facing down.
18. Install the camshaft sprocket (**Figure 58**) and drive chain (**Figure 59**).

*CAUTION*

*Very expensive damage could result from improper camshaft drive chain to camshaft alignment. Recheck your work several times to be sure alignment is correct.*

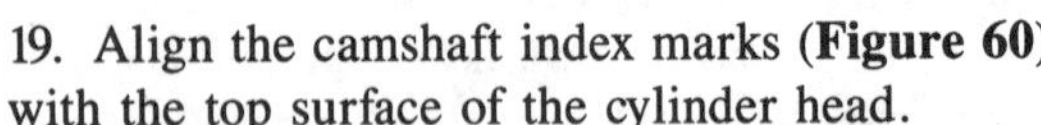

19. Align the camshaft index marks (**Figure 60**) with the top surface of the cylinder head.
20. Align the locating pin on the end of the camshaft with the hole in the camshaft drive sprocket and position the sprocket onto the camshaft (**Figure 61**).
21. Position the lockwasher so it covers the locating pin on the camshaft (**Figure 62**). This is to keep the pin from falling out should it work loose.

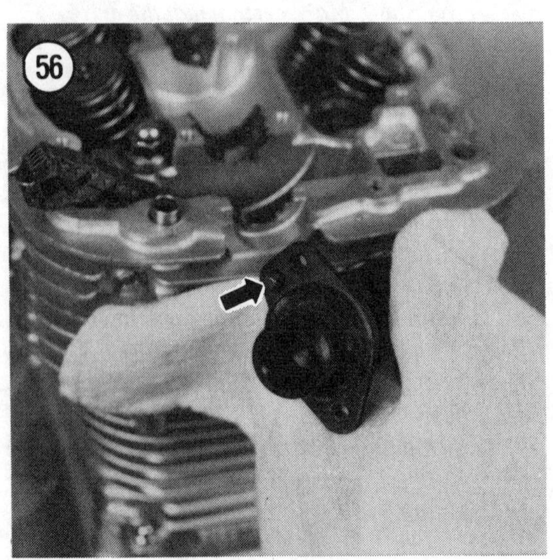

22. Apply red Loctite Threadlocker (No. 271) to the threads of the sprocket bolt and install the bolt. Tighten the bolt to a good finger-tightness at this time. Do *not* completely tighten this bolt until the other bolt is installed.
23. Use a 17 mm wrench on the alternator rotor bolt. Rotate the engine *clockwise,* as viewed from the left-hand side, until the other sprocket bolt hole is exposed.
24. Apply red Loctite Threadlocker (No. 271) to the threads of the remaining sprocket bolt and install the bolt. Tighten the bolt to the torque specification listed in **Table 2**. Bend up a locking tab of the lockwasher against one side of the bolt (**Figure 63**).
25. Use a 17 mm wrench on the alternator rotor bolt. Rotate the engine *clockwise,* as viewed from the left-hand side, until the other sprocket bolt is exposed.
26. Tighten the bolt to the torque specification listed in **Table 2**. Bend up a locking tab of the lockwasher against one side of the bolt (**Figure 64**).
27. Install the camshaft C-ring (**Figure 65**) into the groove in the cylinder head. Push the C-ring down into the groove until the ends are flush with the top surface of the cylinder head.
28. Apply a liberal amount of new engine oil to the top surface of the camshaft and into the pocket in the cylinder head so the cam lobes are submerged in the oil.
29. Do not apply any type of sealant to the cylinder head plug and install the plug into the cylinder head (**Figure 66**).

4

30. Make sure the locating dowels (**Figure 67**) are in place in the cylinder head.
31. Install the loose bolt (**Figure 68**), used to hold the left-hand top cover, into position in the front left-hand corner.

*NOTE*
*The cylinder head sealing surface must be thoroughly cleaned using the following method to help prevent an oil leak.*

32. Clean the sealing surface as follows:
   a. Remove the old gaskets and clean off all gasket sealer residue from the cylinder head cover.
   b. Clean the surface with aerosol electrical contact cleaner and wipe dry with a lint-free cloth.
   c. Apply a coat of Three Bond No. 1216 to sealing surface of the cylinder head cover. Do *not* apply sealant to the rounded surfaces of the camshaft bearing journal surfaces.
33. Install a new O-ring seal (**Figure 69**) in the cylinder head cover.
34. Make sure the wire mesh (**Figure 70**) is in place in the crankcase breather space.
35. Install the cylinder head cover onto the cylinder head.
36. Refer to **Figure 71** for cylinder head cover bolt length placement. Be sure to place a sealing washer under all bolt heads followed by an asterisk (*) in **Figure 71**. Install the bolts securing the cylinder head cover. The only black bolt (length 130 mm) is installed at the right-hand rear corner.

66

67

68

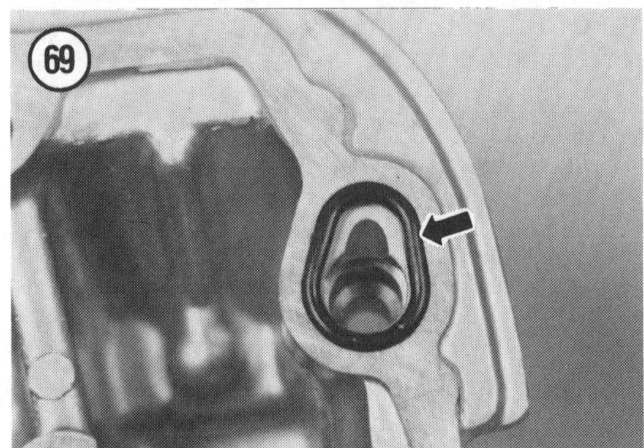
69

70

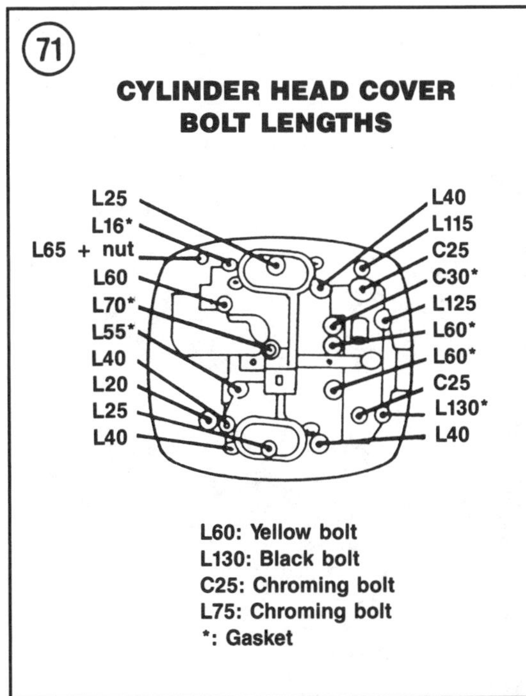


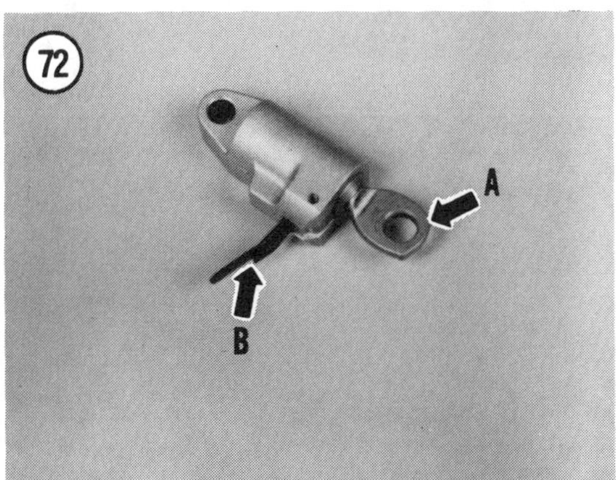

37. Tighten the bolts in a crisscross pattern, starting with the center bolts (surrounding the camshaft) and working outward. Tighten in 2-3 stages to the torque specification listed in **Table 2**.

38. Load the camshaft chain tensioner adjuster in the fully relaxed position as follows:

   a. Cut off about 1/2 inch of a medium length tie wrap and bend it back onto itself.
   b. Using a narrow, flat-bladed screwdriver, release the ratchet and push the plunger back into the camshaft chain tensioner adjuster body until it stops (A, **Figure 72**).
   c. Press the bend over piece of tie wrap (B, **Figure 72**) into the tensioner to hold the plunger in place.

39. Position the rear portion of the tensioner adjuster onto the threaded stud and install the circlip (**Figure 73**). Make sure the circlip is seated securely in the groove.

40. Place an open end wrench (A, **Figure 74**) on the backside of the camshaft chain tensioner adjuster.

41. Install and tighten the bolt (B, **Figure 74**) securing the camshaft chain tensioner adjuster to the camshaft chain tensioner. Tighten the bolt to the torque specification listed in **Table 2**.

42. Remove the piece of tie wrap from the adjuster body. At this time the adjuster will apply the correct amount of tension on the camshaft drive chain. No further adjustment is necessary.

43. Inspect the rubber gasket (**Figure 75**) in the valve adjuster covers, replace if necessary.

44. Adjust the valves as described under *Valve Clearance Measurement and Adjustment* in Chapter Three.

45. Install the bolts (**Figure 76**) securing the valve adjuster covers and tighten securely.
46. Install the spark plug and reconnect the spark plug lead.
47. Install the right- and left-hand crankcase covers as described in this chapter.
48. Make sure the washers under the rubber cushions (**Figure 77**) are in place in the cylinder head right-hand top cover.
49. Install the cylinder head right-hand (**Figure 78**) top cover and the bolts and washers. Tighten the bolts securely.
50. Make sure the rubber cushions (**Figure 79**) are in place in the cylinder head left-hand top cover.
51. Install the cylinder head left-hand (**Figure 80**) top cover and the bolt and nut. Tighten the bolt and nut securely.
52. Install the engine into the frame as described under *Engine Removal/Installation* in this chapter.

**Cylinder Head Cover Inspection**

1. Remove all traces of gasket material from the cylinder head cover gasket surfaces.
2. After the cylinder head cover has been thoroughly cleaned, place the cover on an inspection surface like a piece of plate glass and check for any warpage at several points with a flat feeler gauge.
3. Measure the warp by inserting a flat feeler gauge between the cylinder head cover gasket surface and the plate glass. There should be no

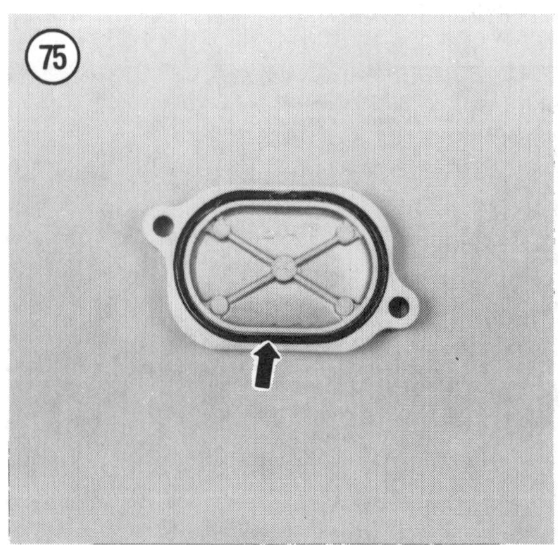


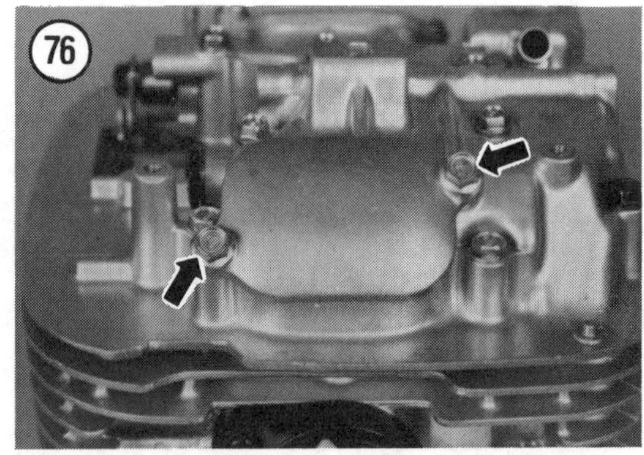

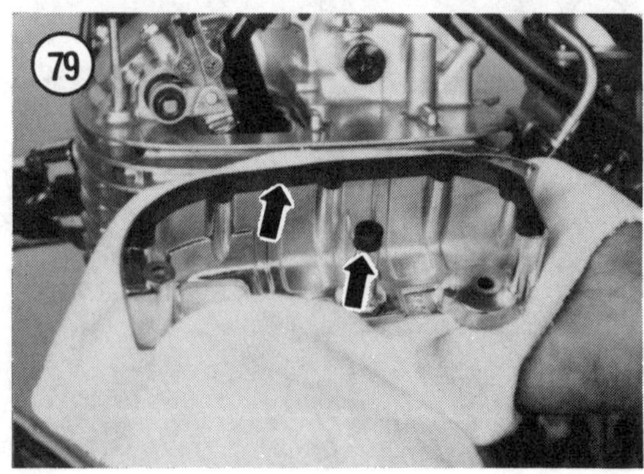

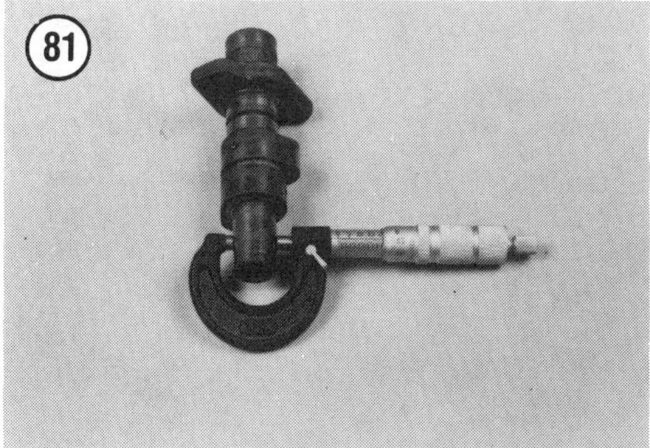

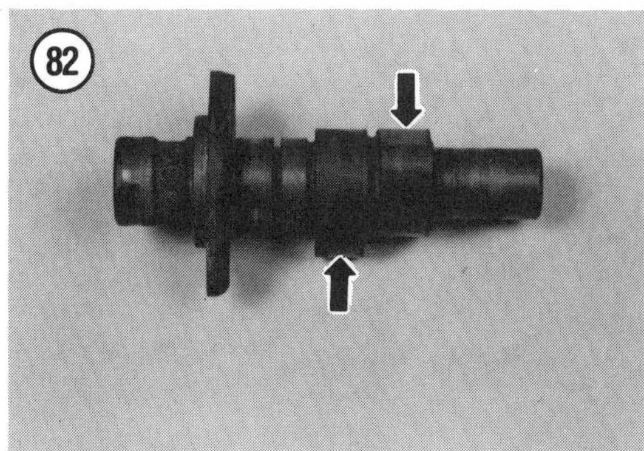

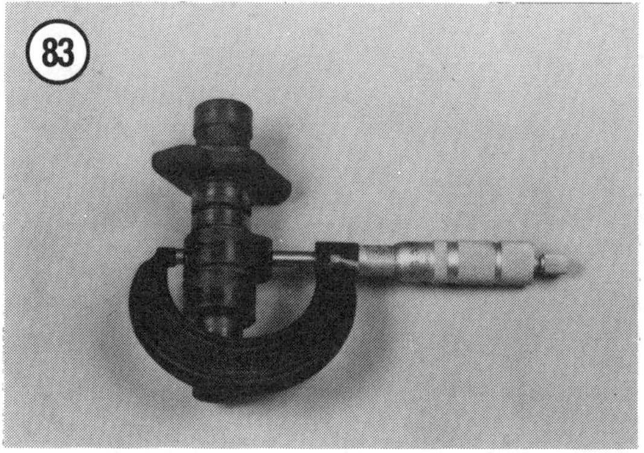

warpage. Replace the cylinder head cover if the gasket surface is warped to or beyond the service limit listed in **Table 1**.

4. Disassemble and inspect the rocker arms as described in this chapter.

## Camshaft Inspection

1. Measure the right, center and left-hand camshaft bearing journals (**Figure 81**) with a micrometer. Compare to the dimensions given in **Table 1**. If worn to the service limit or less, the camshaft must be replaced.
2. Check the camshaft lobes (**Figure 82**) for wear. The lobes should show no signs of scoring and the edges should be square. Slight damage may be removed with a silicone carbide oilstone. Use No. 100-120 grit stone initially, then polish with a No. 280-320 grit stone.
3. Even though the camshaft lobe surface appears to be satisfactory, with no visible signs of wear, the camshaft lobes must be measured with a micrometer (**Figure 83**). Compare to the dimensions given in **Table 1**. If worn to the service limit or less, the camshaft must be replaced.
4. Place the camshaft on a set of V-blocks and check its runout with a dial indicator. Compare to the dimension given in **Table 1**. If the runout is to the service limit or more, the camshaft must be replaced.
5. Make sure the locating pin in the end of the camshaft is a tight fit. If not, replace the pin.
6. Inspect the camshaft bearing surfaces in the cylinder head (**Figure 84**) and cylinder head cover

(**Figure 85**). They should not be scored or excessively worn. Replace the cylinder head and camshaft bearing caps if the bearing surfaces are worn or scored.

7. Inspect the camshaft sprocket teeth (A, **Figure 86**) for wear; replace if necessary.
8. Make sure the camshaft sprocket bolt holes (B, **Figure 86**) are not elongated or damaged. If damaged, replace the camshaft sprocket.

## Camshaft Bearing Clearance Measurement

This procedure requires the use of a Plastigage set. The camshaft must be installed into the cylinder head. Before installing the camshaft, wipe all oil residue from the camshaft bearing journals and bearing surfaces in the cylinder head and cylinder head cover.

1. Install the camshaft into the cylinder head with the lobes facing down. Do not attach the drive sprocket to the camshaft.
2. Install the "C" ring into the groove in the camshaft and cylinder head.
3. Make sure the locating dowels (**Figure 87**) are in place in the cylinder head.
4. Place a strip of Plastigage material on top of each camshaft bearing journal, parallel to the camshaft.
5. Install the cylinder head cover and bolts.
6. Refer to **Figure 71** for cylinder head cover bolt length placement. Be sure to place a sealing washer under all bolt heads followed by an asterisk (*) in **Figure 71**. Install the bolts securing the cylinder head cover. The only black bolt (length 130 mm) is installed at the right-hand rear corner.
7. Tighten the bolts in a crisscross pattern, starting with the center bolts (surrounding the camshaft) and working outward. Tighten in 2-3 stages to the torque specification listed in **Table 2**.

*CAUTION*

*Do not rotate the camshaft with the Plastigage material in place.*

8. Loosen the cylinder head bolts in 2-3 stages in a crisscross pattern, then remove the bolts and sealing washers.
9. Carefully remove the cylinder head cover.
10. Measure the width of the flattened Plastigage material at the widest point, according to the manufacturer's instructions.

*CAUTION*

*Be sure to remove all traces of Plastigage material from the bearing journal grooves in the cylinder head cover. If any material is left in the engine it can plug up an oil control orifice and cause severe engine damage.*

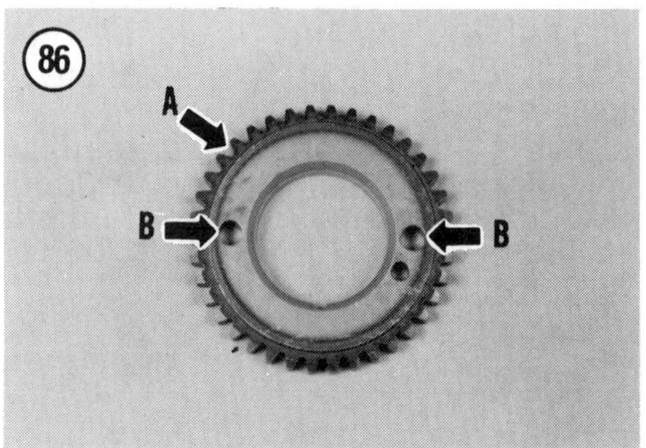

11. Remove *all* Plastigage material from the camshaft and the bearing caps.
12. If the oil clearance is greater than specified in **Table 1**, and the camshaft bearing journal dimensions are within specification in *Camshaft Inspection,* replace the cylinder head and cylinder head cover as a set.
13. Remove the camshaft from the cylinder head.

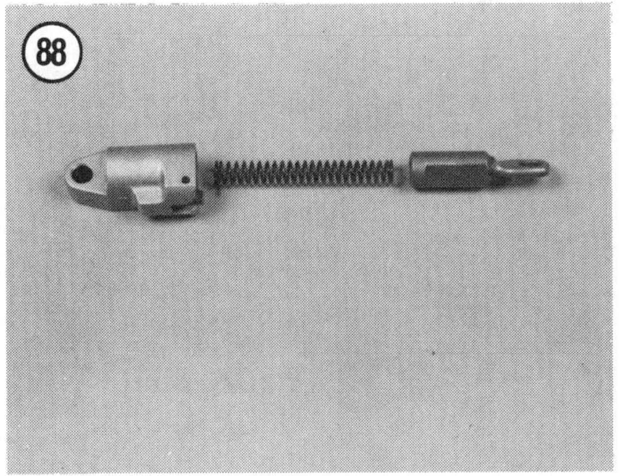
88

89

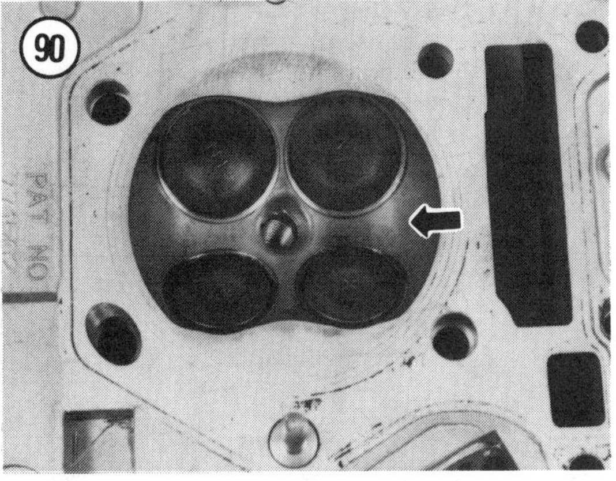
90

### Camshaft Chain Tensioner Adjuster Inspection

Inspect all parts of the camshaft chain tensioner adjuster for wear or damage (**Figure 88**). Suzuki does not provide any service specifications for the tensioner adjuster. If any part of the tensioner adjuster body or rack are worn or damaged, replace the entire assembly. Replacement parts are not available.



### Cylinder Head Inspection

1. Remove all traces of gasket material from the cylinder head cover mating surfaces (**Figure 89**).

2. *Without removing the valves,* remove all carbon deposits from the combustion chambers (**Figure 90**) valve ports with a wire brush. A blunt screwdriver or chisel may be used if care is taken not to damage the head, valves and spark plug threads.

3. After the carbon is removed from the combustion chamber and the valve intake and exhaust ports, clean the entire head in cleaning solvent. Blow dry with compressed air.

4. Check for cracks in the combustion chamber and exhaust ports. A cracked head must be replaced.

5. After the head has been thoroughly cleaned, place a straightedge across the cylinder head/cylinder gasket surface at several points. Measure the warp by inserting a flat feeler gauge between the straightedge and the cylinder head at each location. There should be no warpage. Replace the cylinder head and cylinder head cover as a set if the gasket surface is warped to or beyond the limit listed in **Table 1**.

6. Check the valves and valve guides as described in this chapter.

7. If necessary, remove the screws securing the intake pipe (**Figure 91**) onto the cylinder head. To prevent a vacuum leak, install a new O-ring seal between the intake pipe and the cylinder head. Install the intake pipe and tighten the screws securely.

### Decompressor Linkage Removal/Inspection/Installation

Refer to **Figure 92** for this procedure.

1. Remove the bolt and sealing washer (A, **Figure 93**) securing the actuator shaft assembly in the cylinder head cover.
2. Withdraw the actuator shaft assembly (B, **Figure 93**) from the cylinder head cover.
3. Make sure the nut (**Figure 94**) is tight.
4. Inspect the actuator shaft (A, **Figure 95**) for wear or damage, replace if necessary.
5. Inspect the spring (B, **Figure 95**) for damage or fatigue, replace if necessary.
6. Inspect the oil seal (**Figure 96**) in the cylinder head cover for wear or damage; replace if necessary.
7. Install the actuator shaft assembly into the cylinder head cover. Position the spring end into the recess (**Figure 97**) in the cylinder head cover.
8. Install the bolt and new sealing washer (**Figure 98**) securing the actuator shaft assembly in the cylinder head cover. Tighten the bolt securely.

## ROCKER ARM ASSEMBLIES

Refer to **Figure 99** for this procedure.

### Removal

1. Remove the cylinder head cover as described in this chapter.

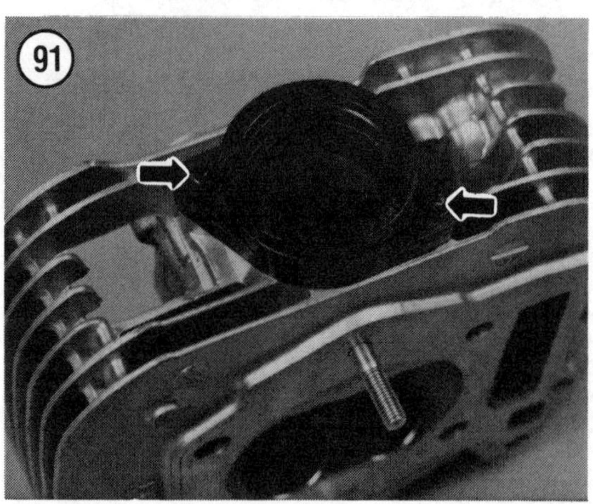


92

**DECOMPRESSOR ASSEMBLY**

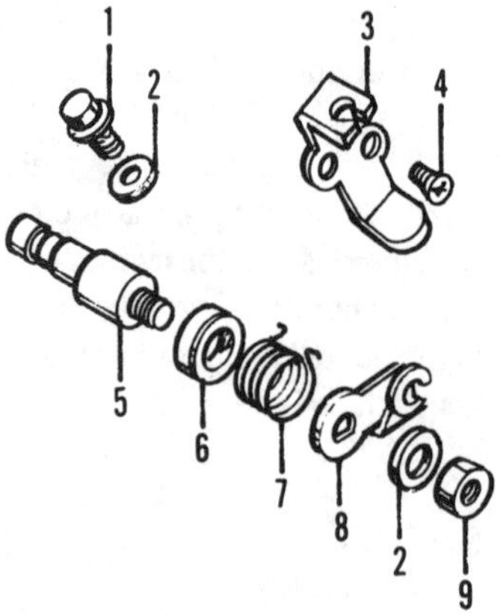

1. Bolt
2. Sealing washer
3. Holder
4. Screw
5. Actuator shaft
6. Oil seal
7. Spring
8. Lever
9. Nut

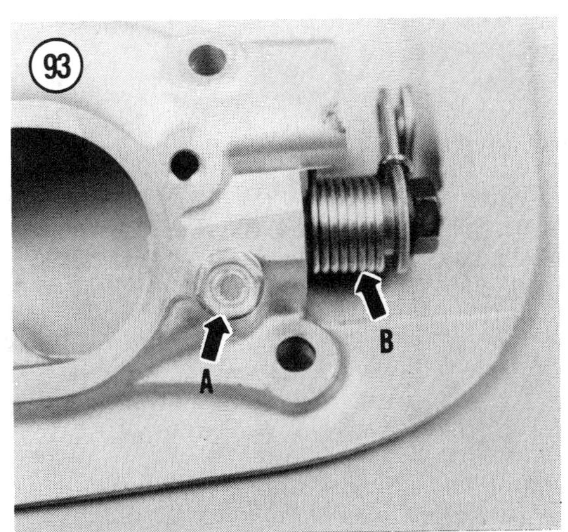
93
A
B

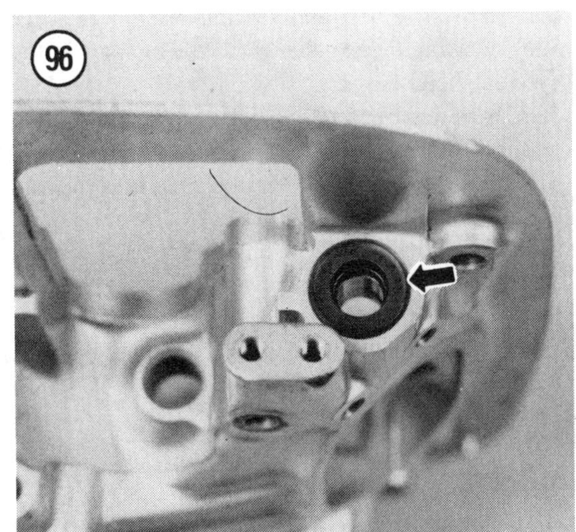
96

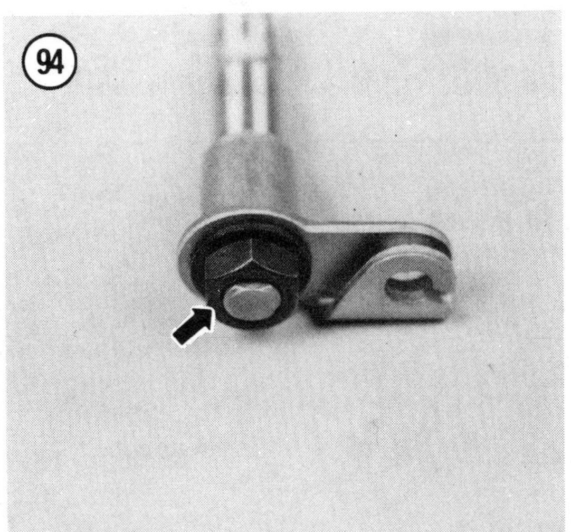
94

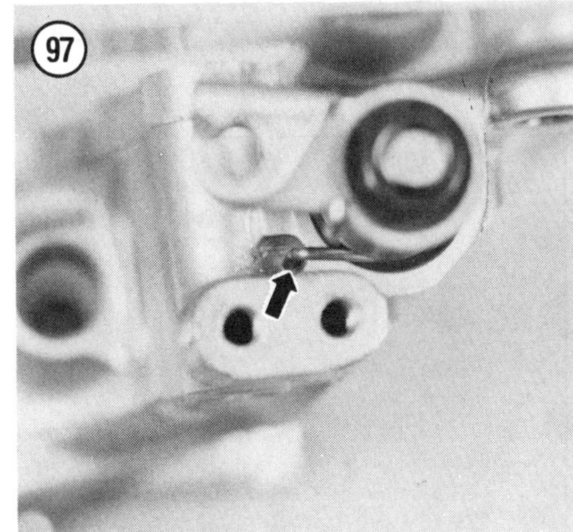
97

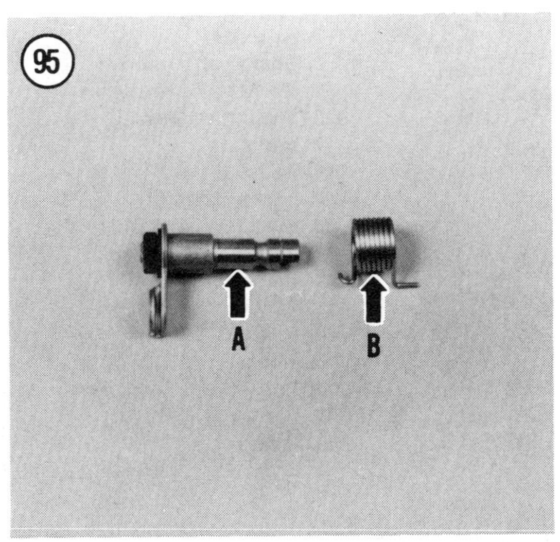
95
A
B

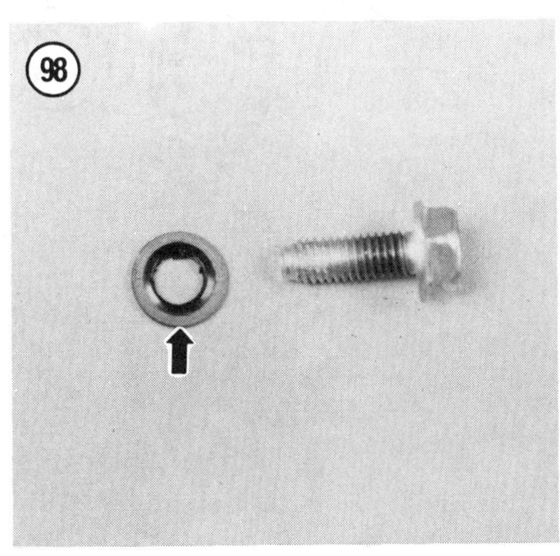
98

2. Remove the bolt and sealing washer (**Figure 100**) securing the exhaust rocker arm shaft in the cylinder head cover.
3. Unscrew the end plug (**Figure 101**) and sealing washer from the end of the intake rocker arm shaft.
4. Screw a 6 mm bolt (**Figure 102**) into the end of the intake rocker arm shaft.
5. Pull the intake rocker arm shaft out and remove the rocker arm and wave washer.
6. Using a pair of pliers, pull the exhaust rocker arm shaft out and remove the rocker arm and wave washer.

*NOTE*
*Note that the rocker arms are a different length and design. The exhaust rocker arm (A, **Figure 103**) is longer and has an O-ring seal on the left-hand end. The intake rocker arm (B, **Figure 103**) is shorter.*

7. Wash all parts in solvent and thoroughly dry with compressed air.

### Inspection

1. Inspect the rocker arm pad where it rides on the cam lobe (**Figure 104**) and where the adjusters

(100)

(99)

**CAMSHAFT AND ROCKER ARMS**

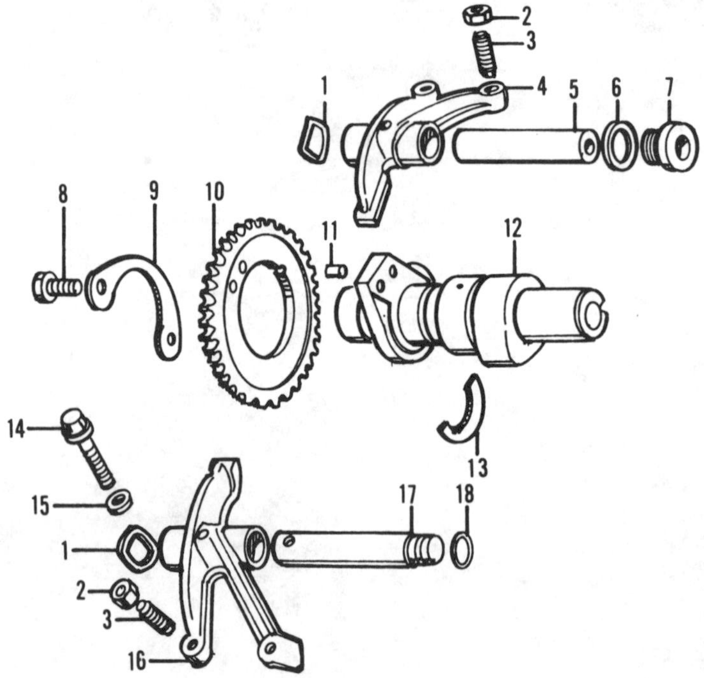

1. Wave washer
2. Locknut
3. Adjuster
4. Rocker arm (intake)
5. Rocker arm shaft
6. Sealing washer
7. End plug
8. Bolt
9. Lockwasher
10. Camshaft sprocket
11. Pin
12. Camshaft
13. "C" ring
14. Bolt
15. Washer
16. Rocker arm (exhaust)
17. Rocker arm shaft
18. O-ring

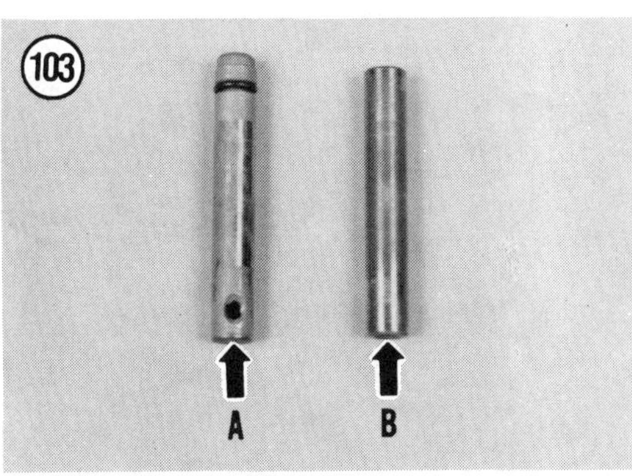


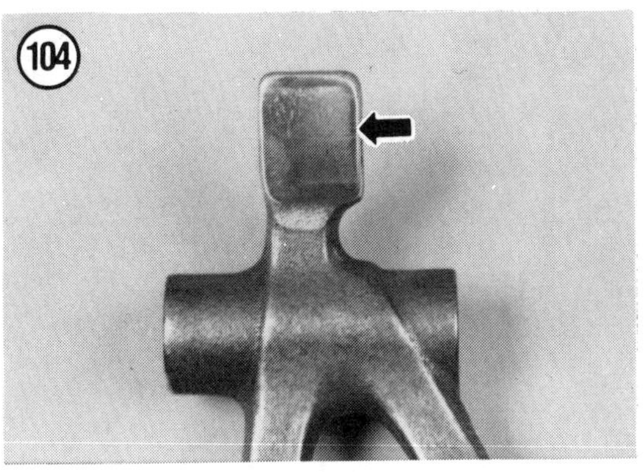


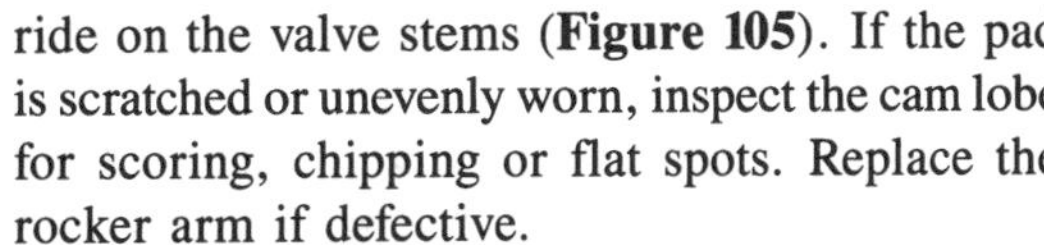
ride on the valve stems (**Figure 105**). If the pad is scratched or unevenly worn, inspect the cam lobe for scoring, chipping or flat spots. Replace the rocker arm if defective.

2. Measure the inside diameter of the rocker arm bore (**Figure 106**) and check against the dimensions in **Table 1**. Replace if worn to the service limit or greater.

3. Inspect the rocker arm shaft for signs of wear or scoring. Measure the outside diameter (**Figure 107**) with a micrometer and check against the

4

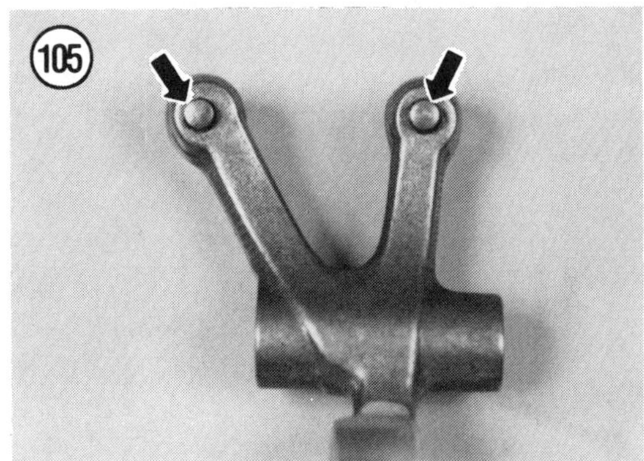


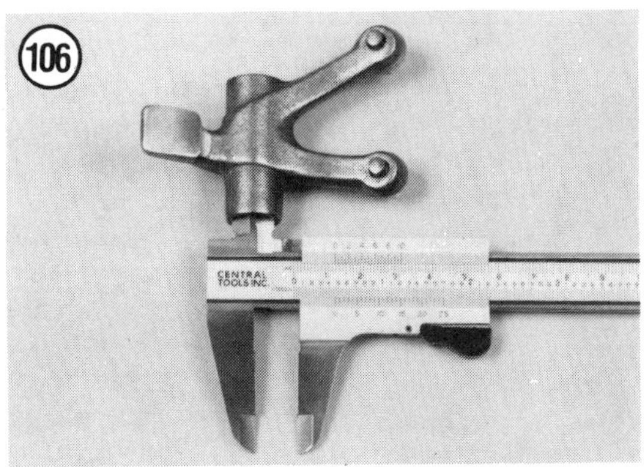


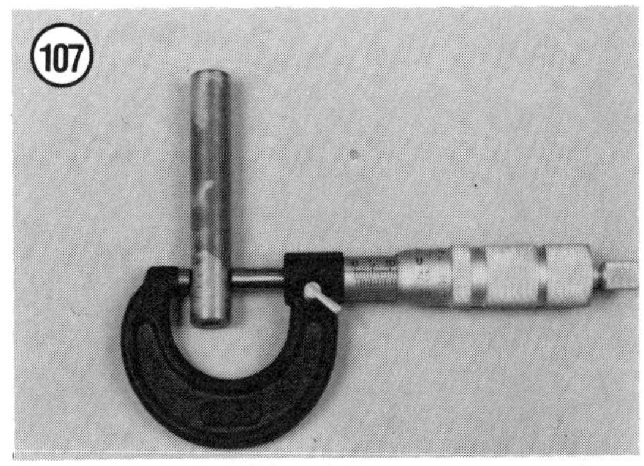

dimensions in **Table 1**. Replace if worn to the service limit or less.

4. Make sure the oil holes in the rocker arm shaft are clean and clear. If necessary, clean out with a piece of wire and thoroughly clean with solvent. Dry with compressed air.
5. Check the wave washers for breakage or distortion; replace if necessary.
6. Inspect the O-ring seal (**Figure 108**) for wear or deterioration, replace if necessary.

### Installation

1. Coat the rocker arm shaft, rocker arm bore and the shaft receptacles in the cylinder head with assembly oil or clean engine oil.

*NOTE*

*The rocker arms are not identical. The exhaust rocker arm has an additional tab (**Figure 109**) on the left-hand side. This tab is for the automatic decompression actuator.*

*NOTE*

*Position the exhaust rocker arm shaft with the O-ring end going in last. Align the bolt hole (A, **Figure 110**) in the up-and-down position so it will be aligned with the holding bolt hole (B, **Figure 110**) in the cylinder head cover.*

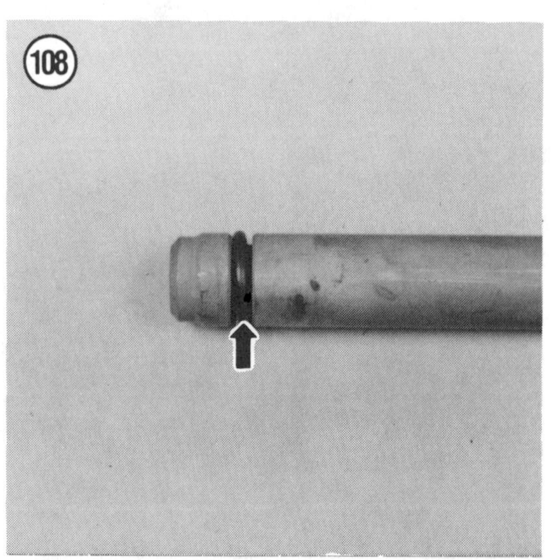

108

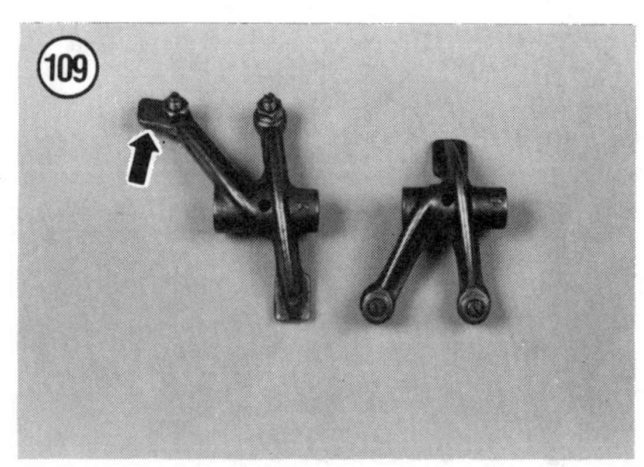

109

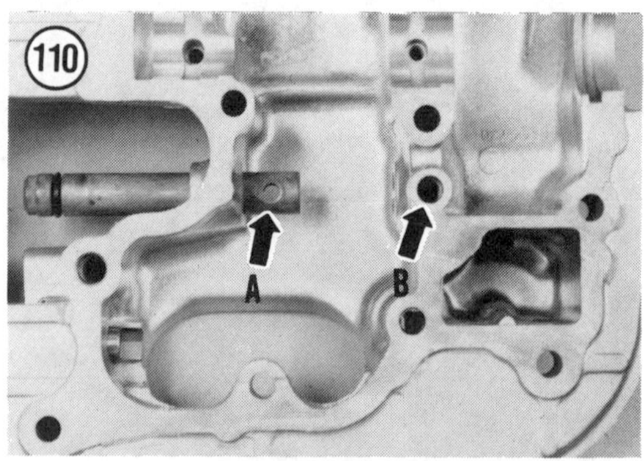


110

111

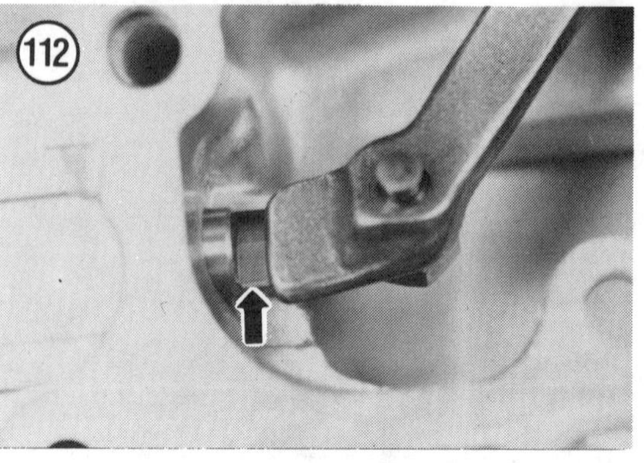

112

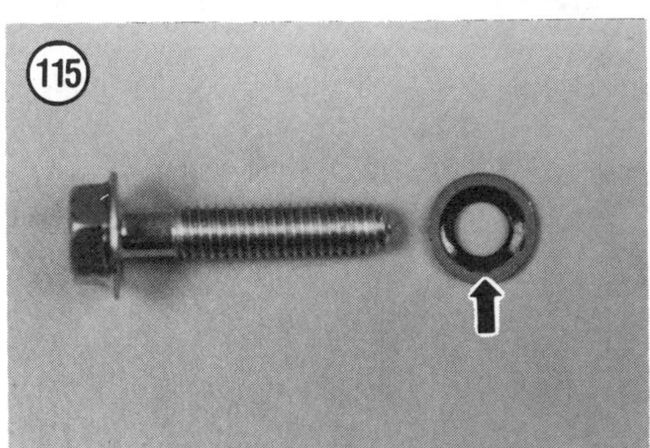

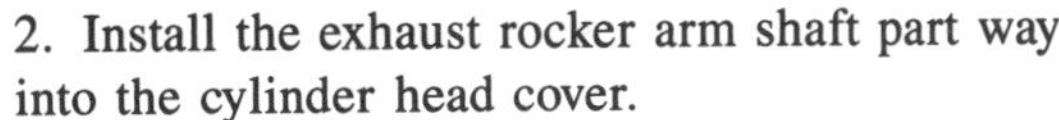

2. Install the exhaust rocker arm shaft part way into the cylinder head cover.

3. Install the exhaust rocker arm (**Figure 111**) and push the rocker arm through it. Make sure the exhaust rocker arm tab is located on the decompression actuator shaft as shown in **Figure 112**.

4. Install the wave washer (**Figure 113**) and push the rocker arm shaft in until it aligns with the bolt hole in the cylinder head cover (**Figure 114**). Don't push the shaft in too far as the hole alignment will be off and you will be unable to install the bolt.

5. Install the bolt and new sealing washer (**Figure 115**) and tighten securely.

6. Install the intake rocker arm shaft part way into the cylinder head cover.

7. Install the intake rocker arm (**Figure 116**) and push the rocker arm through it.

8. Install the wave washer (**Figure 117**) and push the rocker arm shaft in. Don't push the shaft in too far as the bolt hole in the cylinder head cover will be blocked (**Figure 118**) and you will be unable to install the bolt during cylinder head cover installation.

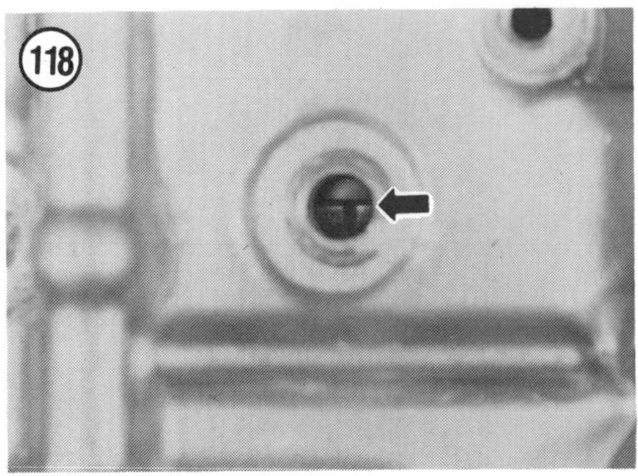

9. Inspect the sealing washer (**Figure 119**); replace if necessary.
10. Install the end plug and sealing washer (**Figure 101**) and tighten securely.

## VALVES AND VALVE COMPONENTS

General practice among those who do their own service is to remove the cylinder head and take it to a machine shop or dealer for inspection and service. Since the cost is relative to the required effort and equipment, this is the best approach even for the experienced mechanic.

This procedure is included for those who choose to do their own valve service.

Refer to **Figure 120** for this procedure.

### Valve Removal

1. Remove the cylinder head as described in this chapter.

*CAUTION*
*To avoid loss of spring tension, do not compress the springs any more than necessary to remove the keepers.*

2. Compress the valve springs with a valve compressor tool (**Figure 121**). Remove the valve keepers (**Figure 122**) and release the compression. Remove the valve compressor tool (**Figure 123**).
3. Remove the valve spring retainer and valve springs.
4. Before removing the valve, remove any burrs from the valve stem (**Figure 124**). Otherwise the valve guide will be damaged.
5. Remove the valve.

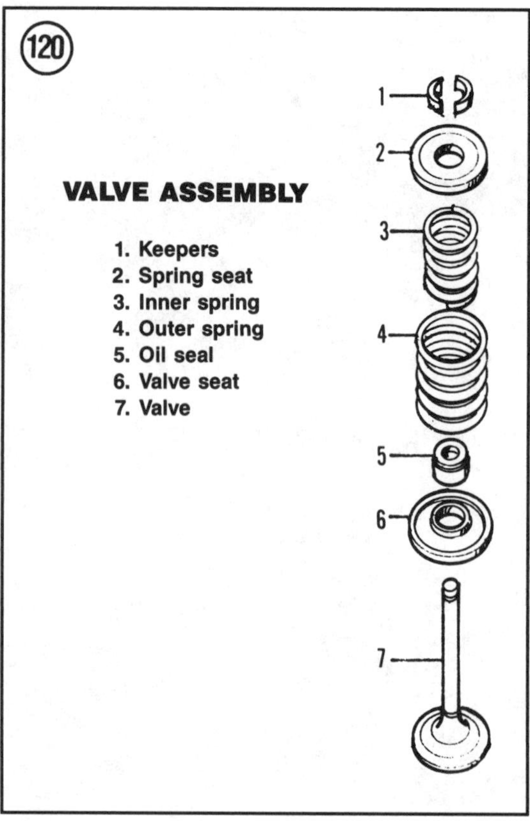


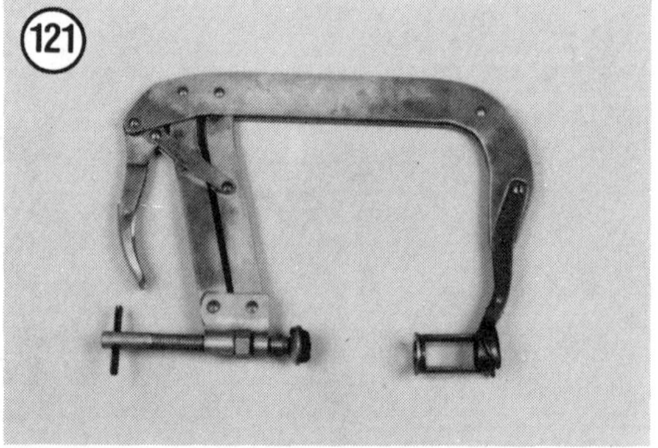


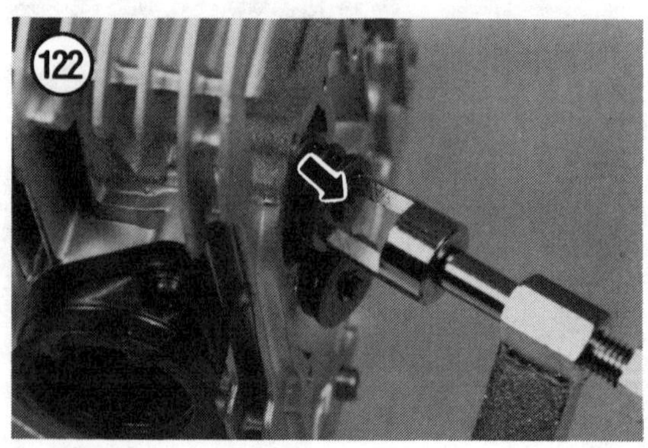

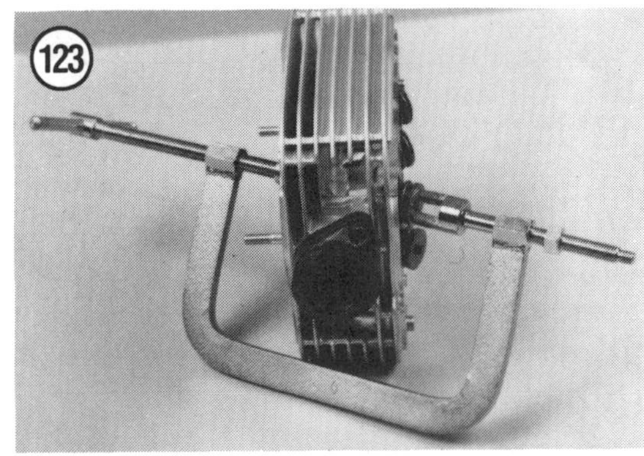

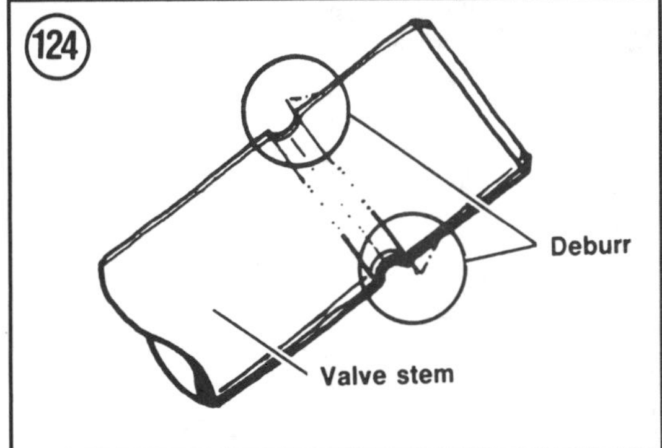


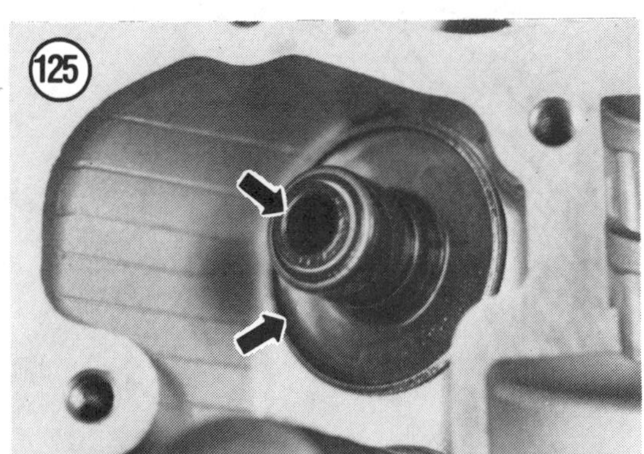

6. Remove the oil seal and spring seat (**Figure 125**) from the valve guide.
7. Repeat Steps 2-6 for all intake and exhaust valves.
8. Mark all parts (**Figure 126**) as they are disassembled so that they will be installed in their same locations. The exhaust valves are at the front of the cylinder head and the intake valves are located at the rear.



### Valve Inspection

1. Clean the valves with a soft wire brush and solvent.
2. Inspect the contact surface of each valve (**Figure 127**) for burning or pitting. Unevenness of the contact surface is an indication that the valve is not serviceable. The valve contact surface can *not* be ground and must be replaced if defective.
3. Inspect each valve stem for wear and roughness and measure the vertical runout of the valve stem as shown in **Figure 128**. The runout should not exceed the service limit listed in **Table 1**.
4. Measure each valve stem for wear (**Figure 129**). If worn to the wear limit listed in **Table 1**, or less, the valve must be replaced.

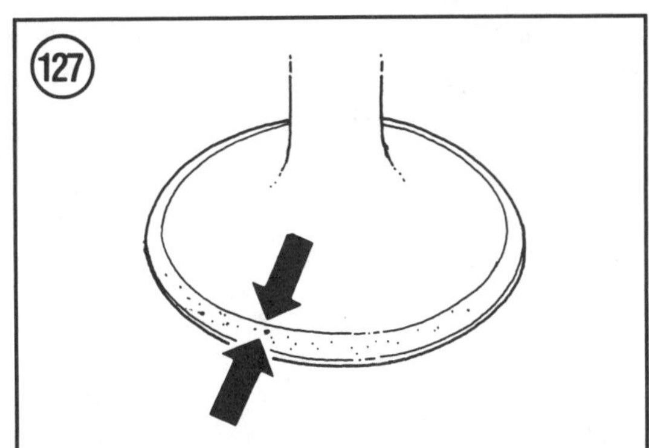

5. Measure each valve seating face for wear (**Figure 130**). If worn to the wear limit listed in **Table 1**, or less, the valve must be replaced.
6. Remove all carbon and varnish from each valve guide with a stiff spiral wire brush.
7. Insert each valve in its guide. Hold the valve with the head just slightly off the valve seat and rock it sideways in 2 directions, "X" and "Y," perpendicular to each other as shown in **Figure 131**. If the valve-to-valve guide clearance measured exceeds the limit listed in **Table 1**, measure the valve stem. If the valve stem is worn, replace the valve. If the valve stem is within tolerances, replace the valve guide.
8. Measure each valve spring free length with a vernier caliper (**Figure 132**). All should be within the length specified in **Table 1** with no signs of bends or distortion (**Figure 133**). Replace defective springs in pairs (inner and outer).
9. Check the valve spring retainer and valve keepers. If they are in good condition, they may be reused; replace as necessary.
10. Inspect the valve seats (**Figure 134**) in the cylinder head. If worn or burned, they must be reconditioned as described in this chapter.
11. Inspect the valve stem end for pitting and wear. If pitted or worn, the end may be resurfaced providing the finished length (**Figure 135**) is not less than length listed in **Table 1**. Replace the valve(s) if the finished length is less than specified.

### Valve Installation

1. Install a new seal on each valve guide.

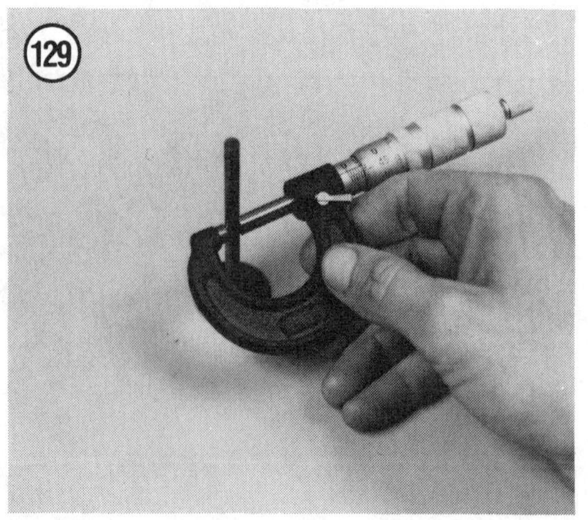


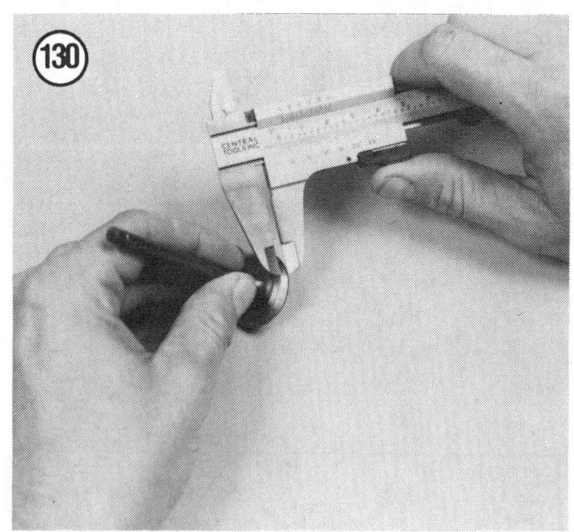


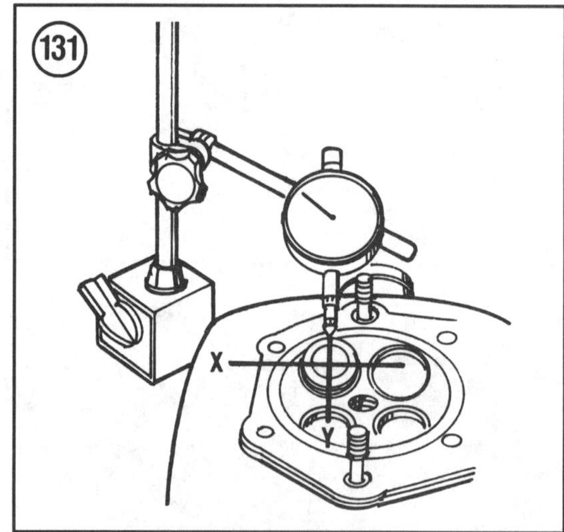


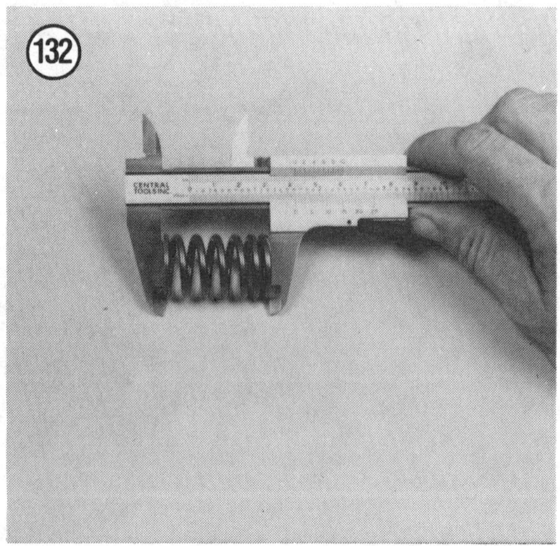

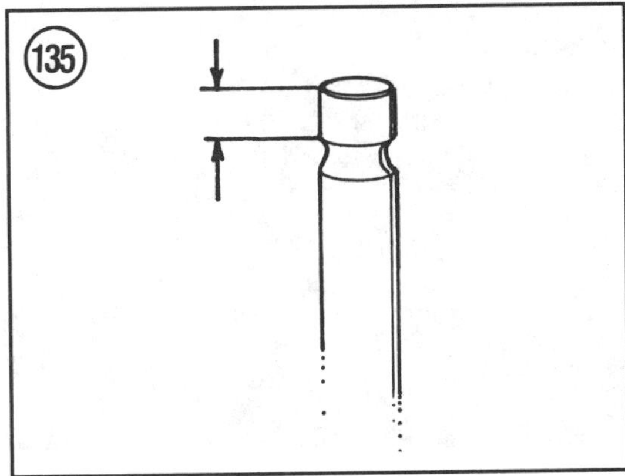

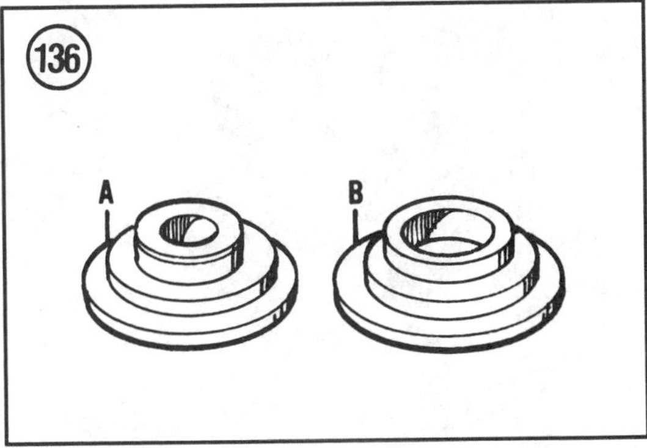


2. Install the valve seat. Do not confuse the valve spring retainer (A, **Figure 136**) seat with the spring seat (B, **Figure 136**). The inner diameter is different.

3. Coat the valve stems with molybdenum disulfide grease. To avoid damage to the valve stem seal, turn the valve slowly while inserting the valve into the cylinder head.

4. Install the valve springs with their closer wound coils (**Figure 137**) facing the cylinder head and install the valve spring retainer.

5. Install the valve spring retainer on top of the valve springs.

*CAUTION*
*To avoid loss of spring tension, do not compress the springs any more than necessary to install the keepers.*

6. Compress the valve springs with a compressor tool (**Figure 123**) and install the valve keepers. Make sure the keepers fit snug into the rounded groove in the valve stem.

7. Remove the compression tool.

8. After all springs have been installed, gently tap the end of the valve stem with a soft aluminum or brass drift and hammer. This will ensure that the keepers are properly seated.

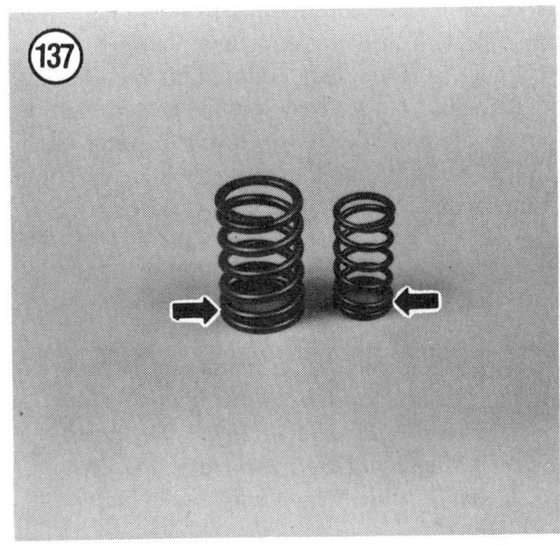

*CAUTION*
*If the valve stem end has been resurfaced, make sure that the valve stem face (A, **Figure 138**) is above the valve retainers (B, **Figure 138**).*

9. Repeat for the other valve assembly.
10. Install the cylinder head as described in this chapter.

**Valve Guide Replacement**

When valve guides are worn so that there is excessive valve stem-to-guide clearance or valve tipping, the guides must be replaced. This job should only be done by a dealer as special tools are required as well as considerable expertise. If the valve guide is replaced; also replace the respective valve.

The following procedure is provided if you choose to perform this task yourself.

*CAUTION*
*There may be a residual oil or solvent odor left in the oven after heating the cylinder head. If you use a household oven, first check with the person who uses the oven for food preparation to avoid getting into trouble.*

1. Remove the screws securing the intake pipe (**Figure 139**) onto the cylinder head. Remove the intake pipe before placing the cylinder head in the oven.
2. The valve guides (**Figure 140**) are installed with a slight interference fit. Place the cylinder head in a heated oven (or on a hot plate). Heat the cylinder head to a temperature between 100-150° C (212-300° F). An easy way to check the proper temperature is to drop tiny drops of water on the cylinder head; if they sizzle and evaporate immediately, the temperature is correct.

*CAUTION*
*Do not heat the cylinder head with a torch (propane or acetylene); never bring a flame into contact with the cylinder head or valve guide. The direct heat will destroy the case hardening of the valve guide and will likely cause warpage of the cylinder head.*

3. Remove the cylinder head from the oven and hold onto it with kitchen pot holders, heavy gloves or heavy shop cloths—it is very *hot*.
4. While heating up the cylinder head, place the new valve guides in a freezer (or refrigerator) if possible. Chilling them will slightly reduce their

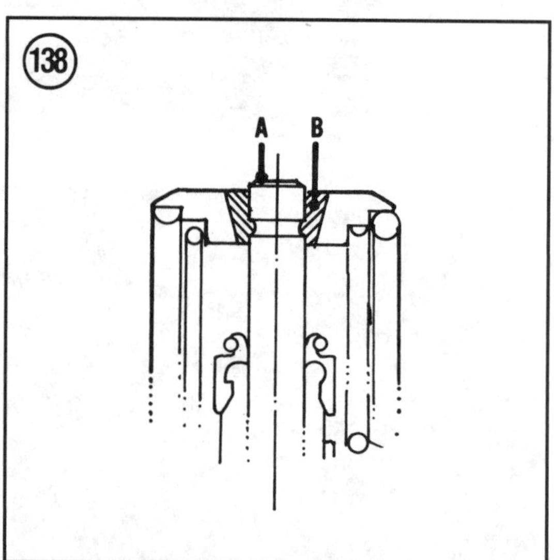


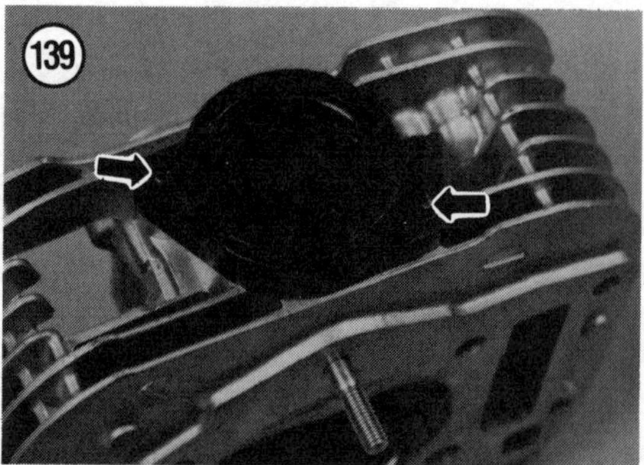


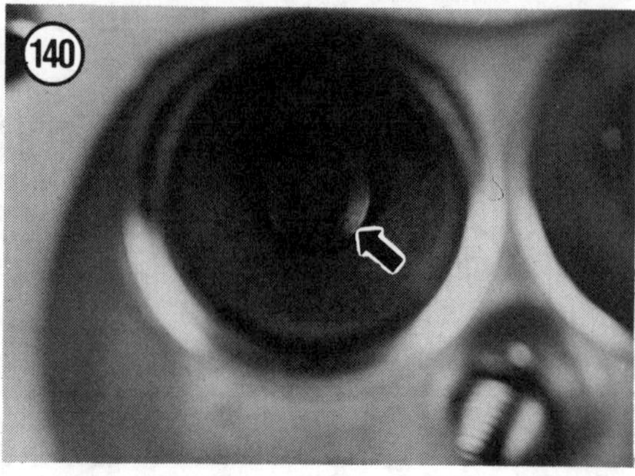

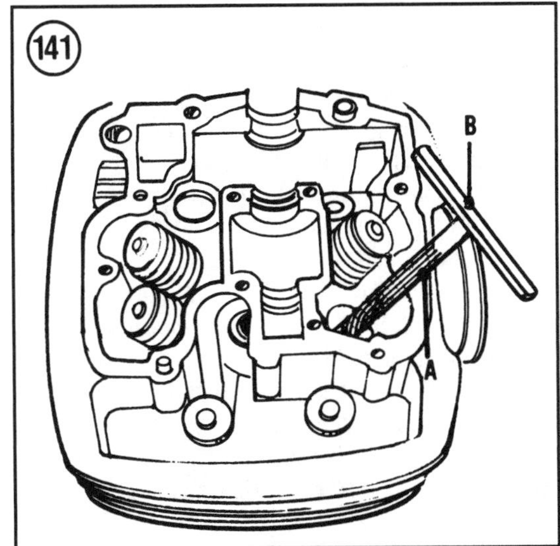


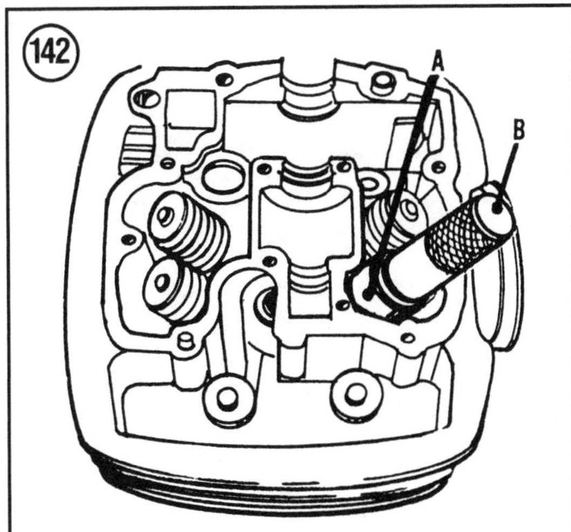


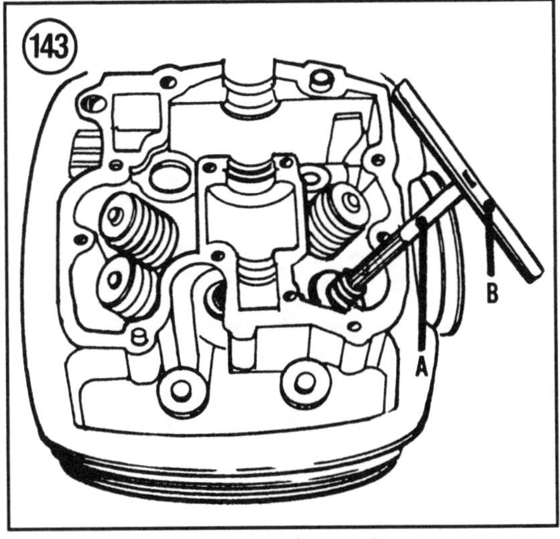


overall diameter while the hot cylinder head is slightly larger due to heat expansion. This will make valve guide installation much easier.

5. Turn the cylinder head upside down on wood blocks. Make sure the cylinder is properly supported on the wood blocks.
6. From the combustion chamber side of the cylinder head, drive out the old valve guide with a hammer and valve guide remover. Use Suzuki special tool, Valve Guide Remover/Installer, part No. 09916-44511. Remove the special tool.
7. Remove and discard the valve guide and ring. *Never* reinstall a valve guide or circlip that has been removed as it is no longer true nor within tolerances.
8. Insert the valve guide reamer into the valve guide hole in the cylinder head. Use Suzuki special tools, Valve Guide Hole 12.3 mm Reamer (A, **Figure 141**), part No. 09916-34531 and Reamer Handle (B, **Figure 141**), part No. 09916-34541. Rotate the reamer *clockwise*. Continue to rotate the reamer and work it down through the entire length of the valve guide hole in the cylinder head.
9. While rotating the reamer *clockwise,* withdraw the reamer from the valve guide hole in the cylinder head. Remove the reamer and handle.
10. Install a new ring onto the valve guide.

*CAUTION*

*Failure to apply fresh engine oil to both the valve guide and the valve guide hole in the cylinder head will result in damage to the cylinder head and/or the new valve guide.*

11. Apply fresh engine oil to the new valve guide and the valve guide hole in the cylinder head.
12. From the top side (valve side) of the cylinder head, drive in the new valve guide. Use Suzuki special tools, Valve Guide Installer Handle (A, **Figure 142**), part No. 09916-57320 and Attachment (B, **Figure 142**), part No. 09916-57311.
13. After installation, ream the new valve guide as follows:
    a. Use Suzuki special tools, Valve Guide 7 mm Reamer (A, **Figure 143**), part No. 09916-34520 and Reamer Handle (B, **Figure 143**), part No. 09916-34541.

b. Apply cutting oil to both the new valve guide and the valve guide reamer.

*CAUTION*

***Always** rotate the valve guide reamer **clockwise**. If the reamer is rotated counterclockwise, damage to a good valve guide will occur.*

c. Rotate the reamer *clockwise*. Continue to rotate the reamer and work it down through the entire length of the new valve guide. Apply additional cutting oil during this procedure.

d. Rotate the reamer *clockwise* until the reamer has traveled all the way through the new valve guide.

e. While rotating the reamer *clockwise*, withdraw the reamer from the valve guide. Remove the reamer.

14. If necessary, repeat Steps 1-13 for any other valve guides.

15. Thoroughly clean the cylinder head and valve guides with solvent to wash out all metal particles. Dry with compressed air.

16. Reface the valve seats as described in this chapter.

17. Install the intake pipe. To prevent a vacuum leak, install a new O-ring seal between the intake pipe and the cylinder head. Install the intake pipes and tighten the screws securely.

### Valve Seat Inspection

1. Remove the valves as described in this chapter.

2. The most accurate method for checking the valve seal is to use Prussian Blue or machinist's dye, available from auto parts stores or machine shops. To check the valve seal with Prussian Blue or machinist's dye, perform the following:

a. Thoroughly clean off all carbon deposits from the valve face with solvent or detergent, then dry thoroughly.

b. Spread a thin layer of Prussian Blue or machinist's dye evenly on the valve face.

c. Moisten the end of a suction cup valve tool (**Figure 144**) and attach it to the valve. Insert the valve into the guide.

d. Using the suction cup tool, tap the valve up and down in the cylinder head. Do *not* rotate the valve or a false indication will result.

e. Remove the valve and examine the impression left by the Prussian Blue or machinist's dye. If the impression left in the dye (on the valve or in the cylinder head) is not even and continuous and the valve seat width (**Figure 145**) is not within specified tolerance listed in **Table 1**, the cylinder head valve seat must be reconditioned.

3. Closely examine the valve seat (**Figure 134**) in the cylinder head. It should be smooth and even with a polished seating surface.

4. If the valve seat is okay, install the valves as described in this chapter.

5. If the valve seat is not correct, recondition the valve seat as described in this chapter.

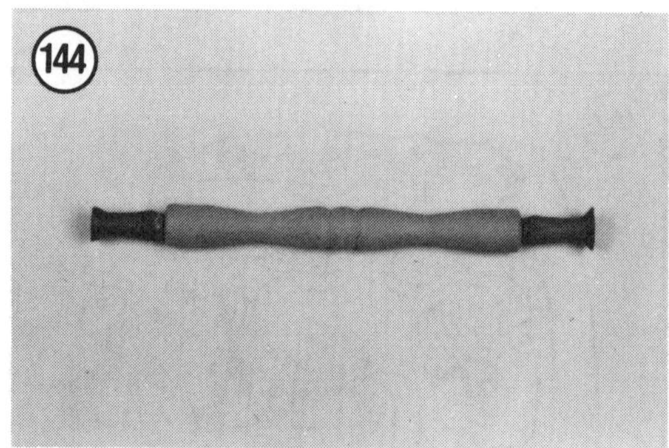


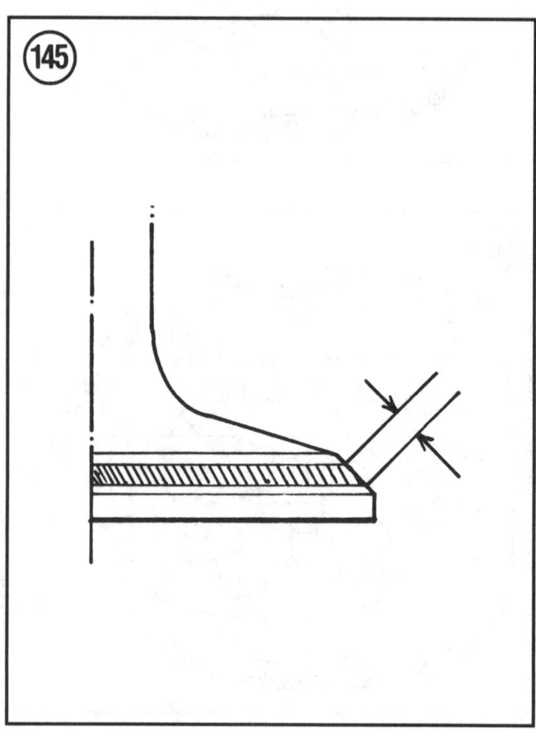

### Valve Seat Reconditioning

Special valve cutter tools and considerable expertise are required to properly recondition the valve seats in the cylinder head. You can save considerable money by removing the cylinder head and taking just the cylinder head to a dealer or machine shop and have the valve seats ground.

The following procedure is provided if you choose to perform this task yourself.

The Suzuki valve seat cutter and T-handle are available from a Suzuki dealer or from machine shop supply outlets. Follow the manufacturer's instruction in regard to operating the cutter. You will need the Suzuki Valve Seat Cutter (N-116), a T-handle and the Solid Pilot (N-100-6.98) or equivalent.

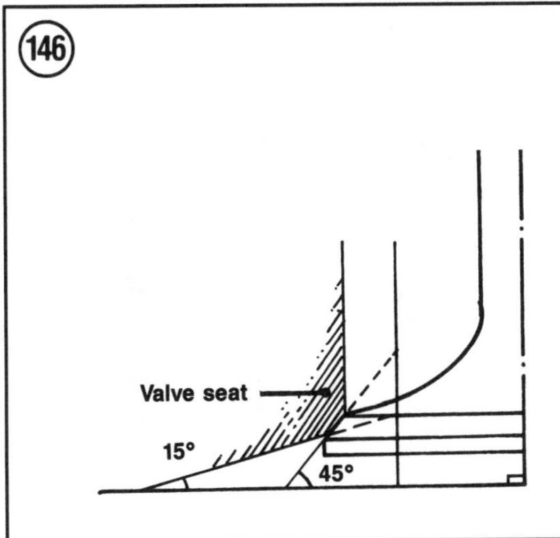


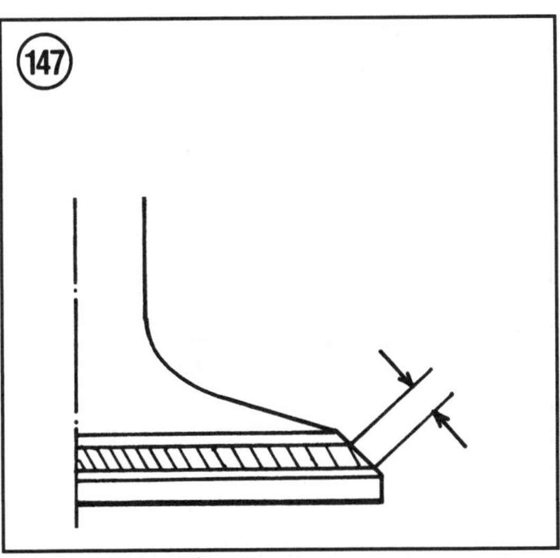


The valve seat for both the intake valves and exhaust valves are machined to the same angles. The valve contact surface is cut to a 45° angle and the area above the contact surface (closest to the combustion chamber) is cut to a 15° angle (**Figure 146**).

1. Carefully rotate and insert the solid pilot into the valve guide. Make sure the pilot is correctly seated.
2. Use the 45° angle side of the cutter, install the cutter and the T-handle onto the solid pilot.
3. Using the 45° cutter, descale and clean the valve seat with one or two turns.

*CAUTION*

*Measure the valve seat contact area in the cylinder head after each cut to make sure the contact area is correct and to prevent removing too much material. If too much material is removed, the cylinder head must be replaced.*

4. If the seat is still pitted or burned, turn the 45° cutter additional turns until the surface is clean. Refer to the previous *CAUTION* to avoid removing too much material from the cylinder head.
5. Remove the valve cutter, T-handle and solid pilot from the cylinder head.
6. Inspect the valve seat-to-valve face impression as follows:

   a. Spread a thin layer of Prussian Blue or machinist's dye evenly on the valve face.
   b. Moisten the end of a suction cup valve tool (**Figure 144**) and attach it to the valve. Insert the valve into the guide.
   c. Using the suction cup tool, tap the valve up and down in the cylinder head. Do *not* rotate the valve or a false indication will result.
   d. Remove the valve and examine the impression left by the Prussian Blue or machinist's dye.
   e. Measure the valve seat width as shown in **Figure 145**. Refer to **Table 1** for the seat width.

7. If the contact area is too *high* on the valve, or if it is too wide, use the 15° side of the cutter and remove a portion of the top area of the valve seat material to lower and narrow the contact area (**Figure 147**).

8. If the contact area is too *low* on the valve, or too narrow, use the 45° cutter and remove a portion of the lower area of the valve seat material to raise and widen the contact area (**Figure 148**).
9. After the desired valve seat position and width is obtained, use the 45° side of the cutter and T-handle and very lightly clean off any burrs that may have been caused by the previous cuts.

*CAUTION*

*Do **not** use any valve lapping compound after the final cut has been made.*

10. Check that the finish has a smooth and velvety surface. It should *not* be shiny or highly polished. The final seating will take place when the engine is first run.
11. Repeat Steps 1-10 for all remaining valve seats.
12. Thoroughly clean the cylinder head and all valve components in solvent or detergent and hot water.
13. Install the valve assemblies as described in this chapter and fill the ports with solvent to check for leaks. If any leaks are present, the valve seats must be inspected for foreign matter or burrs that may be preventing a proper seal.
14. If the cylinder head and valve components were cleaned in detergent and hot water, apply a light coat of engine oil to all bare metal surfaces to prevent any rust formations.

## CYLINDER

Refer to **Figure 149** and **Figure 150** for this procedure.

148

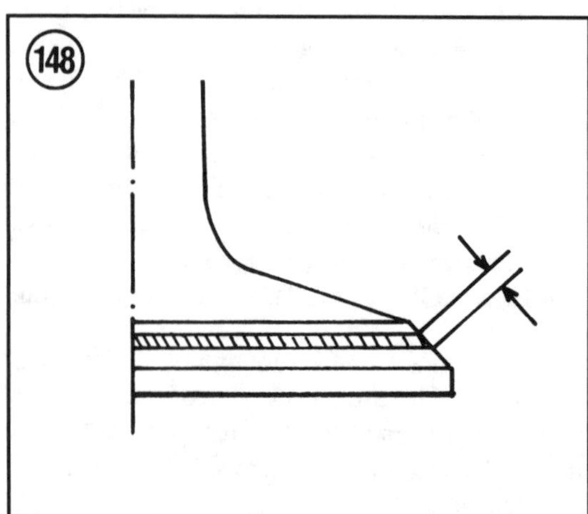

149

**CYLINDER ASSEMBLY**

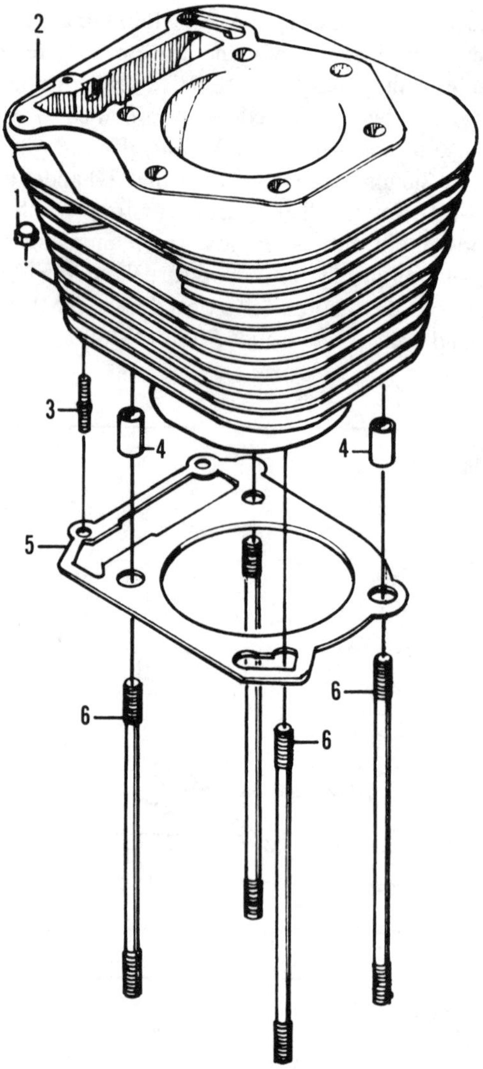

1. Cap nut
2. Cylinder
3. Threaded stud
4. Locating dowel
5. Cylinder gasket
6. Crankcase studs

## CAMSHAFT CHAIN TENSIONER

FRONT

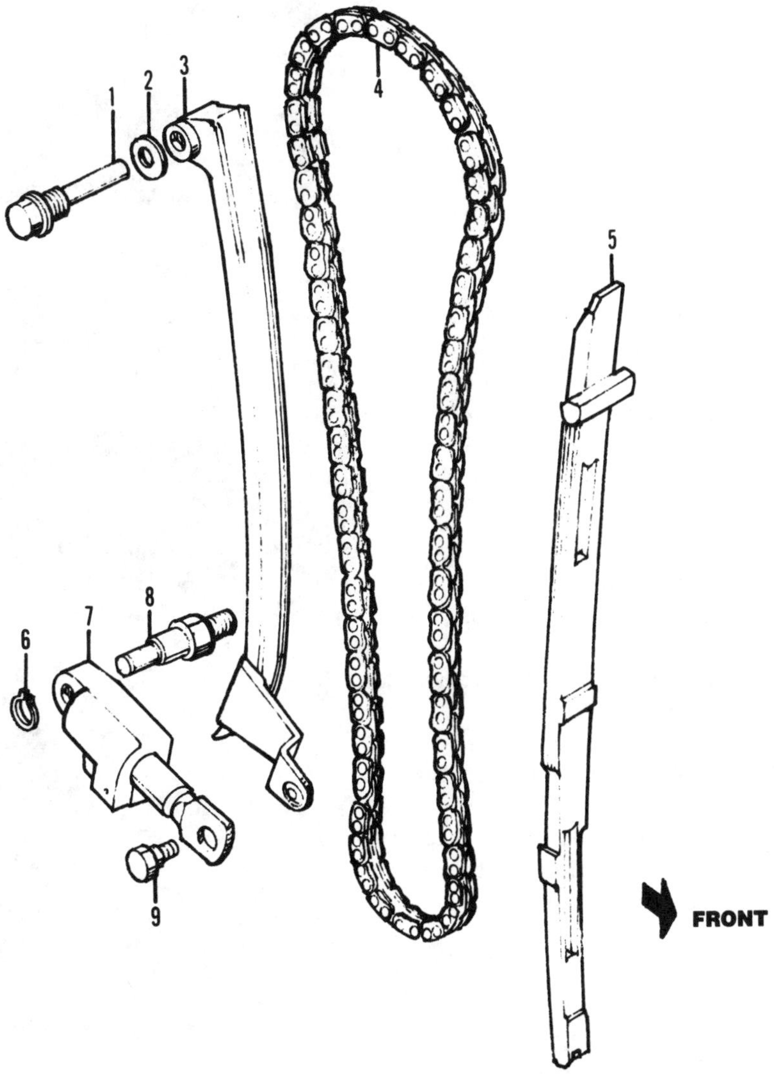

1. Bolt
2. Washer
3. Camshaft chain tensioner
4. Camshaft chain
5. Camshaft chain front guide
6. Circlip
7. Camshaft chain tensioner adjuster
8. Threaded stud
9. Bolt

### Removal

1. Remove the cylinder head as described in this chapter.
2. Remove the camshaft drive chain guide (**Figure 151**).
3. Remove the cylinder head gasket and the locating dowels.
4. Remove the nuts (**Figure 152**) securing the right-hand side of the cylinder to the crankcase.
5. Loosen the cylinder block by tapping around the perimeter with a rubber or plastic mallet. If necessary, *gently* pry the cylinder loose with a broad-tipped screwdriver.

*CAUTION*

*Remember the cooling fins are fragile and may be damaged if tapped on or pried too hard. Never use a metal hammer.*

6. Pull the cylinder (**Figure 153**) straight up and off of the piston and crankcase studs. Work the camshaft chain wire through the opening in the cylinder. Reattach the wire to the exterior of the crankcase (**Figure 154**).
7. Remove the camshaft drive chain tensioner assembly (**Figure 155**).
8. Remove the cylinder base gasket and discard it. Remove the locating dowels from the crankcase studs.
9. Stuff clean shop cloths into the crankcase openings and under the piston to prevent the entry of foreign matter and small objects.

151

152

153

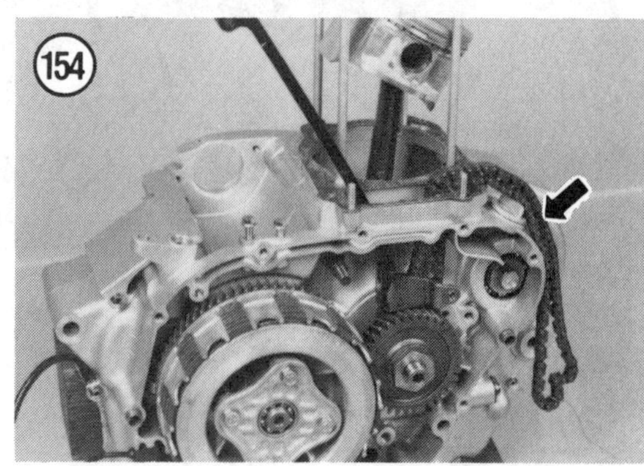

154

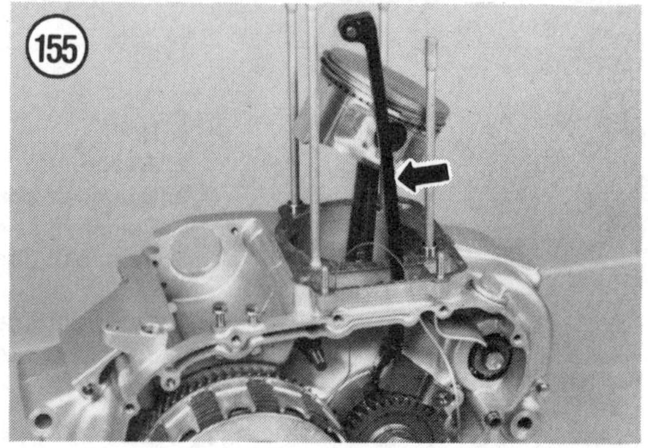

155

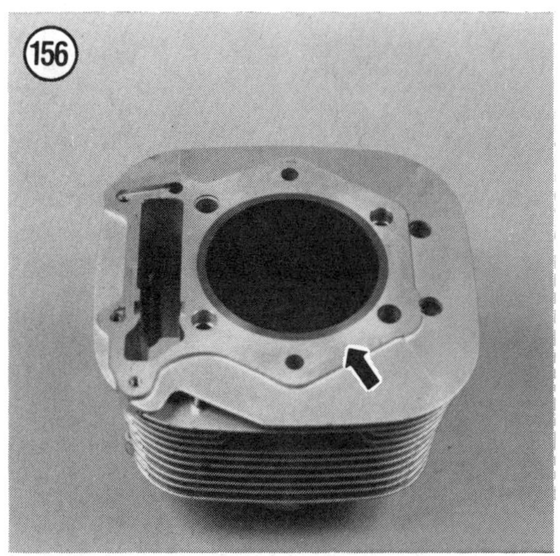

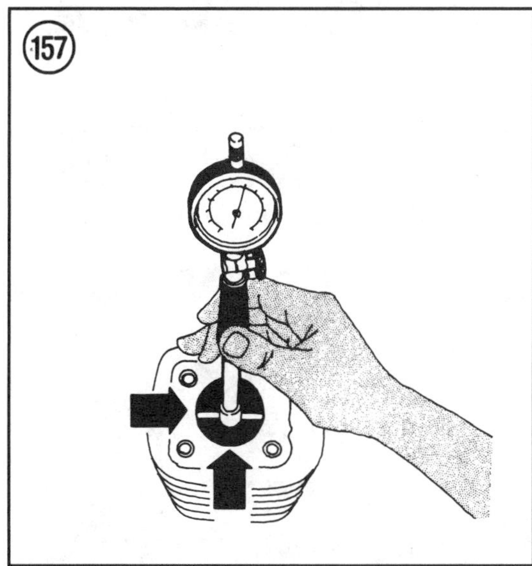

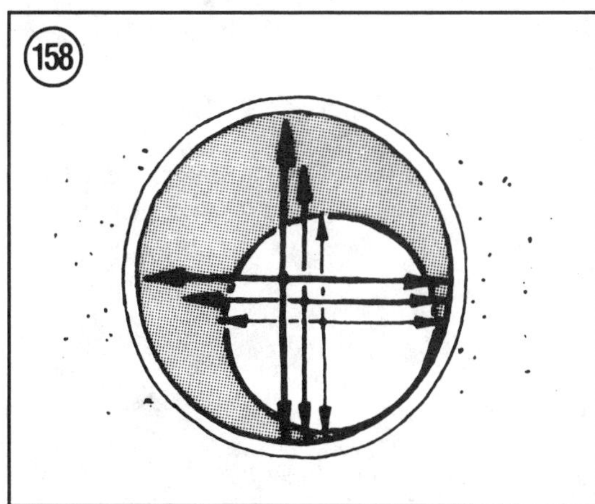

## Inspection

The following procedure requires the use of highly specialized and expensive measuring instruments. If such equipment is not readily available, have the measurements performed by a dealer or qualified machine shop.

1. Soak with solvent any old cylinder head gasket material left on the cylinder (**Figure 156**). If necessary use a broad-tipped *dull* chisel and gently scrape off all gasket residue. Do not gouge the sealing surface as oil leaks will result.



2. Measure the cylinder bore with a cylinder gauge (**Figure 157**) or inside micrometer at the points shown in **Figure 158**. Measure in 2 axes—in line with the piston-pin and at 90° to the pin. If the taper or out-of-round is 0.05 mm (0.002 in.) or greater, the cylinder must be rebored to the next oversize and a new piston and piston rings installed.

*NOTE*

*The new piston should be obtained before the cylinder is rebored so that the piston can be measured; slight manufacturing tolerances must be taken into account to determine the actual size and working clearance.*

3. Check the cylinder walls (**Figure 159**) for scratches; if evident, the cylinder should be rebored.

*NOTE*

*The maximum wear limit on the cylinder is listed in* ***Table 1****. If the*

*cylinder is worn to this limit, the cylinder must be replaced. Never rebore a cylinder if the finished rebore diameter will be this dimension or greater.*

*NOTE*

*After having the cylinder rebored, wash it thoroughly in hot soapy water. This is the best way to clean the cylinder of all fine grit material left from the bore job. After washing the cylinder, run a clean white cloth through the cylinder, the cloth should show no traces of dirt or other debris. If the rag is dirty, the cylinder is not clean enough and must be rewashed. After the cylinder is thoroughly clean, dry and lubricate the cylinder wall with clean engine oil to prevent the cylinder liner from forming rust.*

4. Inspect the camshaft drive chain tensioner assembly and guide (**Figure 160**) for wear or deterioration. Replace if necessary.

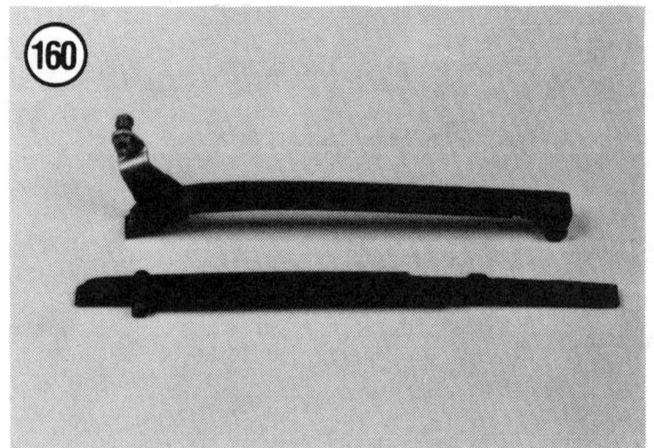
160

161

## Installation

1. Check that the top surface of the crankcase and the bottom surface of the cylinder block are clean before installing a new base gasket.
2. Install the locating dowels (**Figure 161**) on the crankcase studs.
3. Install a new cylinder base gasket (**Figure 162**).
4. Install the camshaft drive chain tensioner assembly (**Figure 155**).
5. Make sure the end gaps of the piston rings are *not* lined up with each other—they must be staggered. Lightly oil the piston rings and the inside of the cylinder bore with assembly oil or engine oil.
6. Carefully feed the camshaft chain and wire up through the opening in the cylinder and tie it to the engine.
7. Start the cylinder down over the piston and crankcase studs (**Figure 163**). Compress each piston ring with your fingers as it enters the cylinder.

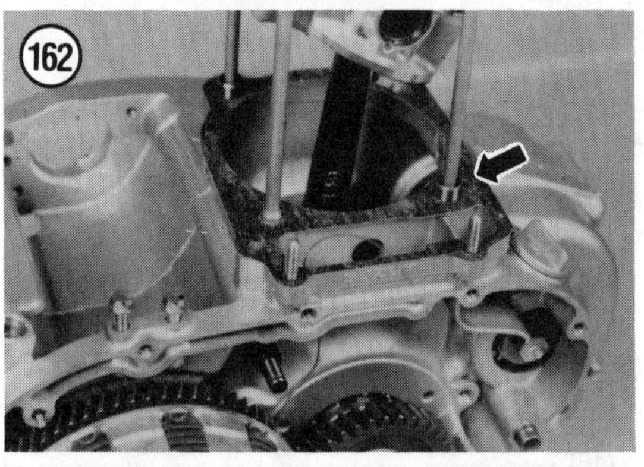
162

163

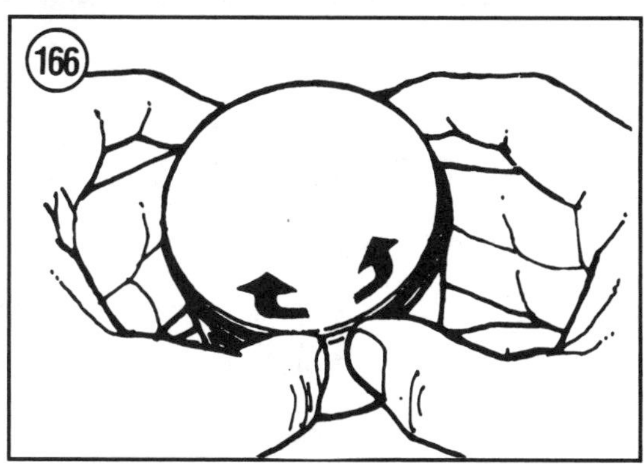

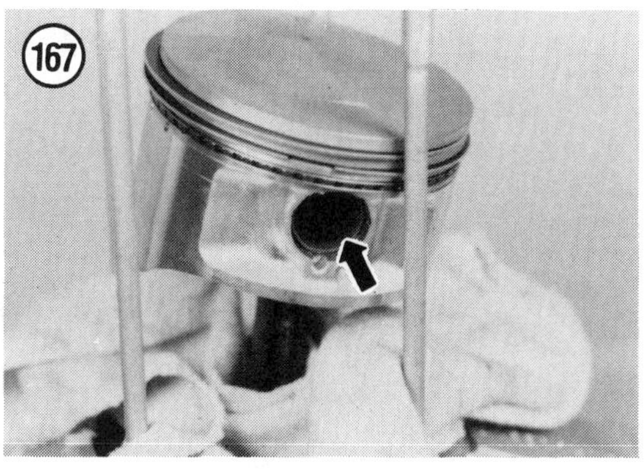

8. Slide the cylinder block down until it bottoms on the crankcase.
9. Install the nuts (**Figure 152**) securing the right-hand side of the cylinder to the crankcase and tighten to the torque specification listed in **Table 2**.
10. Install the camshaft drive chain guide (**Figure 151**). Make sure it is positioned correctly in the lower receptacle (**Figure 164**) in the crankcase and in the upper receptacle in the cylinder (**Figure 165**).
11. Install the cylinder head and cylinder head cover as described in this chapter.
12. Follow the *Break-in Procedure* in this chapter if the cylinder block was rebored or honed or a new piston or piston rings were installed.



## PISTON, PISTON PIN AND PISTON RINGS

The piston is made of an aluminum alloy. The piston pin is made of steel and is a precision fit. The piston pin is held in place by a clip at each end.

### Piston Removal

1. Remove the cylinder head and cylinder as described in this chapter.

*WARNING*

*The edges of all piston rings are very sharp. Be careful when handling them to avoid cutting fingers.*

2. Remove the top ring with a ring expander tool or by spreading the ends with your thumbs just enough to slide the ring up over the piston (**Figure 166**). Repeat for the remaining rings.
3. Before removing the piston, hold the rod tightly and rock the piston. Any rocking motion (do not confuse with the normal sliding motion) indicates wear on the piston pin, piston pin bore or connecting rod small-end bore (more likely a combination of these).

*NOTE*

*Wrap a clean shop cloth under the piston so that the piston pin clip will not fall into the crankcase.*

4. Remove the clip from each side of the piston pin bore (**Figure 167**) with a small screwdriver or

scribe. Hold your thumb over one edge of the clip when removing it to prevent the clip from springing out.

5. Use a proper size wooden dowel or socket extension and push out the piston pin.

*CAUTION*

*Be careful when removing the pin to avoid damaging the connecting rod. If it is necessary to gently tap the pin to remove it, be sure that the piston is properly supported so that lateral shock is not transmitted to the lower connecting rod bearing.*

6. If the piston pin is difficult to remove, heat the piston and pin with a butane torch. The pin will probably push right out. Heat the piston to only about 140° F (60° C), i.e., until it is too warm to touch, but not excessively hot. If the pin is still difficult to push out, use a homemade tool as shown in **Figure 168**.
7. Lift the piston off the connecting rod.
8. If the piston is going to be left off for some time, place a piece of foam insulation tube over the end of the rod to protect it.

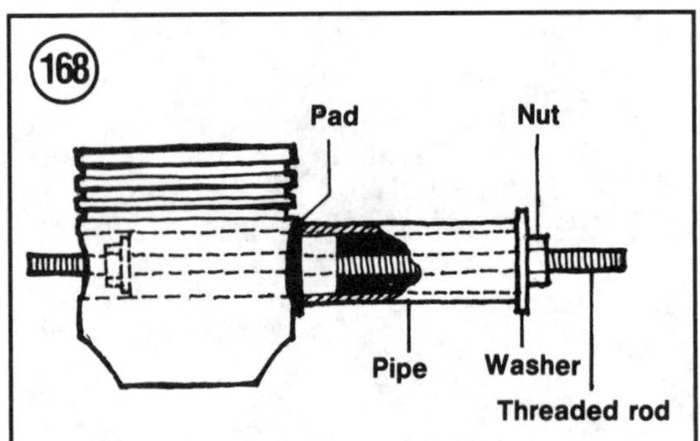


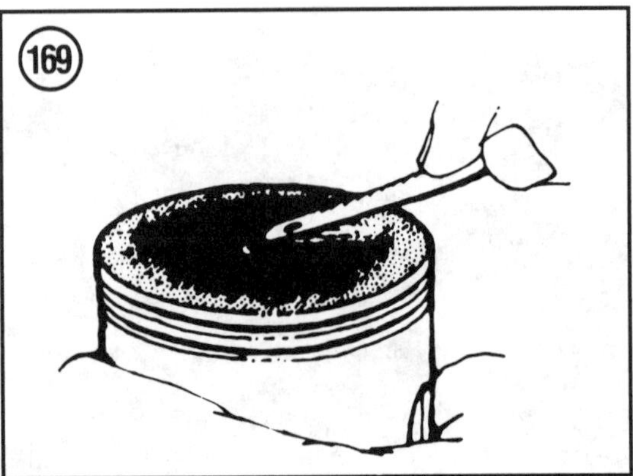


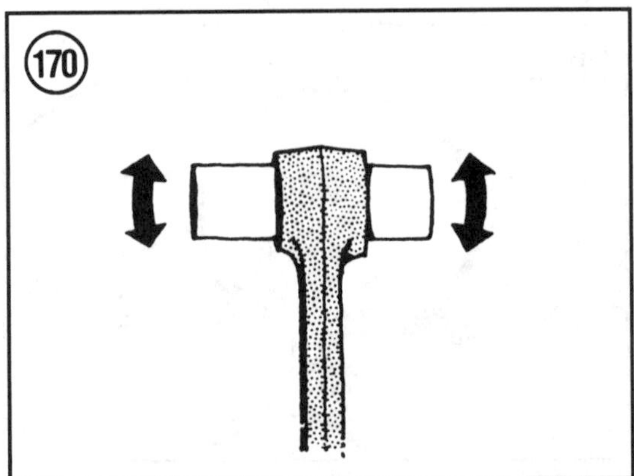


### Inspection

1. Carefully clean the carbon from the piston crown with a chemical remover or with a soft scraper (**Figure 169**). Do not remove or damage the carbon ridge around the circumference of the piston above the top ring. If the piston, rings and cylinder are found to be dimensionally correct and can be reused, removal of the carbon ring from the top of the piston or the carbon ridge from the top of the cylinder wall will promote excessive oil consumption.

*CAUTION*

*Do not wire brush the piston skirts.*

2. Examine each ring groove for burrs, dented edges and wide wear. Pay particular attention to the top compression ring groove as it usually wears more than the other grooves.
3. If damage or wear indicates piston replacement, select a new piston as described under *Piston Clearance* in this chapter.

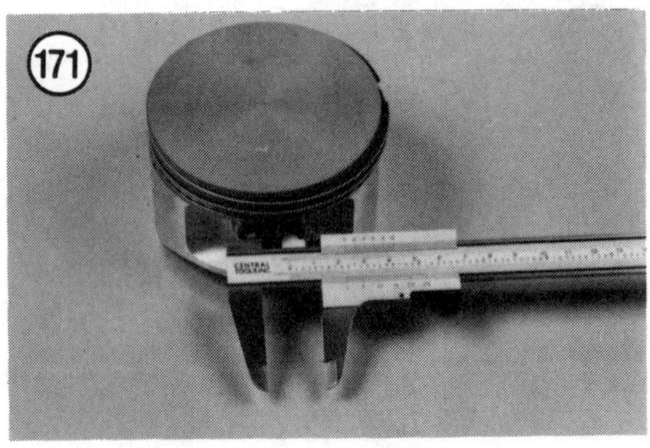

4. Oil the piston pin and install it in the connecting rod. Slowly rotate the piston pin and check for radial and axial play (**Figure 170**). If any play exists, the piston pin should be replaced, providing the rod bore is in good condition.

5. Measure the inside diameter of the piston pin bore with a snap gauge or caliper (**Figure 171**) and measure the outside diameter of the piston pin with a micrometer (**Figure 172**). Compare with dimensions given in **Table 1**. Replace the piston and piston pin as a set if either or both are worn.

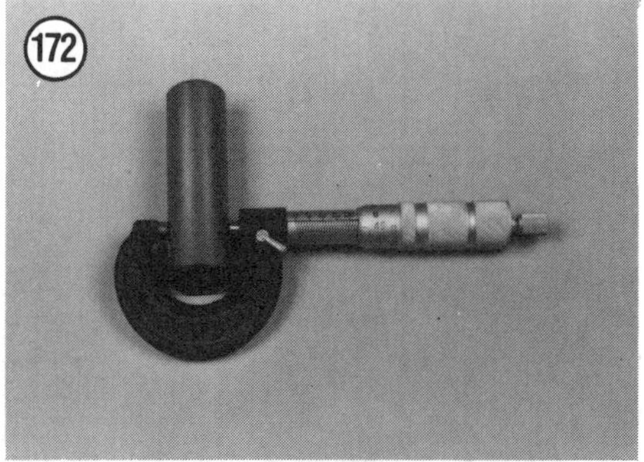

172

173

174

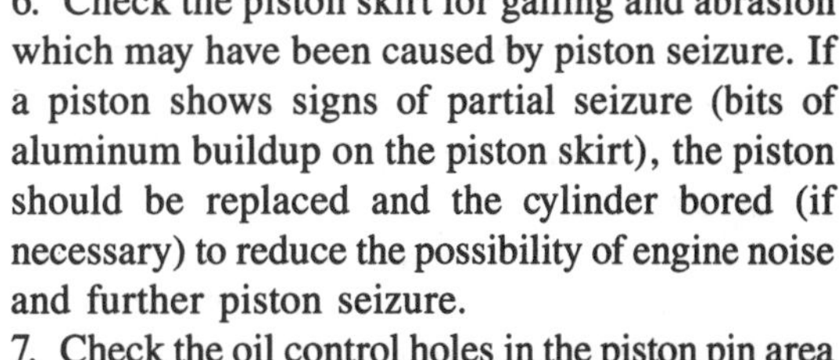

6. Check the piston skirt for galling and abrasion which may have been caused by piston seizure. If a piston shows signs of partial seizure (bits of aluminum buildup on the piston skirt), the piston should be replaced and the cylinder bored (if necessary) to reduce the possibility of engine noise and further piston seizure.

7. Check the oil control holes in the piston pin area (**Figure 173**) for carbon or oil sludge buildup. Clean the holes with a small diameter drill bit and blow out with compressed air.

4

### Piston Clearance

1. Make sure the piston and the cylinder wall is clean and dry.
2. Measure the inside diameter of the cylinder bore at a point 13 mm (1/2 in.) from the upper edge with a bore gauge.
3. Measure the outside diameter of each piston across the skirt at right angles to the piston pin. Measure at a distance 20 mm (0.79 in.) up from the bottom of the piston skirt (**Figure 174**).
4. Piston clearance is the difference between the maximum piston diameter and the minimum cylinder diameter. Subtract the dimension of the piston from the cylinder dimension and compare to the dimension listed in **Table 1**. If the clearance exceeds that specified, the cylinders should be rebored to the next oversize and a new piston installed.
5. To establish a final overbore dimension with a new piston, add the piston skirt measurement to the specified clearance. This will determine the dimension for the cylinder overbore size. Remember, do not exceed the cylinder maximum service limit inside diameter indicated in **Table 1**.

### Piston Installation

1. Apply molybdenum disulfide grease to the inside surface of the connecting rod.

*NOTE*

*New piston pin clips should be installed during assembly. Install the clips with the gap away from the cutout in the piston.*

2. Install one piston pin clip in the piston.
3. Oil the piston pin with assembly oil or fresh engine oil and install the piston pin in the piston until its end extends slightly beyond the inside of the boss (**Figure 175**).
4. Place the piston over the connecting rod. Remember that the arrow on top of the piston (**Figure 176**) must point toward the front of the engine.

*CAUTION*
*When installing the piston pin in Step 5, do not push the pin in too far or the piston pin clip installed in Step 2 will be forced into the piston metal, destroying the clip groove and loosening the clip.*

5. Line up the piston pin with the hole in the connecting rod. Push the piston pin into the connecting rod. It may be necessary to move the piston around until the piston pin enters the connecting rod. Do not use force during installation or damage may occur. Push the piston pin in until it touches the pin clip on the other side of the piston.
6. If the piston pin does not slide easily, use the homemade tool used during removal, but eliminate the piece of pipe. Pull the piston pin in until it stops.
7. After the piston is installed, recheck and make sure that the arrow on top of the piston (**Figure 176**) is pointing toward the front of the engine.

*NOTE*
*In the next step, install the second clip with the gap away from the cutout in the piston.*

8. Install the second piston pin clip in the groove in the piston. Make sure both piston pin clips are seated in the grooves in the piston.
9. Check the installation by rocking the piston back and forth around the pin axis and from side-to-side along the axis. It should rotate freely back and forth, but not from side-to-side.
10. Install the piston rings as described in this chapter.
11. Install the cylinder and cylinder head as described in this chapter.

175

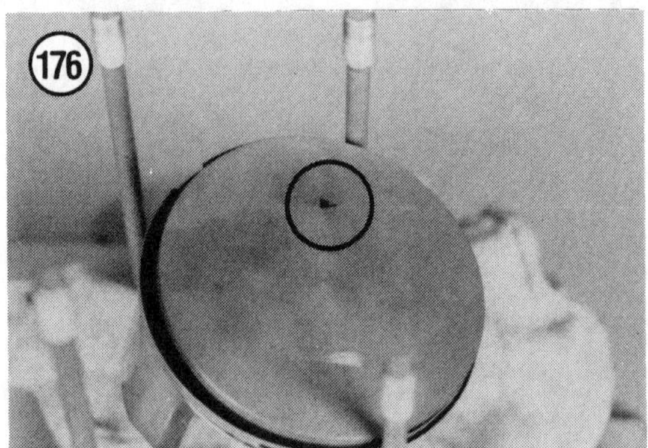
176

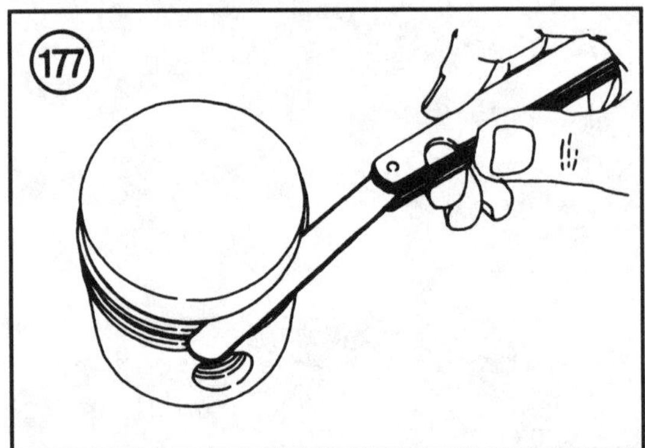
177

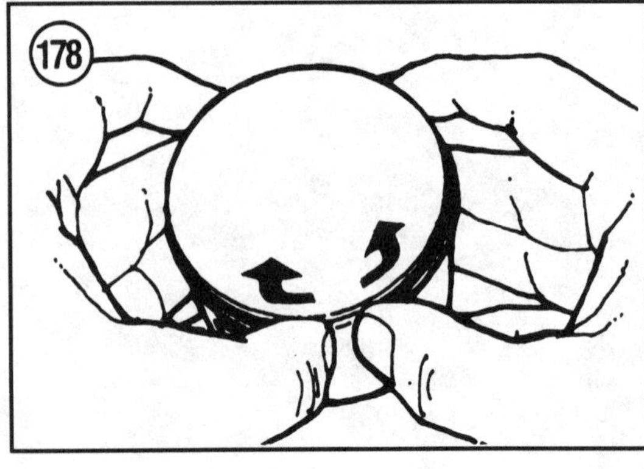
178

### Piston Ring Replacement

*WARNING*
*The edges of all piston rings are very sharp. Be careful when handling them to avoid cutting fingers.*

1. Measure the side clearance of each ring in its groove with a flat feeler gauge (**Figure 177**) and compare to dimensions given in **Table 1**. If the clearance is greater than specified, the rings must be replaced. If the clearance is still excessive with the new rings, the piston must also be replaced.
2. Remove the old top ring by spreading the ends with your thumbs just enough to slide the ring up over the piston (**Figure 178**). Repeat for the remaining rings.
3. Carefully remove all carbon buildup from the ring grooves with a broken piston ring (**Figure 179**). Inspect the grooves carefully for burrs, nicks or broken and cracked lands. Recondition or replace the piston if necessary.
4. Roll each ring around its piston groove as shown in **Figure 180** to check for binding. Minor binding may be cleaned up with a fine-cut file.
5. Measure the thickness of each ring with a micrometer and compare to dimensions given in **Table 1**. If the thickness is less than specified, the ring(s) must be replaced.
6. First, measure the free end gap of each ring with a vernier caliper and compare to dimensions given in **Table 1**. If the end cap is greater than specified, the ring(s) must be replaced.
7. After measuring the free end gap, place each ring, one at a time, into the cylinder and push it in about 20 mm (3/4 in.) with the crown of the piston to ensure that the ring is square in the cylinder bore. Measure the gap with a flat feeler gauge and compare to dimensions in **Table 1**. If the gap is greater than specified, the rings should be replaced.
8. When installing new rings, measure their end gap as described in Step 6 and Step 7 and compare to dimensions given in **Table 1**. If the end cap is greater than specified, return the rings for another set.

*NOTE*
*Install the 2nd and top ring with its "T" mark facing up.*

*CAUTION*
*Do **not** allow the 2 ends of the oil ring spacer to overlap in the piston groove.*

9. Install the oil ring spacer first (A, **Figure 181**), then both side rails (B, **Figure 181**). The new Suzuki factory oil ring side rails do not have top and bottom designations and can be installed either way. If reassembling used parts, install the side rails as they were removed.

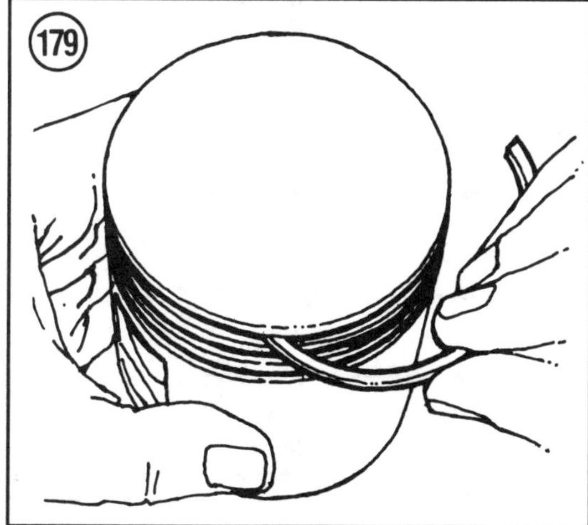


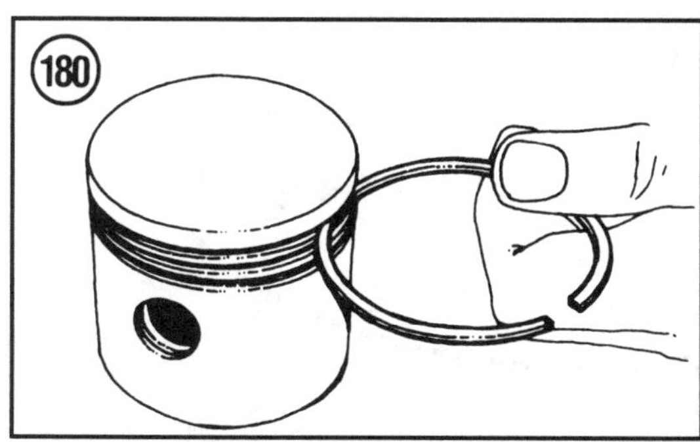


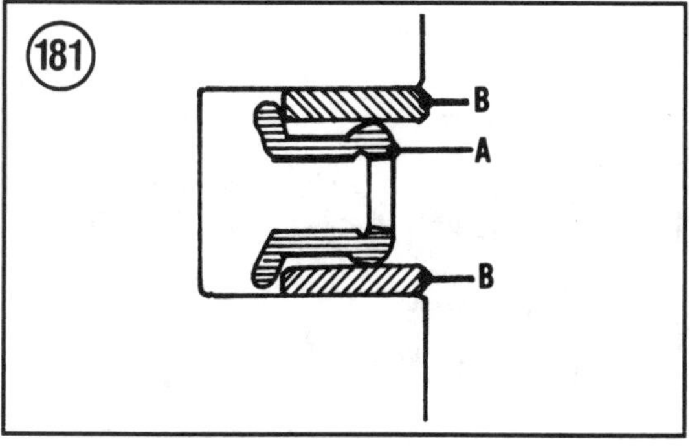


4

10. Install the second compression ring (with slight side taper) (**Figure 182**), then the top—by carefully spreading the ends of the ring with your thumbs and slipping the ring over the top of the piston. Remember that the marks on the piston rings are toward the top of the piston.
11. Make sure the rings are seated completely in their grooves all the way around the piston and that the ends are distributed around the piston. The important thing is that the ring gaps are not aligned with each other when installed to prevent compression pressures from escaping past them.
12. If installing oversized compression rings, check the ring number (A, **Figure 183**) to make sure the correct rings are being installed. The ring oversize numbers should be the same as the piston oversize numbers.
13. If installing oversized oil rings, check the paint color spot (B, **Figure 183**) to make sure the correct oil rings are being installed. The paint color spots are as follows:

a. Red: standard size.
b. Blue: 0.5 mm oversize.
c. Yellow: 1.0 mm oversize.

14. If new rings are installed, the cylinder must be deglazed or honed. This will help to seat the new rings. Refer honing service to a Suzuki dealer or competent machine shop. After honing, measure the end clearance of each ring in the cylinder bore and compare to dimensions in **Table 1**.

*CAUTION*
*If the cylinder was deglazed or honed, clean the cylinder as described under **Cylinder Inspection** in this chapter.*

15. Follow the *Break-in Procedure* in this chapter if a new piston or new piston rings have been installed or the cylinder was rebored or honed.

## OIL PUMP

Refer to **Figure 184** for this procedure.

### Removal/Installation

1. Remove the engine and separate the crankcase as described in this chapter.
2. Remove the circlip (**Figure 185**) securing the oil pump driven sprocket to the oil pump.
3. Remove the oil pump drive sprocket (**Figure 186**) from the oil pump.
4. Remove the drive pin (**Figure 187**) and the thrust washer (**Figure 188**).
5. Turn the crankcase over.
6. Remove the screws (**Figure 189**) securing the oil pump to the crankcase and remove the oil pump assembly.
7. Inspect the oil pump as described in this chapter.
8. Install the oil pump onto the crankcase.
9. Apply red Loctite Threadlocker (No. 271) to the mounting screws prior to installation. Install the screws and tighten securely.

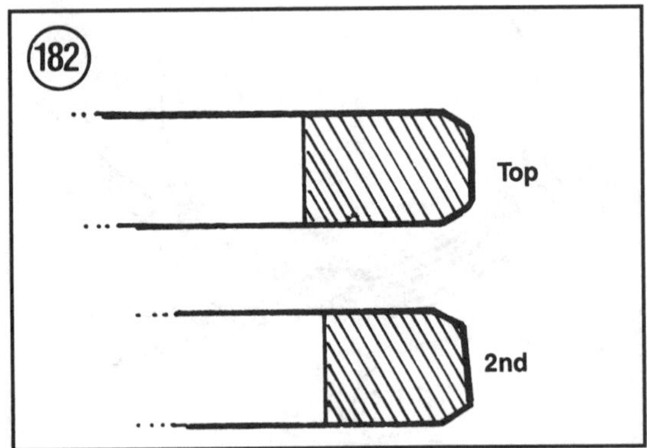


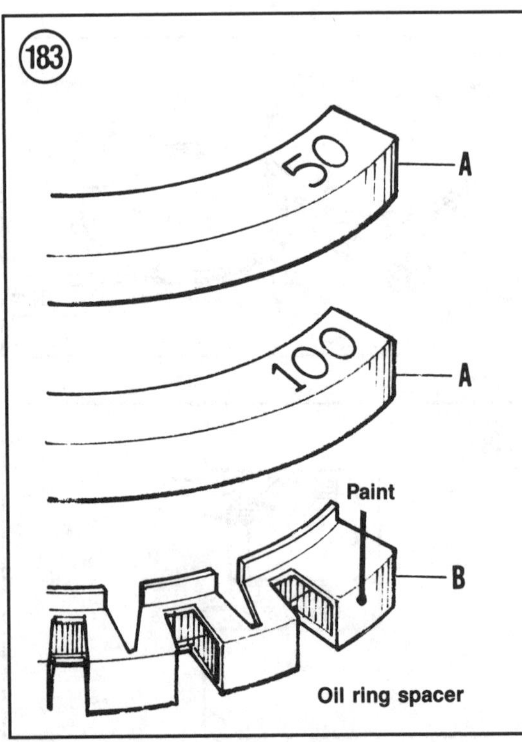

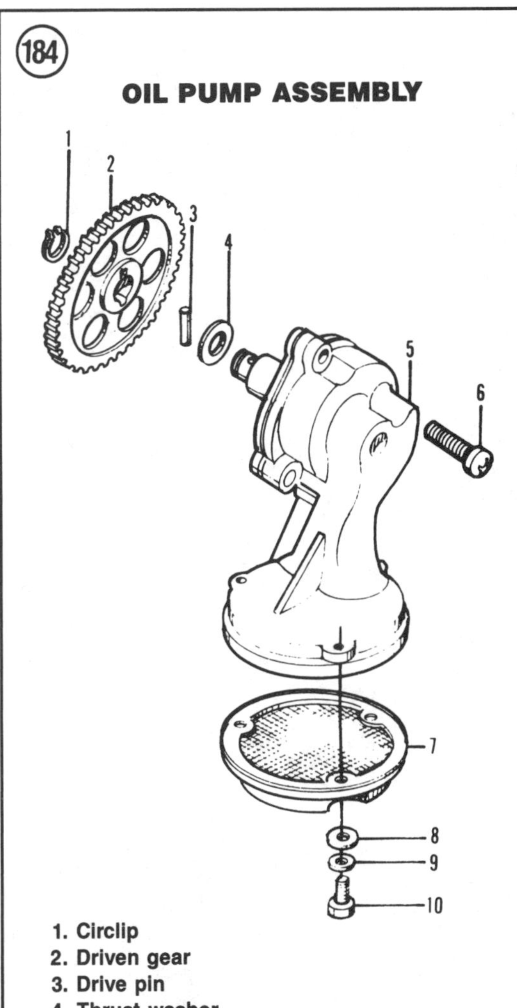
184
OIL PUMP ASSEMBLY
1
2
3
4
5
6
7
8
9
10
1. Circlip
2. Driven gear
3. Drive pin
4. Thrust washer
5. Oil pump assembly
6. Phillips screw
7. Strainer
8. Washer
9. Lockwasher
10. Bolt

186

187

188

185

189

4

10. Install the thrust washer (**Figure 188**) and the drive pin (**Figure 187**).
11. Align the notch in the oil pump drive sprocket with the drive pin and install the oil pump drive sprocket (**Figure 186**) onto the oil pump.
12. Pull up on the shaft and install the circlip (**Figure 185**) securing the oil pump driven sprocket to the oil pump. Make sure the circlip is properly seated in the shaft groove.
13. Assemble the crankcase as described in this chapter.

### Inspection

Replacement parts are *not* available for the oil pump. If the oil pump is not operating properly, the entire oil pump assembly must be replaced.

*CAUTION*
*Do not try to disassemble the oil pump as replacement parts and lockwashers are not available.*

1. Rotate the drive shaft (**Figure 190**). If there is any binding or signs of wear; replace the oil pump assembly.
2. Inspect the oil pump body (**Figure 191**) for cracks or damage.
3. Remove the screws, lockwashers and washers securing the strainer and remove the strainer.
4. Clean the strainer in solvent and blow dry with compressed air. Inspect the strainer screen (**Figure 192**) for breaks, replace if necessary.
5. Install the strainer with the "front" mark (**Figure 193**) facing toward the front of the engine.
6. Install the strainer screws, lockwashers and washers and tighten securely.

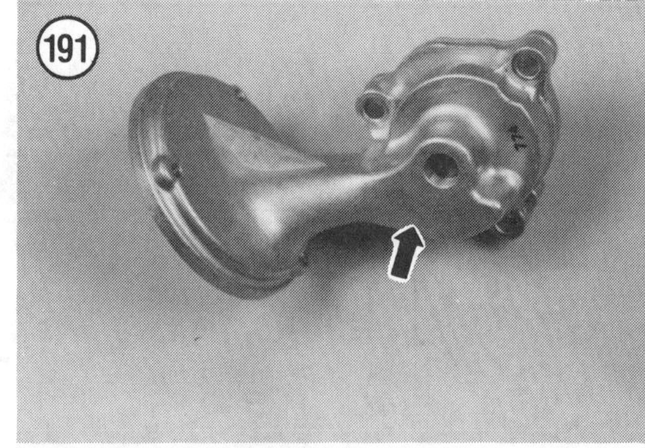


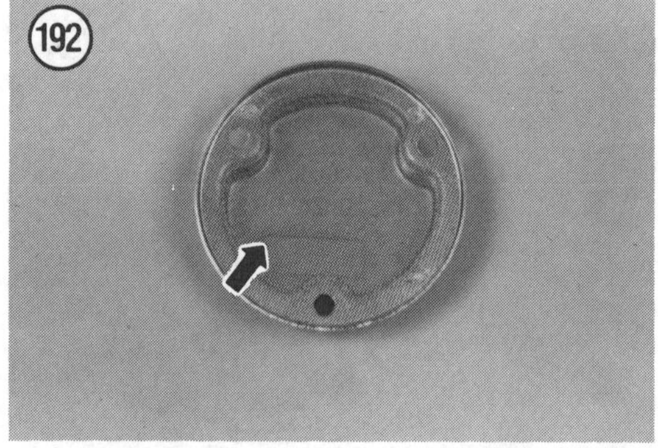

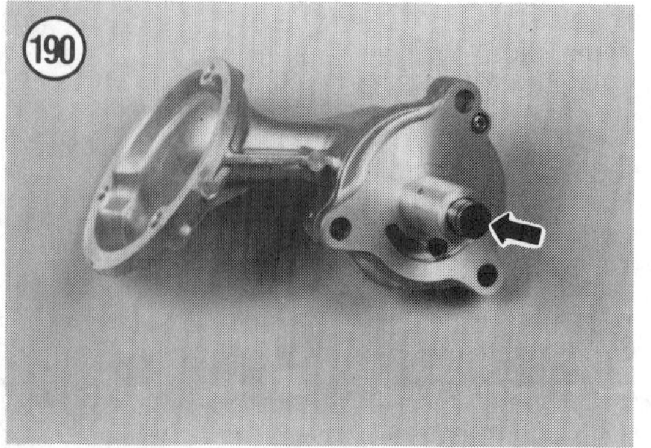

196

7. Inspect the teeth on the driven sprocket (**Figure 194**). Replace the sprocket if the teeth are damaged or any are missing.

## STARTER CLUTCH AND GEARS

Refer to **Figure 195** for this procedure.

### Removal

The starter gears can be removed with the engine in the frame. This procedure is shown with the engine removed for clarity.

1. Remove the left-hand crankcase cover as described in this chapter.
2. Remove the starter idle gears No. 2 and its shaft (**Figure 196**) from the crankcase.



195

**STARTER CLUTCH ASSEMBLY**

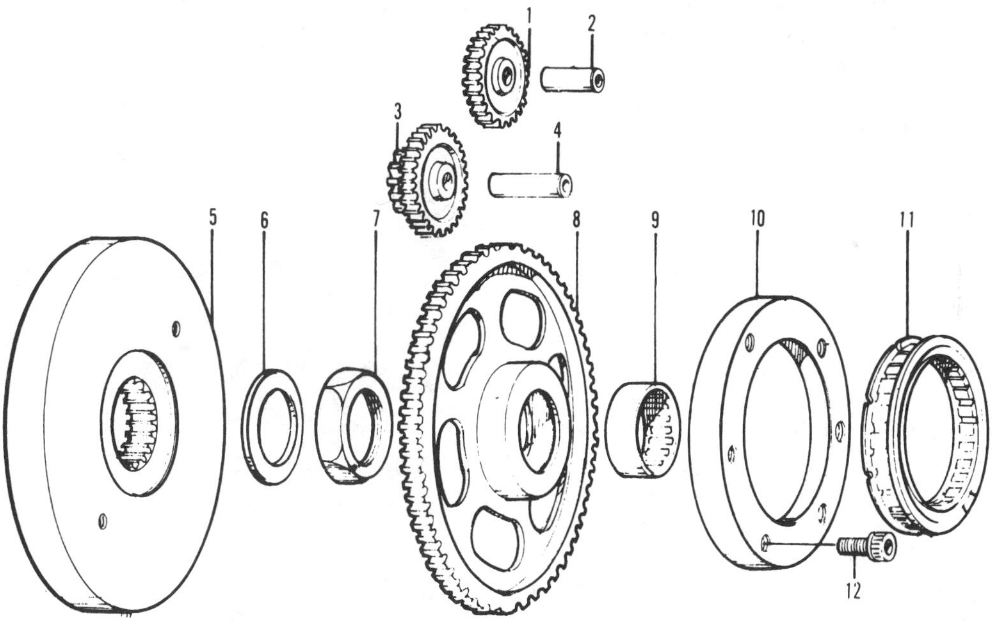

1. Starter idle gear No. 2
2. Shaft (30 mm long)
3. Starter idle gear No. 1
4. Shaft (43 mm long)
5. Flywheel
6. Washer
7. Nut
8. Starter driven gear
9. Needle bearing
10. Bracket
11. One-way clutch
12. Allen bolt

3. Remove the starter idle gears No. 1 and its shaft (**Figure 197**) from the crankcase.

*NOTE*
*The starter driven gear may come off with the alternator rotor in Step 1 or stay on the crankshaft.*

4. If still installed on the crankshaft, remove the starter driven gear (**Figure 198**) from the crankshaft.
5. If removed, install the starter driven gear into the backside of the alternator rotor.
6. Try to rotate the starter driven gear. It should rotate freely in one direction and be locked up in the other direction.
7. If the starter driven gear will rotate in both directions or is locked up in both direction, replace the starter clutch as described in this chapter.
8. Inspect the starter gears (**Figure 199**) for wear or damage. Replace if necessary. Insert the shaft into its respective gear (**Figure 200**) and rotate the gear. Suzuki does not provide specifications for the shafts nor the inside diameter of the gears. If there is a noticeable amount of play, replace the gears and shafts (**Figure 201**).

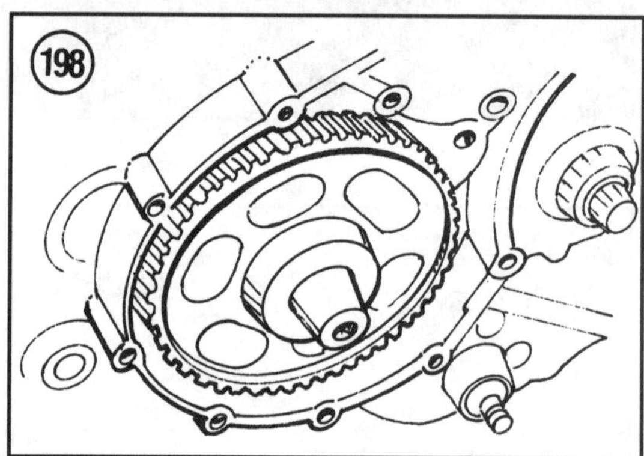

## Installation

1. If removed, install the starter driven gear into the backside of the alternator rotor.
2. Install the starter driven gear and alternator rotor assembly onto the crankshaft. Tighten the rotor bolt as described under *Alternator Rotor Removal/Installation* in Chapter Eight.
3. Install the No. 1 starter idle gear and the long shaft (43 mm) (**Figure 197**) into the crankcase.
4. Position the No. 2 starter idle gear with the shoulder side going on first and install the No. 2 starter idle gear and the short shaft (30 mm) (**Figure 196**) into the crankcase.
5. Install the left-hand crankcase cover as described in this chapter.

## Starter Clutch Replacement

1. If still installed, remove the starter driven gear from the backside of the alternator rotor.
2. Hold onto the center of the rotor with a 36 mm offset wrench.

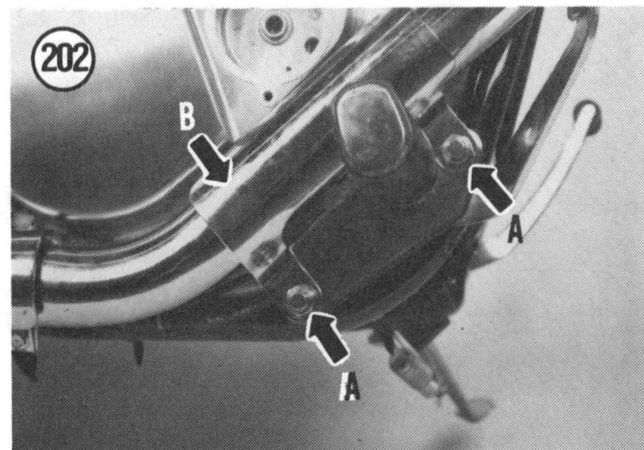


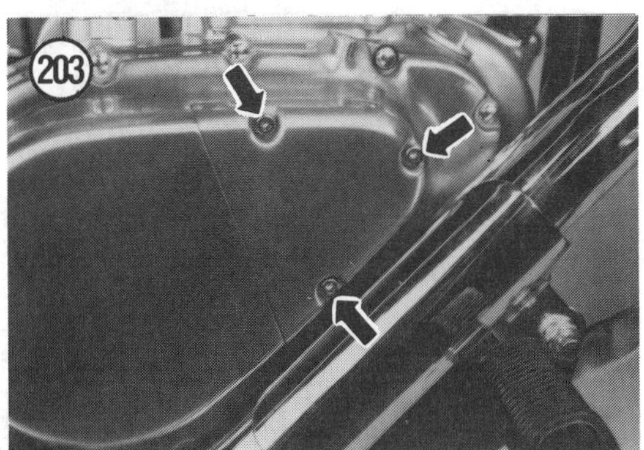

3. Remove the Allen bolts securing the starter clutch assembly to the backside of the rotor.
4. Separate the starter clutch one-way clutch and bracket from the rotor.
5. Install a new one-way clutch with the flange side going on first.
6. Install the bracket and turn the assembly over.
7. Apply red Loctite Threadlocker (No. 271) to the Allen bolt threads prior to installation.
8. Use the same tool set-up used for removal to hold the alternator rotor stationary while tightening the bolts. Tighten the Allen bolts in a crisscross pattern to the torque specification listed in **Table 2**.



## RIGHT-HAND CRANKCASE COVER (CLUTCH COVER)

### Removal

1. Remove the front cap nuts (A, **Figure 202**) and washer from the front through bolts. Remove the exhaust pipe heat shield (B, **Figure 202** )
2. Remove the exhaust system as described under *Exhaust System Removal/Installation* in Chapter Seven.
3. Perform Steps 1-6 of *Engine Oil and Filter Change* as described in Chapter Three.
4. Remove the bolts (**Figure 203**) securing the oil filter cover on the right-hand crankcase cover.
5. Remove the oil filter cover; don't lose the small spring (**Figure 204**) on the center inner surface of the cover. Don't lose the O-ring seal in the cover.
6. Remove the oil filter (**Figure 205**) and place it in a plastic bag to keep the oil from running out of it.

7. At the right-hand crankcase cover, loosen the clutch cable locknuts (A, **Figure 206**) and turn the adjuster (B, **Figure 206**) until there is maximum slack in the cable.
8. Pry open the locking tab (**Figure 207**) on the release arm.
9. Place a 19 mm open end wrench (**Figure 208**) on the clutch release arm and carefully push down on the wrench. This will allow additional slack in the cable.
10. Disengage the clutch cable from the release arm (**Figure 209**) and the receptacle on the right-hand crankcase cover.

*NOTE*
*The following steps are shown with the engine removed from the frame for clarity. It is not necessary to remove the engine for this procedure.*

11. Remove the bolts (**Figure 210** ) securing the right-hand crankcase cover. Note the location of the special washers under 3 of the bolts (W, **Figure 210**). These special washers must be reinstalled in the same location under these specific bolts or the cover will leak oil.
12. Remove the right-hand crankcase cover and gasket. Don't lose the locating dowels.

### Installation

1. Make sure the locating dowels (**Figure 211**) are in place.

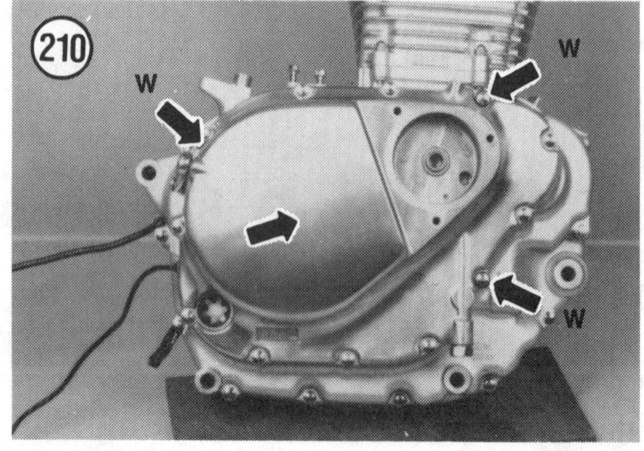

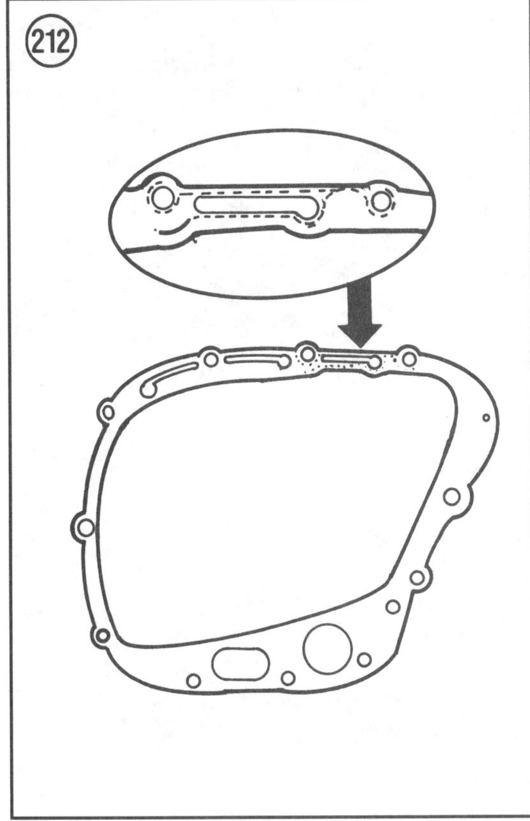

2. If the new gasket does not have a row of gray colored sealant already applied to this area, apply a thin coat of gasket sealant (Three Bond or equivalent) to the right-hand crankcase cover gasket in the area shown in **Figure 212**. This is to provide an oil-tight seal at this portion of the gasket.

3. Install a new right-hand crankcase cover gasket (**Figure 213**).

4. Install the right-hand crankcase cover and the bolts (**Figure 210**). Be sure to install the special washers under the correct bolts as shown in (W, **Figure 210**). If the special washers are not installed, the right-hand crankcase cover will leak oil. Tighten the bolts securely.

5. Install the clutch cable into the receptacle in the right-hand crankcase cover.

6. Place a 19 mm open end wrench (**Figure 208**) on the clutch release arm and carefully push down on the wrench. This will move the arm up in order to easily accept the clutch cable.

7. Install the clutch cable into the release arm (**Figure 209**).

*NOTE*

*If the locking tab has been opened and closed several times, the locking tab may break off. If this happens, insert a small cotter pin through the holes in the release arm receptacle to secure the cable end.*

8. Close the locking tab (**Figure 207**) on the release arm to hold the cable end in place.

9. Perform Steps 12-24 of *Engine Oil and Filter Change* as described in Chapter Three and refill the engine oil.

10. Install the rear brake pedal bracket and right-hand foot rest. Tighten the nuts to the torque specification listed in **Table 1**.

11. Install the exhaust system as described under *Exhaust System Removal/Installation* in Chapter Seven.

12. Adjust the clutch as described under *Clutch Adjustment* in Chapter Three.

4

## LEFT-HAND CRANKCASE COVER AND DRIVE PULLEY

### Removal

1. Remove the seat as described under *Seat Removal/Installation* in Chapter Twelve.
2. Remove the left-hand frame cover.
3. Disconnect the battery negative lead (**Figure 214**).
4. Disconnect the alternator's 3-pin electrical connector (**Figure 215**) containing 3 yellow wires from the voltage regulator located on the rear fender.
5. Drain the engine oil as described under *Engine Oil and Filter Change* in Chapter Three.

*NOTE*

*Prior to removing the shift rod arm from the gearshift shaft, center punch an alignment mark on the end of the shaft aligned with the split in the shift rod arm. This will assure proper alignment during installation.*

6. Remove the bolt and nut (**Figure 216**) securing the gearshift lever to the shift shaft. Remove the lever from the shift shaft. Move the shift lever out of the way.
7. Remove the bolts (**Figure 217**) securing the drive pulley guard and remove the guard.

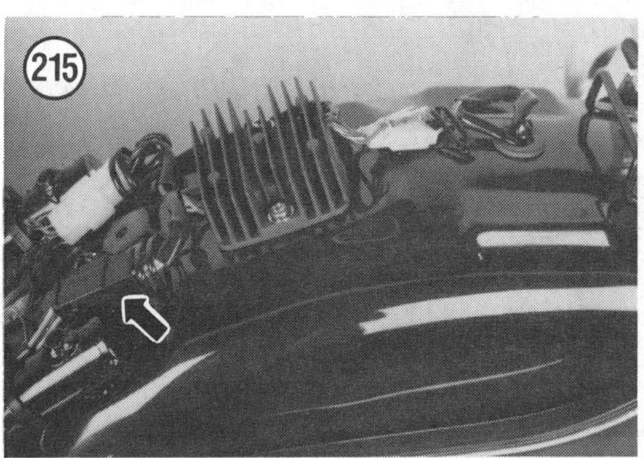

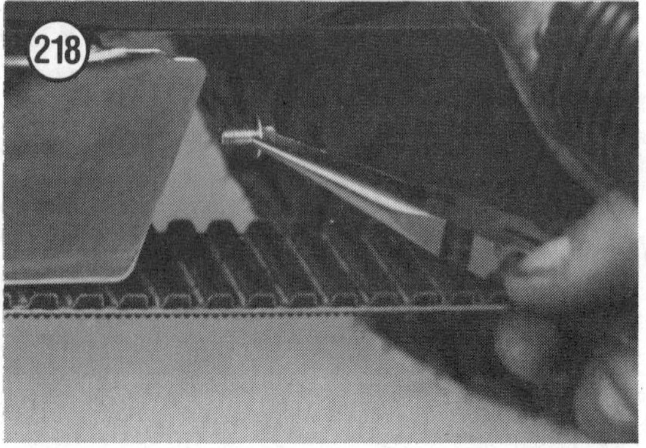

8. Remove the bolt (**Figure 218**) securing the drive belt lower cover at the rear.

9. Remove the bolt and washer (A, **Figure 219**) securing the front of both the drive belt upper and lower covers at the front.

10. Remove the lower cover (B, **Figure 219**).

11. Remove the bolt (**Figure 220**) securing the drive belt upper cover at the rear.

12. Pull the drive belt upper cover (**Figure 221**) up at the rear and remove the upper cover.

13. Shift the transmission into gear.

14. Straighten the tab (**Figure 222**) on the lockwasher.

15. Have an assistant apply the rear brake and loosen the drive pulley nut (**Figure 223**).

16. Remove the nut and lockwasher. Discard the lockwasher.

17. Insert a drift or rod into the hole (**Figure 224**) in the left-hand side of the axle.

18. Loosen the rear axle nut (**Figure 225**).
19. Loosen the drive belt adjuster nut (A, **Figure 226**) and loosen the adjust bolt (B, **Figure 226**) on each side of the swing arm so the wheel can be moved forward for maximum belt slack. Push the rear wheel forward.
20. Carefully pull the drive pulley (A, **Figure 227**) and drive belt (B, **Figure 227**) off the transmission mainshaft.
21. Remove the drive pulley and drive belt.
22. Remove the tie wrap (**Figure 228**) securing the alternator electrical cable and emission control hoses to the frame.

*NOTE*
*Step 23 and Step 24 are shown with the engine removed from the frame for clarity. It is not necessary to remove the engine to perform this procedure.*

23. Remove the bolt (**Figure 229**) securing the stator assembly electrical cable to the external shift mechanism cover.
24. Remove the bolts securing the left-hand crankcase cover (**Figure 230**) assembly and remove the cover and gasket. Don't lose the locating dowels in the crankcase.

### Installation

1. Make sure the locating dowels (**Figure 231**) are in place.
2. Install a new left-hand crankcase cover gasket (**Figure 232**)

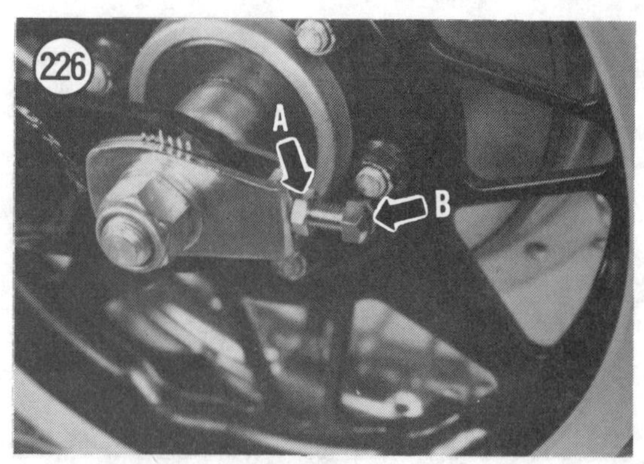

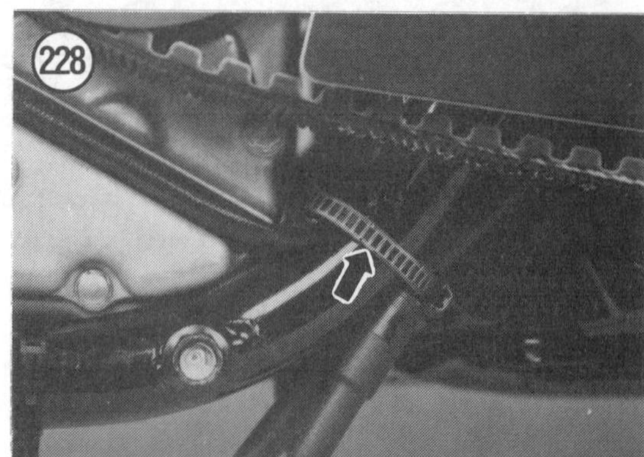

3. Install the left-hand crankcase cover (**Figure 230**) and bolts.
4. Tighten the left-hand crankcase cover bolts securely.
5. Install the bolt (**Figure 229**) securing the stator assembly electrical cable to the external shift mechanism cover.
6. Make sure the drive belt is properly meshed with the driven pulley on the rear wheel.
7. Mesh the drive belt onto the drive pulley and install these 2 parts as an assembly onto the transmission mainshaft (**Figure 233**).
8. Prior to installing the lockwasher, partially bend up one side (**Figure 234**). It is difficult to reach the lockwasher within the recess of the drive pulley once the drive pulley nut is installed.
9. Install a new lockwasher and the nut.

*CAUTION*

*In Step 10, the drive belt must be properly meshed with both the drive and driven pulleys. If not, the belt teeth may be stripped while tightening the drive pulley nut with the rear brake applied.*

10. Pull the rear wheel toward the rear with the drive belt properly engaged with both the drive and driven pulleys. Tighten the drive belt adjuster bolts temporarily.
11. Have an assistant apply the rear brake and tighten the drive pulley nut to the torque specification listed in **Table 1**.
12. Continue to bend up one section of the *new* lockwasher onto one of the flats on the drive pulley nut.

4

13. Install he drive belt upper cover and install the bolt (**Figure 220**) securing the drive belt upper cover at the rear. Tighten the bolt securely (**Figure 235**).
14. Install the lower cover (B, **Figure 219**).
15. Install the bolt and washer (A, **Figure 219**) securing the front of both the drive belt upper and lower covers at the front.
16. Install the bolt (**Figure 218**) securing the drive belt lower cover at the rear and tighten securely.

*WARNING*

*Be sure to secure the alternator electrical cable and emission control hoses back to the frame as shown in (**Figure 228**). If the electrical cable is not secured as shown, it will move over and the drive belt will rub on it. The drive belt will wear through the insulation and an electrical short or open will occur.*

17. Install the tie wrap (**Figure 228**) securing the alternator electrical cable and emission control hoses to the frame.
18. The rubber damper (**Figure 236**) must be installed on each side of the bolt mounting holes in the drive pulley guard as shown in **Figure 237**.
19. Install the bolts (**Figure 217**) securing the drive pulley guard and remove the guard.
20. Adjust the drive belt as described under *Drive Belt Adjustment* in Chapter Three.
21. Install the gearshift lever onto the shift shaft. Install and tighten the bolt and nut (**Figure 216**) securely.
22. Fill the engine with the recommended type and quantity of oil as described under *Engine Oil and Filter Change* in Chapter Three.
23. Connect the alternator's 3-pin electrical connector (**Figure 215**) containing 3 yellow wires to the voltage regulator.
24. Connect the battery negative lead (**Figure 214**).
25. Install the seat as described under *Seat Removal/Installation* in Chapter Twelve.

## CRANKCASE AND CRANKSHAFT

Disassembly of the crankcase—splitting the cases—and removal of the crankshaft assembly requires that the engine be removed from the motorcycle frame.

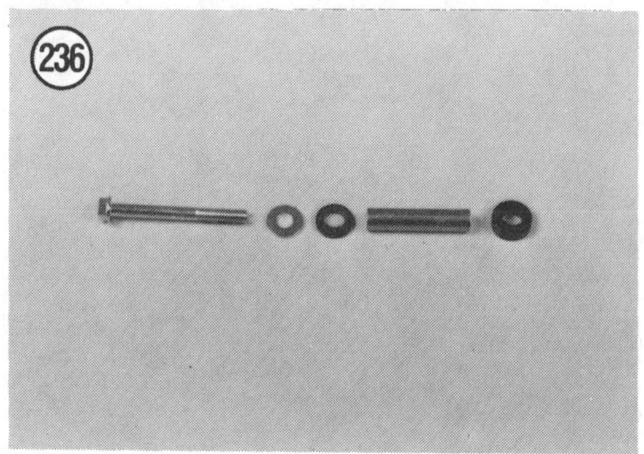


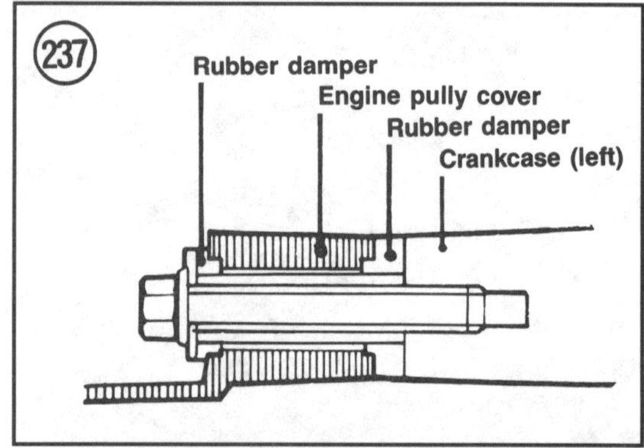

The crankcase is made in 2 halves of precision diecast aluminum and is of the "thin-walled" type. To avoid damage, do not hammer nor pry on any of the exterior or interior projected walls. These areas are easily damaged. They are assembled *without a gasket* and 2 locating dowels align the crankcase halves when they are bolted together.

Since the crankcase is assembled without a gasket, a specific sealant—*Three-Bond No. 1216* is required to seal the case halves together. This specific type of sealant is the only type specified by U.S. Suzuki and is available from most Suzuki dealers. It is a hardening type of sealant but it retains it elasticity even when subjected to engine heat. Other types of sealant, even those manufactured by Three Bond, will eventually become brittle which will lead to an oil leak.

The crankshaft assembly (**Figure 238**) is made up of 2 flywheels pressed together on a hollow crankpin. The connecting rod big end bearing on the crankpin is a needle bearing assembly. The crankshaft is supported on 2 ball bearings in the crankcase. Service to the crankshaft is limited to removal and replacement.



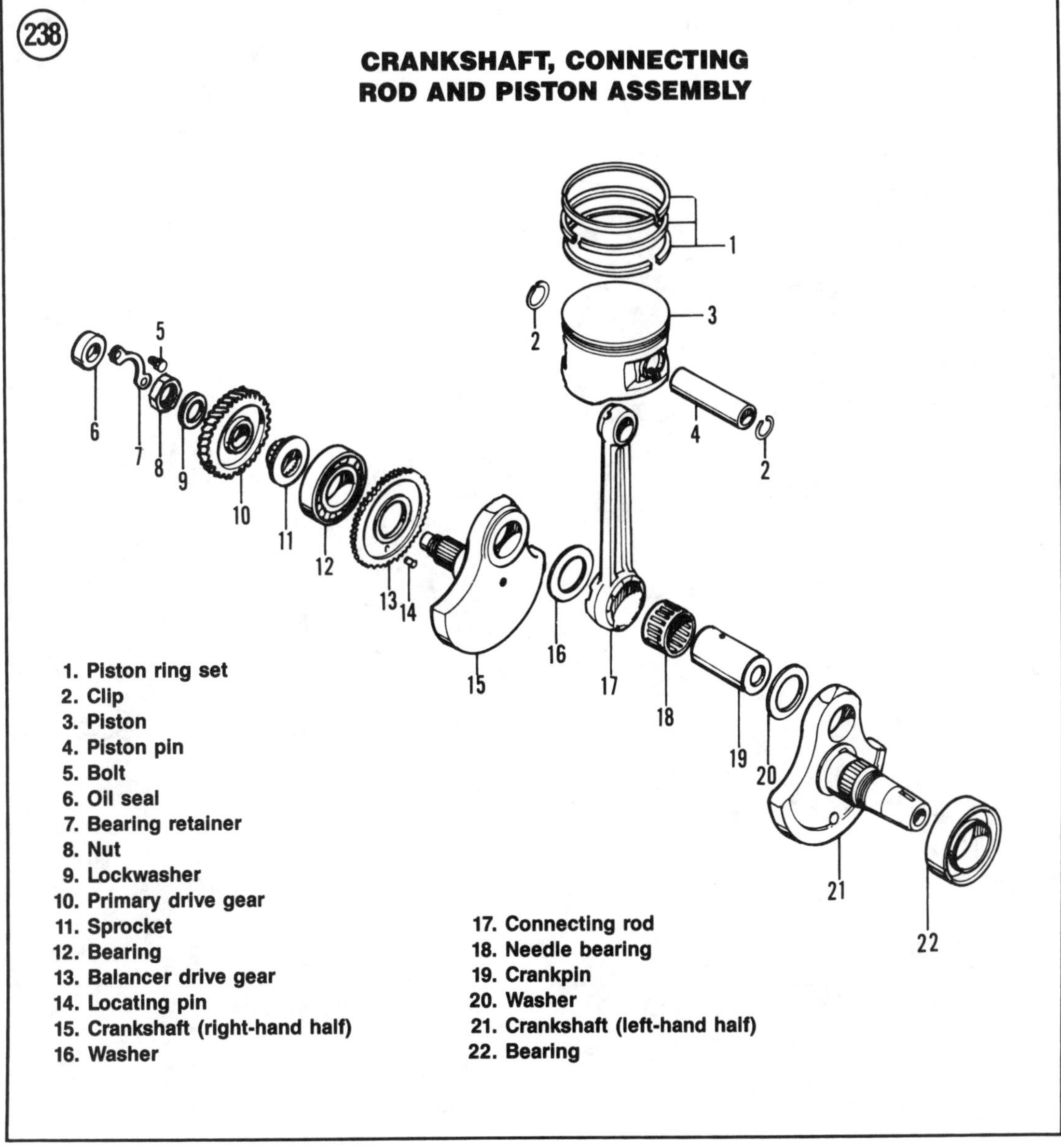

The procedure which follows is presented as a complete, step-by-step, major lower end rebuild that should be followed if an engine is to completely reconditioned. However, if the you're replacing a part that you know is defective, the disassembly should be carried out only until the failed part is accessible. There is no need to disassemble the engine beyond that point so long as you know the remaining components are in good condition and that they were not affected by the failed part.

### Crankcase Disassembly

1. While the engine is still in the frame, remove the starter motor and the alternator as described in Chapter Eight.

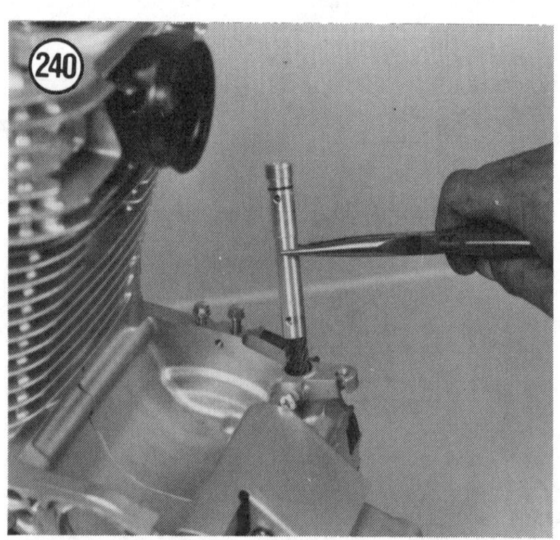

246

247

248

249

2. Remove the engine as described in this chapter.
3. Remove the cylinder head cover, camshaft, cylinder, piston, starter clutch assembly and external gearshift mechanism as described in this chapter.
4. Loosen the bolt (**Figure 239**) securing the speedometer drive shaft assembly. Withdraw the drive shaft assembly (**Figure 240**) from the crankcase.
5. Remove the counterbalancer bolt (**Figure 241**) and washer (**Figure 242**).
6. Remove the oil control orifice (**Figure 243**) from the right-hand crankcase.
7. Place a copper washer (A, **Figure 244**) between the clutch outer housing and the primary drive gear. This will prevent the primary drive gear from rotating while loosening the nut.

*CAUTION*

*The primary drive gear nut has **left-hand threads**.*

8. Turn the wrench *clockwise* and loosen the primary drive gear nut (B, **Figure 244**).
9. Remove the clutch as described under *Clutch Removal/Disassembly* in Chapter Five.
10. Remove the nut (**Figure 245**) and the lockwasher (**Figure 246**).
11. Remove the primary drive gear (**Figure 247**).
12. Remove the camshaft drive chain (**Figure 248**).
13. Remove the camshaft drive chain drive sprocket (**Figure 249**) from the crankshaft.
14. Remove the circlip (**Figure 250**) securing the oil pump driven gear and remove the gear (**Figure 251**).

250

15. Remove the drive pin (**Figure 252**) and washer (**Figure 253**).
16. Remove the screws (A, **Figure 254**) securing the neutral switch. Remove the switch and the rubber grommet (B, **Figure 254**) from the groove in the crankcase. Remove the contact (**Figure 255**) and spring (**Figure 256**).
17. Remove the starter idle gears as described in this chapter.
18. Remove the left-hand crankcase half bolts (**Figure 257**).
19. Remove the alternator rotor as described under *Alternator Rotor Removal/Installation* in Chapter Eight.
20. Remove the flywheel from the left-hand side of the crankshaft as follows:

a. Install Suzuki special tool, Flywheel Holder (part No. 09930-32410) (A, **Figure 258**) onto the flywheel with 2 bolts (A, **Figure 259**).
b. Install Suzuki special tool, 46 mm socket (part No. 09923-12410) (B, **Figure 258**) onto the flywheel nut (B, **Figure 259**).
c. Hold onto the flywheel and loosen the flywheel nut.

251

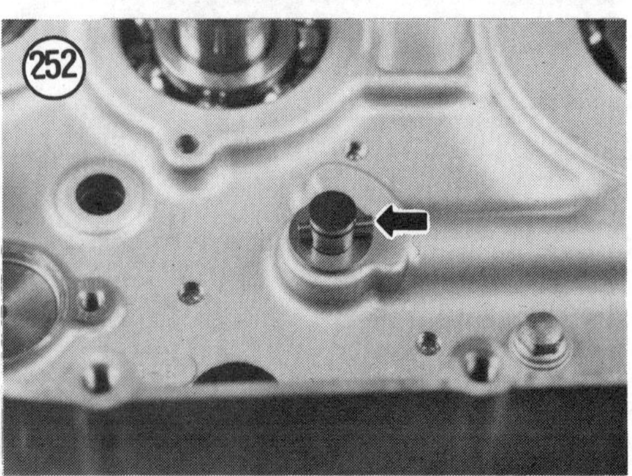
252

253

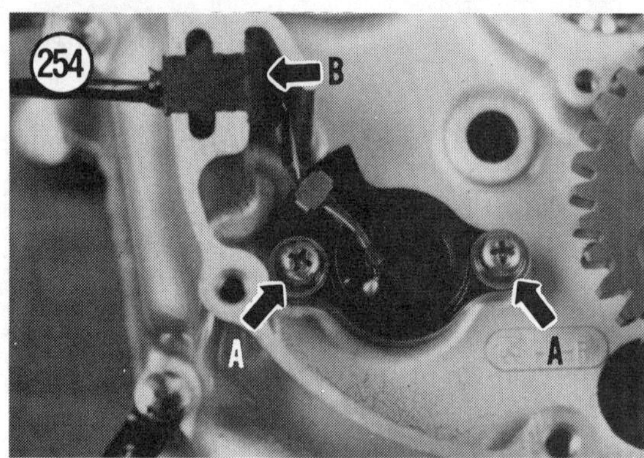

254

255

256

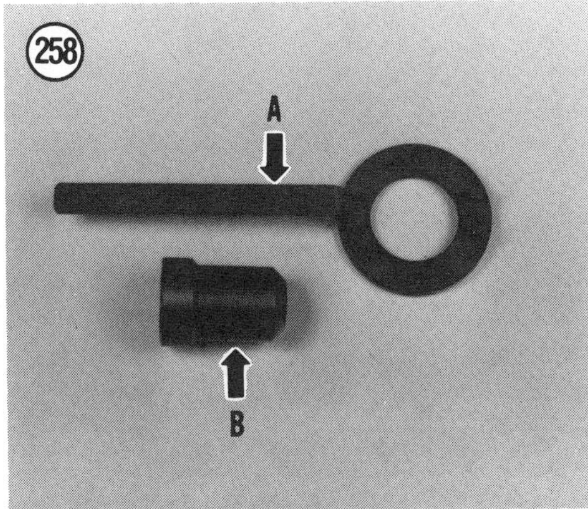


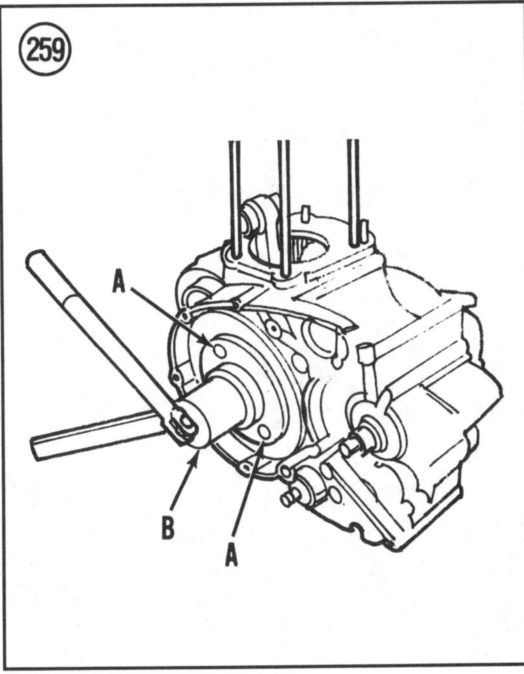


d. Remove the nut and washer.

e. Remove the special tools.

f. Withdraw the flywheel from the crankshaft.

21. Remove the right-hand crankcase half bolts (**Figure 260**).

22. Double check that you have removed all of the right- and left-hand crankcase bolts. Note the location of the engine ground strap and the wire clamp (**Figure 261**). They must be reinstalled in the same location.

23. Tap on the right-hand crankcase with a plastic mallet and separate the 2 halves.

*CAUTION*

*If it is necessary to pry the halves apart, do it very **carefully** so that you do not mar the gasket surfaces. If you do, the cases will leak oil and must be replaced.*

24. Lift the right-hand crankcase off of the left-hand crankcase.

25. Remove both transmission assemblies and the internal shift mechanism from the crankcase as

4

described under *Transmission and Internal Shift Mechanism* in Chapter Six.

26. Remove the balancer driven gear and shaft from the left-hand crankcase half as described in this chapter.

27. Carefully tap on the left-hand end of the crankshaft assembly with a plastic or soft faced mallet and remove the crankshaft assembly from the left-hand crankcase.

28. Remove the internal portion of the oil pump as described in this chapter.

29. Inspect the crankcase halves as described in this chapter.

### Crankcase Assembly

1. Apply assembly oil or engine oil to the inner races of all bearings in both crankcase halves.

*CAUTION*
*Make sure oil pump screen is installed with the "FRONT" arrow (**Figure 262**) facing toward the front of the engine.*

2. Install the inner portion of the oil pump as described in this chapter.
3. Set the left-hand crankcase half on wood blocks or a wood holding fixture.
4. Position the crankshaft assembly with the alternator rotor tapered end going in first into the left-hand crankcase half. Position the connecting rod within the piston clearance area in the top portion of the crankcase half.
5. Install the crankshaft into the left-hand crankcase half. Carefully tap on the right-hand end of the crankshaft to make sure it is properly seated.
6. Install the balancer shaft assembly as described in this chapter.
7. Install the transmission and the internal shift mechanism as described under *Transmission and Internal Shift Mechanism Removal/Installation* in Chapter Six.

*NOTE*
*Prior to installation, coat all bearing surfaces with assembly oil or fresh engine oil.*

8. Make sure both crankcase halves sealing surfaces are perfectly clean and dry. Clean off with electrical contact cleaner and wipe off with a lint-free cloth.
9. Install a new O-ring seal (**Figure 263**) in the left-hand crankcase half.
10. Make sure the locating dowels are in place at the front and rear (**Figure 264**) of the left-hand case half.

*CAUTION*
*Use **Three-Bond No. 1216** to seal the case halves together. Do **not** use a substitute type of gasket sealant as you will end up with an oil leak*

*NOTE*
*Do not apply sealant to the upper outer rear section of the sealing surface, from arrow-to-arrow as shown in A, **Figure 265**. This is the area where the*

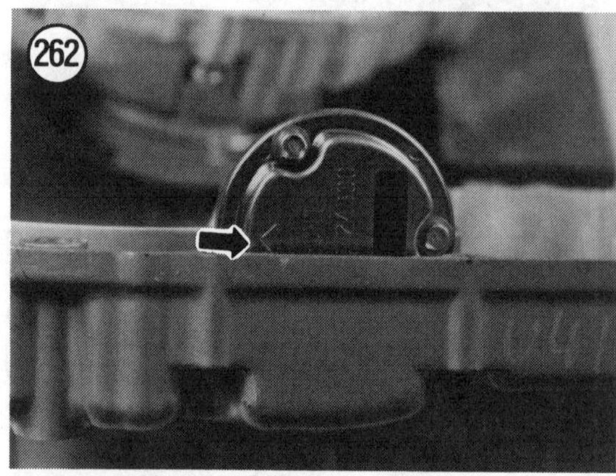

*engine rear mounting through bolt passes through the crankcase halves. Water or moisture frequently enters the crankcase in this area as the bolt is not sealed to the crankcase on either side. By not sealing the external section of this area, any water that enters this area will be able to drain back out. Be sure to apply sealant to the circular sealing surface B,* ***Figure 265*** *inward of this section of the crankcase. This will prevent any water or moisture from entering the crankcase.*

11. Apply a light coat of the recommended type of gasket sealer to the sealing surfaces of the right-hand crankcase half. Cover only flat surfaces, *not curved bearing surfaces*. Make the coating as thin, but still completely covered, or the case can shift and hammer out bearings.

12. Position the right-hand crankcase half onto the left-hand crankcase half. Tap them together lightly with a plastic mallet or soft faced mallet—do not use a metal hammer as it will damage the case.

*CAUTION*

*Crankcase halves should fit together without force. If the crankcase halves do not fit together completely, do not attempt to pull them together with the crankcase bolts. Separate the crankcase halves and investigate the cause of the interference. If the transmission shafts were disassembled, recheck to make sure that a gear is not installed backwards. Do not risk damage by trying to force the cases together.*

13. Before installing the bolts, slowly spin the transmission shafts and shift the transmission through all gears using the shift drum. Make sure the shift forks are operating properly and that you can shift through all gears. Also spin the crankshaft—make sure it moves freely with no binding. This is the time to find that something may be installed incorrectly—not after the crankcase is completely assembled.

14. Install the crankcase bolts in the left-hand side (**Figure 257**) and tighten in a crisscross pattern to the torque specification listed in **Table 2**.

*NOTE*

*Install a new sealing washer under the rear right-hand bolt (W,* ***Figure 260****).*

15. Install the crankcase bolts in the right-hand side (**Figure 260**) and tighten in a crisscross pattern to the torque specification listed in **Table 2**.

16. After the bolts have been tightened, slowly spin the transmission shafts. Also spin the crankshaft, make sure it moves freely with no binding. If there is a small amount of binding, carefully tap on the left-hand end of the crankshaft with a plastic or soft-faced mallet. During the assembly procedure, the crankshaft will "settle-down" into the left-hand crankcase and bearing and needs to be nudged back a little.

4

17. Install the flywheel onto the left-hand side of the crankshaft as follows:

a. Install the flywheel onto the crankshaft.
b. Install the washer with the dished side facing out and install the nut finger-tight.
c. Install Suzuki special tool, Flywheel Holder (part No. 09930-32410) (**Figure 258**) onto the flywheel with 2 bolts (A, **Figure 259**).
d. Install Suzuki special tool, 46 mm socket (part No. 09923-12410) (**Figure 258**) onto the flywheel nut (B, **Figure 259**).
e. Hold onto the flywheel and tighten the flywheel nut to the torque specification listed in **Table 2**.
f. Remove the special tools.

18. Apply blue Loctite Threadlocker (No. 242) to the bolt threads prior to installation. Install the counterbalancer bolt and washer. Tighten the bolt to the torque specification listed in **Table 2**.
19. Install the neutral switch contact as shown in **Figure 266**.
20. Install the neutral switch spring (**Figure 256**).
21. Install the neutral switch and screws (A, **Figure 254**). Tighten the screws securely. Make sure the rubber grommet (B, **Figure 254**) is securely seated in the crankcase groove.
22. Install the starter idle gears as described in this chapter.
23. Install the oil pump washer (**Figure 253**) and drive pin (**Figure 252**).
24. Install the oil pump driven gear (**Figure 251**).
25. Pull up on the oil pump shaft and install and circlip (**Figure 250**). Make sure the circlip is located correctly in the shaft groove.
26. Align the punch marks on the camshaft drive sprocket (A, **Figure 267**) with the crankshaft (B, **Figure 267**) and install the drive sprocket.
27. Install the camshaft drive chain (**Figure 248**) onto the drive sprocket.
28. Install the primary drive gear (**Figure 247**).
29. Position the lockwasher with the dished side facing up and install the lockwasher (**Figure 246**).
30. Install the clutch as described under *Clutch Assembly/Installation* in Chapter Five.

*CAUTION*

*The primary drive gear nut has* ***left-hand threads.***

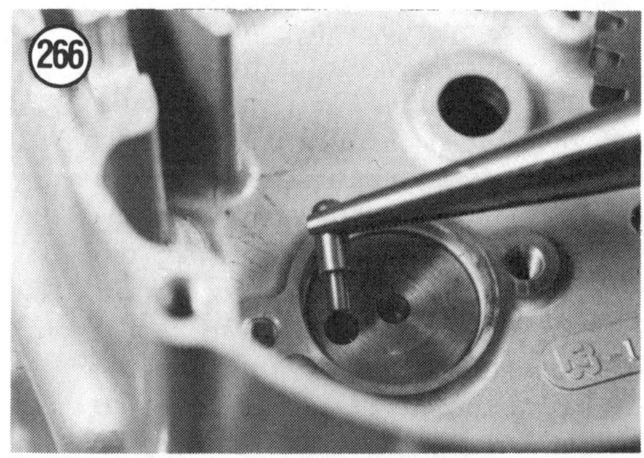

31. Place a copper washer between the clutch outer housing and the primary drive gear. This will prevent the primary drive gear from rotating while tightening the nut.

*CAUTION*
*The primary drive gear nut has **left-hand threads**.*

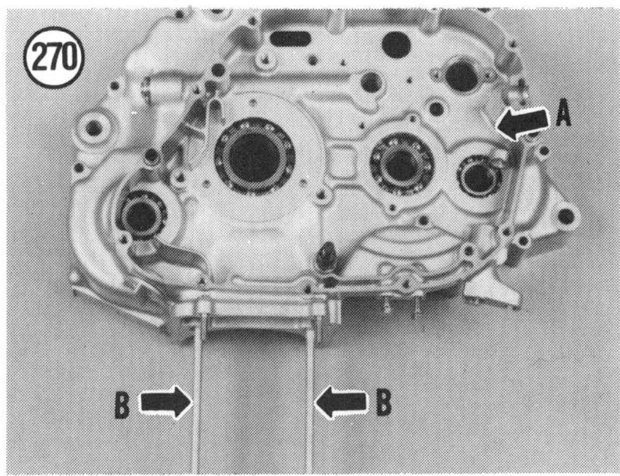


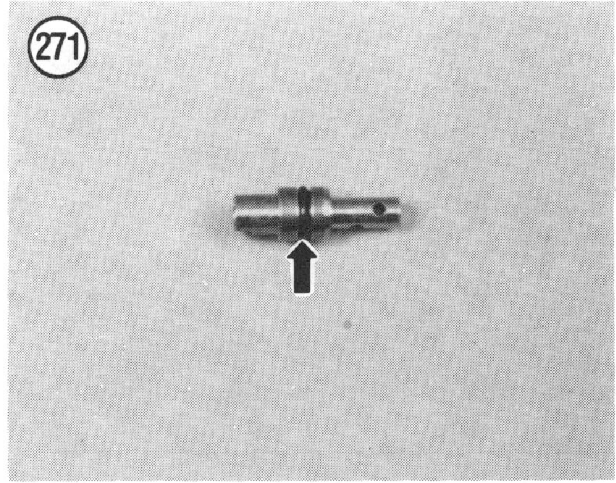

32. Turn the wrench *counterclockwise* and tighten the primary drive gear nut to the torque specification listed in **Table 2**.
33. Make sure the O-ring seal (**Figure 268**) is in place in the engine pulley spacer. Apply a light coat of grease to the O-ring seal after it is in place. Slide the spacer onto the transmission mainshaft with the O-ring side going on first.
34. Install the oil control orifice (**Figure 243**) into the right-hand crankcase.
35. Install the cylinder head cover, camshaft, cylinder, piston, starter clutch assembly and external gearshift mechanism as described in this and other related chapters.
36. Install the speedometer drive shaft assembly (**Figure 240**) into the crankcase. Tighten the bolt (**Figure 239**) securely.
37. Install the engine as described in this chapter.
38. Install the starter motor and the alternator as described in Chapter Eight.



### Crankcase and Crankshaft Inspection

1. Remove the oil gallery plug and gasket (**Figure 269**) from the right-hand crankcase half.
2. Thoroughly clean the inside and outside of both crankcase halves with cleaning solvent. Dry with compressed air. Make sure there is no solvent residue left in the cases as it will contaminate the new engine oil.
3. Remove all old gasket sealing material from both case half mating surfaces.
4. Carefully inspect the cases (A, **Figure 270**) for cracks and fractures. Also check the areas around the stiffening ribs, around bearing bosses and threaded holes. If damage is found, have it repaired by a shop specializing in the repair of precision aluminum castings or replace the crankcase halves as a set.
5. Make sure the crankcase studs are tight (B, **Figure 270**). Suzuki does not provide a torque specification for the studs.
6. Inspect the oil control orifice an its O-ring seal (**Figure 271**) for wear or deterioration. The O-ring cannot be replaced separately. If damaged, the oil control orifice must be replaced.
7. Turn the crankshaft, transmission and shift drum bearings (**Figure 272**) by hand. Check for damaged races and balls. Replace the bearing(s)

if it has excessive side play (**Figure 273**). If the bearings are okay, oil the races and balls with fresh engine oil. If necessary, replace the bearings as described in this chapter.

8. Inspect the cam chain drive sprocket (**Figure 274**) for wear, damage or missing teeth. Replace if damaged.

9. Inspect the primary drive gear (**Figure 275**) for wear, damage or missing teeth. Replace if damaged.

10. Measure the inside diameter of the connecting rod small end (**Figure 276**) with an inside micrometer. Compare to dimensions listed in **Table 1**. If worn to the service limit dimension or greater, the crankshaft assembly must be replaced.

11A. If special tools are not available, check the condition of the connecting rod big end bearing by grasping the rod in one hand and lifting up on it. With the heal of your other hand, rap sharply on the top of the rod. A sharp metallic sound, such as a click, is an indication that the bearing or crankpin or both are worn and the crankshaft assembly should be replaced.

11B. If special tools are available, place the crankshaft assembly on V-blocks. Place a dial indicator against the connecting rod small end (**Figure 277**). Move the connecting rod back and forth; note the reading and compare to the dimension listed in **Table 1**. Replace the crankshaft assembly if worn to the service limit dimension or greater.

12. Place the crankshaft assembly with the bearing journals resting on V-blocks and check the runout. Place a dial indicator against each end of the crankshaft (**Figure 278**). Slowly rotate the crankshaft. Note the reading at each end and

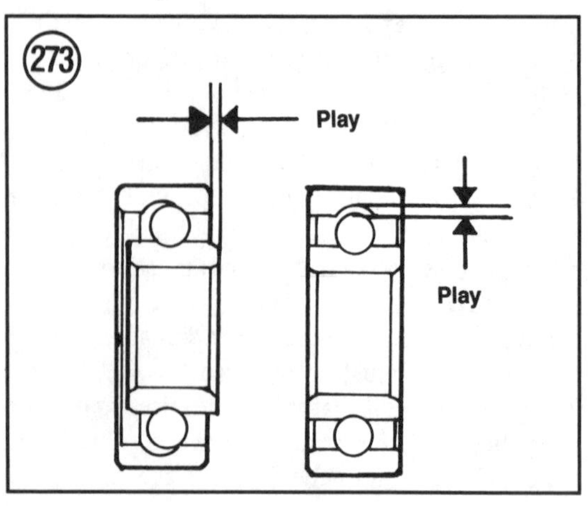

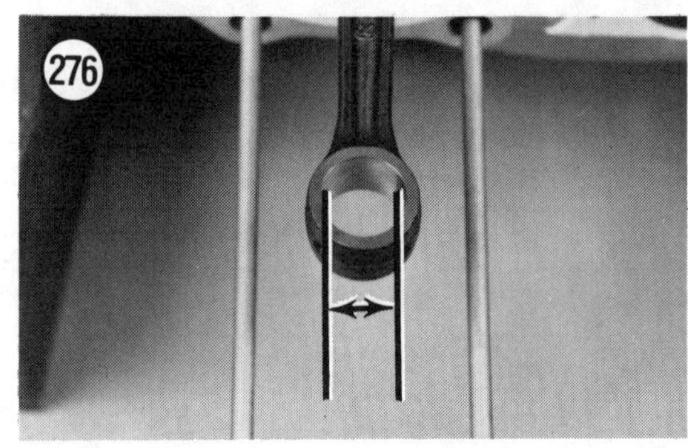


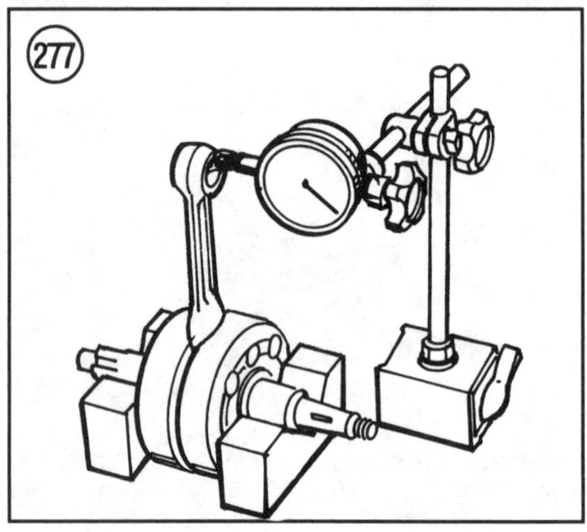

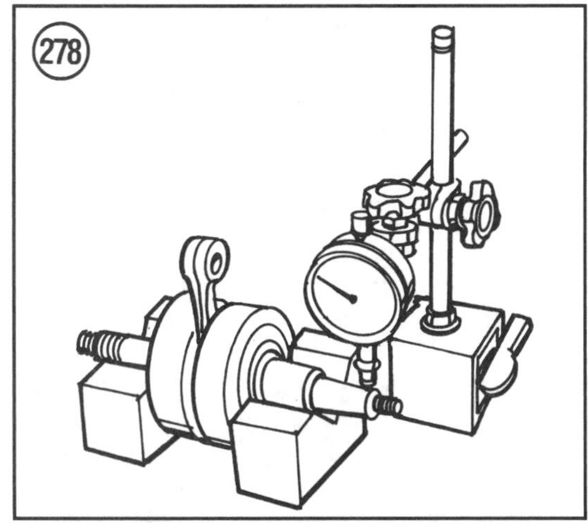

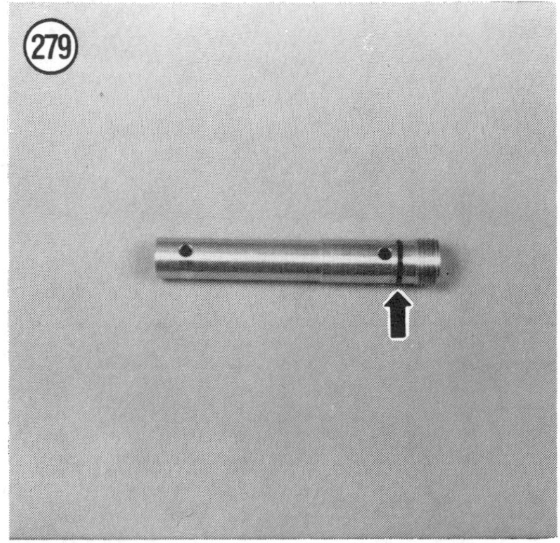

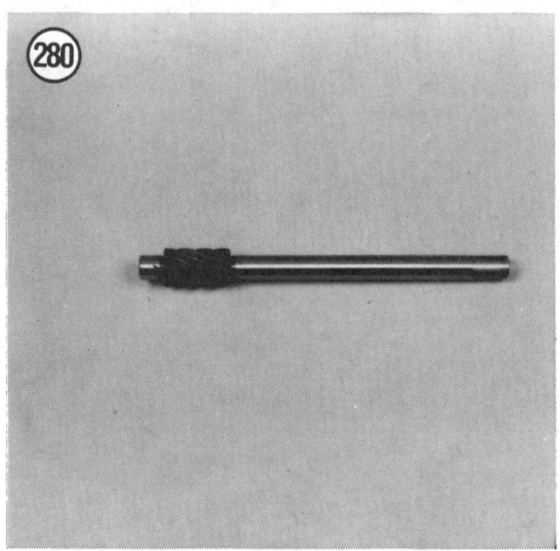

compare to the dimension listed in **Table 1**. Replace the crankshaft assembly if either end is worn to the service limit dimension or greater.

13. Install a new gasket on the oil gallery plug and install the plug (**Figure 269**) into the right-hand crankcase half.

14. Inspect the speedometer drive shaft sleeve for wear or damage. Replace the O-ring seal (**Figure 279**) if worn or deterioration, replace if necessary.

15. Inspect the speedometer drive shaft and gear (**Figure 280**) for wear or damage, replace the drive shaft if necessary.



### Crankcase Bearing and Oil Seal Replacement

1. Turn the crankshaft, transmission and shift drum bearings (**Figure 272**) by hand. Check for damaged races and balls. Replace the bearing(s) if it has excessive side play (**Figure 273**). If the bearings are okay, oil the races and balls with fresh engine oil. If necessary, replace the bearings as follows.

2. To remove the old oil seals, perform the following:

   a. Pry out old oil seals (**Figure 281**) with a small screwdriver, taking care not to damage the crankcase bore.

   b. If the oil seals are old and hard to remove, heat the cases as described in Step 4.

   c. Use an awl to punch a small hole in the steel backing of the seal.

*CAUTION*

*Do not install the screw too deep or it may contact and damage the bearing behind it.*

d. Install a small sheet metal screw part way into the seal and pull the seal out with a pair of pliers.

*NOTE*
*If bearing replacement is required, purchase the new bearing(s) and place them in a freezer for approximately 2 hours before installation. Chilling the bearings will slightly reduce their overall diameter while the hot crankcase is slightly larger due to heat expansion. This will make bearing installation much easier.*

3. On bearings so equipped, remove the screws (**Figure 282**) securing the bearing retainer. Remove the bearing retainer.

*WARNING*
*Prior to heating the crankcase half as described in Step 3, first wash the crankcase thoroughly in soap and water. Make sure there is no gasoline or solvent fumes present.*

*CAUTION*
*Even though the crankcase has been washed, there* ***may*** *be a residual oil or solvent odor left in the oven after heating the crankcase. If you use a household oven, first check with the person who uses the oven for food preparation to avoid getting into trouble.*

4. The bearings are installed with a slight interference fit. The crankcase half must be heated in an oven to a temperature of about 100° C (212° F). An easy way to check the proper temperature is to drop tiny drops of water on the case; if they sizzle and evaporate immediately, the temperature is correct.

*CAUTION*
*Do not heat the cases with a torch (propane or acetylene); never bring a flame into contact with the bearing or case. The direct heat will destroy the case hardening of the bearing and will likely cause warpage of the case.*

*WARNING*
*Wear insulated gloves (insulated kitchen mitts) when handling heated parts.*

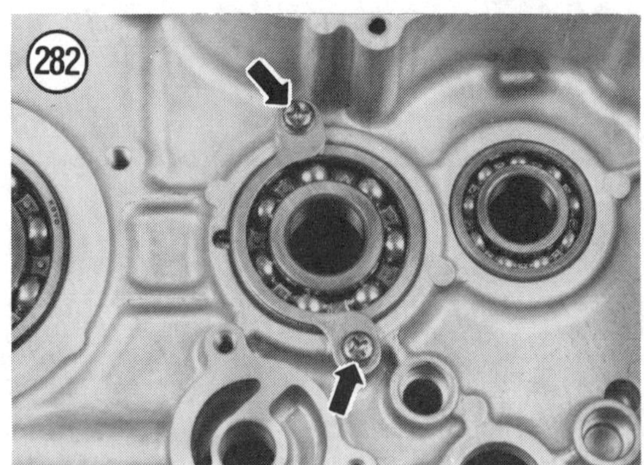

5. Remove the case from the oven and place on wood blocks. Hold onto the crankcase with kitchen mitts or heavy gloves—*it is hot*.

*CAUTION*
*Be sure to tap the crankcase squarely on the piece of wood. Avoid damaging the sealing surface of the crankcase.*

6. Hold the crankcase with the bearing side down and tap it squarely on a piece of soft wood.

Continue to tap until the bearing(s) fall out. Repeat for the other crankcase half.

*NOTE*
*If the bearings are difficult to remove or install, don't take a chance on expensive crankcase damage. Have the work performed by a dealer or competent machine shop.*

7. Reheat the crankcase half in the oven.
8. Remove the case from the oven and place on wood blocks. Hold onto the crankcase with kitchen mitts or heavy gloves—*it is hot*.
9. While the crankcase is still hot, press each new bearing(s) into place in the crankcase by hand until it seats completely. Do not hammer it in. If the bearing will not seat, remove it and cool it again. Reheat the crankcase and try to install the bearing again.
10. On bearings so equipped, install the bearing retainer and screws retaining the ball bearing. Tighten the screws securely.
11. Oil seals are best installed with a special tool available from a Suzuki dealer. However, a proper size socket or piece of pipe can be substituted. Make sure that the bearings and seals are not cocked in the crankcase hole and that they are seated properly.

4

## BALANCER ASSEMBLY

### Removal/Installation

1. Remove the engine from the frame as disassemble the crankcase as described in this chapter.
2. If still installed, remove the balancer drive gear from the crankshaft. Don't lose the locating pin on the backside of the gear.
3. Remove the small washer (**Figure 283**).
4. Remove the large outer washer (**Figure 284**).
5. Remove the balancer gear assembly (**Figure 285**).
6. Remove the large inner washer (**Figure 286**).
7. Withdraw the balancer shaft (**Figure 287**) from the crankcase.
8. Install by reversing these removal steps. Note the following during installation.

9. Make sure the Woodruff key (**Figure 288**) is in place in the balancer shaft.
10. Install the large inner washer and make sure the groove is indexed properly with the Woodruff key on the shaft assembly (**Figure 289**).
11. Install the balancer drive gear onto the crankshaft as follows:
  a. Align the locating pin (A, **Figure 290**) with the locating hole in the crankshaft counterbalance weight.

*CAUTION*
*The alignment of these parts is very critical as they will determine the alignment of the crankshaft to the balancer weight assembly. If this alignment is incorrect, the balancer weight will be "out-of-sinc" with the crankshaft causing extreme vibration that could result in engine damage.*

  b. Align the index marks (B, **Figure 290**) on both the drive and driven gears and install the driven gear.
  c. Make sure that the drive gear is properly engaged with both the driven gear and the locating pin on the crankshaft.
  d. Slowly rotate the crankshaft and make sure the crankshaft and balancer assembly rotate freely with no binding.

288

289

290

### Disassembly/Inspection/Assembly

Refer to **Figure 291** for this procedure.

1. Using a flat bladed screwdriver, carefully pry the springs and pins out from between the inner race and the driven gear. Note that there is a pin in every other slot (**Figure 292**).
2. Inspect the inner race spring slots, the springs and the pins (**Figure 293**) for wear or damage. Replace an damaged part.

*CAUTION*
*The alignment of these parts is very critical as they will determine the alignment of the crankshaft to the balancer weight assembly. If this alignment is incorrect, the balancer weight will be "out-of-sinc" with the crankshaft causing extreme vibration that could result in engine damage.*

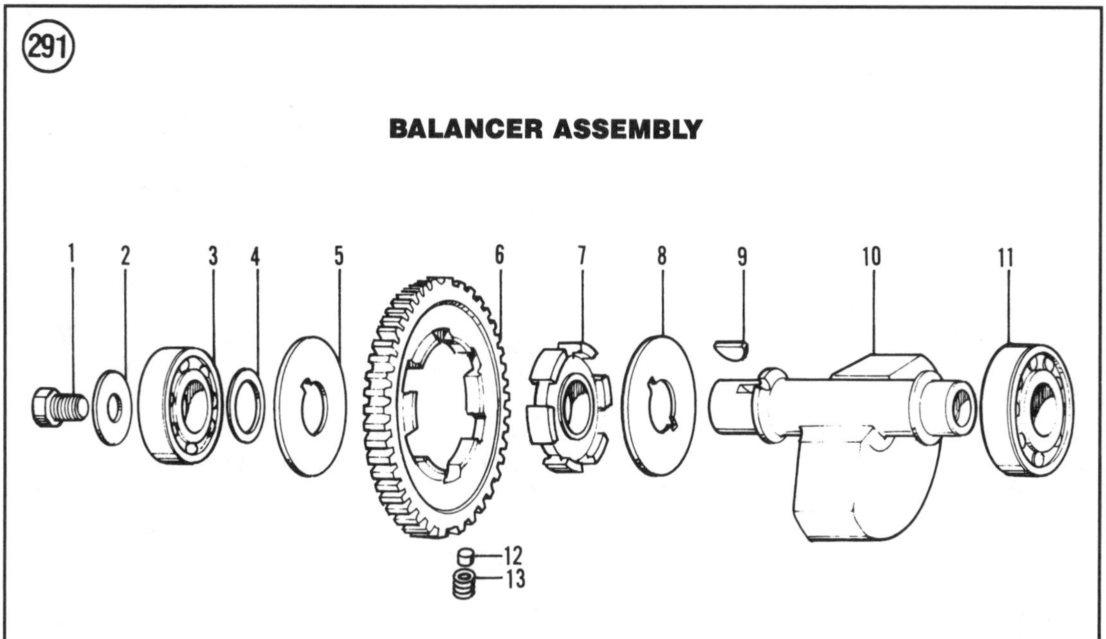

291

**BALANCER ASSEMBLY**

1 2 3 4 5 6 7 8 9 10 11

12
13

1. Bolt
2. Washer
3. Bearing
4. Small washer
5. Washer
6. Balancer driven gear
7. Inner race
8. Washer
9. Woodruff key
10. Balancer shaft
11. Bearing
12. Pin
13. Spring

292

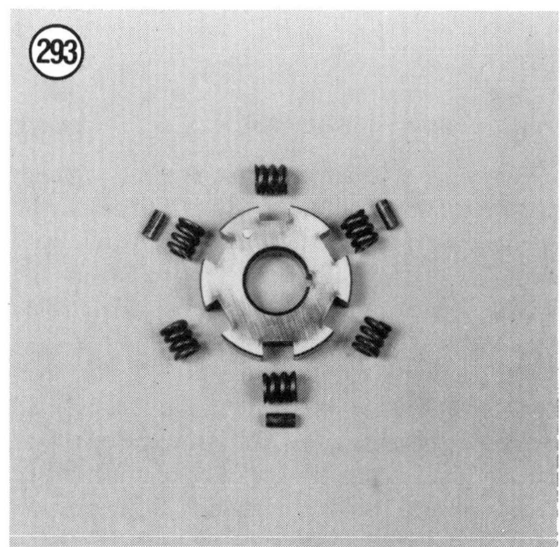
293

3. Install the inner race into the driven gear aligning the index marks (**Figure 294**) on both parts.

*NOTE*
*It doesn't make any difference which slots in the 2 parts have the springs and which slots have both the springs and the pins. The important thing is that the pins are in every other slot.*

*NOTE*
*Using needle nose pliers, compress the springs and press them into the slots in Step 4 and Step 5.*

4. Install a spring only into *every other* slot in both parts. Make sure the springs are pressed in as far as they will go.
5. Install a spring and pin into the remaining slots in both parts. Make sure the springs are pressed in as far as they will go (**Figure 295**).
6. Inspect the gear teeth (A, **Figure 296**) on the balancer drive gear. Also make sure the locating pin (B, **Figure 296**) is securely in place. Replace the gear and/or pin if necessary.
7. Inspect the bearing surfaces at each end of the balancer (**Figure 297**) for wear or damage. Suzuki does not provide service limit outer dimension information. If the surfaces are worn or damaged, replace the balancer.

## BREAK-IN

Following cylinder servicing (boring, honing, new rings, etc.) and major lower end work, the engine should be broken in just as though it were new. The performance and service life of the engine depend greatly on a careful and sensible break-in.

For the first 800 km (500 miles), no more than one-third throttle should be used and speed should be varied as much as possible within the one-third throttle limit. Prolonged, steady running at one speed, no matter how moderate, is to be avoided, as is hard acceleration.

Following the 800 km (500 mile) service, increasingly more throttle can be used but full throttle should not be used until the motorcycle has covered at least 1,600 km (1,000 miles) and then it should be limited to short bursts until 2,410 km (1,500 miles) have been logged.

The mono-grade oils recommended for break-in and normal use provide a more superior bedding pattern for the rings and cylinder than do multi-grade oils. As a result, piston ring and cylinder bore life are greatly increased. During this period, oil consumption will be higher than normal. It is therefore important to frequently check and correct the oil level. At no time, during break-in or later, should the oil level be allowed to drop below the bottom line on the dipstick; if the oil level is low, the oil will become overheated, resulting in insufficient lubrication and increased wear.

### 800 km (500 Mile) Service

It is essential that oil and filter be changed after the first 800 km (500 miles). In addition, it is a good idea to change the oil and filter at the completion of break-in (about 2,410 km/1,500 miles) to ensure that all of the particles produced during break-in are removed from the lubrication system. The small added expense may be considered a smart investment that will pay off in increased engine life.



**Table 1 ENGINE SPECIFICATIONS**

| | Specification | Wear limit |
|---|---|---|
| General | | |
| Type and number of cylinders | Single cylinder, SOHC, air-cooled, 4-stroke | |
| Bore x stroke | 94.0 x 94.0 mm (3.70 x 3.70 in.) | |
| Displacement | 652 cc (39.8 cu. in.) | |
| Compression ratio | 8.5 to 1 | |
| Compression pressure | 1,000-1,400 kPa (145-203 psi) | |
| Camshaft | | |
| Cam lobe height | | |
| Intake | 36.174-36.214 mm (1.4242-1.4257 in.) | 35.880 mm (1.4126 in.) |
| Exhaust | 36.419-36.459 mm (1.4338-1.4354 in.) | 36.120 mm (1.4220 in.) |
| Journal O.D. | | |
| Left | 19.959-19.976 mm (0.7858-0.7865 in.) | — |
| Right and center | 24.959-24.976 mm (0.9826-0.9833 in.) | — |
| Journal oil clearance | 0.032-0.066 mm (0.0013-0.0026 in.) | 0.150 mm (0.0059 in.) |
| Journal holder I.D. | | |
| Left | 20.012-20.025 mm (0.7879-0.7884 in.) | — |
| Right and center | 25.012-25.025 mm (0.9847-0.9852 in.) | — |
| Runout | — | 0.10 mm (0.004 in.) |
| Drive chain (20 pitch length) | — | 128.9 mm (5.07 in.) |
| Rocker assembly (IN and EX) | | |
| Rocker arm bore I.D. | 12.000-12.018 mm (0.4724-0.4731 in.) | — |
| Rocker arm shaft O.D. | 11.966-11.984 mm (0.4711-0.4718 in.) | — |
| Cylinder head distortion | — | 0.05 mm (0.002 in.) |

(continued)

**Table 1 ENGINE SPECIFICATIONS (continued)**

| | Specification | Wear limit |
|---|---|---|
| Valves | | |
| Diameter | | |
| Intake | 33 mm (1.3 in.) | — |
| Exhaust | 28 mm (1.1 in.) | — |
| Valve lift | | |
| Intake and exhaust | 8.5 mm (0.33 in.) | — |
| Valve stem-to-guide clearance | | |
| Intake | 0.025-0.055 mm (0.0010-0.0022 in.) | 0.35 mm (0.014 in.) |
| Exhaust | 0.040-0.070 mm (0.0016-0.0028 in.) | 0.35 mm (0.014 in.) |
| Valve guide I.D. | 7.000-7.015 mm (0.2756-0.2762 in.) | — |
| Valve stem O.D. | | |
| Intake | 6.960-6.975 mm (0.2740-0.2746 in.) | — |
| Exhaust | 6.945-6.960 mm (0.2734-0.2740 in.) | — |
| Valve stem runout | — | 0.05 mm (0.002 in.) |
| Valve head thickness | — | 0.05 mm (0.002 in.) |
| Valve stem end length | — | 2.9 mm (0.11 in.) |
| Valve seat width | 1.0-1.2 mm (0.039-0.047 in.) | — |
| Valve head radial runout | — | 0.03 mm (0.001 in.) |
| Valve spring free length | | |
| Inner | — | 35.6 mm (1.40 in.) |
| Outer | — | 40.4 mm (1.59 in.) |
| Cylinder | | |
| Bore | 94.000-94.015 mm (3.7008-3.7014 in.) | 94.080 mm (3.7039 in.) |
| Cylinder-to-piston clearance | 0.050-0.060 mm (0.0020-0.0024 in.) | 0.120 mm (0.0047 in.) |
| Out-of-round | — | 0.05 mm (0.002 in.) |
| Pistons | | |
| Outer diameter | 93.945-93.960 mm (3.6986-3.6992 in.) | 93.880 mm (3.6961 in.) |
| Clearance in bore | 0.050-0.060 mm (0.0020-0.0024 in. | 0.120 mm (0.0047 in.) |
| Piston pin bore | 23.000-23.006 mm (0.9055-0.9057 in.) | 23.040 mm (0.9071 in.) |
| Piston pin outer diameter | 22.996-23.000 mm (0.9054-0.9055 in.) | 22.980 mm (0.9049 in.) |
| Piston ring groove width | | |
| Top | 1.23-1.25 mm (0.0484-0.0492 in.) | — |
| Second | 1.21-1.23 mm (0.0476-0.0484 in.) | — |
| Oil | 2.81-2.83 mm (0.1106-0.1114 in.) | — |
| Piston rings | | |
| Number per piston | | |
| Compression | 2 | — |
| Oil control | 1 | — |

(continued)

**Table 1 ENGINE SPECIFICATIONS (continued)**

| | Specification | Wear limit |
|---|---|---|
| Piston rings (continued) | | |
| Ring end gap (within cylinder) | | |
| Top and second | 0.30-0.45 mm (0.012-0.018 in.) | 1.0 mm (0.039 in.) |
| Ring end gap (free) | | |
| Top | Approx 11.5 mm (0.45 in.) | 9.2 mm (0.36 in.) |
| Second | Approx 14.0 mm (0.55 in.) | 11.2 mm (0.44 in.) |
| Ring side clearance | | |
| Top | — | 0.180 mm (0.007 in.) |
| Second | — | 0.150 mm (0.006 in.) |
| Ring thickness | | |
| Top | 1.175-1.190 mm (0.0463-0.0469 in.) | — |
| Second | 1.175-1.190 mm (0.0463-0.0469 in.) | — |
| Connecting rods | | |
| Piston pin hole I.D. | 23.006-23.014 mm (0.9057-0.9061 in.) | 23.040 mm (0.9071 in.) |
| Big end side clearance | 0.10-0.65 mm (0.004-0.026 in.) | 1.0 mm (0.039 in.) |
| Big end width | 24.95-25.00 mm (0.982-0.984 in.) | — |
| Crankshaft | | |
| Web-to-web width | 69.9-71.1 (2.752-2.760 in.) | — |
| Runout | — | 0.05 mm (0.002 in.) |
| Balance spring free length | — | 10.0 mm (0.39 in.) |

4

**Table 2 ENGINE TORQUE SPECIFICATIONS**

| Item | N·m | ft.-lb. |
|---|---|---|
| Engine mounting bolts and nuts | | |
| No. 1 bolts and nuts | 37-45 | 27-33 |
| No. 2 bolt | 70-88 | 51-64 |
| No. 3 bolts and nuts | 70-88 | 51-64 |
| No. 4 bolt and nut | 70-88 | 51-64 |
| No. 5 Allen bolts | 20-30 | 15-22 |
| Cylinder head cover | | |
| Bolts | 8-12 | 6-8.5 |
| Cover plug | 25-30 | 18-21.5 |
| Camshaft sprocket bolts | 14-16 | 10-11.5 |
| Camshaft chain tensioner | | |
| Set bolt | 20-25 | 14.5-18.0 |
| Plate bolt | 8-12 | 6-8.5 |
| Rocker arm shaft (exhaust) set bolt | 8-10 | 6-7 |
| Valve adjuster locknut | 13-16 | 9.5-11.5 |
| Cylinder head nuts | | |
| 8 mm | 23-27 | 16.5-19.5 |
| 9 mm | 29-33 | 21-24 |
| Cylinder base nuts | 8-12 | 6-8.5 |

(continued)

**Table 2 ENGINE TORQUE SPECIFICATIONS (continued)**

| Item | N·m | ft.-lb. |
|---|---|---|
| Decompression lever nut | 15-20 | 11-14.5 |
| Alternator rotor bolt | 140-160 | 101-115.5 |
| Primary drive gear nut | 90-110 | 65-80 |
| Gearshift drum stopper | 15-23 | 11-16.5 |
| Oil filter cap nut and oil sump filter cap bolt | 6-8 | 4.5-6 |
| Engine drive pulley nut | 100-130 | 73-94 |
| Starter clutch Allen bolts | 23-28 | 16.5-20 |
| Crankcase bolts (6 mm) | 9-13 | 6.5-9.5 |
| Oil gallery plug | | |
| 10 mm | 12-18 | 8.5-13 |
| 14 mm | 20-25 | 14-18 |
| Crankshaft hold plug (36 mm) | 12-18 | 8.5-13 |
| Oil drain plug | 18-23 | 13-16.5 |
| Starter clutch Allen bolt | 23-28 | 16.5-20 |
| Counterbalancer set bolt | 40-50 | 29-36 |
| Crankshaft right end oil seal retainer bolt | 5-6 | 3.5-4.5 |
| Crankshaft left-hand flywheel nut | 140-160 | 101-115 |
| Transmission shaft oil seal retainer bolt | 9-13 | 6.5-9.5 |

CHAPTER FIVE

# CLUTCH



This chapter provides complete service procedures for the clutch and clutch release mechanism.

The clutch is a wet multi-plate type which operates immersed in the engine oil. It is mounted on the right-hand end of the transmission mainshaft. The inner clutch hub is splined to the mainshaft and the outer housing can rotate freely on the mainshaft. The outer housing is geared to the crankshaft via the primary drive gear.

The clutch release mechanism is mounted within the right-hand crankcase cover and is operated by the clutch cable and hand lever mounted on the left-hand handlebar. This type of clutch *does* require routine adjustment as the cable does stretch with use, refer to Chapter Three for adjustment procedures.

Specifications for the clutch are listed in **Table 1**. **Tables 1-2** are located at the end of this chapter.

## CLUTCH

### Removal/Disassembly

The clutch assembly can be removed with the engine in the frame. This procedure is shown with the engine removed and partially disassembled for clarity.

Refer to **Figure 1** for this procedure.

1. Remove the nuts and washers (A, **Figure 2**) securing the front heat shield (B, **Figure 2**) and the front right-hand footpeg.
2. Remove the heat shield and footpeg assembly (**Figure 3**).
3. Remove the front right-hand footpeg assembly.
4. Reinstall the cap nuts and washer onto the engine front mounting through-bolts.
5. Perform Steps 1-6 of *Engine Oil and Filter Change* as described in Chapter Three.
6. Remove the bolts (**Figure 4**) securing the oil filter cover on the right-hand crankcase cover.
7. Remove the oil filter cover; don't lose the small spring (**Figure 5**) on the center inner surface of the cover. Don't lose the O-ring seal in the cover.
8. Remove the oil filter (**Figure 6**) and place it in a plastic bag to keep the oil from running out of it.
9. Remove the exhaust system as described under *Exhaust System Removal/Installation* in Chapter Seven.
10. Remove the bolts securing the clutch cover (**Figure 7**). Note the location of the special washers under 3 of the bolts (W, **Figure 7**). These special washers must be reinstalled in the same location under these specific bolts or the cover will leak oil.
11. Remove the clutch cover and gasket. Don't lose the locating dowels.

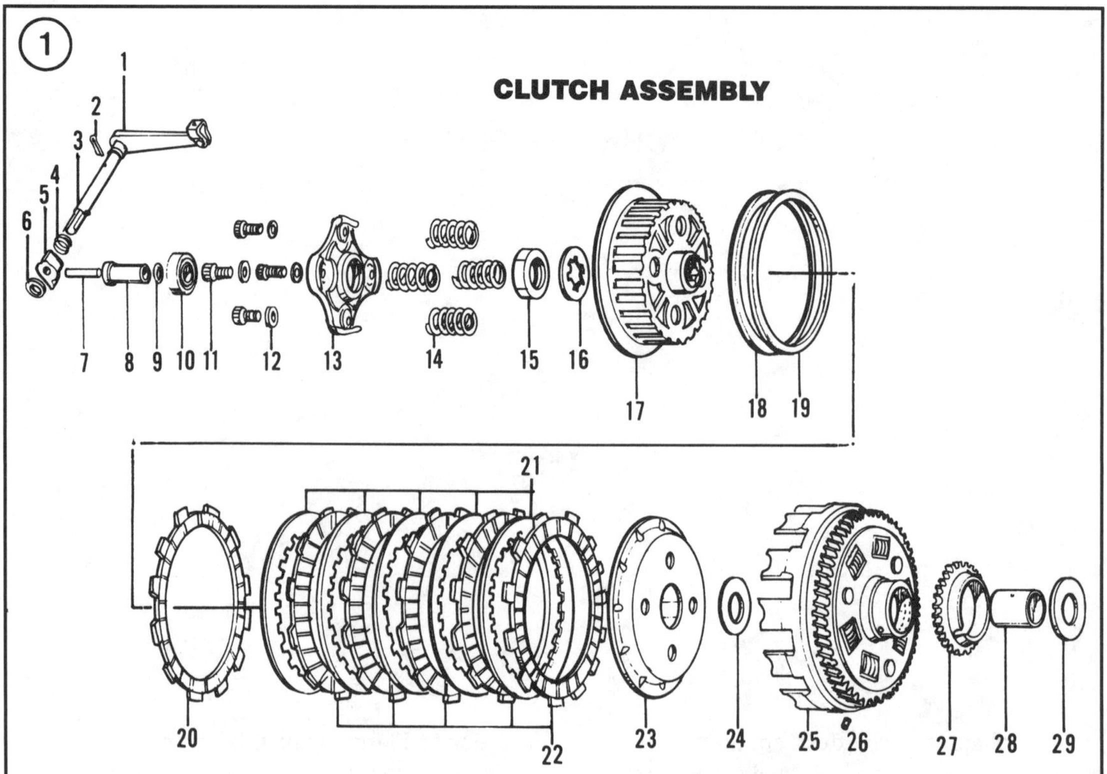

(1)

**CLUTCH ASSEMBLY**

1. Release arm
2. Cotter pin
3. O-ring
4. Spring
5. Release cam
6. Thrust washer
7. Pushrod
8. Push piece
9. O-ring
10. Bearing
11. Bolt
12. Washer
13. Release plate
14. Clutch spring
15. Locknut
16. Lockwasher
17. Clutch hub
18. Wave washer seat
19. Wave washer
20. No. 1 friction disc
21. Clutch plates
22. No. 2 friction discs
23. Pressure plate
24. Thrust washer
25. Clutch outer housing
26. Dowel pin
27. Oil pump drive gear
28. Spacer
29. Thrust washer

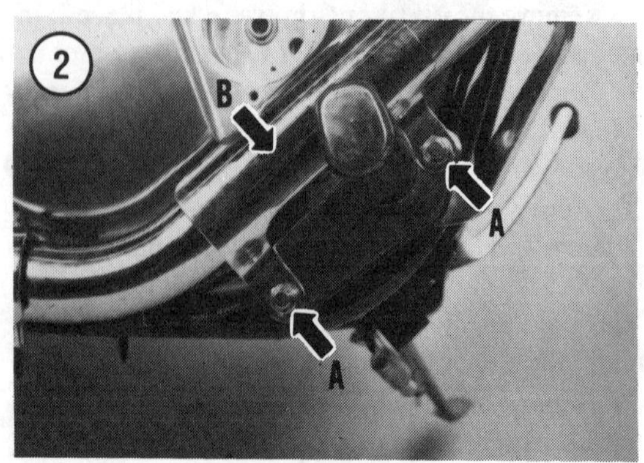


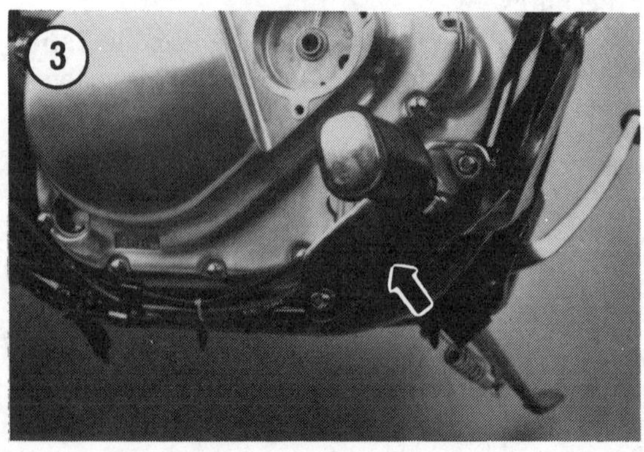

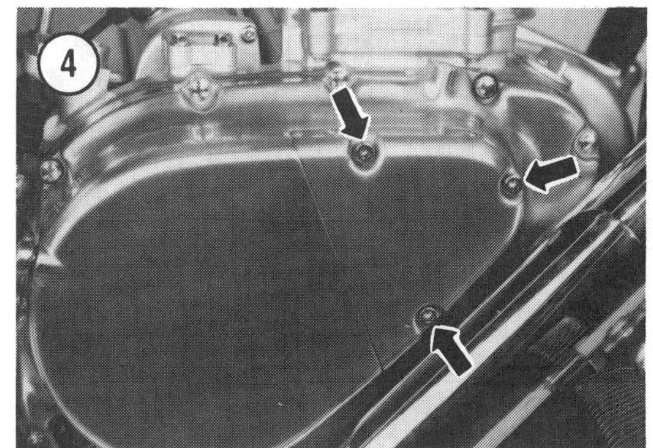

12. Remove the clutch pushrod (**Figure 8**).

13. Using a crisscross pattern, loosen the clutch bolts (**Figure 9**).

14. Remove the bolts, washers and the release plate assembly (**Figure 10**). Don't let the push piece slide out of the release plate and get damaged.

15. Remove the clutch springs (**Figure 11**).
16. Straighten the locking tab (**Figure 12**) on the lockwasher.

*NOTE*
*The following special tool (**Figure 13**) is manufactured for American Honda (not Suzuki) and is very versatile. It can be adjusted to work on almost all types of Japanese motorcycle clutch assemblies—not just Honda. If you work on different motorcycles this is a very handy special tool to have in your tool box.*

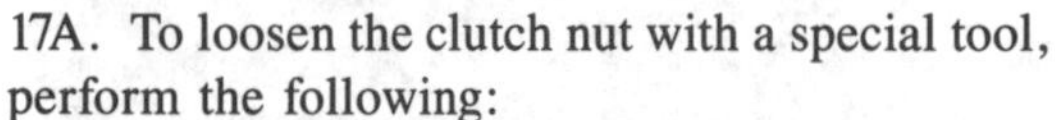

17A. To loosen the clutch nut with a special tool, perform the following:
   a. Hold onto the clutch pressure plate to prevent it from turning. Use Honda special tool (clutch center holder—part No. 07923-4280000) (**Figure 13**) or equivalent. See **Figure 14**.
   b. Loosen the clutch nut (**Figure 15**). Remove the nut and lockwasher.
   c. Remove the special tool from the clutch pressure plate.

17B. To remove the clutch nut without special tool, perform the following:
   a. Hold onto the clutch center to prevent it from turning.
   b. Use an impact driver and loosen the clutch nut. Remove the nut and lockwasher.

18. Slide the entire clutch assembly (outer housing, pressure plate, friction discs, clutch plates and clutch hub) off of the transmission shaft. Don't lose the oil pump drive gear and pin on the backside of the outer housing.
19. Slide off the spacer and the thrust washer.

11

12

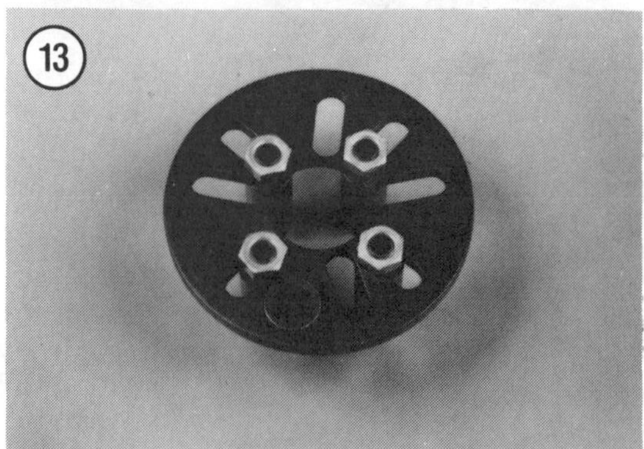
13

14

15

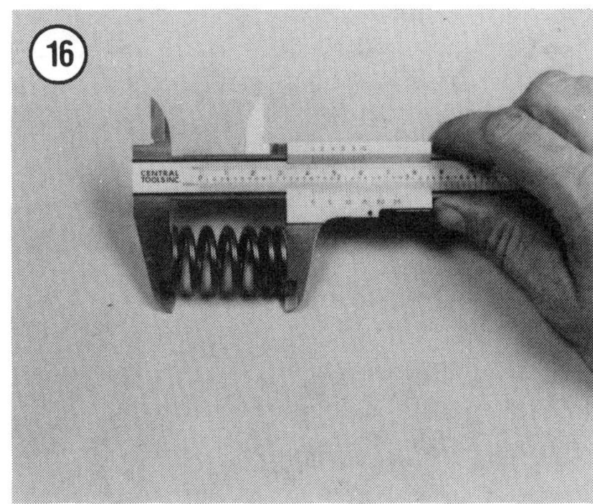
16

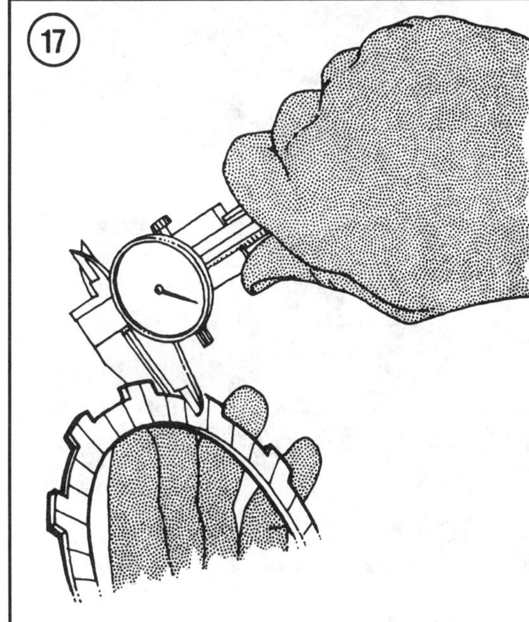
17

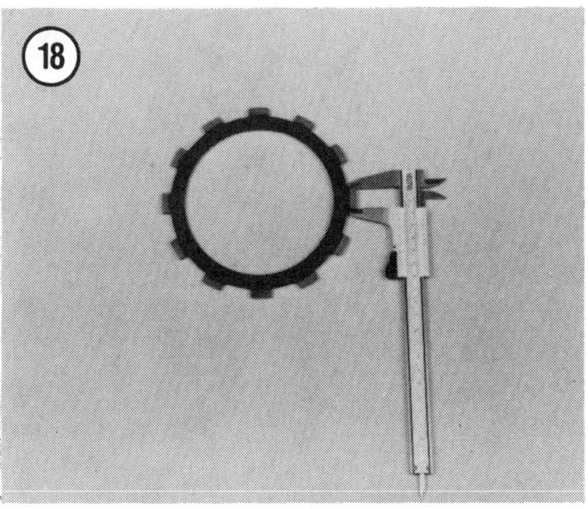
18

20. Disassemble the clutch assembly removed in Step 18. Note that the No. 1 friction disc, next to the clutch hub, is narrower than the No. 2 friction discs. The No. 1 friction disc must be reinstalled in this same location during assembly and installation.
21. Inspect all components as described in this chapter.

## Inspection

Refer to **Table 1** for clutch specifications.

1. Clean all clutch parts in petroleum-based solvent such as kerosene and thoroughly dry with compressed air.
2. Measure the free length of each clutch spring as shown in **Figure 16**. Compare to the specifications listed in **Table 1**. Replace any springs that have sagged to the service limit or less.
3. Measure the thickness of each friction disc at several places around the disc as shown in **Figure 17**. Compare to the specifications listed in **Table 1**. Replace any disc that is worn to the service limit or less.
4. Measure the claw width of all claws on each friction disc as shown in **Figure 18**. Compare to the specifications listed in **Table 1**. Replace any friction disc that is worn to the service limit or less.
5. Check the clutch plates for warpage on a service plate with a flat feeler gauge and a piece of plate glass (**Figure 19**). Compare to the specifications listed in **Table 1**. Replace any plate that is warped to the service limit or more.

*NOTE*
*If any of the friction discs, clutch plates or clutch springs require replacement, you should consider replacing all of them as a set to retain maximum clutch performance.*

19

6. Inspect the slots (**Figure 20**) in the clutch outer housing for cracks, nicks or galling where they come in contact with the friction disc tabs. If any severe damage is evident, the housing must be replaced.
7. Inspect the grooves (A, **Figure 21**) in the clutch hub for cracks, nicks or galling where they come in contact with the friction disc tabs. If any severe damage is evident, the hub must be replaced.
8. Inspect the inner splines (B, **Figure 21**) in the clutch hub for cracks, nicks or galling where they come in contact with the transmission shaft. If any severe damage is evident, the hub must be replaced.
9. Inspect the grooves and studs in the pressure plate (**Figure 22**). If either shows signs of wear or galling, the pressure plate should be replaced.
10. Inspect the gear teeth (**Figure 23**) on the clutch outer housing for damage. Remove any small nicks with an oilstone. If damage is severe, the clutch outer housing must be replaced. Also check the teeth on the primary drive gear (**Figure 24**) on the crankshaft; if damaged, the drive gear may also need replacing.

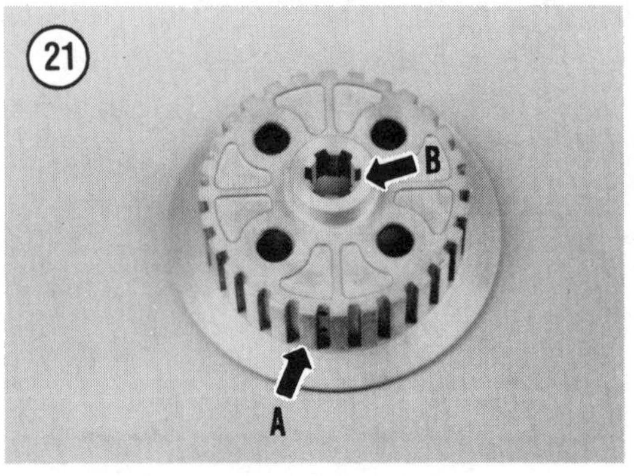


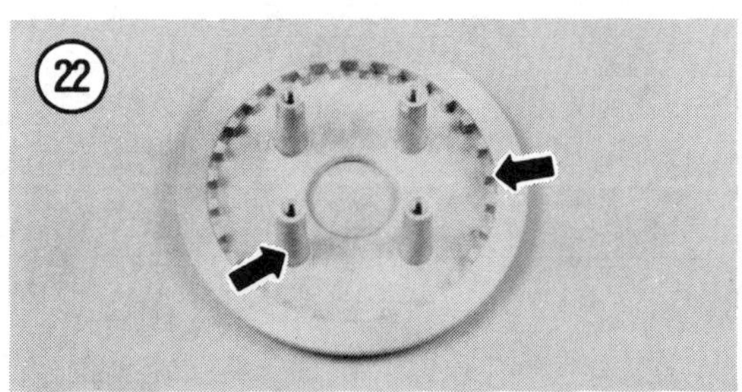

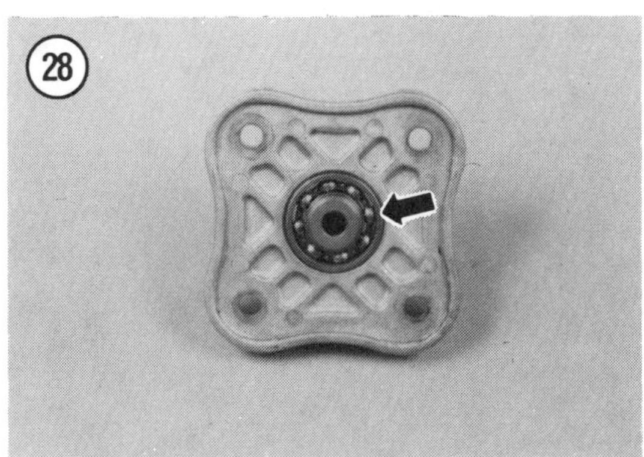

11. Inspect the damper springs (**Figure 25**). If they are sagged or broken the outer housing must be replaced.
12. Inspect the inner surface (**Figure 26**) of the clutch outer housing, where the spacer rides, for wear or damage. If damaged, the outer housing must be replaced.
13. Check the inner and outer surfaces of the spacer (**Figure 27**) for signs of wear or damage. Replace if necessary.
14. Check the clutch push piece bearing (**Figure 28**). Make sure it rotates smoothly with no signs of wear or damage. Replace if necessary.
15. Replace the O-ring seal (**Figure 29**) on the inner end of the push piece.
16. Check the clutch push piece for wear or damage. Replace if necessary.
17. Inspect the gear teeth on the oil pump drive gear for damage. Remove any small nicks with an oilstone. If damage is severe, the gear must be replaced.



### Assembly/Installation

Refer to **Figure 1** for this procedure.

1. If removed, install the dowel pin (**Figure 30**) and the oil pump drive gear (**Figure 31**) onto the backside of the clutch outer housing.

*CAUTION*

*There are 2 different diameter thrust washers used on the clutch assembly. The thrust washers must be installed in their correct location or the oil flow to the center of the clutch assembly will be insufficient and will lead to early clutch failure. Measure the outside diameter of each thrust washer and install it in its correct position.*

2. Install the 44 mm O.D. thrust washer (**Figure 32**) onto the transmission shaft.

3. Hold onto the oil pump drive gear and install the clutch outer housing onto the transmission shaft (A, **Figure 33**). Align the oil pump drive gear with the oil pump driven gear (B, **Figure 33**). Align the clutch outer housing gear with the primary drive gear (C, **Figure 33**) on the crankshaft.

4. Apply clean engine oil to the inner and outer surfaces of the spacer and slide the spacer (**Figure 34**) onto the transmission shaft.

5. Install the 40 mm O.D. thrust washer (**Figure 35**) onto the transmission shaft.

6. Install the pressure plate (**Figure 36**) onto the clutch outer housing.

*NOTE*
*If new friction discs and clutch plates are being installed, apply new engine*

*oil to all surfaces to avoid having the clutch lock up when used for the first time.*

7. Install a No. 2 friction disc (**Figure 37**) and a clutch plate (**Figure 38**).
8. Continue to install the friction discs and clutch plates, alternating them until all are installed. The last item installed is the No. 1 (narrow) friction disc (**Figure 39**).
9. Install the wave washer (**Figure 40**) with the concave side facing outward.
10. Install the wave washer seat (**Figure 41**).
11. Align the tabs on the clutch disc in order to accept the clutch hub.
12. Install the clutch hub (**Figure 42**). Push the clutch hub down through the clutch discs while slightly wiggling it back and forth.

13. The stack-up of parts installed in Steps 7-12 should be arranged as those shown in **Figure 43**.
14. Install a new lockwasher (**Figure 44**) and locknut (**Figure 45**).
15. Use the same special tool (**Figure 46**) setup used in Step 17A of *Removal/Disassembly* to hold the pressure plate for the following step.
16. Tighten the clutch locknut to the torque specification listed in **Table 2**.
17. Remove the special tool from the pressure plate.
18. Bend up one of the tabs of the lockwasher against one side of the clutch nut (**Figure 47**).
19. Install the clutch springs.
20. Install the clutch release plate assembly.
21. Install the spring bolts.
22. Using a crisscross pattern, tighten the clutch bolts to the torque specification listed in **Table 2**.
23. Install the clutch pushrod into the push piece.
24. Make sure the crankcase locating dowels (**Figure 48**) are in place.
25. If the new gasket does not have a row of gray colored sealant already applied to this area, apply a thin coat of gasket sealant (Three Bond or equivalent) to the right-hand crankcase cover gasket in the area shown in **Figure 49**. This is to provide an oil-tight seal at this portion of the gasket.
26. Install a new clutch cover gasket (**Figure 50**).

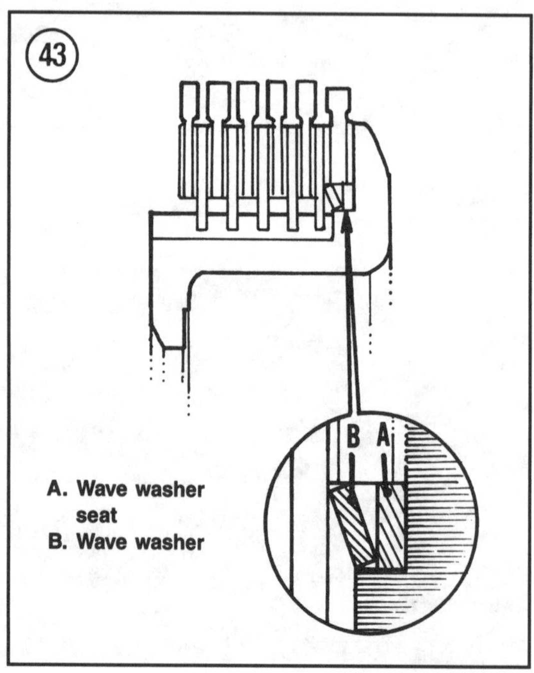

49

5

27. Install the clutch cover and the bolts. Be sure to install the special washers under the correct bolts as shown in (W, **Figure 51**). If the special washers are not installed, the right-hand crankcase cover will leak oil. Tighten the bolts securely.

28. Perform Steps 12-24 of *Engine Oil and Filter Change* as described in Chapter Three and refill the engine oil.

29. Install the exhaust system as described under *Exhaust System Removal/Installation* in Chapter Seven.

30. Install the rear brake pedal bracket and right-hand foot rest. Tighten the nuts to the torque specification listed in **Table 2**.

### Clutch Release Mechanism Removal/Inspection/Installation

1. Perform Steps 1-12 of *Clutch Removal/ Disassembly* in this chapter.
2. Remove the cotter pin (**Figure 52**) securing the release arm in the right-hand crankcase cover.
3. Partially withdraw the release arm and remove the thrust washer (**Figure 53**) from the end of the release arm.
4. Disengage the spring (A, **Figure 54**) from the release cam (B, **Figure 54**) and withdraw the release arm (**Figure 55**) from the right-hand crankcase cover.
5. Inspect the release arm (A, **Figure 56**) for wear or damage. Replace release arm if necessary.

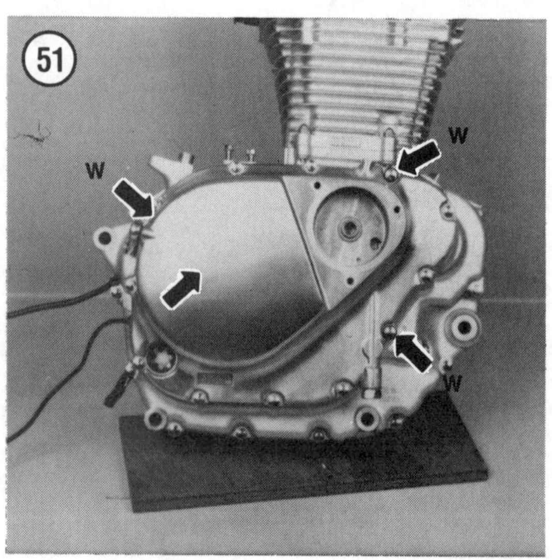


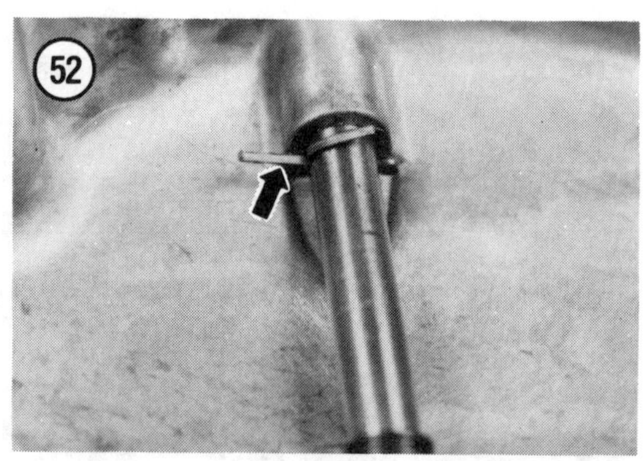

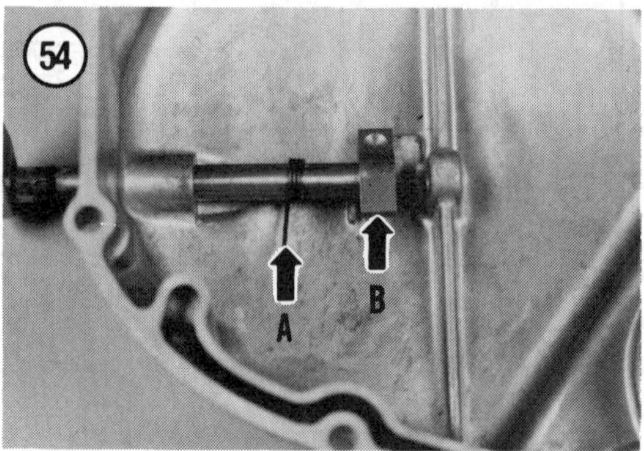

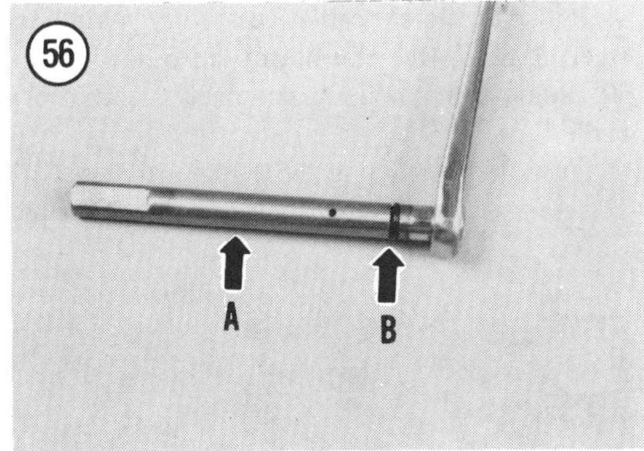


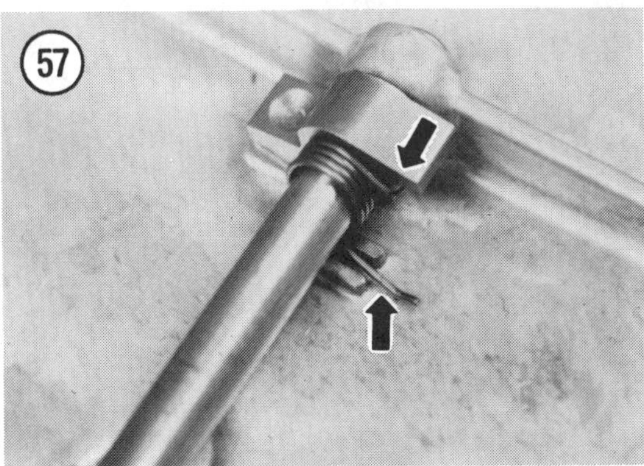


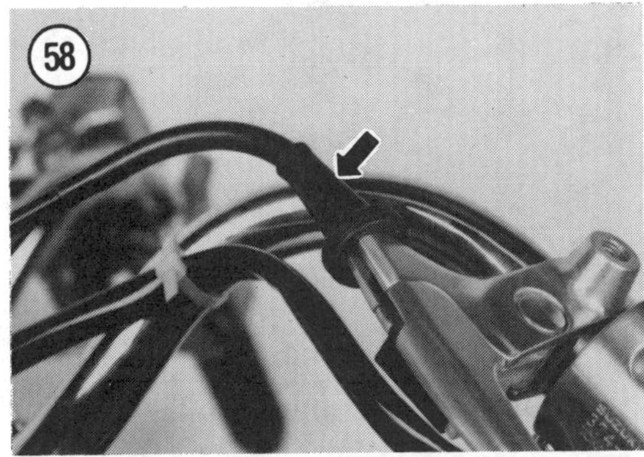


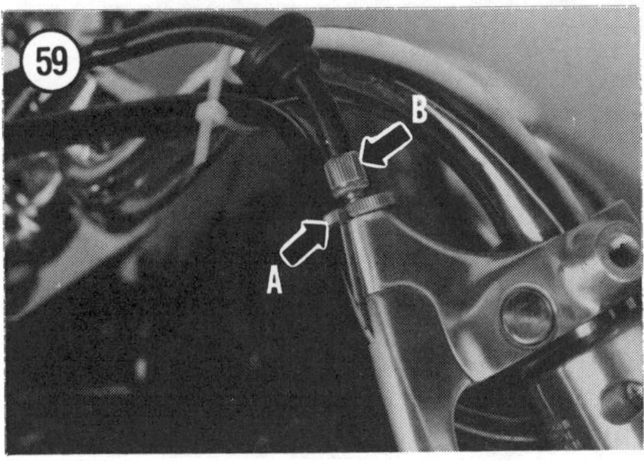


6. Inspect the O-ring seal (B, **Figure 56**) on the release arm for wear or deterioration. Replace if necessary.
7. Install by reversing these removal steps. Note the following during installation.
8. Engage the spring with the release cam and the groove in the right-hand crankcase cover as shown in **Figure 57**.

## CLUTCH CABLE



### Replacement

In time, the clutch cable will stretch to the point where it is no longer useful and will have to be replaced.

1. Remove the seat as described in Chapter Twelve.
2. Remove the fuel tank as described in Chapter Seven.
3. At the clutch lever, perform the following:

   a. Slide back the rubber boot (**Figure 58**).
   b. Loosen the locknut (A, **Figure 59**) and turn the adjuster (B, **Figure 59**) in all the way toward the hand grip.

4. At the right-hand crankcase cover, loosen the locknuts (A, **Figure 60**) and turn the adjuster (B, **Figure 60**) until there is maximum slack in the cable.

5. Pry open the locking tab (**Figure 61**) on the release arm.
6. Place a 19 mm open end wrench (**Figure 62**) on the clutch release arm and carefully push down on the wrench. This will allow additional slack in the cable.
7. Disengage the clutch cable from the release arm (**Figure 63**) and the receptacle on the right-hand crankcase cover.
8. Remove any straps securing the clutch cable to the frame.

*NOTE*
*Before removing the cable, make a drawing of the cable routing through the frame. It is very easy to forget how it was, once it has been removed. Replace the cable exactly as it was, avoiding any sharp turns.*

9. Pull the clutch cable out from behind the steering head area and out of the frame.
10. Remove the cable and replace it with a new cable.
11. Install by reversing these removal steps.
12. Adjust the clutch as described in Chapter Three.

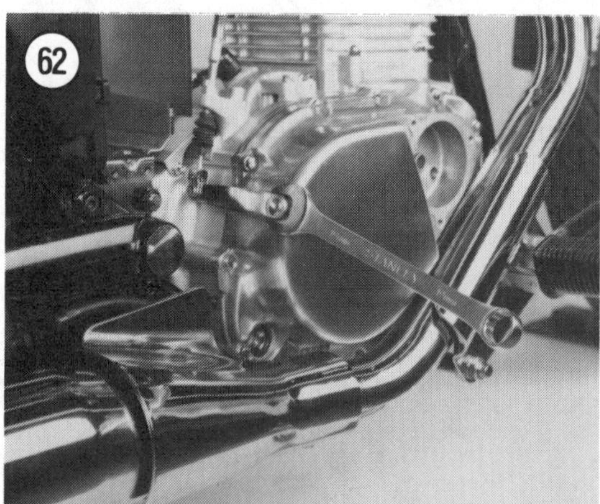

**Table 1 CLUTCH SPECIFICATIONS**

| Item | Standard | Wear limit |
|---|---|---|
| Friction disc thickness | | |
| No. 1 | 2.92-3.08 mm (0.115-0.121 in.) | 2.62 mm (0.103 in.) |
| No. 2 | 3.45-3.55 mm (0.136-0.140 in.) | 3.15 mm (0.124 in.) |
| Friction disc claw width | 15.8-16.0 mm (0.622-0.630 in.) | 15.0 mm (0.591 in.) |
| Clutch plate warpage | — | 0.10 mm (0.004 in.) |
| Clutch spring free lenth | — | 33.0 mm (1.30 in.) |

**Table 2 CLUTCH TORQUE SPECIFICATIONS**

| Item | N·m | ft.-lb. |
|---|---|---|
| Clutch locknut | 50-70 | 36-51 |
| Clutch spring bolts | 11-13 | 8-10 |
| Front foot rest nuts | 50-80 | 36-58 |

CHAPTER SIX

# TRANSMISSION AND GEARSHIFT MECHANISMS

This chapter provides complete service procedures for the transmission and the external and the internal gearshift mechanism.

## GEARSHIFT LINKAGE

### Removal/Installation

Refer to **Figure 1** for this procedure.

*NOTE*
*Before removing the shift rod arm from the gearshift shaft, centerpunch an alignment mark on the end of the shaft aligned with the split in the shift rod arm. This will assure proper alignment during installation.*

1. Remove the bolt (**Figure 2**) securing the shift rod arm to the gearshift shaft.
2. Remove the shift rod arm from the gearshift shaft.

*NOTE*
*Unless the entire external shift mechanism is to be removed, it is not necessary to proceed any further.*

3. Place a suitable size jack under the engine with a piece of plywood between the jack and the engine. Apply a small amount of jack pressure up on the engine.

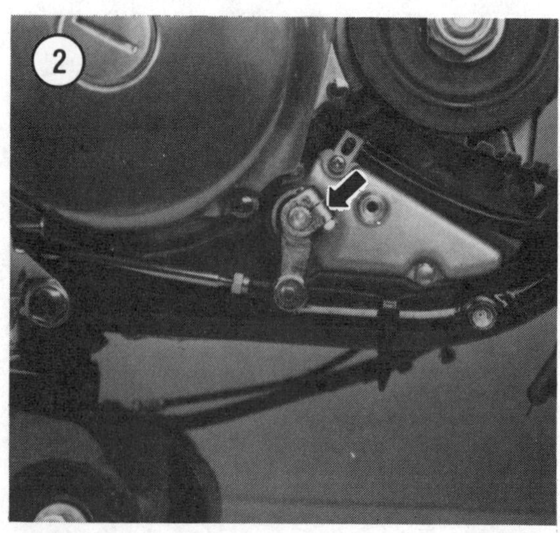

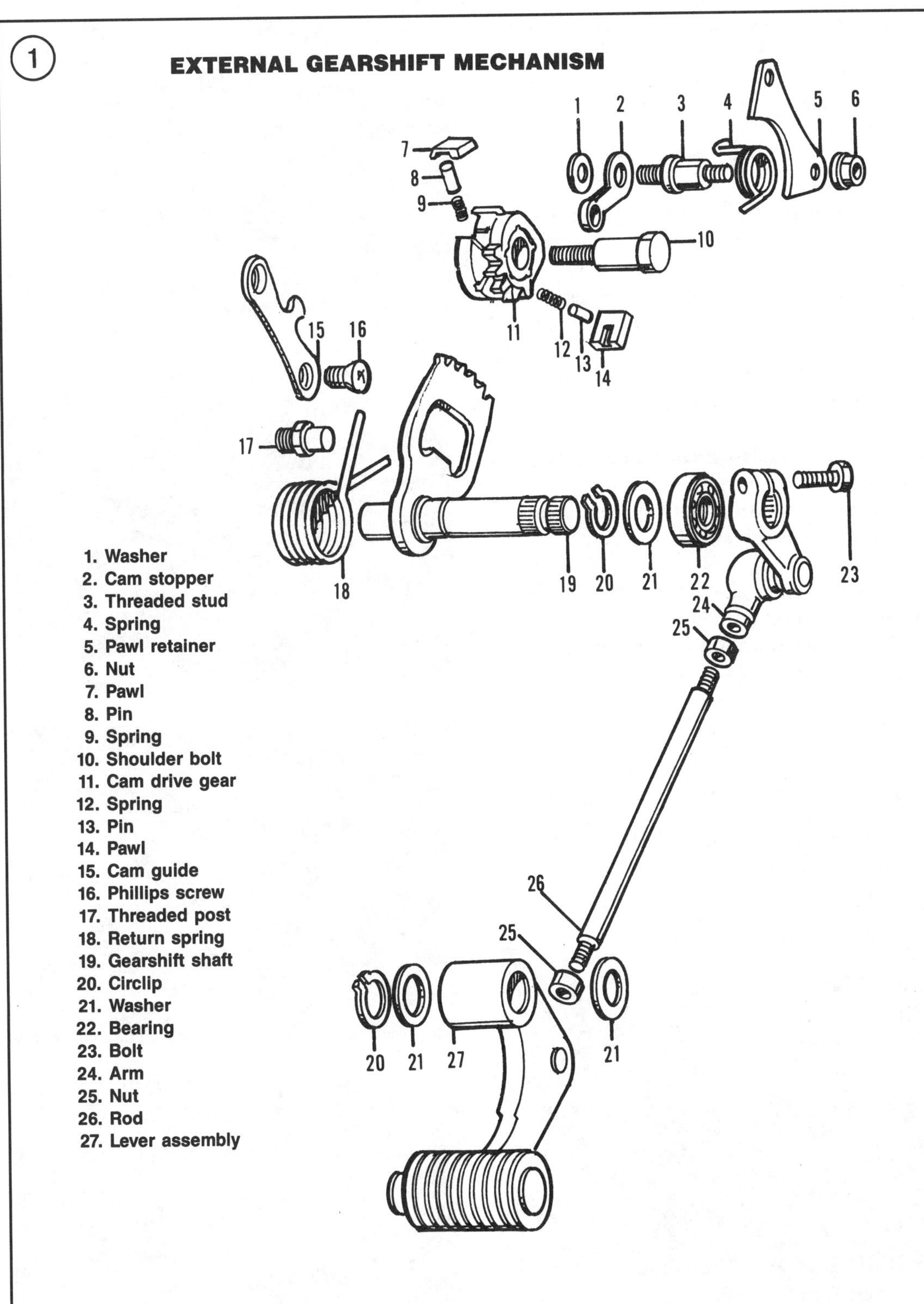
1
EXTERNAL GEARSHIFT MECHANISM
1. Washer
2. Cam stopper
3. Threaded stud
4. Spring
5. Pawl retainer
6. Nut
7. Pawl
8. Pin
9. Spring
10. Shoulder bolt
11. Cam drive gear
12. Spring
13. Pin
14. Pawl
15. Cam guide
16. Phillips screw
17. Threaded post
18. Return spring
19. Gearshift shaft
20. Circlip
21. Washer
22. Bearing
23. Bolt
24. Arm
25. Nut
26. Rod
27. Lever assembly

6

4. Remove the nuts and washers (A, **Figure 3**) securing the front heat shield (B, **Figure 3**) and the front right-hand footpeg.
5. Remove the heat shield and footpeg assembly (**Figure 4**).
6. Remove the engine front mounting through-bolts (**Figure 5**).
7. Remove the front right-hand footpeg assembly.
8. Reinstall the engine front mounting through-bolts and screw the cap nuts on.
9. Remove the circlip and washer securing the shift lever assembly to the backside of the right-hand footpeg assembly.
10. Slide the shift lever assembly off of the pivot pin on the right-hand footpeg assembly. Remove the other washer.
11. Install by reversing these removal steps. Note the following during installation.
12. Apply a light coat of multipurpose grease to the pivot pin before installing the shift lever assembly.
13. Make sure the circlip is correctly seated in the groove in the pivot pin.
14. Tighten the engine front mounting through-bolts and nuts to 70-88 N•m (50-63 ft.-lb.).

## EXTERNAL GEARSHIFT MECHANISM

The external gearshift mechanism is located on the left-hand side of the crankcase to the rear of the alternator.

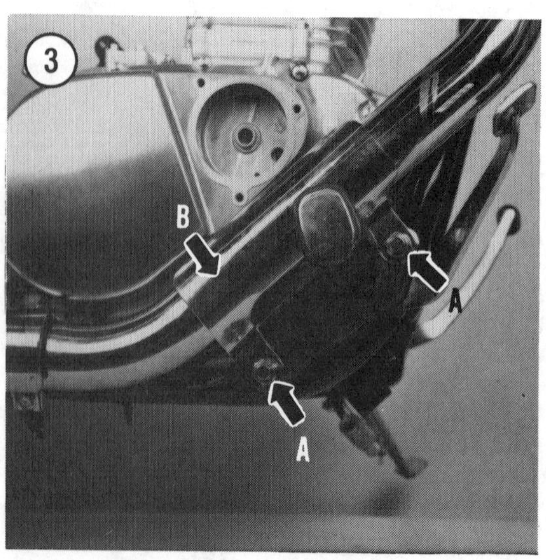

3

4

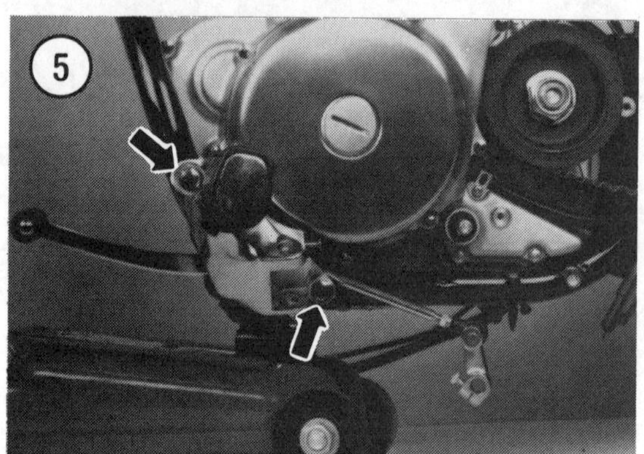
5

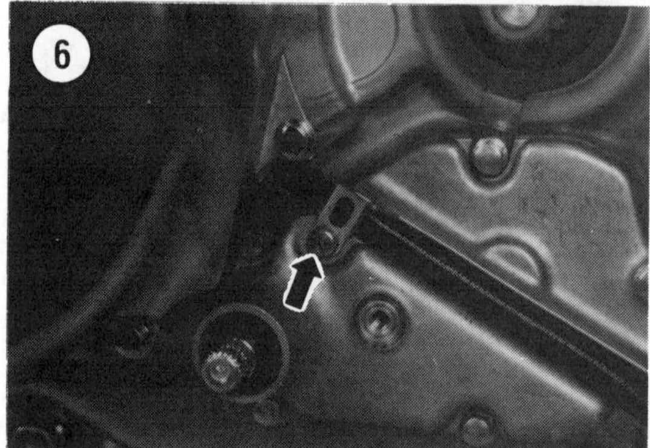
6

7

To remove the external shift mechanism, it is necessary to remove the engine from the frame.

**Removal**

1. Remove the engine from the frame as described under *Engine Removal/Installation* in Chapter Four.
2. Remove the bolt (**Figure 6**) securing the alternator stator electrical cable strap to the external shift mechanism cover.
3. Remove the bolts securing the left-hand crankcase cover (**Figure 7**) and remove the cover and gasket.

4A. If only the external gearshift mechanism is going to be removed, place duct tape over the starter idle gears and shaft to hold them in place in the crankcase. If not taped in place, they will fall out of their receptacles in the crankcase.

4B. If the entire engine is going to be disassembled, remove the starter idle gears as described under *Starter Idle Gears Removal/ Installation* in Chapter Four.

5. Remove the upper bolt (**Figure 8**) securing the transmission mainshaft oil seal retainer.
6. Remove the bolts securing the transmission mainshaft oil seal retainer (A, **Figure 9**) and the external gearshift mechanism cover (B, **Figure 9**). Remove the retainer, the cover (**Figure 10**) and gasket. Don't lose the locating dowels.
7. Remove the gearshift shaft (**Figure 11**), washer and return spring. Don't lose the washer on the end of the gearshift shaft.
8. Remove the nuts securing the pawl retainer (**Figure 12**) and remove the pawl retainer.

9. Remove the screws securing the cam guide (**Figure 13**) and remove the cam guide.
10. Using needlenose pliers, remove the cam stopper spring (**Figure 14**).
11. Unscrew the threaded stud and remove the cam stopper and washer (A, **Figure 15**).
12. Remove the shoulder bolt (B, **Figure 15**) securing the cam driven gear and stopper plate.
13. Remove the cam driven gear assembly (**Figure 16**) from the stopper plate. Don't lose the pawls, springs and pins in the assembly. Store the cam gear assembly in a spray paint can top to keep all components together until they are disassembled and cleaned.
14. Remove the stopper plate (**Figure 17**) and the spacer (**Figure 18**) from the end of the shift drum.

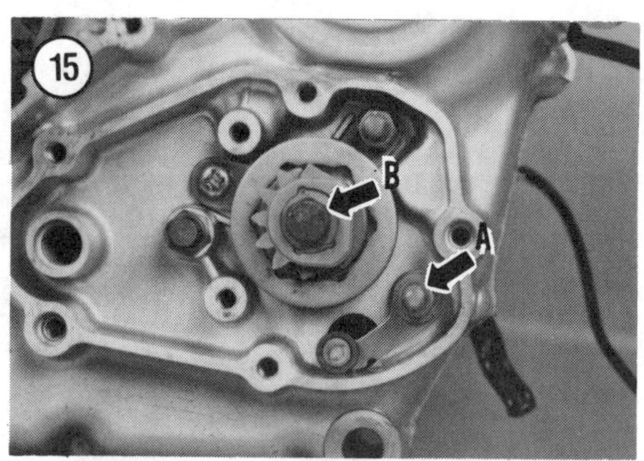

19

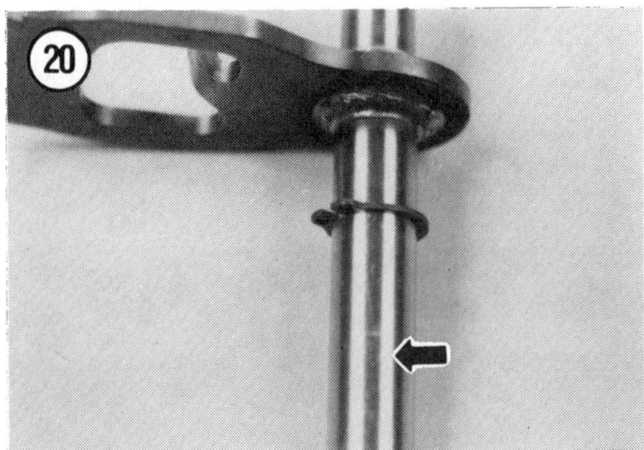
20

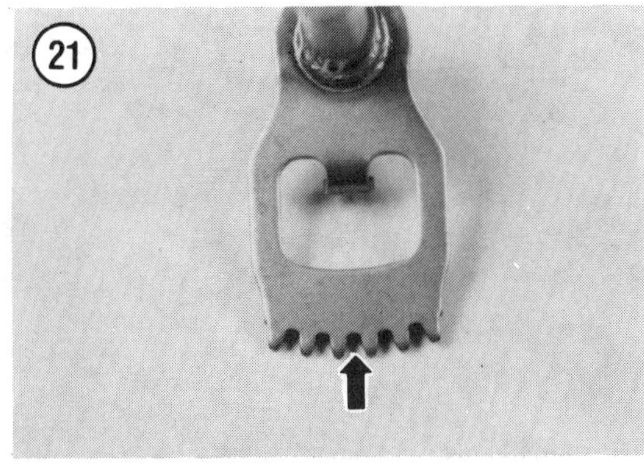
21

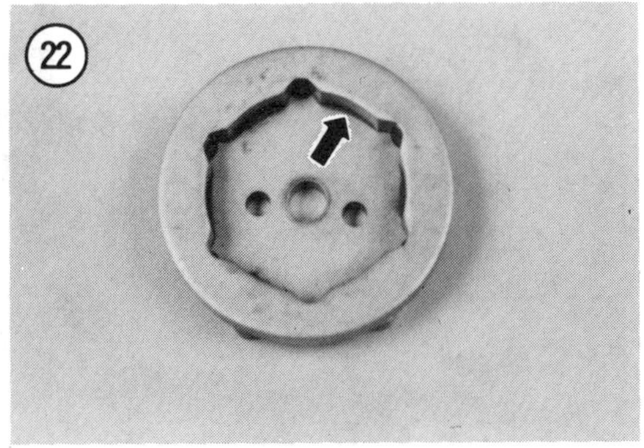
22

## Inspection

1. Clean all parts in solvent and dry thoroughly.
2. Inspect the gearshift shaft return spring (**Figure 19**). If broken or weak, it must be replaced.
3. Inspect the gearshift shaft (**Figure 20**) for bending, wear or other damage; replace if necessary.
4. Inspect the sector gear teeth (**Figure 21**) on the gearshift shaft. If broken or damaged the gearshift shaft must be replaced.
5. Inspect the cam driven gear receptacle (**Figure 22**) in the stopper plate for wear or damage. Replace the stopper plate if necessary.
6. Inspect the ramps (**Figure 23**) on the backside of the stopper plate for wear or damage. Replace the stopper plate if necessary.
7. Inspect the roller (**Figure 24**) on the end of the cam stopper. If worn or damaged, replace the cam stopper.



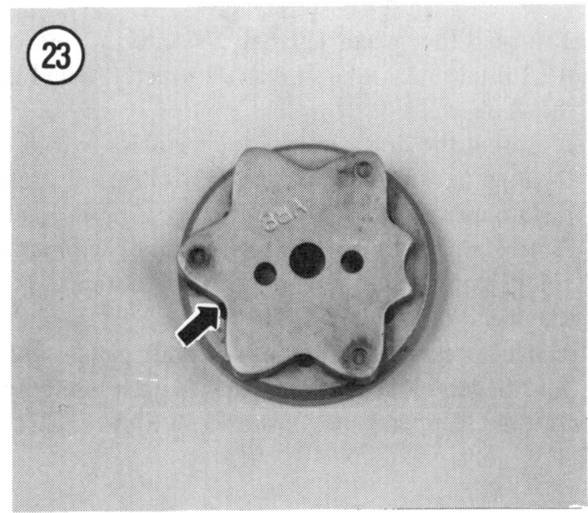
23

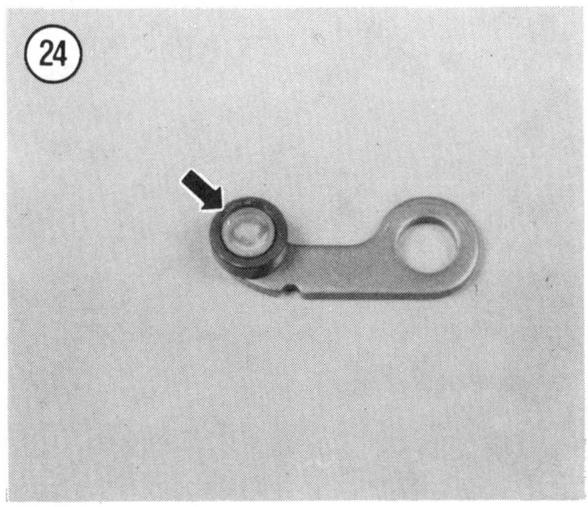
24

8. Disassemble the cam driven gear assembly (**Figure 25**) and inspect the pawls, springs and pins for wear or damage.
9. Assemble the cam driven gear assembly as follows:
   a. Install the springs into the cam gear body.
   b. Position the pawl pins with the rounded end facing out and install them onto the springs.
   c. Install the pawls onto the pins and into the cam gear body.
   d. The pin grooves in the pawls are offset. When the pawls are installed correctly, the wider shoulder (W, **Figure 26**) must face toward the outside.
   e. Hold the pawls in place and place the assembly into the spray paint can top.
10. Inspect the gearshift shaft oil seal (**Figure 27**) in the cover. If worn or damaged, replace the seal.

### Installation

1. Install the spacer (**Figure 28**) into the end of the shift drum. Make sure it is correctly seated in the shift drum.
2. Install the holes in the stopper plate with the locating pins in the end of the shift drum. Install the stopper plate.
3. Remove the cam driven gear assembly from the spray paint can top and keep all components together.
4. Compress the spring-loaded shift pawls with your fingers. Install the cam driven gear assembly into the stopper plate as shown in **Figure 16**.

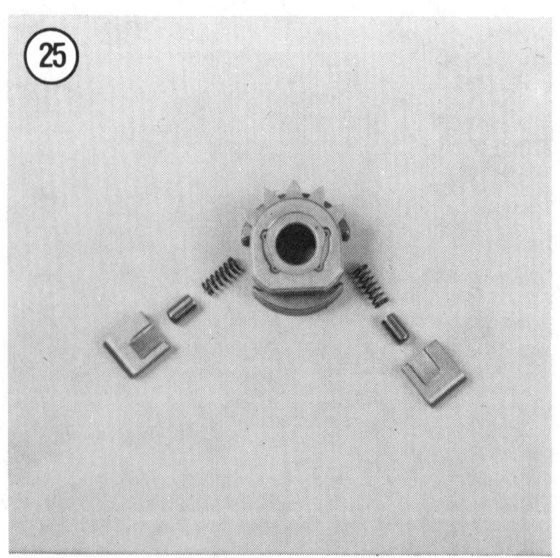


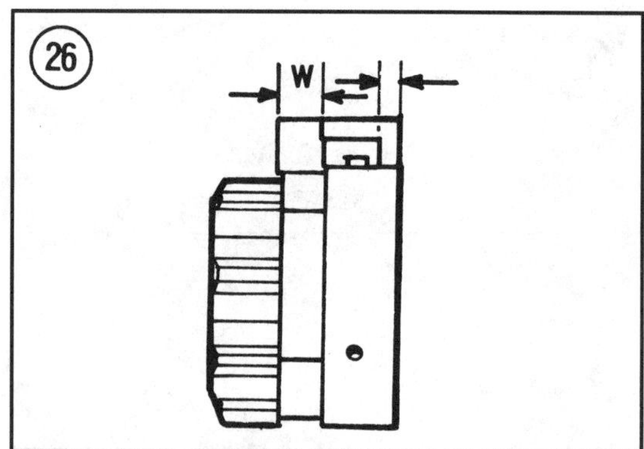


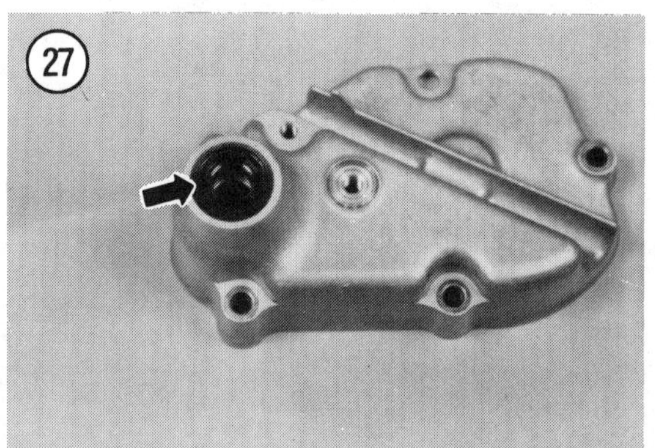

5. Apply red Loctite Threadlocker No. 271 to the shoulder bolt threads prior to installation. Install the shoulder bolt (**Figure 29**) and tighten securely.
6. Position the cam stopper (roller side out) onto the backside of the threaded stud and install the washer (**Figure 30**).
7. Install the threaded stud and tighten securely.
8. Install the spring onto the cam stopper.
9. Using needlenose pliers, hook the spring into the notch in cam stopper (**Figure 14**). Push the lower end of the spring into position on the shelf of the crankcase (**Figure 31**).
10. Install the cam guide (**Figure 13**). Apply a small amount of blue Loctite Threadlocker No. 242 to the cam guide screw threads prior to installation.
11. Install the cam guide screws and tighten securely.
12. Install the pawl retainer (**Figure 12**). Apply a small amount of blue Loctite Threadlocker No. 242 to the pawl retainer screw threads prior to installation.
13. Install the pawl retainer screws and tighten securely.
14. Apply clean engine oil to the gearshift shaft and partially install the gearshift shaft and spring (**Figure 32**) into the crankcase.
15. Align the center of the cam driven gear with the center of the gearshift shaft gear (**Figure 33**), then push the shaft assembly all the way in until it bottoms out.
16. Install the washer (**Figure 34**) onto the gearshift shaft.
17. Apply a light coat of multipurpose grease to the gearshift shaft oil seal (**Figure 27**) in the external gearshift mechanism cover.

6

18. Make sure the locating dowels (**Figure 35**) are in place.
19. Install a new gasket (**Figure 36**) and the external gearshift mechanism cover.
20. Install the transmission mainshaft oil seal retainer (A, **Figure 37**) and the upper bolt (B, **Figure 37**).
21. Install the bolts securing the oil seal retainer and the cover. Tighten the bolts securely in a crisscross pattern.
22A. If duct tape was used to hold the starter idle gears and shaft in place; remove the duct tape.
22B. If the starter idle gears were removed; install them as described under *Starter Idle Gears Removal/Installation* in Chapter Four.
23. Install the left-hand crankcase cover and gasket. Install the bolts and tighten securely in a crisscross pattern.
24. Install the bolt securing the alternator stator electrical cable strap to the external shift mechanism cover.
25. Install the engine into the frame as described under *Engine Removal/Installation* in Chapter Four.

## TRANSMISSION AND INTERNAL SHIFT MECHANISM

To gain access to the transmission and internal shift mechanism, it is necessary to remove the engine and split the crankcase as described in Chapter Four.

Refer to **Table 1** for transmission and gearshift mechanism specifications.

### Removal

1. Remove the engine and split the crankcase as described under *Crankcase Disassembly* in Chapter Four.
2. Withdraw the shift fork shaft (**Figure 38**).
3. Remove the mainshaft shift fork (**Figure 39**).
4. Remove the countershaft shift fork (**Figure 40**).
5. Remove the shift drum (**Figure 41**).
6. Remove both transmission shaft assemblies.
7. Inspect the transmission shaft assemblies as described under *Transmission Preliminary Inspection* in this chapter.

### Assembly

1. Install the 2 transmission assemblies by meshing them together in their proper relationship to each other.
2. Install both transmission assemblies into the left-hand crankcase half (**Figure 42**).
3. After both assemblies are installed, tap on the end of both shafts (**Figure 43**) with a plastic or soft-faced mallet to make sure they are completely seated.
4. Coat all bearing and sliding surfaces of the shift drum with engine or assembly oil.
5. Install the shift drum (**Figure 41**).
6. Install the countershaft shift fork (**Figure 40**) into position in its gear.
7. Install the mainshaft shift fork (**Figure 39**) into position in its gear.
8. Mesh the shift forks with the shift drum and install the shift fork shaft (**Figure 38**). Apply a liberal coat of engine oil onto the shift fork shaft and let the oil run down the shaft and onto the shift forks.
9. Make sure the cam pin followers are in mesh with the grooves in the shift drum.
10. Make sure the thrust washer (**Figure 44**) is still installed on the mainshaft.

*NOTE*

*The next procedure is best done with the aid of a helper as the transmission assemblies are loose and won't spin very easily. Have a helper hold the crankcase and spin the transmission shaft while you turn the shift drum through all of the gears.*

11. Turn the crankcase to a near a vertical position. Do not try this step with the crankcase horizontal as the gears are loaded by their own weight, in an abnormal way and will not shift easily, or in some cases not at all. This may give a false impression that something is installed incorrectly.
12. Spin the transmission shafts and shift through all 4 gears using the shift drum. Make sure you can shift into all gears. This is the time to find that something may be installed incorrectly—not after the crankcase is completely assembled.
13. Reassemble the crankcase as described under *Crankcase Assembly* and install the engine as described in Chapter Four.

## Transmission Preliminary Inspection

After the transmission shaft assemblies have been removed from the crankcase, clean and inspect the assemblies before disassembling them. Place the assembled shaft into a large can or plastic bucket and thoroughly clean with a petroleum-based solvent such as kerosene and a stiff brush. Dry with compressed air or let it sit on rags to drip dry. Repeat for the other shaft assembly.

1. After they have been cleaned, visually inspect the components of the assemblies for excessive wear. Any burrs, pitting or roughness on the teeth of a gear will cause wear on the mating gear. Minor roughness can be cleaned up with an oilstone but there's little point in attempting to remove deep scars.

*NOTE*
*Defective gears should be replaced. It's a good idea to replace the mating gear on the other shaft even though it may not show as much wear or damage.*

2. Carefully check the engagement dogs. If any are chipped, worn, rounded or missing, the affected gear must be replaced.
3. Rotate the transmission bearings (**Figure 45**) in the crankcase halves by hand. Check for roughness, noise and radial play. Any bearing that shows wear or other damage should be replaced as described in this chapter.
4. If the transmission shafts are satisfactory and are not going to be disassembled, apply assembly oil or engine oil to all components and reinstall them in the crankcase as described in this chapter.

*NOTE*
*If disassembling a used, well run-in (high mileage) transmission for the first time by yourself, pay particular attention to any additional shims that may have been added by a previous owner. These may have been added to take up the tolerance of worn components and must be reinstalled in the same position since the shims have developed a wear pattern. If new parts are going to be installed, these shims can be eliminated. This is something you will have to determine upon reassembly.*

## Mainshaft Disassembly/Inspection

Refer to **Figure 46** for this procedure.

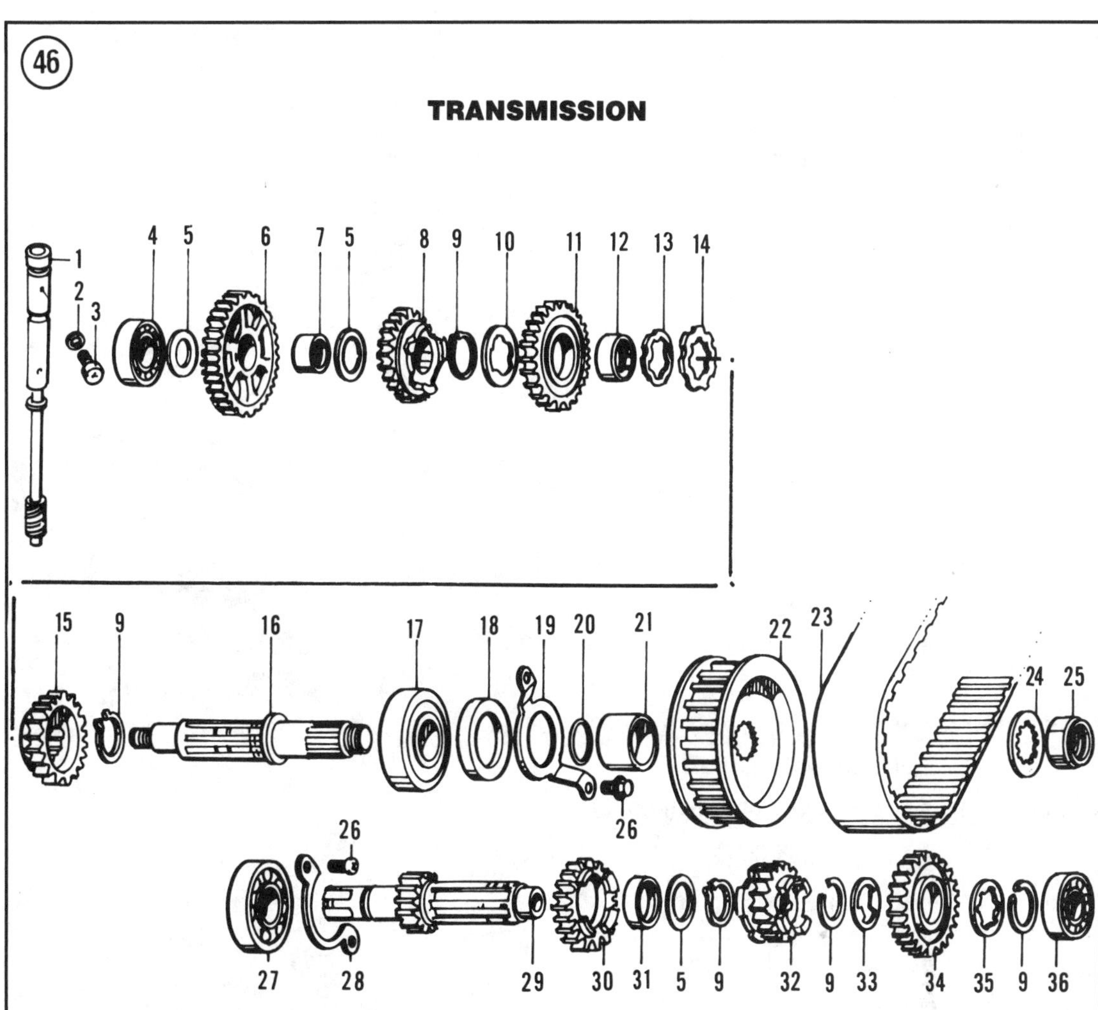


1. Speedometer drive assembly
2. Washer
3. Bolt
4. Bearing
5. Thrust washer
6. Mainshaft 1st gear
7. Mainshaft 1st gear bushing
8. Mainshaft 3rd gear
9. Circlip
10. Splined washer
11. Mainshaft 2nd gear
12. Mainshaft 2nd gear bushing
13. Splined lockwasher
14. Splined washer
15. Mainshaft 4th gear
16. Mainshaft
17. Bearing
18. Oil seal
19. Bearing seal retainer
20. O-ring
21. Spacer
22. Drive pulley
23. Drive belt
24. Lockwasher
25. Nut
26. Bolt
27. Bearing
28. Bearing retainer
29. Countershaft/1st gear
30. Countershaft 3rd gear
31. Countershaft 3rd gear bushing
32. Countershaft 2nd gear
33. Splined washer (thin with 3 dogs)
34. Countershaft 4th gear
35. Splined washer (thick with 6 dogs)
36. Bearing

*NOTE*
*A helpful "tool" that should be used for transmission disassembly is a large egg flat (the type that restaurants get their eggs in) as shown in* ***Figure 47****. As you remove a part from the shaft, set it in one of the depressions in the same position from which it was removed. This is an easy way to remember the correct relationship of all parts.*

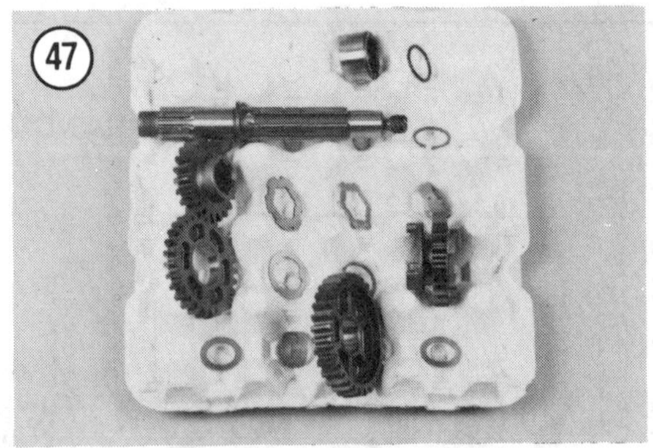


1. If not cleaned in the *Preliminary Inspection* sequence, place the assembled shaft into a large can or plastic bucket and thoroughly clean with solvent and a stiff brush. Dry with compressed air or let it sit on rags to dry.
2. Slide off the thrust washer.
3. Slide off the 1st gear, 1st gear bushing and thrust washer.
4. Slide off the 3rd gear.
5. Remove the circlip and splined washer.
6. Slide off the 2nd gear and 2nd gear bushing.
7. Slide off the splined lockwasher.
8. Rotate the splined washer in either direction to disengage the tangs from the grooves on the transmission shaft. Slide off the splined washer.
9. Slide off the 4th gear.
10. Remove the circlip.
11. Check each gear for excessive wear, burrs, pitting or chipped or missing teeth (A, **Figure 48**). Make sure the lugs (B, **Figure 48**) on the gears are in good condition.
12. Check the 1st and 2nd gear bushings for excessive wear, pitting or damage.
13. Inspect the shift fork-to-gear clearance as described under *Internal Gearshift Mechanism* in this chapter.

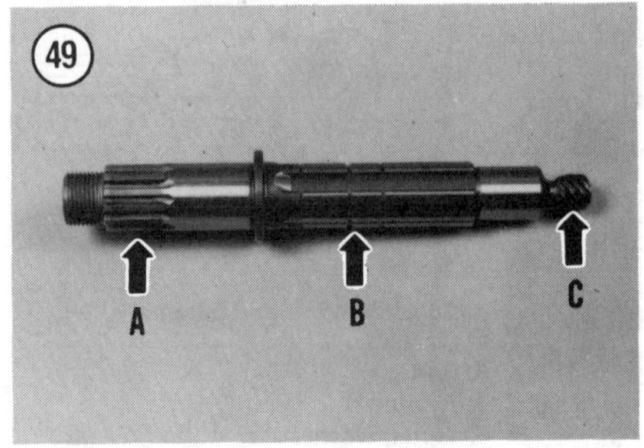


*NOTE*
*Defective gears should be replaced. It is a good idea to replace the mating gear on the countershaft even though it may not show as much wear or damage.*

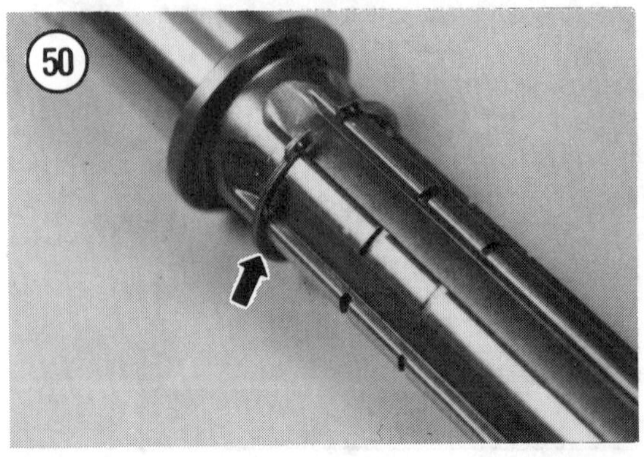

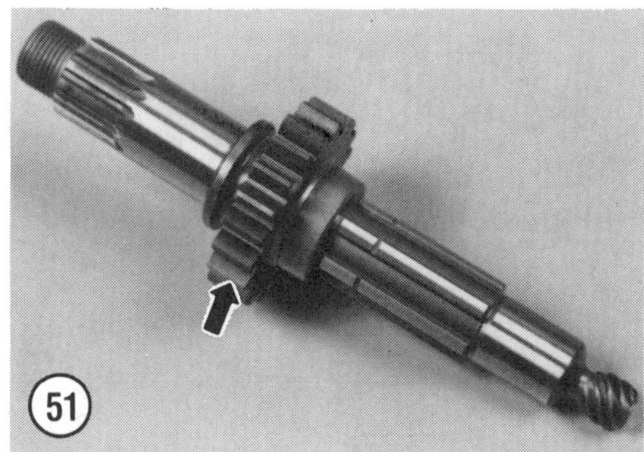


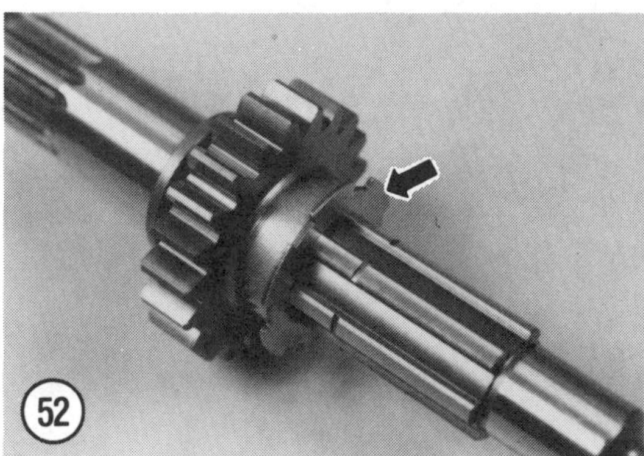

14. Make sure that all gears and bushings slide smoothly on the mainshaft splines.

*NOTE*
*It is recommended that all circlips be replaced every time the transmission is disassembled to ensure proper gear alignment. When installing circlips, slide them onto the shaft with the rounded side going on first. This will position the sharp side outward to take the gear thrust correctly. Do not expand a circlip more than necessary to slide it over the shaft.*

15. Inspect the drive pulley splines (A, **Figure 49**), the gear splines (B, **Figure 49**), the speedometer drive gear (C, **Figure 49**) and the circlip grooves of the mainshaft. If any are damaged, the shaft must be replaced.



**Mainshaft Assembly**

1. Apply a light coat of clean engine oil to all sliding surfaces before installing any parts.
2. Install the circlip (**Figure 50**).
3. Slide on the 4th gear (**Figure 51**).
4. Slide on the splined washer (**Figure 52**). Rotate the splined washer in either direction to engage the tangs into the grooves on the transmission shaft (**Figure 53**).
5. Slide on the splined lockwasher (**Figure 54**) and push it on until the tangs go into the open areas of the splined washer (**Figure 55**) and lock the washer into place.

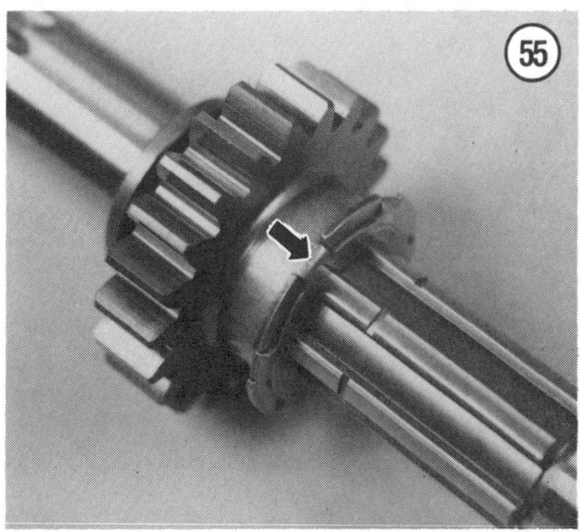

6. Align the oil hole in the 2nd gear bushing with the oil hole in the shaft (**Figure 56**) and slide on the bushing. This alignment is necessary for proper oil flow.
7. Slide on the 2nd gear (**Figure 57**).
8. Slide on the thrust washer (**Figure 58**) and install the circlip (**Figure 59**).
9. Slide on the 3rd gear (**Figure 60**) and the thrust washer (**Figure 61**).
10. Slide on the 1st gear bushing (**Figure 62**) and the 1st gear (**Figure 63**).
11. Install the thrust washer (**Figure 64**).
12. Refer to **Figure 65** for correct placement of all gears. Make sure all circlips are seated correctly in the mainshaft grooves.
13. Make sure each gear engages properly to the adjoining gear where applicable.

**Countershaft Disassembly/Inspection**

Refer to **Figure 46** for this procedure.

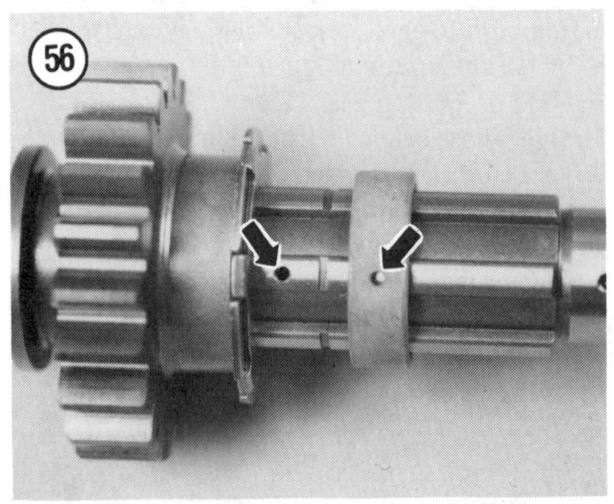

*NOTE*
*Use the same large egg flat (used on the mainshaft disassembly) during the countershaft disassembly (**Figure 66**). This is an easy way to remember the correct relationship of all parts.*

1. If not cleaned in the *Preliminary Inspection* sequence, place the assembled shaft into a large can or plastic bucket and thoroughly clean with solvent and a stiff brush. Dry with compressed air or let it sit on rags to dry.
2. Remove the circlip and slide off the thrust washer.
3. Slide off the 4th gear.
4. Slide off the splined washer and remove the circlip.
5. Slide off the 2nd gear.
6. Remove the circlip and slide off the thrust washer.
7. Slide off the 3rd gear and 3rd gear bushing.
8. Check each gear for excessive wear, burrs, pitting or chipped or missing teeth (A, **Figure 67**). Make sure the lugs (B, **Figure 67**) on the gears are in good condition.

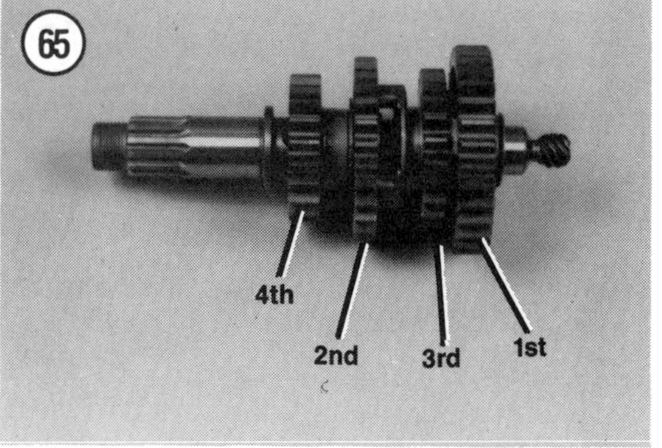


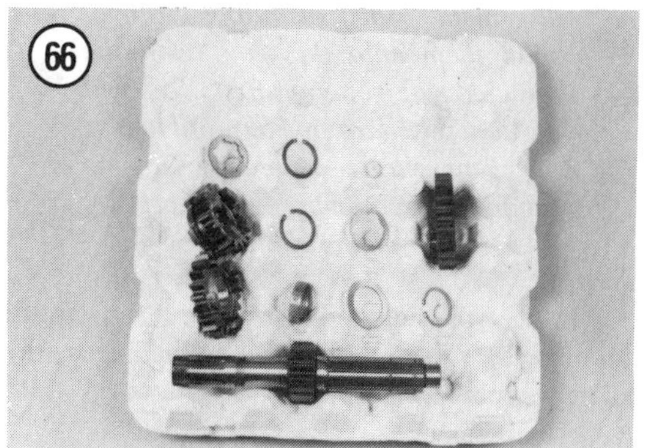


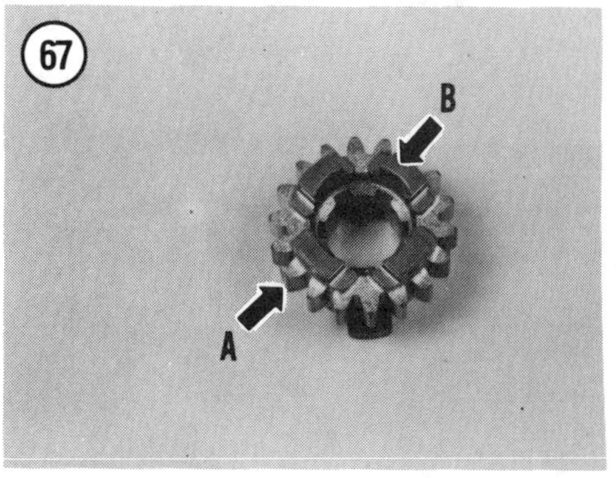

9. Check the 3rd gear bushing for excessive wear, pitting or damage.
10. Inspect the shift fork-to-gear clearance as described under *Internal Gearshift Mechanism* in this chapter.

*NOTE*
*Defective gears should be replaced. It is a good idea to replace the mating gear on the mainshaft even though it may not show as much wear or damage.*

*NOTE*
*The 1st gear (A,* ***Figure 68****) is part of the countershaft. If the gear is defective, the countershaft must be replaced.*

11. Make sure that all gears and bushings slide smoothly on the countershaft splines.

*NOTE*
*It is recommended that all circlips be replaced every time the transmission is disassembled to ensure proper gear alignment. When installing circlips, slide them onto the shaft with the rounded side going on first. This will position the sharp side outward to take the gear thrust correctly. Do not expand a circlip more than necessary to slide it over the shaft.*

12. Inspect the countershaft splines and circlip grooves (B, **Figure 68**). If any are damaged, the shaft must be replaced.

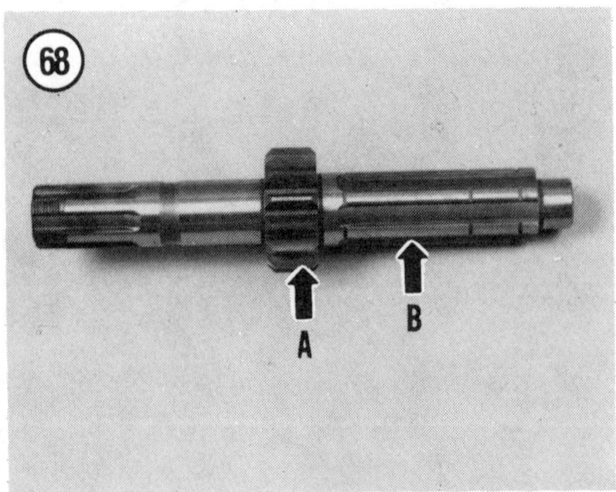


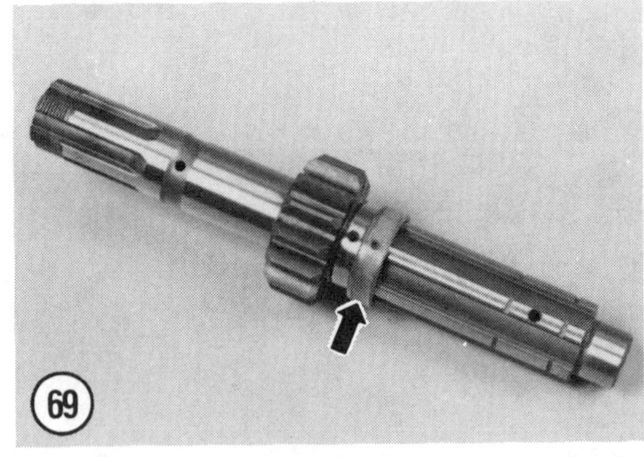


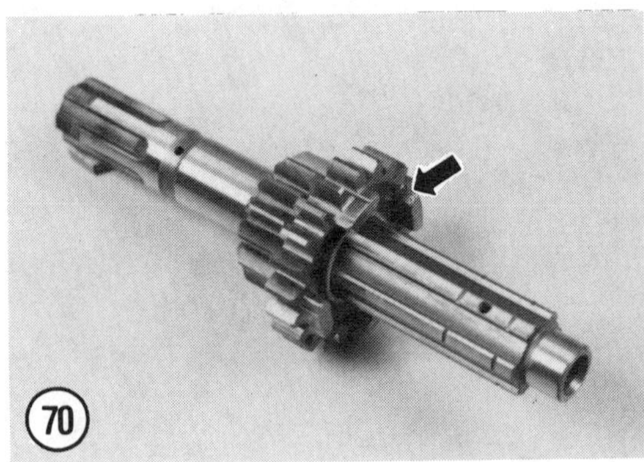


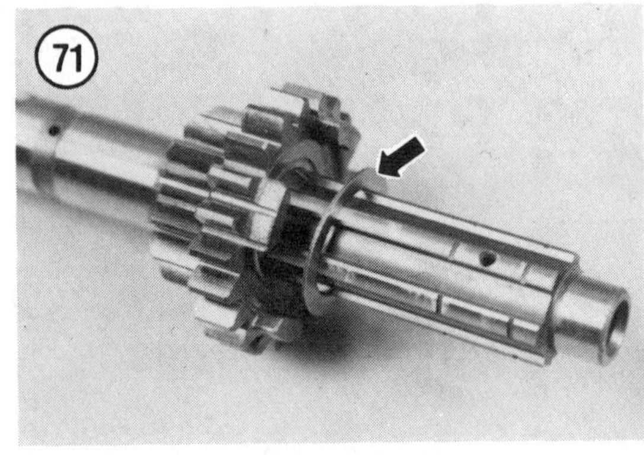

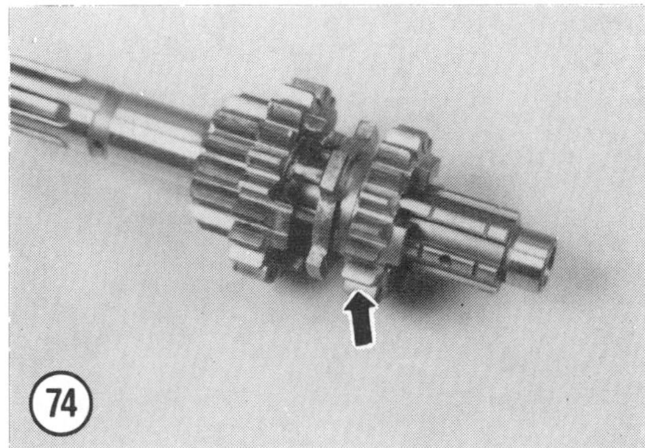


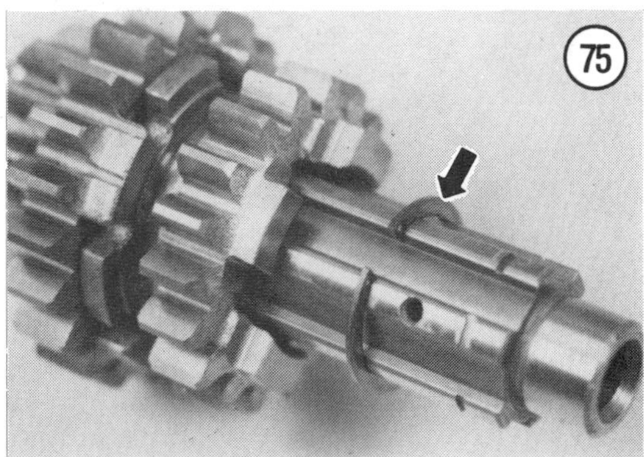

**Countershaft Assembly**

1. Apply a light coat of clean engine oil to all sliding surfaces before installing any parts.
2. Slide on the 3rd gear bushing (**Figure 69**) and install the 3rd gear (**Figure 70**).
3. Slide on the thrust washer (**Figure 71**).
4. Install the circlip (**Figure 72**). Make sure it is correctly seated in the countershaft groove (**Figure 73**).
5. Slide on the 2nd gear (**Figure 74**).
6. Install the circlip (**Figure 75**). Make sure it is correctly seated in the countershaft groove.

*CAUTION*

*There are 2 splined washers used on this shaft. One has 3 dogs and is **thin**. The other has 6 dogs and is **thick**. These splined washers must be installed in the correct position or damage to the transmission components will result.*

7. Slide on the *thin 3-dog* splined washer (**Figure 76**).
8. Slide on the 4th gear (**Figure 77**).
9. Slide on the *thick 6-dog* splined washer (**Figure 78**).
10. Install the circlip (**Figure 79**). Make sure it is correctly seated in the countershaft groove.
11. Refer to **Figure 80** for correct placement of all gears. Make sure all circlips are seated correctly in the countershaft grooves.
12. Make sure each gear engages properly to the adjoining gear where applicable.

6

## Internal Gearshift Mechanism Inspection

Refer to **Figure 81** for this procedure.

1. Inspect each shift fork (A, **Figure 82**) for signs of wear or cracking. Check for bending and make sure each fork slides smoothly on the shaft (B, **Figure 82**). Replace any worn or damaged forks.
2. Check for any arc-shaped wear or burned marks on the shift fork fingers (**Figure 83**). This indicates that the shift fork has come in contact with the gear. Thus, the fork fingers have become excessively worn and the fork must be replaced.
3. Check the grooves in the shift drum (**Figure 84**) for wear or roughness. If any of the groove profiles have excessive wear or damage, replace the shift drum.
4. Check the neutral switch contact plunger and spring (**Figure 85**) for wear or damage. If the spring has sagged, replace it.
5. Make sure the locating pins (**Figure 86**) are a tight fit in the shift drum. If the pins are loose, replace them.

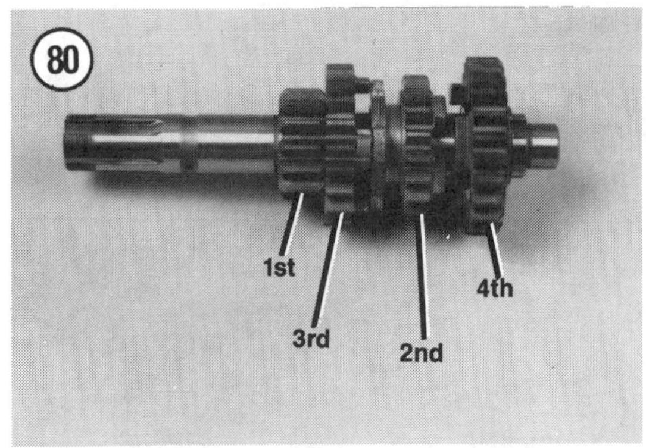


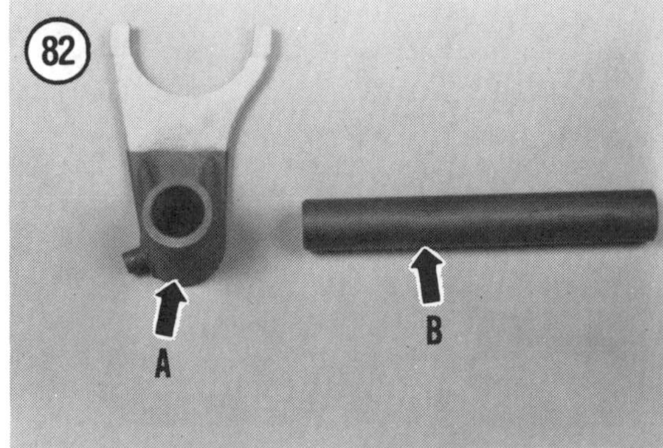


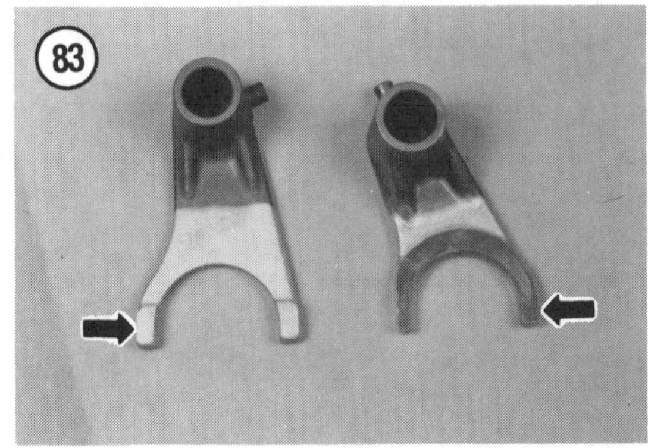


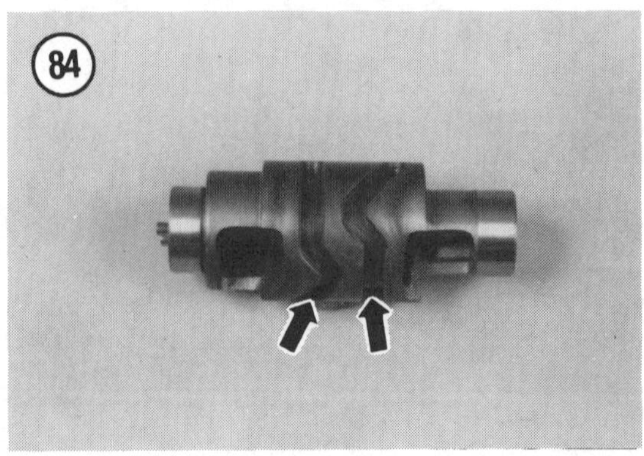

81

**INTERNAL SHIFT MECHANISM**

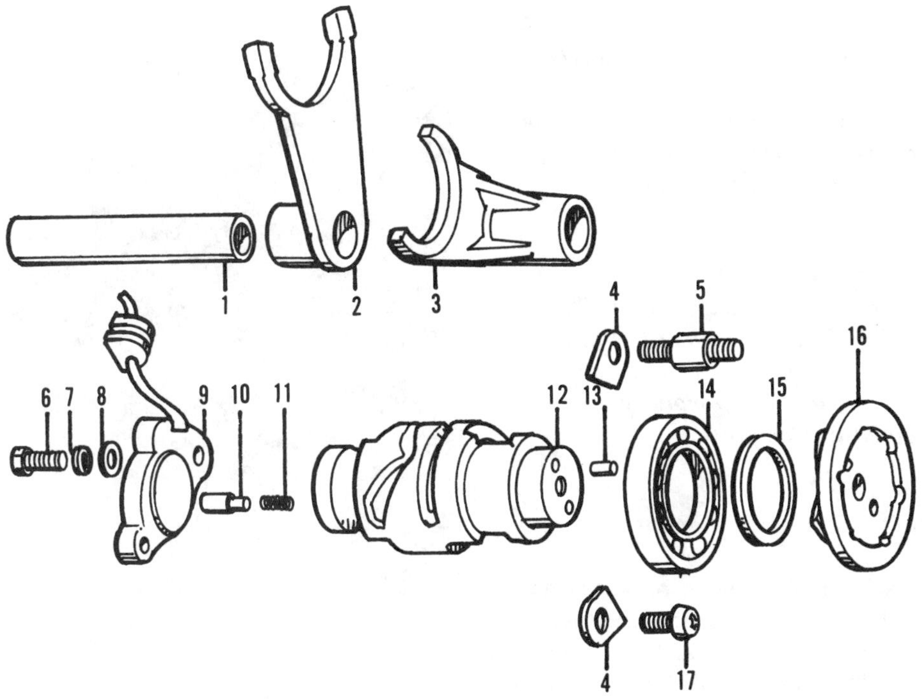

1. Shift drum shaft
2. Shift fork No. 1
3. Shift fork No. 2
4. Bearing retainer
5. Threaded stud
6. Bolt
7. Lockwasher
8. Washer
9. Neutral switch
10. Switch contact
11. Spring
12. Shift drum
13. Pin
14. Bearing
15. Spacer
16. Stopper plate
17. Phillips screw



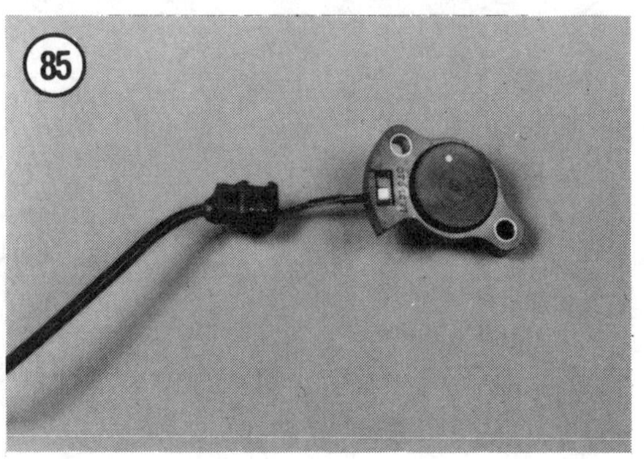

6. Check the shift drum bearing (**Figure 87**). Make sure it operates smoothly with no signs of wear or damage. If damaged, replace as described under *Crankcase Bearings Removal/Installation* in Chapter Four.
7. Check the cam pin followers (**Figure 88**) on each shift fork, that rides in the shift drum, for wear or damage. Replace the shift fork(s) as necessary.
8. Roll the shift fork shaft on a flat surface such as a piece of plate glass and check for any bends. If the shaft is bent, it must be replaced.

*CAUTION*
*It is recommended that marginally worn shift forks be replaced. Worn forks can cause the transmission to slip out of gear, leading to more serious and expensive damage.*

9. Inspect the shift fork-to-gear clearance as follows:
   a. Install each shift fork into its respective gear. Use a flat feeler gauge and measure the clearance between the fork and gear as shown in **Figure 89**. Compare to the specifications listed in **Table 1**.
   b. If the clearance is greater than specified in **Table 1**, measure the width of the gearshift fork fingers with a micrometer (**Figure 90**). Replace the shift fork(s) worn to the service limit listed in **Table 1** or less.
   c. If the shift fork finger width is within tolerance, measure the shift fork groove width in the gears with a vernier caliper. Compare to the specifications listed in **Table 1**. Replace the gear(s) if the groove is worn to the service limit or more.

87

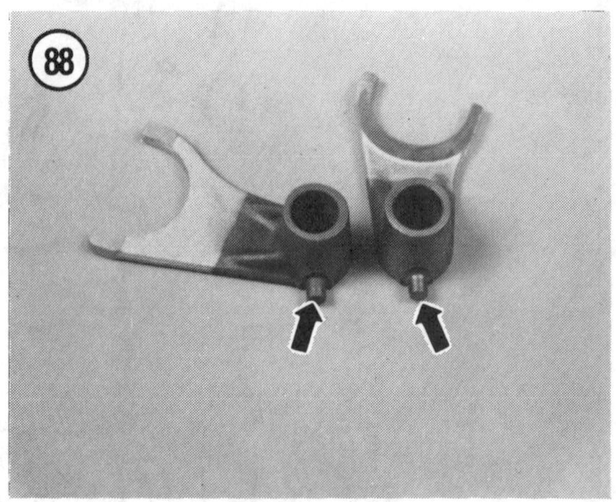
88

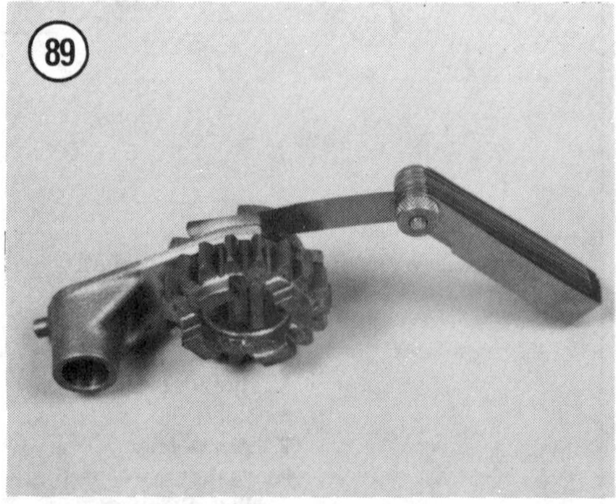
89

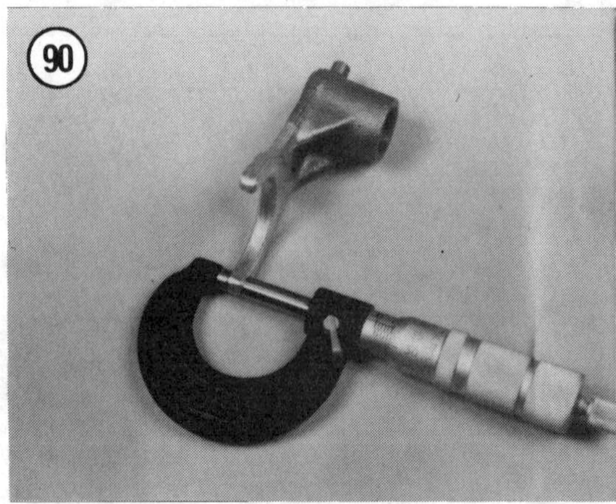
90

**Table 1 TRANSMISSION, GEARSHIFT AND DRIVE BELT SPECIFICATIONS**

| Item | Specifications | Wear limit |
|---|---|---|
| Shift fork-to-groove | | |
| in gear clearance | 0.1-0.3 mm (0.004-0.012 in.) | 0.50 mm (0.02 in.) |
| Shift fork groove width in gear | | |
| 2nd gear countershaft | 5.5-5.6 mm (0.217-0.220 in.) | — |
| 3rd gear mainshaft | 5.5-5.6 mm (0.217-0.220 in.) | — |
| Shift fork finger thickness | | |
| Shift fork No. 1 | | |
| and No. 2 | 5.3-5.4 mm (0.209-0.220 in.) | — |
| Transmission gear ratios | | |
| 1st gear | 2.214 | |
| 2nd gear | 1.500 | |
| 3rd gear | 1.095 | |
| 4th gear | 0.875 | |
| Drive belt | | |
| Type | Bando 133U-14M 40.0 | |
| Number of teeth | 133 | |

# CHAPTER SEVEN

# FUEL, EMISSION CONTROL AND EXHAUST SYSTEMS

The fuel system consists of the fuel tank, the shutoff valve, a single carburetor and an air filter. The exhaust system consists of an exhaust pipe and a muffler assembly.

The emission controls consist of crankcase emission system and on California models, an evaporative emission control system.

This chapter includes service procedures for all parts of the fuel system and exhaust system. Air filter service is covered in Chapter Three.

Carburetor specifications are covered in **Table 1** located at the end of this chapter. **Table 1** and **Table 2** are located at the end of this chapter.

## CARBURETOR OPERATION

For proper operation, a gasoline engine must be supplied with fuel and air mixed in proper proportions by weight. A mixture in which there is an excess of fuel is said to be rich. A lean mixture is one which contains insufficient fuel. A properly adjusted carburetor supplies the proper mixture to the engine under all operating conditions.

The carburetor consists of several major systems. A float and float valve mechanism maintain a constant fuel level in the float bowl. The pilot system supplies fuel at low speeds. The main fuel system supplies fuel at medium and high speeds. A starter (choke) system supplies the very rich mixture needed to start a cold engine.

## CARBURETOR SERVICE

Major carburetor service (removal and cleaning) should be performed at the intervals indicated in **Table 2** in Chapter Three or when poor engine performance, hesitation and little or no response to mixture adjustment is observed. Alterations in jet size, needle position, etc., should be attempted only if you're experienced in this type of "tuning" work; a bad guess could result in costly engine damage or, at least, poor performance. If, after servicing the carburetor and making the adjustments described in this chapter, the bike does not perform correctly (and assuming that other factors affecting performance are correct, such as proper compression and ignition component condition, etc.), the bike should be checked by a Suzuki dealer or a qualified performance tuning specialist.

## CARBURETOR

### Removal/Installation

1. Remove the seat as described in Chapter Twelve.
2. Remove the fuel tank as described in this chapter.
3. Remove the frame left-hand side cover.
4. Disconnect the battery negative lead (**Figure 1**).

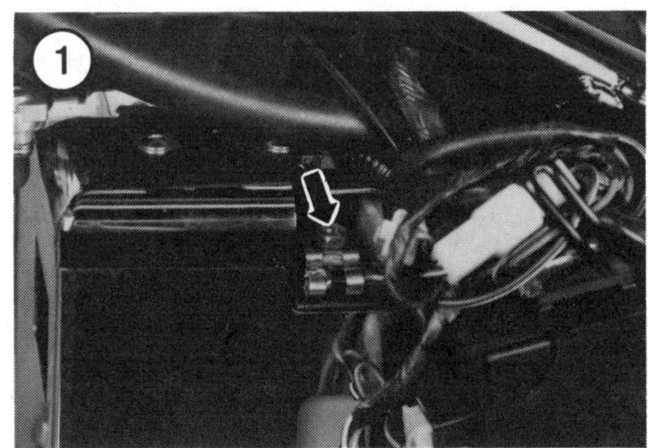


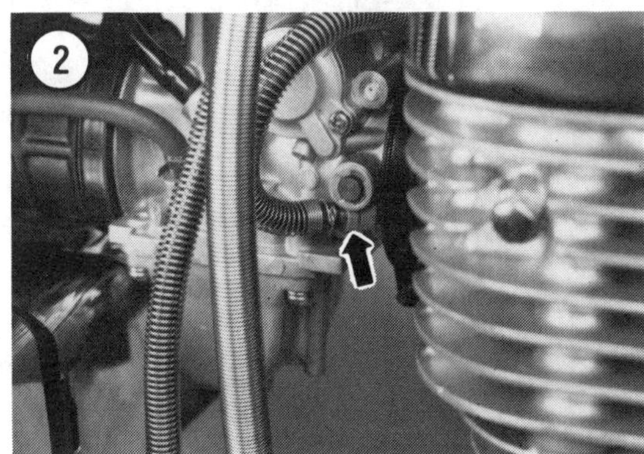

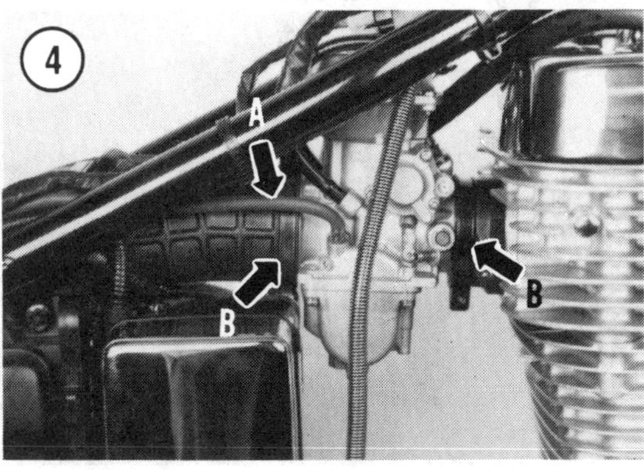


5. Disconnect the fuel shutoff valve vacuum hose (**Figure 2**) from the right-hand side of the carburetor.
6. Remove the clip (A, **Figure 3**) securing the throttle cable and unhook the throttle cable from the throttle wheel (B, **Figure 3**).
7. On California models, disconnect the evaporative emission tube (A, **Figure 4**) from the carburetor.
8. Loosen the screw on the clamping bands (B, **Figure 4**) on each end of the carburetor. Slide the clamping bands away from the carburetor.
9. Pull the carburetor toward the rear and free it from the intake tube on the cylinder head.
10. Carefully remove the carburetor from the engine and frame and take it to a workbench for disassembly and cleaning.
11. Install by reversing these removal steps. Note the following during installation.
12. Make sure the carburetor is fully seated forward in the rubber holder in the cylinder head. You should feel a solid "bottoming out" when it is correctly seated.
13. Make sure the screws on the clamping bands are tight to avoid a vacuum loss and possible valve damage due to a lean fuel mixture.
14. Hook the throttle cable onto the throttle wheel (B, **Figure 3**).
15. Position the clip with the flat section (**Figure 5**) facing toward the front and install the clip securing the throttle cable to the bracket. Make sure it is seated in the slot correctly so that it will not work free.
16. Adjust the throttle cable as described in Chapter Three.

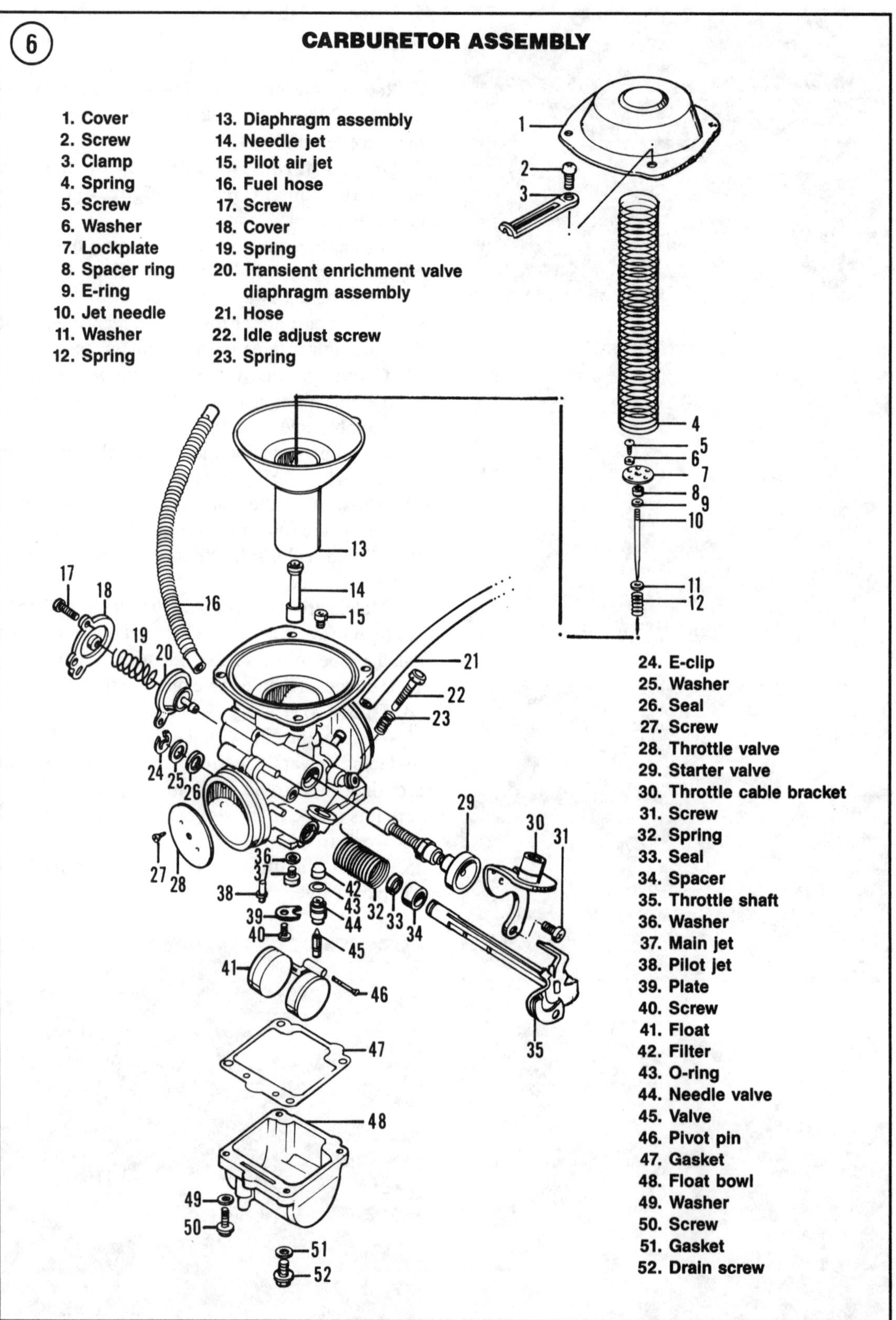
6
CARBURETOR ASSEMBLY
1. Cover
2. Screw
3. Clamp
4. Spring
5. Screw
6. Washer
7. Lockplate
8. Spacer ring
9. E-ring
10. Jet needle
11. Washer
12. Spring
13. Diaphragm assembly
14. Needle jet
15. Pilot air jet
16. Fuel hose
17. Screw
18. Cover
19. Spring
20. Transient enrichment valve diaphragm assembly
21. Hose
22. Idle adjust screw
23. Spring
24. E-clip
25. Washer
26. Seal
27. Screw
28. Throttle valve
29. Starter valve
30. Throttle cable bracket
31. Screw
32. Spring
33. Seal
34. Spacer
35. Throttle shaft
36. Washer
37. Main jet
38. Pilot jet
39. Plate
40. Screw
41. Float
42. Filter
43. O-ring
44. Needle valve
45. Valve
46. Pivot pin
47. Gasket
48. Float bowl
49. Washer
50. Screw
51. Gasket
52. Drain screw

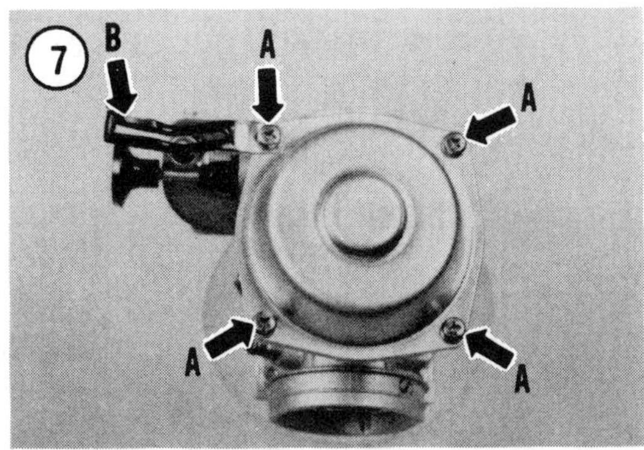

## CARBURETOR

### Disassembly

Refer to **Figure 6** for this procedure.

1. Remove the screws (A, **Figure 7**) securing the top cover and remove the cover. Note the location of the throttle cable clamp (B, **Figure 7**). It must be reinstalled in the same location during assembly.
2. Remove the spring (A, **Figure 8**) and the diaphragm assembly (B, **Figure 8**) from the carburetor.
3. Unscrew the pilot air jet (**Figure 9**).
4. Remove the screws (**Figure 10**) securing the float bowl and remove the float bowl.
5. Remove the gasket (**Figure 11**) from the float bowl.
6. Remove the float pivot pin (A, **Figure 12**).
7. Remove the float (B, **Figure 12**) and needle valve.

8. Remove the screw (**Figure 13**) and plate securing the needle valve assembly and remove the assembly (**Figure 14**).
9. Unscrew the pilot jet (**Figure 15**).
10. Unscrew the main jet (**Figure 16**) and remove the main jet washer (**Figure 17**).
11. Turn the carburetor over and gently tap the side of the body. Catch the needle jet (**Figure 18**) as it falls out into your hand. If the needle jet does not fall out, use a plastic or fiber tool and gently push the needle jet out. Do not use any metal tools for this purpose.
12. Remove the screws securing the transient enrichment valve cover (**Figure 19**). Remove the cover, the spring (**Figure 20**) and the diaphragm assembly (A, **Figure 21**).
13. Unscrew and remove the starter (choke) plunger assembly (**Figure 22**).
14. Remove the idle adjust screw and spring (**Figure 23**).

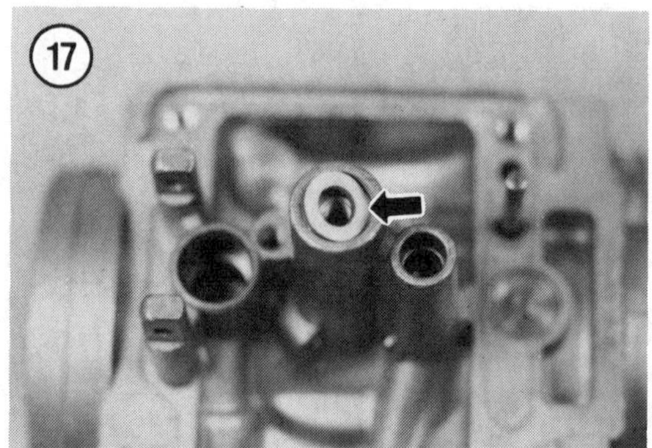


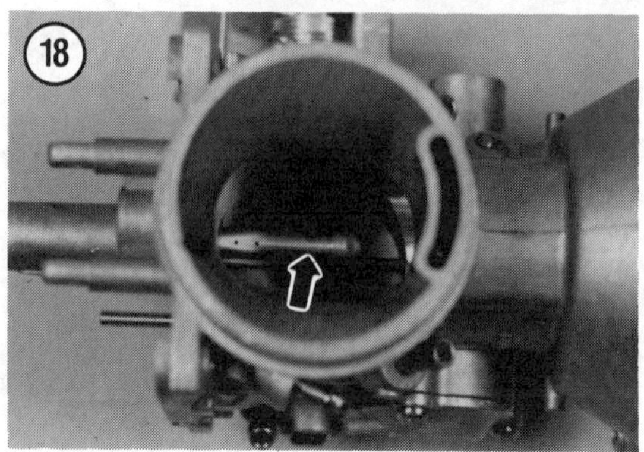

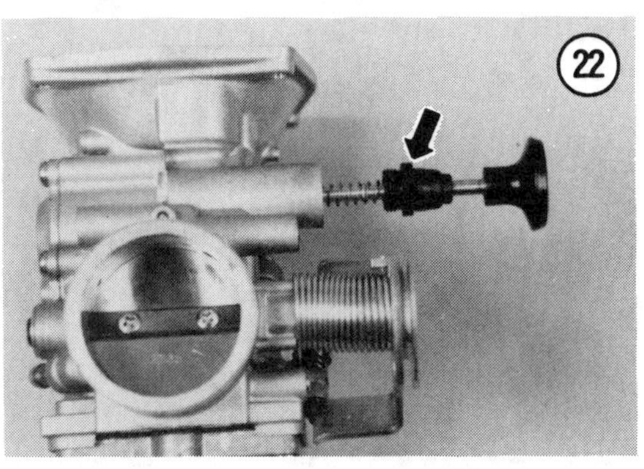


15. To disassemble the diaphragm assembly, perform the following:
   a. Remove the screws (A, **Figure 24**) and washers securing the lock plate to the diaphragm.
   b. Remove the lock plate (A, **Figure 25**), the jet needle, washer and spring (B, **Figure 25**).

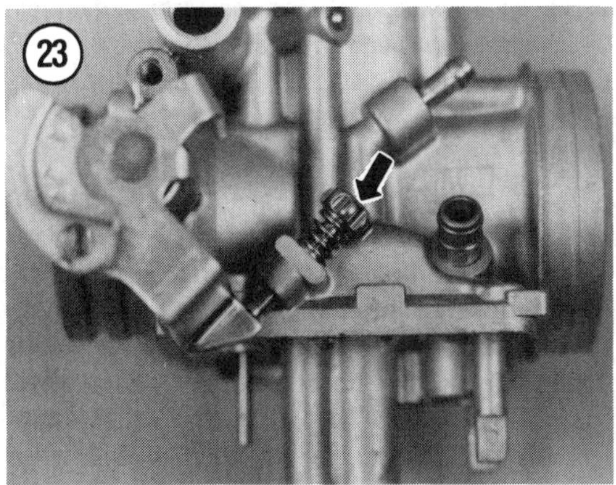


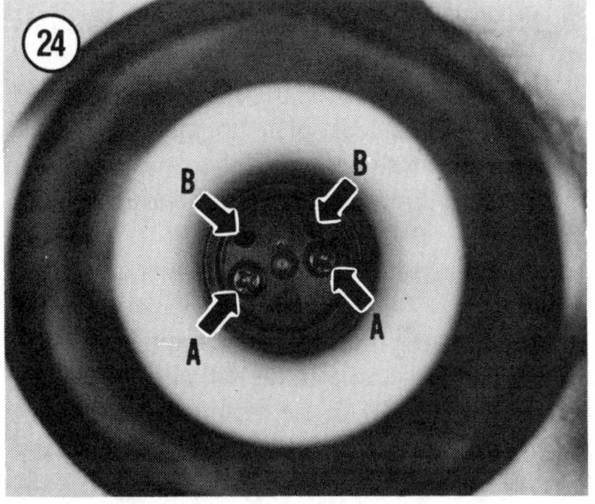


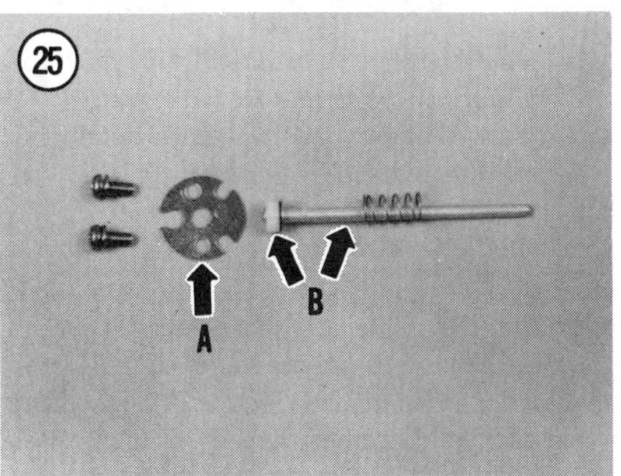

*NOTE*
*Further disassembly is neither necessary nor recommended. If throttle or choke shaft or butterfly (**Figure 26**) are damaged, take the carburetor body to a dealer for replacement.*

16. Clean and inspect all parts as described under *Cleaning and Inspection* in this chapter.

## Assembly

1. To assemble the diaphragm assembly, perform the following:
   a. Install the washer, spring and spacer ring (**Figure 27**) onto the jet needle.
   b. Install the jet needle assembly (A, **Figure 28**) into the diaphragm assembly.
   c. Install the lock plate (B, **Figure 28**) and position the lock plate so its holes align with the holes (B, **Figure 24**) in the diaphragm assembly.
   d. Make sure the lock plate's protrusion is pushing down on the spacer ring.
   e. Install the screws (C, **Figure 28**) and washers securing the lock plate to the diaphragm. Tighten the screws securely.
2. Install the idle adjust screw and spring (**Figure 23**).
3. Install the starter (choke) plunger assembly (**Figure 22**).
4. Install the transient enrichment valve diaphragm so the hole in the tab aligns with the hole (B, **Figure 21**) in the carburetor body.
5. Install the transient enrichment valve spring (**Figure 20**) and cover (**Figure 19**).

*CAUTION*
*In the next step, make sure that the flat portion on the needle jet is correctly aligned with the protrusion in the main jet stanchion. If alignment is not correct, you will be unable to screw the main jet into the needle jet.*

6. Position the needle jet with the threaded portion going in last. Install the needle jet so the groove aligns with the protrusion (**Figure 29**) in the main jet stanchion of the carburetor body. Carefully push the needle jet all the way in until it bottoms out.

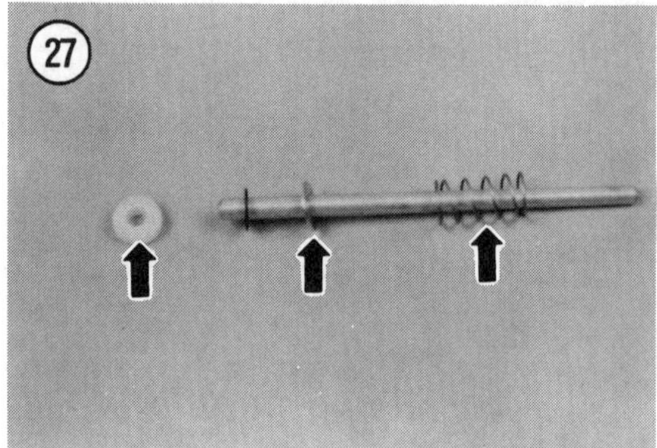


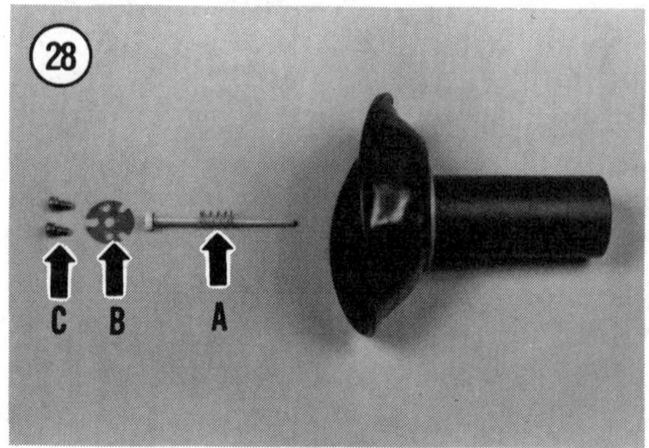

30

31

32

33

7. Install the main jet washer (**Figure 17**) and the main jet (**Figure 16**).
8. Install the pilot jet with the threaded end (**Figure 30**) going in last and tighten securely.
9. Make sure the O-ring seal (**Figure 31**) is in place on the needle valve assembly and install the assembly.
10. Install the needle valve plate and screw (**Figure 13**). Tighten the screw securely.
11. Hook the valve needle (**Figure 32**) on the float and install the float assembly.

*NOTE*
*The float pivot pin right-hand stanchion in the carburetor body has a slight chamfer to accept the float pivot pin head.*

12. Install the float pivot pin in from the right-hand side of the carburetor (**Figure 33**). Push the pin in until it stops.
13. Check the float height and adjust if necessary as described in this chapter.
14. Install a new float bowl gasket and install the float bowl. Tighten the screws securely.
15. Install the pilot air jet.

*CAUTION*
*In Step 16, if the tab on the diaphragm assembly is **not** positioned correctly in the groove in the carburetor body (**Figure 34**) there will be a vacuum leak that could lead to very poor performance and possible serious engine damage.*

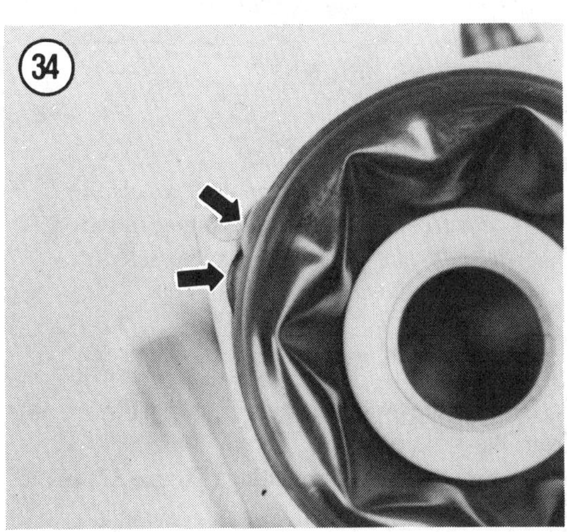
34

16. Make sure the tab on the diaphragm assembly is positioned correctly in the groove in the carburetor body (**Figure 35**). Push up on the piston valve just enough so there is no crease in the diaphragm lip.
17. Install the diaphragm assembly spring.
18. Install the carburetor top cap and screws. Be sure to install the throttle cable clamp (B, **Figure 7**) in the correct place as noted during disassembly.

### Cleaning and Inspection

1. Clean all parts, except rubber or plastic parts, in a good grade of carburetor cleaner. This solution is available at most automotive or motorcycle supply stores in a small, resealable tank with a dip basket for just a few dollars. If it is tightly sealed when not in use, the solution will last for several cleanings. Follow the manufacturer's instructions for correct soak time (usually about 1/2 hour).
2. Remove all parts from the cleaner and blow dry with compressed air. Blow out the jets and needle jet holder with compressed air.

*CAUTION*
*If compressed air is not available, allow the parts to air dry or use a clean, lint-free cloth. Do **not** use a paper towel to dry carburetor parts, as small paper particles may plug openings in the carburetor body or jets.*

*CAUTION*
*Do **not** use a piece of wire to clean carburetor jets as minor gouges in the jet can alter flow rate and upset the fuel/air mixture.*

3. Remove the drain screw and gasket (**Figure 36**) from the float bowl.
4. Be sure to clean out opening (**Figure 37**) in the float bowl.

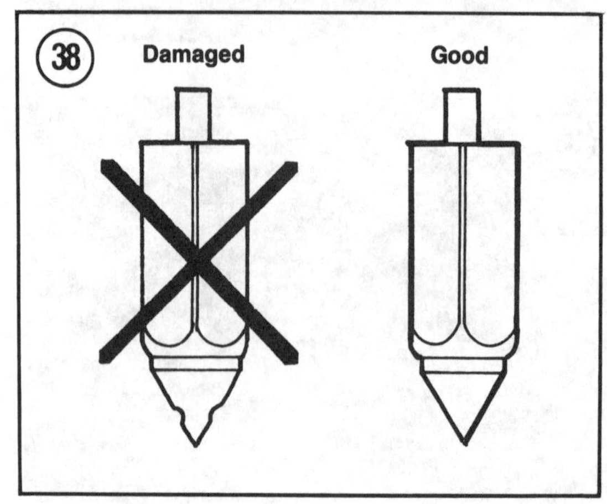

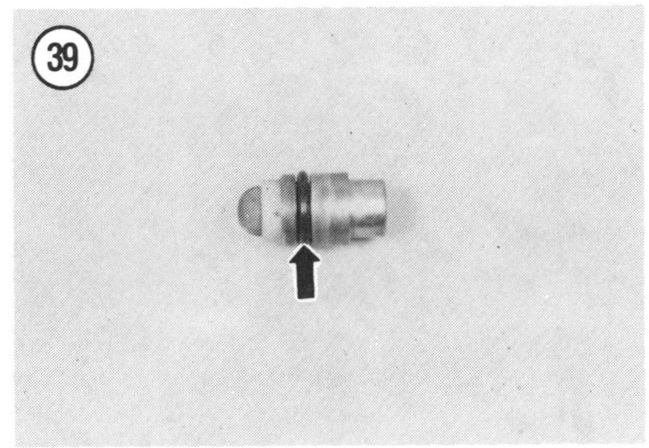


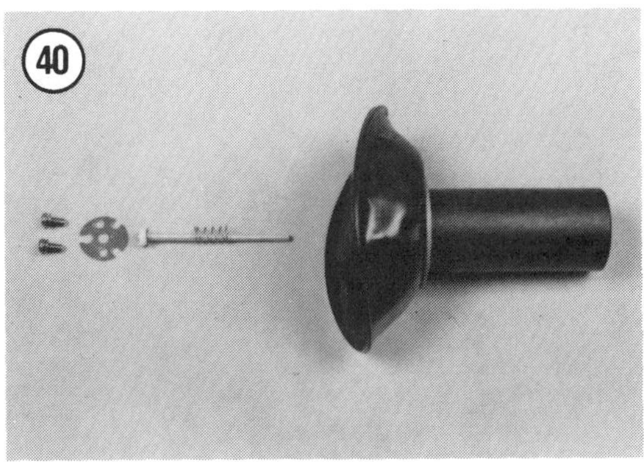


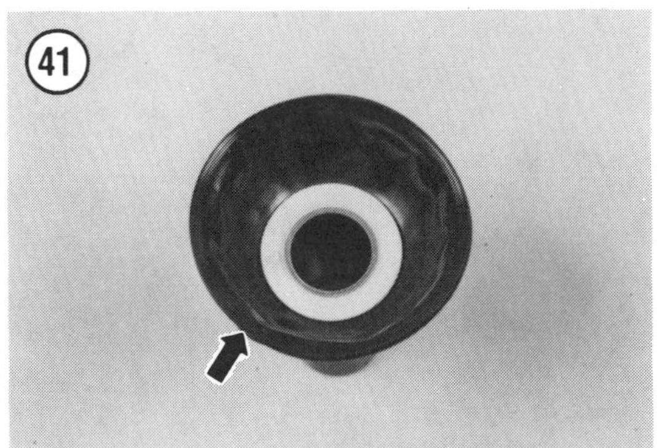


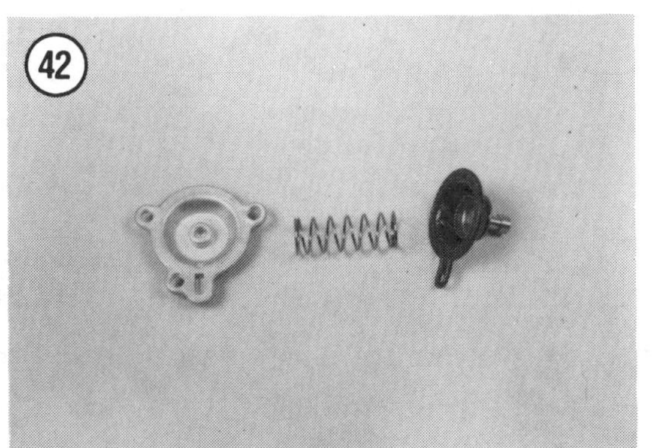


5. Inspect the end of the float valve needle (**Figure 38**) for wear or damage. Also check the inside of the needle valve body. If either part is damaged, replace as a set. A damaged needle valve or a particle of dirt or grit in the needle valve assembly will cause the carburetor to flood and overflow fuel.
6. Inspect all O-ring seals (**Figure 39**). O-ring seals tend to become hardened after prolonged use and heat and therefore lose their ability to seal properly.
7. Examine all parts of the diaphragm assembly (**Figure 40**) for wear or damage. Make sure the diaphragm (**Figure 41**) is not torn or cracked. Replace any damaged or worn parts.
8. Examine all parts of the transient enrichment valve assembly (**Figure 42**) for wear or damage. Make sure the diaphragm (**Figure 43**) is not torn or cracked. Replace any damaged or worn parts.
9. Make sure the holes in the needle jet (**Figure 44**) are clear. Clean out if they are plugged in any way. Replace the needle jet if you cannot unplug the holes.

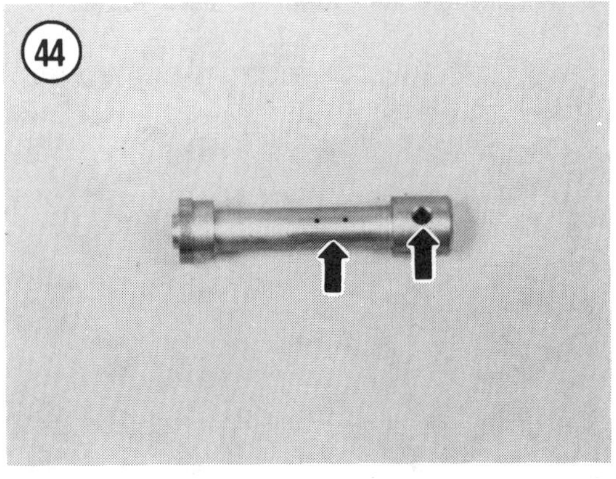

10. Make sure the holes in the remaining jets (**Figure 45**) are clear. Clean out if they are plugged in any way. Replace the jet(s) if you cannot unplug the hole(s).
11. Make sure all openings in the carburetor body are clear. Refer to **Figure 46**, **Figure 47** and **Figure 48**. Clean out if they are plugged in any way.
12. Shake the float assembly (**Figure 49**) and listen for any fuel sloshing around within either of the floats. If any fuel is present, replace the float assembly.
13. Inspect the starter (choke) plunger assembly (**Figure 50**) for wear or damage. Replace as a unit if necessary; replacement parts are not available even though the assembly can be disassembled.

## CARBURETOR ADJUSTMENT

### Float Adjustment

The carburetor has to be removed and partially disassembled for this adjustment.

1. Remove the carburetor as described in this chapter.
2. Remove the screws (**Figure 51**) securing the float bowl and remove it.
3. Hold the carburetor upside down so that the float arm is just touching the float needle—not pushing it down.
4. Use a vernier caliper or small ruler and measure the distance "A" from the carburetor body to the bottom surface of the float body (**Figure 52**). The correct height is listed in **Table 1**.
5. Adjust by carefully bending the tang (**Figure 53**) on the float arm. If the float level is too high, the result will be a rich fuel/air mixture. If it is too low, the mixture will be too lean.
6. Reassemble and install the carburetor.

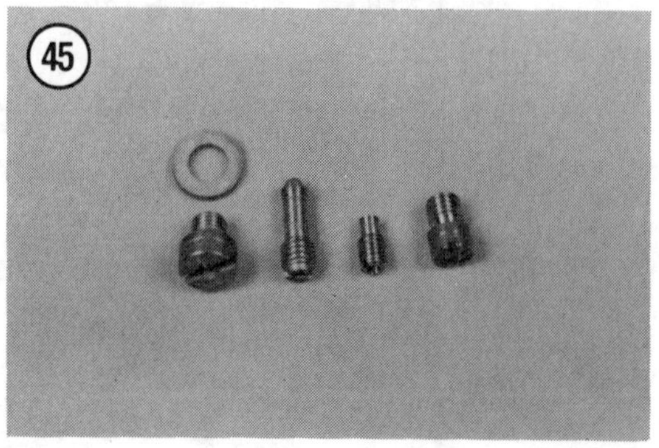

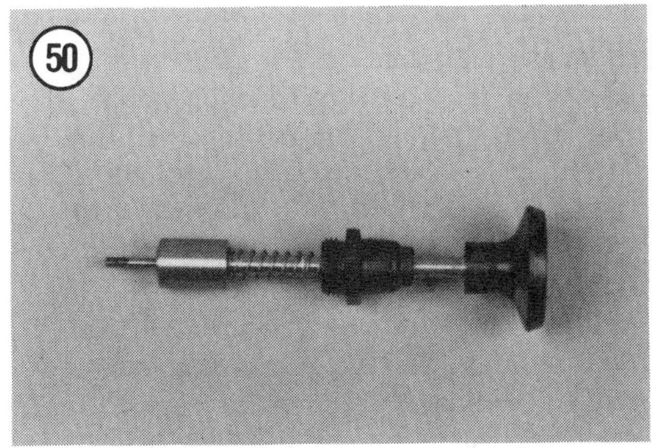

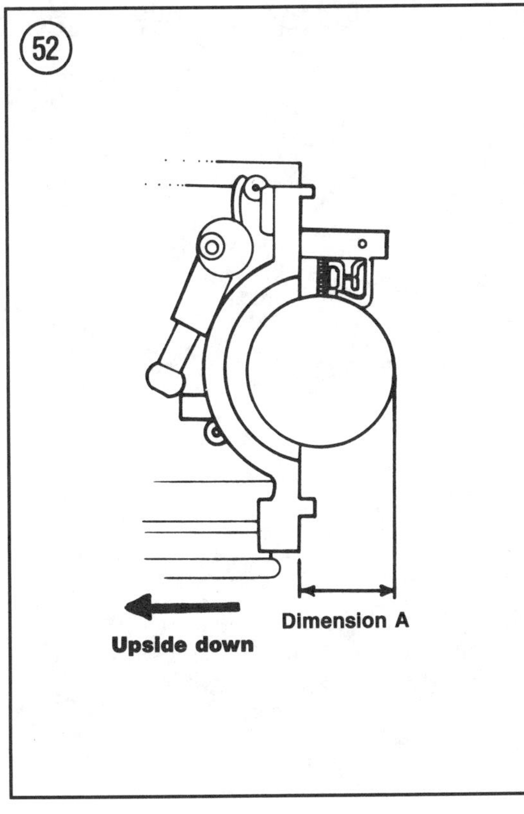


## Rejetting the Carburetor

Do not try to solve a poor running engine problem by rejetting the carburetor if all of the following conditions hold true:

a. The engine has held a good tune in the past with the standard jetting.
b. The engine has not been modified.
c. The motorcycle is being operated in the same geographical region under the same general climatic conditions as in the past.
d. The motorcycle was and is being ridden at average highway speeds.

If those conditions all hold true, the chances are that the problem is due to a malfunction in the carburetor or in another component that needs to be adjusted or repaired. Changing carburetor jet size probably won't solve the problem. Rejetting the carburetor may be necessary if any of the following conditions hold true:

a. A non-standard type of air filter element is being used.
b. A non-standard exhaust system is installed on the motorcycle.
c. Any of the top end components in the engine (piston, camshaft, valves, compression ratio, etc.) have been modified.
d. The motorcycle is in use at considerably higher or lower altitudes or in a considerably hotter or colder climate than in the past.
e. The motorcycle is being operated at considerably higher speeds than before and changing to colder spark plugs does not solve the problem.
f. Someone has previously changed the carburetor jetting.
g. The motorcycle has never held a satisfactory engine tune.

If it is necessary to rejet the carburetors, check with a dealer or motorcycle performance tuner for recommendations as to the size of jets to install for your specific situation.

If you do change the jets, do so only one size at a time. After rejetting, test ride the bike and perform a spark plug test; refer to *Reading Spark Plugs* in Chapter Three.

## THROTTLE CABLE REPLACEMENT

1. Remove the seat as described in Chapter Twelve.
2. Remove the fuel tank as described in this chapter.
3. Remove the clip (A, **Figure 54**) securing the throttle cable and unhook the throttle cable from the throttle wheel (B, **Figure 54**).
4. Remove the screws securing the right-hand switch assembly (**Figure 55**) together, then disengage the throttle cable from the throttle grip.
5. Remove any tie wraps or metal clamps securing the throttle cable to the frame.

*NOTE*
*The piece of string attached in the next step will be used to pull the new throttle cable back through the frame so it will be routed in exactly the same position as the old one was.*

6. Tie a piece of heavy string or cord (approximately 7 ft./2 m long) to the carburetor end of both throttle cables. Wrap this end with masking or duct tape. Do not use an excessive amount of tape as it must be pulled through the frame during removal. Tie the other end of the string to the frame or air box.
7. At the throttle grip end of the cable, carefully pull the cable (and attached string) out through the frame. Make sure the attached string follows the same path as the cable through the frame.
8. Remove the tape and untie the string from the old cable.
9. Lubricate the new cable as described under *Control Cable* in Chapter Three.
10. Tie the string to the new throttle cable and wrap it with tape.
11. Carefully pull the string back through the frame routing the new cable through the same path as the old cable.
12. Remove the tape and untie the string from the cable and the frame.
13. Attach the throttle cable to the throttle wheel and turn the clip to hold the cable in place.
14. Attach the throttle cable to the throttle grip on the handlebar.
15. Install the right-hand switch housing and tighten the screws securely.
16. Operate the throttle grip and make sure the carburetor throttle linkage is operating correctly, with no binding. If operation is incorrect or there is binding, carefully check that the cable is attached correctly and there are no tight bends in the cable.
17. Install the fuel tank and seat.
18. Adjust the throttle cable as described in Chapter Three.
19. Test ride the bike slowly at first and make sure the throttle is operating correctly.

## AIR FILTER AIR BOX

### Removal/Installation

Refer to **Figure 56** for this procedure.

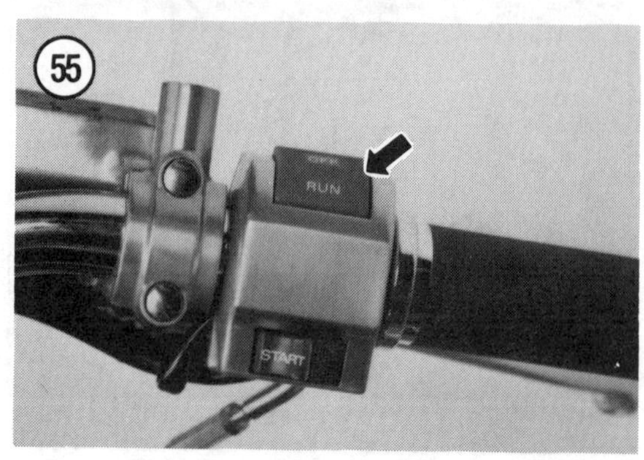

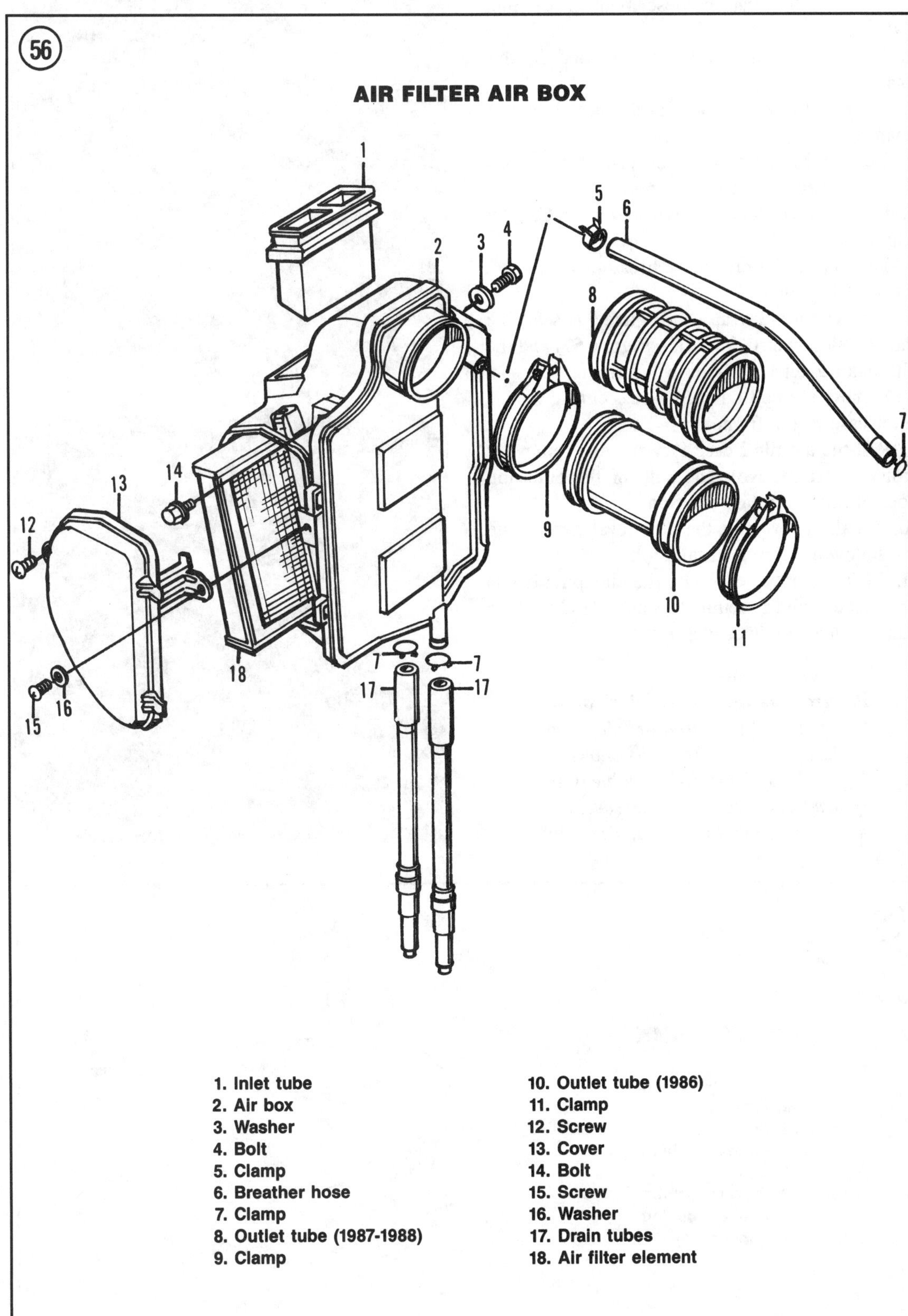
56
AIR FILTER AIR BOX
1. Inlet tube
2. Air box
3. Washer
4. Bolt
5. Clamp
6. Breather hose
7. Clamp
8. Outlet tube (1987-1988)
9. Clamp
10. Outlet tube (1986)
11. Clamp
12. Screw
13. Cover
14. Bolt
15. Screw
16. Washer
17. Drain tubes
18. Air filter element

1. Remove the seat as described in Chapter Twelve.
2. Remove the fuel tank as described in this chapter.
3. Remove the carburetor as described in this chapter.
4. Remove the air filter as described under *Air Filter Element* in Chapter Three.
5. Remove the battery case as described in Chapter Eight.
6. Disconnect the crankcase breather hose from the air filter air box.
7. Remove the tie wrap (A, **Figure 57**) securing the emission control hoses (B, **Figure 57**) and the alternator electrical cable to the frame.
8. Remove the bolt on each side securing the air filter case to the frame.
9. Pull the air filter case forward and remove it from the frame. Note the path of the emission control hoses through the frame.
10. Install by reversing these removal steps. Note the following during installation.
11. Make sure the screws on the clamping bands are tight to avoid a vacuum loss and possible valve damage due to a lean fuel mixture.

*WARNING*

*Be sure to secure the emission control hoses and the alternator electrical cable back to the frame as shown in* ***Figure 58****. If the electrical cable is not secured as shown, it will move over and the drive belt will rub on it. The drive*

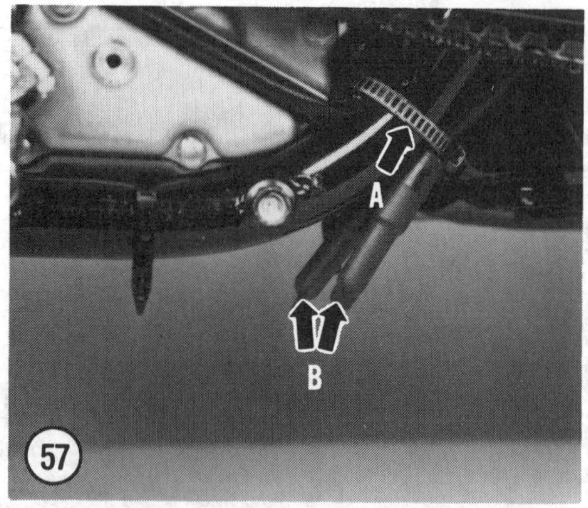


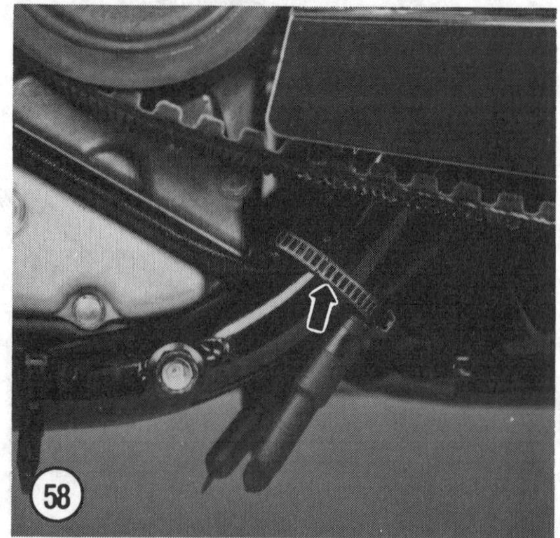

**FUEL TANK**

1. Filler cap and key
2. Fuel tank
3. Bolt
4. Rubber cushion
5. Collar
6. Rubber cushion
7. Rubber cushion
8. Rubber strip

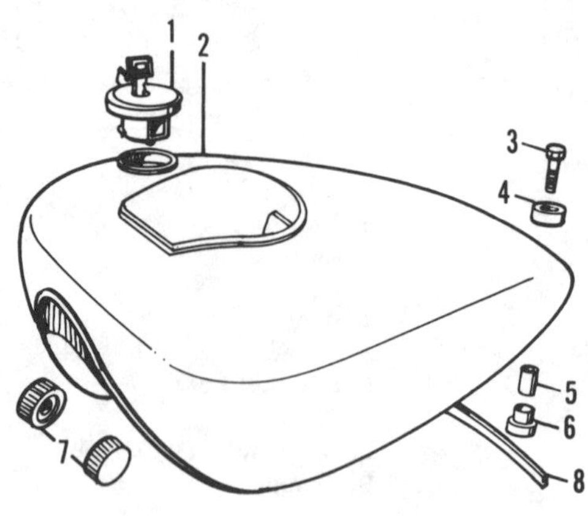

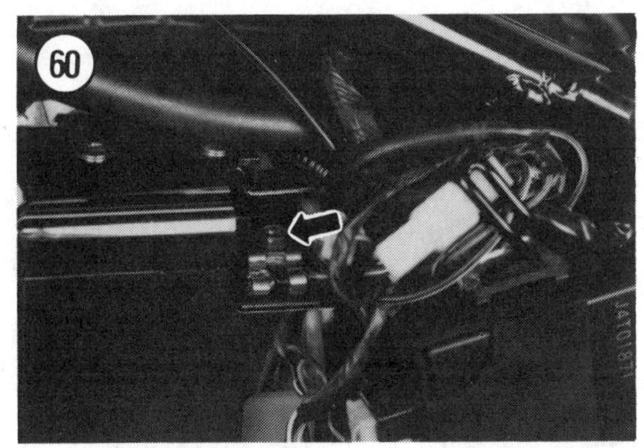

*belt will wear through the insulation and an electrical short or open will occur.*

12. Install the tie wrap (**Figure 58**) securing the alternator electrical cable and emission control hoses to the frame.

## FUEL TANK

### Removal/Installation

Refer to **Figure 59** for this procedure.

1. Remove the seat as described in Chapter Twelve.
2. Remove the frame left-hand side cover.
3. Disconnect the battery negative lead (**Figure 60**).
4. Disconnect the speedometer cable (**Figure 61**) from the top of the crankcase on the right-hand side.
5. Turn the fuel shutoff valve (A, **Figure 62**) to the OFF position.
6. Disconnect the fuel line (B, **Figure 62**) to the carburetor assembly. Plug the end of the line with a golf tee (**Figure 63**) to prevent the entry of foreign matter and prevent the dribbling of fuel.
7. Disconnect the vacuum line (**Figure 64**) to the carburetor assembly. Plug the end of the line with a golf tee to prevent the entry of foreign matter.

7

8. On California models, disconnect the evaporative emission system vent line at the connector (**Figure 65**).
9. Remove the bolts and washers (**Figure 66**) securing the rear of the fuel tank. Don't lose the seat hold down strap that is held in place with the same bolts.
10. Carefully slide the fuel tank toward the rear to gain access to the electrical connector.
11. Disconnect the indicator light electrical connector (**Figure 67**).
12. Lift up and pull the tank to the rear and remove the fuel tank. Carefully guide the speedometer cable out through the frame.
13. Install by reversing these removal steps. Note the following during installation.
14. Inspect the rubber cushions (**Figure 68**) where the front of the fuel tank attaches to the frame. Replace the cushions if damaged or starting to deteriorate.
15. Turn the fuel shutoff valve ON and check for fuel leaks.

## FUEL FILTER

The bike is equipped with a small fuel filter screen in the fuel shutoff valve. Considering the dirt and residue that is often found in today's gasoline, it is a good idea to install an inline fuel filter to help keep the carburetor clean.

A good quality inline fuel filter (A.C. part No. GF453 or equivalent) is available at most auto and motorcycle supply stores. Just cut the fuel line from the fuel tank to the carburetor and install the filter. Cut out a section of the fuel line the length of the filter so the fuel line does not kink and restrict fuel flow. Insert the fuel filter and make sure the fuel line is secured to the filter at each end.

## GASOLINE/ALCOHOL BLEND TEST

Gasoline blended with alcohol is available in many areas. Most states and most fuel suppliers require labeling of gasoline pumps that dispense gasoline containing a certain percentage of alcohol (methyl or wood). If in doubt, ask the service station operator if their fuel contains any alcohol. A gasoline/alcohol blend, even if it contains cosolvents and corrosion inhibitors for methanol, may be damaging to the fuel system. It may also cause poor performance, difficult hot engine restart or hot engine running problems.

If you are not sure if the fuel you purchased contains alcohol, run this simple and effective test. A blended fuel doesn't look any different from straight gasoline so it must be tested.

*WARNING*

*Gasoline is very volatile and presents an extreme fire hazard. Be sure to work*

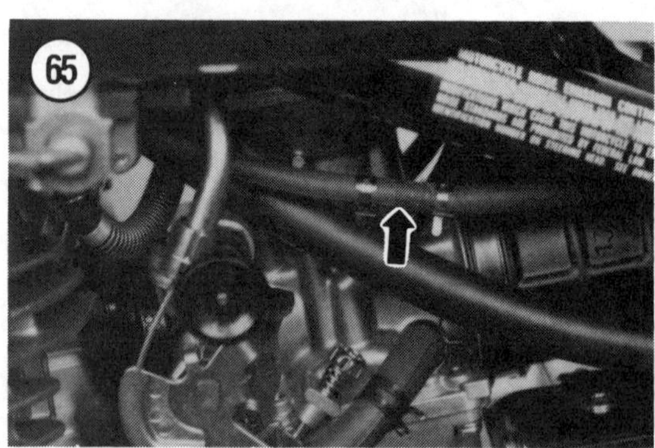

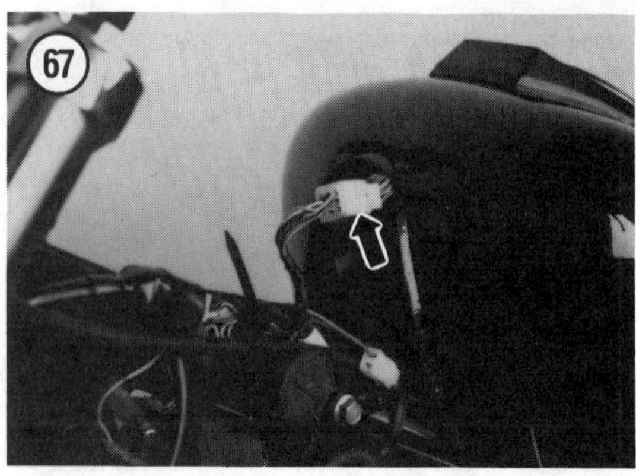

*in a well-ventilated area away from any open flames (including pilot lights on household appliances). Do not allow anyone to smoke in the area and have a fire extinguisher rated for gasoline fires handy.*

During this test, keep the following facts in mind:

a. Alcohol and gasoline mix together.
b. Alcohol mixes *easier* with water.
c. Gasoline and water do *not* mix.

NOTE

*If cosolvents have been used in the gasoline, this test may not work with water. Repeat this test using automotive antifreeze instead of water.*

Use an 8 oz. transparent baby bottle with a sealable cap.

1. Set the baby bottle on a level surface and add water up to the 1.5 oz. mark. Mark this line on the bottle with a fine-line permanent marking pen. This will be the reference line used later in this test.
2. Add the suspect fuel into the baby bottle up to the 8 oz. mark.

68

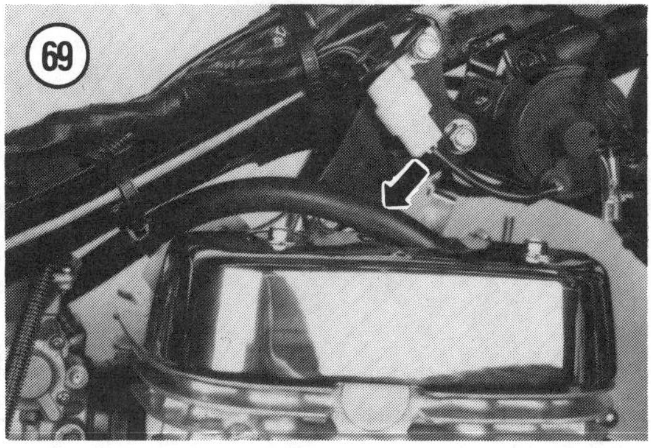
69

3. Install the sealable cap and shake the bottle vigorously for about 10 seconds.
4. Set the baby bottle upright on the level surface used in Step 1 and wait for a few minutes for the mixture to settle down.
5. If there is *no* alcohol in the fuel, the gasoline/water separation line will be exactly on the 1.5 oz. reference line made in Step 1.
6. If there *is* alcohol in the fuel, the gasoline/water separation line will be *above* the 1.5 oz. reference line made in Step 1. The alcohol has separated from the gasoline and mixed in with the water (remember it is easier for the alcohol to mix with water than gasoline).

WARNING

*After the test, discard the baby bottle or place it out of reach of small children. There will always be a gasoline and alcohol residue in it and should* ***not*** *be used to drink out of.*

## CRANKCASE BREATHER SYSTEM (U.S. ONLY)

To comply with air pollution standards, all models are equipped with a closed crankcase breather system. The system routes the engine combustion gases into the air filter air box where they are burned in the engine.

### Inspection/Cleaning

Make sure the hose clamps at each end of the breather hose (**Figure 69**) are tight. Check the hose for deterioration and replace as necessary.

Squeeze the ends of the air box drain hoses (B, **Figure 57**) and drain out all residue. This cleaning procedure should be done more frequently if a considerable amount of riding is done at full throttle or in the rain.

## EVAPORATIVE EMISSION CONTROL SYSTEM (CALIFORNIA MODELS ONLY)

Fuel vapor from the fuel tank is routed through the breather valve and into the charcoal canister. This vapor is stored when the engine is not running. When the engine is running these vapors are drawn from the canister through the purge hose and into the carburetor (**Figure 70**).

7

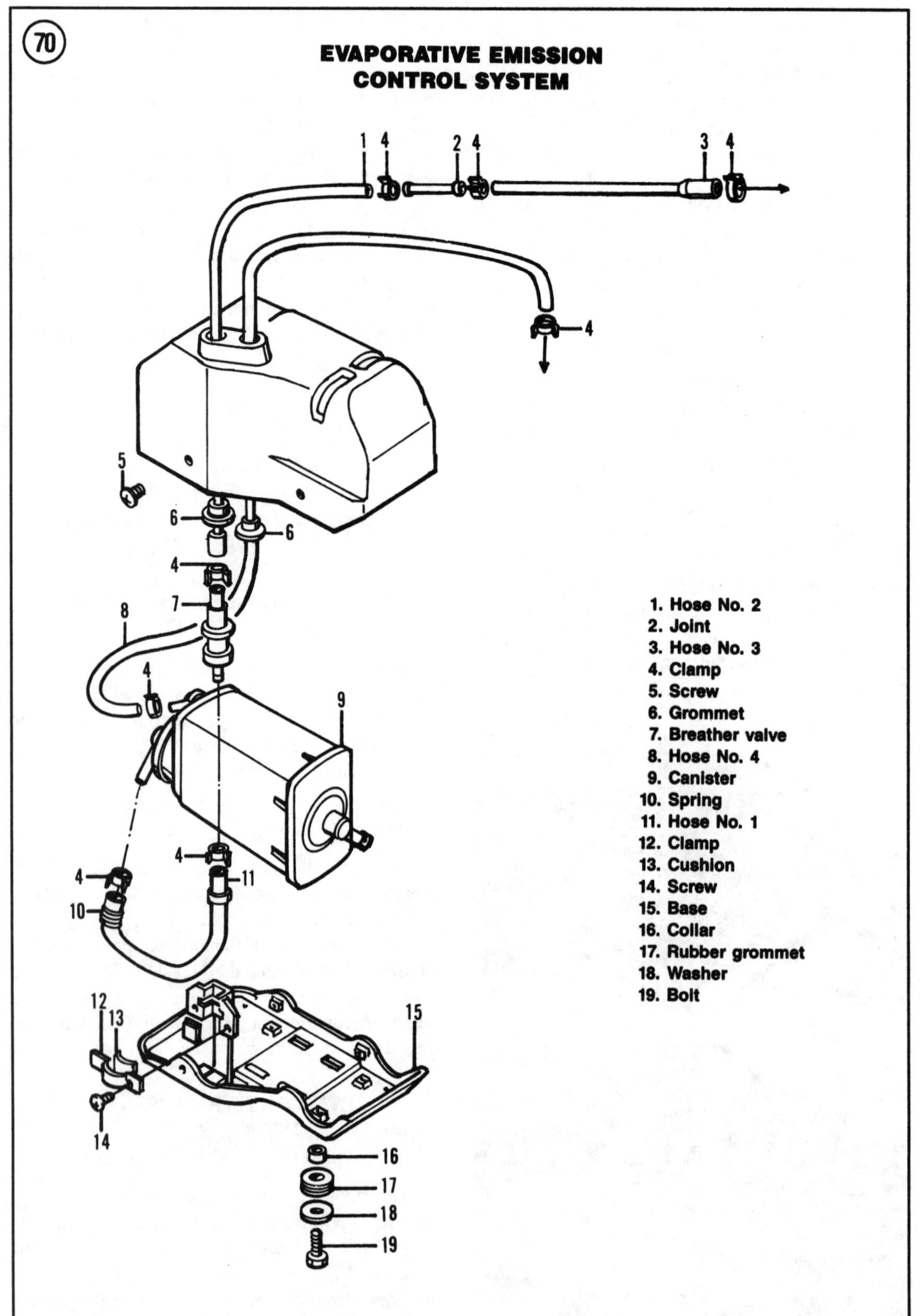
70
EVAPORATIVE EMISSION
CONTROL SYSTEM
1. Hose No. 2
2. Joint
3. Hose No. 3
4. Clamp
5. Screw
6. Grommet
7. Breather valve
8. Hose No. 4
9. Canister
10. Spring
11. Hose No. 1
12. Clamp
13. Cushion
14. Screw
15. Base
16. Collar
17. Rubber grommet
18. Washer
19. Bolt

Make sure all hose clamps are tight. Check all hoses for deterioration and replace as necessary.

When removing the hoses from any component in the system, mark each hose and the fitting with a piece of masking tape and identify where the hose goes. There are so many vacuum hoses on these models that reconnecting the hoses can be very confusing.

The charcoal canister is located just forward of the rear wheel. Refer to **Figure 71** and **Figure 72** for canister hose routing.

### Charcoal Canister Removal/Installation

*NOTE*
*Before removing the hoses from the charcoal canister, mark each hose and the fitting with a piece of masking tape and identify where the hose goes.*

1. Remove the seat as described in Chapter Twelve.

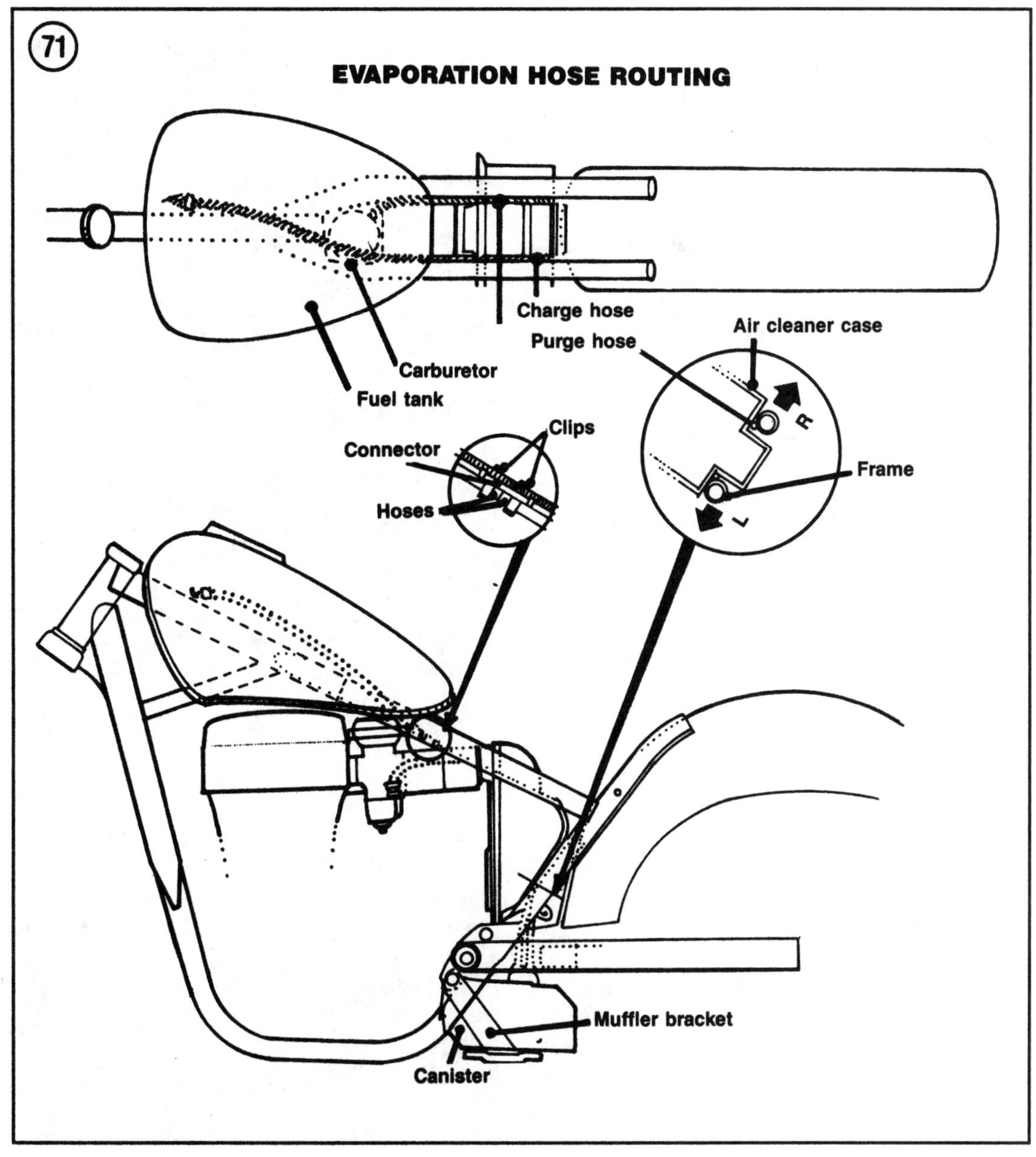

2. Disconnect the hose at the connector (**Figure 65**), going to the fuel tank, at the rear of the fuel tank.
3. Disconnect the hose (**Figure 73**) going to the carburetor.
4. Remove the bolts, washers and rubber cushions securing the charcoal canister assembly (**Figure 74**) to the frame and remove the canister assembly. Don't lose the spacer located within each rubber cushion.
5. To replace the canister, perform the following:
   a. Remove the screws securing the canister cover and move the cover up off of the base.
   b. Disconnect the vacuum hose No.1 and No. 4 from the old charcoal canister and transfer them to the new charcoal canister.
   c. Slide the cover back down and reinstall the screws.
6. Install by reversing these removal steps.
7. Be sure to install the hoses to their correct fitting on the charcoal canister and the vacuum control valves.
8. Make sure the hoses are not kinked, twisted or in contact with any sharp surfaces.

## EXHAUST SYSTEM

The exhaust system is a vital performance component and frequently, because of its design, it is a vulnerable piece of equipment. Check the exhaust system for deep dents and fractures and repair or replace them immediately. Check the cylinder head mounting flanges for tightness. A loose exhaust pipe connection can rob the engine of power.

### Removal/Installation

Refer to **Figure 75** for this procedure.

*WARNING*
*Do not work on the exhaust system when it is hot. Allow the system to cool down before working on it.*

1. Remove the nuts and washers (A, **Figure 76**) securing the front heat shield (B, **Figure 76**) and the front right-hand footpeg. Remove the heat shield and footpeg assembly. Reinstall the nuts and washers onto the bolts as these are engine mounting bolts and must be kept in place.
2. Remove the bolts (**Figure 77**) securing the exhaust pipe clamp to the cylinder head. Remove and discard the cylinder head gasket.
3. Remove the nuts, washers and rubber cushions securing the muffler to the muffler hanger. Don't lose the spacer located within each rubber cushion.
4. Move the exhaust system forward and withdraw the system out from the frame.
5. To separate the muffler from the exhaust pipe, perform the following:
   a. Remove the bolt and clamp securing the rear heat shield and remove the heat shield.

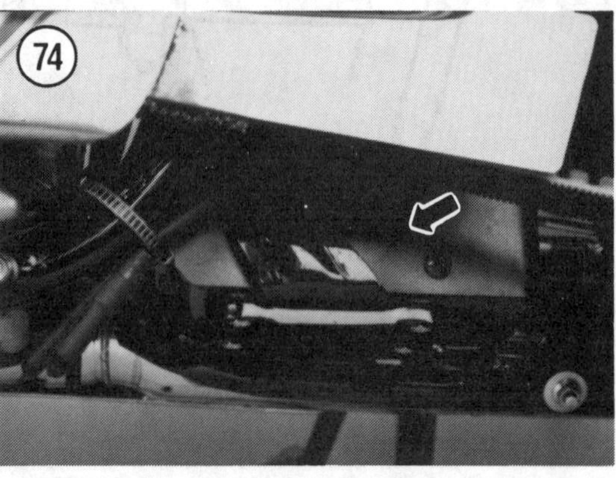

75

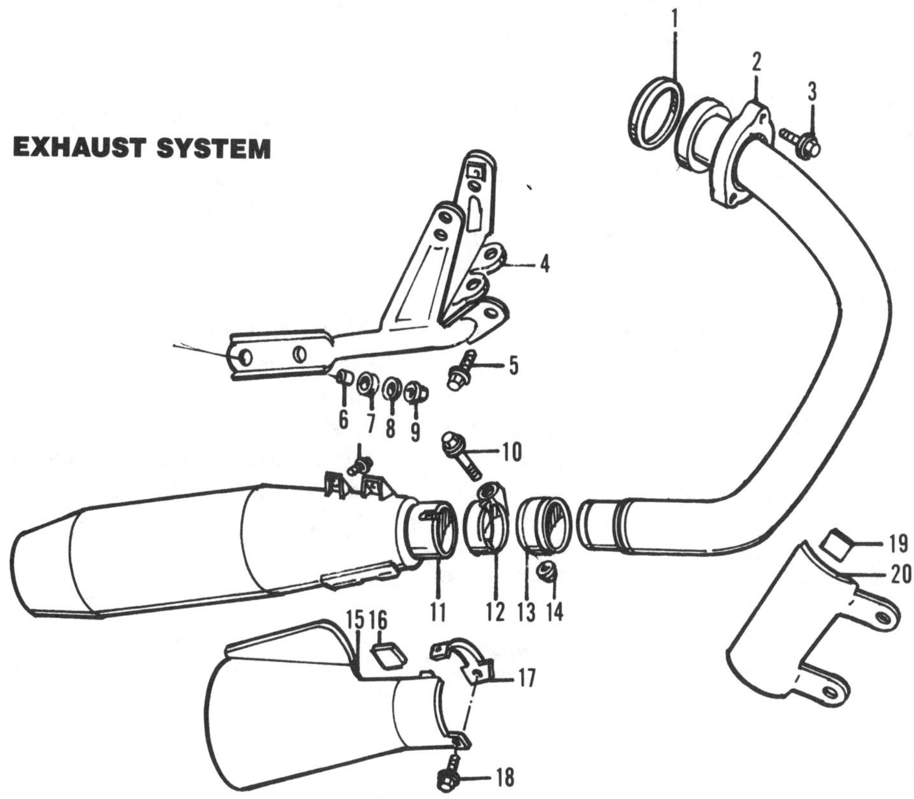

**EXHAUST SYSTEM**

1. Gasket
2. Clamp
3. Bolt
4. Muffler bracket
5. Bolt
6. Spacer
7. Cushion
8. Washer
9. Nut
10. Bolt
11. Muffler
12. Clamp
13. Connector
14. Nut
15. Rear heat shield
16. Pad
17. Clamp
18. Bolt
19. Pad
20. Front heat shield

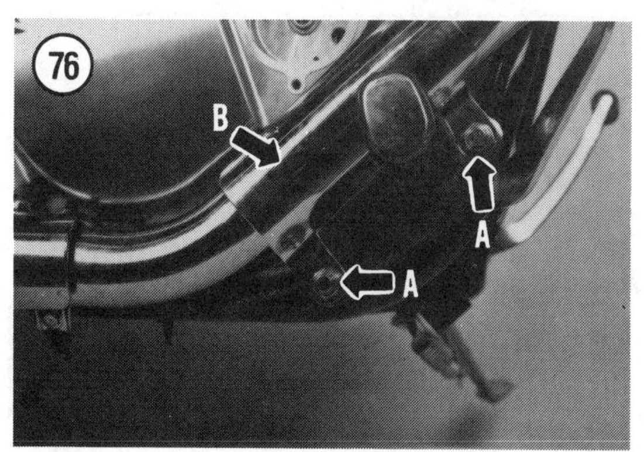

b. Loosen the bolt on the muffler clamp.
c. Withdraw the muffler from the exhaust pipe.
d. Inspect the connector on the exhaust pipe and replace if necessary.
e. Assemble by reversing these disassembly steps.

6. Install a new gasket in the exhaust port in the cylinder head.
7. Install the exhaust system onto the frame and engine.
8. Install the exhaust pipe clamp bolts (on the cylinder head) only finger-tight until the rest of the nuts and washers are installed.
9. Install the nuts, washers and rubber cushions securing the muffler to the muffler hanger. Don't forget the spacer located within each rubber cushion. Tighten the nuts only finger-tight at this time.
10. Tighten the exhaust pipe clamp bolts to the torque specification listed in **Table 2**.

*NOTE*
*Tightening the exhaust pipe bolts at the cylinder head first will minimize exhaust leaks at the cylinder head.*

11. Tighten the muffler mounting nuts securely.
12. After installation is complete, start the engine and make sure there are no exhaust leaks.
13. Remove the nuts and washers from the engine front mounting bolts.
14. Install the front footpeg assembly and the front heat shield onto the bolts. Reinstall the washers and nuts and tighten to the torque specification listed in **Table 2**.

**Table 1 CARBURETOR SPECIFICATIONS**

| | |
|---|---|
| Carburetor type | Mikuni BS40SS |
| Model No. | |
| 49-state | 24B00 |
| California | 24B20 |
| Venturi diameter | 40 mm (1.57 in.) |
| Fuel level | 6.5-7.5 mm (0.256-0.296 in.) |
| Float level | 26.95-28.95 mm (1.06-1.14 in.) |
| Needle clip position | fixed |
| Jet needle | 5C17 |
| Needle jet | X-6 |
| Main jet No. | 155 |
| Main air jet No. | 0.6 mm |
| Pilot jet No. | 47.5 |
| Pilot outlet | 1.3 mm |
| Starter jet No. | 22.5 |
| Pilot screw | pre-set |
| Pilot air jet No. | |
| No. 1 | 67.5 |
| No. 2 | 2.0 mm |

**Table 2 EXHAUST SYSTEM TORQUE SPECIFICATIONS**

| Item | N·m | ft.-lb. |
|---|---|---|
| Exhaust pipe clamp bolts | 18-28 | 13-20 |
| Engine front mounting bolt nuts | 70-88 | 51-63 |

# CHAPTER EIGHT

# ELECTRICAL SYSTEM

This chapter contains operating principles and the service and test procedures for all electrical and ignition components. Information regarding the battery and spark plug are covered in Chapter Three.

The electrical system includes the following systems:

a. Charging system.
b. Ignition system.
c. Lighting system.

**Tables 1-3** are at the end of this chapter.

8

## CHARGING SYSTEM

The charging system consists of the battery, alternator and a solid-state voltage regulator/ rectifier (**Figure 1**). Alternating current generated

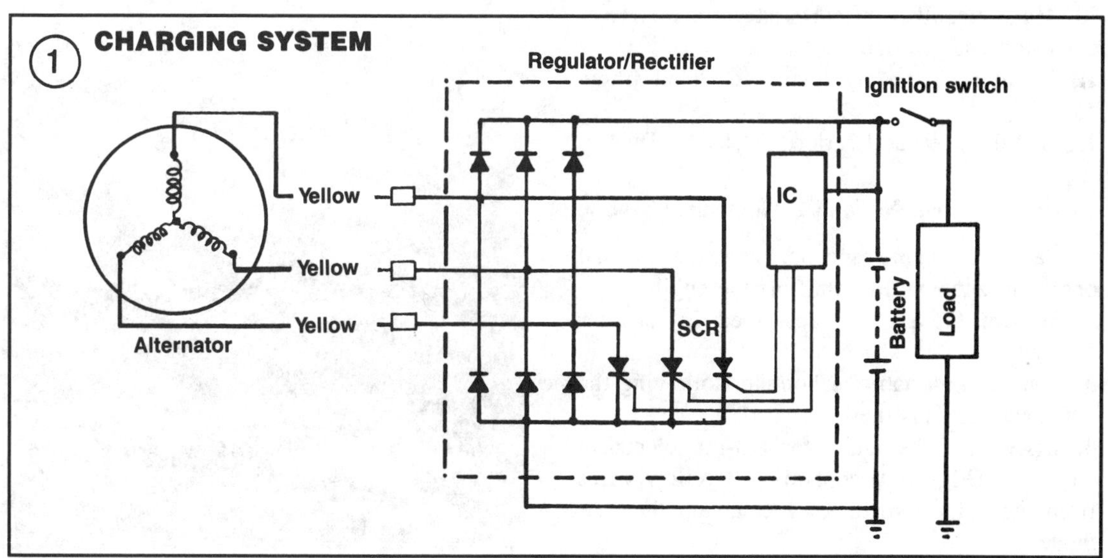

by the alternator is rectified to direct current. The voltage regulator maintains the voltage to the electrical load (lights, ignition, etc.) at a constant voltage regardless of variations in engine speed and load.

### Charging System Output Test

Whenever charging system trouble is suspected, make sure the battery is fully charged and in good condition before going any further. Clean and test the battery as described in Chapter Three. Make sure all electrical connectors are tight and free of corrosion.

1. Start the engine and let it reach normal operating temperature. Shut off the engine.
2. Remove the seat as described in Chapter Twelve.
3. Remove both the right- and left-hand frame covers (**Figure 2**).
4. Connect a portable tachometer following the manufacturer's instructions.
5. Turn the headlight dimmer switch to the HI position.
6. Start the engine and let it idle.
7. Connect a 0-30 DC voltmeter to the battery negative (–) and positive (+) terminals (**Figure 3**).
8. Increase engine speed to 5,000 rpm. The voltage reading should be between 14.0-15.5 volts. If the voltage is under 14.0 volts or above 15.5 volts, test the alternator with the *Charging System No-load Performance Test* procedure in this chapter.
9. After the test is completed, disconnect the voltmeter and tachometer and shut off the engine.
10. Make sure all electrical connectors are free of corrosion and are tight.
11. Install both the right- and left-hand frame covers.
12. Install the seat as described in Chapter Twelve.

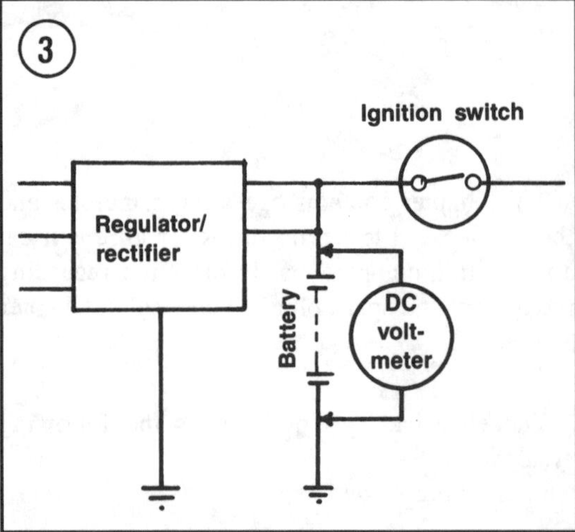


### Charging System No-load Performance Test

1. Start the engine and let it reach normal operating temperature. Shut off the engine.
2. Remove the seat as described in Chapter Twelve.
3. Connect a portable tachometer following the manufacturer's instructions.
4. Disconnect the alternator's 3-pin electrical connector (**Figure 4**) containing 3 yellow wires from the voltage regulator located on the rear fender.

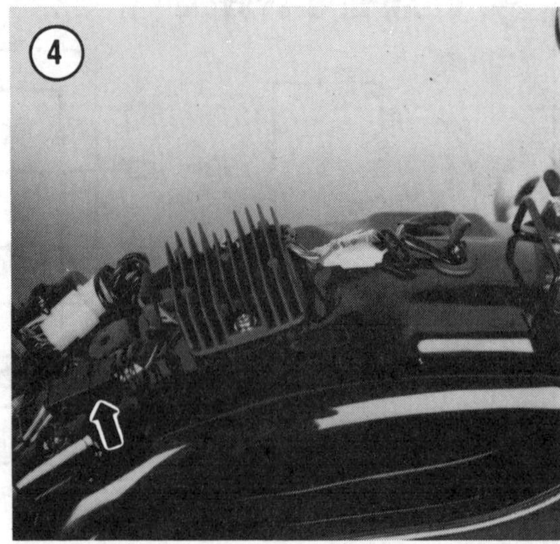

5. Start the engine and let it idle, then increase engine speed to 5,000 rpm.

*NOTE*

*In Step 6 connect the voltmeter test leads to the alternator stator side of the electrical connector disconnected in Step 4.*

6. Connect a 0-150 AC voltmeter between each of the yellow wire electrical connectors as shown in (**Figure 5**).
7. The voltage reading should be above 100 volts at each of the 3 test points. If the voltage is less than specified, the alternator is faulty and must be replaced.
8. After the test is completed, disconnect the voltmeter and portable tachometer and shut off the engine.
9. Reconnect the alternator's 3-pin electrical connector (**Figure 4**) containing 3 yellow wires to the voltage regulator.

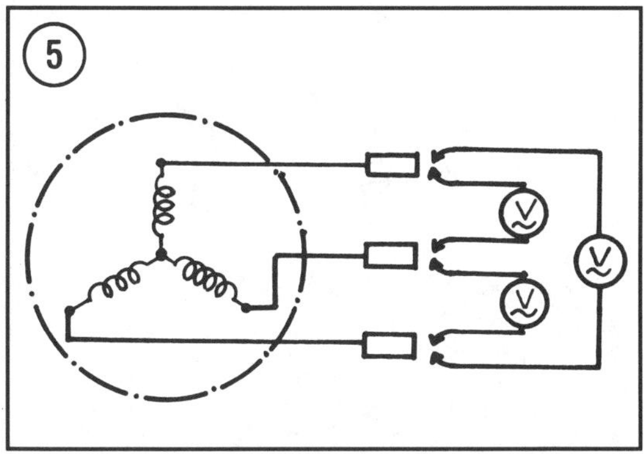


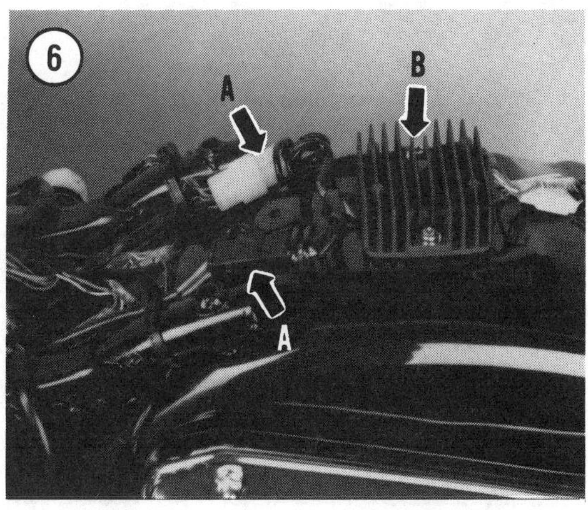


10. Make sure all electrical connectors are free of corrosion and are tight.
11. Install the seat as described in Chapter Twelve.

## VOLTAGE REGULATOR/RECTIFIER

### Testing

Complete testing of the voltage regulator/rectifier requires a special Suzuki tester and should be tested by a Suzuki dealer.

The dealer will either test the voltage regulator/rectifier with the special tool or perform a "remove and replace" test to see if the voltage regulator/rectifier is faulty. This type of test is expensive if performed by yourself. Remember if you purchase a new voltage regulator/rectifier and it does *not* solve your particular charging system problem, you cannot return the unit for refund. Most motorcycle dealers will *not* accept returns on any electrical component since they could be damaged internally even though they look okay externally.

Make sure all connections between the various components are clean and tight. Be sure that the wiring connectors are pushed together firmly to help keep out moisture.

### Removal/Installation

1. Remove the seat as described in Chapter Twelve.
2. Disconnect both alternator's 3-pin electrical connectors (A, **Figure 6**) from the voltage regulator located on the rear fender.
3. Remove the screws and washers securing the voltage regulator/rectifier unit (B, **Figure 6**) to the rear fender and remove the unit.
4. Install by reversing these removal steps. Note the following during installation.
5. Make sure all electrical connectors are free of corrosion and are tight.

## ALTERNATOR

### Stator Continuity Check

1. Start the engine and let it reach normal operating temperature. Shut off the engine.

2. Remove the seat as described in Chapter Twelve.
3. Disconnect the alternator's 3-pin electrical connector (**Figure 4**) containing 3 yellow wires from the voltage regulator located on the rear fender.
4. Use an ohmmeter set at R × 10 and check for continuity between each stator yellow wire (**Figure 7**).
5. There should be continuity (low resistance). If there is no continuity (infinite resistance) the stator assembly is faulty and must be replaced as described in this chapter.
6. Make sure all electrical connectors are free of corrosion and are tight.
7. Reconnect the alternator's 3-pin electrical connector (**Figure 4**) containing 3 yellow wires to the voltage regulator.
8. Make sure all electrical connectors are free of corrosion and are tight.
9. Install the seat as described in Chapter Twelve.

**Stator Assembly Removal/Installation**

Refer to **Figure 8** for this procedure.
1. Remove the seat as described in Chapter Twelve.
2. Remove the left-hand frame cover.
3. Disconnect the battery negative lead (**Figure 9**).

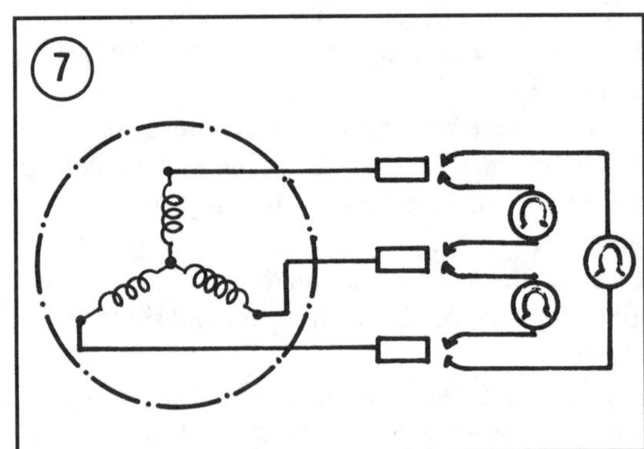


8

**ALTERNATOR**

1 2 1 3

4 5 6 7 8 1 9

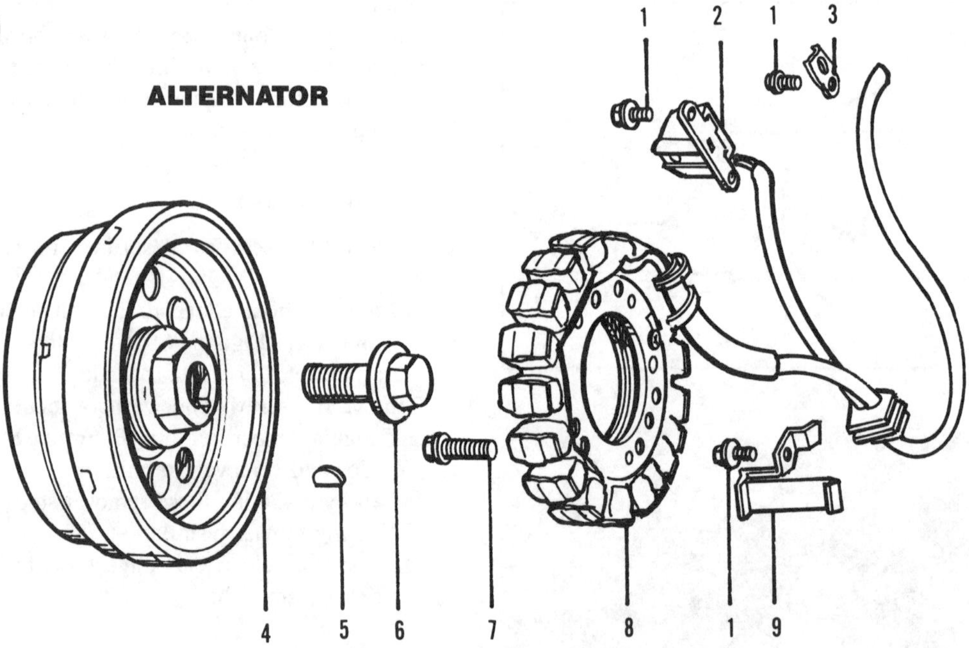

1. Bolt
2. Pulse generator
3. Clamp
4. Rotor
5. Woodruff key
6. Bolt
7. Bolt
8. Stator assembly
9. Clamp

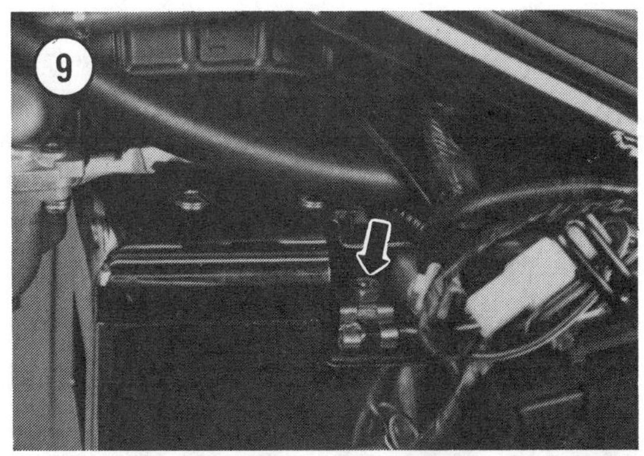


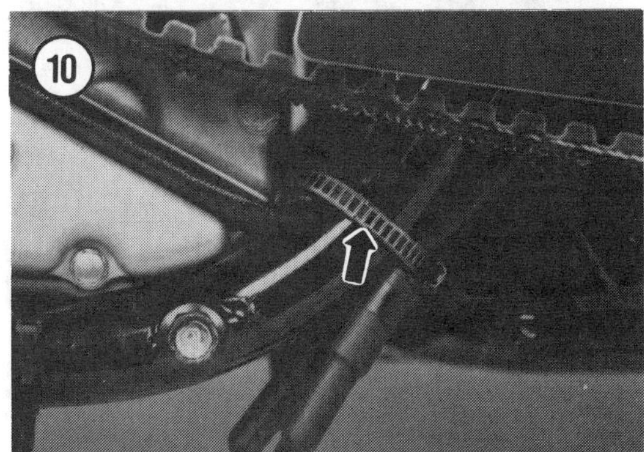


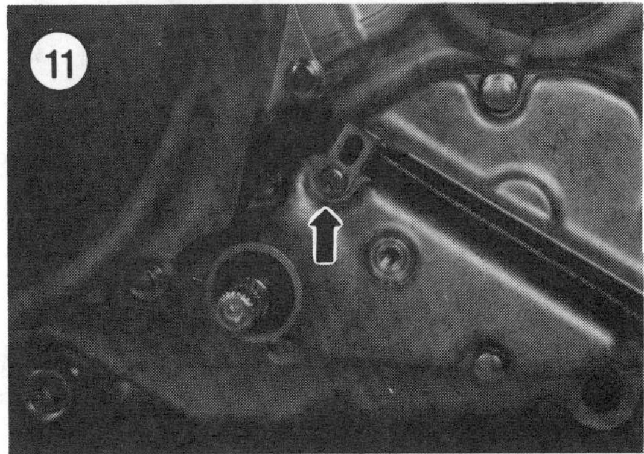

4. Disconnect the alternator's 3-pin electrical connector (**Figure 4**) containing 3 yellow wires from the voltage regulator located on the rear fender.
5. Drain the engine oil as described under *Engine Oil and Filter Change* in Chapter Three.
6. Remove the drive pulley guard and the drive pulley as described under *Left-hand Crankcase Cover and Drive Pulley Removal/Installation* in Chapter Four.
7. Remove the tie wrap (**Figure 10**) securing the alternator electrical cable and emission control hoses to the frame.

*NOTE*

***Figure 11*** *is shown with the engine removed from the frame for clarity. It is not necessary to remove the engine to perform this procedure.*

8. Remove the bolt (**Figure 11**) securing the stator assembly electrical cable to the external shift mechanism cover.
9. Remove the engine left-hand crankcase cover as described in Chapter Four.
10. To remove the alternator stator assembly from the left-hand crankcase cover, perform the following:
    a. Turn the alternator cover upside down on several shop cloths to protect the finish.
    b. Remove the bolts (A, **Figure 12**) securing the stator assembly to the alternator cover.
    c. Remove the screws securing the pickup coil (B, **Figure 12**) and the wiring harness strap and clamp.
    d. Remove the bolt and wire clamp (C, **Figure 12**) securing the electrical wire harness to the left-hand crankcase cover.
    e. Remove the rubber grommet (D, **Figure 12**) from the receptacle in the alternator cover and remove the stator assembly from the cover.
11. Install by reversing these removal steps. Note the following during installation.
12. Apply blue Loctite Threadlocker No. 242 to the screw and bolt threads prior to installation. Tighten all screws and bolts securely.
13. Install a new cover gasket.

14. Tighten the cover bolts securely.

*WARNING*
*Be sure to secure the alternator electrical cable and emission control hoses back to the frame as shown in **Figure 10**. If the electrical cable is not secured as shown, it will move over and the drive belt will rub on it. The drive belt will wear through the insulation and an electrical short or open will occur.*

15. Install the tie wrap (**Figure 10**) securing the alternator electrical cable and emission control hoses to the frame.
16. Make sure the electrical connector is free of corrosion and is tight.
17. Fill the engine with the recommended type and quantity of oil as described under *Engine Oil and Filter Change* in Chapter Three.

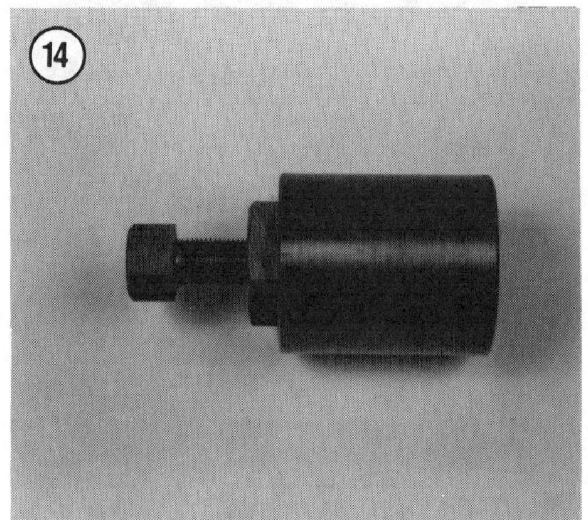


### Rotor Testing

The rotor is permanently magnetized and cannot be tested except by replacement of a rotor known to be good. A rotor can lose magnetism from old age or a sharp blow. If defective, the rotor must be replaced; it cannot be remagnetized.

### Rotor Removal/Installation

*NOTE*
*This procedure is shown with the engine remove from the frame and partially disassembled for clarity. It is not necessary to remove the engine to remove the rotor assembly.*

1. Remove the stator assembly as described in this chapter.
2. Using a 36 mm offset wrench, hold onto the flats on the rotor (A, **Figure 13**).

*NOTE*
*In Step 3, do not remove the rotor bolt. Loosen it several turns and leave it in place. The bolt must remain installed as it is used in conjunction with the rotor remover tool in Step 4.*

3. Loosen the rotor bolt (B, **Figure 13**) several turns.

*CAUTION*
*Do not try to remove the rotor without a puller; any attempt to do so will lead to some form of damage to the engine and/or the rotor. Many aftermarket types of pullers are available from most motorcycle dealers or mail order houses. The puller is relatively inexpensive and makes an excellent addition to any mechanic's tool box. If you can't purchase or borrow one, have a dealer remove the rotor for you.*

4. Screw the Suzuki special tool (Rotor remover, part No. 09930-30720) (**Figure 14**) onto the rotor.
5. Hold onto the rotor remover with the 36 mm offset wrench and turn the center bolt (**Figure 15**) of the rotor remover. Turn the center bolt until the rotor disengages from the crankshaft.
6. Unscrew the special tool from the rotor.
7. Unscrew the rotor bolt.
8. Remove the rotor from the crankshaft. Don't lose the Woodruff key on the crankshaft.

*CAUTION*
*Carefully inspect the inside of the rotor for small bolts, washers, other metal "trash" that may have been picked up by the magnets. These small metal bits can cause severe damage to the stator assembly components as the rotor revolves around it.*

9. Make sure the Woodruff key is in place on the crankshaft.
10. Align the keyway in the rotor with the Woodruff key on the crankshaft while installing the rotor. Push the rotor on until it bottoms out.
11. Apply red Loctite Threadlocker No. 271 to the rotor bolt threads prior to installation. Screw on the rotor bolt.
12. Using a 36 mm offset wrench, hold onto the flats on the rotor.
13. Use a wrench on the rotor bolt and tighten to the torque specification listed in **Table 1**.
14. Install the stator assembly as described in this chapter.

## TRANSISTORIZED IGNITION SYSTEM

The Savage is equipped with a transistorized ignition system, a solid-state system that uses no breaker points. The ignition circuit is shown in **Figure 16**.

The signal generator consists of a raised tab on the alternator rotor and a pickup coil attached to the alternator cover next to the alternator stator coil assembly. As the alternator rotor is turned by the crankshaft, the raised tab passes by the pickup coil and a signal is sent to the ignitor unit. This signal turns the ignitor unit transistor alternately on and off. As the transistor is turned on and off, the current passing through the primary windings of the ignition coil, is also turned on and off. This induces the secondary current on the ignition coils secondary windings to produce the current necessary to fire the spark plug.

A decompression control unit is built into the ignition circuit. This control unit is described in this chapter.



### Transistorized Ignition System Precautions

Certain measures must be taken to protect the ignition system. Instantaneous damage to the semiconductors in the system will occur if the following precautions are not observed.

1. Never disconnect any of the electrical connections while the engine is running.
2. Keep all connections between the various units clean and tight. Be sure that the wiring connectors are pushed together firmly to help keep out moisture.
3. Do not substitute another type of ignition coil.

### Troubleshooting

Problems with the transistorized ignition system fall into one of the following categories. See **Table 2**.

a. Weak spark.
b. No spark.

### Signal Generator (Pickup Coil) Testing

1. Remove the seat as described in Chapter Twelve.

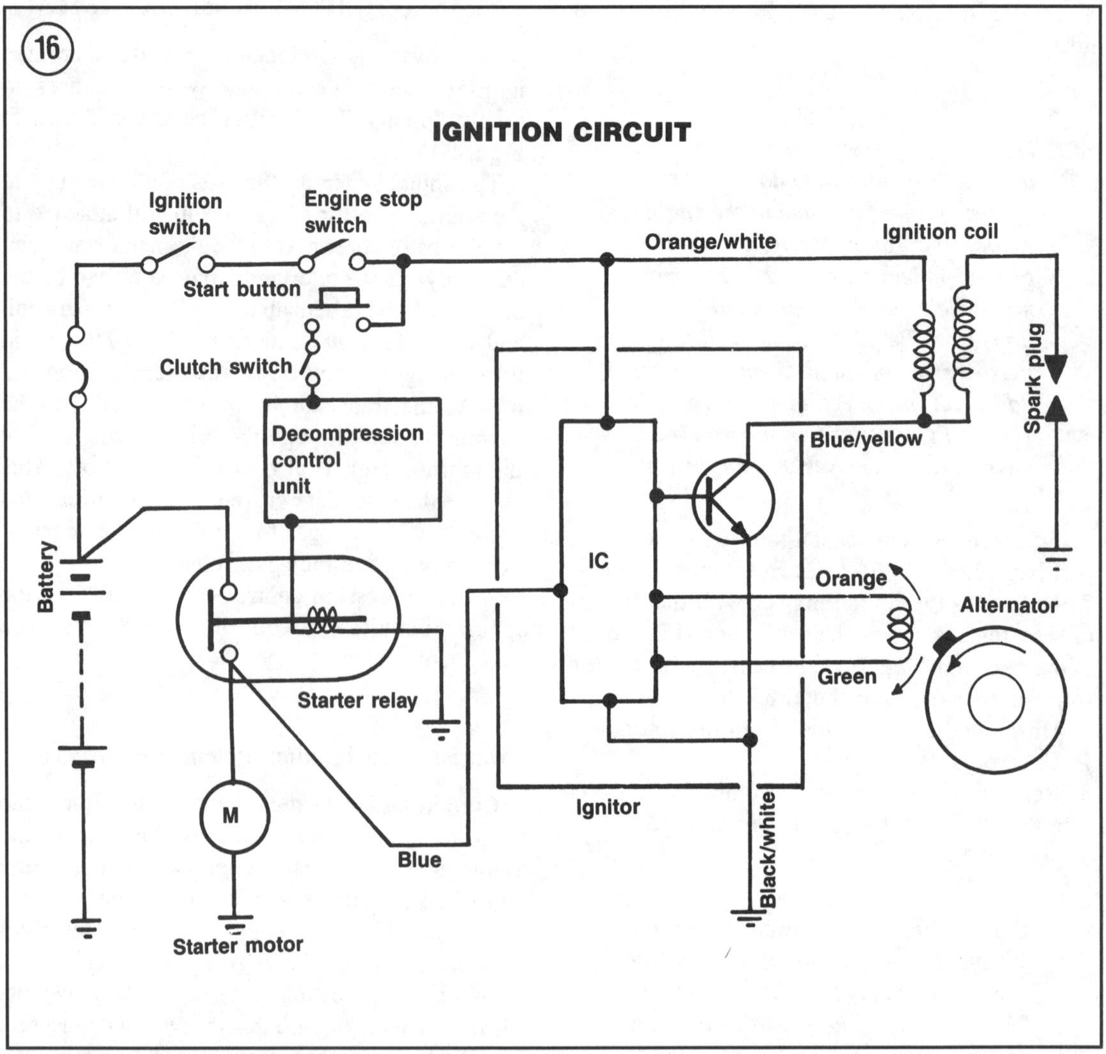

16
IGNITION CIRCUIT
Ignition switch
Engine stop switch
Start button
Clutch switch
Decompression control unit
Orange/white
Ignition coil
Spark plug
Blue/yellow
IC
Orange
Alternator
Green
Battery
Starter relay
Ignitor
M
Blue
Black/white
Starter motor

17
A
B

18

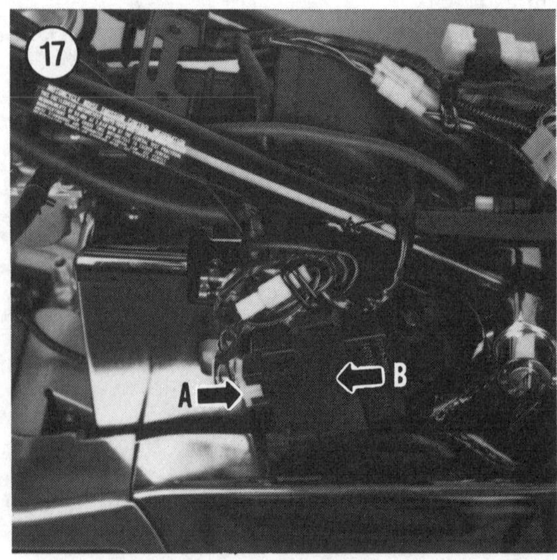

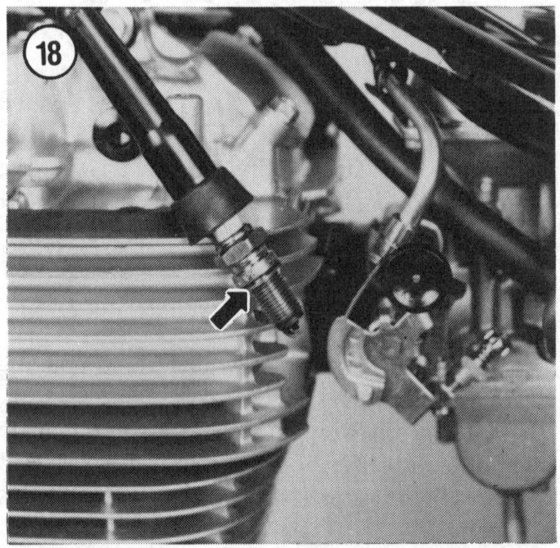

2. Remove the left-hand frame cover.
3. Disconnect the 2-pin electrical connector (1 orange and 1 green wire) from the signal generator (A, **Figure 17**).
4. Use an ohmmeter set at R × 1000 and check the resistance between both wires in the electrical connector. The specified resistance is 200-240 ohms.
5. If the resistance shown is less than specified or there is no indicated resistance (infinite resistance) between the 2 wires, the signal generator has an open or short and must be replaced as described in this chapter.
6. If the signal generator checks out okay, reconnect the electrical connector. Make sure the electrical connector is free of corrosion and is tight.
7. Install the left-hand frame cover and the seat.

### Signal Generator Removal/Installation

The signal generator is part of the alternator stator coil assembly and cannot be replaced separately. If the signal generator is faulty, the alternator stator assembly must be replaced as described in this chapter.

### Ignition Coil Testing

The ignition coil is a form of transformer which develops the high voltage required to jump the spark plug gap. The only maintenance required is that of keeping the electrical connections clean and tight and occasionally checking to see that the coil is mounted securely.

If the condition of the coil is doubtful, there are several checks which may be made.

*NOTE*
*The spark plug must ground out against a piece of bare metal on the engine or frame.*

First as a quick check of coil condition, perform the following:

a. Remove the spark plug from the cylinder as described under *Spark Plug Removal/Cleaning* in Chapter Three.
b. Connect the spark plug wire and connector to the spark plug and touch the spark plug's base to a good ground such as the engine cylinder head (**Figure 18**). Make sure the spark plug is against bare metal, not a painted surface. Position the spark plug so you can see the electrodes.

*WARNING*
*If it is necessary to hold the high voltage lead, do so with an insulated pair of pliers. The high voltage generated by the signal generator could produce serious or fatal shocks.*

c. Turn the engine over with the starter. If a fat blue spark occurs, the coil is in good condition; if not, proceed as follows. Make sure that you are using a known good spark plug for this test. If the spark plug used is defective, the test results will be incorrect.
d. Reinstall the spark plug in the cylinder head and connect the high voltage lead.

8

*NOTE*
*In order to get accurate resistance measurements, the coil must be warm (minimum temperature is 20° C/68° F). If necessary, start the engine and let it warm up to normal operating temperature.*

1. Remove the seat as described in Chapter Twelve.
2. Remove the fuel tank as described in Chapter Seven.
3. Disconnect all ignition coil wires (including the spark plug lead from the spark plug) before testing.

*NOTE*
*In Step 4 and Step 5, the resistance specification is not as important as the fact that there is continuity between the terminals. If the ignition coil windings are in good condition, the resistance values will be close to those specified.*

4. Use an ohmmeter set at R × 1 and measure the primary coil resistance between the positive (+) and the negative (-) terminals on the top of the ignition coil (**Figure 19**). The specified resistance value is 1-7 ohms.
5. Use an ohmmeter set at R × 150,000 to measure the secondary coil resistance between the spark plug lead and one of the primary coil terminals. The specified resistance value is 10,000-25,000 ohms.
6. If the coil resistance does not meet (or come close to) either of these specifications, the coil must be replaced. If the coil exhibits visible damage, it should be replaced as described in this chapter.
7. Reconnect all ignition coil wires to the ignition coil.
8. Install the fuel tank as described in Chapter Seven.
9. Install the seat as described in Chapter Twelve.

## Ignition Coil Removal/Installation

1. Remove the seat as described in Chapter Twelve.
2. Remove the fuel tank as described in Chapter Seven.
3. Remove the frame left-hand side cover.
4. Disconnect the battery negative lead (**Figure 9**).
5. Disconnect the high voltage lead (A, **Figure 20**) from the spark plug.
6. Remove the screws securing the ignition coil (C, **Figure 20**) to the frame.
7. Carefully pull the ignition coil away from the frame and disconnect the primary electrical wires (B, **Figure 20**) from the coil.
8. Install by reversing these removal steps. Note the following during installation.
9. Make sure all electrical connections are free of corrosion and are tight.

## Ignitor Unit Testing

Complete testing of the ignitor unit requires a special Suzuki tool and should be tested by a Suzuki dealer. If the signal generator and the ignition coils are working correctly, then this simple test can be run to check if the ignition unit is working.

The dealer will either test the ignitor unit with the special tool or perform a "remove and replace" test to see if the ignitor unit is faulty. This type of test is expensive to perform yourself. Remember if you purchase a new ignitor unit and it does *not* solve your particular ignition system problem, you cannot return the ignitor unit for refund. Most motorcycle dealers will *not* accept returns on any electrical component since they could be damaged internally even though they look okay externally.

Make sure all connections between the various components are clean and tight. Be sure that the wiring connectors are pushed together firmly to help keep out moisture.

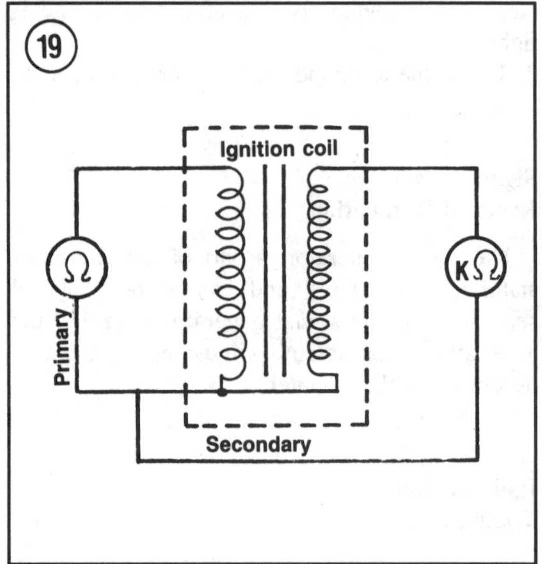


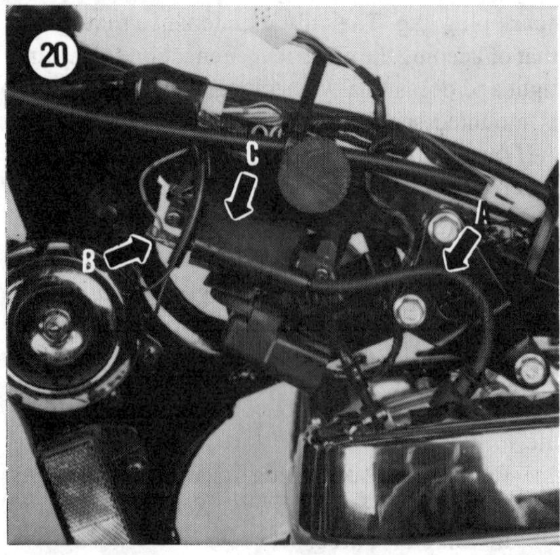

1. Test the signal generator and the ignition coil as described in this chapter before performing this test. If either of these units are faulty, this test will *not* provide any usable test results.
2. Test the ignitor's unit ability to produce a spark. Perform the following:
   a. Remove the spark plug from the cylinder as described in Chapter Three.
   b. Connect the spark plug wire and connector to the spark plug and touch the spark plug's base to a good ground such as the engine cylinder head (**Figure 18**). Make sure the spark plug is against bare metal, not a painted surface. Position the spark plug so you can see the electrodes.

*WARNING*

*If it is necessary to hold the high voltage lead, do so with an insulated pair of pliers. The high voltage generated by the signal generator could produce serious or fatal shocks.*

   c. Turn the engine over with the starter. If a fat blue spark occurs the ignition unit is in good condition.
   d. If a weak spark or no spark is obtained and the signal generator and ignition coil are okay, have the ignitor unit tested by a Suzuki dealer.
   e. Reinstall the spark plug and connect the high voltage lead to the spark plug.
3. If all of the ignition components are okay, then check the following:
   a. Check for an open or short in the wire harness between each component in the system.
   b. Again, make sure all connections between the various components are clean and tight. Be sure that the wiring connectors are pushed together firmly to help keep out moisture.

### Ignitor Unit Replacement

1. Remove the seat as described in Chapter Twelve.
2. Remove the left-hand frame cover.
3. Disconnect the battery negative lead (**Figure 9**).
4. Carefully pull the ignitor unit and its rubber mount (B, **Figure 17**) from the mounting tab on the frame.
5. Disconnect the ignition unit's electrical connector (A, **Figure 17**).
6. Remove the ignitor unit.
7. Attach the electrical connector to the unit. Make sure the electrical connector is free of corrosion and is tight.
8. Install a new ignitor unit onto the frame.
9. Connect the battery negative lead.
10. Install the left-hand frame cover.
11. Install the seat as described in Chapter Twelve.

## STARTING SYSTEM

The starter system includes an ignition switch, a starter switch, clutch interlock switch, sidestand interlock switch (1987-1988 models), automatic decompression control unit, starter solenoid, battery and starter motor as shown in (**Figure 21**). Each component of this system is covered separately in this chapter except for the battery that is covered in Chapter Three.

## ELECTRIC STARTER

8

### Removal/Installation

1. Remove the seat as described in Chapter Twelve.
2. Remove the left-hand frame cover.
3. Disconnect the battery negative lead (**Figure 9**).
4. Slide back the rubber boot (A, **Figure 22**) on the electrical cable connector.
5. Disconnect the starter electrical cable from the starter.
6. Remove the bolts securing the starter (B, **Figure 22**) to the crankcase.
7. Lift up the right-hand end of the starter and withdraw it from the top of the crankcase.
8. Install by reversing these removal steps. Note the following during installation.
9. Make sure the O-ring seal (A, **Figure 23**) is in good condition and is in place on the left-hand end of the starter.
10. Make sure the electrical connector is free of corrosion and is tight.

### Preliminary Inspection

The overhaul of a starter motor is best left to an expert. This procedure shows how to detect a defective starter.

21

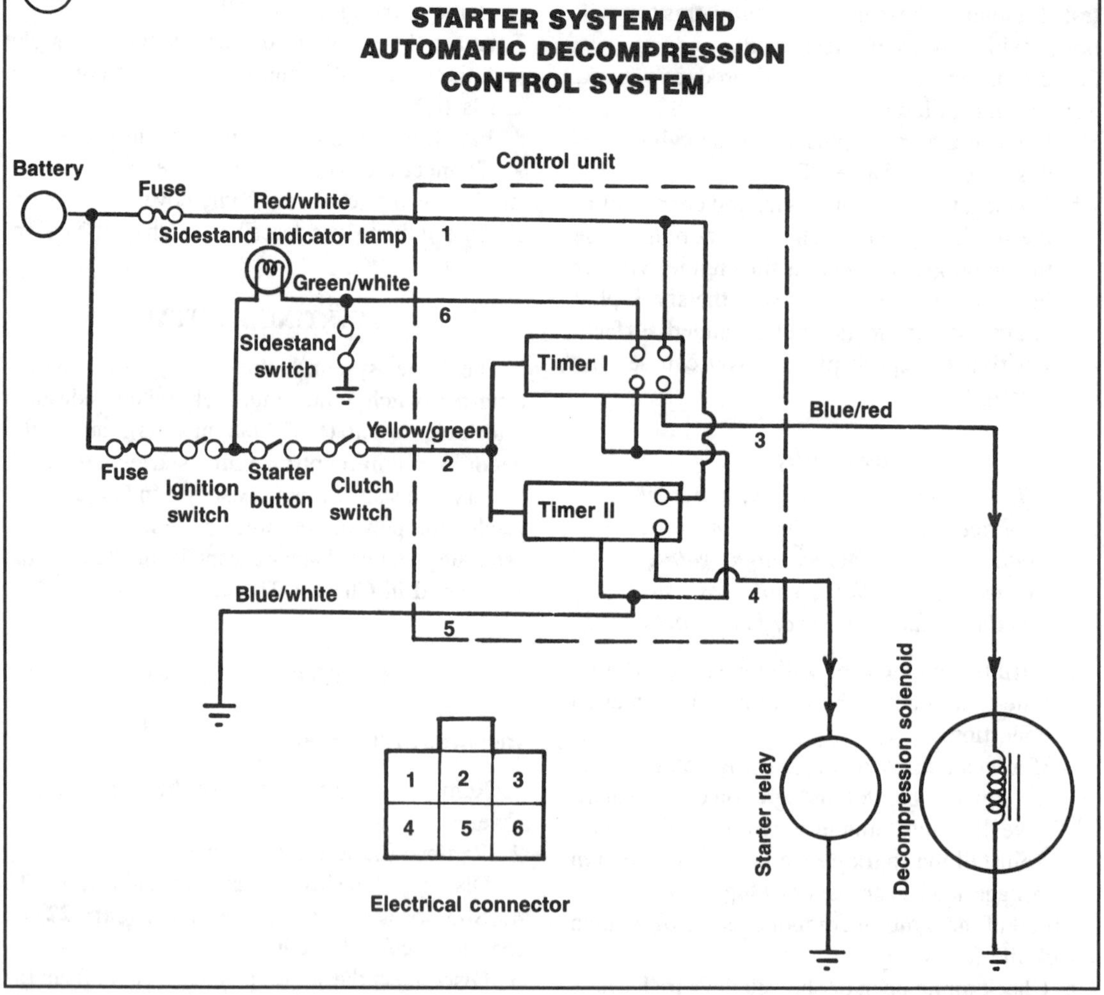

**STARTER SYSTEM AND AUTOMATIC DECOMPRESSION CONTROL SYSTEM**

Battery
Fuse
Red/white
Sidestand indicator lamp
Control unit
1
Green/white
6
Sidestand switch
Timer I
Blue/red
Yellow/green
3
Fuse
Ignition switch
Starter button
Clutch switch
2
Timer II
Blue/white
4
5
Starter relay
Decompression solenoid

| 1 | 2 | 3 |
|---|---|---|
| 4 | 5 | 6 |

Electrical connector

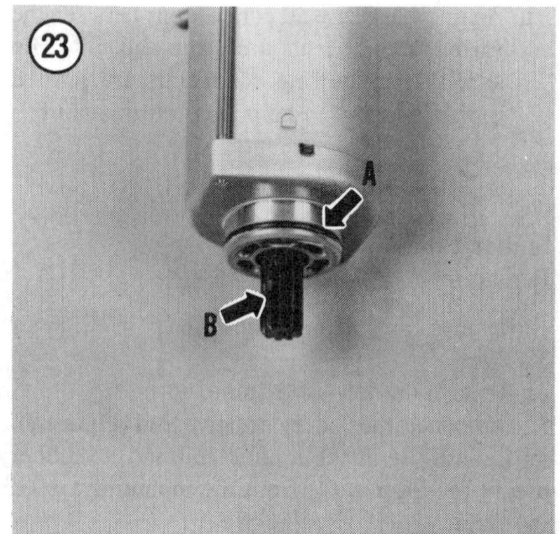

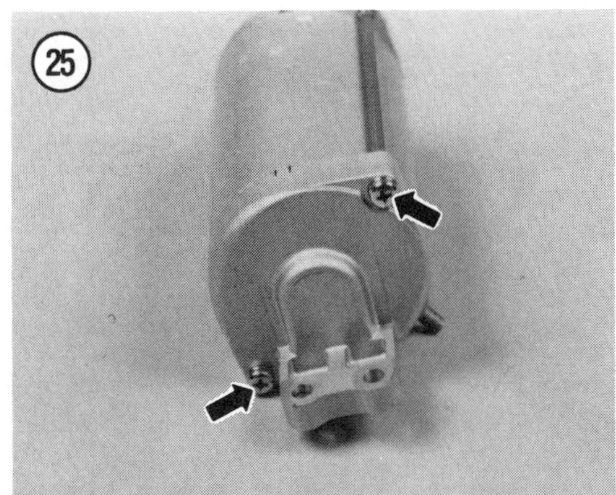

Inspect the O-ring seal (A, **Figure 23**). O-ring seals tend to harden after prolonged use and heat and therefore lose their ability to seal properly. Replace as necessary.

Inspect the gear (B, **Figure 23**) for chipped or missing teeth. If damaged, the starter assembly must be replaced.

### Disassembly

Refer to **Figure 24** for this procedure.

1. Remove the case screws and washers (**Figure 25**), then separate the front and rear covers from the case.

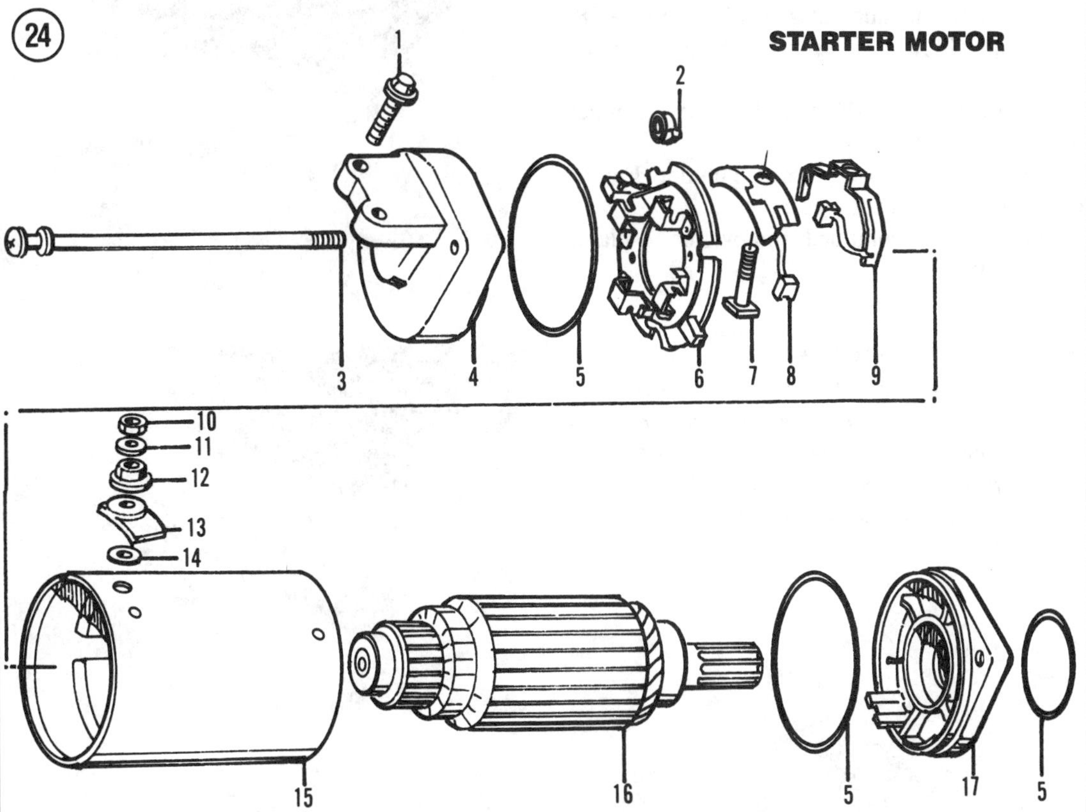

(24)

**STARTER MOTOR**

1. Bolt
2. Brush spring
3. Bolt
4. Right-hand end cap
5. O-ring
6. Brush holder (–)
7. Bolt
8. Inner holder
9. Brush holder (+)
10. Nut
11. Lockwasher
12. Nut
13. Outer bushing
14. O-ring
15. Case (field coils)
16. Armature
17. Left-hand end cap

2. Remove the left-hand end cap and O-ring seal.
3. Remove the right-hand end cap and O-ring seal.
4. Remove the negative (–) brush holder (**Figure 26**) from the case.
5. Withdraw the armature coil assembly (**Figure 27**) from the case.

*NOTE*
*Before removing the nuts and washers, write down their description and order. They must be reinstalled in the same order to insulate this set of brushes from the case.*

6. Remove the nut and outer bushing (**Figure 28**) and O-ring (**Figure 29**) securing the positive and negative brush sets.
7. Remove the bolt (**Figure 30**) and the inner bushing (**Figure 31**).
8. Remove the positive (+) brush holder (**Figure 32**) from the end of the case.
9. On models so equipped, remove the insulator ring (**Figure 33**).

*CAUTION*
*Do not immerse the wire windings in the case or the armature coil in solvent as the insulation may be damaged. Wipe the windings with a cloth lightly moistened with solvent and thoroughly dry.*

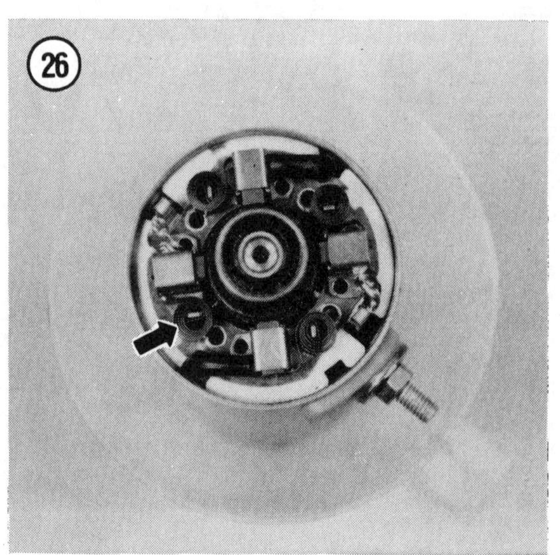
26

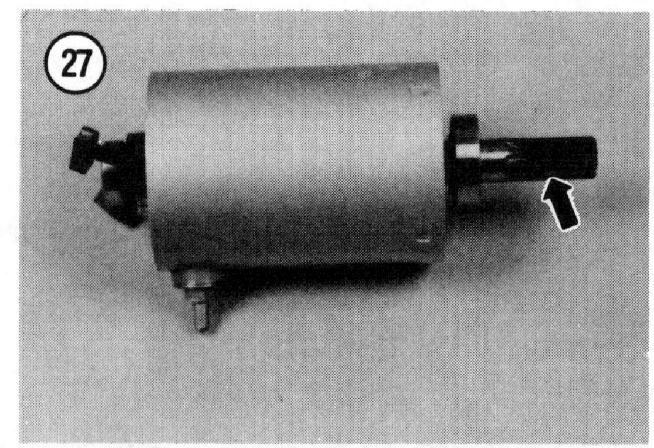
27

28

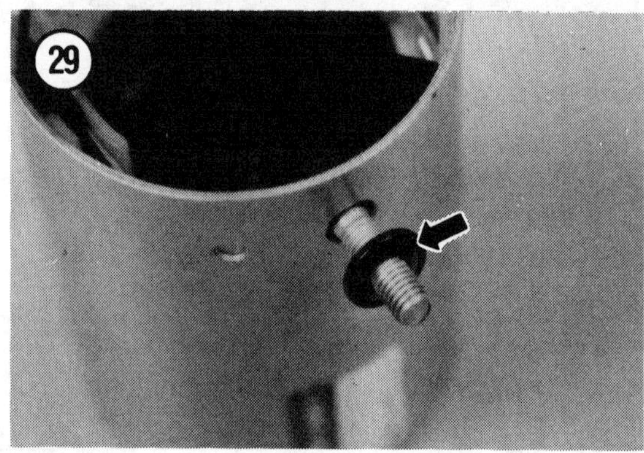
29

30

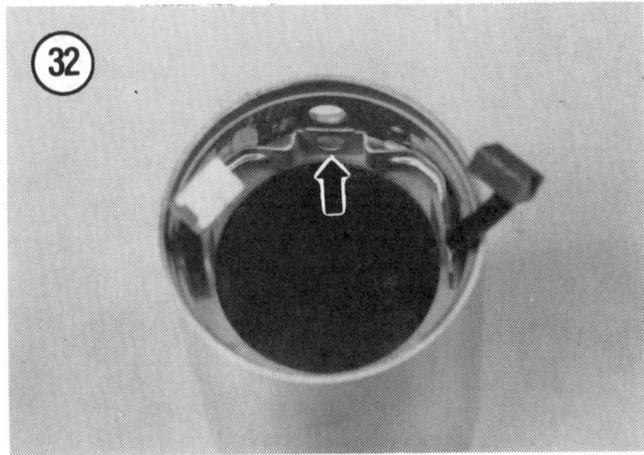

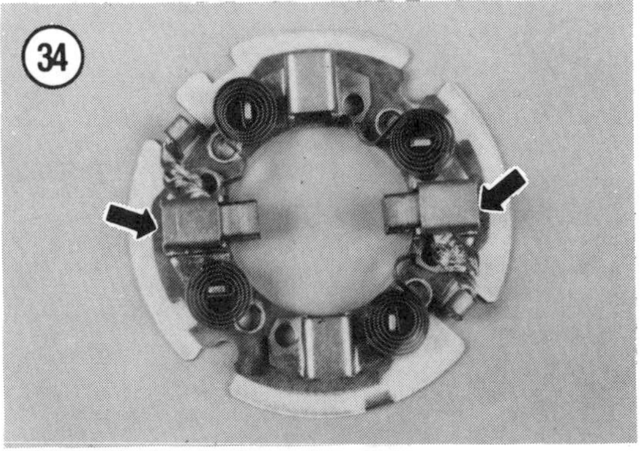

10. Clean all grease, dirt and carbon from all components.
11. Inspect the starter components as described in this chapter.

**Assembly**

1. On models so equipped, install the insulator ring and align the notch with the locating tab on the case (**Figure 33**).
2. Install the positive (+) brush holder (**Figure 32**).
3. Install the inner insulator (**Figure 31**).
4. Install the bolt (**Figure 30**) and install the O-ring (**Figure 29**).
5. Install the outer bushing and nut (**Figure 28**) securing the brush assembly to the case.
6. Insert the armature coil assembly (**Figure 27**) into the left-hand end of the case.
7. Release the springs from the brushes (**Figure 34**) in the negative (-) brush holder.
8. Move the positive (+) brushes out so the negative (-) brush holder can be installed over them. Carefully align the positive brush wires with the notches in the negative brush holder.
9. Install the negative (-) brush holder into the end of the case. Align the notch in the holder with the locating tab (**Figure 35**) in the case.
10. Install the positive (+) brushes into their receptacles in the negative brush holder.
11. Rotate the end of the spring *counterclockwise* and index the spring end into the backside of the brush. Repeat for all 4 brushes.

8

12. Inspect the O-ring seal (**Figure 36**) in the right-hand end cap; replace if necessary.
13. Install the right-hand end cap.
14. Inspect the O-ring seal (**Figure 37**) in the left-hand end cap; replace if necessary.
15. Align the raised tab on the negative (–) brush holder with the locating notch (**Figure 38**) in the right-hand end cap and install the end cap.
16. Align the raised marks on the right hand end cap with the notch on the left-hand end cap (**Figure 39**).
17. Apply blue Loctite Threadlocker No. 242 to the case screw threads prior to installation. Install the case screws (**Figure 40**) and washers, then tighten securely.

### Inspection

1. Measure the length of each brush (**Figure 41**) with a vernier caliper. If the length is 9.0 mm (0.35 in.) or less for any one of the brushes, the brush sets must be replaced. The brushes cannot be replaced individually.
2. Inspect the commutator (A, **Figure 42**). The mica in a good commutator is below the surface of the copper bars. On a worn commutator, the mica and copper bars may be worn to the same level (**Figure 43**). If necessary, have the commutator serviced by a dealer or electrical repair shop.
3. Inspect the commutator copper bars for discoloration. If a pair of bars are discolored, grounded armature coils are indicated.

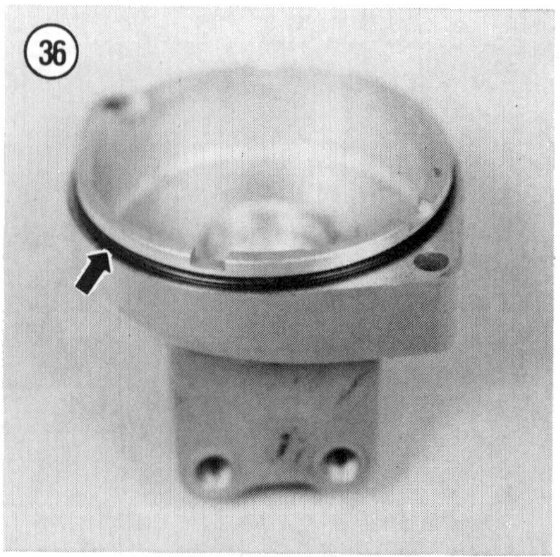
36

37

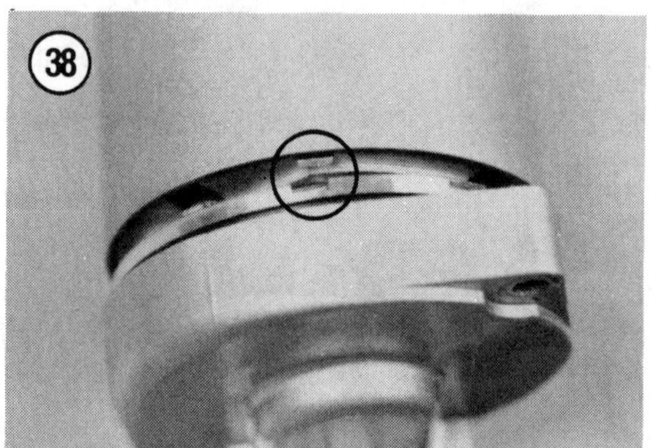
38

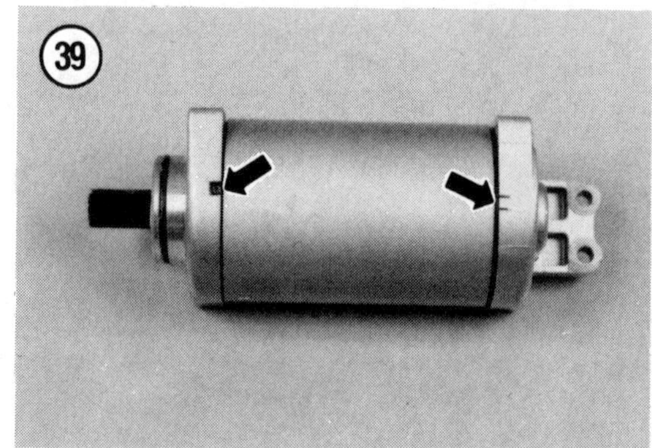
39

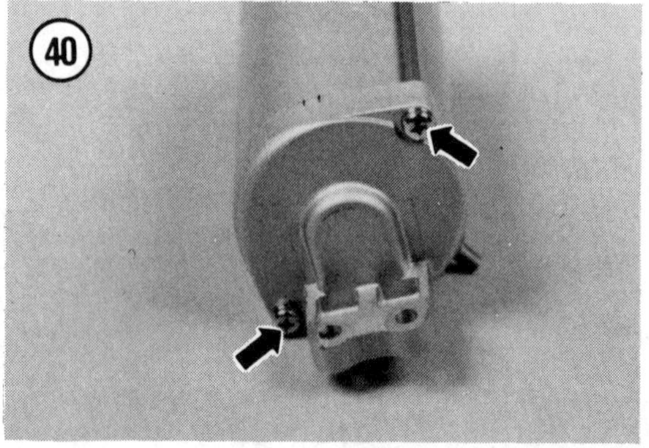
40

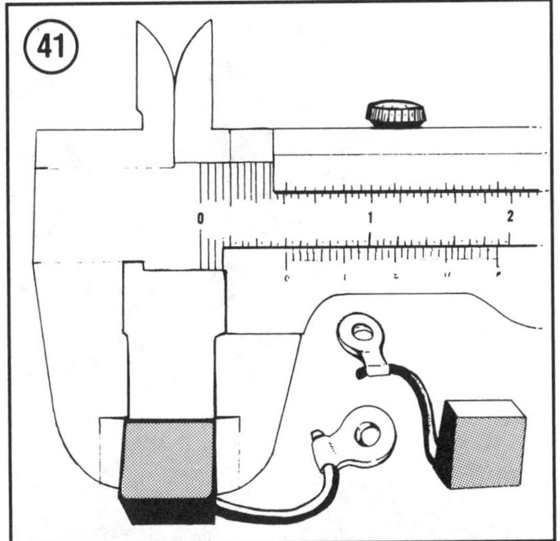


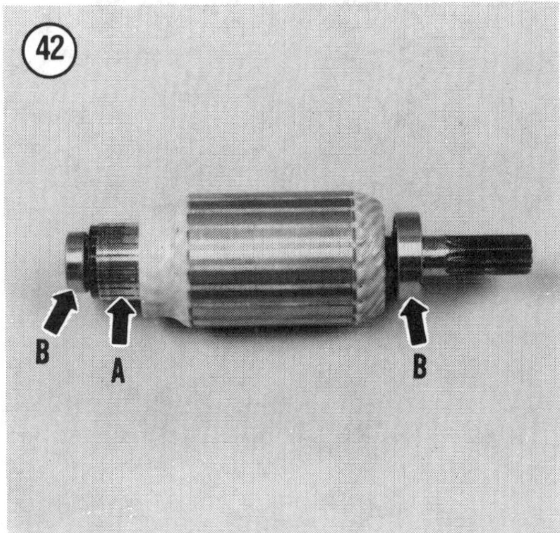


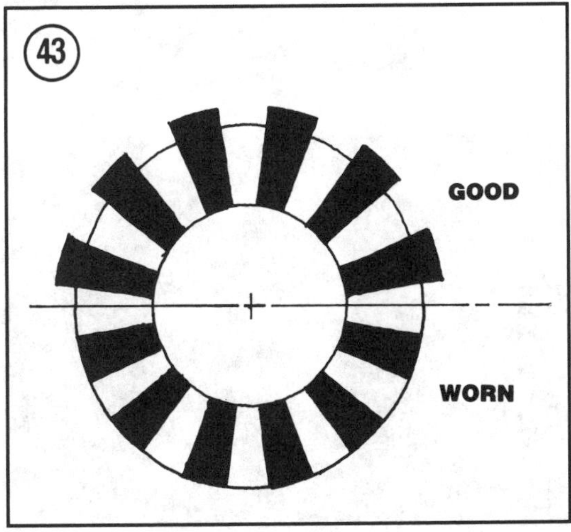


4. Use an ohmmeter and perform the following:
   a. Check for continuity between the commutator bars (**Figure 44**). There should be continuity (indicated resistance) between pairs of bars.
   b. Check for continuity between the commutator bars and the shaft (**Figure 45**). There should be *no* continuity (infinite resistance).
   c. If the unit fails either of these tests, the starter assembly must be replaced. The armature cannot be replaced individually.
5. Use an ohmmeter and perform the following:
   a. Check for continuity between the starter cable terminal and the starter case. There should be continuity (indicated resistance).
   b. Check for continuity between the starter cable terminal and the brush wire terminal; there should be *no* continuity (infinite resistance).
   c. If the unit fails either of these tests, the starter assembly must be replaced. The case/field coil assembly cannot be replaced individually.
6. Inspect the bearings (B, **Figure 42**) on each end of the armature coil assembly. They must rotate



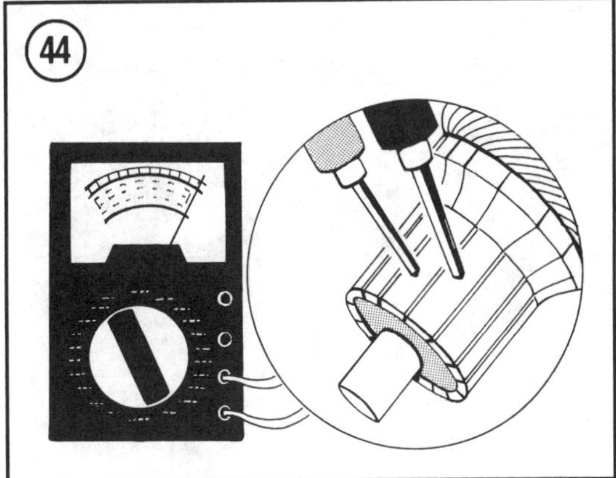


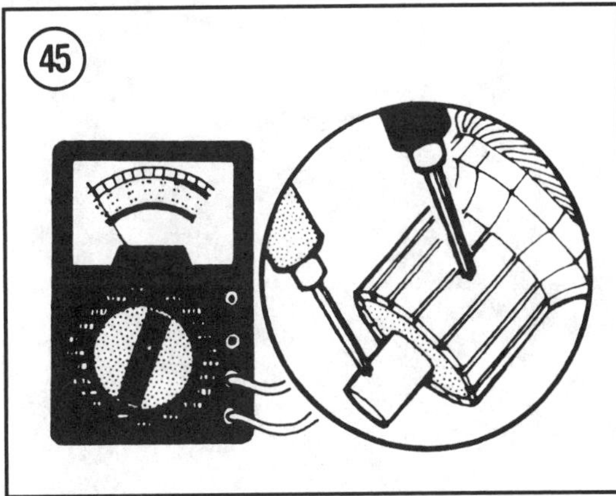

freely with no signs of wear. If the bearings are worn, replace the armature coil assembly. The bearings cannot be replaced individually.

7. Inspect the oil seal (**Figure 46**) in the left-hand end cap for wear, damage or deterioration. The oil seal cannot be replaced. If damaged, replace the left-hand end cap.

8. Inspect the right-hand end cap (**Figure 47**) for wear or damage; replace if necessary.

9. Inspect the case assembly for wear or damage. Make sure the field coils (**Figure 48**) are bonded securely in place. If damaged, or any field coils are loose, replace the case assembly.

10. Inspect the positive (+) brush holder and related parts (**Figure 49**) for wear or damage; replace any damaged parts.

11. Inspect the negative (–) brush holder and brush springs (**Figure 50**) assembly for wear or damage. The springs are the only replacement parts available for this assembly.

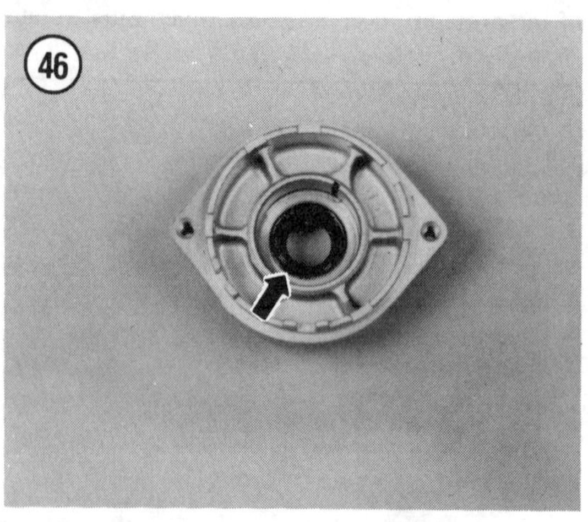


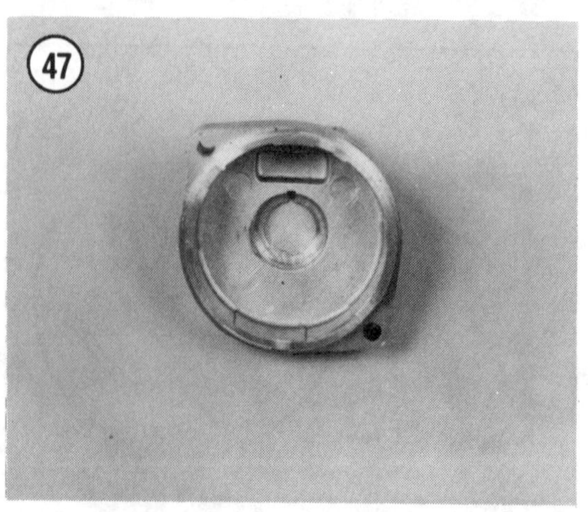

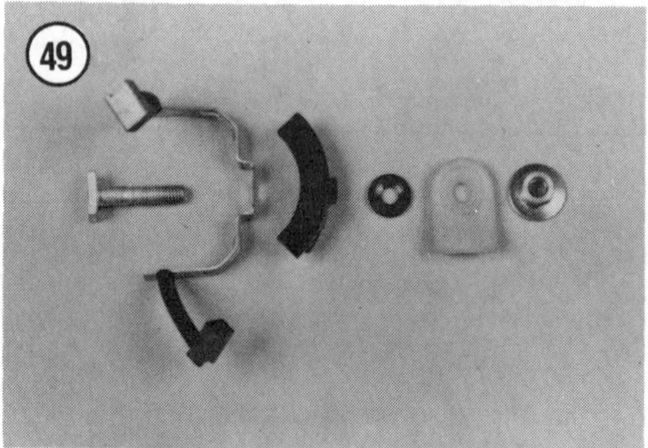

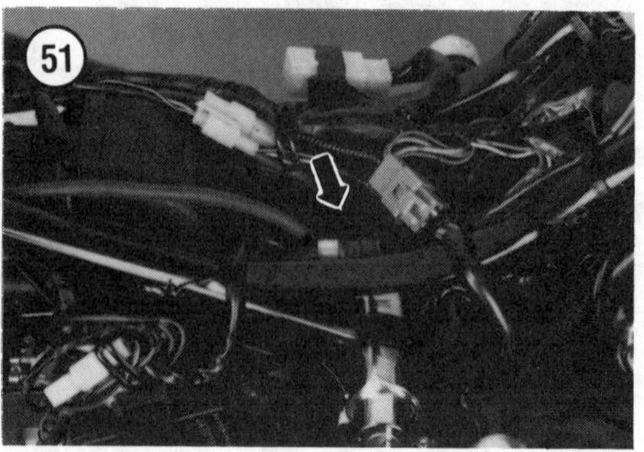

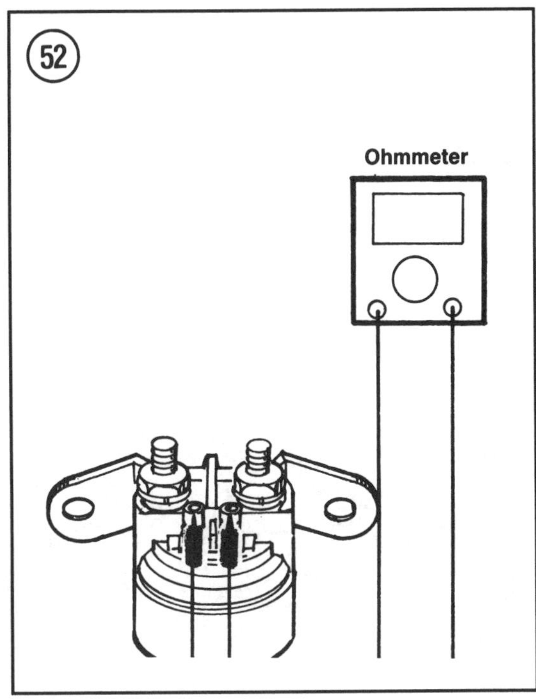


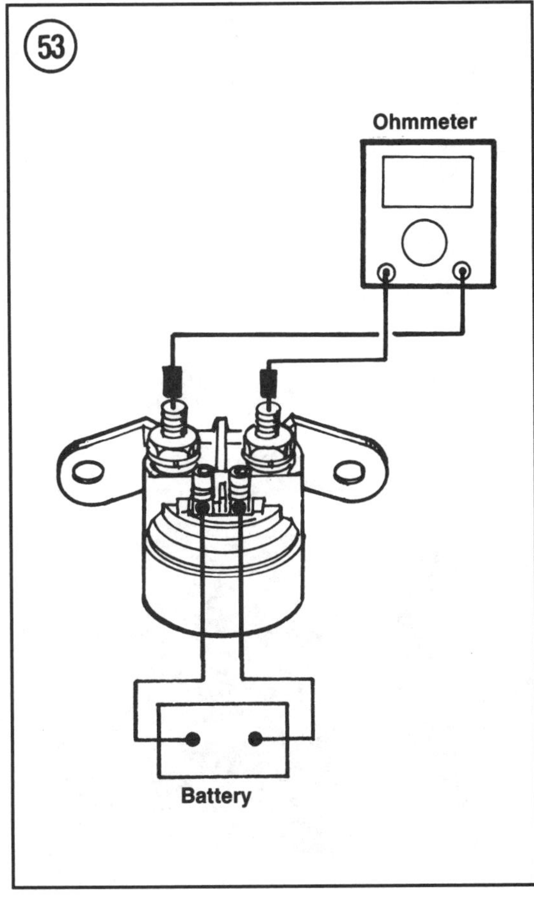


## STARTER SOLENOID

### Testing

1. Remove the seat as described in Chapter Twelve.

*CAUTION*
*When disconnecting the starter electrical wire from the starter solenoid, do **not** touch the other electrical terminal on the starter solenoid—this would result in a short.*

*NOTE*
*The starter solenoid (**Figure 51**) is located behind the ignition switch.*

2. Disconnect the electrical wire going from the starter solenoid to the starter. Leave the other electrical wire connected to the solenoid.
3. Shift the transmission into NEUTRAL.
4. Turn the ignition switch ON.
5. Pull in on the clutch lever until it bottoms out.
6. Press the START button.
7. Have an assistant connect an ohmmeter between the positive and negative small terminals (**Figure 52**) on top of the solenoid and check for continuity. If there is continuity (low resistance) the solenoid is okay. If there is no continuity (infinite resistance), the solenoid is faulty, proceed to Step 8.
8. Disconnect the battery (+) wire and the ground (-) wire from the large terminals on the solenoid.
9. Using small jumper wires, connect a 12-volt battery to the small terminals on the solenoid.
10. Connect an ohmmeter to the 2 large terminals (**Figure 53**) and check the resistance. The specified resistance is 2-6 ohms. If the resistance is not within specified range, the solenoid is faulty and must be replaced.
11. If the solenoid checks out okay, install all electrical wires to the solenoid and on the large terminals, tighten the nuts securely. Make sure the electrical connectors are on tight and that the rubber boot is properly installed to keep out moisture.
12. Install the seat as described in Chapter Twelve.

8

54

**HEADLIGHT ASSEMBLY**

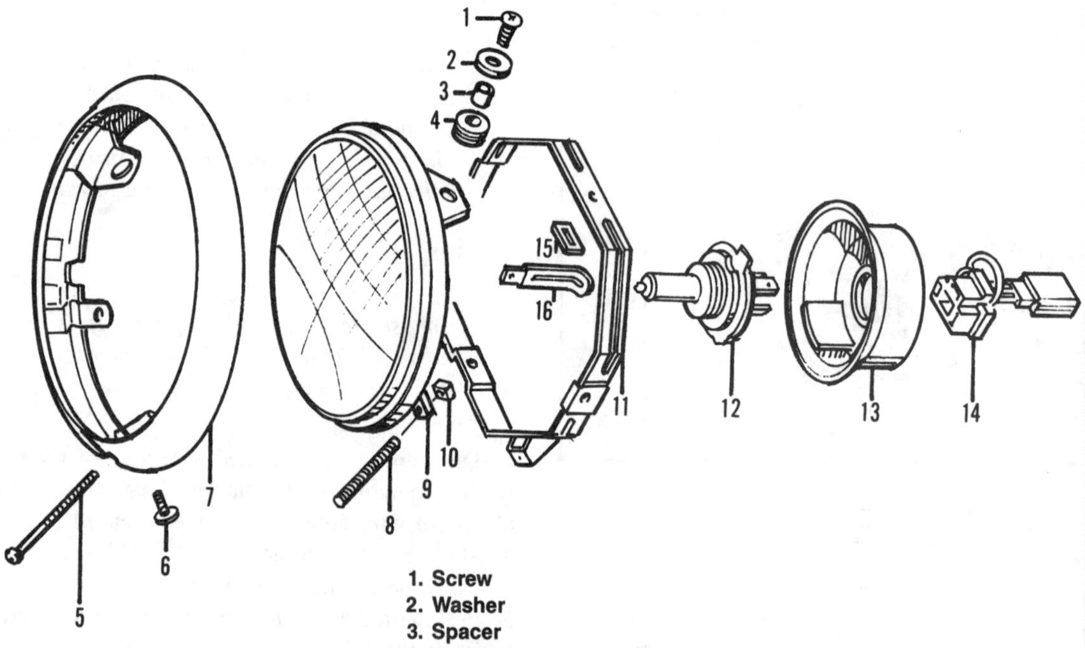


1. Screw
2. Washer
3. Spacer
4. Rubber grommet
5. Adjust screw
6. Screw
7. Trim ring
8. Spring
9. Lens unit
10. Nut
11. Mounting unit
12. Bulb
13. Rubber cap
14. Electrical connector

55

56

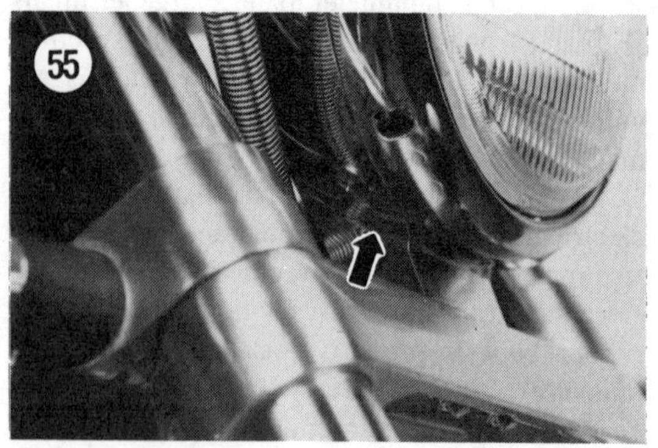

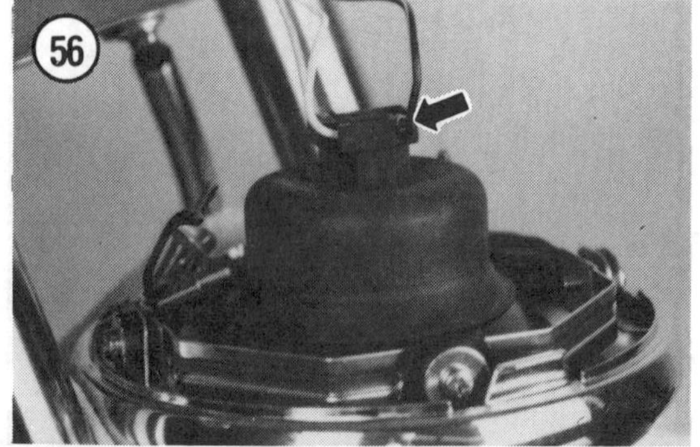

**Removal/Installation**

1. Remove the seat as described in Chapter Twelve.

*NOTE*
*The starter solenoid (**Figure 51**) is located behind the ignition switch.*

2. Slide off the rubber protective boot and disconnect the large electrical wires from the top terminals of the solenoid.

3. Disconnect the 2 small electrical wires from the top of the solenoid.
4. Remove the screws securing the solenoid to the frame and remove the solenoid.
5. Replace by reversing these removal steps. Note the following during installation.
6. Install all electrical wires to the solenoid and on the large terminals, tighten the nuts securely. Make sure the electrical connectors are on tight and that the rubber boot is properly installed to keep out moisture.

## LIGHTING SYSTEM

The lighting system consists of a headlight, taillight/brake light, directional lights, indicator lights and a speedometer illumination light. **Table 3** lists replacement bulbs for these components.

Always use the correct wattage bulb as indicated in this section. The use of a larger wattage bulb will give a dim light and a smaller wattage bulb will burn out prematurely.

8

### Headlight Bulb and Lens Replacement

Refer to **Figure 54** for this procedure.

1. Remove the screw (**Figure 55**) on each side, at the bottom of the headlight case.
2. Pull out on the bottom of the headlight trim ring and disengage it from the headlight case. Remove the trim ring and headlight lens unit assembly.
3. Disconnect the electrical connector (**Figure 56**) from the backside of the bulb.
4. Remove the rubber cover (**Figure 57**) from the back of the headlight bulb.

*CAUTION*
*Carefully read all instructions shipped with the replacement quartz bulb. Do not touch the bulb glass with your fingers as any traces of skin oil on the quartz halogen bulb will drastically reduce bulb life. Clean any traces of oil from the bulb with a cloth moistened in alcohol or lacquer thinner.*

5. Unhook the clip (**Figure 58**) and remove the light bulb (**Figure 59**). Replace with a new bulb.

6. To remove the headlight lens unit, perform the following:
   a. Remove the adjustment screws (**Figure 60**).
   b. Remove the screws, washers and spacers (**Figure 61**) securing the lens unit to the mounting ring and remove the mounting ring and trim ring from the lens unit.
7. Install by reversing these removal steps. Note the following during installation.
8. Install the rubber cover with the TOP arrow (**Figure 62**) facing upward.
9. Make sure the electrical connector is on tight and that the rubber cover is properly installed to keep out moisture.
10. Adjust the headlight as described in this chapter.

### Headlight Case Removal/Installation

1. Remove the screw (**Figure 55**) on each side at the bottom of the headlight case.
2. Pull out on the bottom of the headlight trim ring and disengage it from the headlight case. Remove the trim ring and headlight lens unit assembly.
3. Disconnect the electrical connector (**Figure 56**) from the backside of the bulb.
4. Disconnect the electrical wire connectors (A, **Figure 63**) within the headlight case and withdraw the wires from the case (B, **Figure 63**).
5. Remove the nuts (A, **Figure 64**) securing the headlight case to the lower fork bridge and remove the case assembly.
6. Install by reversing these removal steps.
7. Adjust the headlight as described in this chapter.

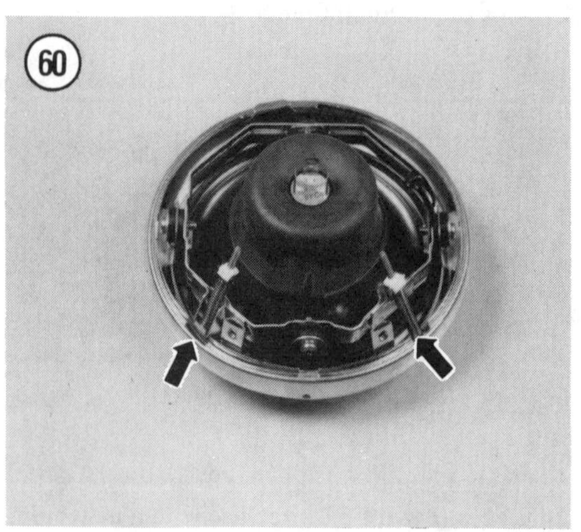


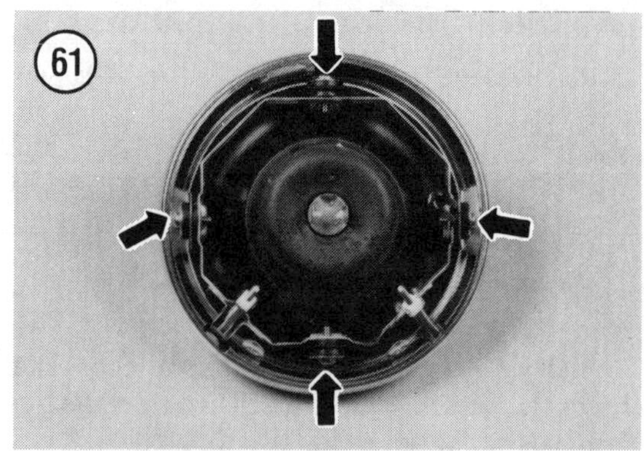

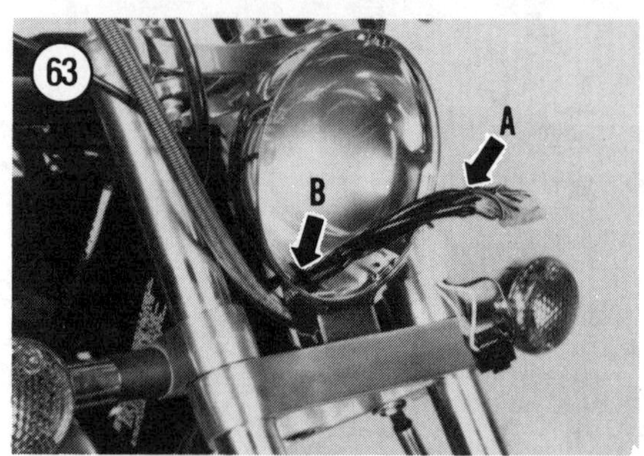

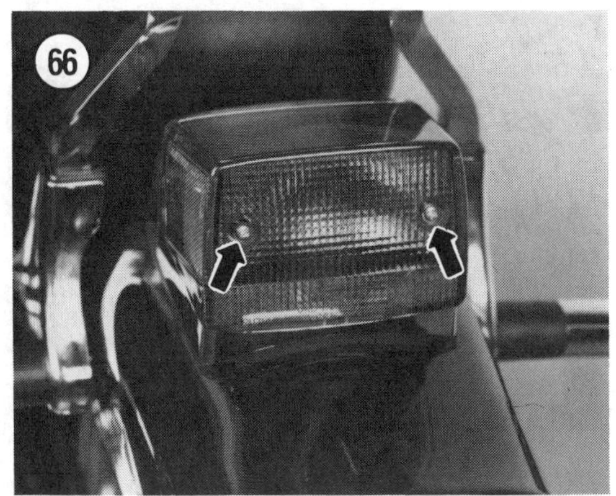


### Headlight Adjustment

Adjust the headlight horizontally and vertically according to Department of Motor Vehicles regulations in your area.

To adjust the headlight horizontally and vertically, turn the screws (B, **Figure 64**) on the bottom of the trim ring, until the aim is correct.

### Taillight/Brake Light Replacement

Refer to **Figure 65** for this procedure.

1. Remove the screws (**Figure 66**) securing the lens and remove the lens and gasket.



(65)

**TAILLIGHT/BRAKE LIGHT/ LICENSE PLATE LIGHT**

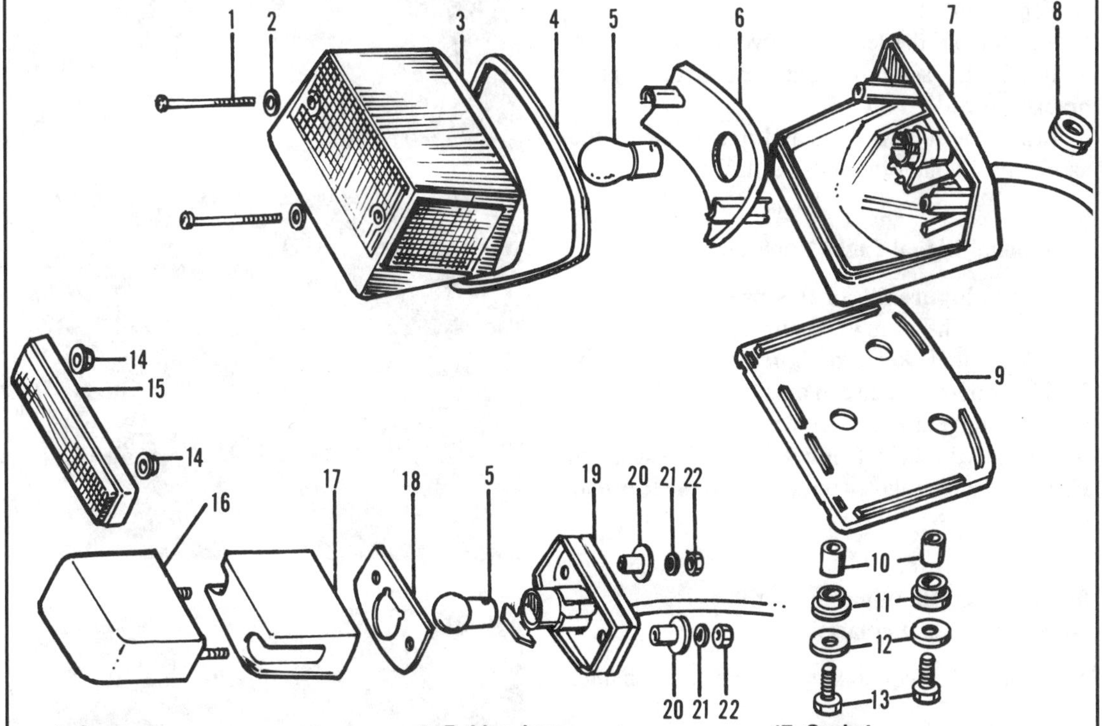

1. Screw
2. Washer
3. Taillight/brake light lens
4. Gasket
5. Bulb
6. Reflector
7. Housing
8. Rubber grommet
9. Rubber base
10. Collars
11. Rubber cushions
12. Washers
13. Bolts
14. Nut
15. License plate light cover
16. License plate lens
17. Gasket
18. Gasket
19. Base
20. Spacer
21. Washer
22. Nut

2. Wash out the inside and outside of the lens with a mild detergent and wipe dry.
3. Inspect the lens gasket and replace it if damaged or deteriorated.
4. Replace the bulb (**Figure 67**) and install the lens; do not overtighten the screws as the lens may crack.

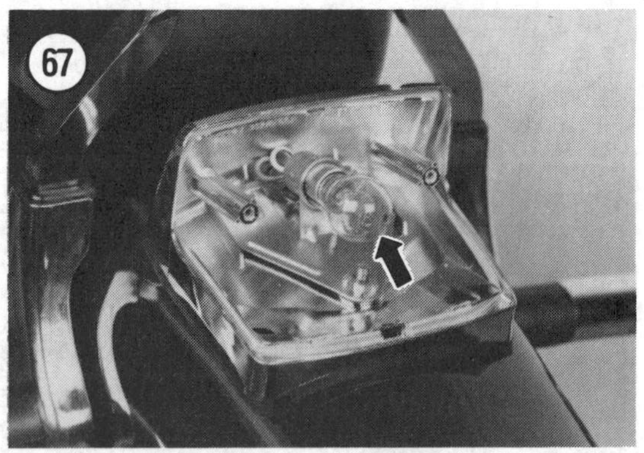
67

### License Plate Light Replacement

Refer to **Figure 65** for this procedure.

1. Remove the nuts and lockwasher securing the light assembly (**Figure 68**) and remove the assembly from the license plate bracket. Don't lose the mounting hole spacers in the bracket.
2. Separate the cover and lens from the base.
3. Wash out the inside and outside of the lens with a mild detergent and wipe dry.
4. Inspect the lens gasket and replace it if damaged or deteriorated.
5. Replace the bulb.
6. Reassemble the lens and cover onto the base.
7. Install the assembly onto the license plate bracket.
8. Install the lockwashers and nuts securing the assembly. Tighten the nuts securely.

68

### Directional Signal Light Replacement

Refer to **Figure 69** for this procedure.

1. Remove the screws securing the lens and remove the lens. Refer to **Figure 70** or **Figure 71**.
2. Wash out the inside and outside of the lens with a mild detergent and wipe dry.
3. Replace the bulb (**Figure 72**) and install the lens. Do not overtighten the screws as the lens may crack.

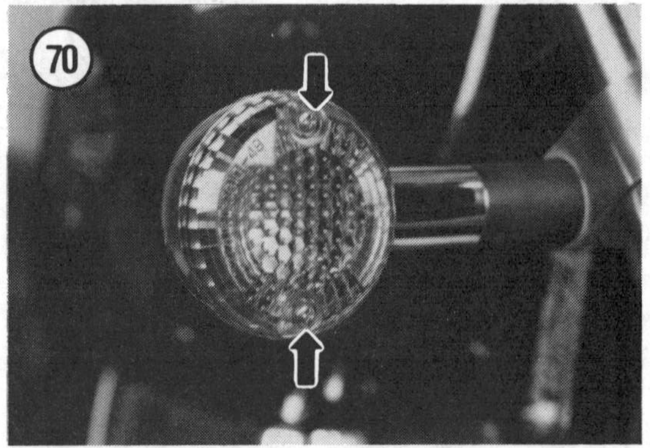
70

### Speedometer Illumination Light Indicator Light Replacement

1. Remove the fuel tank as described in Chapter Seven.
2. Carefully pull the defective lamp holder/electrical wire assembly (**Figure 73**) from the backside of the housing.
3. Remove and replace the defective bulb.

*NOTE*
*If a new bulb will not work, check the wire connections for loose or broken*

71

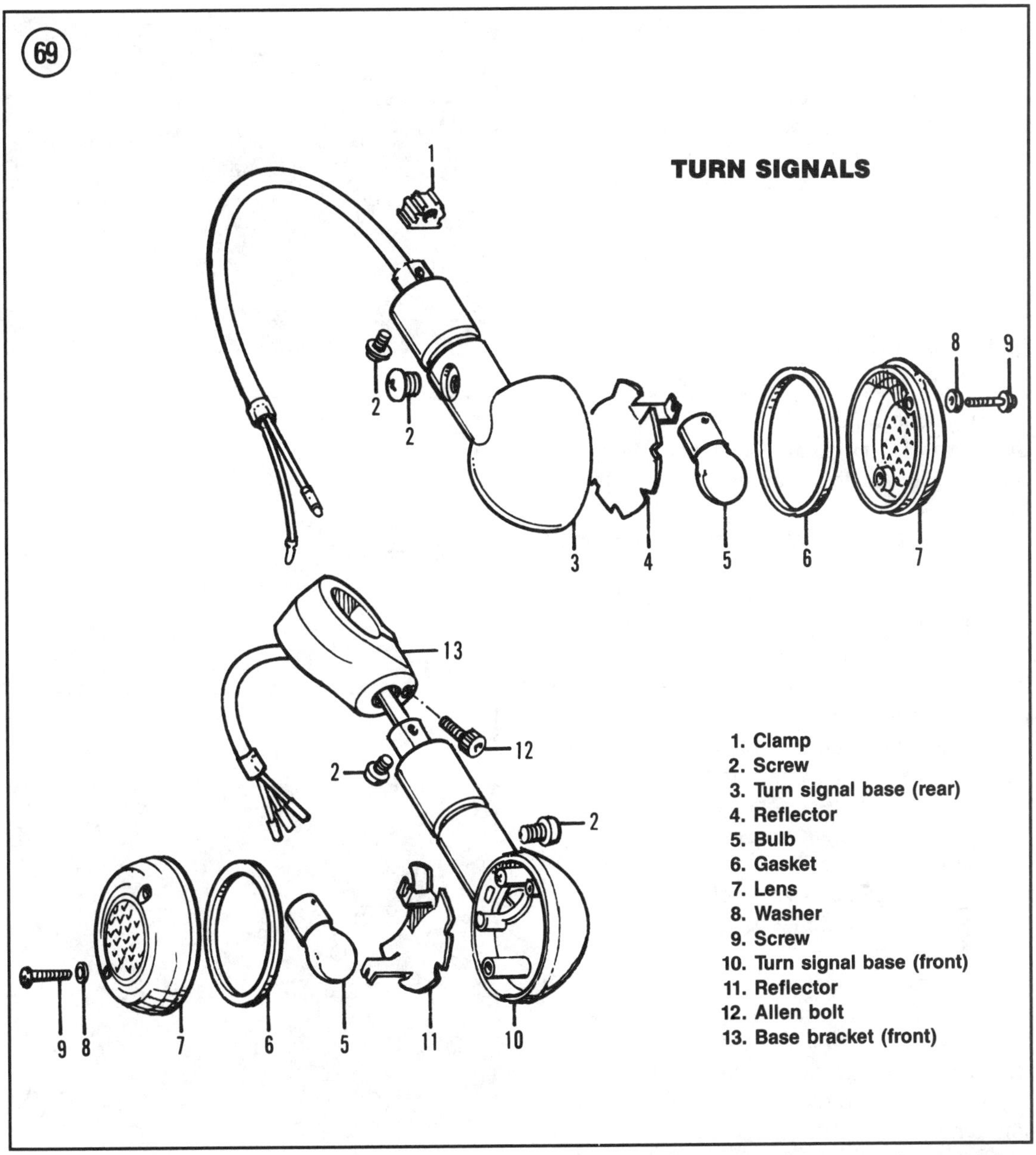

69

**TURN SIGNALS**

1 2 2 3 4 5 6 7 8 9

13 12 2 2 9 8 7 6 5 11 10

1. Clamp
2. Screw
3. Turn signal base (rear)
4. Reflector
5. Bulb
6. Gasket
7. Lens
8. Washer
9. Screw
10. Turn signal base (front)
11. Reflector
12. Allen bolt
13. Base bracket (front)

8

72

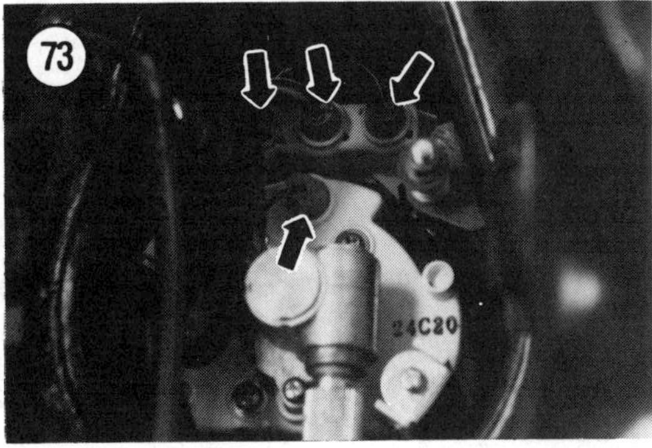

73

*wires. Also check the bulb socket for corrosion; replace as necessary.*

4. Push the lamp socket/electrical wire assembly back into the housing. Make sure it is completely seated to prevent the entry of water and moisture.
5. Install the fuel tank as described in Chapter Twelve.

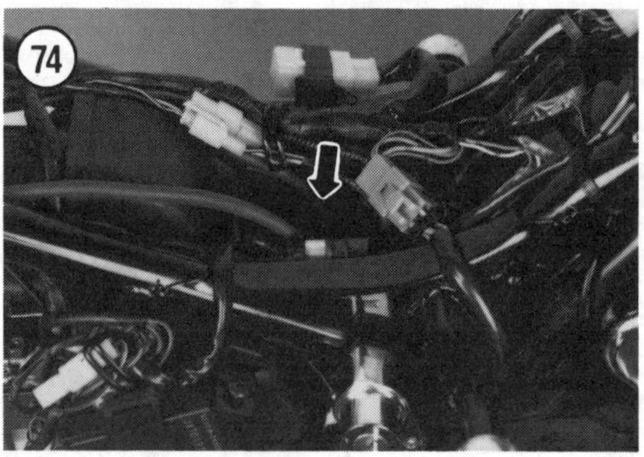

## SWITCHES

### Ignition Switch Continuity Test

The ignition switch cannot be separated. If either the electrical or mechanical portions of the switch become defective, the entire switch assembly must be replaced.

1. Remove the seat as described in Chapter Twelve.
2. Disconnect the ignition switch 4-pin electrical connector (**Figure 74**) containing 4 wires (1 red, 1 orange, 1 gray and 1 brown).
3. Use an ohmmeter and check for continuity. Connect the test leads to the ignition switch side of the electrical connector (**Figure 75**) as follows:
   a. Turn the ignition switch to the ON position: there should be continuity (low resistance) between the red and orange wires and between the gray and brown wires.
   b. Turn the ignition switch off: there should be *no* continuity (infinite resistance) between any of these wires.
   c. Turn the ignition switch to the "P" position: there should be continuity (low resistance) between the red and brown wires.
4. If the ignition switch fails any one of these tests, the switch must be replaced as described in this chapter.
5. Reconnect the 4-pin electrical connector. Make sure the electrical connector is free of corrosion and is tight.
6. Install the seat as described in Chapter Twelve.

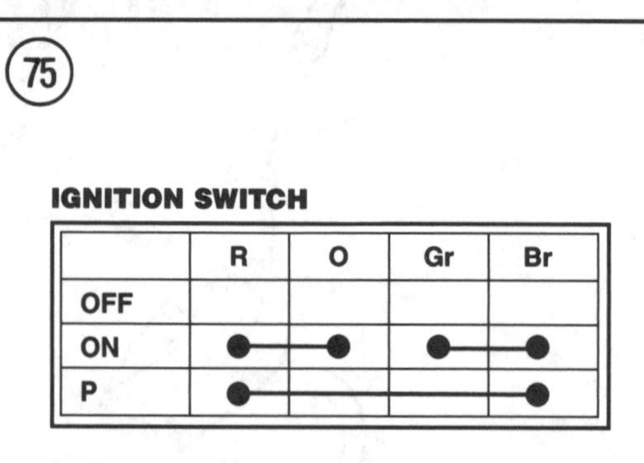

**IGNITION SWITCH**

| | R | O | Gr | Br |
|---|---|---|---|---|
| OFF | | | | |
| ON | ● | ● | ● | ● |
| P | ● | | | ● |

### Ignition Switch Removal/Installation

1. Remove the seat as described in Chapter Twelve.
2. Disconnect the ignition switch 4-pin electrical connector (**Figure 74**) containing 4 wires (1 red, 1 orange, 1 gray and 1 brown).

3. Remove the mounting screw and washer (**Figure 76**) securing the ignition switch to the frame on the left-hand side.
4. Remove the switch assembly from the frame.
5. Install the new ignition switch onto the frame and tighten the screw securely.
6. Reconnect the 4-pin electrical connector. Make sure the electrical connector is free of corrosion and is tight.
7. Install the seat as described in Chapter Twelve.

### Right-hand Combination Switch Testing (Engine Start and Stop Switch and Front Brake Light Switch)

The right-hand combination switch assembly contains both the engine start and engine stop switch. The front brake light switch shares the same electrical harness, but is a separate switch that is connected to the front master cylinder. If any of the switches are faulty, then both switch assemblies must be replaced.

1. Remove the seat as described in Chapter Twelve.

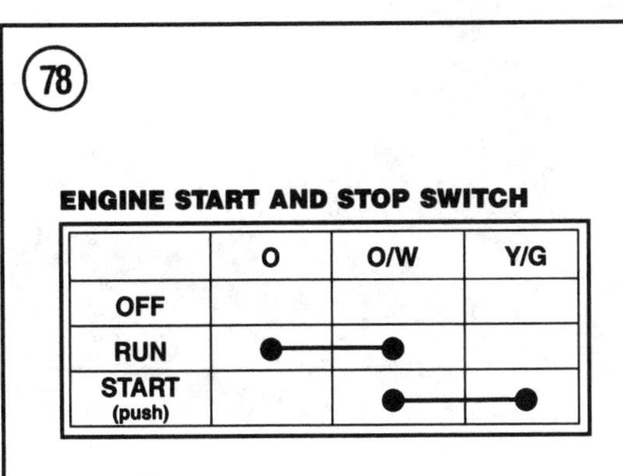


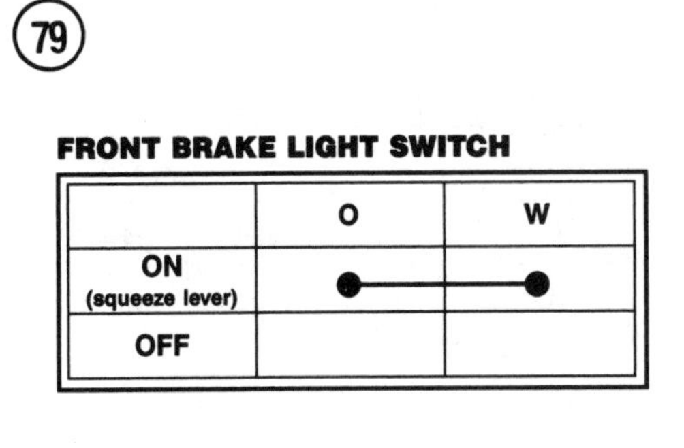


2. Remove the fuel tank as described in Chapter Seven.
3. Unhook the tie wrap and locate the engine start and stop switch 6-pin electrical connector containing 6 wires (1 yellow/green, 1 orange, 1 white/black [one side] white [other side], 1 orange/white, 1 green, 1 yellow/white). Disconnect this electrical connector (**Figure 77**).
4. Use an ohmmeter and check for continuity. Connect the test leads to the right-hand combination switch side of the electrical connector (**Figure 78**) as follows:

   a. Turn the engine stop switch to the RUN position: there should be continuity (low resistance) between the orange and the orange/white wires.

   b. Turn the engine stop switch to the OFF position: there should be *no* continuity (infinite resistance) between the orange, orange/white or yellow/green wires.

   c. Press the START switch: there should be continuity (low resistance) between the orange/white and the yellow/green wires.

5. To test the front brake light switch (**Figure 79**), perform the following:

   a. Squeeze the front brake lever to the fully applied position: there should be continuity (low resistance) between the orange and the white wires.

   b. Release the brake lever: there should be no continuity (infinite resistance) between the orange and white wires.

6. If the right-hand combination switch fails any one of these tests, the switch must be replaced as described in this chapter.
7. Reconnect the 6-pin electrical connector containing 6 wires.
8. Make sure the electrical connector is free of corrosion and is tight. Install the tie wrap to hold the electrical wires to the front of the frame. The wires must be retained in this manner to allow room for the fuel tank.
9. Install the fuel tank as described in Chapter Seven.
10. Install the seat as described in Chapter Twelve.

### Right-hand Combination Switch Removal/Installation (Engine Start and Stop Switch and Front Brake Light Switch)

The right-hand combination switch assembly contains both the engine start and engine stop switch. The front brake light switch shares the same electrical harness, but is a separate switch connected to the front master cylinder. If any of the switches are faulty, both switch assemblies must be replaced.

1. Remove the seat as described in Chapter Twelve.
2. Remove the fuel tank as described in Chapter Seven.
3. Unhook the tie wrap and locate the engine start and stop switch 6-pin electrical connector containing 6 wires (1 yellow/green, 1 orange, 1 white/black [one side] white [other side], 1 orange/white, 1 green, 1 yellow/white). Disconnect this electrical connector (**Figure 77**).
4. Remove the screws securing the front brake light switch to the front master cylinder and remove the electrical wires from the switch assembly.
5. Remove the screws securing the right-hand combination switch together and remove the switch assembly (**Figure 80**).
6. Install a new switch and tighten the screws securely. Do not overtighten the screws or the plastic switch housing may crack.
7. Install the front brake light switch to the front master cylinder and connect the electrical wires to the switch assembly.
8. Reconnect the 6-pin electrical connector.
9. Make sure the electrical connector is free of corrosion and is tight. Install the tie wrap to hold the electrical wires to the front of the frame. The wires must be retained in this manner to allow room for the fuel tank.
10. Install the fuel tank as described in Chapter Seven.
11. Install the seat as described in Chapter Twelve.

### Left-hand Combination Switch Testing (Headlight Dimmer Switch, Turn Signal Switch and Horn Switch)

The left-hand combination switch assembly contains the headlight dimmer switch, turn signal switch and horn switch. If any of the switches are faulty, the entire switch assembly must be replaced.

1. Remove the seat as described in Chapter Twelve.
2. Remove the fuel tank as described in Chapter Seven.
3. Unhook the tie wrap and locate the engine start and stop switch 10-pin electrical connector containing 9 wires (1 yellow, 1 green/white, 1 black, 1 light green, 1 black/white, 1 blue, 1 orange, 1 green). Disconnect this electrical

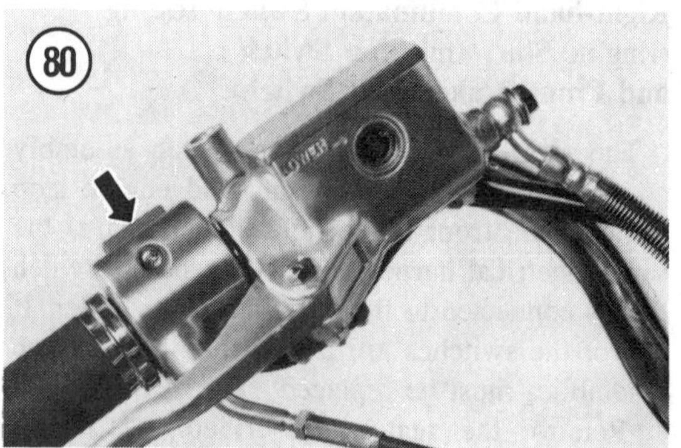


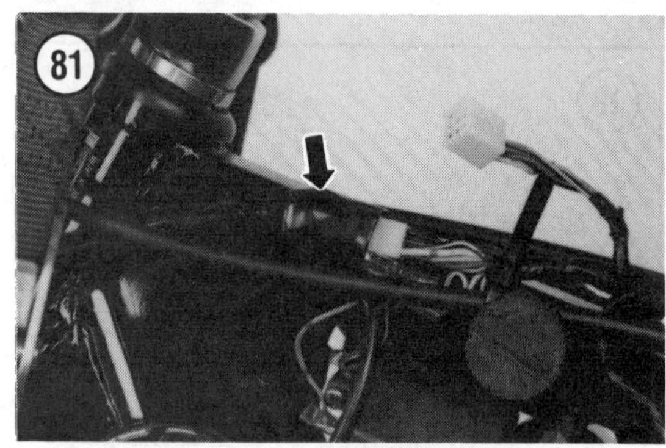


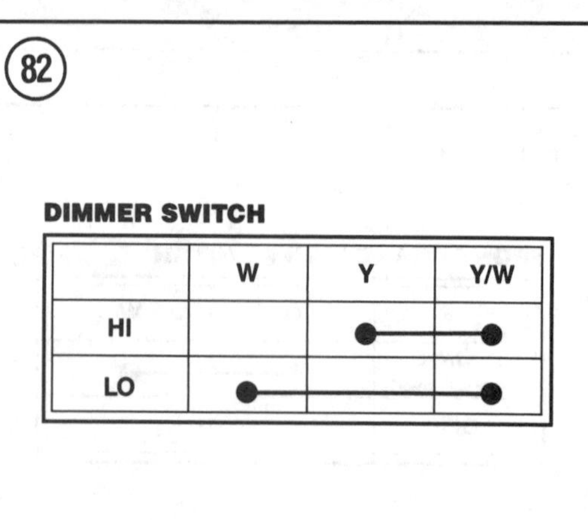


**DIMMER SWITCH**

| | W | Y | Y/W |
|---|---|---|---|
| HI | | ● | ● |
| LO | ● | | ● |

connector (**Figure 81**) plus the 2 individual wires (1 light green and 1 black). One additional wire for the horn (dark green) is attached to the horn; disconnect it from the horn.

*NOTE*

*In the following tests, connect the test leads to the left-hand combination switch side of the electrical connector.*

4. To test the headlight dimmer switch (**Figure 82**), perform the following:
   a. Use an ohmmeter and check for continuity.
   b. Turn the headlight dimmer switch to the HI position: there should be continuity (low resistance) between the yellow and the yellow/white wires.
   c. Turn the headlight dimmer switch to the LO position: there should be continuity (low resistance) between the white and the yellow/white blue wires.
5. To test the turn signal switch (**Figure 83**), perform the following:
   a. Use an ohmmeter and check for continuity.

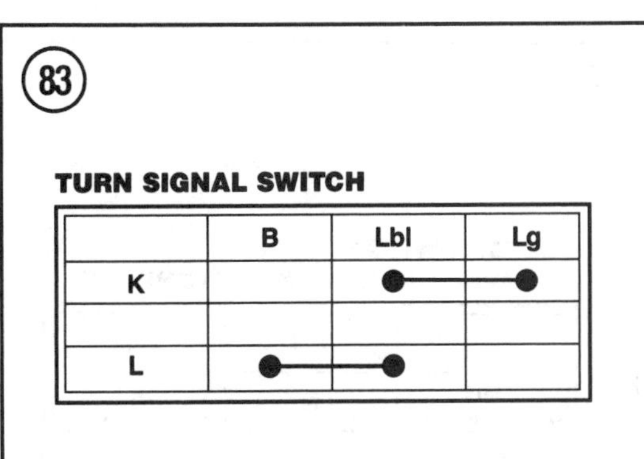

83

TURN SIGNAL SWITCH

| | B | Lbl | Lg |
|---|---|---|---|
| K | | ● | ● |
| | | | |
| L | ● | ● | |

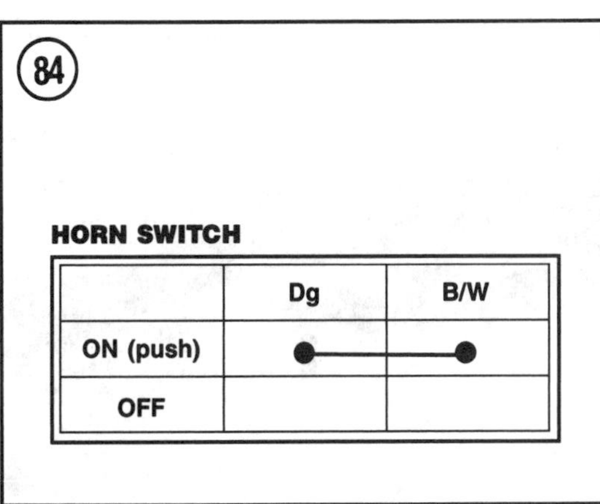

84

HORN SWITCH

| | Dg | B/W |
|---|---|---|
| ON (push) | ● | ● |
| OFF | | |

   b. Turn the turn signal switch to the "R" position: there should be continuity (low resistance) between the light blue and the light green wires.
   c. Turn the turn signal switch to the "L" position: there should be continuity (low resistance) between the black and the light blue wires.
6. To test the horn switch (**Figure 84**), perform the following:
   a. Use an ohmmeter and check for continuity.
   b. Press the HORN button: there should be continuity (low resistance) between the dark green and the black/white wires.
7. If the left-hand combination switch fails any one of these tests, the switch must be replaced as described in this chapter.
8. Reconnect the 10-pin electrical connector, the 2 individual wire connectors and the one to the horn.
9. Make sure the electrical connectors are free of corrosion and are tight. Install the tie wrap to hold the electrical wires to the front of the frame. The wires must be retained in this manner to allow room for the fuel tank.
10. Install the fuel tank as described in Chapter Seven.
11. Install the seat as described in Chapter Twelve.

### Left-hand Combination Switch Removal/Installation (Headlight Dimmer Switch, Turn Signal Switch and Horn Switch)

The left-hand combination switch assembly contains the headlight dimmer switch, turn signal switch and horn switch. If any of the switches are faulty the entire switch assembly must be replaced.

1. Remove the seat as described in Chapter Twelve.
2. Remove the fuel tank as described in Chapter Seven.
3. Unhook the tie wrap and locate the engine start and stop switch 10-pin electrical connector containing 9 wires (1 yellow, 1 green/white, 1 black, 1 light green, 1 black/white, 1 blue, 1 orange, 1 green). Disconnect this electrical connector (**Figure 81**) plus the 2 individual wires (1 light green and 1 black). One additional wire for the horn (dark green) is attached to the horn; disconnect it from the horn.

4. Remove the screws securing the left-hand combination switch together and remove the switch assembly (**Figure 85**).
5. Remove the electrical wire harness from any clips on the frame and carefully pull the harness out from the frame.
6. Install a new switch and tighten the screws securely. Do not overtighten the screws or the plastic switch housing may crack.
7. Reconnect the 10-pin electrical connector, the 2 individual wire connectors and the one to the horn.
8. Make sure the electrical connectors are free of corrosion and are tight. Install the tie wrap to hold the electrical wires to the front of the frame. The wires must be retained in this manner to allow room for the fuel tank.
9. Install the fuel tank as described in Chapter Seven.
10. Install the seat as described in Chapter Twelve.

### Starter Interlock Switch (Clutch Lever) Testing

1. Remove the seat as described in Chapter Twelve.
2. Remove the fuel tank as in Chapter Seven.
3. Unhook the tie wrap and locate the starter interlock switch's 2 individual yellow/green wires. Disconnect these 2 individual electrical connectors (**Figure 81**).
4. Use an ohmmeter and check for continuity (**Figure 86**). Connect the test leads to the starter interlock switch side of the electrical connectors as follows:
   a. Squeeze the clutch lever to the fully applied position: there should be continuity (low resistance) between the 2 yellow/green wires.
   b. Release the clutch lever: there should be no continuity (infinite resistance) between the 2 yellow/green wires.
5. If the starter interlock switch fails any one of these tests, the switch must be replaced as described in this chapter.
6. Reconnect the 2 individual electrical connectors.
7. Make sure the electrical connectors are free of corrosion and are tight. Install the tie wrap to hold the electrical wires to the front of the frame. The wires must be retained in this manner to allow room for the fuel tank.
8. Install the fuel tank as described in Chapter Seven.
9. Install the seat as described in Chapter Twelve.

### Starter Interlock Switch (Clutch Lever) Removal/Installation

1. Remove the seat as described in Chapter Twelve.
2. Remove the fuel tank as described in Chapter Seven.

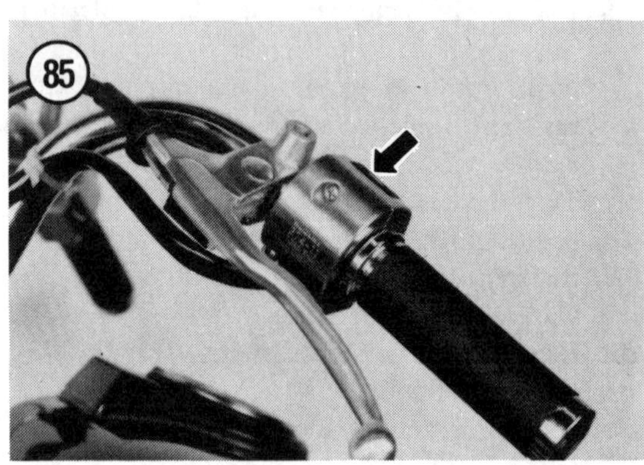


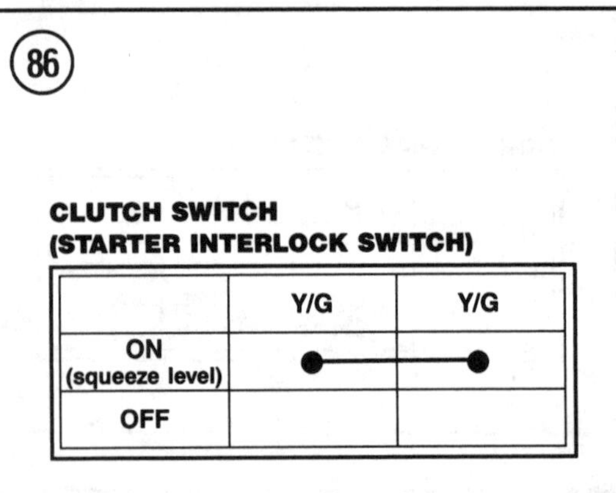


**CLUTCH SWITCH (STARTER INTERLOCK SWITCH)**

| | Y/G | Y/G |
|---|---|---|
| ON (squeeze level) | ● | ● |
| OFF | | |

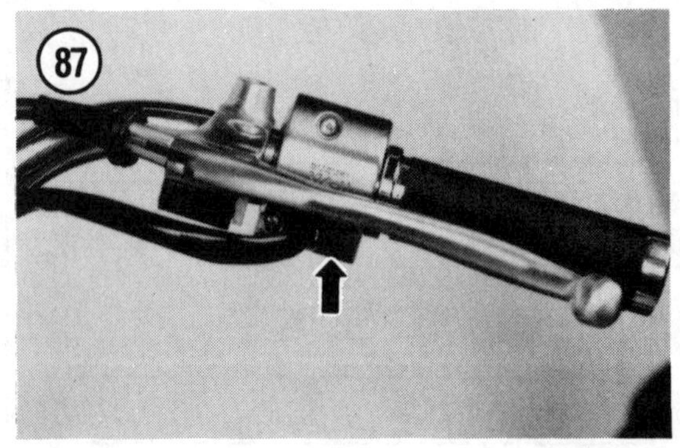

3. Unhook the tie wrap and locate the starter interlock switch's 2 individual yellow/green wires. Disconnect these 2 individual electrical connectors (**Figure 81**).
4. Remove the screws securing the starter interlock switch to the clutch lever housing and remove the switch assembly (**Figure 87**).
5. Remove the electrical wire harness from any clips on the frame and carefully pull the harness out from the frame.
6. Install a new switch and tighten the screws securely.
7. Reconnect the 2 individual electrical connectors.
8. Make sure the electrical connectors are free of corrosion and are tight. Install the tie wrap to hold the electrical wires to the front of the frame. The wires must be retained in this manner to allow room for the fuel tank.
9. Install the fuel tank as described in Chapter Seven.
10. Install the seat as described in Chapter Twelve.

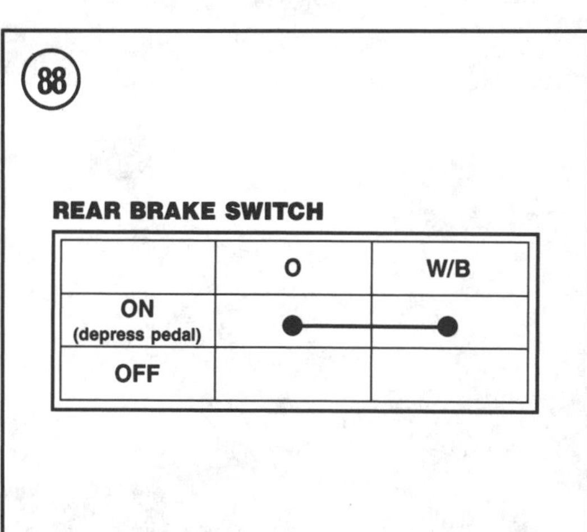
88

REAR BRAKE SWITCH

| | O | W/B |
|---|---|---|
| ON (depress pedal) | ●——— | ———● |
| OFF | | |

89

### Rear Brake Light Switch Testing

The rear brake light switch is mounted on the right-hand side of the frame just behind the swing arm's right-hand pivot point.
1. Disconnect the electrical connector wires on top of the rear brake pedal switch.
2. Have an assistant apply the rear brake. Use an ohmmeter set at R × 1 and connect the 2 leads of the ohmmeter to the electrical terminals on top of the rear brake light switch (**Figure 88**).
3. If the switch is good, there will be continuity (very low resistance).
4. If the switch fails to pass this test, the switch is faulty and must be replaced.
5. To remove the switch, refer to *Rear Brake Pedal and Cable Removal/Installation* in Chapter Eleven.
6. Install a new switch and adjust as described in this chapter.
7. Connect the electrical connector wires to the rear brake pedal switch.

### Rear Brake Light Switch Adjustment

1. Turn the ignition switch to the ON position.
2. Depress the brake pedal. The brake light should come on just as the brake begins to work.
3. To make the brake light come on earlier, hold the brake light switch body and turn the adjusting nut *clockwise* as viewed from the top. Turn the adjusting nut *counterclockwise* to delay the light from coming on.

*NOTE*
*Some riders prefer the brake light to come on a little early. This way, they can tap the pedal without braking to warn drivers who are following too closely.*

### Neutral Indicator Light Switch Testing

1. Remove the seat as described in Chapter Twelve.
2. Shift the transmission into NEUTRAL.
3. Disconnect the neutral indicator light switch individual blue wire connector (**Figure 89**).

4. Use an ohmmeter and check for continuity (**Figure 90**). Connect one of the test leads to the blue wire and connect the other test lead to ground.
5. If the switch is good, there will be continuity (very low resistance).
6. If the switch fails to pass this test, the switch is faulty and must be replaced.
7. Remove the switch as described in this chapter.
8. Reconnect the individual electrical connector.
9. Make sure the electrical connector is free of corrosion and is tight. Install the tie wrap to hold the electrical wires to the frame.
10. Install the seat as described in Chapter Twelve.

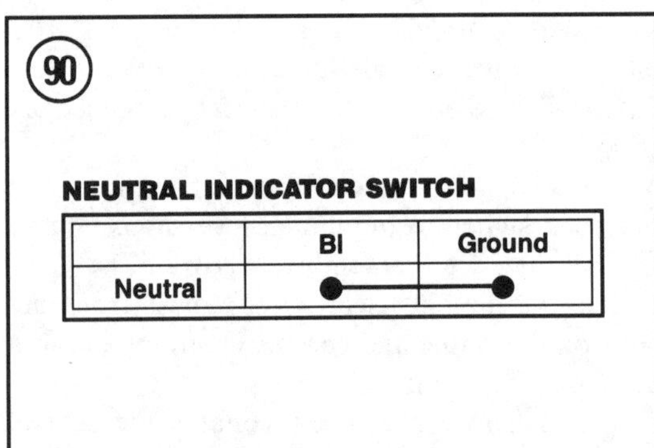
90

NEUTRAL INDICATOR SWITCH

| | Bl | Ground |
|---|---|---|
| Neutral | ● | ● |

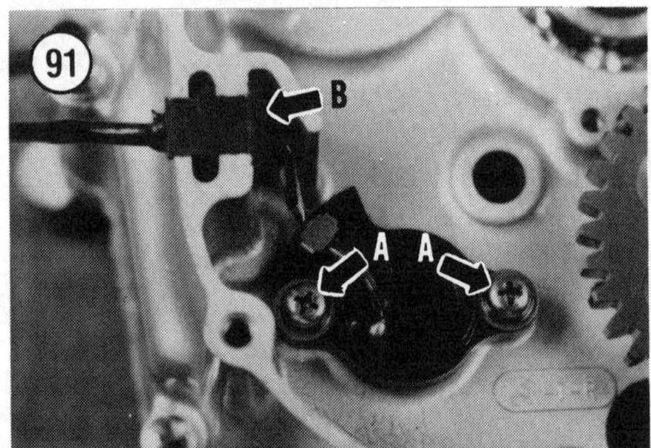

91

### Neutral Switch Removal/Installation

1. Remove the right-hand side cover as described in Chapter Four.
2. Remove the screws, lockwashers and washers (A, **Figure 91**) securing the neutral switch and remove the neutral switch assembly.
3. Remove the switch contact plunger (**Figure 92**) and spring (**Figure 93**) from the end of the gearshift drum.
4. Carefully remove the electrical wire and rubber grommet from the right-hand crankcase half (B, **Figure 91**).
5. Install by reversing these removal steps. Note the following during installation.
6. Install the plunger as shown in **Figure 94**.
7. Make sure the rubber grommet is correctly seated in the groove in the crankcase. If not seated correctly, there will be an oil leak.
8. Make sure the electrical connector is free of corrosion and is tight.

92

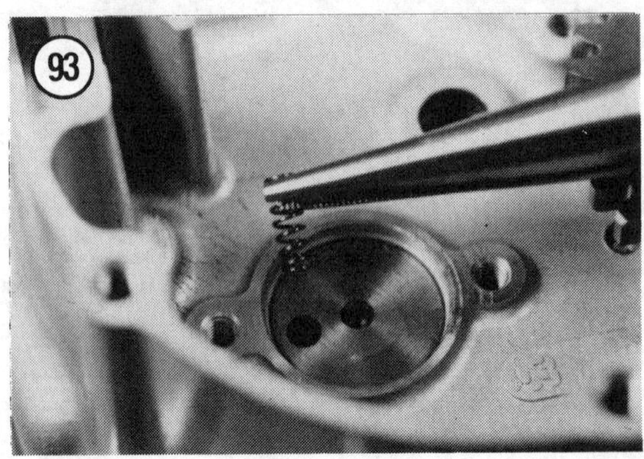
93

### Sidestand Check Switch Testing (1986 Models)

*NOTE*
*On 1987-1988 models, refer to **Sidestand Interlock** in this chapter for test procedures.*

1. Remove the seat as described in Chapter Twelve.
2. Disconnect the sidestand check switch 2-pin electrical connector containing 2 wires (1 green/white wire and 1 black/white wire).

3. Use an ohmmeter and check for continuity (**Figure 95**). Connect the test leads to the sidestand check switch side of the electrical connectors as follows:

a. Place the sidestand in the down position: there should be continuity (low resistance) between the green/white and the black/white wires.
b. Have an assistant hold the bike in the upright position, raise the sidestand and check for continuity: there should be no continuity (infinite resistance) between the green/white and black/white wires.

94

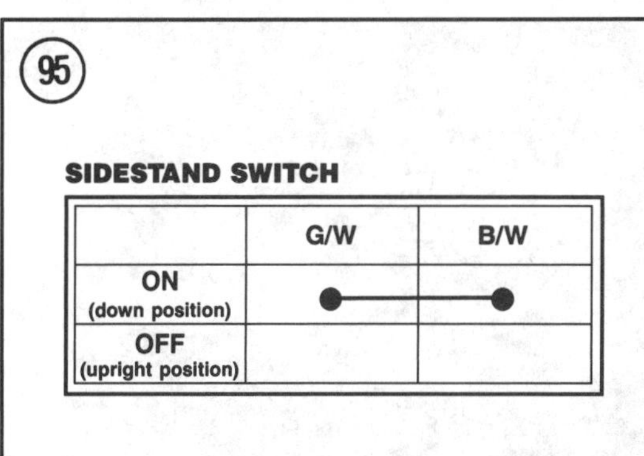

95

SIDESTAND SWITCH

| | G/W | B/W |
|---|---|---|
| ON (down position) | ● | ● |
| OFF (upright position) | | |

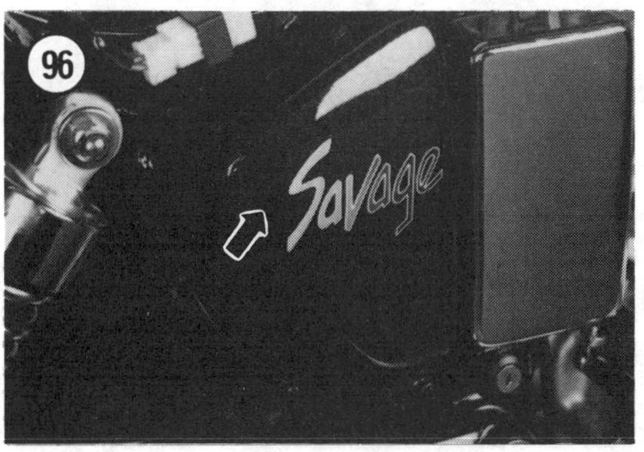


96

4. If the sidestand check switch fails either one of these tests, the switch must be replaced as described in this chapter.
5. Reconnect the 2-pin electrical connector.
6. Remove the switch as described in this chapter.
7. Reconnect the individual electrical connector.
8. Make sure the electrical connector is free of corrosion and is tight. Install the tie wrap to hold the electrical wires to the frame.
9. Install the seat as described in Chapter Twelve.

### Sidestand Check Switch Removal/Installation

1. Remove the seat as described in Chapter Twelve.
2. Disconnect the sidestand check switch 2-pin electrical connector containing 2 wires (1 green/white wire and 1 black/white wire).
3. Unhook the tie-wraps securing the electrical wire harness to the frame.
4. Have an assistant hold the bike in the upright position.
5. Disconnect the spring from the switch.
6. Remove the screws and lockwashers securing the sidestand check switch to the frame and remove the switch.
7. Install a new sidestand check switch and tighten the screws securely.
8. Route the electrical wire harness through the frame and install the tie wraps securing the harness to the frame.
9. Reconnect the 2-pin electrical connector.
10. Make sure the electrical connector is free of corrosion and is tight. Install the tie wrap to hold the electrical wires to the frame.
11. Install the seat as described in Chapter Twelve.

## ELECTRICAL COMPONENTS

This section contains information on all electrical components except switches.

### Battery Case Removal/Installation

1. Remove the seat as described in Chapter Twelve.
2. Remove the screws securing the right-hand and left-hand frame covers (**Figure 96**).

8

3. First disconnect the battery negative (-) lead (**Figure 97**).
4. Using the ignition key, unlock and remove the tool holder cover (**Figure 98**).
5. Remove the tool pouch from the tool holder.
6. Remove the screws (**Figure 99**) securing the tool holder and remove the tool holder (**Figure 100**).
7. Disconnect the breather tube (**Figure 101**) from the battery. Leave the breather tube routed through the frame.
8. Pull back the rubber boot (A, **Figure 102**) and disconnect the battery positive lead (+) (B, **Figure 102**).
9. Carefully slide the battery out of the battery case.
10. Remove the bolts, washers and spacers (**Figure 103**) securing the battery case to the frame.
11. Carefully slide the battery case out of the frame.
12. Install by reversing these removal steps.

### Instrument Cluster Removal/Installation

Refer to **Figure 104** for this procedure.

1. Remove the seat as described in Chapter Twelve.
2. Remove the fuel tank as described in Chapter Seven.

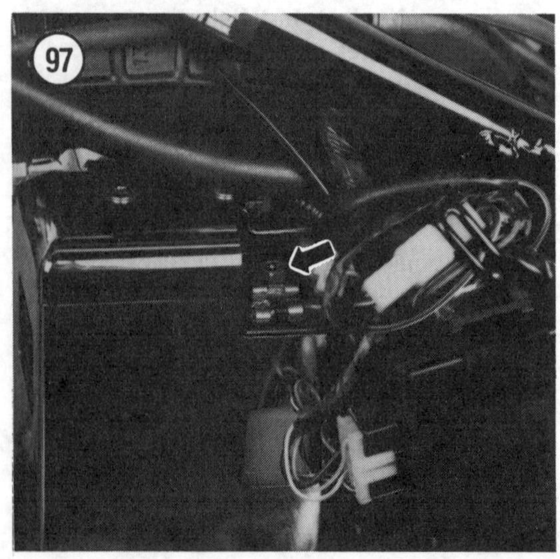
97

98

99

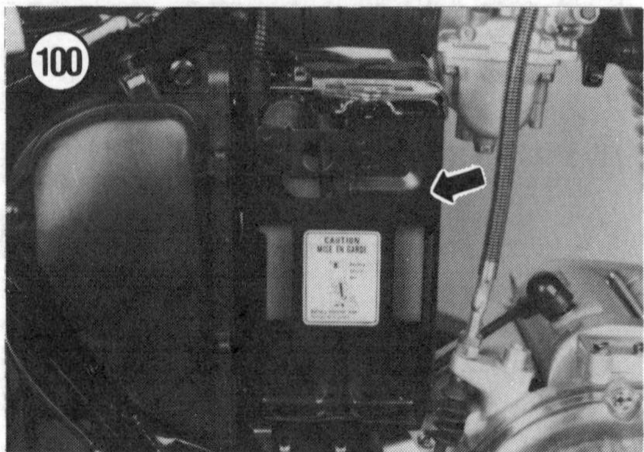
100

101

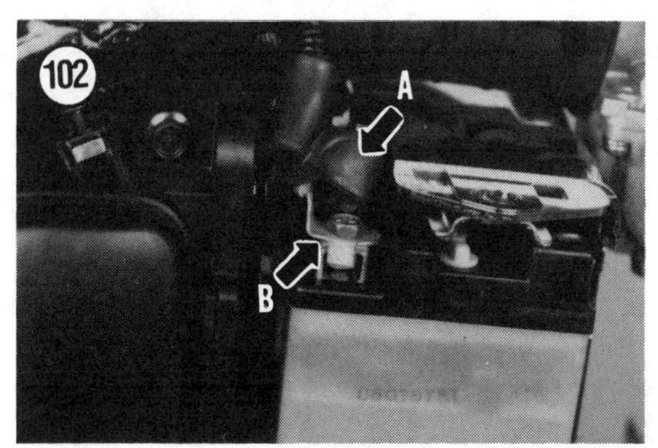


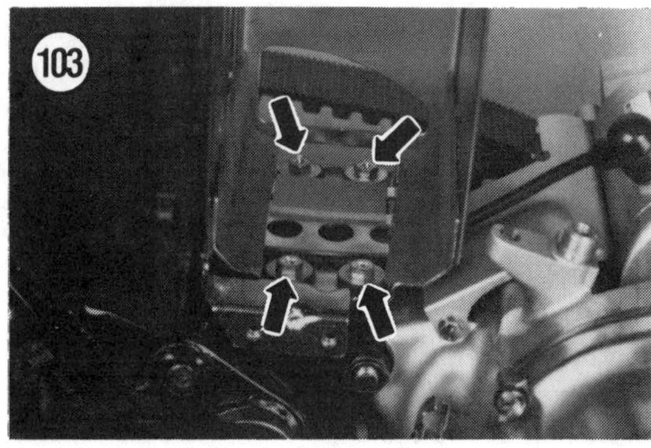


104

**INSTRUMENT CLUSTER**

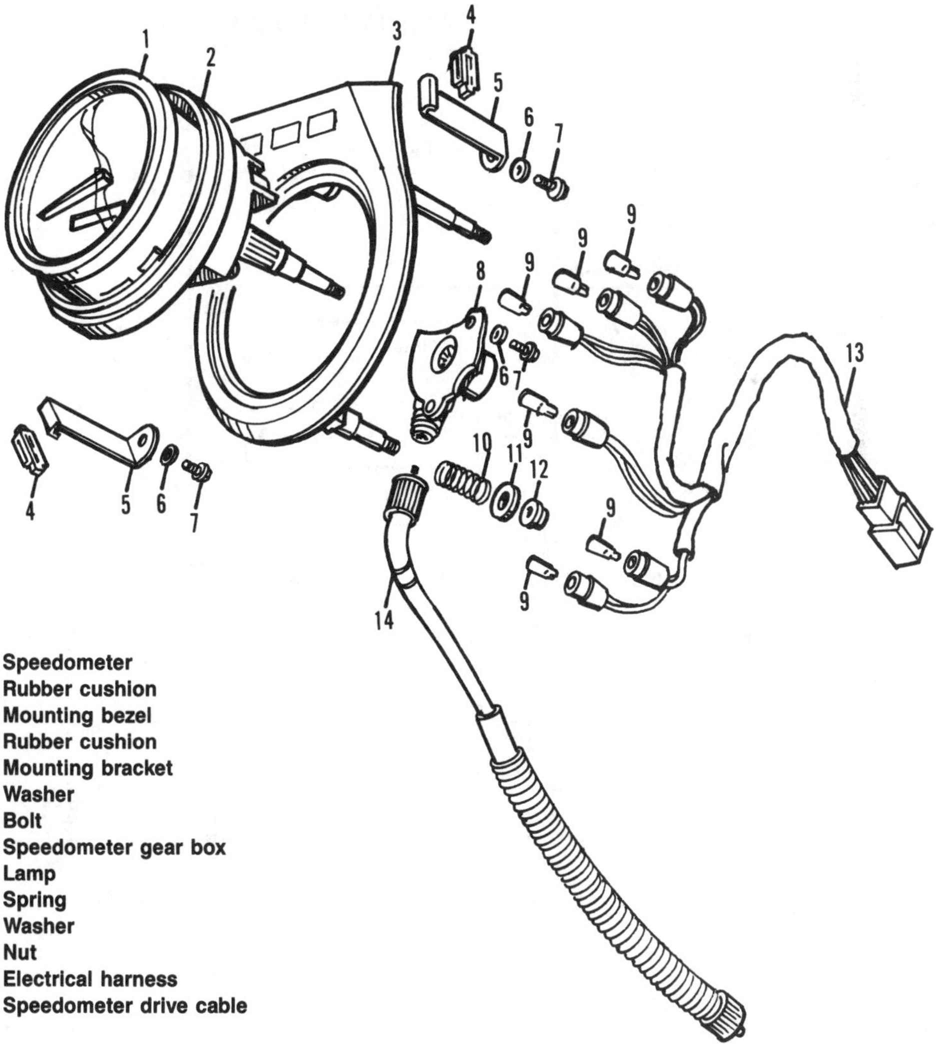

1. Speedometer
2. Rubber cushion
3. Mounting bezel
4. Rubber cushion
5. Mounting bracket
6. Washer
7. Bolt
8. Speedometer gear box
9. Lamp
10. Spring
11. Washer
12. Nut
13. Electrical harness
14. Speedometer drive cable

3. Unscrew the speedometer drive cable (A, **Figure 105**) from the back of the speedometer.
4. Remove the nuts, washer and springs (B, **Figure 105**) securing the instrument cluster to the mounting brackets in the fuel tank.
5. Carefully remove the instrument cluster assembly from the recess in the fuel tank.
6. Install by reversing these removal steps. Note the following during installation.
7. Make sure the electrical connector is free of corrosion and is tight.

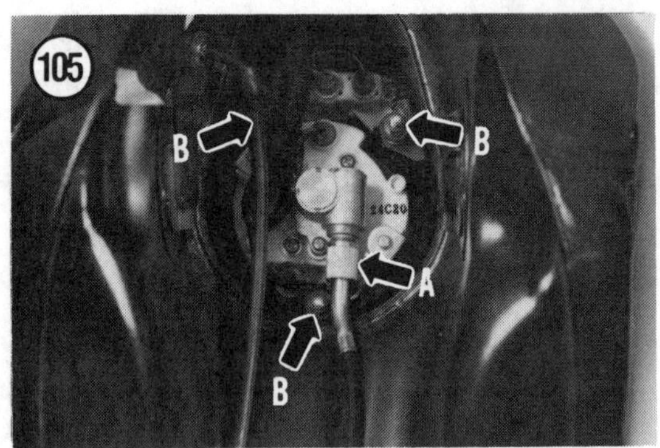


106

**AUTOMATIC DECOMPRESSION CONTROL AND STARTER SYSTEM**

Battery
Fuse
Red/white
Control unit
Sidestand indicator lamp
1
Green/white
6
Sidestand switch
Timer I
Blue/red
Yellow/green
3
2
Fuse
Ignition switch
Starter button
Clutch switch
Timer II
Blue/white
4
5
Starter relay
Decompression solenoid

| 1 | 2 | 3 |
|---|---|---|
| 4 | 5 | 6 |

Electrical connector

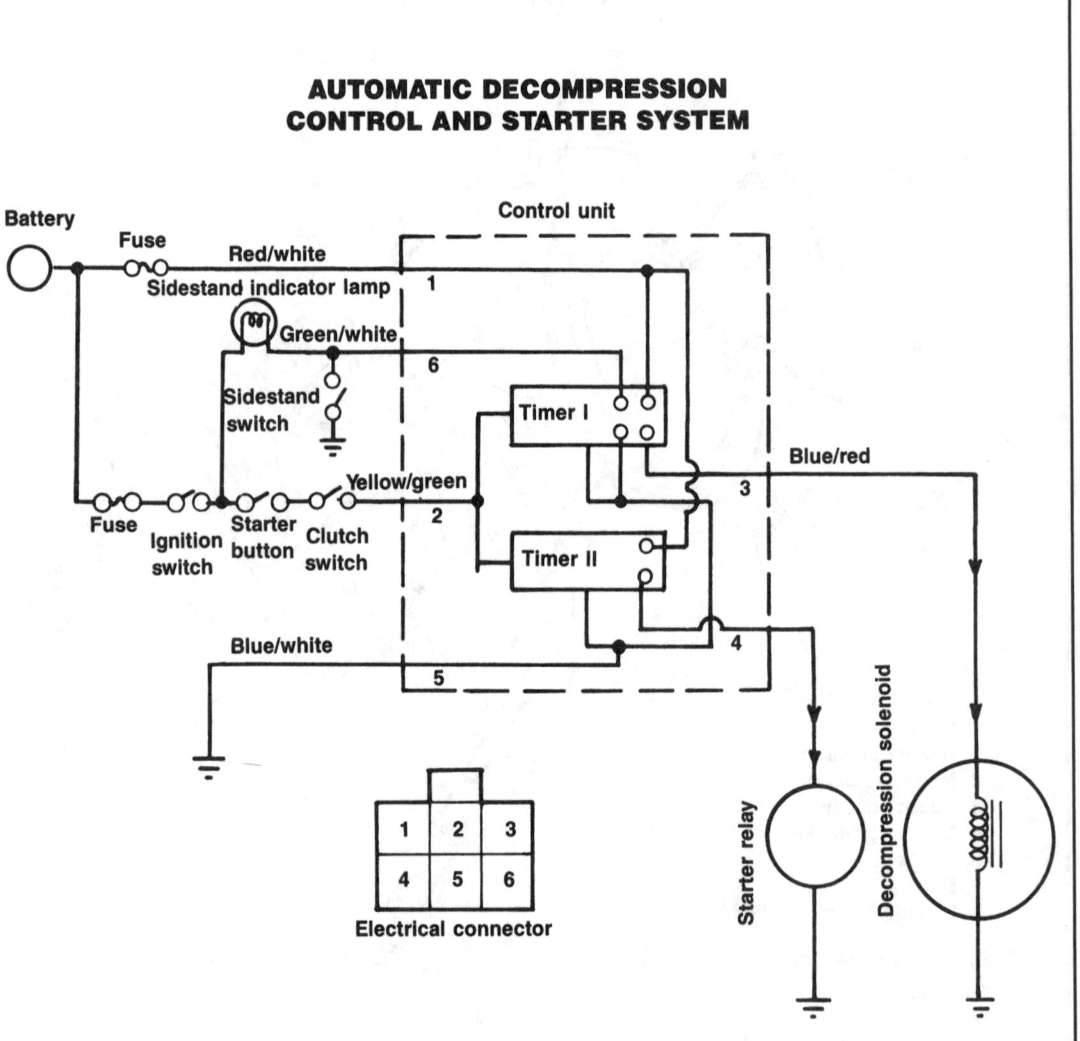

## Automatic Decompression Control System

The automatic decompression control system (**Figure 106**) automatically operates a solenoid that actuates the decompression lever. The decompression lever opens the exhaust valves a small amount in order to relieve compression during the starting cycle. This makes it easier for the starter to turn the engine over initially.

107

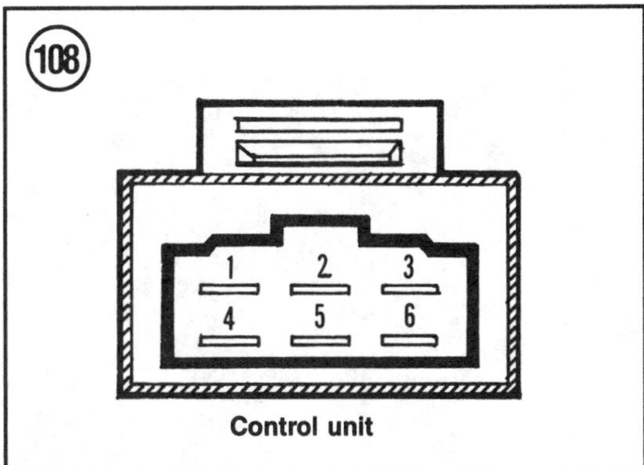

108
Control unit

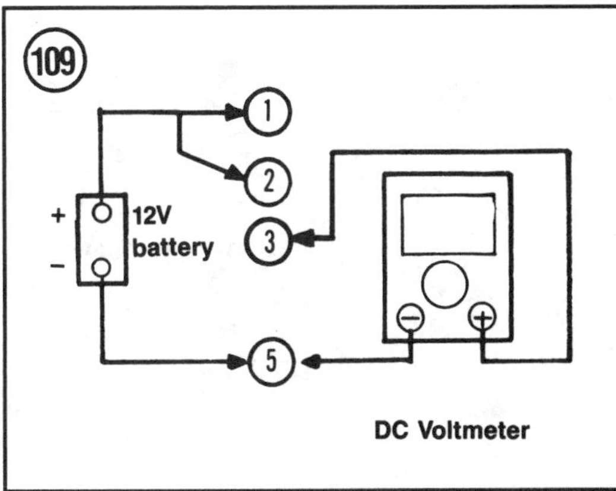

109

With the ignition switch ON, the clutch lever pulled in and starter button pressed in, the circuit from the battery is completed and 12 volts are applied to the No. 2 terminal of the control unit. When the 12 volts reach the Timer I, it is activated allowing the 12 volts to reach the No. 3 terminal of the control unit. At this time, the control unit activates the decompression solenoid which operates the decompression lever. About 0.2 seconds after the starter button is pressed, the Timer II is activated and 12 volts reach the No. 4 terminal on the control unit. At this time, the starter solenoid is energized and the starter motor starts to turn. The operation of the Timer I is 0.7 seconds and the Timer II shuts off the solenoid 0.5 seconds after starter motor starts turning. This allows the decompression lever to return to its normal position.

### *Control unit testing*

1. Remove the seat as described Chapter Twelve.
2. Remove the fuel tank as described in Chapter Seven.
3. Disconnect the electrical connector from the control unit (**Figure 107**).

*NOTE*

*The following tests are to be made on the terminals of the control unit (**Figure 108**).*

4. To test the Timer I portion of the control unit, refer to **Figure 109** and perform the following:
   a. Set a DC voltmeter to the DC 25 V range.
   b. Connect the voltmeter's positive (+) lead to the No. 3 terminal and the negative (-) lead to the No. 5 terminal.
   c. Using small jumper wires, connect a 12-volt battery as follows; positive (+) to the No. 1 and No. 2 terminals and the negative (-) to the No. 5 terminal.
   d. The voltmeter should read 12 volts for 0.7 seconds and then return to 0 volts.
   e. If this does not occur, the Timer I portion of the control unit is faulty and the control unit must be replaced.

8

5. To test the Timer II portion of the control unit, refer to **Figure 110** and perform the following:
   a. Set a DC voltmeter to the DC 25 V range.
   b. Connect the voltmeter's positive (+) lead to the No. 4 terminal and the negative (–) lead to the No. 5 terminal.
   c. Using small jumper wires, connect a 12-volt battery as follows; positive (+) to the No. 1 and No. 2 terminals and the negative (–) to the No. 5 terminal.
   d. The voltmeter should read 0 volts for 0.2 seconds and then 12 volts thereafter.
   e. If this does not occur, the Timer II portion of the control unit is faulty and the control unit must be replaced.
6. Disconnect the voltmeter and battery from the control unit.
7. Either replace the control unit as described in this chapter, or reconnect the electrical connector to the control unit. Make sure the electrical connector is free of corrosion and is tight.
8. Install the fuel tank as described in Chapter Seven.
9. Install the seat as described in Chapter Twelve.

*Control unit removal/installation*

1. Remove the seat as described in Chapter Twelve.
2. Remove the fuel tank as described in Chapter Seven.
3. Disconnect the electrical connector from the control unit (**Figure 107**).
4. Pull the control unit and its rubber mount from the mounting tab on the frame.
5. Reinstall the control unit and rubber mount onto the frame.
6. Reconnect the electrical connector to the control unit. Make sure the electrical connector is free of corrosion and is tight.
7. Install the fuel tank as described in Chapter Seven.
8. Install the seat as described in Chapter Twelve.

*Solenoid testing*

1. Remove the seat as described in Chapter Twelve.
2. Remove the fuel tank as described in Chapter Seven.
3. Remove the bolt and cap nut securing the cylinder head left-hand cover (**Figure 111**). Remove the cover and rubber cushions.
4. Shift the transmission into NEUTRAL.
5. Turn the ignition switch to the ON position.
6. Press the starter button.
7. Observe that the solenoid pulls the decompression cable properly and operates the lever (**Figure 112**).
8. If the solenoid does not operate correctly, perform the following test:
   a. Disconnect the solenoid electrical connector (**Figure 107**).

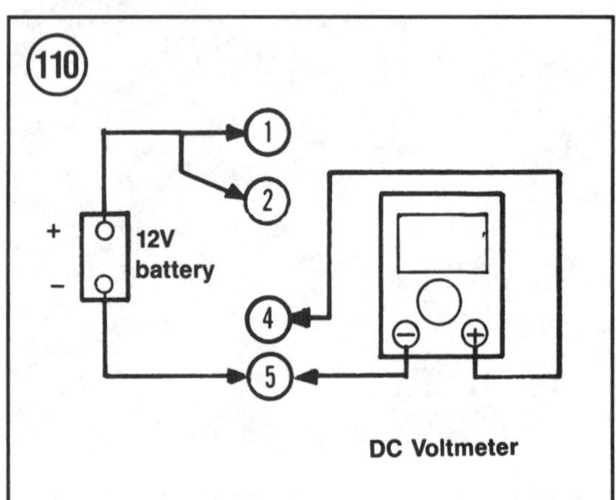

b. Use an ohmmeter and check for continuity between the 2 terminals on the solenoid side of the connector. There should be continuity (0.1-1.0 ohms). Disconnect the ohmmeter.

c. Using jumper wires, connect a 12-volt battery to the solenoid electrical connector as follows; positive (+) to the black/red and negative (-) to the black/white terminal (**Figure 113**).

d. With the battery connected, the solenoid should operate.
If the solenoid does not operate, replace the solenoid as described in this chapter.

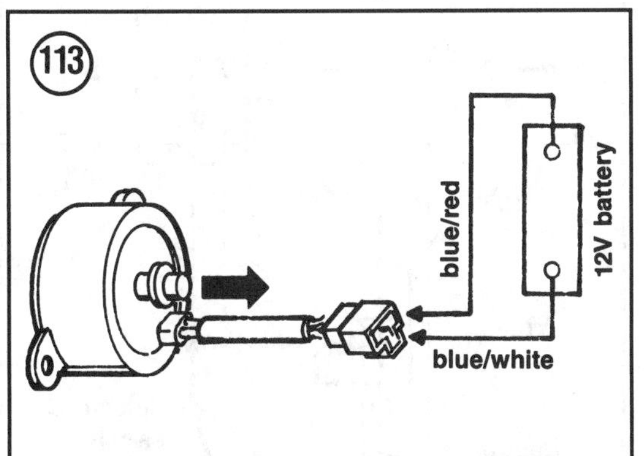


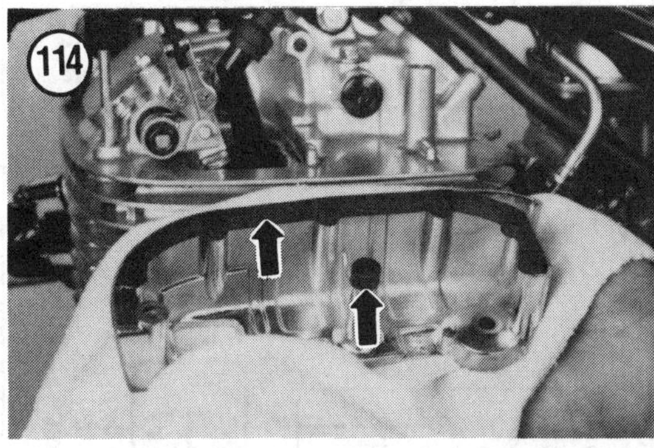


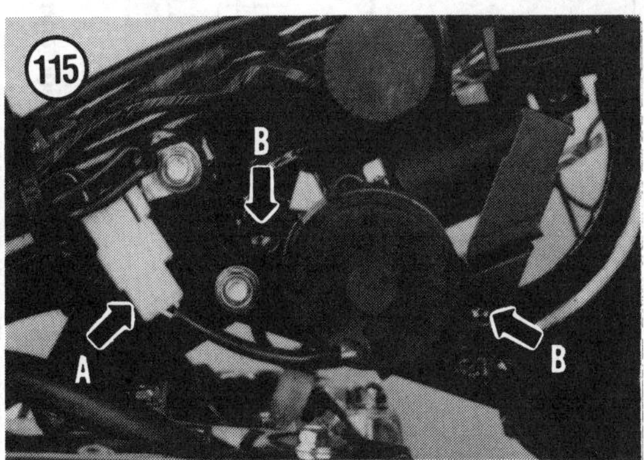


9. Disconnect the 12-volt battery.
10. Either replace the solenoid as described in this chapter or reconnect the electrical connector to the solenoid. Make sure the electrical connector is free of corrosion and is tight.
11. Make sure the rubber cushions (**Figure 114**) are in place on the cylinder head left-hand cover and install the cover.
12. Install the bolt and cap nut securing the cylinder head left-hand cover (**Figure 111**). Tighten the bolt and cap nut securely.
13. Install the fuel tank as described in Chapter Seven.
14. Install the seat as described in Chapter Twelve.

***Solenoid removal/installation***

1. Remove the seat as described in Chapter Twelve.
2. Remove the fuel tank as described in Chapter Seven.
3. Remove the bolt and cap nut securing the cylinder head left-hand cover (**Figure 111**). Remove the cover and rubber cushions.
4. Disconnect the solenoid electrical connector (A, **Figure 115**).
5. Disconnect the solenoid cable from the decompression lever (**Figure 112**).
6. Remove the bolts (B, **Figure 115**) securing the solenoid and cable to the frame. Remove the solenoid and cable from the frame.
7. Remove the E-clip from the pivot pin and disconnect the cable from the solenoid.
8. Install by reversing these removal steps. Note the following during installation.
9. Make sure the electrical connector is free of corrosion and is tight.
10. Adjust the cable as described under *Automatic Decompression Cable Adjustment* in Chapter Three.



## Sidestand Interlock (1987-1988)

The sidestand interlock system is equipped on 1987-1988 models. This system prevents the engine from being started with the sidestand in down position and the transmission in gear. A special circuit between the battery and ignition coil, consisting of a relay, lamp, diode and switches, decide whether the ignition circuit can be completed, thus allowing the engine to be started.

The ignition circuit is completed under the 2 following different situations:

a. The transmission in NEUTRAL and the sidestand DOWN (**Figure 116**).
b. The transmission in GEAR and the sidestand UP (**Figure 117**).

### *Switch testing*

1. Remove the seat as described in Chapter Twelve.
2. Disconnect the sidestand interlock switch electrical connector.
3. Use an ohmmeter and check for continuity between the 2 terminals on the switch side of the connector (**Figure 118**) as follows:
   a. With the sidestand DOWN, there should be no continuity (infinite resistance).
   b. With the sidestand UP, there should be continuity (low resistance).
4. Either replace the switch as described in this chapter or reconnect the electrical connector to the switch. Make sure the electrical connector is free of corrosion and is tight.
5. Install the seat as described in Chapter Twelve.

### *Switch removal/installation*

1. Remove the seat as described in Chapter Twelve.
2. Remove the left-hand frame cover.
3. Disconnect the sidestand interlock switch electrical connector.
4. Remove the clamps securing the electrical wires to the frame.
5. Remove the screws and lockwashers securing the switch to the frame and remove the switch.
6. Install by reversing these removal steps. Note the following during installation.
7. Make sure the electrical connector is free of corrosion and is tight.

### *Relay removal/installation*

1. Remove the seat as described in Chapter Twelve.
2. Remove the fuel tank as described in Chapter Seven.
3. Disconnect the electrical connector from the relay.
4. Pull the relay and its rubber mount from the mounting tab on the frame.
5. Reinstall the relay and rubber mount onto the frame.
6. Reconnect the electrical connector to the relay. Make sure the electrical connector is free of corrosion and is tight.
7. Install the fuel tank as described in Chapter Seven.
8. Install the seat as described in Chapter Twelve.

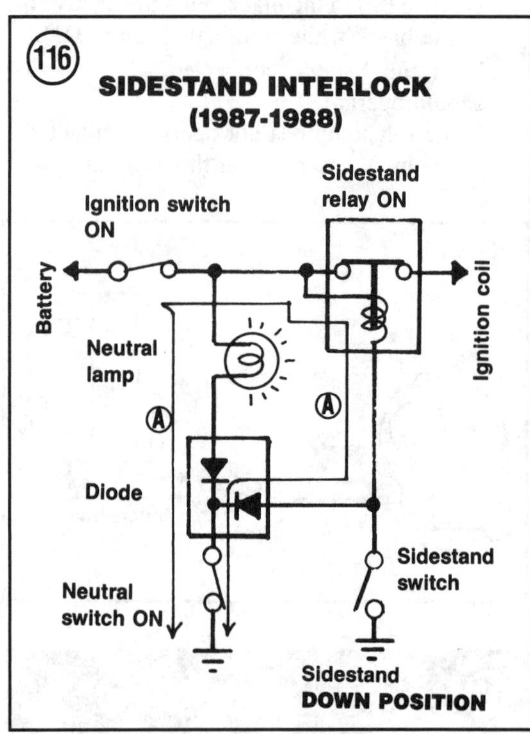


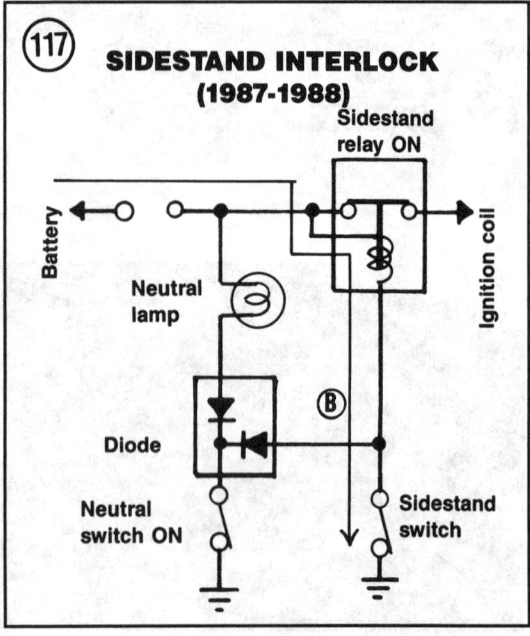

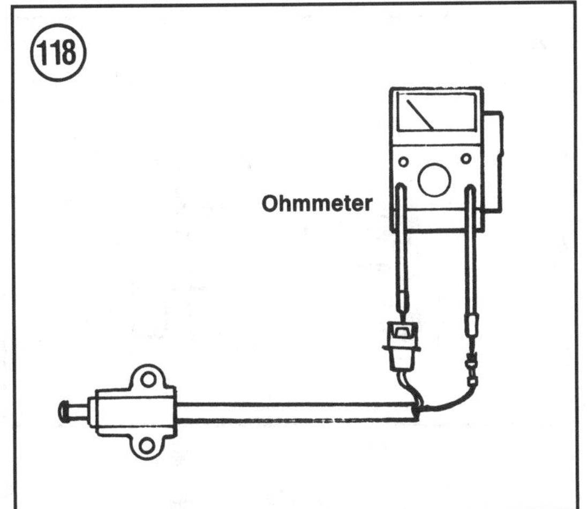


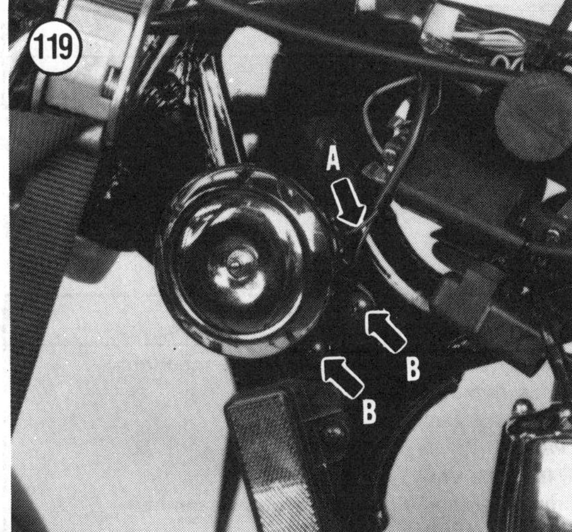


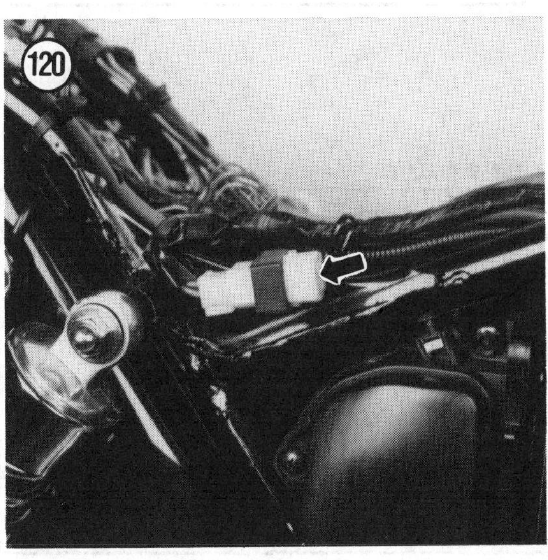


### Horn Testing

1. Disconnect horn wires from harness.
2. Connect a 12-volt battery to the horn.
3. If the horn is good, it will sound. If not, replace it.

### Horn Removal/Installation

1. Disconnect the electrical connector (A, **Figure 119**) from the horn.
2. Remove the screws and washers securing the horn (B, **Figure 119**) to the frame. Remove the horn.
3. Install by reversing these removal steps. Note the following during installation.
4. Make sure the electrical connector is free of corrosion and is tight.

## FUSES



The fuses are located under the seat. Whenever the fuse blows, find out the reason for the failure before replacing the fuse. Usually, the trouble is a short circuit in the wiring. This may be caused by worn-through insulation or a disconnected wire shorted to ground.

*CAUTION*

*Never substitute metal foil or wire for a fuse. Never use a higher amperage fuse than specified. An overload could result in a fire and complete loss of the bike.*

*CAUTION*

*When replacing a fuse, make sure the ignition switch is in the OFF position. This will lessen the chance of a short circuit.*

### Fuse Replacement

1. Remove the seat as described in Chapter Twelve.
2. Disconnect the fuse holder (**Figure 120**) from the wiring harness.

*NOTE*

*These fuses (**Figure 121**) are not the typical glass tube with metal ends. Carry extra fuses in your tool box.*

3. Remove the fuse and install a new one.
4. Attach the fuse holder to the wiring harness.
5. Install the seat as described in Chapter Twelve.

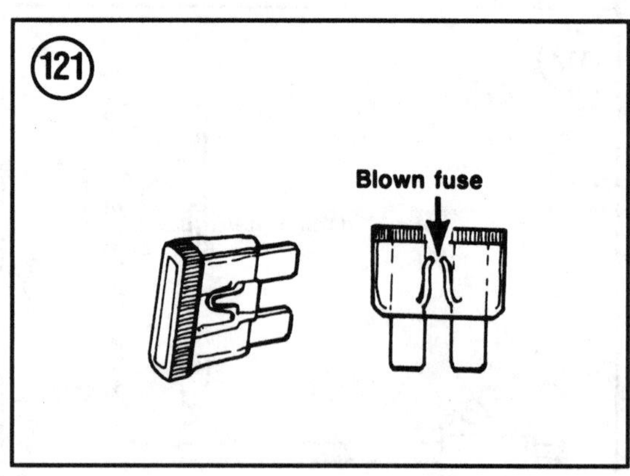


## WIRING DIAGRAMS

Wiring diagrams for all models are located at the end of this book.

**Table 1 ELECTRICAL SYSTEM TORQUE SPECIFICATIONS**

| Item | N·m | ft.-lb. |
|---|---|---|
| Alternator rotor bolt | 140-160 | 103-118 |

**Table 2 IGNITION TROUBLESHOOTING**

| Symptoms | Probable cause |
|---|---|
| Weak spark | Poor connections in circuit (clean and retighten all connections) |
| | High voltage leak (replace defective wire) |
| | Defective ignition coil (replace coil) |
| No spark | Broken wire (replace wire) |
| | Defective ignition coil (replace coil) |
| | Defective signal generator (replace signal generator assembly) |
| | Defective ignitor unit (replace ignitor unit) |
| | Faulty engine stop switch (replace switch) |

**Table 3 REPLACEMENT BULBS**

| Item | Voltage/wattage |
|---|---|
| Headlight | 12V 55/60W |
| Taillight/brake light | 12V 8/23W |
| License plate light | 12V 8W |
| Turn signal light | 12V 23W |
| Front position light | 12V 8W |
| Speedometer | |
| Illumination light | 12V 3W |
| Indicator light | |
| Sidestand check light, | |
| turn signal, neutral | 12V 3W |
| High beam | 12V 1.7W |

CHAPTER NINE

# FRONT SUSPENSION AND STEERING

This chapter describes procedures for the repair and maintenance of the front wheel, front forks and steering components.

Front suspension torque specifications are covered in **Table 1**. **Tables 1-3** are at the end of this chapter.

9

## FRONT WHEEL

### Removal

1. Loosen the front axle pinch bolt (**Figure 1**) and the front axle (**Figure 2**) on the right-hand side.
2. Place wood block(s) under the engine and frame to support the bike securely with the front wheel off the ground.
3. Remove the front caliper assembly as described under *Front Brake Caliper Removal/Installation* in Chapter Eleven.
4. Completely unscrew and withdraw the front axle (**Figure 2**) from the right-hand side.
5. Pull the wheel down and forward to remove.
6. Remove the wheel. Don't lose the spacers on each side.

*CAUTION*

*Do not set the wheel down on the disc surface as it may get scratched or warped. Set the sidewalls on 2 wood blocks (**Figure 3**).*

*NOTE*
*Insert a piece of vinyl tubing or wood in the caliper in place of the brake disc. That way if the brake lever is inadvertently squeezed, the piston will not be forced out of the cylinder. If this does happen, the caliper may have to be disassembled to reseat the piston and the system will have to be bled. By using the wood, bleeding the brake is not necessary when installing the wheel.*

### Installation

1. Make sure the axle bearing surfaces of the fork sliders and axle are free from burrs and nicks.
2. Remove the vinyl tubing or pieces of wood from the brake caliper.
3. Position the wheel in place and carefully insert the brake disc between the brake pads in the caliper assembly.
4. Make sure the wheel spacer is in place on each side of the hub.
5. Apply a light coat of grease to the front axle. Insert the front axle from the left-hand side through the wheel hub.
6. Tighten the front axle to the torque specification listed in **Table 1**.
7. Install the front caliper assembly as described under *Front Brake Caliper Removal/Installation* in Chapter Eleven.
8. Remove the wood block(s) from under the engine and frame.
9. With the front brake applied, push down hard on the handlebars and pump the forks several times to seat the front axle.
10. Tighten the front axle and front axle pinch bolt to the torque specification listed in **Table 1**.
11. After the wheel is completely installed, rotate it several times to make sure that it rotates freely. Apply the front brake as many times as necessary to make sure the brake pads are against the brake disc correctly.

## WHEEL INSPECTION

Measure the axial (end play) and radial (side play) runout of the wheel with a dial indicator as shown in **Figure 4**. The maximum axial and radial runout is 2.0 mm (0.08 in.). If the runout exceeds this dimension, check the wheel bearing condition. Check the front axle runout as described under *Front Hub* in this chapter.

## FRONT HUB

### Inspection

Inspect each wheel bearing before removing it from the wheel hub.

*CAUTION*
*Do not remove the wheel bearings for inspection purposes as they will be damaged during the removal process. Remove wheel bearings only if they are to be replaced.*

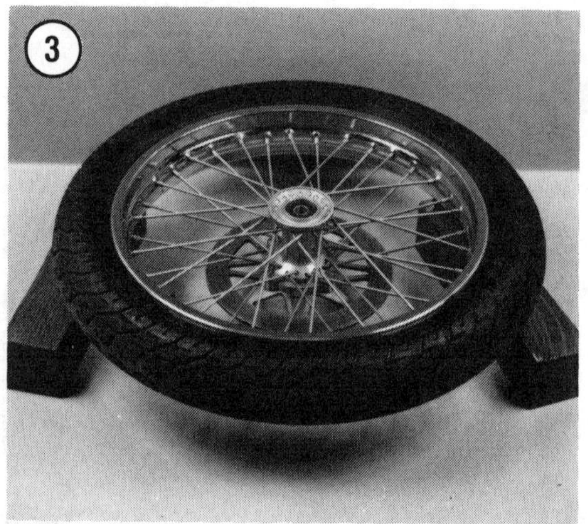
3

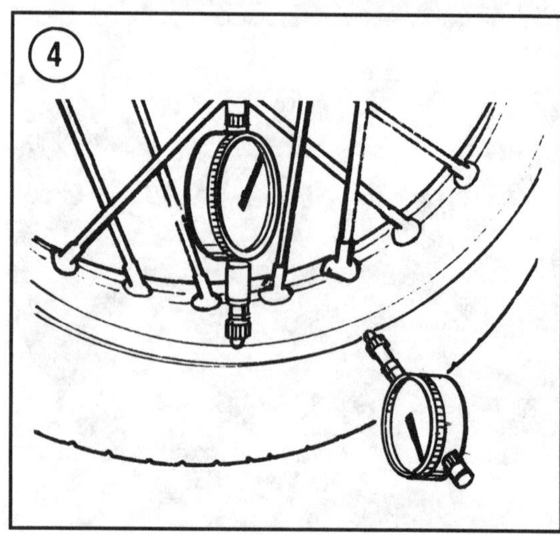
4

1. Perform Steps 1-3 of *Disassembly* in this chapter.
2. Turn each bearing by hand. Make sure bearings turn smoothly.
3. Inspect the play of the inner race (**Figure 5**) of each wheel bearing. Check for excessive axial (side play) and radial (end play) play. Replace the bearing if it has an excess amount of free play.
4. On non-sealed bearings, check the balls for evidence of wear, pitting or excessive heat (bluish tint). Replace the bearings if necessary; always replace as a complete set. When replacing the bearings, be sure to take your old bearings along to ensure a perfect matchup.

*NOTE*
*Fully sealed bearings are available from many bearing specialty shops. Fully sealed bearings provide better protection from dirt and moisture that may get into the hub.*

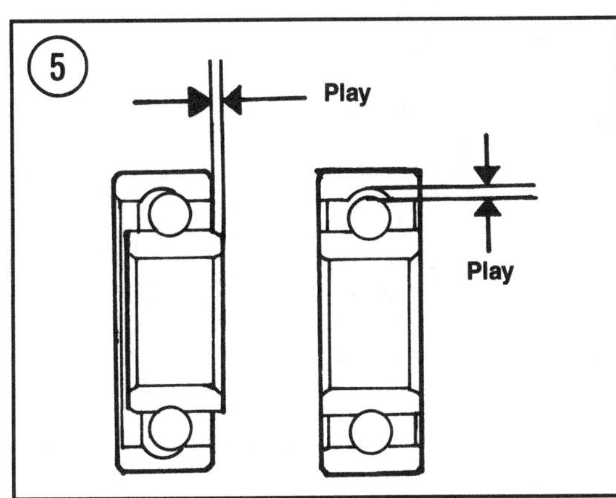

5. Check the axle for wear and straightness. Use V-blocks and a dial indicator as shown in **Figure 6**. If the runout is 0.2 mm (0.01 in.) or greater, the axle should be replaced.

### Disassembly

Refer to **Figure 7** for this procedure.

1. Remove the front wheel as described in this chapter.
2. Remove the spacer, from the right-hand side and left-hand side, from the hub.
3. Remove the bolts (A, **Figure 8**) securing the brake disc and remove the disc.
4. Before proceeding further, inspect the wheel bearings as described in this chapter. If they must be replaced, proceed as follows.

5A. A special Suzuki tool setup (Suzuki part No. 09941-50110) can be used to remove the wheel bearings as follows:

a. Insert the adaptor (A, **Figure 9**) into one of the wheel bearings from the outer surface of the wheel.
b. Turn the wheel over and insert the wedge bar (B, **Figure 9**) into the backside of the adaptor. Tap the wedge bar and force it into the slit in the adaptor. This will wedge the adaptor against the inner bearing race.
c. Tap on the end of the wedge bar with a hammer (**Figure 10**) and drive the bearing out of the hub. Remove the bearing and the distance collar.
d. Repeat for the bearing on the other side.

5B. If the special tools are not used, perform the following:

a. To remove the right- and left-hand bearings and distance collar, insert a soft-aluminum or brass drift into one side of the hub.
b. Push the distance collar over to one side and place the drift on the inner race of the lower bearing.
c. Tap the bearing out of the hub with a hammer, working around the perimeter of the inner race.
d. Repeat for the bearing on the other side.

6. Clean the inside and the outside of the hub with solvent. Dry with compressed air.

9

7

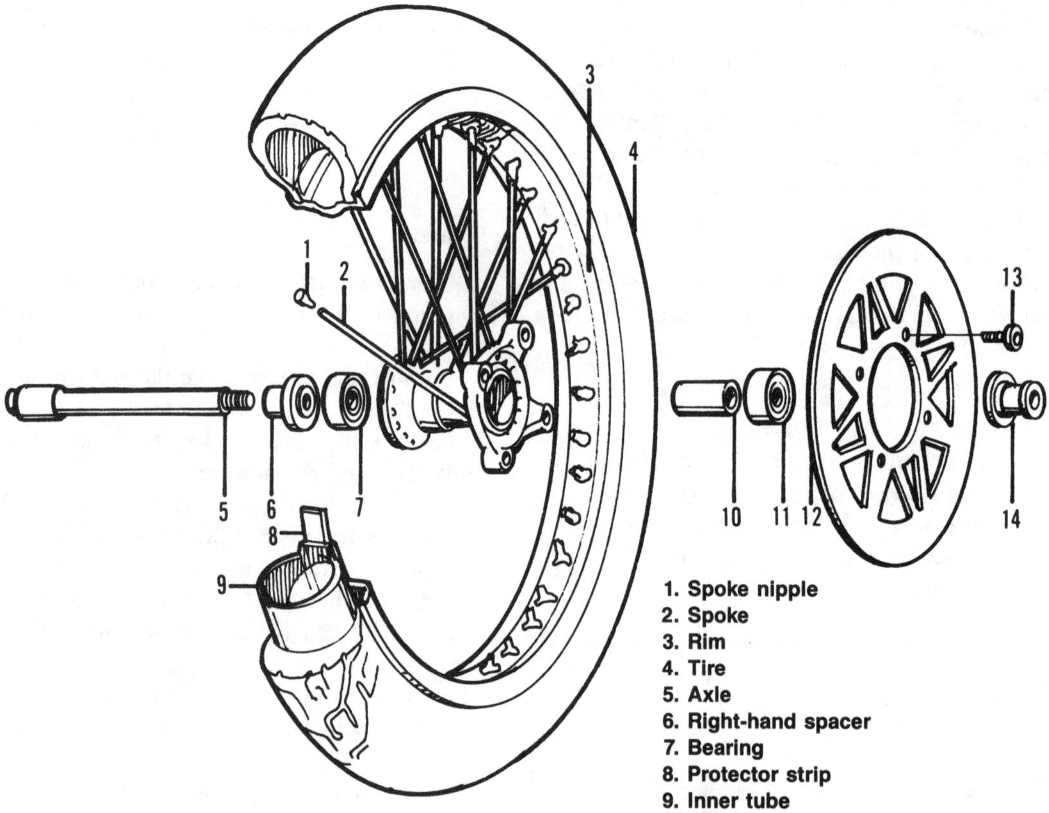

1. Spoke nipple
2. Spoke
3. Rim
4. Tire
5. Axle
6. Right-hand spacer
7. Bearing
8. Protector strip
9. Inner tube
10. Distance collar
11. Bearing
12. Brake disc
13. Disc bolts
14. Left-hand spacer

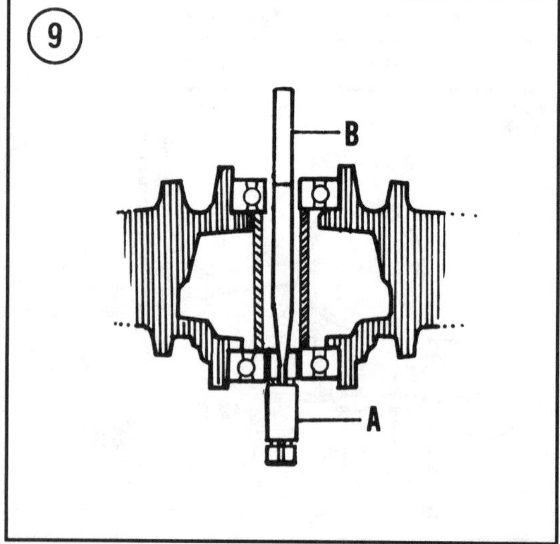

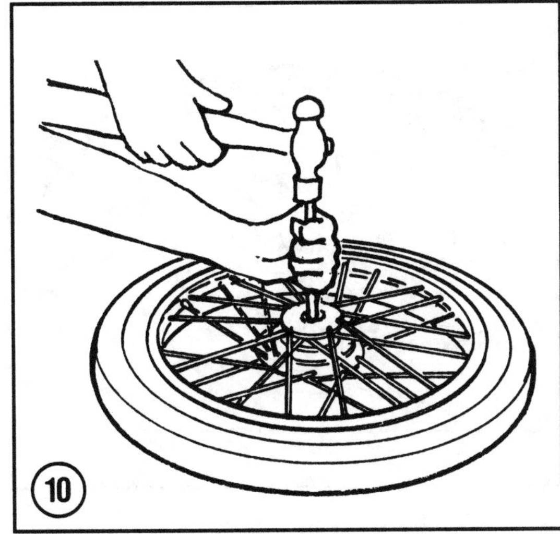
10

## Assembly

1. On non-sealed bearings, pack the bearings with a good-quality bearing grease. Work the grease in between the balls thoroughly; turn the bearing by hand a couple of times to make sure the grease is distributed evenly inside the bearing.
2. Blow any dirt or foreign matter out of the hub before installing the bearings.

*CAUTION*

*Install non-sealed bearings with the single sealed side facing outward. Tap the bearings squarely into place and tap on the outer race only. Do not tap on the inner race or the bearing might be damaged. Be sure that the bearings are completely seated.*

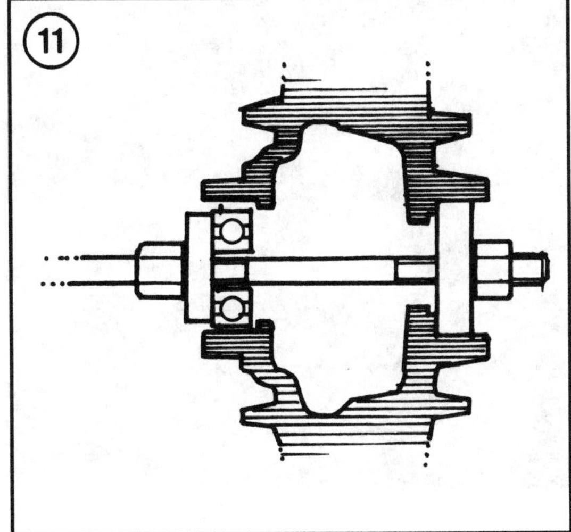
11

3A. A special Suzuki tool setup (Suzuki part No. 99924-84510) can be used to install the wheel bearings as follows:

a. Install the left-hand bearing into the hub first.
b. Set the bearing with the sealed side facing out and install the bearing installer as shown in **Figure 11**.
c. Tighten the bearing installer (**Figure 12**) and pull the bearing into the hub until it is completely seated (B, **Figure 8**). Remove the bearing installer.
d. Turn the wheel over (right-hand side up) on the workbench and install the distance collar.
e. Set the bearing with the sealed side facing out and install the bearing installer as shown in **Figure 13**.

12

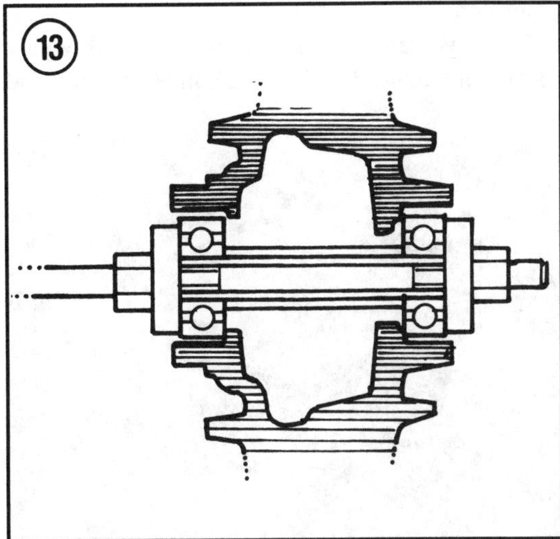
13

f. Tighten the bearing installer (**Figure 12**) and pull the bearing into the hub until it is completely seated (**Figure 14**).

g. Remove the bearing installer.

3B. If special tools are not used, perform the following:

a. Tap the left-hand bearing squarely into place and tap on the outer race only. Use a socket (**Figure 15**) that matches the outer race diameter. Do not tap on the inner race or the bearing might be damaged. Be sure that the bearing is completely seated.

b. Turn the wheel over (right-hand side up) on the workbench and install the distance collar.

c. Use the same tool setup and drive in the right-hand bearing.

4. Apply red Loctite Threadlocker No. 271 to the brake disc bolts prior to installation.

5. Install the brake disc and bolts (**Figure 16**). Tighten to the torque specifications listed in **Table 1**.

6. Install the front wheel as described in this chapter.

## WHEELS

### Wheel Balance

An unbalanced wheel is unsafe. Depending on the degree of unbalance and the speed of the motorcycle, the rider may experience anything from a mild vibration to a violent shimmy which may even result in loss of control.

The balance weights are attached to the wheel spokes on the light side of the wheel to correct this condition.

Before you attempt to balance the wheel, check to be sure that the wheel bearings are in good

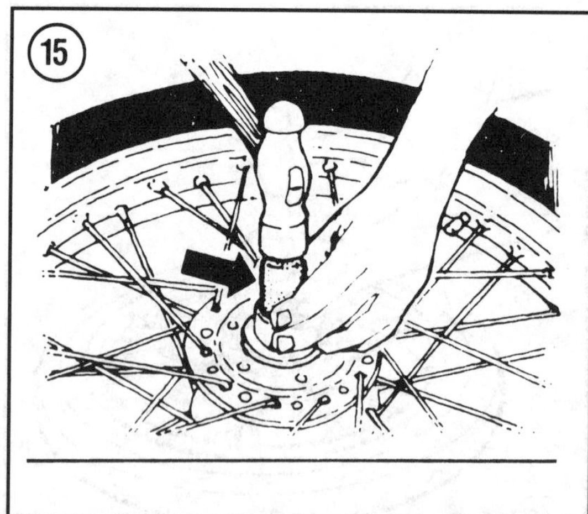

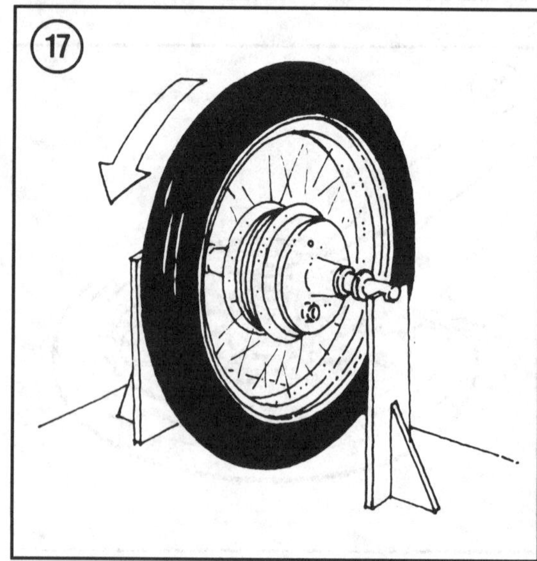

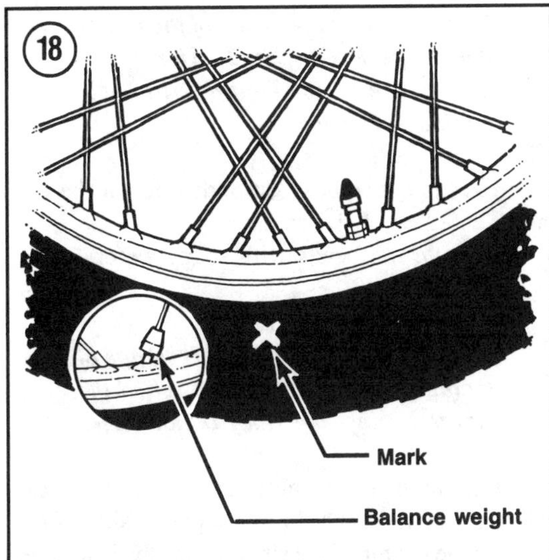


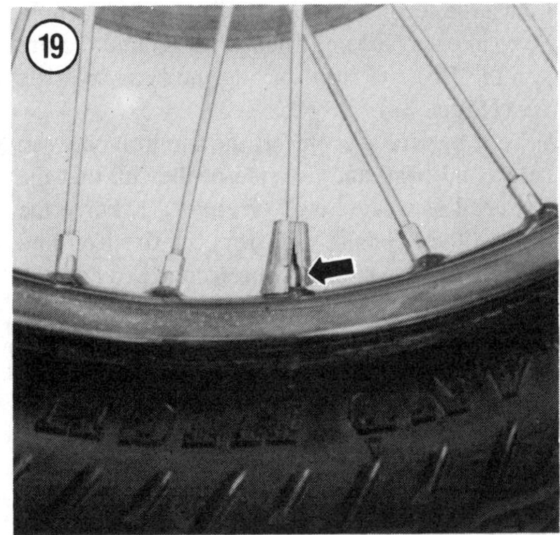


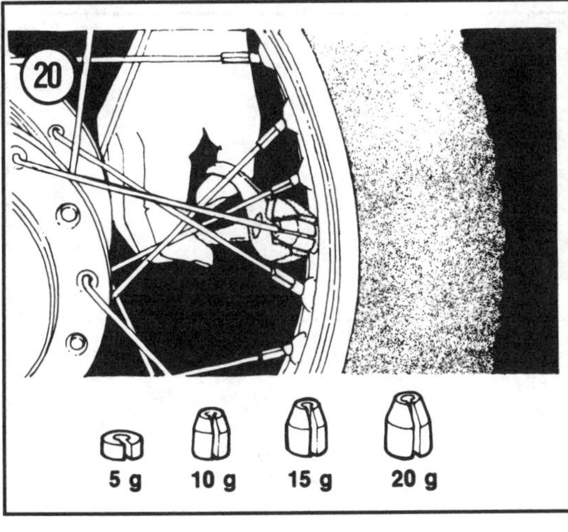


condition and properly lubricated and that the brakes do not drag. The wheel must rotate freely.

*NOTE*
*When balancing the wheels, do so with the brake disc attached to the front wheel and with the driven pulley assembly attached to the rear wheel. These components rotate with the wheels and they affect the balance.*

1. Remove the wheel as described in this chapter or Chapter Ten.
2. Mount the wheel on a fixture such as the one shown in **Figure 17** so it can rotate freely.
3. Give the wheel a spin and let it coast to a stop. Mark the tire at the lowest point (**Figure 18**).
4. Spin the wheel several more times. If the wheel keeps coming to rest at the same point, it is *out of balance*.
5. Attach a weight (**Figure 19**) to the upper (or light) side of the wheel at the spoke (**Figure 20**). Weights are crimped onto the spoke with ordinary gas pliers.
6. Experiment with different weights until the wheel, when spun, comes to a rest at a different position each time.

9

### Spoke Adjustment

Spokes loosen with use and should be checked periodically. If all appear loose, tighten all spokes on one side of the hub, then tighten all the spokes on the other side with a 6 mm spoke wrench (**Figure 21**). One-half to one turn should be sufficient; do not overtighten. If you have a torque wrench spoke wrench, tighten the spokes to the torque specification listed in **Table 1**.

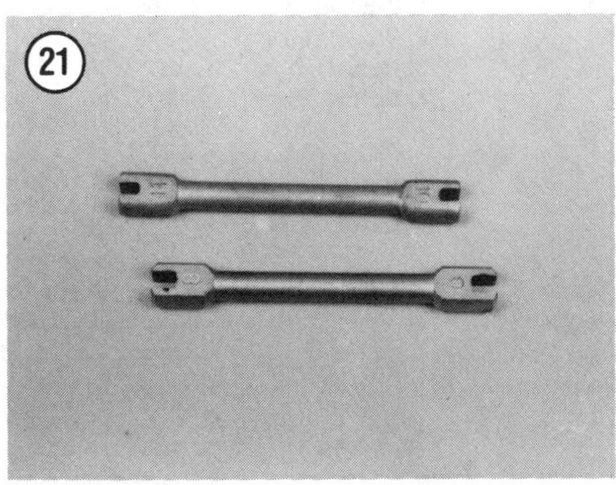

After tightening the spokes, check rim runout to be sure you haven't pulled the rim out of shape. One way to check rim runout is to mount a dial indicator to the front fork (or swing arm) so that it bears on the rim.

If you don't have a dial indicator, improvise one as shown in **Figure 22**. Adjust the position of the bolt until it just clears the wheel rim. Rotate the wheel and note whether the clearance between the bolt and rim increases or decreases. Mark the tire with chalk or crayon in areas that produce significantly large or small clearances. Clearance must not change by more than 2 mm (0.08 in.).

To pull the rim out, tighten the spokes which terminate on the opposite side of the hub (**Figure 23**). In most cases, only a slight amount of adjustment is necessary to true the rim. After adjustment, rotate the wheel and make sure another area has not been pulled out of true. Continue adjusting and checking until the runout does not exceed 2 mm (0.08 in.).

## TIRE CHANGING

### Removal

1. If you are going to reinstall the existing tire, mark the valve stem location on the tire (**Figure 24**). This will ensure that the tire will be installed in the same position for easier balancing.
2. Remove the valve core to deflate the tire.

*CAUTION*
*The inner rim and tire bead area are sealing surfaces on the tubeless tire. Do not scratch the inside of the rim or damage the tire bead. Use good-quality tire irons (**Figure 25**) to help minimize damage.*

3. Press the entire bead on both sides of the tire into the center of the rim.
4. Lubricate the beads with soapy water.

*CAUTION*
*Use rim protectors or insert scraps of leather between the tire irons and the rim to protect the rim from damage.*

5. Insert the tire iron under the bead next to the valve. Force the bead on the opposite side of the tire into the center of the rim and pry the bead over the rim with the tire iron.
6. Insert a second tire iron next to the first to hold the bead over the rim. Then work around the tire with the first tire iron, prying the bead over the rim (**Figure 26**).
7. Turn the tire over. Insert the tire iron between the second bead and the side of the rim that the first bead was pried over (**Figure 27**). Force the bead on the opposite side from the tire iron into the center of the rim. Pry the second bead off the rim, working around as with the first.
8. Inspect the valve stem seal. Because rubber deteriorates with age, it is advisable to replace the valve stem when replacing the tire.
9. Remove the old valve stem and discard it. Inspect the valve stem hole in the rim. Remove any dirt or corrosion from the hole and wipe dry with a clean cloth.

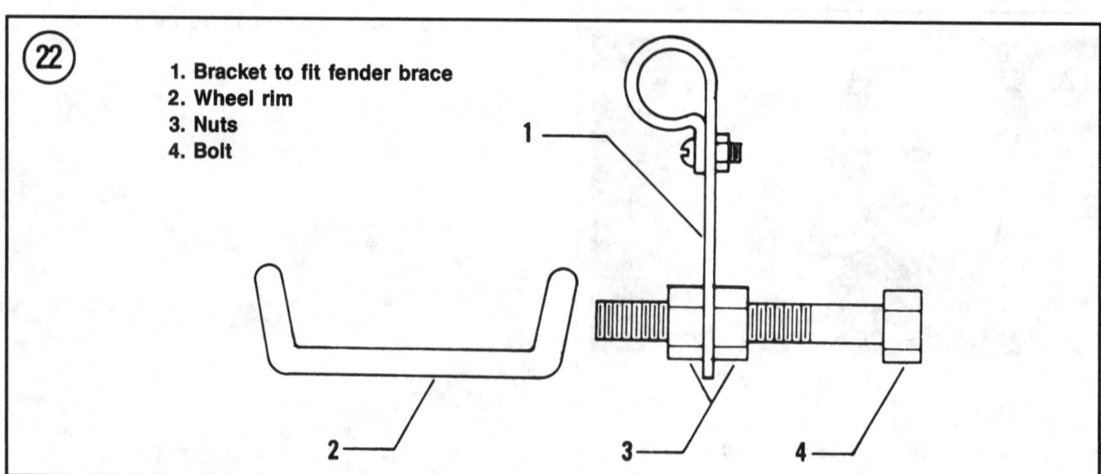

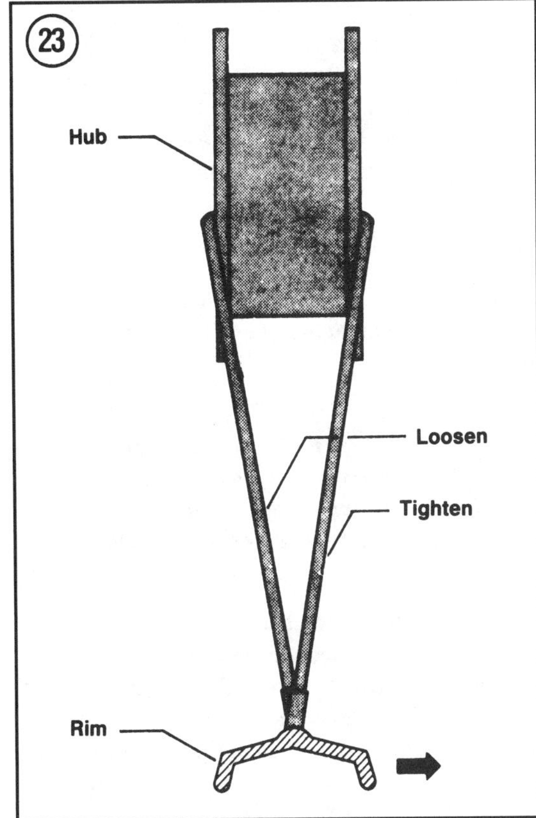


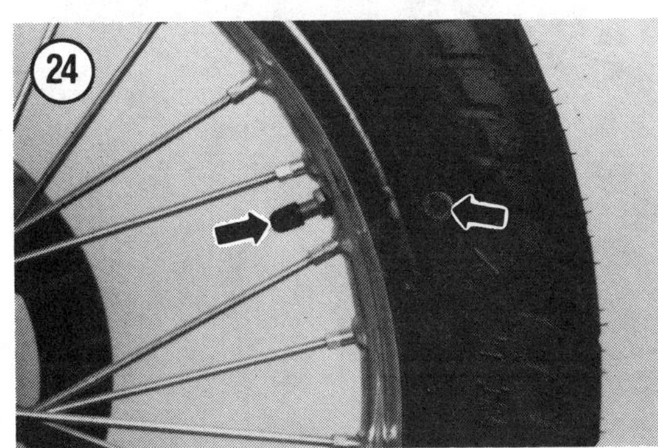


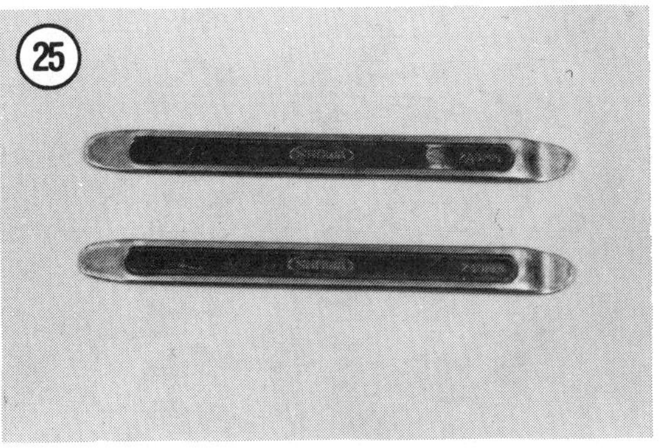


## Tire and Rim Inspection

1. Wipe off the inner surfaces of the wheel rim. Clean off any rubber residue or any oxidation.
2. If a can of pressurized tire sealant was used for a temporary fix of a flat, thoroughly clean off all sealant residue. Any remaining residue will present a problem when reinstalling the tire and achieving a good seal of the tire bead against the rim.

*WARNING*
*Carefully consider whether a tire should be patched or replaced. If there is any doubt about the quality of the existing tire,* ***replace it with a new one****. Don't take a chance on a tire failure.*

3. If a tire is going to be patched, thoroughly inspect the tire. If any one of the following is observed, do not repair the tire; *replace it with a new one*:

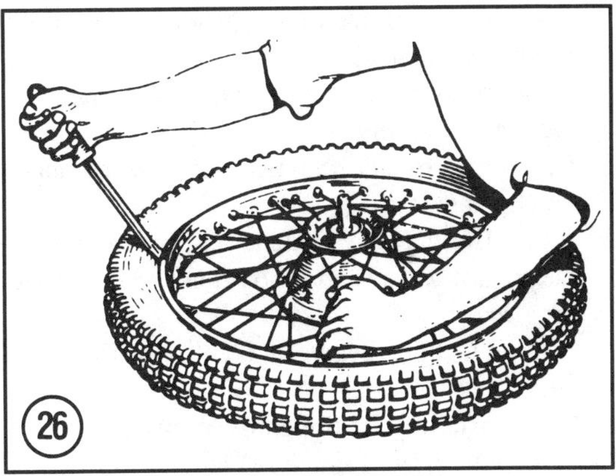


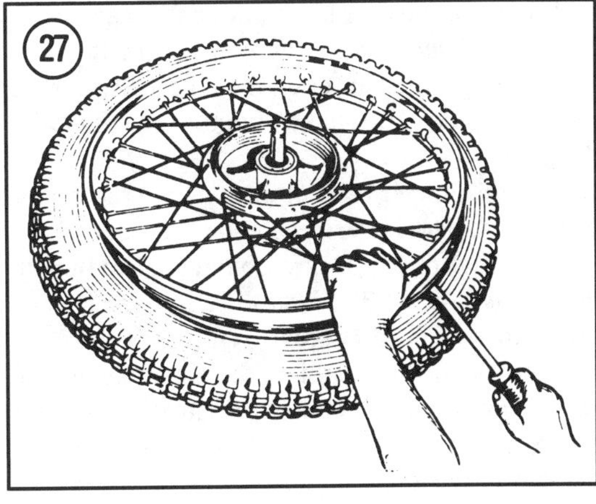


9

a. A puncture or split whose total length or diameter exceeds 6 mm (0.24 in.).
b. A scratch or split on the side wall.
c. Any type of ply separation.
d. Tread separation or excessive abnormal wear pattern.
e. Tread depth of less than 1.6 mm (0.06 in.) in the front tire or less than 2.0 mm (0.08 in.) in the rear tire on original equipment tires. Aftermarket tires tread depth minimum may vary.
f. Scratches on either sealing bead.
g. The cord is cut in any place.
h. Flat spots in the tread from skidding.
i. Any abnormality in the inner liner.

### Installation

1. Install a new valve stem as follows:
   a. Insert the new valve stem into the rim.
   b. Install the nut and tighten with your fingers only. Do not use pliers and overtighten the nut as it may distort the rubber grommet that could cause an air leak.
   c. Hold onto the nut and install and tighten the locknut securely.
2. Carefully inspect the tire for any damage, especially inside.
3. A new tire may have balancing rubbers inside. These are not patches and should not be disturbed or removed.
4. Lubricate both beads of the tire with soapy water.
5. When installing the tire onto the rim, make sure the direction arrow (**Figure 28**) faces the direction of wheel rotation.
6. If remounting the old tire, align the mark made in Step 1, *Removal* with the valve stem. If a new tire is being installed, align the colored spot near the bead (indicating a lighter point on the tire) with the valve stem.
7. Place the upper bead of the tire into the center of the rim. The lower bead should go outside of the rim (**Figure 29**). Work around the tire in both directions (**Figure 30**). Use a tire iron for the last few inches of bead (**Figure 31**).
8. Press the upper bead into the rim opposite the valve stem. Pry the bead into the rim on both sides of the initial point with a tire iron, working around the rim to the valve (**Figure 32**).
9. Check the bead on both sides of the tire for an even fit around the rim.
10. Bounce the wheel several times, rotating it each time. This will force the tire beads against the rim flanges. After the tire beads are in contact with the rim evenly, inflate the tire to seat the beads.
11. Place an inflatable band around the circumference of the tire. Slowly inflate the band until the tire beads are pressed against the rim. Inflate the tire enough to seat it, deflate the band and remove it.

*WARNING*

*In the next step never exceed 45 psi (310 kPa) inflation pressure as the tire could burst causing severe injury. Never stand directly over a tire while inflating it.*

12. After inflating the tire, check to see that the beads are fully seated and that the tire rim lines are the same distance from the rim all the way around the tire. If the beads won't seat, deflate the tire and relubricate the rim and beads with soapy water.

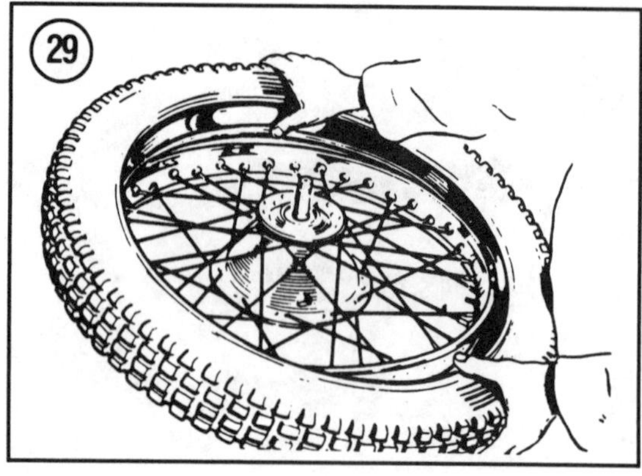

13. Reinflate the tire to the required pressure listed in **Table 2**. Install the valve stem cap.
14. Balance the wheel as described in this chapter.

*WARNING*
*If you have repaired a tire, do not ride the bike any faster than 30 mph (50 km/h) for the first 24 hours. It takes at least 24 hours for a patch to cure. Also* ***never*** *ride the bike faster than 80 mph (130 km/h) with a repaired tire.*

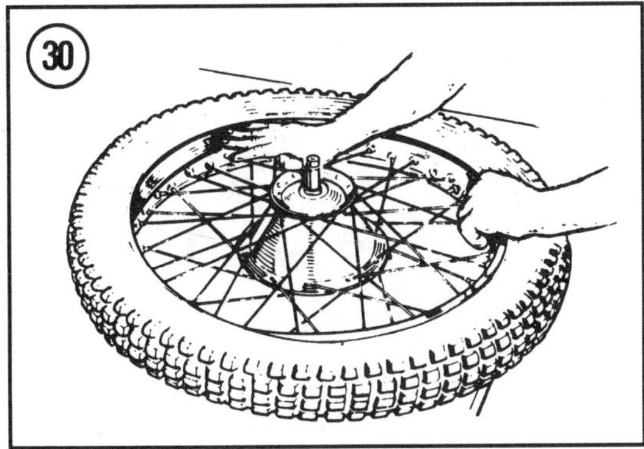


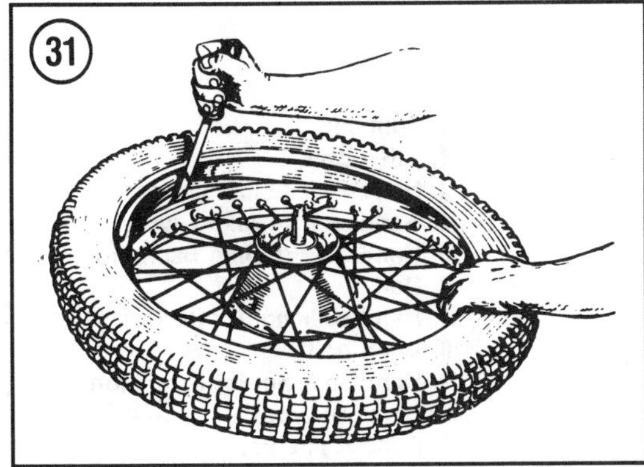

## TIRE REPAIRS

Patching a tubeless tire on the road is very difficult. If both beads are still against the rim, a can of pressurized tire sealant may inflate the tire and seal the hole, although this is only a temporary fix. The beads must be against the rim for this method to work. Another solution is to carry a spare inner tube that could be installed and inflated. This will enable you to get to a service station where the tire can be correctly repaired. Be sure that the inner tube is designed for use with tubeless tires.

Suzuki (and the tire industry) recommends that the tubeless tire be patched from the inside. Use a combination plug/patch applied from the inside the tire. Do not patch the tire with an external type plug. If you find an external patch on the tire, it is recommended that it be patch-reinforced from the inside.

Due to the variations of material supplied with different tubeless tire repair kits, follow the instructions and recommendations supplied with the repair kit.

9

## HANDLEBAR

### Removal/Installation

*WARNING*
*There are 2 different types of handlebars available for the Savage: the straight type and the pulled back type. If you choose to change the type of handlebar from the type that the bike was originally equipped with to the other type, Suzuki suggests the following: The throttle cable, clutch cable and hydraulic brake hose must also be changed. The lengths of these parts differ between the 2 different types of handlebars and for the proper and safe operation of the bike, these items must also be replaced.*

Refer to **Figure 33** and **Figure 34** for this procedure.

1. Disconnect the brake light switch electrical connector from the brake lever.

(33)

**STEERING STEM AND HANDLEBAR**

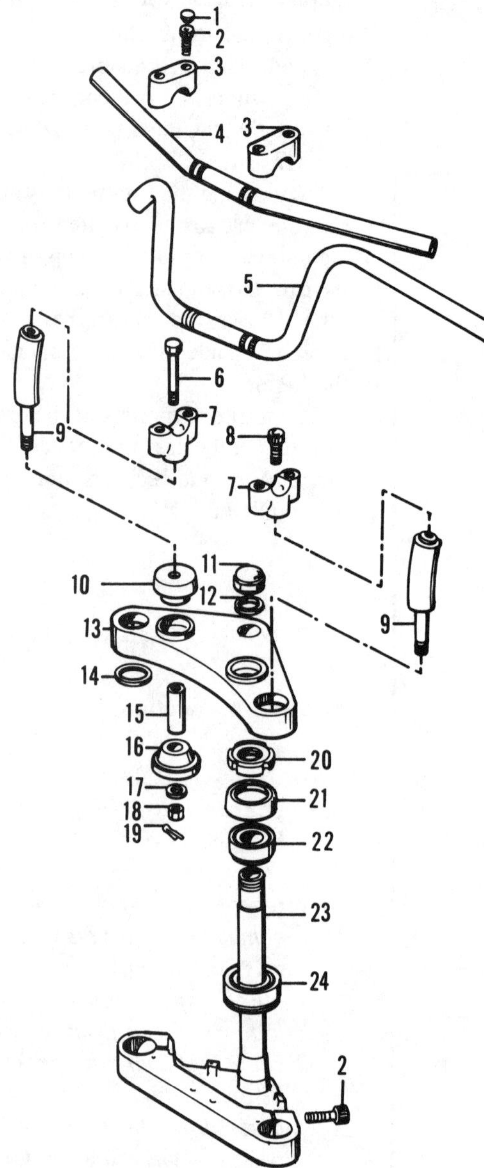


1. Trim cap
2. Allen bolt
3. Handlebar holder (upper)
4. Handlebar (straight type)
5. Handlebar (pulled back type)
6. Bolt
7. Handlebar holder (lower)
8. Allen bolt
9. Handlebar holder extension (straight type)
10. Rubber cushion
11. Steering stem cap nut
12. Washer
13. Upper fork bridge
14. Washer
15. Spacer
16. Rubber cushion
17. Washer
18. Nut
19. Cotter pin
20. Steering stem adjust nut
21. Dust seal
22. Upper bearing
23. Steering stem
24. Lower bearing

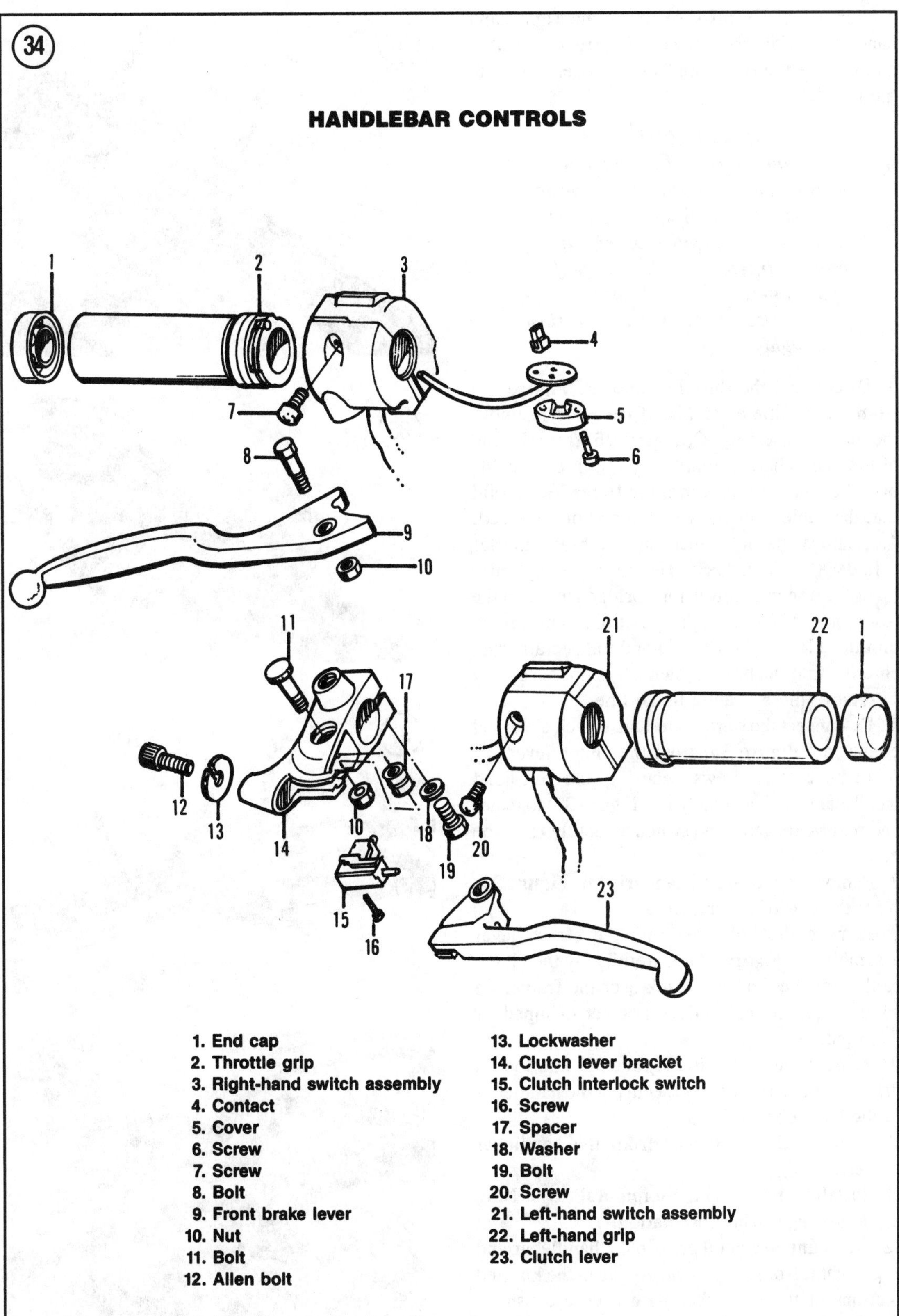
34
HANDLEBAR CONTROLS
1
2
3
4
5
6
7
8
9
10
11
21
22
1
17
12
13
14
10
18
19
20
15
16
23
1. End cap
2. Throttle grip
3. Right-hand switch assembly
4. Contact
5. Cover
6. Screw
7. Screw
8. Bolt
9. Front brake lever
10. Nut
11. Bolt
12. Allen bolt
13. Lockwasher
14. Clutch lever bracket
15. Clutch interlock switch
16. Screw
17. Spacer
18. Washer
19. Bolt
20. Screw
21. Left-hand switch assembly
22. Left-hand grip
23. Clutch lever

2. Remove the screws securing the right-hand handlebar switch assembly (A, **Figure 35**) together and remove the right-hand switch assembly from the handlebar.

*CAUTION*
*Cover the frame and fuel tank with a heavy cloth or plastic tarp to protect it from accidental spilling of brake fluid. Wash any spilled brake fluid off any painted or plated surface immediately, as it will destroy the finish. Use soapy water and rinse thoroughly.*

3. Disconnect the throttle cable (B, **Figure 35**) from the throttle assembly. If necessary, remove the throttle assembly (C, **Figure 35**) from the end of the handlebar. Carefully lay the throttle cable over the fender or back over the frame. Be careful that the cable does not get crimped or damaged.
4. Remove the bolts securing the brake master cylinder (D, **Figure 35**). Tie the master cylinder up to the upper or lower fork bridge and keep the reservoir in the upright position. This is to minimize loss of brake fluid and to keep air from entering into the brake system. It is not necessary to remove the hydraulic brake line.
5. Disconnect the starter interlock switch electrical connector (**Figure 36**) from the clutch lever.
6. Remove the screws securing the left-hand handlebar switch assembly (A, **Figure 37**) together and remove the left-hand switch assembly from the handlebar.
7. Remove the left-hand handgrip (B, **Figure 37**) from the end of the handlebar.
8. Remove the bolts securing the clutch lever assembly (C, **Figure 37**). Carefully lay the clutch cable over the fender or back over the frame. Be careful that the cable does not get crimped or damaged.
9. Remove the trim caps (**Figure 38**) and loosen the Allen bolts (**Figure 39**) securing the handlebar to the handlebar holders.
10. Remove the handlebar from the handlebar holders.
11. Install by reversing these removal steps. Note the following during installation.
12. To maintain a good grip on the handlebar and to prevent it from slipping down, clean the knurled sections of the handlebar with a wire brush. It should be kept rough so it will be held securely

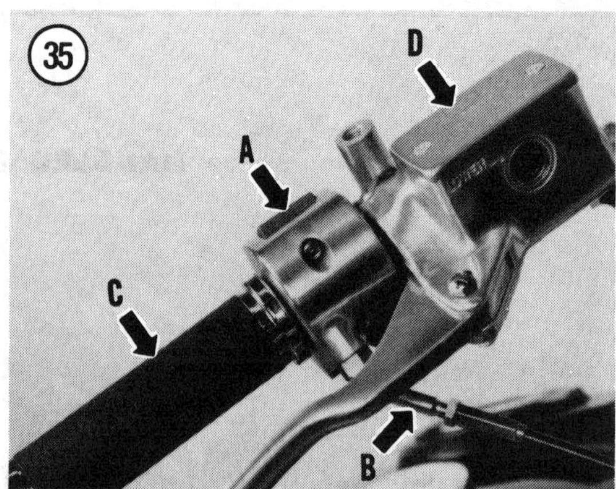


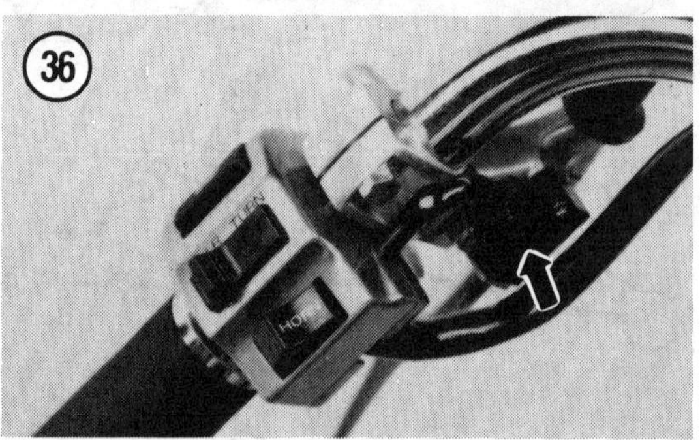


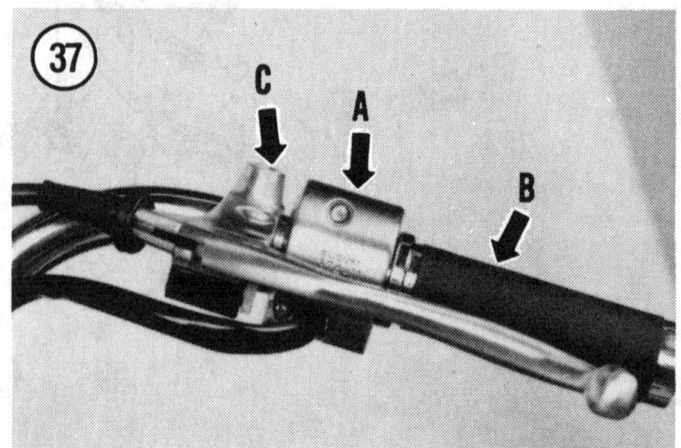


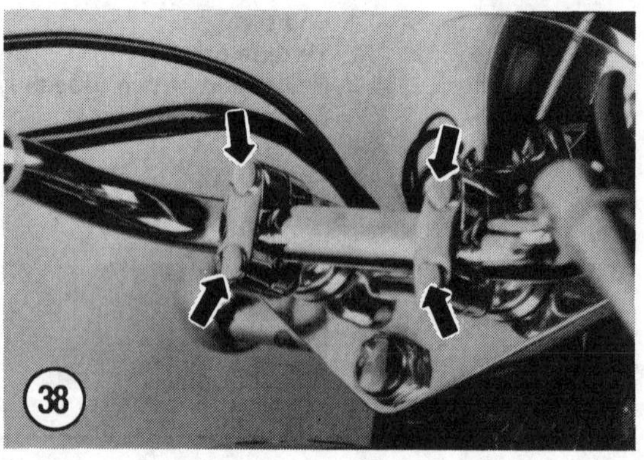

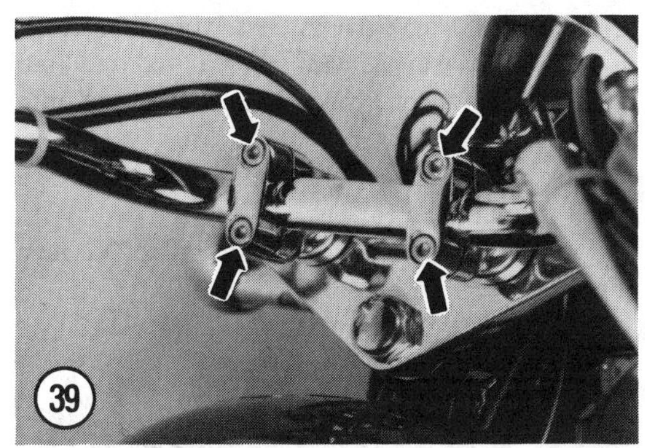
39

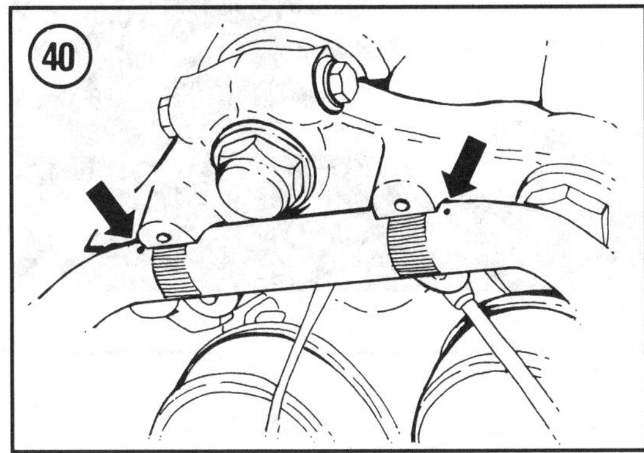
40

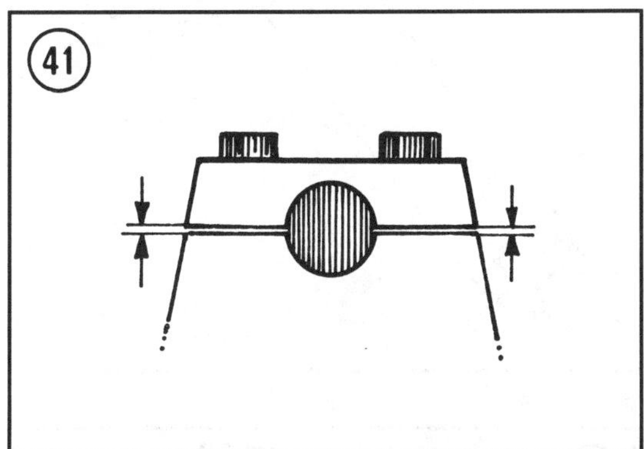
41

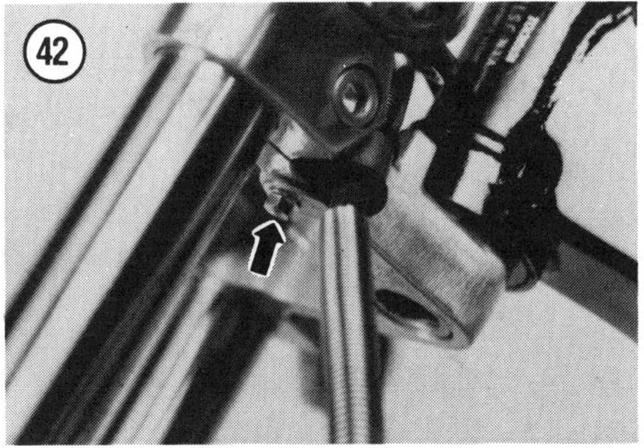
42

by the holders. The holders should also be kept clean and free of any metal that may have been gouged loose by handlebar slippage.

13. Position the handlebar on the lower holder so the punch mark on the handlebar is aligned with the top surface of the handlebar lower holders (**Figure 40**).

14. Tighten the handlebar holder bolts to the torque specification listed in **Table 3**. There should be an even space on the front and rear of the holders (**Figure 41**).

15. Apply a light coat of multipurpose grease to the throttle grip area on the handlebar before installing the throttle grip assembly.

16. Install the brake master cylinder onto the handlebar. Install the clamp with the rear view mirror receptacle facing up and align the clamp mating surface with the punch mark on the handlebar. Tighten the upper bolt first and then the lower bolt.

*WARNING*

*After installation is completed, make sure the brake lever does not come in contact with the throttle grip assembly when it is pulled on fully. If it does, the brake fluid may be low in the reservoir; refill as necessary. Refer to **Front Disc Brakes** in Chapter Eleven.*

17. Adjust the throttle operation and clutch free play as described in Chapter Three.

## STEERING HEAD AND STEM

### Disassembly

Refer to **Figure 33** for this procedure.

1. Remove the front wheel as described in this chapter.
2. Remove the handlebars as described in this chapter.
3. Remove the front forks as described in this chapter.
4. Remove the bolt (**Figure 42**) securing the brake hose clamp to the lower fork bridge. Move the hose out of the way.

9

5. Remove the steering stem cap nut and washer (A, **Figure 43**).
6. Remove the upper fork bridge (B, **Figure 43**).
7. Loosen the steering stem adjust nut. To loosen the adjust nut, use a large drift and hammer or use the easily improvised tool shown in **Figure 44**.
8. Hold onto the lower end of the steering stem assembly and remove the steering stem adjust nut (C, **Figure 43**).
9. Lower the steering stem assembly down and out of the steering head. Don't worry about catching any loose steel balls as the steering stem is equipped with assembled roller bearings.
10. Remove the dust seal from the top of the headset.
11. Remove the upper bearing from the top of the headset area of the frame.

### Inspection

1. Clean the bearing outer races in the steering head and the bearings with solvent.
2. Check the welds around the steering head for cracks and fractures. If any are found, have them repaired by a competent frame shop or welding service that is knowledgeable in the welding of aluminum.
3. Check the rollers for pitting, scratches or discoloration indicating wear or corrosion. Replace them in sets if any are bad.
4. Check the races for pitting, galling and corrosion. If any of these conditions exist, replace the races (and the bearings) as described in this chapter.
5. Check the steering stem for cracks, damage or wear. If damaged in any way, replace the steering stem.

### Steering Stem Assembly

Refer to **Figure 33** for this procedure.

1. Make sure the steering head outer races are properly seated.
2. Apply an even coat of wheel bearing grease completely to the steering head outer races (**Figure 45**) and to both bearings.
3. Install the upper bearing into the steering head.
4. Install the steering stem into the head tube and hold it firmly in place.
5. Install the dust seal onto the top of the headset.
6. Install the steering stem adjust nut and tighten it to the initial torque specification listed in **Table 1**.
7. Turn the steering stem from lock-to-lock 5-6 times to seat the bearings.
8. Loosen the steering stem nut 1/4 to 1/2 turn (**Figure 46**).

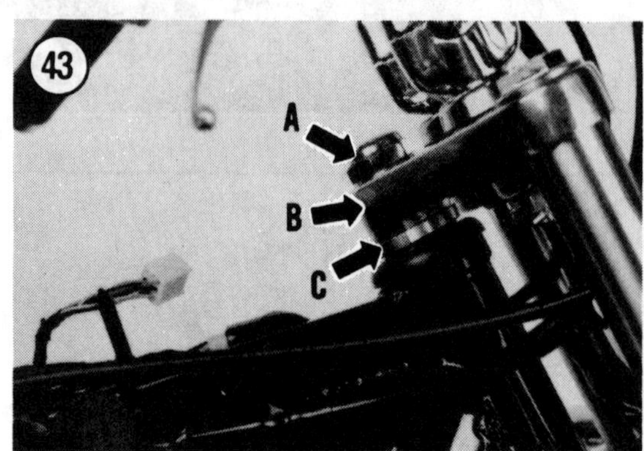


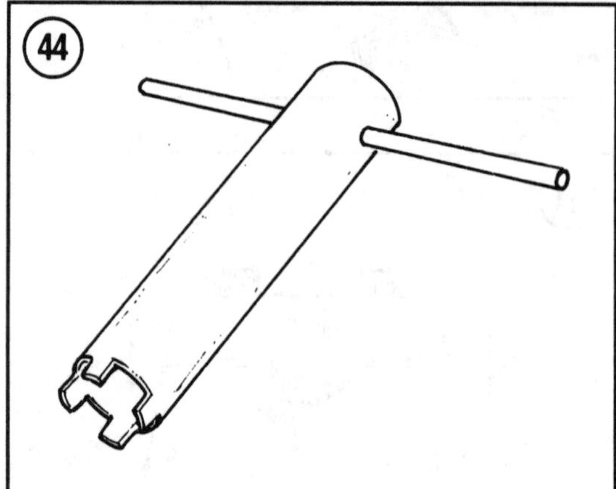


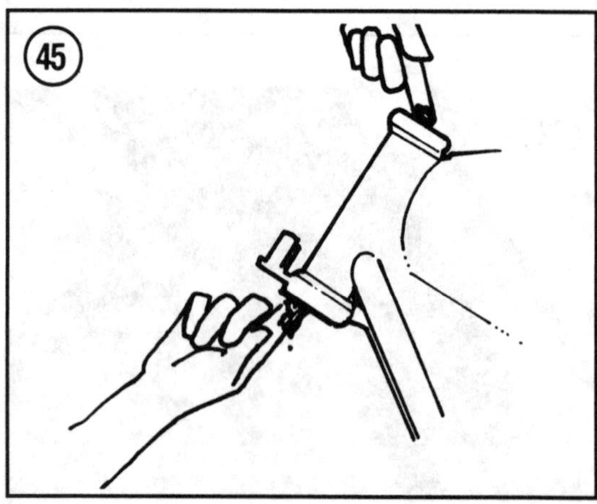

*NOTE*
*If during Step 6 and Step 8 the adjust nut will not tighten or loosen, remove the nut and inspect both the nut and the steering stem threads for dirt and/or burrs. Clean both parts with a tap and die if necessary, then repeat Steps 6-8.*

9. Install the upper fork bridge, washer and steering stem cap nut only finger-tight at this time.

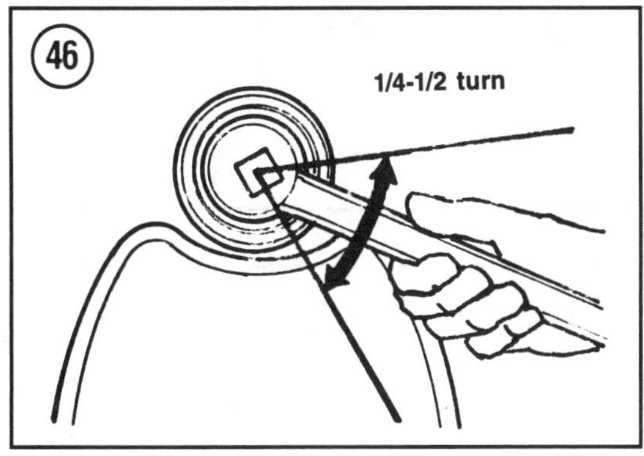


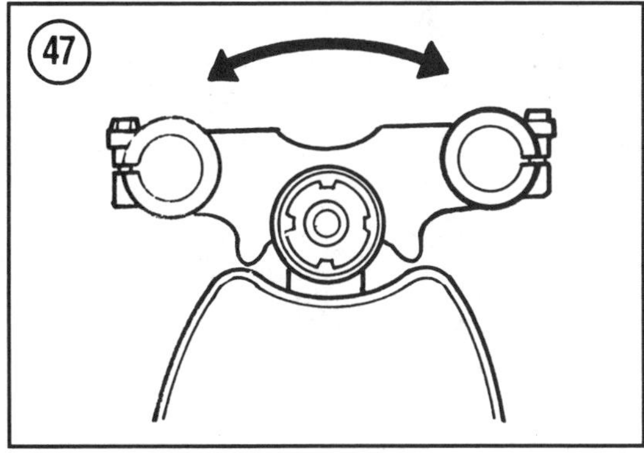


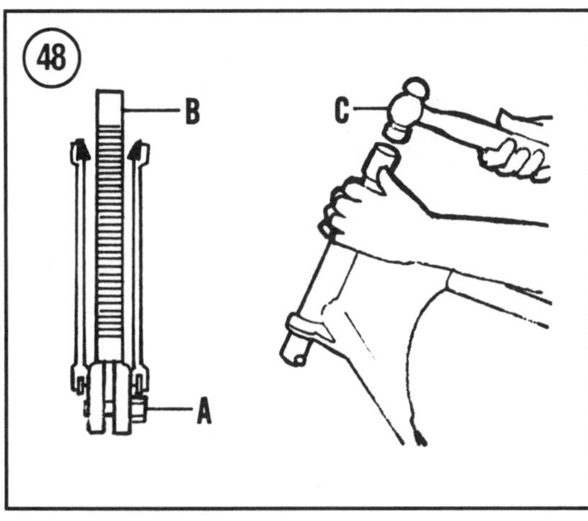


10. Move the steering stem back and forth from side-to-side (**Figure 47**). The steering stem should move freely from side-to-side with no looseness or stiffness. If necessary, repeat Step 6 and Step 8 and readjust the steering stem adjust nut.

*NOTE*
*Steps 11-13 must be performed in this order to assure proper upper and lower fork bridge to fork alignment.*

11. Install the front forks as described in this chapter.
12. Tighten the lower fork bridge bolts to the torque specification listed in **Table 1**.
13. Tighten the steering stem cap nut to the torque specification listed in **Table 1**.
14. Install the bolt securing the brake hose clamp to the lower fork bridge.
15. Install the handlebars as described in this chapter.
16. Install the front wheel as described in this chapter.

## STEERING HEAD BEARING RACES

The headset and steering stem bearing outer races are pressed into place. Because they are easily bent, do not remove them unless they are worn and require replacement.

### Headset Bearing Race Removal/Installation

1. Remove the steering stem as described in this chapter.
2A. A special Suzuki tool setup (Suzuki bearing outer race remover part No. 09941-54911, steering bearing remover/installer part No. 09941-74910) can be used to remove the headset bearing race as follows:
   a. Install the outer race remover (A, **Figure 48**) into one of the outer races.
   b. Insert the bearing remover (B, **Figure 48**) into the backside of the outer race remover.
   c. Tap on the end of the bearing remover with a hammer (C, **Figure 48**) and drive the bearing outer race out of the steering head. Remove the special tool from the outer race.
   d. Repeat for the bearing outer race on the other end of the headset.

2B. If the special tools are not used, perform the following:

a. Insert a hardwood stick or soft punch into the head tube and carefully tap the outer race out from the inside.
b. After it is started, work around the outer race in a crisscross pattern so that neither the race nor the head tube is damaged.

3A. A special Suzuki tool setup (Suzuki bearing installer part No. 09941-34513) can be used to install the headset bearing race as follows:

a. Position the outer races into the headset and just start them into position lightly with a soft-faced mallet. Just tap them in enough to hold them in place until the special tool can be installed.
b. Install the bearing installer (**Figure 49**) into both of the outer races.
c. Tighten the nuts on the bearing installer and pull the outer races into place in the headset. Tighten the nuts until both bearing outer races are completely seated in the head set and are flush with the steering head surface.
d. Remove the special tool.

3B. If the special tools are not used, perform the following:

a. Position one of the outer races into the headset and just start it into position lightly with a soft-faced mallet. Just tap it in enough to hold it in place.
b. Tap the outer race in slowly with a block of wood, a suitable size socket or piece of pipe (**Figure 50**). Make sure that the race is squarely seated in the headset race bore before tapping it into place. Tap the race in until it is flush with the steering head surface.
c. Repeat for the other outer race.

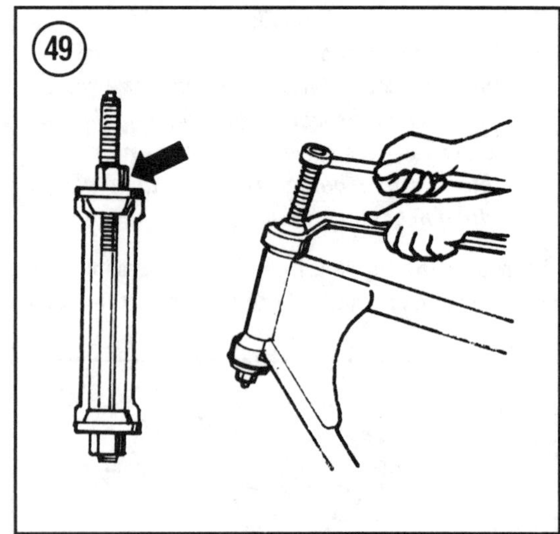


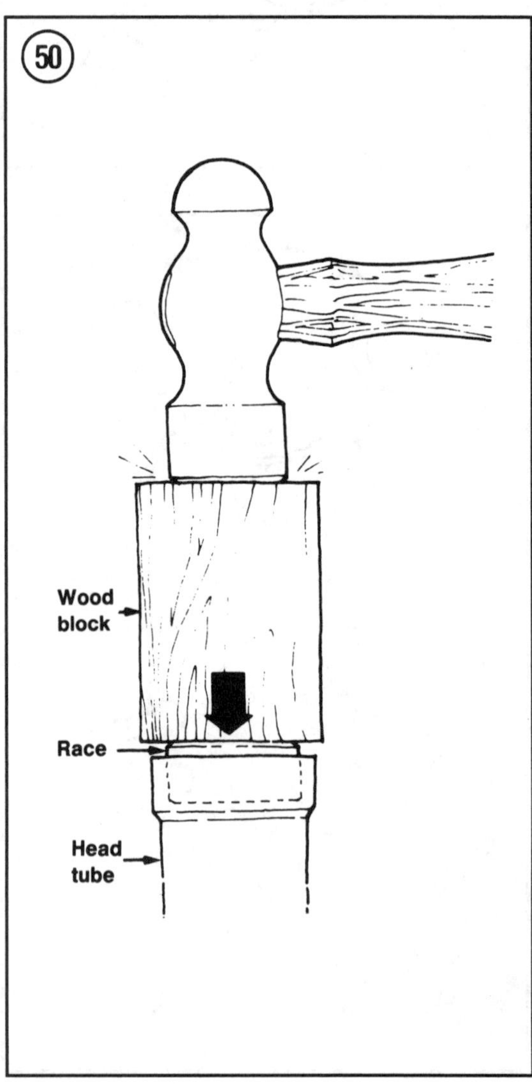


### Steering Stem Lower Bearing Removal/Installation

1. Install the Suzuki special tool (bearing remover part No. 09941-84510) (A, **Figure 51**) onto the steering stem assembly (B, **Figure 51**).
2. Tighten the upper bolt (C, **Figure 51**) and withdraw the lower bearing from the steering stem.
3. Remove the special tool and the lower bearing from the steering stem.

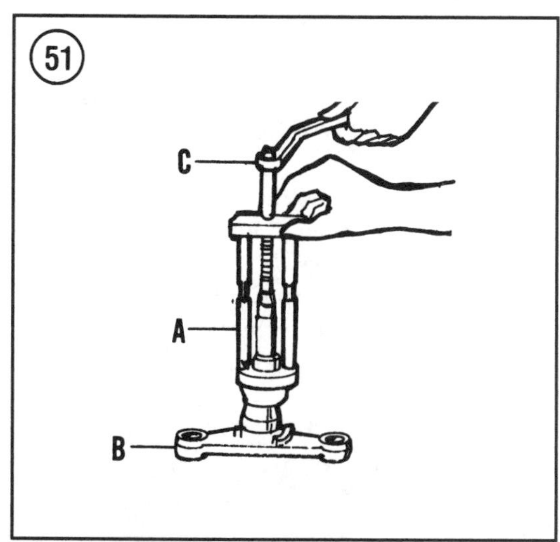


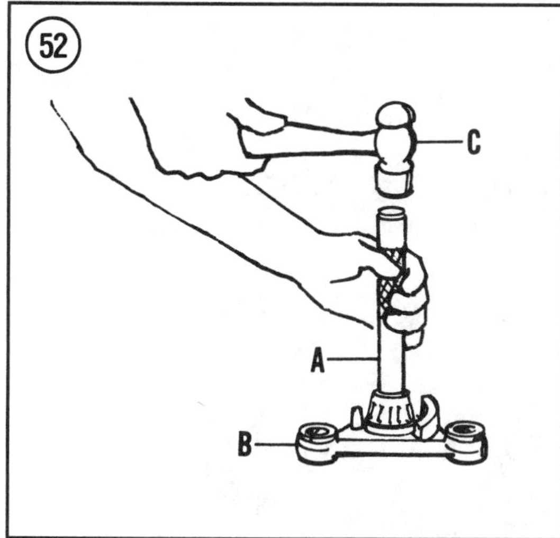


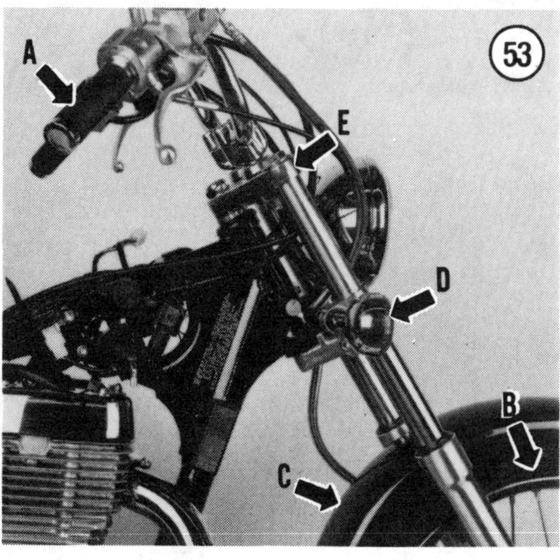


4. Install the lower bearing onto the steering stem and slide it down onto the top of the shoulder at the base of the steering stem.
5. Install the Suzuki special tool (steering stem bearing installer, part No. 09941-74910) (A, **Figure 52**) on top of the lower bearing (B, **Figure 52**).
6. Using a hammer (C, **Figure 52**), carefully tap on the bearing installer and drive the lower bearing into place.
7. Remove the bearing installer.
8. Make sure it is seated squarely and is all the way down.

## FRONT FORK

The front suspension uses a spring controlled, hydraulically damped, telescopic fork.

### Front Fork Service

Before suspecting major trouble, drain the front fork oil and refill with the proper type and quantity; refer to *Front Fork Oil Change* in Chapter Three. If you still have trouble, such as poor damping, a tendency to bottom or top out or leakage around the rubber seals, follow the service procedures in this section.

To simplify fork service and to prevent the mixing of parts, the legs should be removed, serviced and installed individually.

9

### Removal/Installation

1. Remove the handlebars (A, **Figure 53**) as described in this chapter.
2. Remove the brake caliper as described in Chapter Eleven.
3. Remove the front wheel (B, **Figure 53**) as described in this chapter.
4. Remove the screws securing the front fender (C, **Figure 53**) to the front forks.

*NOTE*

*The Allen bolt at the base of the slider has been secured with Loctite and is often very difficult to remove because the damper rod will turn inside the slider. It sometimes can be removed with an air impact driver. If you are unable to remove it, take the fork tubes to a dealer and have the bolts removed.*

5. If the fork assembly is going to be disassembled, slightly loosen the Allen bolt at the base of the slider with an Allen wrench. If the bolt is loosened too much, fork oil may start to drain out of the slider.
6. Remove the fork cap bolt (**Figure 54**) and the spacer.
7. Remove the screw (A, **Figure 55**) securing the front turn signal mounting bracket on the front fork tube.
8. Loosen the lower fork bridge bolt (B, **Figure 55**).

*CAUTION*
*The fork leg also goes through the turn signal mounting bracket (D, **Figure 53**) as well as the upper and lower fork bridges. Remember this while sliding the fork tube in and out of the fork bridges.*

9. Slide the fork tube from the upper and lower fork bridges (E, **Figure 53**). It may be necessary to slightly rotate the fork tube while pulling it down and out.
10. Install by reversing these removal steps. Note the following during installation.
11. Align the front turn signal mounting bracket locating tab with the notch in the lower fork bridge.
12. Install the fork tube into the top of the fork tube until it bottoms out on the stop.
13. Tighten the lower fork bridge bolt and the fork cap bolt to the torque specifications listed in **Table 1**.

**Disassembly**

Refer to **Figure 56** during the disassembly procedures.

1. Clamp the slider in a vise with soft jaws.
2. If not loosened during the fork removal sequence, loosen the Allen bolt on the bottom of the slider as follows:
   a. Reinstall the fork spacer into the fork tube.
   b. Install the fork top cap and tighten securely.
   c. Loosen the Allen bolt (**Figure 57**) on the bottom of the slider.

*NOTE*
*If you have the special Suzuki tools used for fork disassembly, loosen the Allen bolt in Step 10.*

*NOTE*
*This bolt has been secured with Loctite and is often very difficult to remove because the damper rod will turn inside the slider. It sometimes can be removed with an air impact driver. If*

54

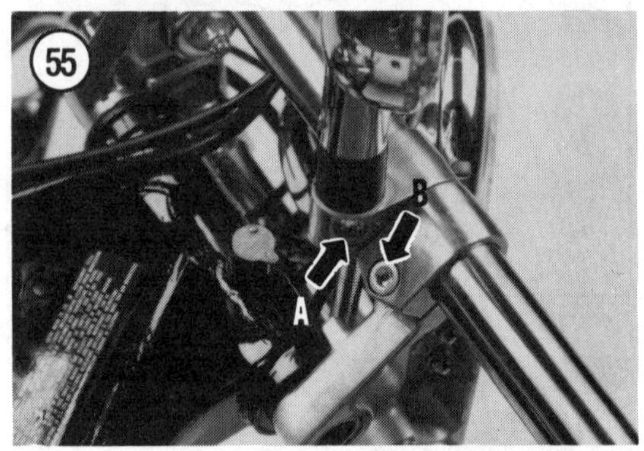

55

57

## FRONT FORK ASSEMBLY

1. Fork cap bolt
2. O-ring
3. Spacer
4. Spring seat
5. Fork spring
6. Piston ring
7. Damper rod
8. Fork tube
9. Fork tube bushing
10. Oil lock piece
11. Dust seal
12. Stopper ring
13. Oil seal
14. Washer
15. Slider bushing
16. Fork slider
17. Gasket
18. Allen bolt
19. Drain screw

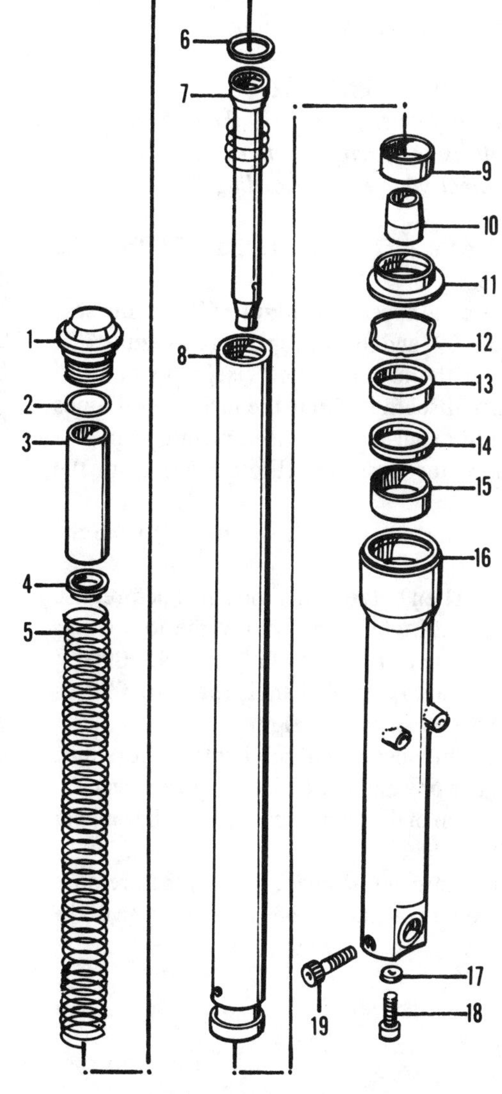

*you are unable to remove it, take the fork tubes to a Suzuki dealer and have the bolts removed.*

3. Remove the Allen bolt and gasket from the slider.
4. Hold the upper fork tube in a vise with soft jaws and loosen the fork cap bolt (if it was not loosened during the fork removal sequence).

*WARNING*
*Be careful when removing the fork cap bolt as the spring is under pressure. Protect your eyes accordingly.*

5. Remove the fork cap bolt (**Figure 58**) from the fork tube.
6. Remove the spacer (A, **Figure 59**), spring seat (B, **Figure 59**) and the fork spring (C, **Figure 59**).
7. Remove the fork from the vise, pour the fork oil out and discard it. Pump the fork several times by hand to expel most of the remaining oil.
8. Remove the dust seal (**Figure 60**) from the slider.
9. Remove the stopper ring (**Figure 61**) from the slider.
10. If the Allen bolt was not loosened before, use special Suzuki tools and perform the following:
   a. Install the attachment "G" (part No. 09940-34592) onto the "T" handle (part No. 09940-34520) as shown in **Figure 62**.
   b. Insert this special tool setup into the fork tube (**Figure 63**) and index it into the hex receptacle in the top of the damper rod to hold the damper rod in place.
   c. Using an Allen wrench, loosen, then remove the Allen bolt and washer from the base of the slider.

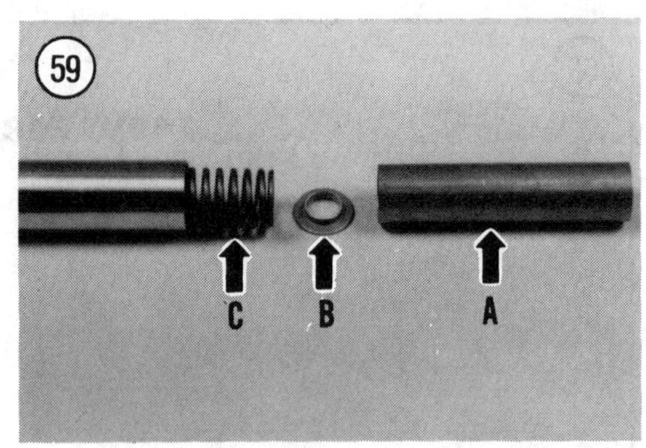


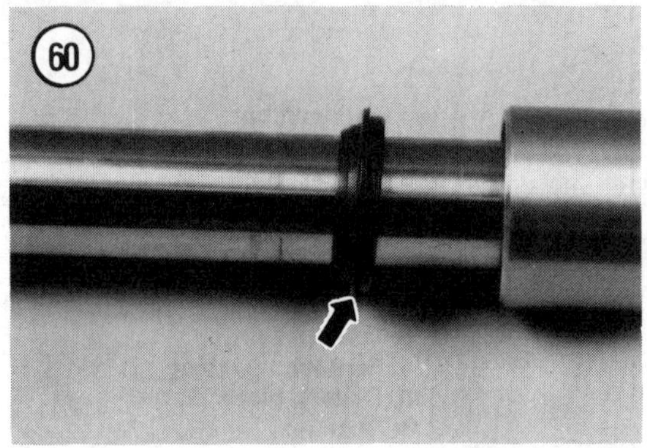

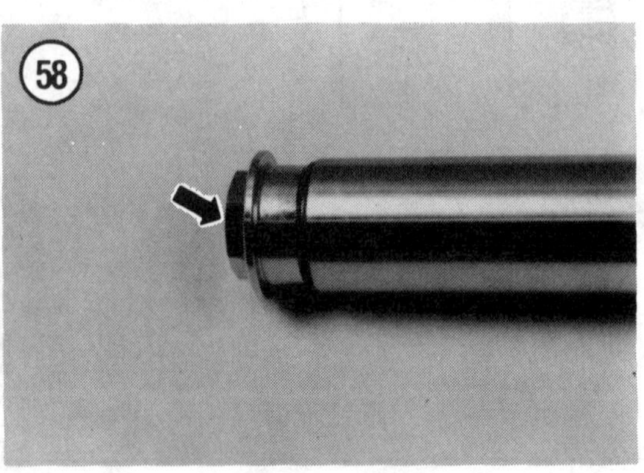


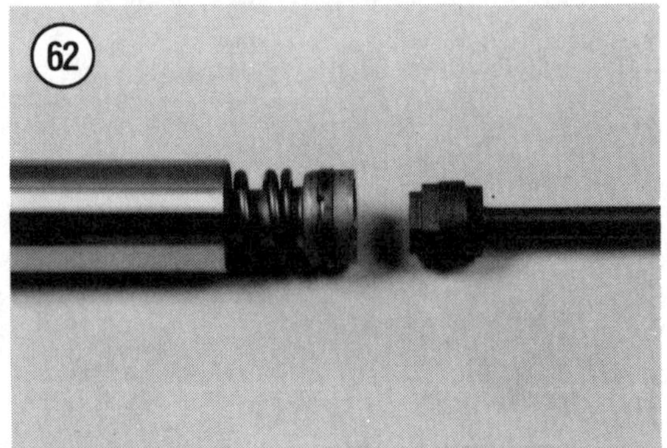

*NOTE*
*On this type of fork, force is needed to remove the fork tube from the slider.*

11. Install the fork tube in a vise with soft jaws.
12. There is an interference fit between the bushing in the fork slider and the bushing on the fork tube. In order to remove the fork tube from the slider, pull hard on the fork tube using quick in-and-out strokes (**Figure 64**). Doing so will withdraw the bushing, washer and the oil seal from the slider.

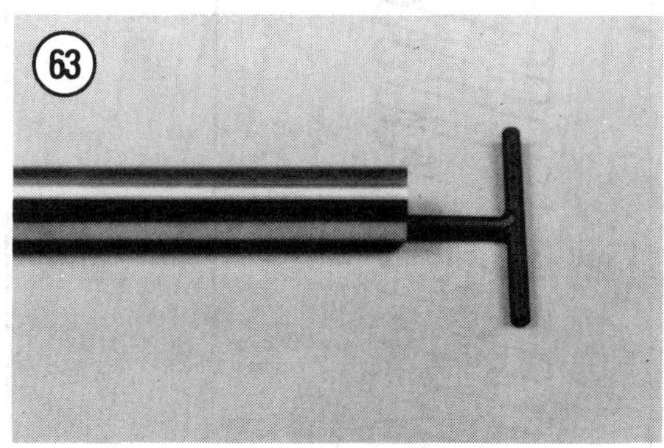

63

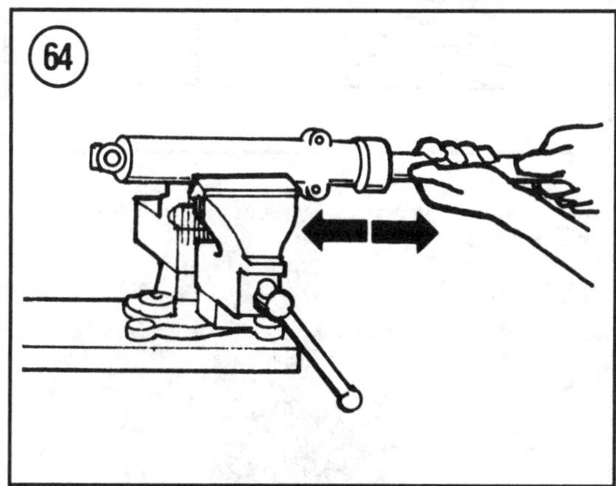

64

65

*NOTE*
*It may be necessary to slightly heat the area on the slider around the oil seal prior to removal. Use a rag soaked in hot water. Do not apply a flame directly to the fork slider.*

13. Withdraw the fork tube from the slider.

*NOTE*
*Do not remove the fork tube bushing unless it is going to be replaced. Inspect it as described in this chapter.*

14. Remove the oil lock piece from the damper rod.
15. Remove the damper rod and rebound spring from the slider.
16. Inspect the components as described in this chapter.

9

**Inspection**

1. Thoroughly clean all parts in solvent and dry them. Check the fork tube for signs of wear or scratches.
2. Check the damper rod for straightness. **Figure 65** shows one method. The damper rod should be replaced if the runout is 0.2 mm (0.008 in.) or greater.
3. Make sure the oil holes (**Figure 66**) in the damper rod are clear. Clean out if necessary.

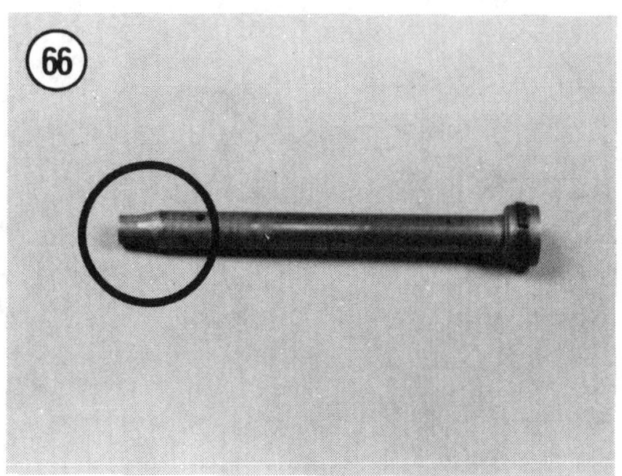

66

4. Inspect the damper rod and piston ring (**Figure 67**) for wear or damage. Replace as necessary.
5. Check the upper fork tube for straightness. If bent or severely scratched, it should be replaced.
6. Check the lower slider for dents or exterior damage that may cause the upper fork tube to hang up during riding. Replace if necessary.
7. Measure the uncompressed length of the fork spring (not rebound spring) as shown in **Figure 68**. If the spring has sagged to the service limit dimensions listed in **Table 3**, the spring must be replaced.
8. Inspect the slider (**Figure 69**) and fork tube bushings (**Figure 70**). If either is scratched or scored, they must be replaced. If the Teflon coating is worn off so that the copper base material is showing on approximately 3/4 of the total surface, the bushing must be replaced. Also check for distortion on the check points of the backup ring; replace as necessary. Refer to **Figure 71**.
9. Inspect the gasket on the Allen bolt (**Figure 72**); replace if damaged.
10. Any parts that are worn or damaged should be replaced. Simply cleaning and reinstalling unserviceable components will not improve performance of the front suspension.

### Assembly

Refer to **Figure 56** during the assembly procedures.
1. Coat all parts with fresh DEXRON automatic transmission fluid or SAE 15W fork oil prior to installation.

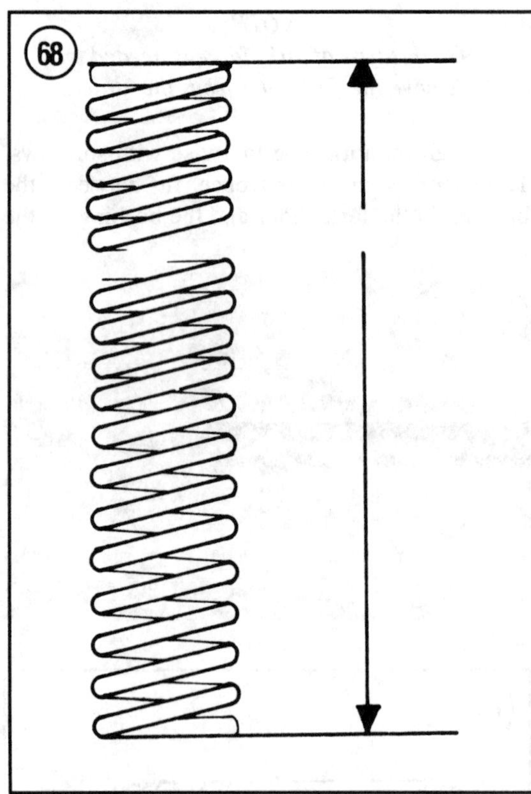

68

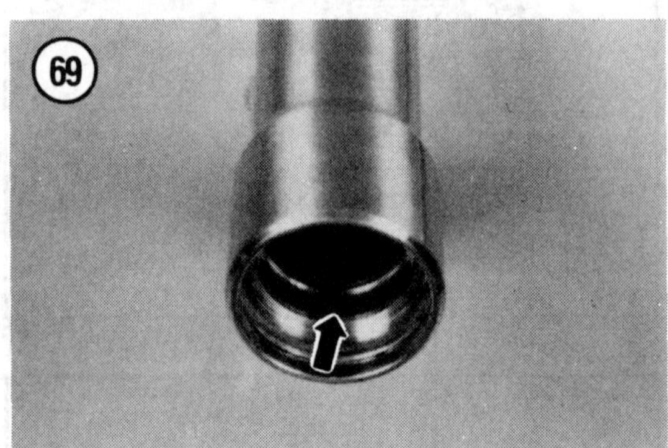

69

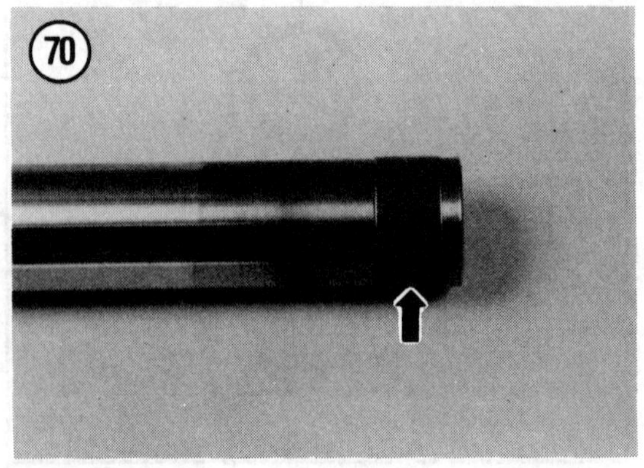

70

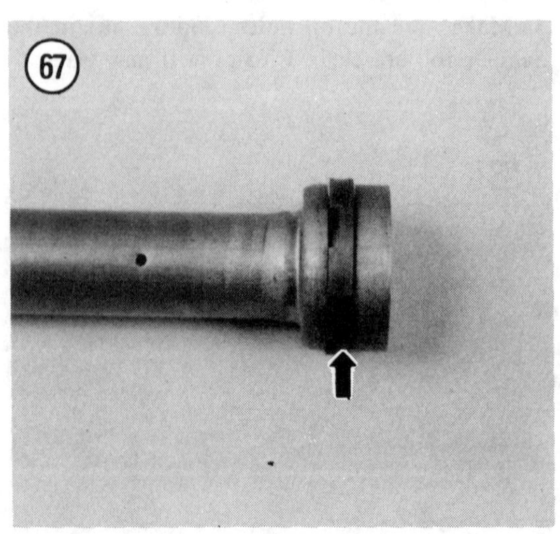

67

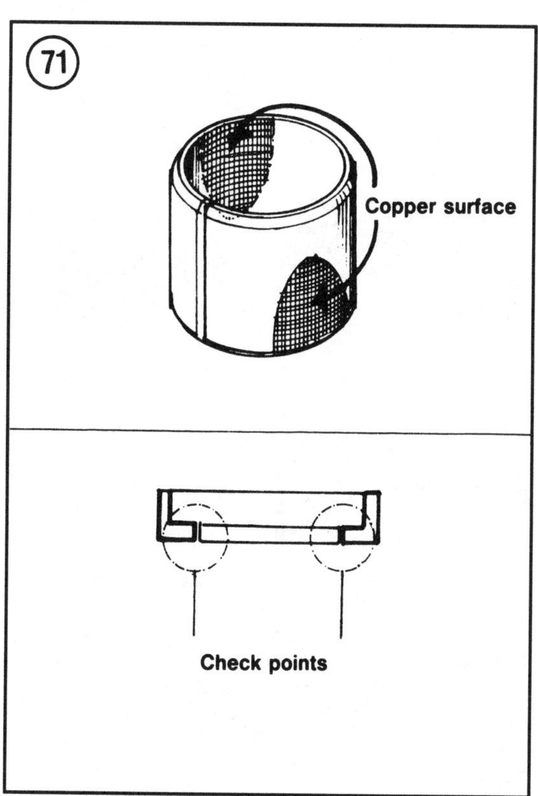


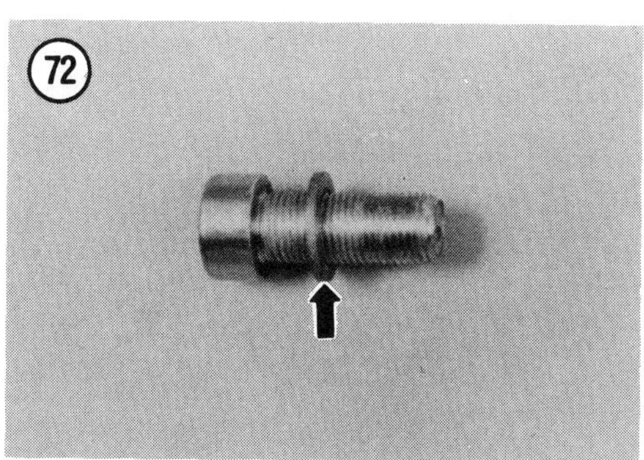


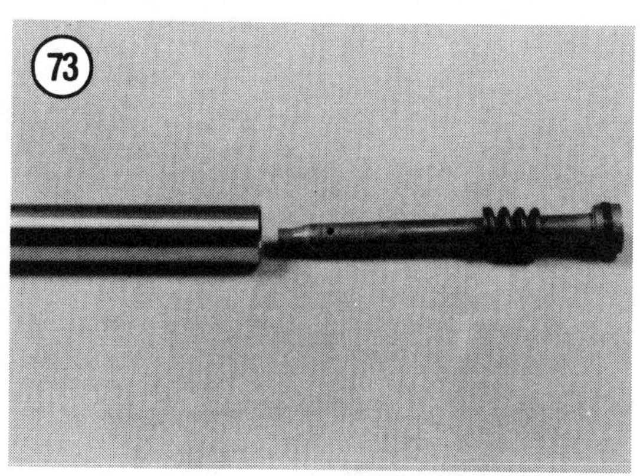


2. Install the rebound spring onto the damper rod and insert this assembly into the fork tube (**Figure 73**).

3. Temporarily install the fork spring, spring seat (**Figure 74**) and fork cap bolt (**Figure 75**) to hold the damper rod in place. Tighten the fork cap bolt securely.

4. Install the oil lock piece onto the damper rod (**Figure 76**).

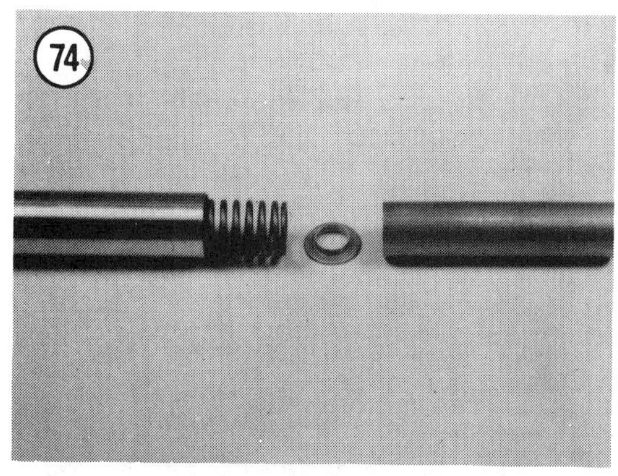


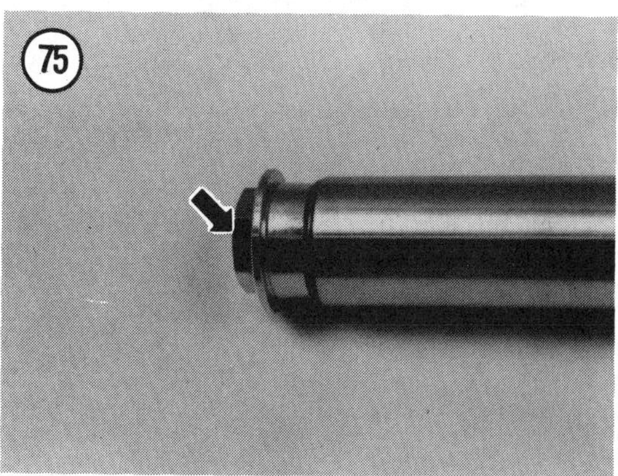


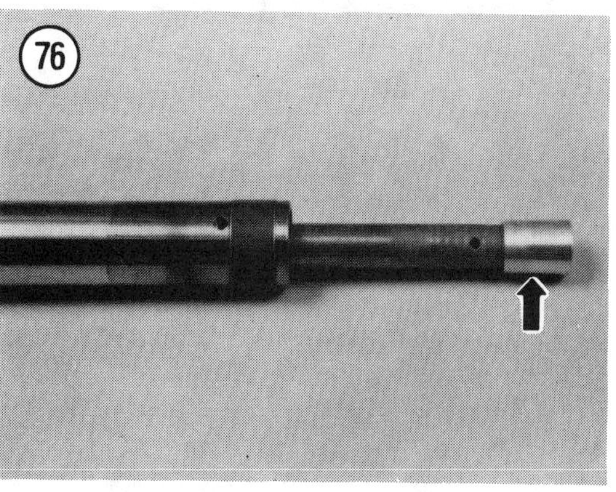


9

5. Install the upper fork assembly into the slider (**Figure 77**).
6. Make sure the gasket (**Figure 72**) is on the Allen bolt.
7. Apply blue Loctite Threadlocker No. 242 to the threads of the Allen bolt prior to installation. Install it in the fork slider (**Figure 78**) and tighten to the torque specification listed in **Table 1**.
8. Slide the fork slider bushing (A, **Figure 79**) and the washer (B, **Figure 79**) down the fork tube and rest it on top of the fork slider.
9. Install the new oil seal as follows:
   a. Coat the new seal with ATF (automatic transmission fluid).
   b. Position the seal with the open groove facing upward (**Figure 80**) and slide the oil seal (C, **Figure 79**) down onto the fork tube.

*NOTE*
*The following Suzuki special tool (**Figure 81**) is **very expensive**. If you work on a lot of different bikes, this special tool is a must for your tool box. It is adjustable and will work on almost all Japanese fork assemblies (including Japanese "Showa" forks equipped on some late model Harleys).*

   c. Slide the Suzuki special tool Front Fork Oil Seal Installer (part No. 09940-50112) down the fork tube (**Figure 82**).
   d. Drive the seal into the slider with Suzuki special tool (**Figure 83**).

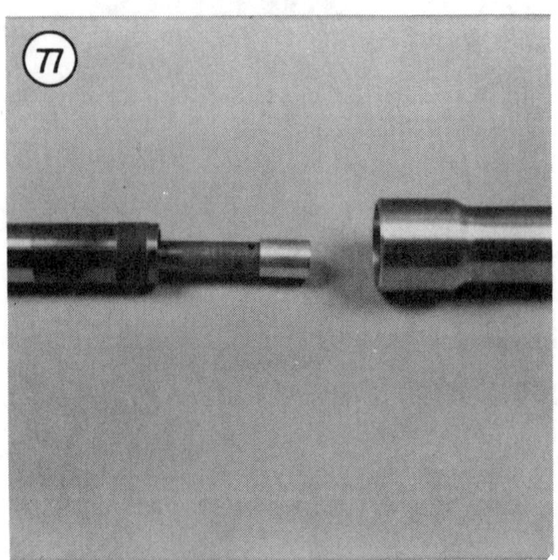


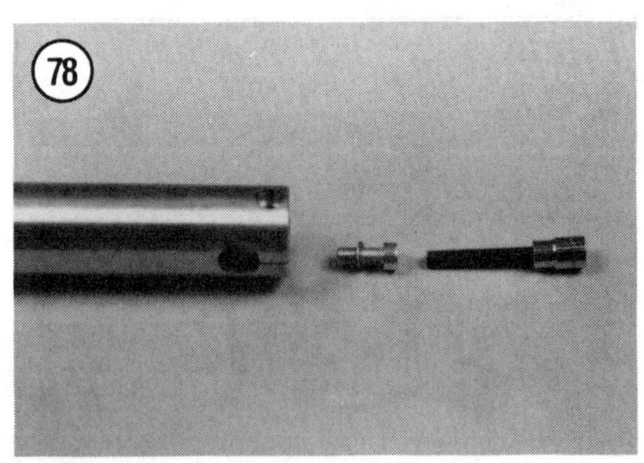


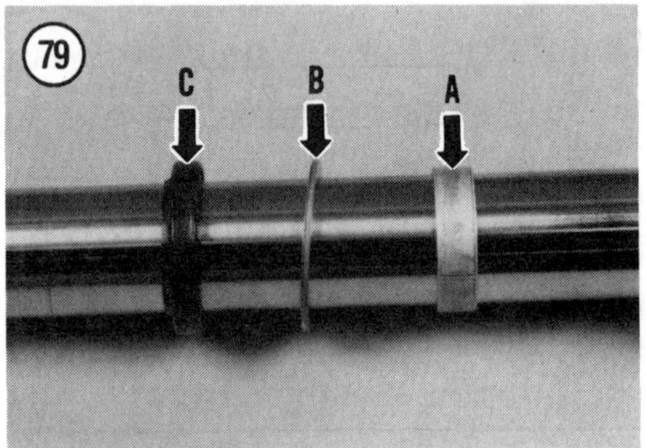

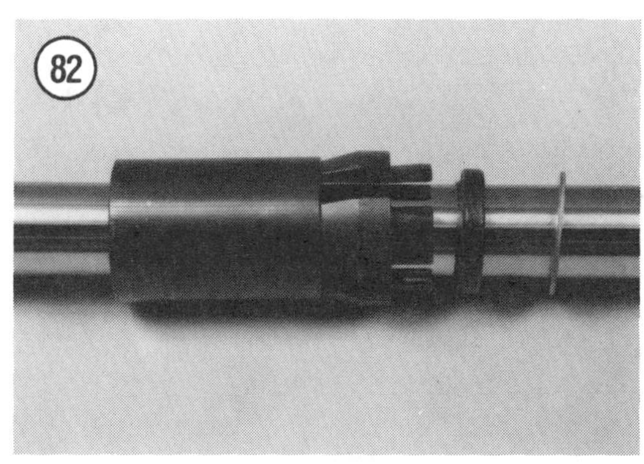

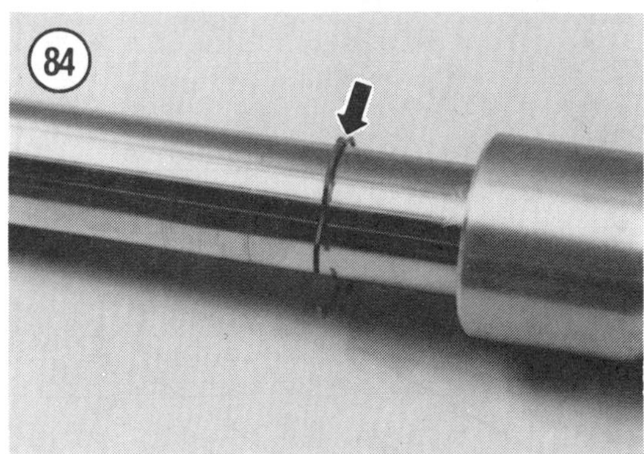

e. Drive the oil seal in until the groove in the slider can be seen above the top surface of the upper washer.

10. Install the stopper ring (**Figure 84**). Make sure the stopper ring (**Figure 85**) is completely seated in the groove in the fork slider.

11. Install the dust seal (**Figure 86**) into the slider. Press it in until it is completely seated.

12. Remove the fork cap bolt, spacer, spring seat and the fork spring from the fork assembly.

*NOTE*

*Suzuki recommends that the fork oil level be measured, if possible, to ensure a more accurate filling.*

*NOTE*

*To measure the correct amount of fluid, use a plastic baby bottle. These bottles have measurements in fluid ounces (oz.) and cubic centimeters (cc) on the side.*

13. Compress the fork completely.

14. Add 441 cc (14.91 oz.) of DEXRON ATF or SAE 15W fork oil to the fork assembly.

15. Hold the fork assembly as close to vertical as possible.

16. Use an accurate ruler or the Suzuki oil level gauge (part No. 09943-74111), or equivalent (**Figure 87**), to achieve the correct oil level of 75 mm (2.95 in.). Refer to **Figure 88**.

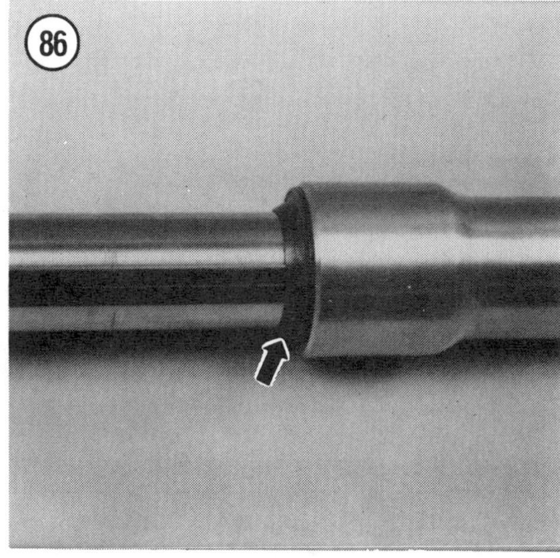

*NOTE*

*An oil level measuring devise can be made as shown in* ***Figure 89****. Position the lower edge of the hose clamp the specified oil level distance up from the small diameter hole. Fill the fork with a few cc more than the required amount of oil. Position the hose clamp on the top edge of the fork tube and draw out the excess oil. Oil is sucked out until the level reaches the small diameter hole. A precise oil level can be achieved with this simple device.*

17. Allow the oil to settle completely and recheck the oil level measurement. Adjust the oil level if necessary.
18. Install the fork spring (**Figure 90**) with the wide pitch coils (**Figure 91**) going in first.
19. Inspect the O-ring seal (**Figure 92**) on the fork cap bolt; replace if necessary.
20. Install the spring seat and spacer (**Figure 93**).
21. Do not install the top fork cap bolt at this time. Hold the fork assembly upright so the fork oil will not drain out. Tighten the fork cap bolt to the torque specification listed in **Table 1** after the front fork assembly is installed.
22. Install the fork assemblies as described in this chapter.
23. Repeat this procedure for the other fork assembly.

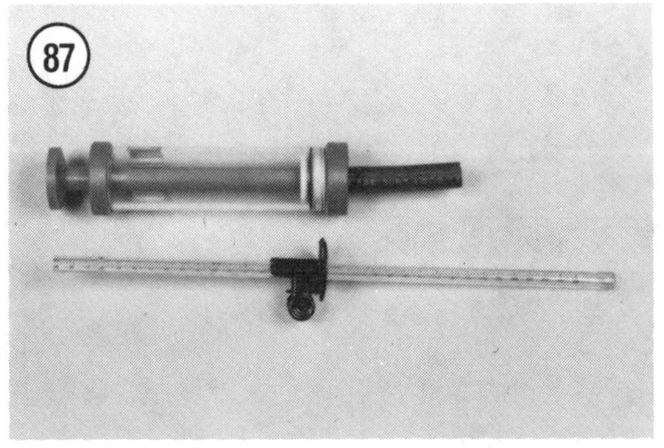


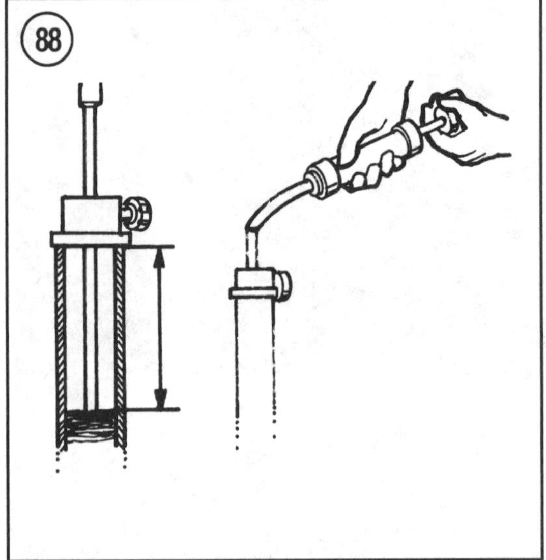


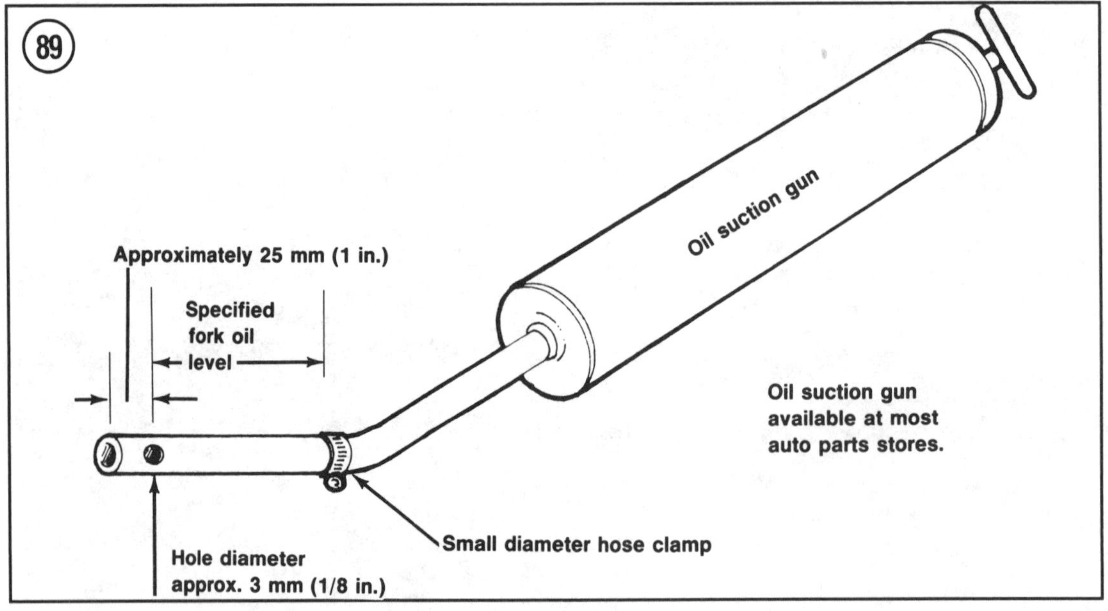

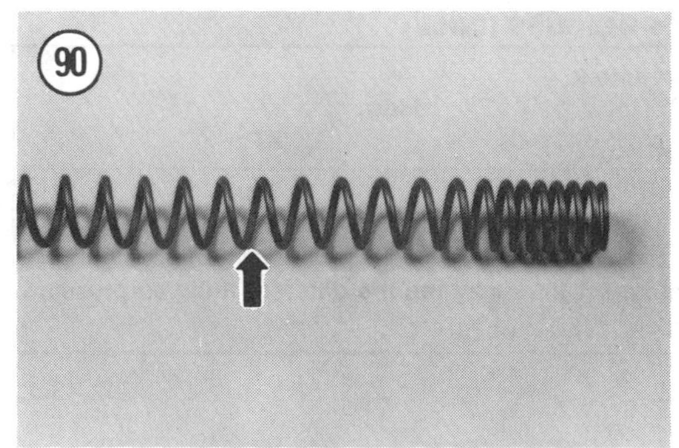

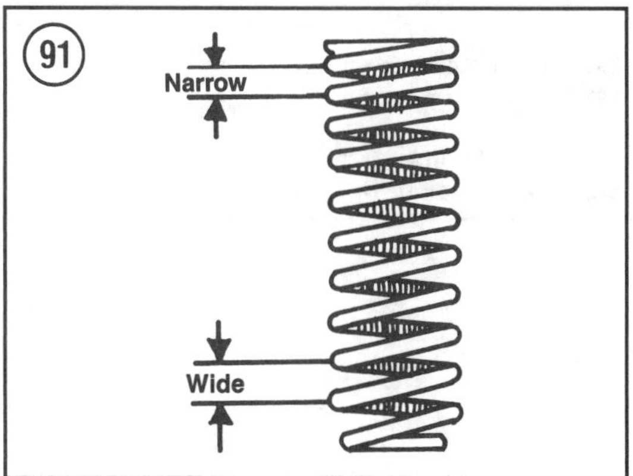


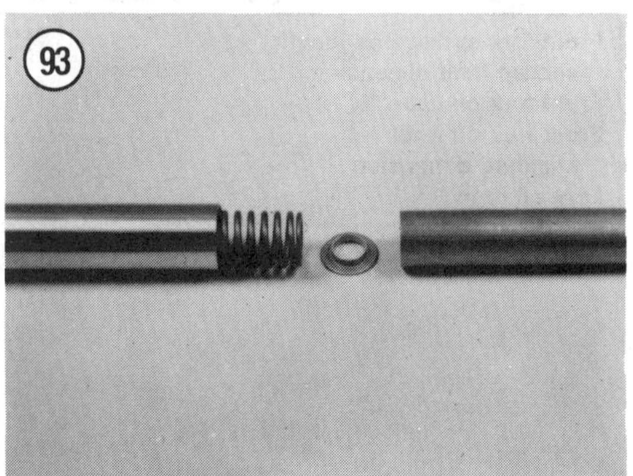



**Table 1 FRONT SUSPENSION TORQUE SPECIFICATIONS**

| Item | N·m | ft.-lb. |
|---|---|---|
| Front axle nut | 36-52 | 26-38 |
| Front axle pinch bolt and nut | 15-25 | 11-18 |
| Brake disc bolts | 18-28 | 13-20 |
| Spoke nipples | 4-5 | 3-3.5 |
| Handlebar holder | | |
| Bolts | 20-30 | 14-22 |
| Nuts | 20-30 | 14-22 |
| Handlebar clamp bolt | 12-20 | 8-14 |
| Fork bridge clamp bolts | 25-35 | 18-26 |
| Steering stem adjust nut | | |
| Initial torque | 40-50 | 29-36 |
| Steering stem cap nut | 30-40 | 21-29 |
| Front fork bolt | 35-55 | 26-40 |
| Front fork Allen bolt | 25-35 | 18-26 |

**Table 2 TIRE INFLATION PRESSURE (COLD)***

| | Tire pressure | | | |
|---|---|---|---|---|
| | Front | | Rear | |
| Load | psi | kPa | psi | kPa |
| Solo riding | 28 | 200 | 28 | 200 |
| Dual riding | 32 | 225 | 36 | 250 |

* Tire inflation pressure for factory equipped tires. Aftermarket tires may require different inflation pressure.

**Table 3 FRONT SUSPENSION SPECIFICATIONS**

| | |
|---|---|
| Front fork spring free length | |
| service limit dimension | 392.5 mm (15.45 in.) |
| Front fork oil capacity | 441 cc (14.91 U.S. oz.) |
| Front fork oil level | |
| standard dimension | 75.0 mm (2.95 in.) |
| Fork oil type | SAE 15W fork oil or DEXRON ATF |

CHAPTER TEN

# REAR SUSPENSION

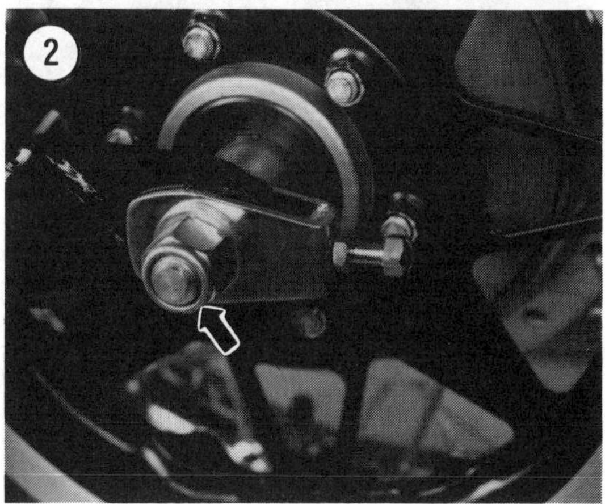


This chapter includes repair and replacement procedures for the rear wheel and rear suspension components. Tire changing and wheel balancing are covered in Chapter Nine.

Refer to **Table 1** for rear suspension torque specifications. **Table 1** is located at the end of this chapter.



## REAR WHEEL

### Removal/Installation

1. Insert a drift or rod into the hole (**Figure 1**) in the left-hand side of the axle to keep the axle from turning.
2. Loosen the rear axle nut (**Figure 2**).
3. Shift the transmission into NEUTRAL.
4. Place wood block(s) under the engine and frame to support the bike securely with the rear wheel off the ground.
5. Loosen the drive belt adjuster nut (A, **Figure 3**) and loosen the adjust bolt (B, **Figure 3**) on each side of the swing arm so the wheel can be moved forward for maximum belt slack.
6. Completely unscrew the rear brake adjusting nut (**Figure 4**).
7. Depress the brake pedal and remove the brake cable from the pivot joint in the brake arm. Install the pivot joint and adjusting nut onto the end of the brake cable to avoid misplacing them.

8. Remove the bolts (**Figure 5**) securing the drive pulley guard and remove the guard.
9. Remove the bolt (**Figure 6**) securing the drive belt lower cover at the rear.
10. Remove the bolt and washer (A, **Figure 7**) securing the front of both the drive belt upper and lower covers at the front.
11. Remove the lower cover (B, **Figure 7**).
12. Remove the bolt (**Figure 8**) securing the drive belt upper cover at the rear.
13. Pull the drive belt upper cover (**Figure 9**) up at the rear and remove the upper cover.
14. Push the rear wheel forward until it stops.
15. Carefully disengage the drive belt from the driven sprocket.
16. Remove the rear axle nut and washer (**Figure 2**) and withdraw the rear axle (**Figure 1**) from the right-hand side and lower the wheel and drive belt. Don't lose the right-hand spacer between the brake panel and the swing arm—it will fall off when the rear axle is withdrawn.
17. Roll the rear wheel to the rear and remove it. Don't lose the spacer on each side of the wheel hub.

*CAUTION*

*Do not set the wheel down on the driven pulley surface as it may get damaged. Set the sidewalls on 2 wood blocks.*

18. Inspect the rear hub and driven pulley as described in this chapter.
19. Install by reversing these removal steps. Note the following during installation.

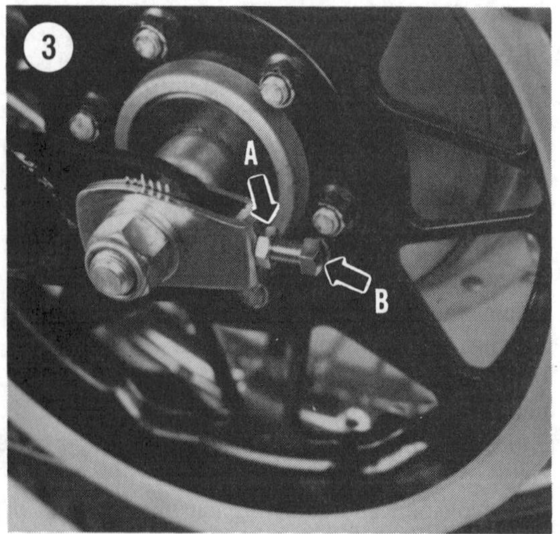


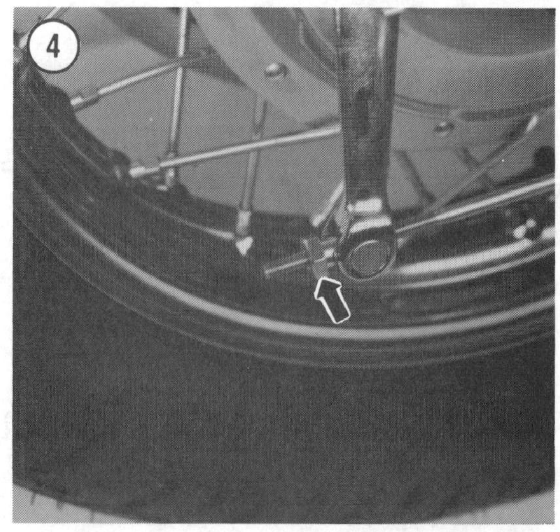

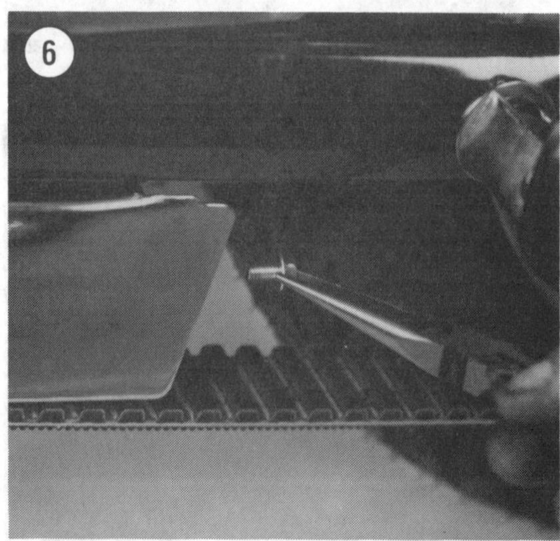

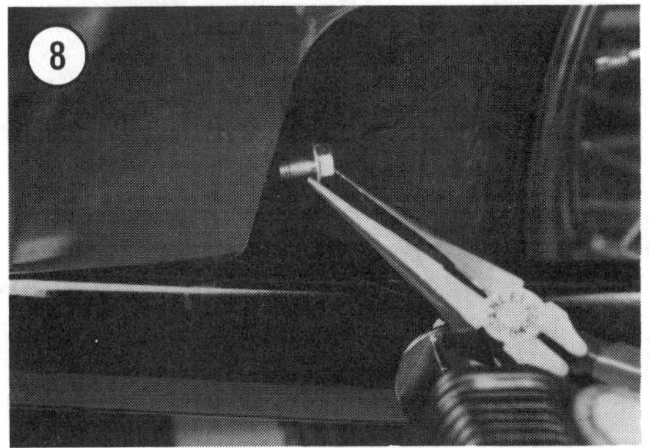

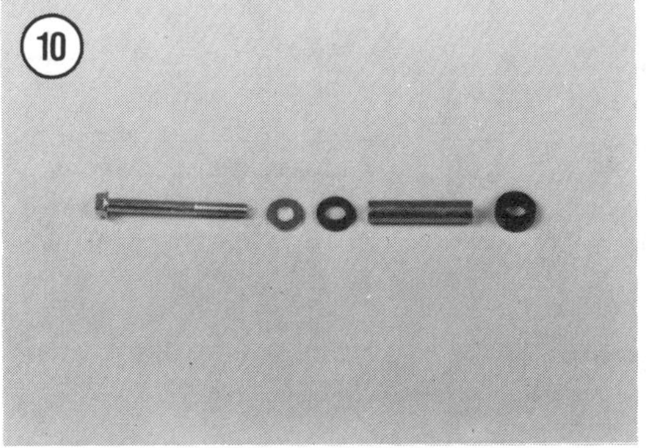


20. Make sure the drive belt adjuster assembly is in place on each side of the swing arm.
21. Install the left-hand spacer into the rear hub.
22. Install the spacer between the rear brake panel and the right-hand side of the swing arm while installing the rear axle.
23. Be sure to properly index the brake panel groove with the raised tab on the right-hand side of the swing arm.
24. The rubber damper (**Figure 10**) must be installed on each side of the bolt mounting holes in the drive pulley guard as shown in **Figure 11**.
25. Adjust the drive belt as described in Chapter Three.
26. Tighten the rear axle nut to the torque specification listed in **Table 1**.
27. Adjust the rear brake as described under *Rear Brake Pedal Height and Freeplay Adjustment* in Chapter Three.
28. After the wheel is completely installed, rotate it several times to make sure that it rotates freely. Apply the rear brake several times to make sure it is operating correctly.

### Inspection

Measure the axial and radial runout of the wheel with a dial indicator as shown in **Figure 12**. The maximum axial (end play) and radial (side play) runout is 2.0 mm (0.08 in.).

Check axle runout as described in this chapter.

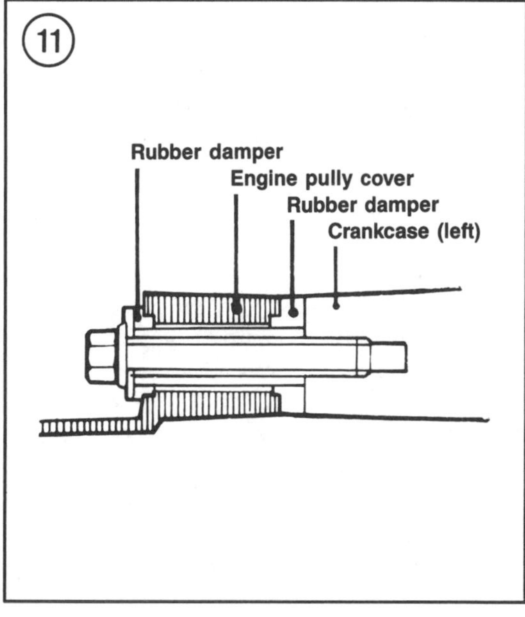


10

## REAR HUB

### Inspection

Inspect each wheel bearing before removing it from the wheel hub.

*CAUTION*
*Do not remove the wheel bearings for inspection purposes as they will be damaged during the removal process. Remove wheel bearings only if they are to be replaced.*

1. Perform Steps 1-7 of *Disassembly* in this chapter. 2. Turn each bearing by hand. Make sure the bearings turn smoothly.
3. Inspect the play of the inner race (**Figure 13**) of each wheel bearing. Check for excessive axial (side play) and radial (end play) play. Replace the bearing if it has an excessive amount of free play.
4. On non-sealed bearings, check the balls for evidence of wear, pitting or excessive heat (bluish tint). Replace the bearings if necessary; always replace as a complete set. When replacing the bearings, be sure to take your old bearings along to ensure a perfect matchup.

*NOTE*
*Fully sealed bearings are available from many bearing specialty shops. Fully sealed bearings provide better protection from dirt and moisture that may get into the hub.*

5. Check the axle for wear and straightness. Use V-blocks and a dial indicator as shown in **Figure 14**. If the runout is 0.2 mm (0.01 in.) or greater, the axle should be replaced.
6. Inspect the raised webs (**Figure 15**) where the rubber dampers fit. Check for cracks or wear. If any damage is visible, replace the wheel.
7. Inspect the driven pulley as described in this chapter.
8. Inspect the drive belt as described in Chapter Three.

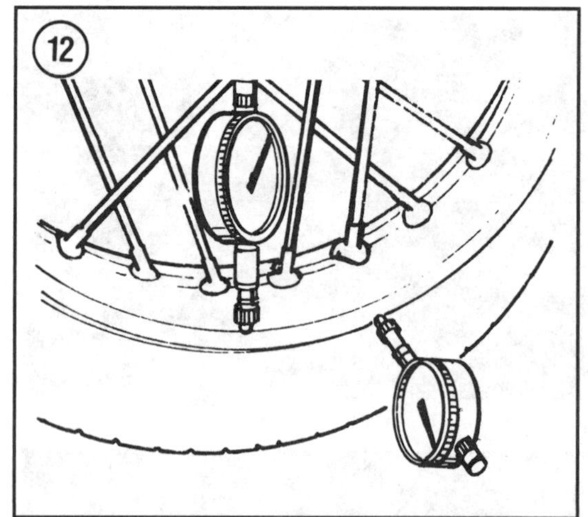


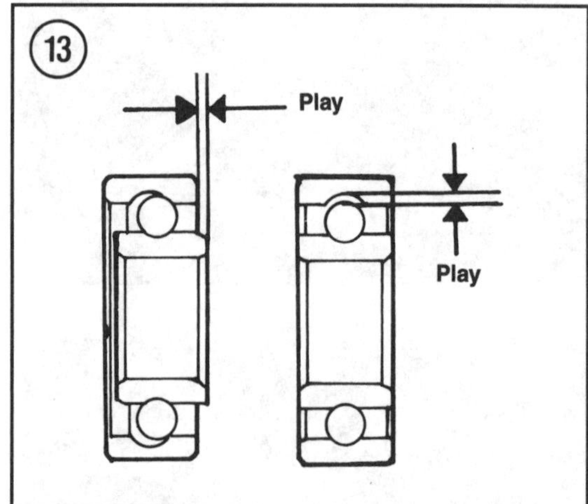


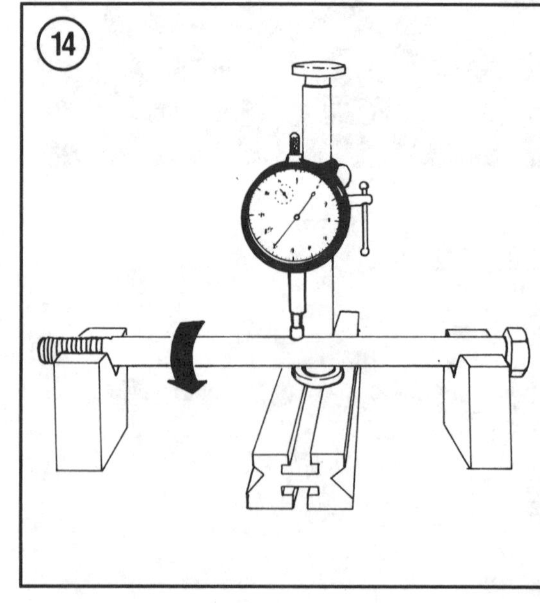

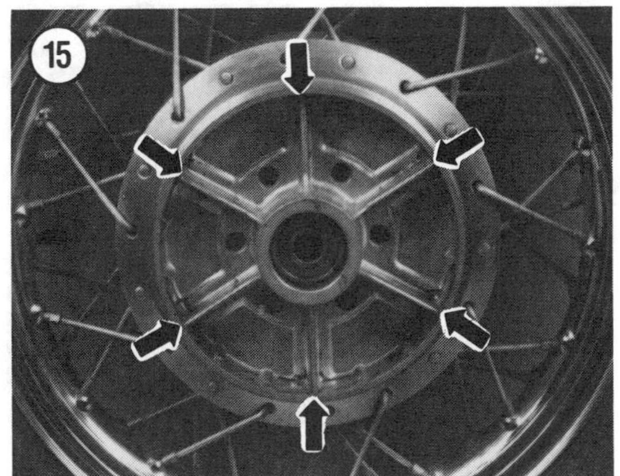

## Disassembly

Refer to **Figure 16** for this procedure.

1. Remove the rear wheel as described in this chapter.
2. Pull straight up and remove the brake assembly from the right-hand side.
3. Remove the spacer from the left-hand side.
4. If the driven pulley assembly is going to be serviced, loosen the mounting nuts at this time. The wheel makes a great holding fixture.
5. If the driven pulley is difficult to remove, tap on the backside of the pulley with a wooden hammer handle through the spokes from the opposite side. Work around the perimeter of the pulley until the pulley is loose.
6. Lift up and remove the driven pulley assembly from the left-hand side. Don't lose the drum spacer (**Figure 17**) in the backside of the driven pulley drum.
7. Remove the rubber dampers (**Figure 18**) from the rear hub.
8. Before proceeding further, inspect the wheel bearings as described in this chapter. If they must be replaced, proceed as follows.

9A. A special Suzuki tool setup (Suzuki part No. 09941-50110) can be used to remove the wheel bearings as follows:



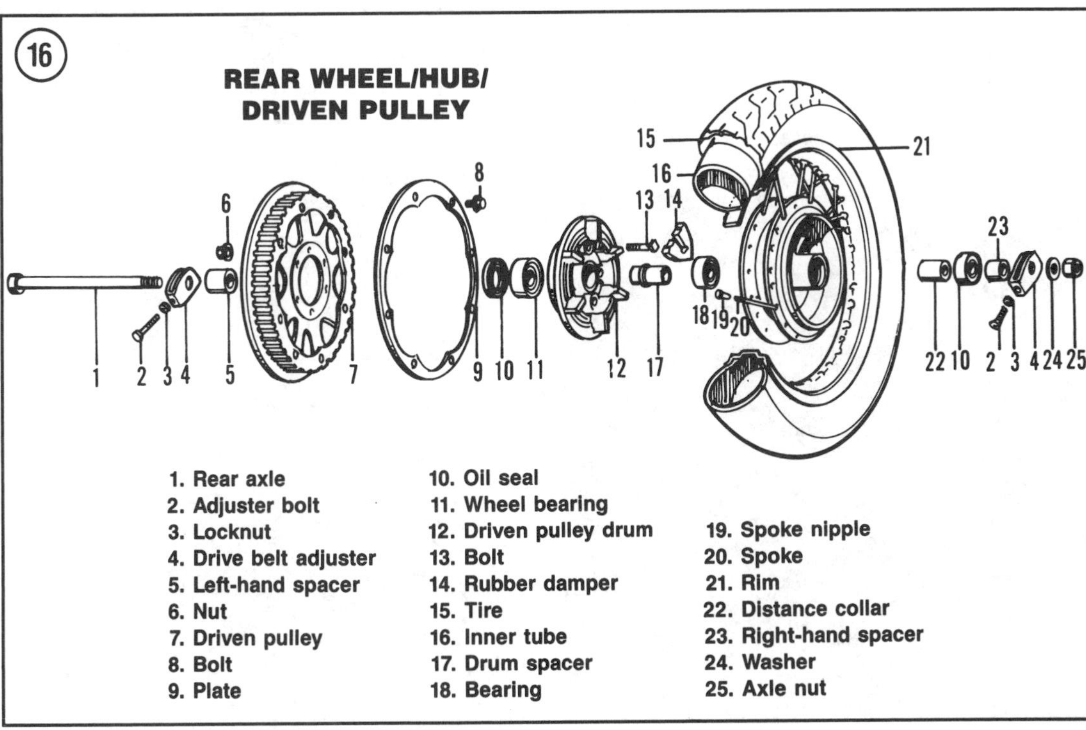


1. Rear axle
2. Adjuster bolt
3. Locknut
4. Drive belt adjuster
5. Left-hand spacer
6. Nut
7. Driven pulley
8. Bolt
9. Plate
10. Oil seal
11. Wheel bearing
12. Driven pulley drum
13. Bolt
14. Rubber damper
15. Tire
16. Inner tube
17. Drum spacer
18. Bearing
19. Spoke nipple
20. Spoke
21. Rim
22. Distance collar
23. Right-hand spacer
24. Washer
25. Axle nut

a. Insert the adaptor (A, **Figure 19**) into one of the wheel bearings from the outer surface of the wheel.
b. Turn the wheel over and insert the wedge bar into the backside of the adaptor. Tap the wedge bar and force it into the slit in the adaptor (B, **Figure 19**). This will wedge the adaptor against the inner bearing race.
c. Tap on the end of the wedge bar with a hammer (**Figure 20**) and drive the bearing out of the hub. Remove the bearing and the distance collar.
d. Repeat for the bearing on the other side.

9B. If the special tools are not used, perform the following:

a. To remove the right- and left-hand bearings and distance collar, insert a soft-aluminum or brass drift into one side of the hub.
b. Push the distance collar over to one side and place the drift on the inner race of the lower bearing.
c. Tap the bearing out of the hub with a hammer, working around the perimeter of the inner race.
d. Repeat for the other bearing.

10. Clean the inside and the outside of the hub with solvent. Dry with compressed air.

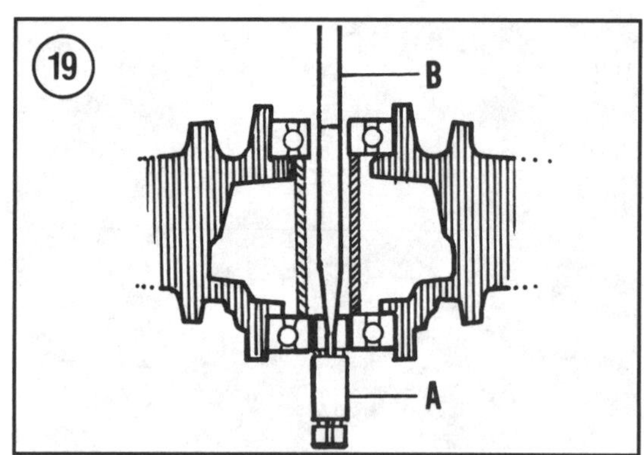


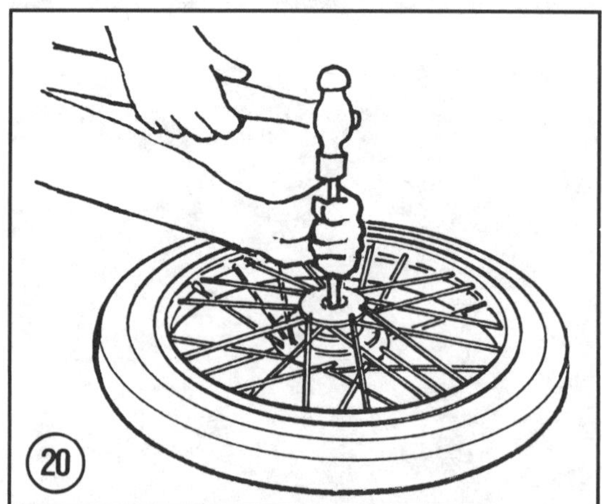


### Assembly

1. On non-sealed bearings, pack the bearings with a good-quality bearing grease. Work the grease in

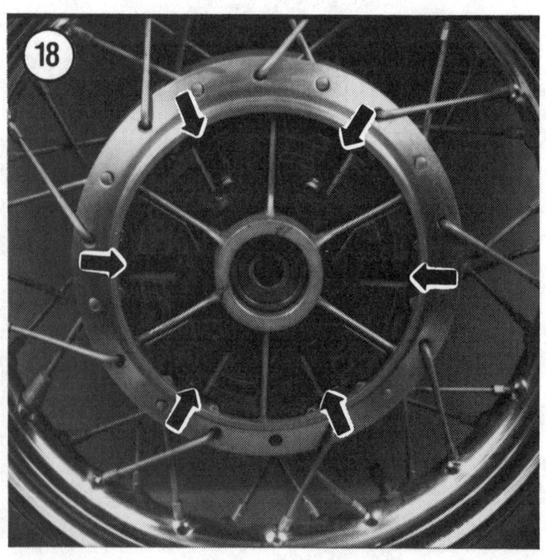


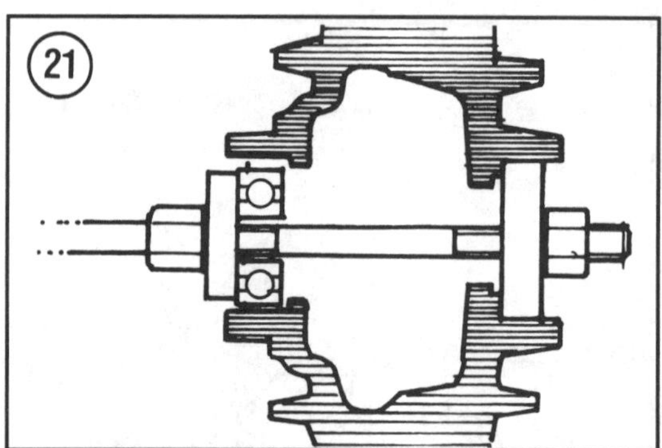

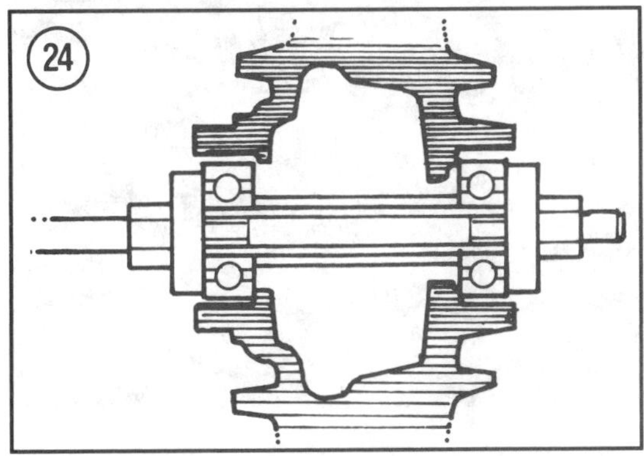

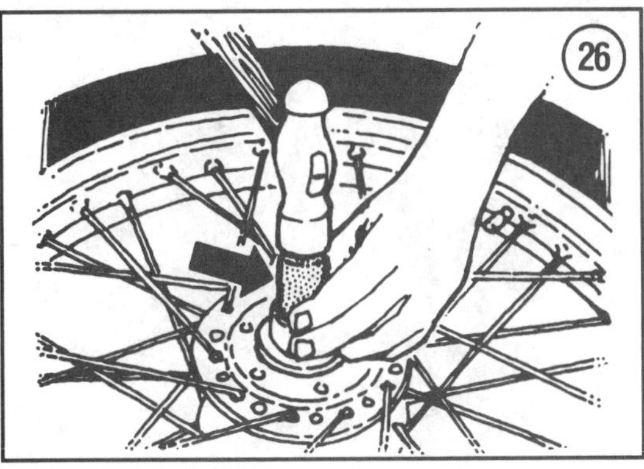

between the balls thoroughly; turn the bearing by hand a couple of times to make sure the grease is distributed evenly inside the bearing.

2. Blow any dirt or foreign matter out of the hub before installing the bearings.

*CAUTION*

*Install non-sealed bearings with the single-sealed side facing outward. Tap the bearings squarely into place and tap on the outer race only. Do not tap on the inner race or the bearing might be damaged. Be sure that the bearings are completely seated.*

3A. A special Suzuki tool setup (Suzuki part No. 09924-84510) can be used to install the wheel bearings as follows:

a. Install the left-hand bearing into the hub first.
b. Set the bearing with the sealed side facing out and install the bearing installer as shown in **Figure 21**.
c. Tighten the bearing installer (**Figure 22**) and pull the bearing into the hub until it is completely seated (**Figure 23**). Remove the bearing installer.
d. Turn the wheel over (right-hand side up) on the workbench and install the distance collar.
e. Set the right-hand bearing with the sealed side facing out and install the bearing installer as shown in **Figure 24**.
f. Tighten the bearing installer (**Figure 22**) and pull the bearing into the hub until it is completely seated (**Figure 25**).
g. Remove the bearing installer.

3B. If special tools are not used, perform the following:

a. Tap the left-hand bearing squarely into place and tap on the outer race only. Use a socket (**Figure 26**) that matches the outer race diameter. Do not tap on the inner race or the bearing might be damaged. Be sure that the bearing is completely seated.
b. Turn the wheel over (right-hand side up) on the workbench and install the distance collar.
c. Use the same tool setup and drive in the right-hand bearing.

4. Install the rubber dampers (**Figure 18**) into the rear hub.

5. If removed, install the drum spacer with the short side (**Figure 27**) going in first and install the drum spacer (**Figure 17**) into the backside of the driven pulley drum.
6. Install the driven pulley assembly into the left-hand side.
7. If the driven pulley assembly was serviced, tighten the nuts at this time to the torque specification listed in **Table 1**.
8. Install the brake assembly into the right-hand side.
9. Install the left-hand spacer into the hub.
10. Install the rear wheel as described in this chapter.

## DRIVEN PULLEY

### Removal/Installation

1. Remove the rear wheel as described in this chapter.
2. If the driven pulley assembly is going to be serviced, loosen the mounting nuts at this time. The wheel makes a great holding fixture.

NOTE

*If the driven pulley assembly is difficult to remove, tap on the backside of the pulley (from the opposite side of the wheel through the wheel spokes) with a wooden handle of a hammer. Tap evenly around the perimeter of the pulley until the assembly is free.*

3. Lift up and remove the driven pulley assembly from the left-hand side. Don't lose the drum spacer (**Figure 17**) in the backside of the driven pulley drum.
4. Make sure the rubber dampers (**Figure 18**) are in place in the rear hub.
5. If removed, install the drum spacer with the short side (**Figure 27**) going in first and install the drum spacer (**Figure 17**) into the backside of the driven pulley drum.
6. Install the driven pulley assembly into the left-hand side.
7. If the driven pulley assembly was serviced, tighten the nuts at this time to the torque specification listed in **Table 1**.
8. If removed, install the left-hand spacer into the hub.
9. Install the rear wheel as described in this chapter.

### Disassembly/Assembly

Refer to **Figure 16** for this procedure.

1. Remove the driven pulley as described in this chapter.

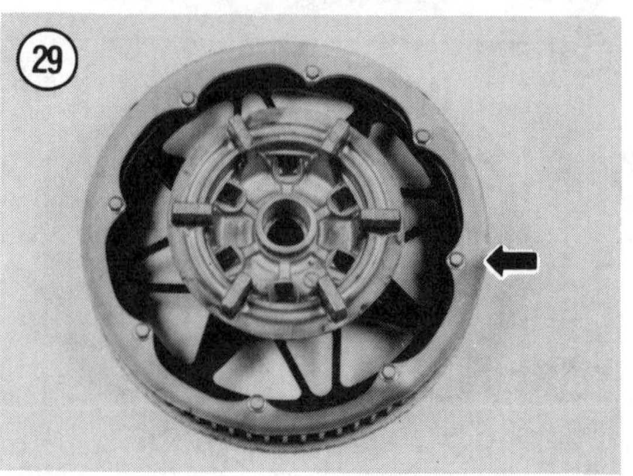

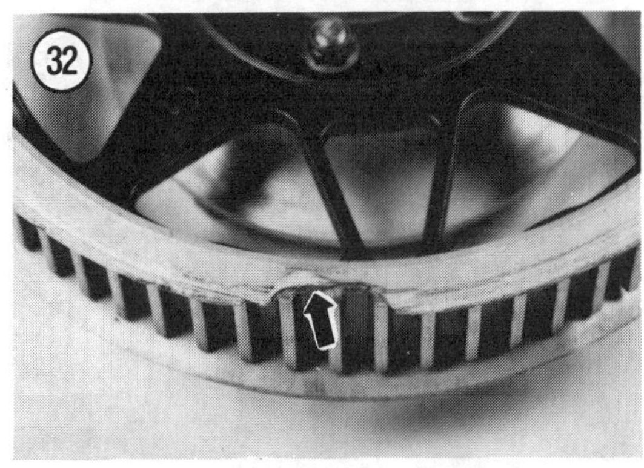

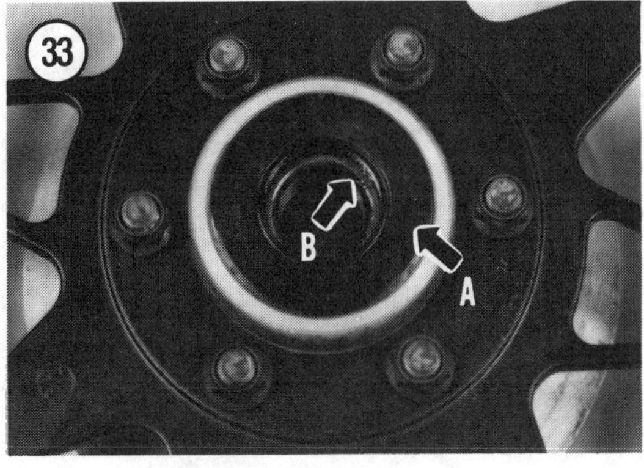


2. Remove the drum spacer (**Figure 17**) from the backside of the driven pulley drum.
3. Remove the nuts (**Figure 28**) securing the driven pulley to the driven pulley drum and separate the 2 parts.
4. If necessary, remove the bolts securing the side plate (**Figure 29**) to the driven pulley and remove the side plate.
5. Inspect all parts as described in this chapter.
6. Install by reversing these removal steps. Note the following during installation.
7. If the side plate was removed, tighten the bolts to the torque specification listed in **Table 1**.
8. Position the drum spacer with the short side (**Figure 27**) going in first and install the drum spacer into the backside of the driven pulley drum.

### Inspection

1. Visually inspect the rubber dampers (**Figure 30**) for signs of damage or deterioration. Replace dampers as a complete set.
2. Inspect the teeth on the driven pulley (**Figure 31**) assembly for cracks or damage or missing teeth; replace if necessary.
3. Inspect the driven pulley for damage (**Figure 32**).
4. If the driven pulley requires replacement, also inspect the drive belt and the drive pulley on the engine. They also may be worn and need replacing.
5. Inspect the bearing, turn the bearing by hand. Make sure it turns smoothly. Replace if necessary as described in this chapter.
6. On non-sealed bearings, check the balls for evidence of wear, pitting or excessive heat (bluish tint). Replace the bearings if necessary; always replace as a complete set. When replacing the bearings, be sure to take your old bearings along to ensure a perfect matchup.

*NOTE*
*Fully sealed bearings are available from many bearing specialty shops. Fully sealed bearings provide better protection from dirt and moisture that may get into the hub.*

### Bearing Replacement

1. Remove the grease seal (A, **Figure 33**) from the driven pulley drum.

2. To remove the bearing, insert a soft-aluminum or brass drift into one side of the drum.
3. Place the drift on the inner race of the bearing (B, **Figure 33**).
4. Tap the bearing out of the drum with a hammer, working around the perimeter of the inner race.
5. On a non-sealed bearing, pack the bearing with a good-quality bearing grease. Work the grease in between the balls thoroughly; turn the bearing by hand a couple of times to make sure the grease is distributed evenly inside the bearing.
6. Blow any dirt or foreign matter out of the driven pulley drum before installing the bearing.
7. Tap the bearing squarely into place and tap on the outer race only. Use a socket that matches the outer race diameter. Do not tap on the inner race or the bearing might be damaged. Be sure that the bearing is completely seated.
8. Install the grease seal.

## DRIVE PULLEY AND DRIVE BELT

### Removal

1. Remove the bolts (**Figure 34**) securing the drive pulley guard and remove the guard.
2. Remove the bolt (**Figure 35**) securing the drive belt lower cover at the rear.
3. Remove the bolt and washer (A, **Figure 36**) securing the front of both the drive belt upper and lower covers at the front.

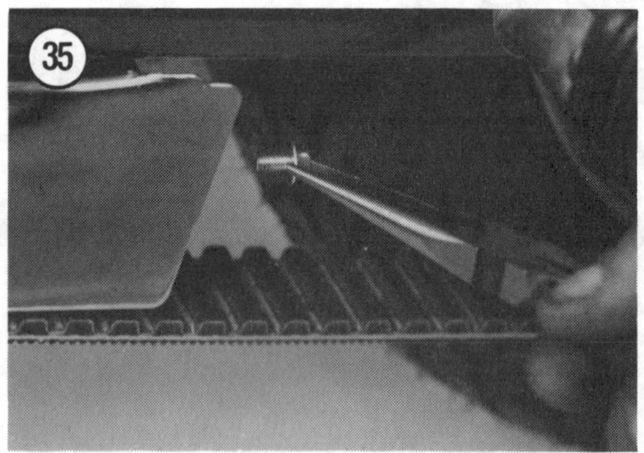

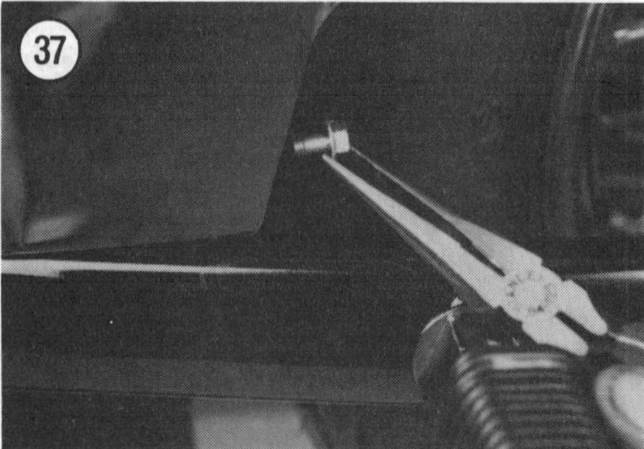

39

40

41

42

4. Remove the lower cover (B, **Figure 36**).
5. Remove the bolt (**Figure 37**) securing the drive belt upper cover at the rear.
6. Remove the left-hand shock absorber as described in this chapter.
7. Pull the drive belt upper cover (**Figure 38**) up at the rear and remove the upper cover.
8. Straighten the tab (**Figure 39**) on the lockwasher.
9. Have an assistant apply the rear brake and loosen the drive pulley nut (**Figure 40**).
10. Remove the nut and lockwasher. Discard the lockwasher.
11. Remove the left-hand shock absorber as described in this chapter.
12. Insert a drift or rod into the hole (**Figure 41**) in the left-hand side of the axle.
13. Loosen the rear axle nut (**Figure 42**).
14. Shift the transmission into NEUTRAL.
15. Loosen the drive belt adjuster nut (A, **Figure 43**) and loosen the adjust bolt (B, **Figure 43**) on each side of the swing arm so the wheel can be moved forward for maximum belt slack.
16. Push the rear wheel forward until it stops.
17. Carefully pull the drive pulley (A, **Figure 44**) and drive belt (B, **Figure 44**) off the transmission mainshaft.
18. Carefully disengage the drive belt from the driven sprocket.
19. Remove the drive pulley and drive belt.



### Installation

1. Make sure the drive belt is properly meshed with the driven pulley on the rear wheel.

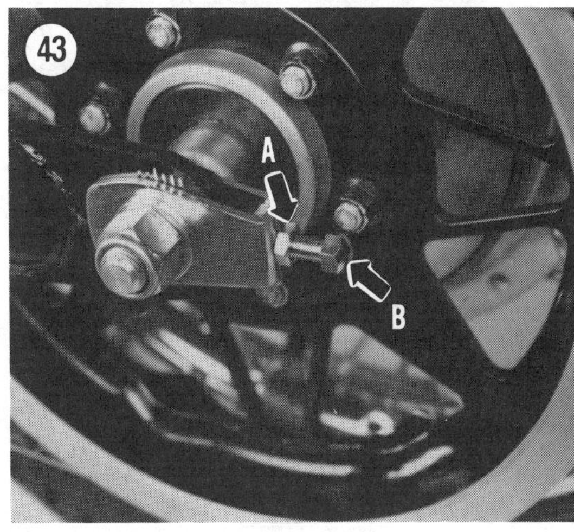

43

2. Mesh the drive belt onto the drive pulley and install these 2 parts as an assembly onto the transmission mainshaft.
3. Before installing the new lockwasher, partially bend up one side (**Figure 45**).
4. Install a new lockwasher and the drive pulley nut.
5. Have an assistant apply the rear brake. Tighten the drive pulley nut to the torque specification listed in **Table 1**.
6. Continue to bend up one section of the *new* lockwasher onto one of the flats on the drive pulley nut.
7. Install the drive belt upper cover (**Figure 38**).
8. Install the left-hand shock absorber as described in this chapter.
9. Install the bolt (**Figure 37**) securing the drive belt upper cover at the rear and tighten securely (**Figure 46**).
10. Install the lower cover (B, **Figure 36**).
11. Install the bolt and washer (A, **Figure 36**) securing the front of both the drive belt upper and lower covers at the front.
12. Install the bolt (**Figure 35**) securing the drive belt lower cover at the rear and tighten securely.
13. The rubber damper (**Figure 47**) must be installed on each side of the bolt mounting holes in the drive pulley guard as shown in **Figure 48**.
14. Install the bolts (**Figure 34**) securing the drive pulley guard and remove the guard.
15. Adjust the drive belt as described in Chapter Three.

## SHOCK ABSORBER

The shock absorbers are spring controlled and hydraulically dampened. Spring pre-load can be adjusted by rotating the spring lower seat at the base of the shock absorber. Insert a drift into the receptacle (**Figure 49**) in the spring lower seat and rotate it to any one of the 5 settings. The No. 1 setting is the softest while the No. 5 setting is the stiffest.

The spring lower seat on each shock absorber must be indexed on the same detent. The shock absorbers are sealed and cannot be rebuilt. Service is limited to removal and installation as no replacement parts are available.

### Removal/Installation

Removal and installation of the shock absorbers is easier if done one shock at a time. The remaining

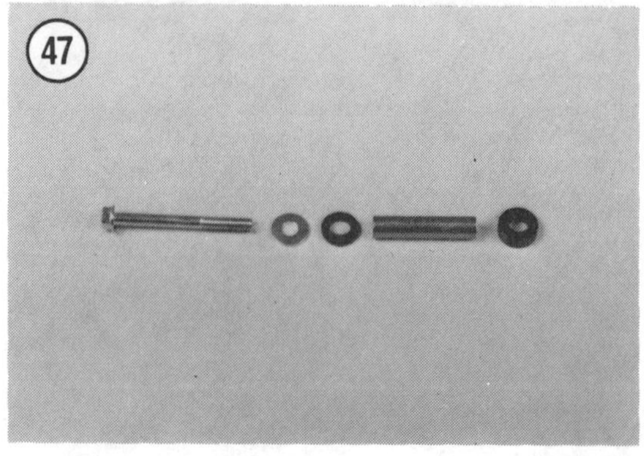

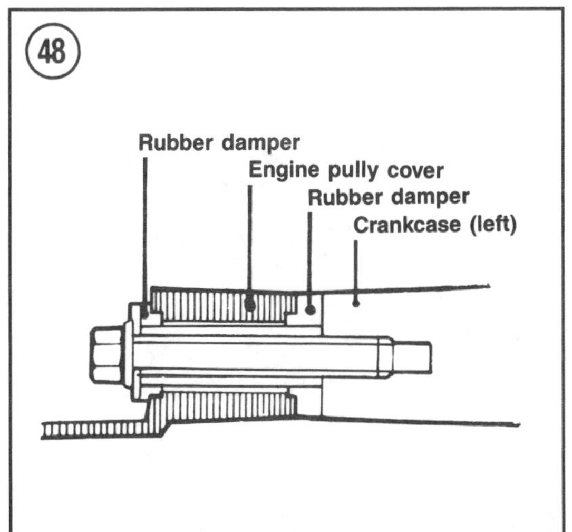

unit will support the rear of the bike and maintain correct relationship between the swing arm and the frame shock mounting points.

*NOTE*

*It is not necessary to remove the seat, but it is very close to the shock's upper mount on the frame. If a tool should slip during this removal and installation of the upper nut, the seat may be damaged.*

1. Remove the seat as described in Chapter Twelve.
2. Adjust the shocks to their softest settings, completely *counterclockwise*.
3. Remove the cap nuts and washers (**Figure 50**) from the upper and lower mounts on the frame and swing arm.
4. Pull the shock absorber straight off the upper and lower mounts and remove the unit.
5. Don't lose the inner washer on the upper mount, it must be reinstalled in the same place.
6. Install by reversing these removal steps. Note the following during installation.
7. Tighten the upper and lower mounting nuts to the torque specification listed in **Table 1**.

### Inspection

The shock absorber cannot be disassembled. As it cannot be serviced, there are *no* replacement parts available.

If the bike has a lot of miles on it and one of the shock absorbers is faulty, replace both units to maintain maximum handling performance.

1. Inspect the rubber bushings in the upper and lower mounting joints (**Figure 51**) for wear or damage. If worn or damaged, replace the shock absorber unit.
2. Check the damper unit for leakage and make sure the damper rod is straight (**Figure 52**).
3. Inspect the rubber stopper. If it is worn, damaged or starting to deteriorate, replace the shock absorber unit.

## SWING ARM

In time, the needle bearings will wear and will have to be replaced. The condition of the bearings can greatly affect handling performance. If worn parts are not replaced, they can produce erratic and dangerous handling. Common symptoms are wheel hop, pulling to one side during acceleration and pulling to the other side during braking.

### Removal

1. Place wood block(s) under the engine and frame to support the bike securely with the rear wheel off the ground.
2. Remove the drive belt (A, **Figure 53**) as described in this chapter.
3. Remove the cap (B, **Figure 53**) from each side of the frame covering the pivot bolt and nut.
4. Remove the shock absorbers as described in this chapter.
5. Remove the rear wheel as described in this chapter.
6. Grasp the rear end of the swing arm and try to move it from side-to-side in a horizontal arc. There should be no noticeable side play. If play is evident and the pivot bolt is tightened correctly, the needle bearings should be replaced.
7. Loosen the locknuts (A, **Figure 54**) on the rear brake cable and remove the cable from the receptacle (B, **Figure 54**) on the swing arm. Be careful not to kink or damage the brake cable.
8. Remove the self-locking nut and withdraw the pivot bolt from the left-hand side.
9. Pull back on the swing arm, free it from the drive belt and remove the swing arm from the frame.
10. Inspect the swing arm as described in this chapter.

*NOTE*
*Don't lose the dust seal and thrust washer on each side of the pivot points; they may fall off when the swing arm is removed.*

### Installation

1. Make sure the washer and dust seal are correctly installed at each side of the swing arm.
2. Position the swing arm into the mounting area of the frame. Align the holes in the swing arm with

51

52

53

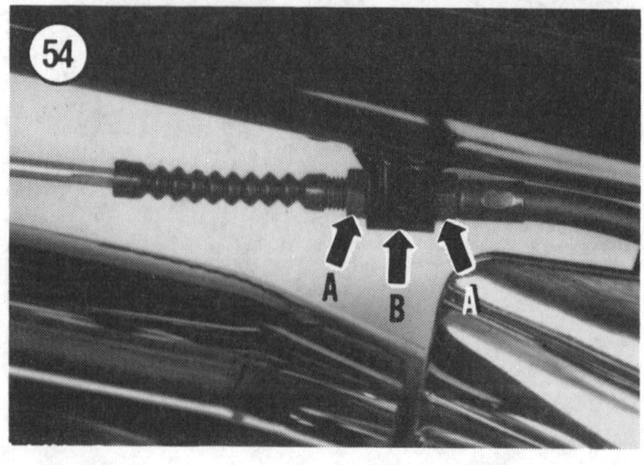

54

the holes in the frame. To help align the holes, insert a drift in from the right-hand side.

3. Apply a light coat of molybdenum disulfide grease to the pivot bolt and install the pivot bolt from the left-hand side.
4. Install the self-locking nut and tighten to the torque specification listed in **Table 1**.
5. Move the swing arm up and down several times to make sure all components are properly seated.
6. Insert the brake cable through the receptacle in the swing arm and tighten the locknut.
7. Install the rear wheel as described in this chapter.
8. Install the drive belt as described in this chapter.
9. Install the shock absorbers as described in this chapter.
10. Install the cap on each side of the frame covering the pivot bolt and nut.
11. Adjust the drive belt as described in Chapter Three.
12. Adjust the rear brake as described under *Rear Brake Pedal Height and Freeplay Adjustment* in Chapter Three.

### Disassembly/Inspection/Assembly

Refer to **Figure 55** for this procedure.

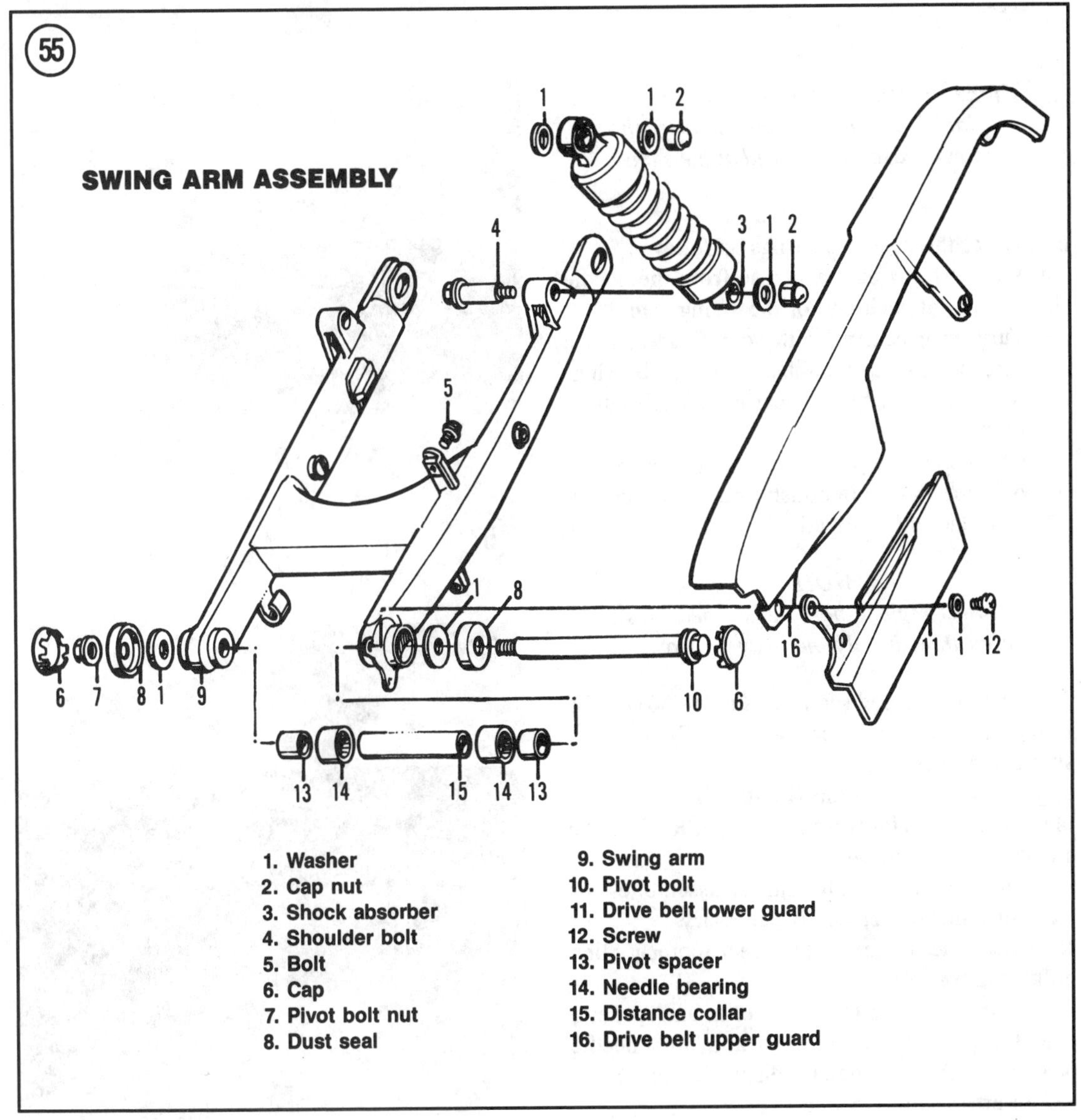

1. Remove the swing arm as described in this chapter.
2. Remove both dust seals and washers if they have not already fallen off during the removal sequence.
3. Withdraw the pivot spacer and pivot collar from the frame.
4. Clean all parts in solvent and dry thoroughly.

*NOTE*
*There are no factory specifications for the outside diameter of the pivot spacers or pivot collar.*

5. Inspect the spacers and the pivot collar for abnormal wear, scratches or score marks. Replace if necessary.

*NOTE*
*If the spacers and the pivot collar are replaced, the needle bearing at each end must also be replaced at the same time.*

6. Inspect the needle bearings as follows:
   a. Wipe off any excess grease from the needle bearing at each end of the swing arm.
   b. Turn each bearing with your fingers; make sure they rotate smoothly. The needle bearings wear very slowly and wear is very difficult to measure.
   c. Check the rollers for evidence of wear, pitting or color change (a bluish tint indicating heat from lack of lubrication).

*NOTE*
*Always replace both needle bearings even though only one may be worn.*

7. Check the welded sections (**Figure 56**) on the swing arm for cracks or fractures. Replace the swing arm if necessary.
8. Inspect the pivot points (**Figure 57**) at the front of the swing arm for wear or damage. Replace the swing arm if necessary.
9. Inspect the drive belt adjuster assemblies for wear or damage, replace if necessary.
10. Check the tightness of the rear footpeg Allen bolts (**Figure 58**).
11. Before installing the pivot collar and spacers, coat the pivot collar, spacers and both needle bearings with molybdenum disulfide grease.
12. Insert the pivot collar.

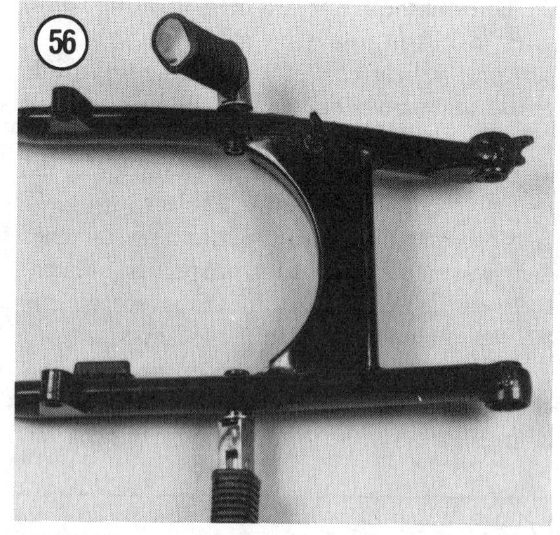
56

57

58

13. Insert the pivot spacer into each end.
14. Coat the inside of both dust caps and the thrust washers with molybdenum disulfide grease and install them onto the ends of the swing arm.
15. Install the swing arm as described in this chapter.

### Pivot Point Needle Bearing Replacement

The swing arm pivot point needle bearings are located in the frame and not in the swing arm as the usual practice. The bearings are pressed into place and have to be removed with force. The bearings will become distorted when removed, so don't remove them unless absolutely necessary.

The bearings must be removed and installed from the frame with special tools that are available from a Suzuki dealer.

1. Remove the swing arm as described in this chapter.
2. Withdraw the spacers and pivot collar.
3. Either the right- or left-hand bearing can be removed first.
4. Install the swing arm in a vise with soft jaws.

*NOTE*
*The special tool grabs the inner surface of the bearing and then withdraws it from the swing arm.*

5. Install the bearing remover (Suzuki bearing puller, part No. 09923-73210) through the hole in the bearing and expand the tool behind the bearing.
6. Attach the sliding shaft (Suzuki sliding shaft, part No. 09930-30102) to the bearing puller. Using quick in and out movement of the weight on the sliding shaft, withdraw the needle bearing from the frame.
7. Remove the bearing and the special tool.
8. Turn the swing arm over in the vise and repeat Steps 6-8 for the other bearing.
9. Thoroughly clean out the inside of the swing arm with solvent and dry with compressed air.
10. Apply a light coat of molybdenum disulfide grease to all parts prior to installation.

*NOTE*
*Either the right- or left-hand bearing race can be installed first.*

*CAUTION*
*Never reinstall a needle bearing that has been removed. During removal it becomes slightly damaged and is no longer true to alignment. If installed, it will damage the pivot collar and create an unsafe riding condition.*

11. Position the new needle bearing with its marks facing up (toward the outside).
12. Install the bearing installer (Suzuki steering outer race installer, part No. 09941-34513) through the hole in the bearing and through the frame.
13. Turn the nut on the installer and push the new needle bearing into the frame.
14. Remove the installer from the frame.
15. Repeat Steps 12-14 for the other bearing. 10
16. Before installing the pivot collar and spacers, coat the pivot collar, spacers and both needle bearings with molybdenum disulfide grease.
17. Insert the pivot collar.
18. Insert the spacer into each end.
19. Coat the inside of both dust caps and the washers with molybdenum disulfide grease and install them onto the ends of the swing arm.
20. Install the swing arm as described in this chapter.

**Table 1 REAR SUSPENSION TORQUE SPECIFICATIONS**

| Item | N·m | ft.-lb. |
|---|---|---|
| Rear axle nut | 55-88 | 40-63 |
| Driven pulley | | |
| Mounting nuts | 50-70 | 36-51 |
| Side plate bolt | 9-13 | 6-10 |
| Drive pulley nut | 100-130 | 73-94 |
| Swing arm pivot bolt and nut | 50-80 | 36-58 |
| Shock absorber mounting nuts | 20-30 | 15-22 |

# CHAPTER ELEVEN

# BRAKES

The brake system consists of a single disc on the front wheel and a drum brake on the rear. This chapter describes repair and replacement procedures for all brake components.

Table 1 contains the brake system torque specifications and **Table 2** contains brake system specifications. **Table 1** and **Table 2** are located at the end of this chapter.

## DISC BRAKES

The disc brake is actuated by hydraulic fluid and is controlled by a hand lever that is attached to the front master cylinder. As the brake pads wear, the brake fluid level drops in the reservoir and automatically adjusts for wear.

When working on hydraulic brake systems, it is necessary that the work area and all tools be absolutely clean. Any tiny particles of foreign matter and grit in the caliper assembly or the master cylinder can damage the components. Also, sharp tools must not be used inside the calipers or on the piston. If there is any doubt about your ability to correctly and safely carry out major service on the brake components, take the job to a Suzuki dealer or brake specialist.

*WARNING*

*When working on the brake system, do **not** inhale brake dust. It may contain asbestos, which can cause lung injury and cancer. Wear a disposable face mask and wash your hands thoroughly after completing the work.*

When adding brake fluid, use only a brake fluid clearly marked DOT 3 or DOT 4 from a sealed container. Other types may vaporize and cause brake failure. Always use the same brand name; do not intermix as many brands are not compatible. Brake fluid will draw moisture which greatly reduces its ability to perform correctly, so it is a good idea to purchase brake fluid in small containers.

*WARNING*

*Do not intermix silicone based (DOT 5) brake fluid as it can cause brake component damage leading to brake system failure.*

Whenever *any* component has been removed from the brake system, the system is considered "opened" and must be bled to remove air bubbles.

If the brake feels "spongy," this usually means there are air bubbles in the system and it must bled. For safe operation, refer to *Bleeding the System* in this chapter.

*CAUTION*

*Disc brake components rarely require disassembly, so do not disassemble them unless necessary. Do not use solvents of any kind on the brake system's internal components. Solvents will cause the seals to swell and distort and require replacement. When disassembling and cleaning brake components (except brake pads), use new brake fluid.*

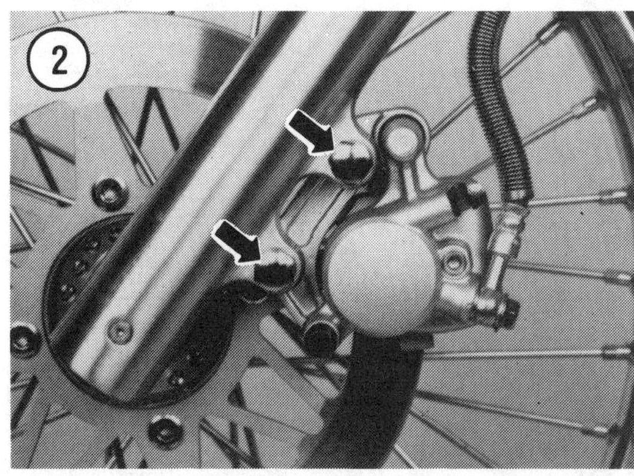

## FRONT BRAKE PAD REPLACEMENT

There is no recommended mileage interval for changing the friction pads in the disc brake. Pad wear depends greatly on riding habits and conditions. The pads should be checked for wear every 6 months and replaced when the wear indicator reaches the edge of the brake disc. To maintain an even brake pressure on the disc, always replace both pads in the caliper at the same time.

Disconnecting the hydraulic brake hose from the brake caliper is not necessary for brake pad replacement. Disconnect the hose only if the caliper assembly is going to be removed.

*CAUTION*

*Check the pads more frequently when the wear line approaches the disc. On some pads, the wear line is very close to the metal backing plate. If pad wear happens to be uneven for some reason, the backing plate may come in contact with the disc and cause damage.*

1. Loosen the pad pin bolt (**Figure 1**).
2. Remove the bolts, washers and lockwashers (**Figure 2**) securing the caliper assembly to the front fork slider.
3. Carefully remove the brake caliper assembly off the brake disc and remove the caliper assembly from the fork slider and brake disc.
4. Completely unscrew the pad pin bolt.
5. Withdraw both brake pads and shims from the caliper assembly.
6. Clean the pad recess and the end of the piston (**Figure 3**) with a soft brush. Do not use solvent, a wire brush or any hard tool which would damage the cylinders or pistons.
7. Carefully remove any rust or corrosion from the disc.
8. Lightly coat the end of the piston and the backs of the new pads (*not* the friction material) with disc brake lubricant.

*NOTE*

*When purchasing new pads, check with your dealer to make sure the friction compound of the new pad is compatible with the disc material. Remove any roughness from the backs of the new pads with a fine-cut file; wipe them clean with a lint-free cloth.*

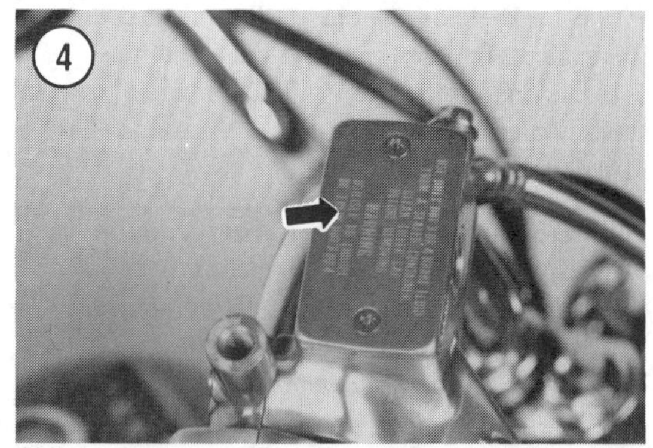

9. When new pads are installed in the caliper, the master cylinder brake fluid level will rise as the caliper piston is repositioned. Perform the following:
   a. Clean the top of the master cylinder of all dirt and foreign matter.
   b. Remove the screws securing the cover (**Figure 4**). Remove the cover and the diaphragm from the master cylinder and slowly push the caliper piston into the caliper. Constantly check the reservoir to make sure brake fluid does not overflow. Remove fluid, if necessary, before it overflows.
   c. The pistons should move freely. If they do not and there is evidence of them sticking in the cylinder, the caliper should be removed and serviced as described in this chapter.

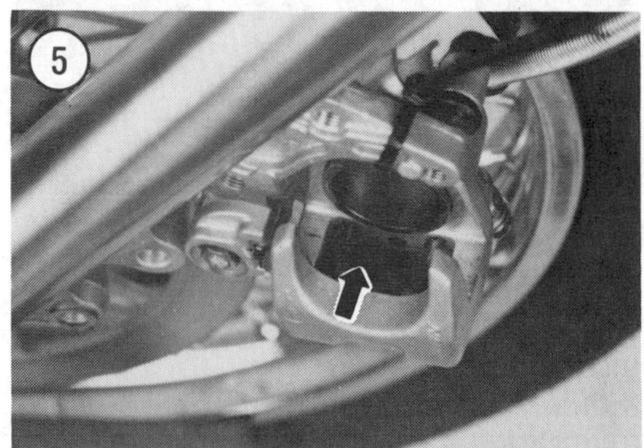

10. Push the caliper piston in all the way to allow room for the new pads.
11. If removed, install the anti-rattle spring (**Figure 5**) into the caliper.
12. Install the outboard pad (**Figure 6**) into the caliper.
13. Install the inboard pad (**Figure 7**) into the caliper.

14. Push both brake pads down against the anti-rattle spring and install the pad bolt through both pads and screw it into the other side of the caliper assembly. Tighten it only finger-tight at this time.
15. Install the brake caliper assembly onto the disc, being careful not to damage the leading edge of the brake pads.
16. Install the caliper mounting bolts, lockwashers and washers and tighten to the torque specification listed in **Table 1**.
17. Tighten the pad pin bolt to the torque specification listed in **Table 1**.
18. Place wood block(s) under the engine and the frame to support the bike securely with the front wheel off the ground. Spin the front wheel and

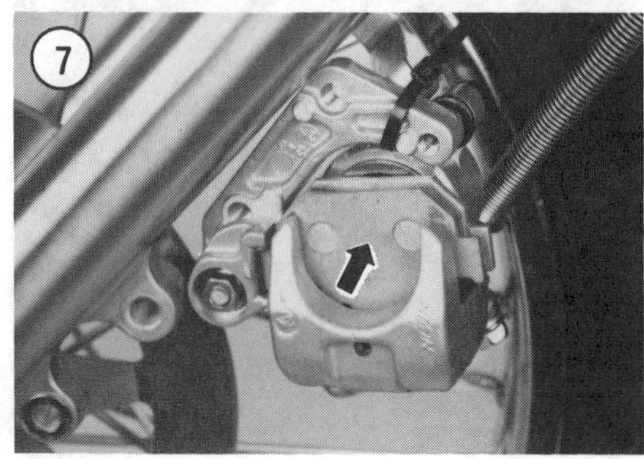

activate the front brake lever as many times as it takes to refill the cylinder in the caliper and correctly locate the pads.

*WARNING*
*Use brake fluid clearly marked DOT 3 or DOT 4 from a sealed container. Other types may vaporize and cause brake failure. Always use the same brand name; do not intermix as many brands are not compatible. Do not intermix silicone based (DOT 5) brake fluid as it can cause brake component damage leading to brake system failure.*

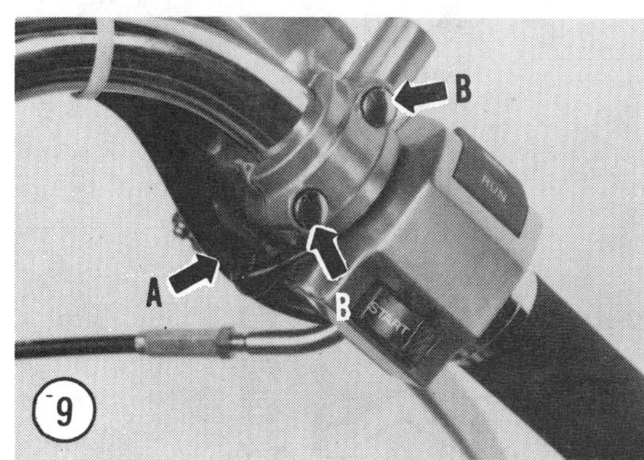


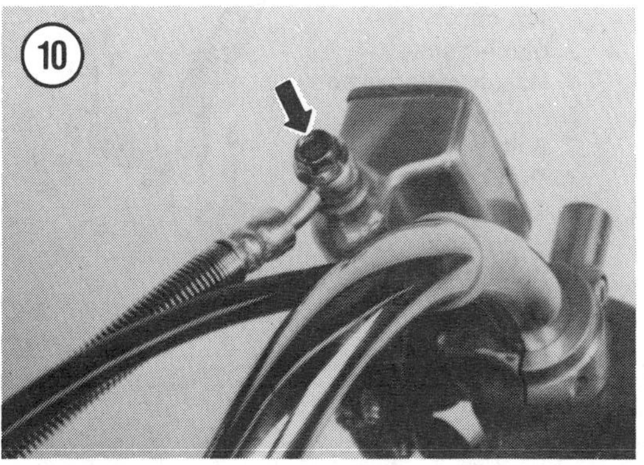


19. Refill the master cylinder reservoir, if necessary, to maintain the correct fluid level as seen through the viewing port on the side (**Figure 8**). Install the diaphragm and cover. Tighten the screws securely.

*WARNING*
*Do not ride the motorcycle until you are sure the brakes are operating correctly with full hydraulic advantage. If necessary, bleed the brake as described under **Bleeding the System** in this chapter.*

20. Bed the pads in gradually for the first 10 days of riding by using only light pressure as much as possible. Immediate hard application will glaze the new friction pads and greatly reduce the effectiveness of the brake.

## FRONT MASTER CYLINDER

### Removal/Installation

1. Remove the rear view mirror from the master cylinder.

*CAUTION*
*Cover the fuel tank and front fender with a heavy cloth or plastic tarp to protect them from accidental brake fluid spills. Wash brake fluid off any painted or plated surfaces or plastic parts immediately, as it will destroy the finish. Use soapy water and rinse completely.*

2. Disconnect the brake light switch electrical connector (A, **Figure 9**) from the main wiring harness.
3. Place a shop cloth under the union bolt to catch any spilled brake fluid that will leak out.
4. Unscrew the union bolt (**Figure 10**) securing the brake hose to the master cylinder. Don't lose the sealing washer on each side of the hose fitting.

5. Tie the loose end of the hose up to the handlebar. Place the hose end in a resealable plastic bag and zip the bag closed around the hose to prevent the entry of moisture and foreign matter.
6. Remove the trim plug (B, **Figure 9**) from each clamp bolt.
7. Remove the clamping bolts (**Figure 11**) and clamp securing the master cylinder to the handlebar and remove the master cylinder.
8. Install by reversing these removal steps. Note the following during installation.
9. Install the clamp with the rear view mirror receptacle facing up. Align the face of the clamp with the punch mark on the handlebar. Tighten the upper bolt first, then the lower to the torque specification listed in **Table 1**.
10. Place a sealing washer on each side of the brake hose fitting and install the union bolt.
11. Tighten the union bolt to the torque specification listed in **Table 1**.
12. Bleed the front brakes as described under *Bleeding the System* in this chapter.

### Disassembly

Refer to **Figure 12** for models with straight handlebars or **Figure 13** for models with pulled back handlebars for this procedure. The only difference between the 2 models is the location of the union bolt hole in the reservoir.

1. Remove the master cylinder as described in this chapter.

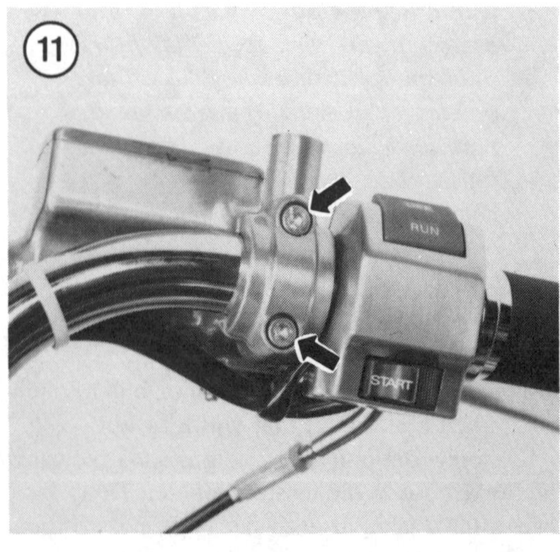


**FRONT MASTER CYLINDER (STRAIGHT HANDLEBAR)**

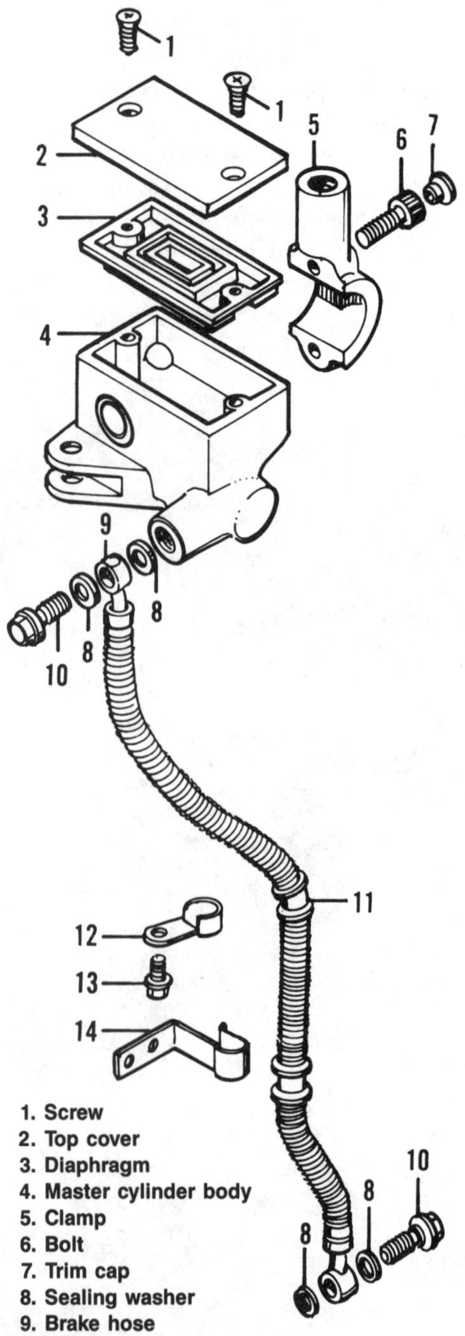

1. Screw
2. Top cover
3. Diaphragm
4. Master cylinder body
5. Clamp
6. Bolt
7. Trim cap
8. Sealing washer
9. Brake hose
10. Union bolt
11. Rubber grommet
12. Bracket
13. Bolt
14. Bracket

(12)

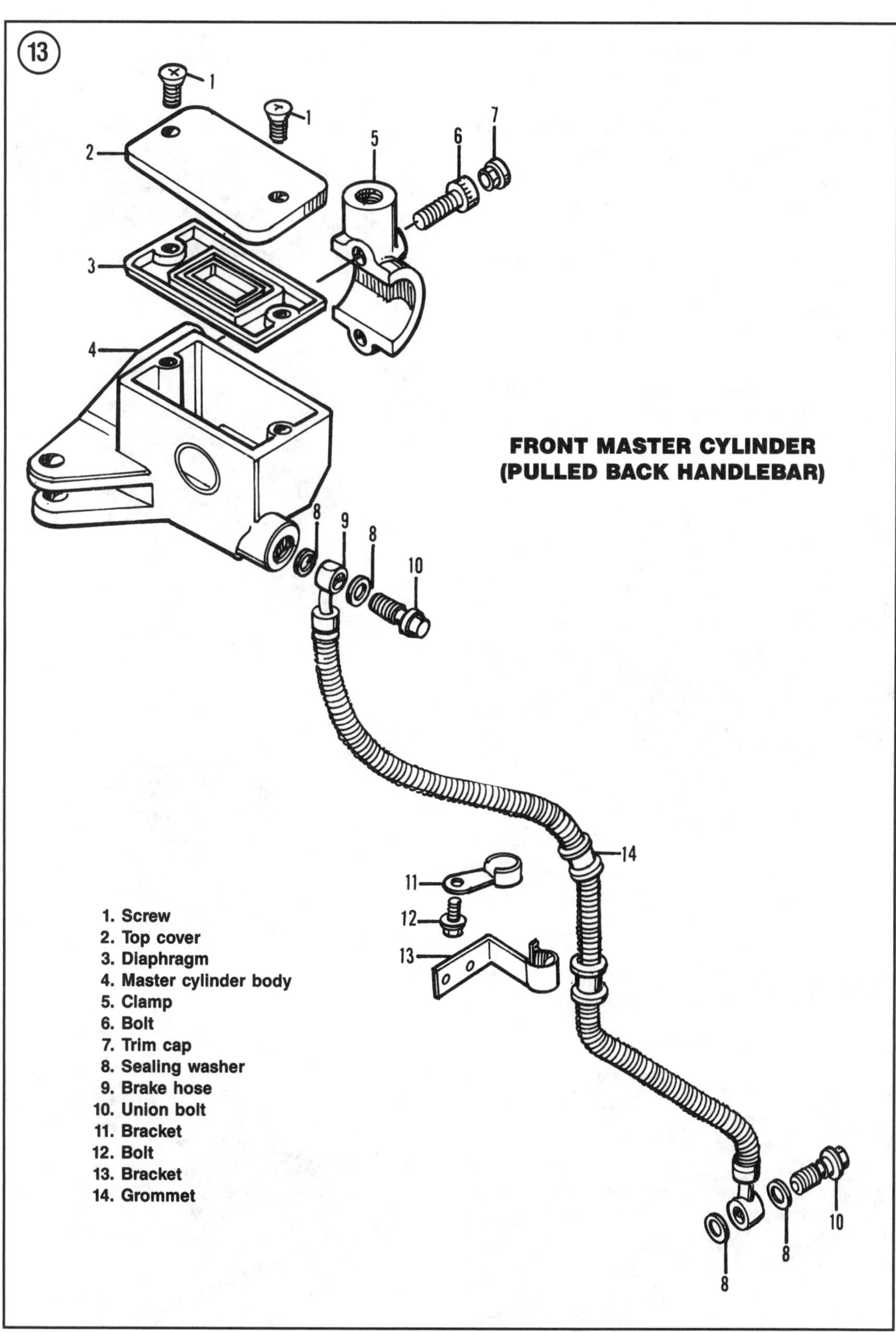
13
1
1
2
3
4
5
6
7
8
9
8
10
14
11
12
13
10
8
8
FRONT MASTER CYLINDER
(PULLED BACK HANDLEBAR)
1. Screw
2. Top cover
3. Diaphragm
4. Master cylinder body
5. Clamp
6. Bolt
7. Trim cap
8. Sealing washer
9. Brake hose
10. Union bolt
11. Bracket
12. Bolt
13. Bracket
14. Grommet

2. Remove the screws and cover (**Figure 14**) securing the brake light switch to the master cylinder. Remove the switch assembly and the switch contact (**Figure 15**).
3. Remove the bolt and nut (**Figure 16**) securing the hand lever and remove the lever.
4. Remove the screws (**Figure 17**) securing the top cover and remove the top cover and the diaphragm (**Figure 18**).
5. Pour out any residual hydraulic fluid and discard it. *Never* reuse hydraulic fluid.
6. Remove the rubber boot (**Figure 19**) from the area where the hand lever actuates the piston assembly.
7. Using circlip pliers, remove the internal circlip (**Figure 20**) from the body.
8. Remove the piston assembly and the spring (**Figure 21**).

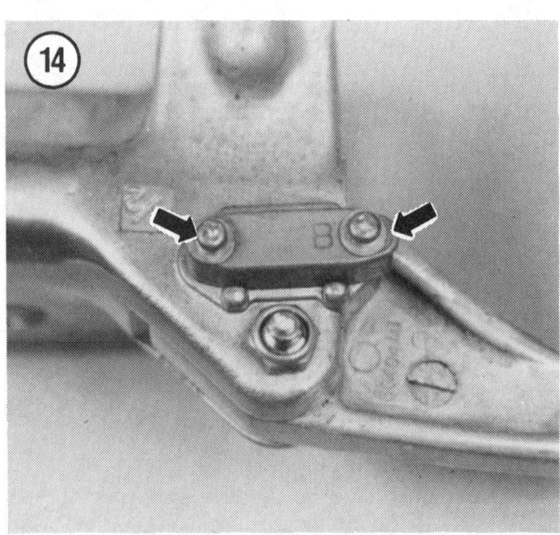
14

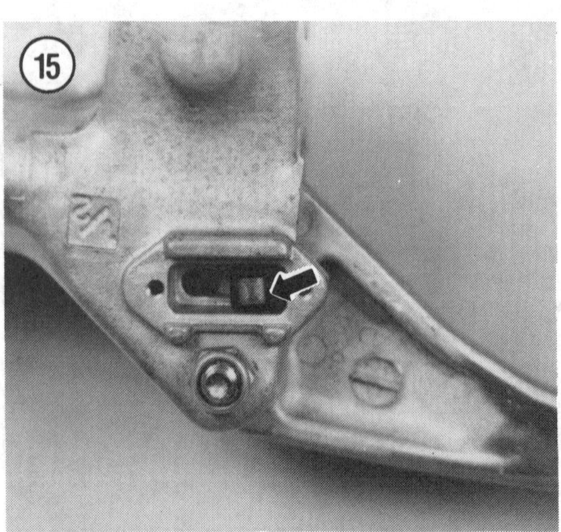
15

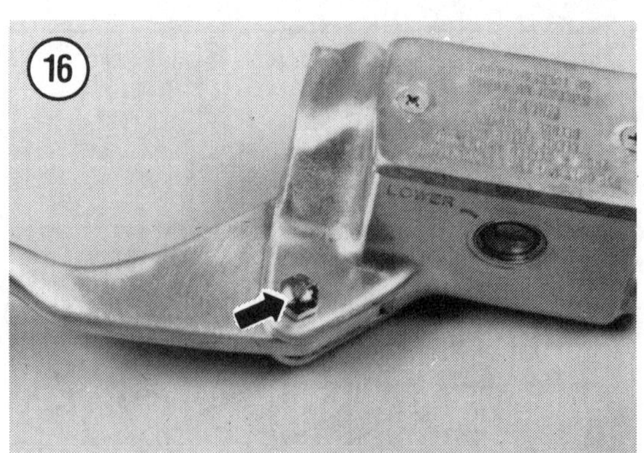
16

17

18

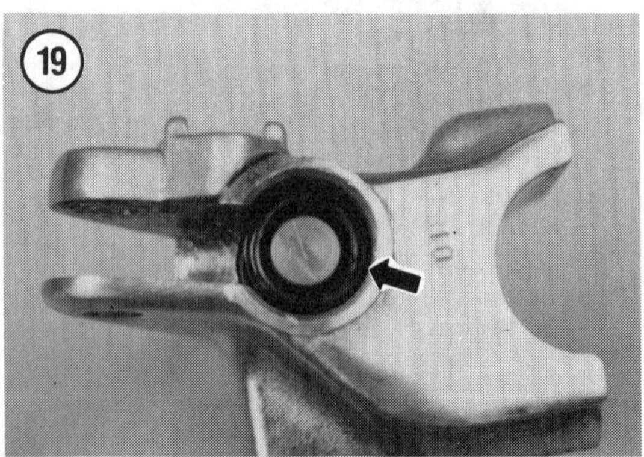
19

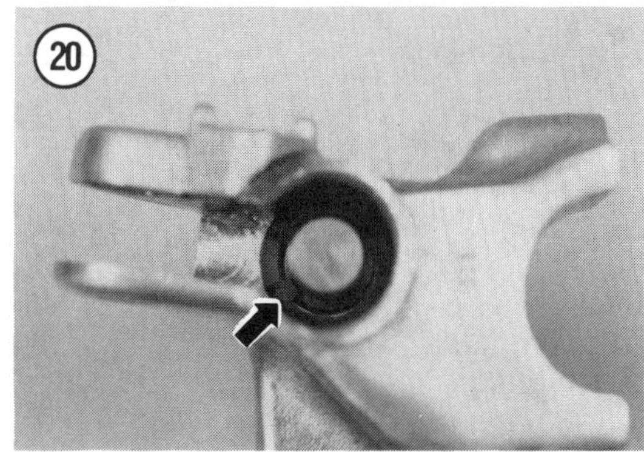


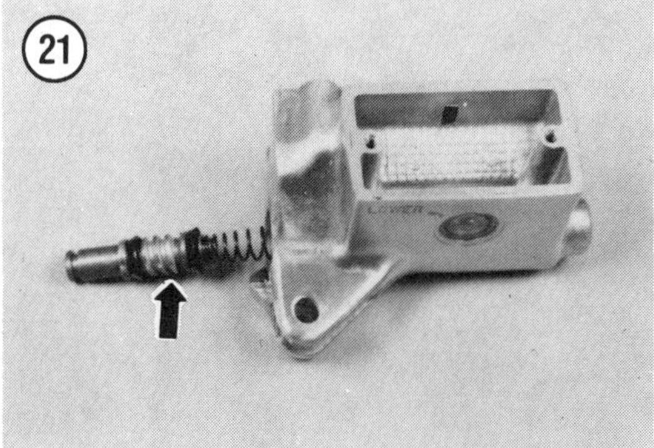


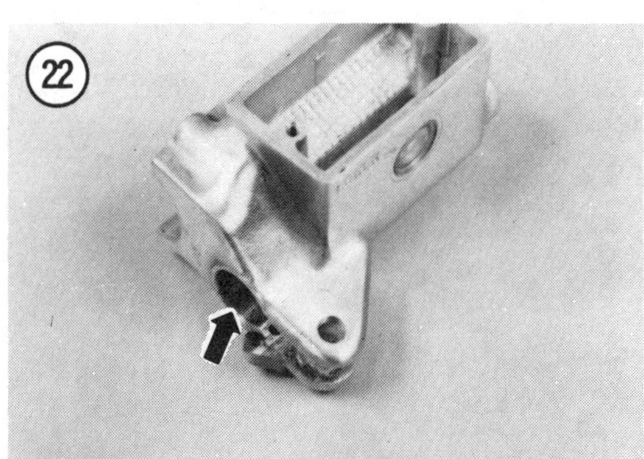

### Inspection

1. Clean all parts in denatured alcohol or fresh hydraulic fluid.
2. Inspect the body cylinder bore (**Figure 22**) surface for signs of wear and damage. If less than perfect, replace the master cylinder assembly. The body cannot be replaced separately.
3. Inspect the body (**Figure 23**) for wear, damage or cracks. If less than perfect, replace the master cylinder assembly. The body cannot be replaced separately.
4. Inspect the piston primary or secondary cups (A, **Figure 24**) for signs of wear and damage. Replace the piston assembly if either the primary or secondary cup requires replacement.
5. Check the end of the piston (B, **Figure 24**) for wear caused by the hand lever. If worn, replace the piston assembly.
6. Inspect the pivot hole (**Figure 25**) in the hand lever. If worn or elongated, it must be replaced.
7. Make sure the passages in the bottom of the master cylinder body are clear.

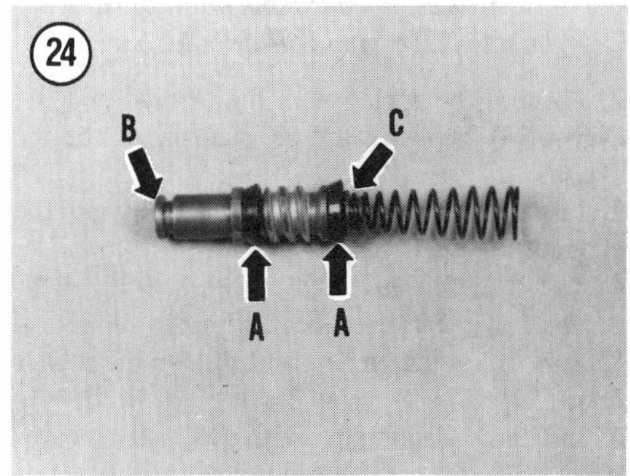


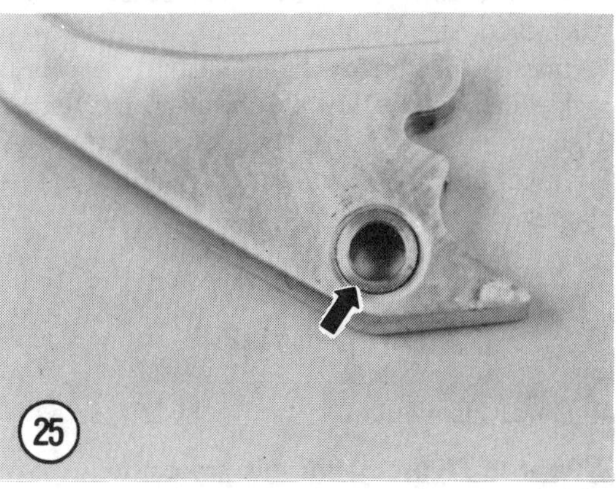

8. Check the top cover and diaphragm (**Figure 26**) for damage and deterioration and replace as necessary.
9. Inspect the threads in the bore (**Figure 27**) for the union bolt. If worn or damaged, clean out with a thread tap or replace the master cylinder assembly.
10. Check the hand lever pivot lugs (**Figure 28**) on the master cylinder body for cracks. If damaged, replace the master cylinder assembly.
11. Make sure the opening (**Figure 29**) in the union bolt is clear. Clean out if necessary.

### Assembly

1. Soak the new cups in fresh brake fluid for at least 15 minutes to make them pliable. Coat the inside of the cylinder bore with fresh hydraulic fluid before assembling parts.

*CAUTION*
*When installing the piston assembly, do not allow the cups to turn inside out as they will be damaged and allow brake fluid leakage within the cylinder bore.*

2. Position the spring with the tapered end (C, **Figure 24**) facing toward the primary cup on the piston.
3. Install the spring and piston assembly into the cylinder together (**Figure 21**).
4. Install the circlip (**Figure 20**).
5. Position the rubber boot with the raised rib (**Figure 30**) going on first and slide in the rubber boot.
6. Install the diaphragm (**Figure 18**) and top cover (**Figure 17**). Do not tighten the cover screws at this time as hydraulic fluid will have to be added later when the system is bled.
7. Install the brake light switch, washers, lockwashers and screws to the master cylinder. Tighten the screws securely.
8. Install the master cylinder as described in this chapter.

## FRONT CALIPER

### Removal/Installation

Refer to **Figure 31** for this procedure.

26

27

28

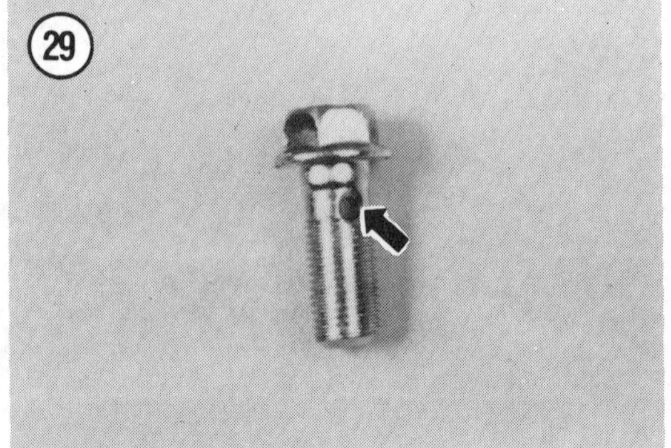

29

It is not necessary to remove the front wheel in order to remove the caliper assembly.

*CAUTION*
*Do not spill any brake fluid on the front fork or front wheel. Wash off any spilled brake fluid immediately, as it will destroy the finish. Use soapy water and rinse completely.*

1. Clean the top of the master cylinder of all dirt and foreign matter.
2. Loosen the screws (**Figure 32**) securing the master cylinder cover. Pull up and loosen the cover and the diaphragm. This will allow air to enter the reservoir and allow the brake fluid to drain out more quickly in the next steps.
3. Place a container under the brake line at the caliper.

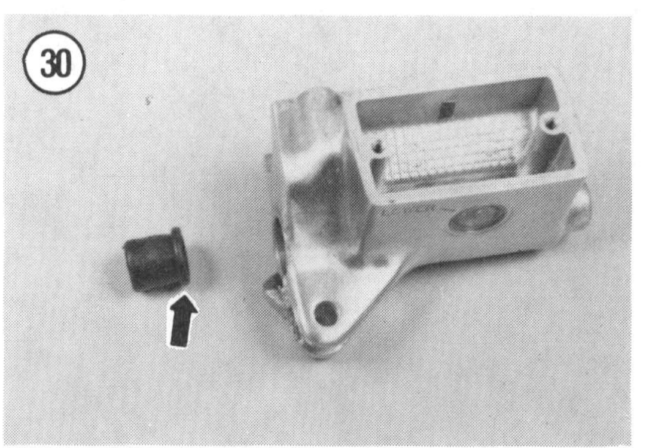


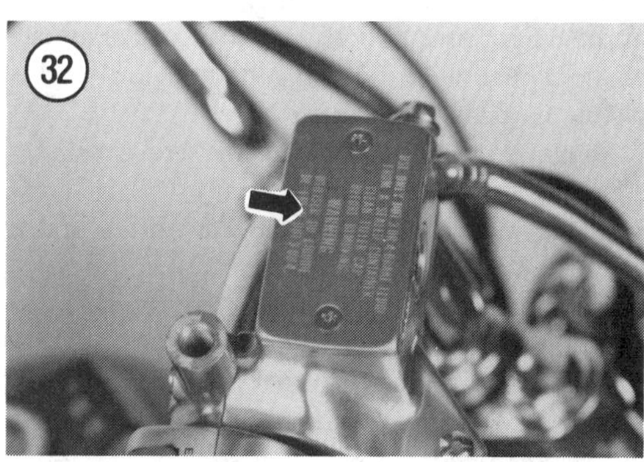


(31)

**FRONT BRAKE CALIPER ASSEMBLY**

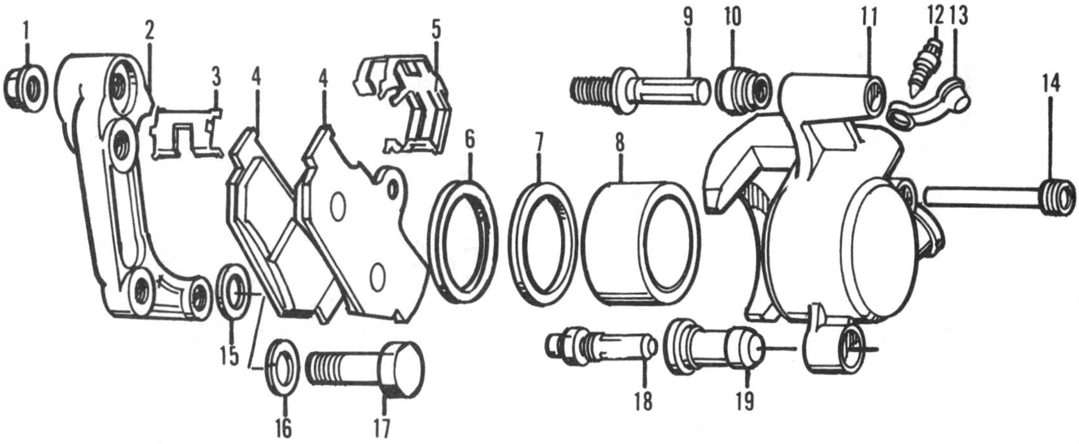

1. Nut
2. Caliper bracket
3. Retainer
4. Brake pads
5. Anti-rattle spring
6. Dust seal
7. Piston seal
8. Piston
9. Special bolt
10. Rubber boot
11. Caliper body
12. Bleed valve
13. Dust cap
14. Pad pin bolt
15. Washer
16. Lockwasher
17. Mounting bolt
18. Special bolt
19. Rubber boot

4. Remove the union bolt (A, **Figure 33**) securing the brake hose to the caliper assembly. Don't lose the sealing washer on each side of the hose fitting. Apply the brake lever as many times as necessary to pump the brake fluid out of the brake hose.
5. Tie the loose end of the hose up to the lower fork bridge. Place the hose end in a resealable plastic bag and zip the bag closed around the hose to prevent the entry of moisture and foreign matter.
6. Loosen the bolts (B, **Figure 33**) securing the brake caliper assembly to the front fork. Push in on the caliper while loosening the bolts to push the piston back into the caliper bores.
7. Remove the bolts securing the brake caliper assembly to the front fork.
8. Remove the caliper assembly from the brake disc.
9. Install by reversing these removal steps. Note the following during installation.
10. Carefully install the caliper assembly onto the disc being careful not to damage the leading edge of the brake pads.
11. Install the bolts securing the brake caliper assembly to the front fork and tighten to the torque specifications listed in **Table 1**.
12. Install the brake hose onto the caliper.
13. Place a sealing washer on each side of the brake hose fitting and install the union bolt.
14. Tighten the union bolt to the torque specification listed in **Table 1**.
15. Remove the master cylinder top cover and diaphragm.

*WARNING*

*Use brake fluid clearly marked DOT 3 or DOT 4 from a sealed container. Other types may vaporize and cause brake failure. Always use the same brand name; do not intermix as many brands are not compatible. Do not intermix silicone-based (DOT 5) brake fluid as it can cause brake component damage leading to brake system failure.*

16. Place wood block(s) under the engine and the frame to support the bike securely with the front wheel off the ground.
17. Spin the front wheel several times and activate the front brake lever as many times as it takes to refill the cylinder in the caliper and correctly locate the pads.

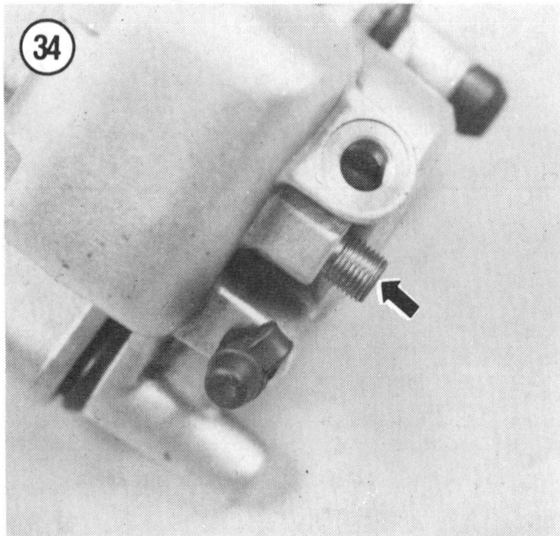


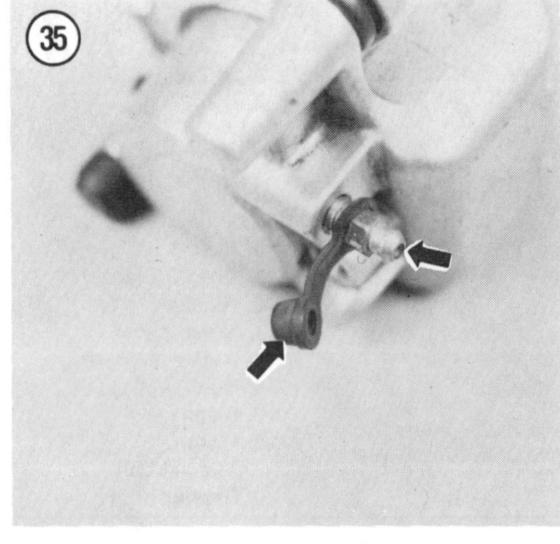

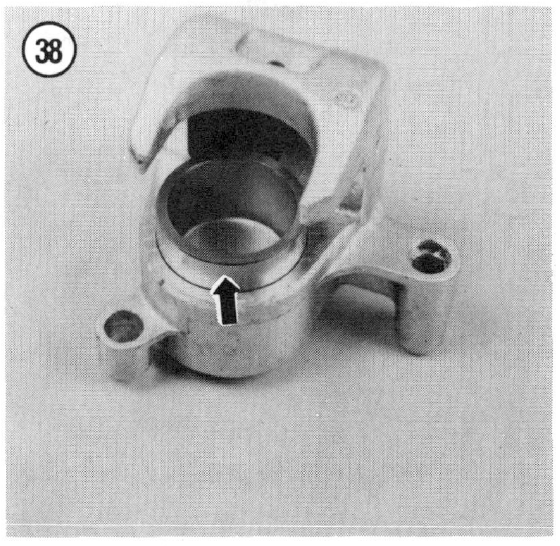

18. Refill the master cylinder reservoir. Install the diaphragm and cover. Do not tighten the screws at this time.
19. Bleed the brake as described under *Bleeding the System* in this chapter.

*WARNING*
*Do not ride the motorcycle until you are sure that the brakes are operating properly.*

**Caliper Rebuilding**

Refer to **Figure 31** for this procedure.

1. Remove the caliper assembly as described in this chapter.
2. Unscrew and remove the pad pin bolt (**Figure 34**) from the caliper.
3. Remove the brake pads from the caliper.
4. Remove the anti-rattle spring from the caliper.
5. Unscrew the bleed screw and cap (**Figure 35**).
6. Carefully separate the caliper body from the caliper bracket (**Figure 36**).
7. Remove the retainer from the caliper bracket.
8. Remove both rubber boots from the caliper body.
9. Place a shop cloth or piece of soft wood over the end of the piston.
10. Perform this step over and close down to a workbench top. Hold the caliper body with the piston facing away from you.

*WARNING*
*In the next step, the piston may shoot out of the caliper body like a bullet. Keep your fingers out of the way. Wear shop gloves and apply air pressure gradually. Do **not** use high pressure air or place the air hose nozzle directly against the hydraulic line fitting inlet in the caliper body. Hold the air nozzle away from the inlet allowing some of the air to escape.*

11. Apply the air pressure in short spurts to the union bolt hole (**Figure 37**) and force the piston out (**Figure 38**). Use a service station air hose if you don't have an air compressor.

*CAUTION*

*In the following step, do not use a sharp tool to remove the dust and piston seals from the caliper cylinders. Do not damage the cylinder surface.*

12. Use a piece of plastic or wood and carefully push the dust seal and the piston seal in toward the caliper cylinder and out of their grooves. Remove the dust and piston seals from the cylinder and discard both seals.
13. Inspect the seal grooves in the caliper body (**Figure 39**) for damage. If damaged or corroded, replace the caliper assembly.
14. Inspect the caliper body (**Figure 40**) for damage. Replace the caliper body if necessary.
15. Inspect the hydraulic fluid passageways (A, **Figure 41**). Make sure they are clean and open. Apply compressed air to the openings and make sure they are clear. Clean out, if necessary, with fresh brake fluid.

*NOTE*

*The caliper body cannot be replaced separately. If it is damaged in any way, the entire caliper assembly must be replaced.*

16. Inspect the cylinder wall (B, **Figure 41**) and the piston (**Figure 42**) for scratches, scoring or other damage. If either is rusty or corroded, replace either the piston or the caliper assembly.
17. Inspect the caliper mounting bolt holes on the caliper bracket. If worn or damaged, replace the caliper bracket.

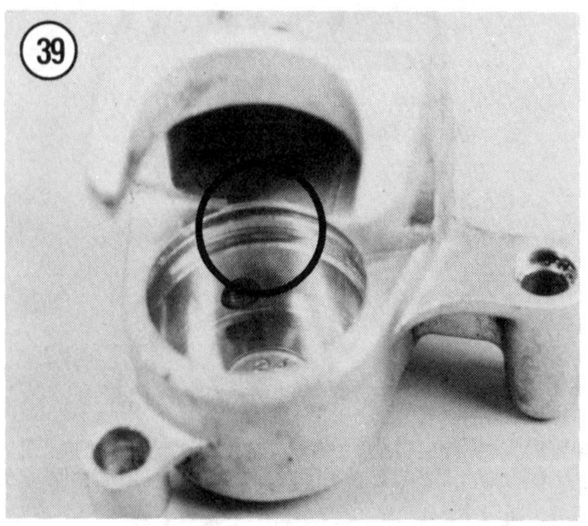


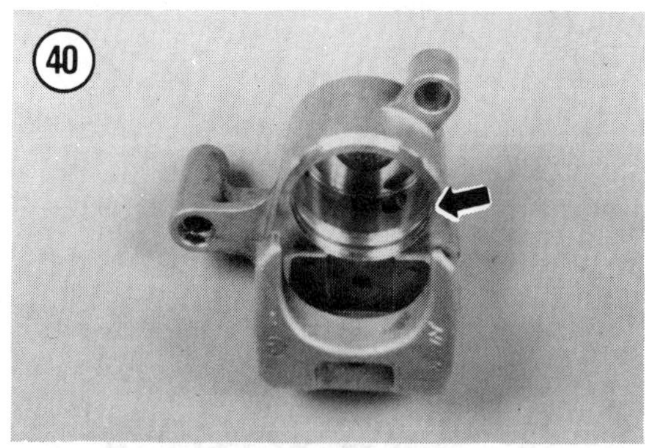


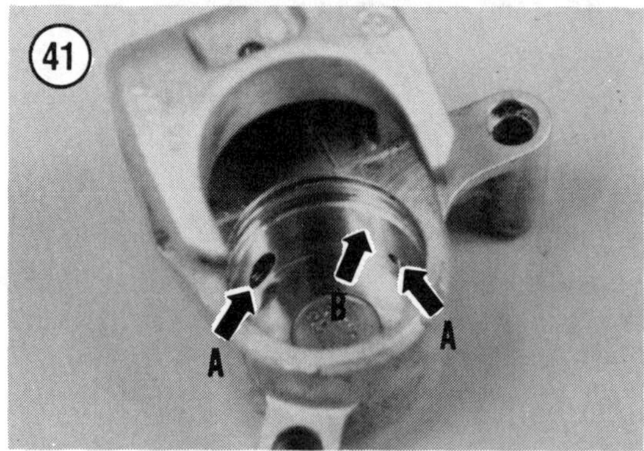

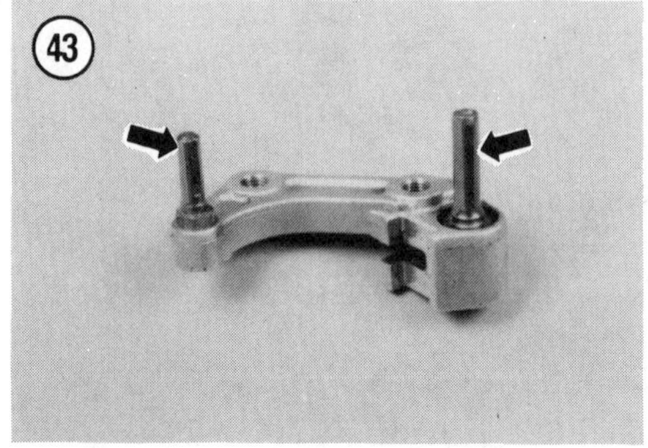

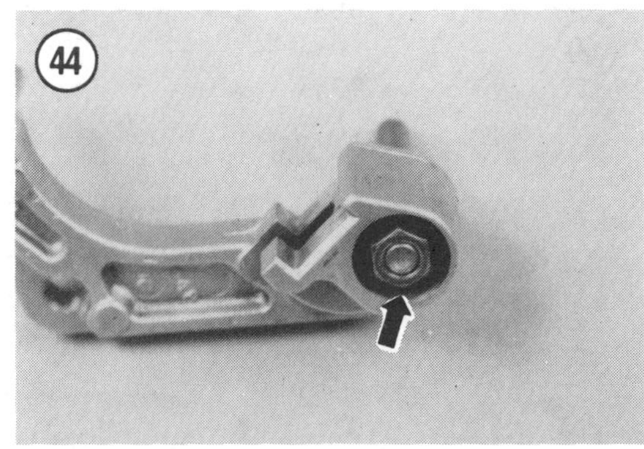

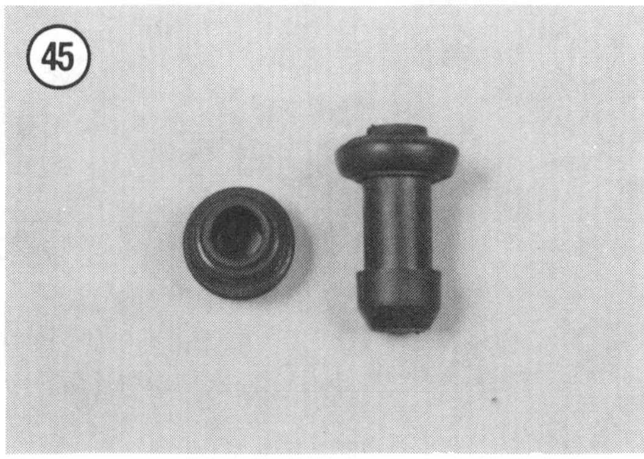

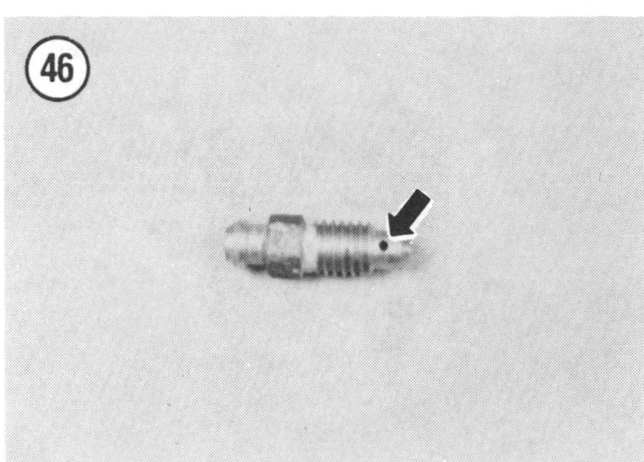

18. Inspect the special bolts (**Figure 43**) on the caliper bracket for wear or damage. Replace if necessary. Make sure the nut (**Figure 44**) is securely tightened.
19. Inspect the rubber boots (**Figure 45**) for damage or deterioration. Replace boots if necessary.
20. Make sure the hole in the bleed screw (**Figure 46**) is clean and open. Apply compressed air to the opening and make sure it is clear. Clean out if necessary with fresh brake fluid.
21. If serviceable, clean the caliper body with rubbing alcohol and rinse with clean brake fluid.

*NOTE*
*Never reuse a dust seal or piston seal that has been removed. Very minor damage or age deterioration can make the seals useless.*

22. Coat the new dust and piston seals with fresh DOT 3 or DOT 4 brake fluid.
23. Carefully install the new piston seal (**Figure 47**) and new dust seal (**Figure 48**) in the grooves in the caliper cylinder. Make sure the seals are properly seated in their respective grooves.
24. Coat the piston and the caliper cylinder with fresh DOT 3 or DOT 4 brake fluid.
25. Position the piston with the *open end facing out* toward the brake pads and install the piston into the caliper cylinder (**Figure 38**). Push the piston in until it bottoms out.



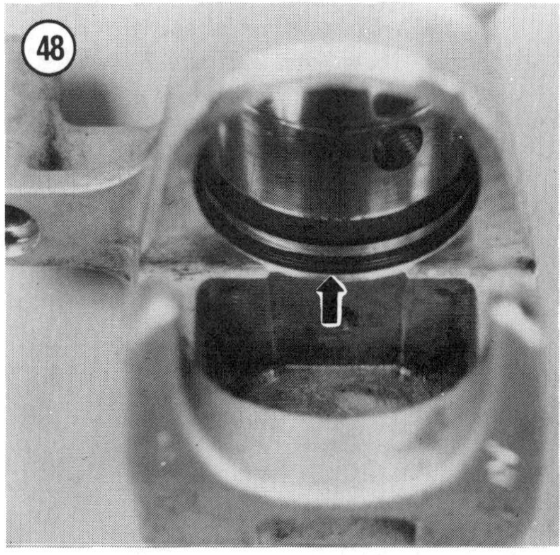

26. Install the retainer (**Figure 49**) onto the caliper bracket.
27. Install the rubber boots (**Figure 50**) into the receptacles in the caliper bracket.
28. Apply silicone grease to the special bolts on the caliper bracket and to the inner surfaces of the rubber boots in the caliper body.
29. Assemble the caliper bracket onto the caliper body. Push the 2 parts together until they bottom out.
30. Install the bleed screw and cap (**Figure 35**).
31. Install the anti-rattle spring (**Figure 51**) into the caliper.
32. Install the outboard (**Figure 52**) and inboard (**Figure 53**) brake pads into the caliper.
33. Push down on both brake pads and install the pad pin bolt (**Figure 34**) through both brake pads and into the caliper. Tighten the pad pin bolt to the torque specification listed in **Table 1**.
34. Install the brake caliper as described in this chapter.

## FRONT BRAKE HOSE REPLACEMENT

Suzuki recommends replacing all brake hoses every four years or when they show signs of cracking or damage.

Refer to **Figure 54** for models with straight handlebars or **Figure 55** for models with pulled back handlebars for this procedure.

*CAUTION*
*Cover the fuel tank and front fender with a heavy cloth or plastic tarp to protect them from accidental brake fluid spills. Wash brake fluid off any*

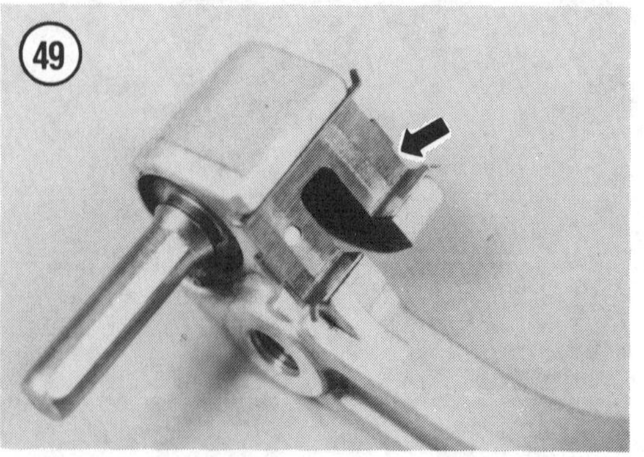


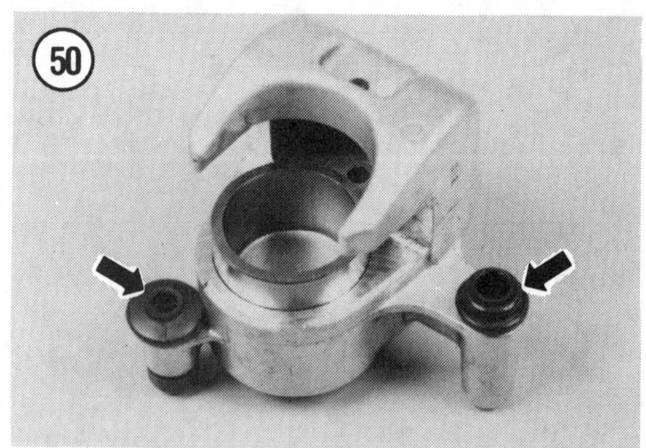

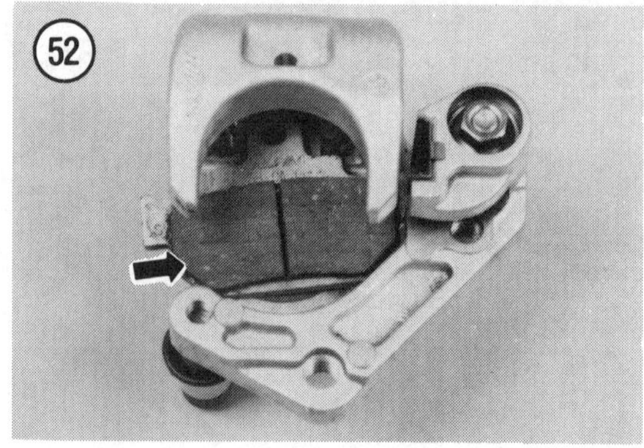


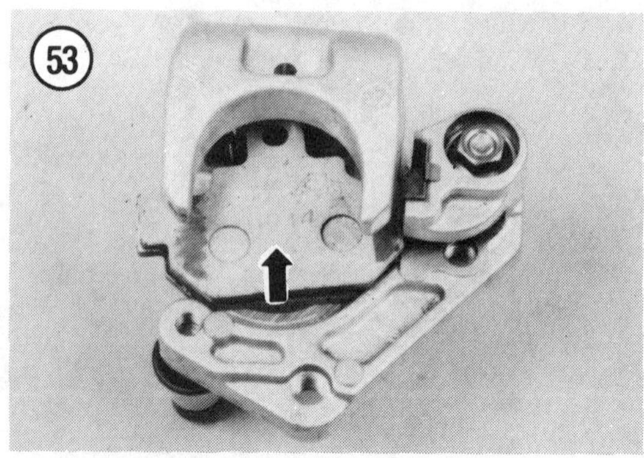

## FRONT MASTER CYLINDER (STRAIGHT HANDLEBAR)

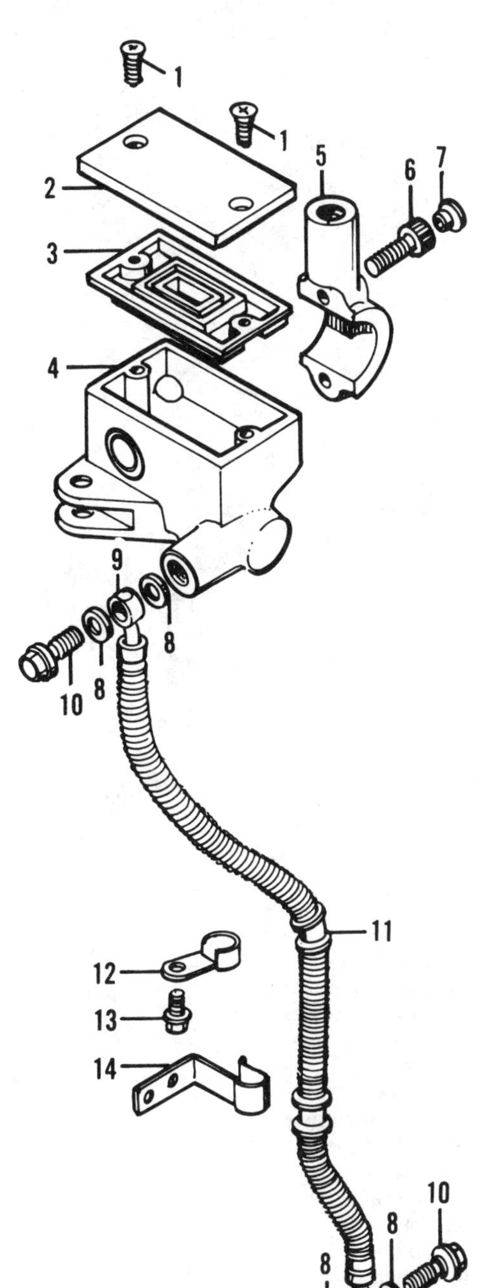


1. Screw
2. Top cover
3. Diaphragm
4. Master cylinder body
5. Clamp
6. Bolt
7. Trim cap
8. Sealing washer
9. Brake hose
10. Union bolt
11. Rubber grommet
12. Bracket
13. Bolt
14. Bracket

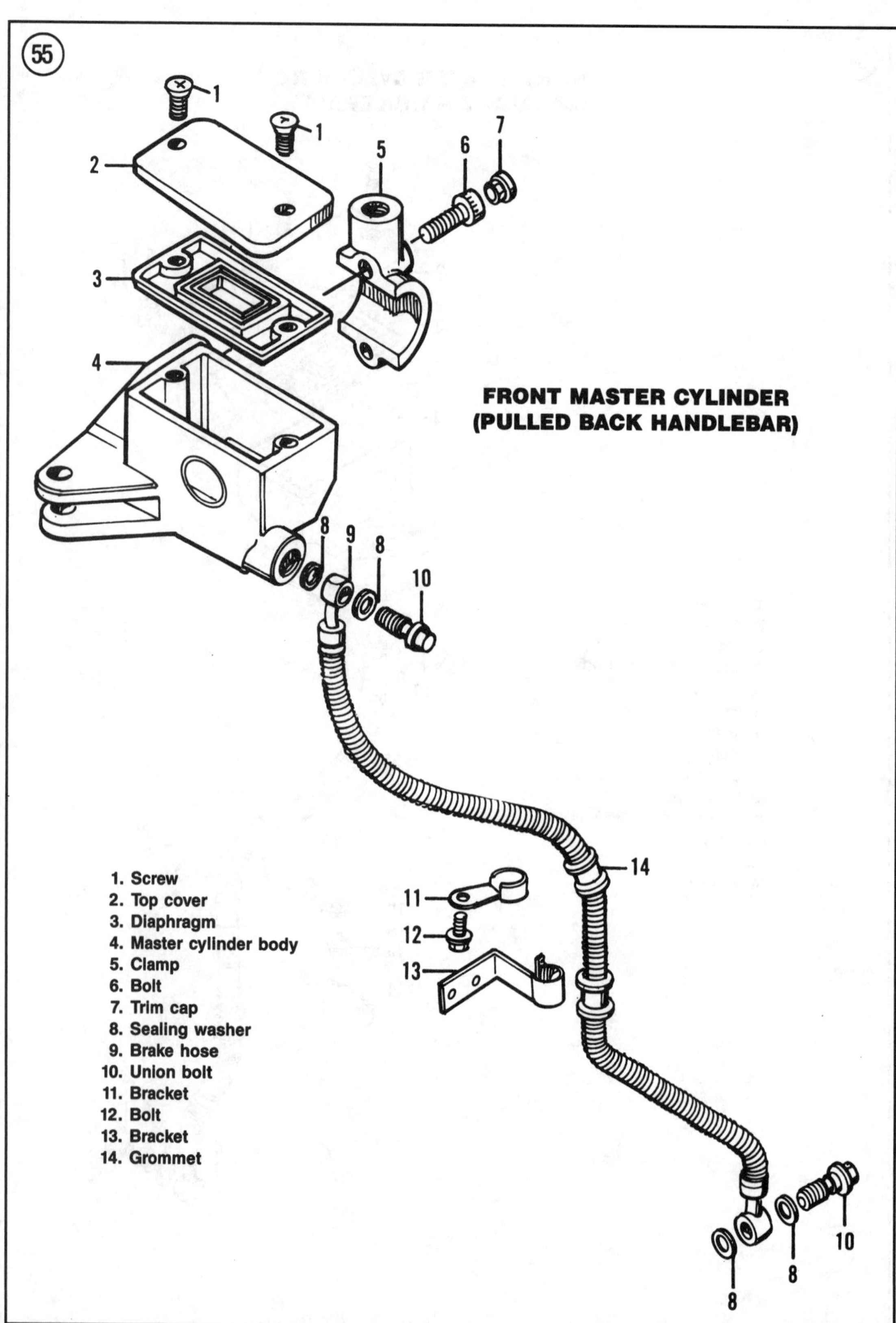
55
1
1
2
3
4
5
6
7
FRONT MASTER CYLINDER
(PULLED BACK HANDLEBAR)
8
9
8
10
14
11
12
13
10
8
8
1. Screw
2. Top cover
3. Diaphragm
4. Master cylinder body
5. Clamp
6. Bolt
7. Trim cap
8. Sealing washer
9. Brake hose
10. Union bolt
11. Bracket
12. Bolt
13. Bracket
14. Grommet

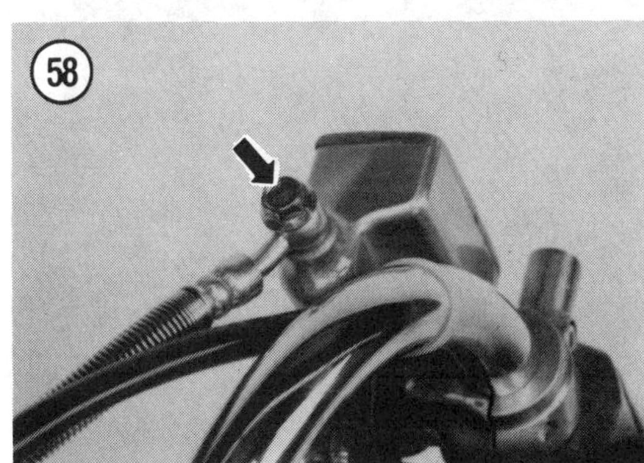


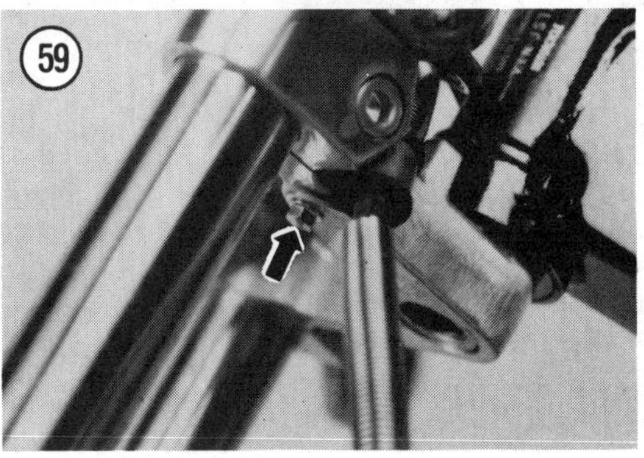


*painted or plated surfaces or plastic parts immediately, as it will destroy the finish. Use soapy water and rinse completely.*

1. Clean the top of the master cylinder of all dirt and foreign matter.
2. Loosen the screws securing the master cylinder cover (**Figure 56**). Pull up and loosen the cover and the diaphragm. This will allow air to enter the reservoir and allow the brake fluid to drain out more quickly in the next step.
3. Unscrew the union bolt (**Figure 57**) securing the brake hose to the brake caliper. Don't lose the sealing washer on each side of the hose fitting.
4. Remove the brake hose from the caliper assembly and let the brake fluid drain out into the container. Dispose of this brake fluid. *Never* reuse brake fluid.
5. Place a shop cloth under the union bolt on the master cylinder to catch any spilled brake fluid that will leak out.
6. Unscrew the union bolt (**Figure 58**) securing the brake hose to the master cylinder. Don't lose the sealing washer on each side of the hose fitting.
7. Remove the bolt (**Figure 59**) securing the brake hose to the lower fork bridge.
8. Carefully pull the brake hose from the hose clamp on the fork slider (A, **Figure 60**). Remove the hose (B, **Figure 60**) from the front fork area.
9. Install a new hose, sealing washers and union bolts in the reverse order of removal. Be sure to install new sealing washers in their correct positions.

10. Tighten the union bolts to the torque specifications listed in **Table 1**.

*WARNING*
*Use brake fluid clearly marked DOT 3 or DOT 4 from a sealed container. Other types may vaporize and cause brake failure. Always use the same brand name; do not intermix as many brands are not compatible. Do not intermix silicone-based (DOT 5) brake fluid as it can cause brake component damage leading to brake system failure.*

11. Refill the master cylinder reservoir, if necessary, to maintain the correct fluid level as seen through the viewing port on the side (**Figure 61**). Install the diaphragm and cover. Do not tighten the screws at this time.

*WARNING*
*Do not ride the motorcycle until you are sure that the brakes are operating properly.*

12. Bleed the brake as described in this chapter.

## FRONT BRAKE DISC

### Removal/Installation

1. Remove the front wheel as described in Chapter Nine.

*NOTE*
*Place a piece of wood or vinyl tube in the caliper in place of the disc. This way, if the brake lever is inadvertently squeezed the piston will not be forced out of the cylinder. If this does happen, the caliper might have to be disassembled to reseat the pistons and the system will have to be bled. By using the wood or vinyl tube, bleeding the system is not necessary when installing the wheel.*

2. Remove the bolts (**Figure 62**) securing the brake disc to the hub and remove the disc.
3. Install by reversing these removal steps. Note the following during installation.
4. Apply red Loctite Threadlocker No. 271 to the disc mounting bolt threads prior to installation. Tighten the disc mounting bolts to the torque specifications listed in **Table 1**.

### Inspection

It is not necessary to remove the disc from the wheel to inspect it. Small marks on the disc are not important, but radial scratches deep enough to snag a fingernail reduce braking effectiveness and

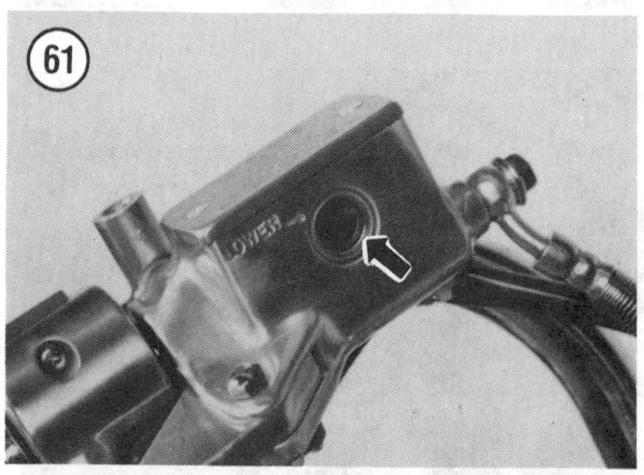

increase brake pad wear. If these grooves are found, the disc should be replaced.

1. Measure the thickness of the disc at several locations around the disc with a micrometer (**Figure 63**) or vernier caliper. The disc must be replaced if the thickness in any area is less than that specified in **Table 2**.
2. Make sure the disc mounting bolts are tight before running this check. Check the disc runout with a dial indicator as shown in **Figure 64**.
3. Slowly rotate the wheel and watch the dial indicator. If the runout exceeds that listed in **Table 2**, the disc must be replaced.
4. Clean the disc of any rust or corrosion and wipe clean with lacquer thinner. Never use an oil-based solvent that may leave an oil residue on the disc.

## BLEEDING THE SYSTEM

This procedure is not necessary unless the brakes feel spongy, there has been a leak in the system, a component has been replaced or the brake fluid has been replaced.

### Brake Bleeder Process

This procedure uses a brake bleeder that is available from motorcycle or automotive supply stores or from mail order outlets.

1. Remove the dust cap (**Figure 65**) from the bleed valve on the caliper assembly.
2. Connect the brake bleeder to the bleed valve on the caliper assembly (**Figure 66**).

*CAUTION*

*Cover the front wheel with a heavy cloth or plastic tarp to protect it from the accidental spilling of brake fluid. Wash any brake fluid off of any plastic, painted or plated surface immediately; as it will destroy the finish. Use soapy water and rinse completely.*

3. Clean the top of the master cylinder of all dirt and foreign matter.
4. Remove the screws securing the reservoir cover (**Figure 56**) and remove the reservoir cover and diaphragm.

11

5. Fill the reservoir almost to the top lip; insert the diaphragm and the cover loosely. Leave the cover in place during this procedure to prevent the entry of dirt.

*WARNING*
*Use brake fluid from a sealed container marked DOT 3 or DOT 4 only (specified for disc brakes). Other types may vaporize and cause brake failure. Do not intermix different brands or types as they may not be compatible. Do not intermix a silicone-based (DOT 5) brake fluid as it can cause brake component damage leading to brake system failure.*

6. Open the bleed valve about one-half turn and pump the brake bleeder.

*NOTE*
*If air is entering the brake bleeder hose from around the bleed valve, apply several layers of Teflon tape to the bleed valve. This should make a good seal between the bleed valve and the brake bleeder hose.*

7. As the fluid enters the system and exits into the brake bleeder the level will drop in the reservoir. Maintain the level at about 9.5 mm (3/8 in.) from the top of the reservoir to prevent air from being drawn into the system.
8. Continue to pump the lever on the brake bleeder until the fluid emerging from the hose is completely free of bubbles. At this point, tighten the bleed valve.

*NOTE*
*Do not allow the reservoir to empty during the bleeding operation or more air will enter the system. If this occurs, the entire procedure must be repeated.*

9. When the brake fluid is free of bubbles, tighten the bleed valve, remove the brake bleeder tube and install the bleed valve dust cap.
10. If necessary, add fluid to correct the level in the reservoir. It should be to the upper level line (**Figure 61**).
11. Install the diaphragm and the reservoir cover. Tighten the screws securely.
12. Test the feel of the brake lever. It should be firm and should offer the same resistance each time it's operated. If it feels spongy, it is likely that there is still air in the system and it must be bled again. When all air has been bled from the system and the fluid level is correct in the reservoir, double-check for leaks and tighten all fittings and connections.

*WARNING*
*Before riding the bike, make certain that the brake is operating correctly by operating the lever several times.*

13. Test ride the bike slowly at first to make sure that the brakes are operating properly.

**Without a Brake Bleeder**

1. Remove the dust cap (**Figure 65**) from the bleed valve on the caliper assembly.
2. Connect the bleed hose to the bleed valve on the caliper assembly (**Figure 67**).
3. Place the other end of the tube into a clean container. Fill the container with enough fresh brake fluid to keep the end submerged. The tube should be long enough so that a loop can be made higher than the bleed valve to prevent air from being drawn into the caliper during bleeding.

*CAUTION*
*Cover the front fender and front wheel with a heavy cloth or plastic tarp to protect it from the accidental spilling of brake fluid. Wash any brake fluid off of any plastic, painted or plated surface immediately; as it will destroy the finish. Use soapy water and rinse completely.*

4. Clean the top of the master cylinder of all dirt and foreign matter.
5. Remove the screws securing the reservoir cover (**Figure 56**) and remove the reservoir cover and diaphragm.
6. Fill the reservoir almost to the cover lip; insert the diaphragm and the cover loosely. Leave the cover in place during this procedure to prevent the entry of dirt.

*WARNING*
*Use brake fluid from a sealed container marked DOT 3 or DOT 4 only (specified for disc brakes). Other types may vaporize and cause brake failure. Do not intermix different brands or types as they may not be compatible. Do not intermix a silicone-based (DOT 5) brake fluid as it can cause brake component damage leading to brake system failure.*

7. Slowly apply the brake lever several times as follows:
   a. Pull the lever in. Hold the lever in the applied position.

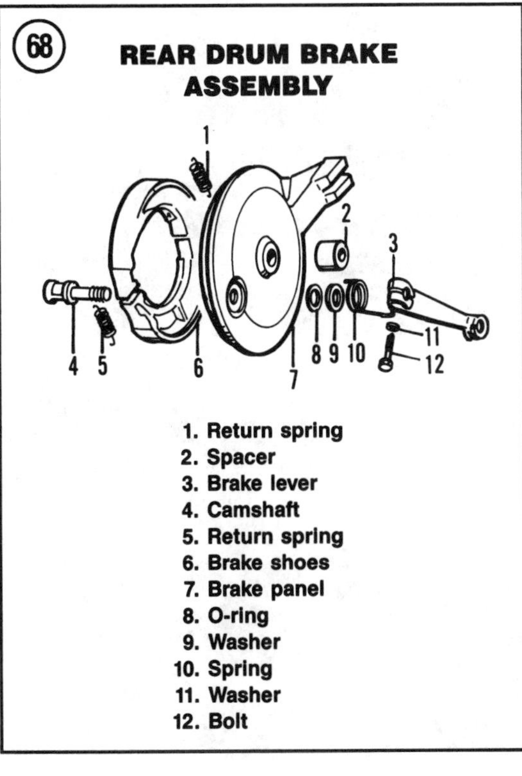


**68 REAR DRUM BRAKE ASSEMBLY**

1. Return spring
2. Spacer
3. Brake lever
4. Camshaft
5. Return spring
6. Brake shoes
7. Brake panel
8. O-ring
9. Washer
10. Spring
11. Washer
12. Bolt

   b. Open the bleed valve about one-half turn. Allow the lever to travel to its limit.
   c. When this limit is reached, tighten the bleed screw.
8. As the fluid enters the system, the level will drop in the reservoir. Maintain the level at about 9.5 mm (3/8 in.) from the cover of the reservoir to prevent air from being drawn into the system.
9. Continue to pump the lever and fill the reservoir until the fluid emerging from the hose is completely free of bubbles.

*NOTE*
*Do not allow the reservoir to empty during the bleeding operation or more air will enter the system. If this occurs, the entire procedure must be repeated.*

10. Hold the lever in, tighten the bleed valve, remove the bleed tube and install the bleed valve dust cap.
11. If necessary, add fluid to correct the level in the reservoir (**Figure 61**).
12. Install the diaphragm and reservoir cover. Tighten the screws securely.
13. Test the feel of the brake lever. It should be firm and should offer the same resistance each time it's operated. If it feels spongy, it is likely that there is still air in the system and it must be bled again. When all air has been bled from the system and the fluid level is correct in the reservoir, double-check for leaks and tighten all fittings and connections.

*WARNING*
*Before riding the bike, make certain that the front brake is operating correctly by operating the lever several times.*

14. Test ride the bike slowly at first to make sure that the front brake is operating properly.



## REAR DRUM BRAKE

Refer to **Figure 68** for this procedure.

### Disassembly

1. Remove the rear wheel as described in Chapter Ten.

2. Pull the brake assembly straight up and out of the brake drum.
3. Using a vernier caliper, measure the thickness of the brake linings (**Figure 69**). They should be replaced if the lining portion is worn to the service limit listed in **Table 2**.

*NOTE*
*If the brake linings are in good condition and are going to be reinstalled; place a clean shop cloth on the linings to protect them from oil and grease during removal.*

4. Pull up on the center of each brake shoe and remove the linings from the backing plate.
5. Remove the return springs and separate the brake shoes.
6. Remove the bolt and nut securing the brake arm and remove the brake arm.
7. Remove the return spring, washer and O-ring from the brake camshaft.

### Inspection

1. Thoroughly clean and dry all parts except the brake linings.
2. Check the contact surface of the brake drum (**Figure 70**) for scoring. If there are grooves deep enough to snag a fingernail, the drum should be reground.
3. Measure the inside diameter of the brake drum with a vernier caliper (**Figure 71**). If the dimension is greater than the service limit listed in **Table 2**, the brake drum/hub must be replaced.
4. If the drum can be reground and still stay within the maximum service limit dimension diameter, the linings will have to be replaced and the linings arced to conform to the new drum contour.

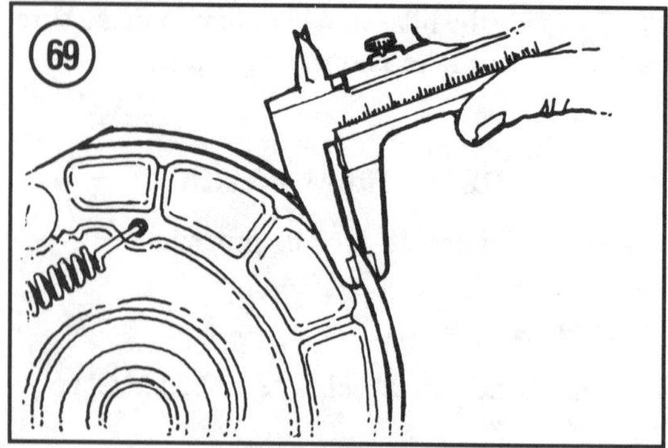
69

70

71

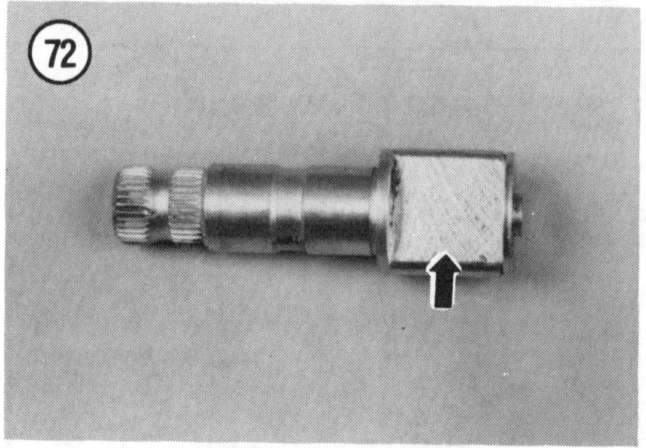
72

73

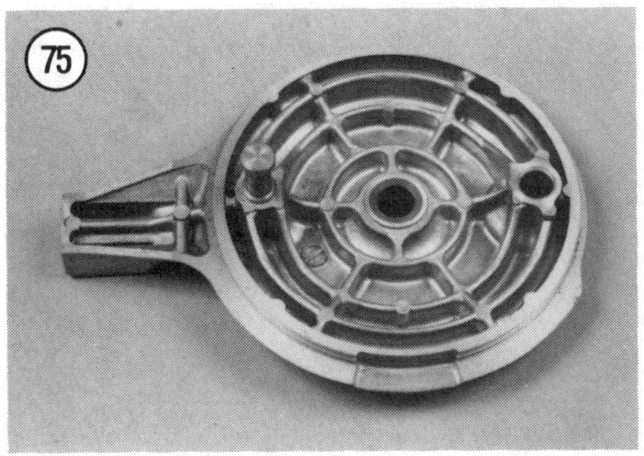

5. Inspect the linings for embedded foreign material. Dirt can be removed with a stiff wire brush. Check for any traces of oil or grease; if they are contaminated they must be replaced.
6. Inspect the camshaft lobe (**Figure 72**) and the pivot post (**Figure 73**) on the backing plate for wear or corrosion. Minor roughness can be removed with fine emery cloth.
7. Inspect the brake shoe return springs (**Figure 74**) for wear or weakness. If they are stretched, they will not fully retract the brake shoes leading to premature wear. Replace the springs as a pair if necessary.
8. Inspect the backing plate (**Figure 75**) for wear, damage or cracks. Replace if necessary.

### Assembly

1. Apply a light coat of molybdenum disulfide grease to the camshaft. Install the camshaft (**Figure 76**) into the backside of the brake panel.
2. Apply a light coat of high-temperature grease to the camshaft and pivot post; avoid getting any grease on the brake backing plate where the brake linings may come in contact with it.

*NOTE*

*If new linings are being installed, file off the leading edge of each shoe a little so that the brake will not grab when applied for the first few times.*

3. Hold the shoes in a "V" formation with the return springs attached and snap one of the shoes into place (**Figure 77**) on the brake panel.
4. Pivot the other shoe down into place (**Figure 78**). Make sure both brake shoes are firmly seated on the brake panel.

11

5. Install the O-ring seal (**Figure 79**) and washer (**Figure 80**).
6. Install one end of the spring into the hole in the backing plate and install the spring (**Figure 81**).
7. Align the brake lever with the camshaft and install the brake lever.
8. Install the bolt and nut (**Figure 82**) and tighten securely.
9. Install the brake panel assembly into the brake drum.
10. Install the rear wheel as described in Chapter Ten.
11. Adjust the rear brake as described under *Rear Brake Height and Freeplay Adjustment* in Chapter Three.

## REAR BRAKE PEDAL AND CABLE

### Removal/Installation

Refer to **Figure 83** for this procedure.

1. Completely unscrew the rear brake adjusting nut (**Figure 84**).
2. Depress the brake pedal and remove the brake cable from the pivot joint in the brake arm. Install the pivot joint and adjusting nut onto the end of the brake cable to avoid misplacing them.
3. Remove the cap nuts and washers (A, **Figure 85**) on the engine front mounting through-bolts.
4. Remove the exhaust pipe heat shield (B, **Figure 85**).

79

80

81

82

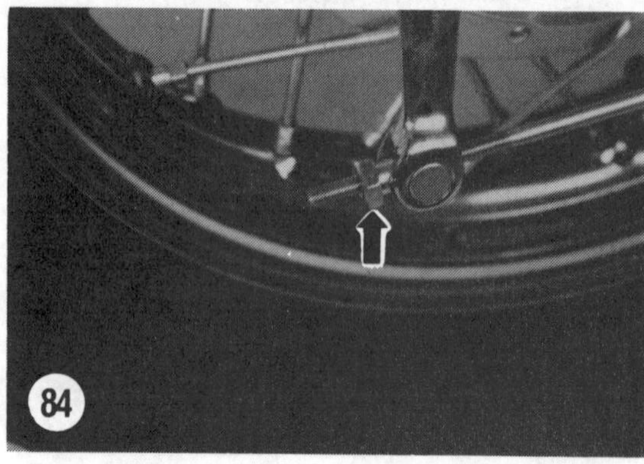

84

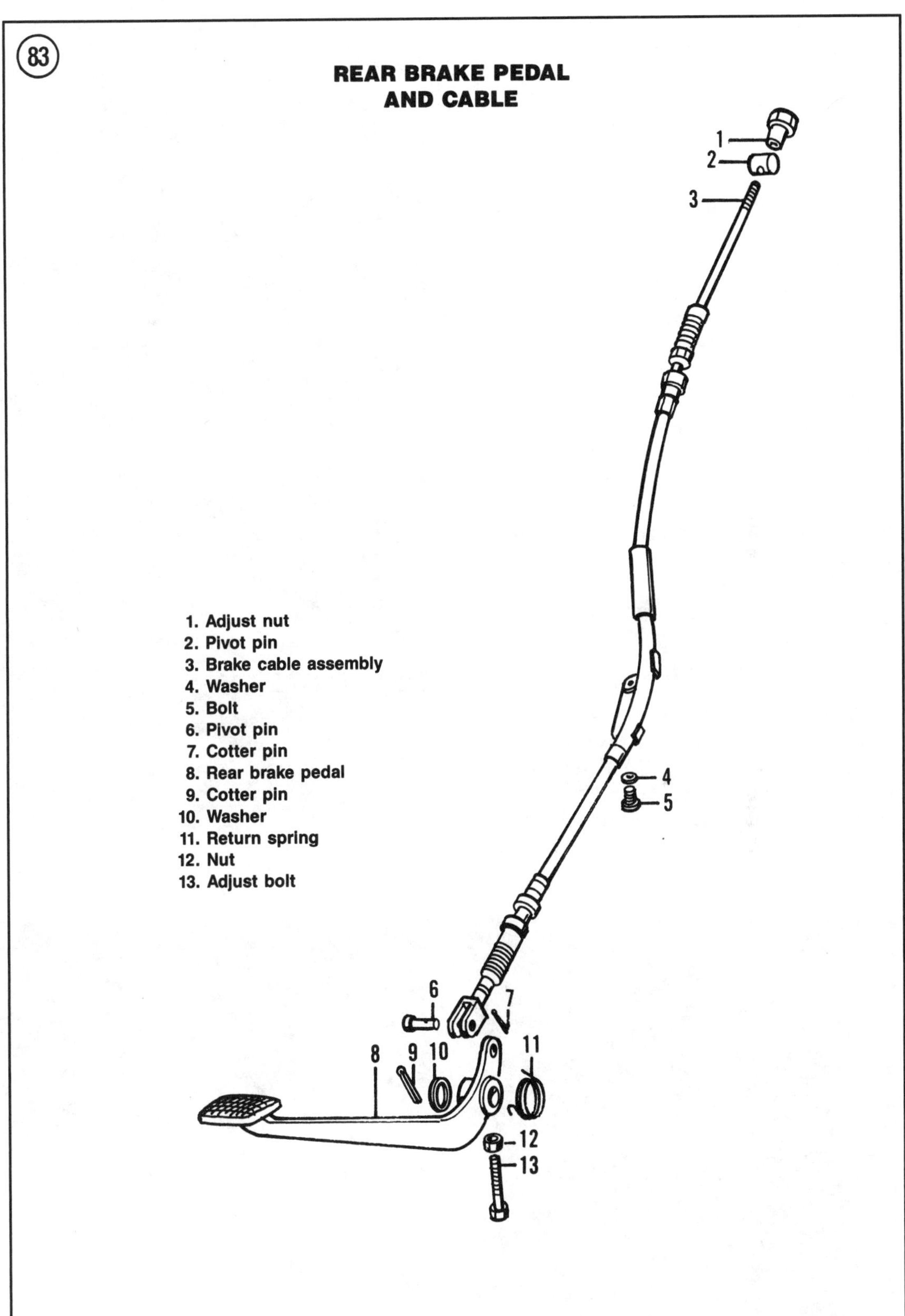
83
REAR BRAKE PEDAL
AND CABLE
1. Adjust nut
2. Pivot pin
3. Brake cable assembly
4. Washer
5. Bolt
6. Pivot pin
7. Cotter pin
8. Rear brake pedal
9. Cotter pin
10. Washer
11. Return spring
12. Nut
13. Adjust bolt
1
2
3
4
5
6
7
8
9
10
11
12
13

*NOTE*
**Figure 86** *is shown with the exhaust system removed for clarity. It is not necessary to remove the system for this procedure.*

5. Pull the front right-hand footpeg and front brake pedal assembly (**Figure 86**) off the through-bolts.

*NOTE*
*If the footpeg and brake pedal assembly is going to be left off for some time, reinstall the washers and cap nuts onto the through-bolts.*

6. Remove the cotter pin (A, **Figure 87**) and withdraw the pivot pin securing the brake cable and rear brake light switch cable to the brake pedal.
7. Remove the cotter pin and washer (B, **Figure 87**) and slide the brake pedal (C, **Figure 87**) and return spring off the pivot post on the backside of the right-hand footpeg bracket.
8. Loosen the locknuts (D, **Figure 87**) on the brake cable on the footpeg assembly and remove the brake cable from the receptacle on the footpeg assembly.
9. Remove the screws and nuts (**Figure 88**) securing the brake cable and bracket to the frame.
10. Loosen the locknuts (A, **Figure 89**) on the brake cable on the swing arm.
11. Remove the brake cable from the receptacle (B, **Figure 89**) on the swing arm and remove the brake cable.

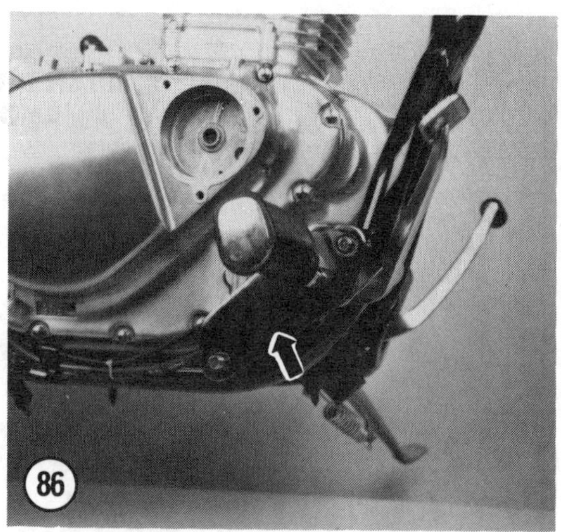
86

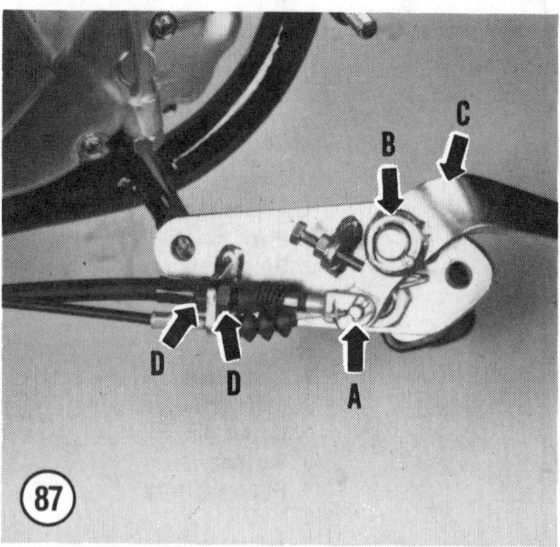

87

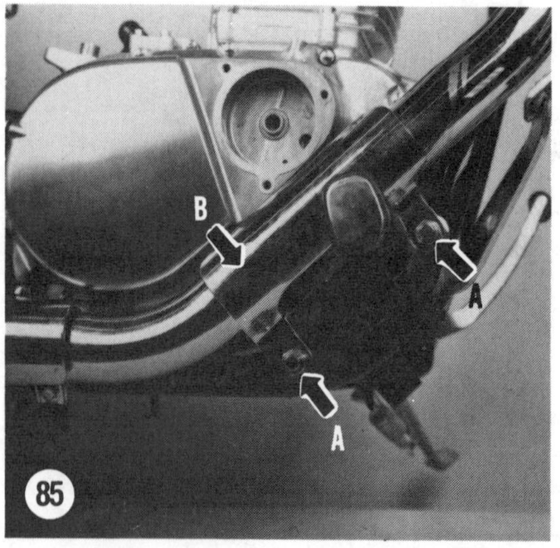

85

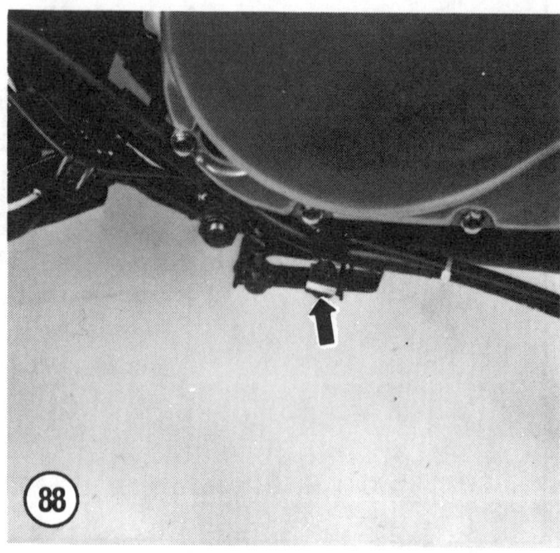
88

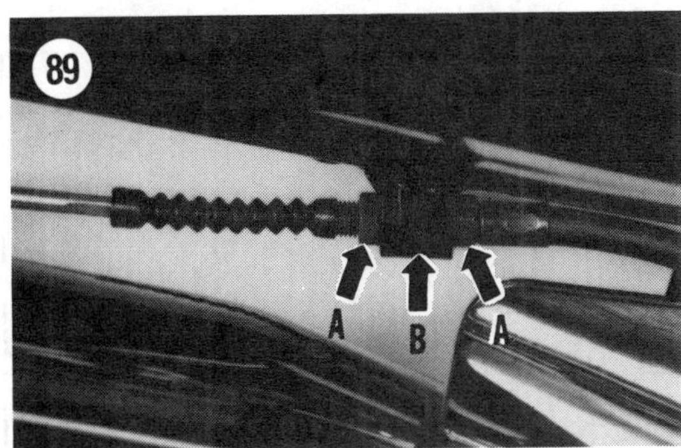


12. Install by reversing these removal steps. Note the following during installation.
13. Apply grease to the pivot post on the backside of the right-hand footpeg bracket.
14. Route the brake cable as shown in **Figure 90**.
15. Tighten the cap nuts (A, **Figure 85**) on the engine front mounting through-bolts to the torque specification listed in **Table 1**.
16. Adjust the rear brake as described under *Rear Brake Height and Freeplay Adjustment* in Chapter Three.

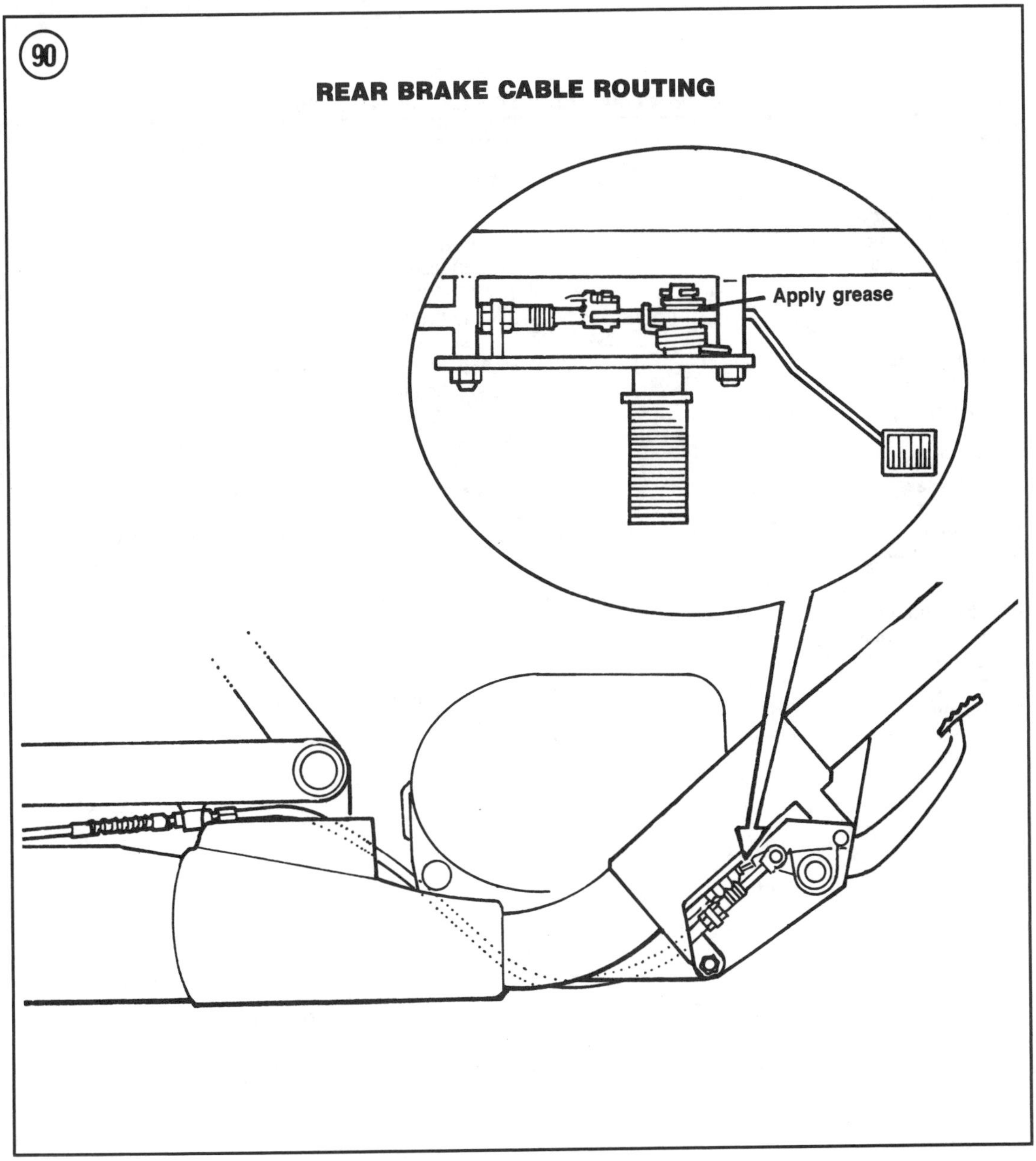

(90)

**REAR BRAKE CABLE ROUTING**

Apply grease

**Table 1 BRAKE SYSTEM TORQUE SPECIFICATIONS**

| Item | N·m | ft.-lb. |
|---|---|---|
| Front master cylinder | | |
| Clamping bolts | 5-8 | 3-6 |
| Union bolt | 20-25 | 14-18 |
| Front caliper | | |
| Mounting bolts | 25-40 | 18-28 |
| Pad pin bolt | 10-15 | 7-11 |
| Bleed valve | 6-9 | 4-7 |
| Brake disc mounting bolt | 18-28 | 13-20 |
| Engine front mounting through-bolt nuts | 77-88 | 50-63 |

**Table 2 BRAKE SYSTEM SPECIFICATIONS**

| Item | Specification | Wear limit |
|---|---|---|
| | **Disc Brake** | |
| Front master cylinder | | |
| Cylinder bore I.D | 12.700-12.743 mm (0.5000-0.5017 in.) | — |
| Piston O.D. | 12.657-12.684 mm (0.4983-0.4994 in.) | — |
| Front caliper | | |
| Cylinder bore I.D. | 42.850-42.926 mm (1.6870-1.6900 in.) | — |
| Piston O.D. | 42.770-42.820 mm (1.6839-1.6858 in.) | — |
| Front disc | | |
| Thickness | 4.3-4.7 mm (0.17-0.19 in.) | 4.0 mm (0.16 in.) |
| Runout | — | 0.30 mm (0.012 in.) |
| | **Drum Brake** | |
| Brake drum I.D. | — | 160.7 mm (6.33 in.) |
| Brake lining thickness | — | 1.5 mm (0.06 in.) |
| Rear brake pedal | | |
| Free play | 20-30 mm (0.8-1.2 in.) | |
| Height | 60 mm (2.4 in.) | |

## CHAPTER TWELVE

# BODY AND FRAME

This chapter contains removal and installation procedures for the seat, fenders and frame components.

## SEAT

### Removal/Installation

Refer to **Figure 1** for this procedure.

1. Remove the bolt, lockwasher and washer (**Figure 2**) on each side of the main seat.
2. Pull up on the rear of the main seat and move the main seat toward the rear and remove the main seat (**Figure 3**).
3. Remove the bolt, lockwasher and washer (A, **Figure 4**) at the front of the pillion seat.
4. Pull up on the front of the pillion seat and remove the pillion seat assembly (B, **Figure 4**).
5. Install by reversing these removal steps. Note the following during installation.
6. Make sure the locating tab on the front of the main seat is correctly hooked onto the metal seat hook on the frame.

*WARNING*

*After the seat is installed, pull up on it firmly to make sure it is securely locked in place. If the seat is not correctly locked in place it may slide to one side or the other when riding the bike. This could lead to the loss of control and a possible accident.*

## REAR HANDLE

Refer to **Figure 5** for this procedure.

1. Remove the seat as described in this chapter.
2. Disconnect the electrical connectors for both rear turn signals. The electrical connectors are individual and consist of a black wire and a black/white wire for each turn signal assembly.
3. Remove the screw on the bottom of the turn signal base and remove the turn signal assembly (A, **Figure 6**) from the side handle.
4. Repeat Step 3 for the other turn signal assembly.
5. Remove the upper bolts (**Figure 7**) and lower bolts (under the rear fender) securing the back support to the side handles. Remove the back support (B, **Figure 6**).
6. Remove the bolts and nuts securing the right- and left-hand side handles (C, **Figure 6**) and remove both side handles.
7. Install by reversing these removal steps.
8. Tighten all bolts and nuts securely.



## FRONT FENDER

### Removal/Installation

1. Remove the front wheel as described in Chapter Nine.
2. Remove the bolts securing the front fender to the front fork sliders and remove the fender.
3. Install by reversing these removal steps.
4. Tighten the bolts securely.

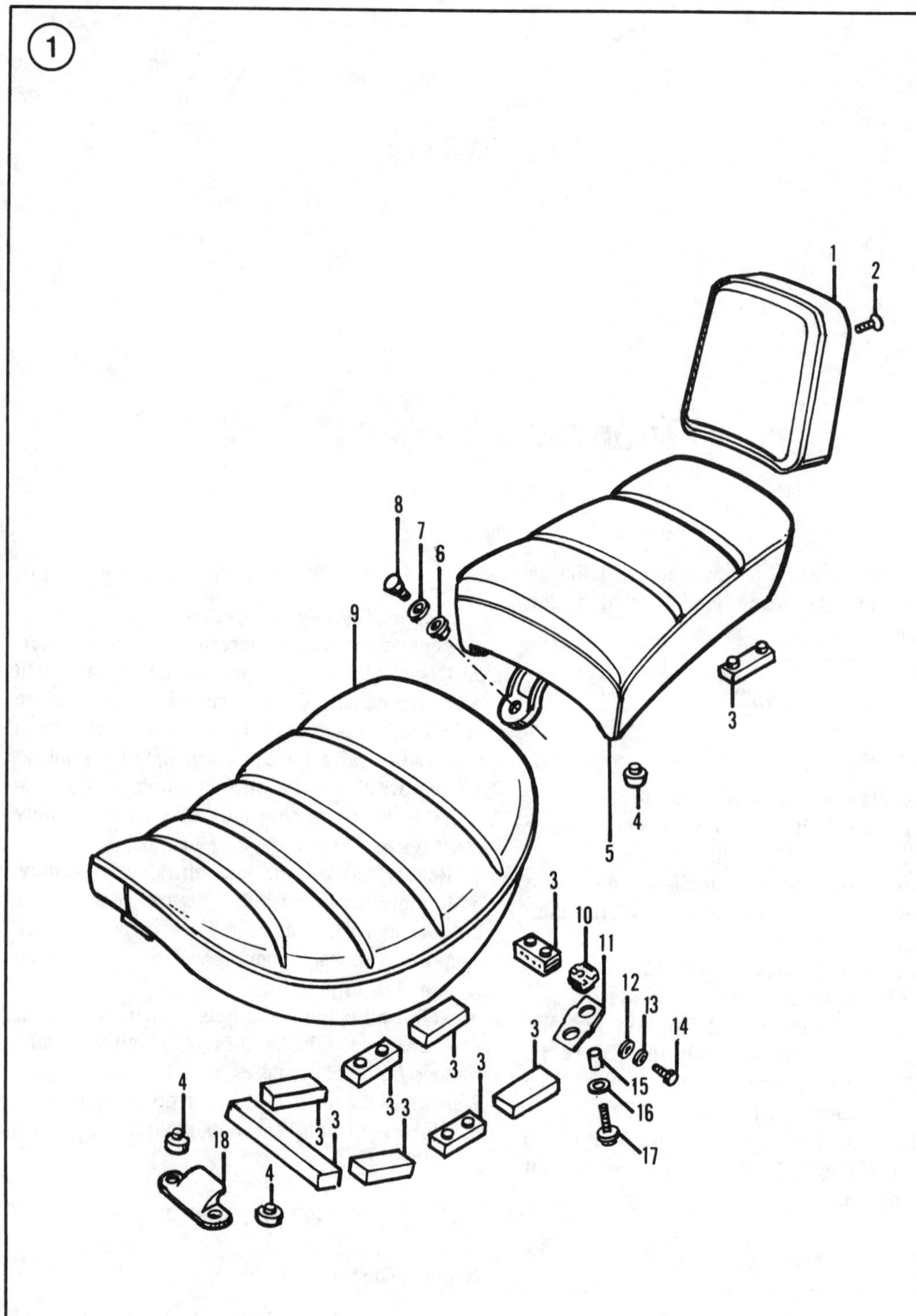
1
1
2
8
7
6
9
3
4
5
3
10
11
12
13
14
15
16
17
3
3
3
3
3
4
3
3
18
4

## SEATS

1. Back pad
2. Screw
3. Cushion
4. Rubber stopper
5. Pillion seat
6. Flange washer
7. Lockwasher
8. Bolt
9. Main seat
10. Rubber cushion
11. Seat bracket
12. Washer
13. Lockwasher
14. Screw
15. Spacer
16. Washer
17. Bolt
18. Seat hook

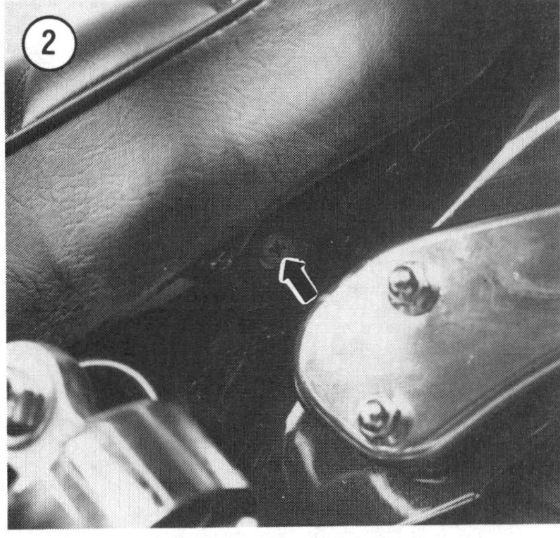

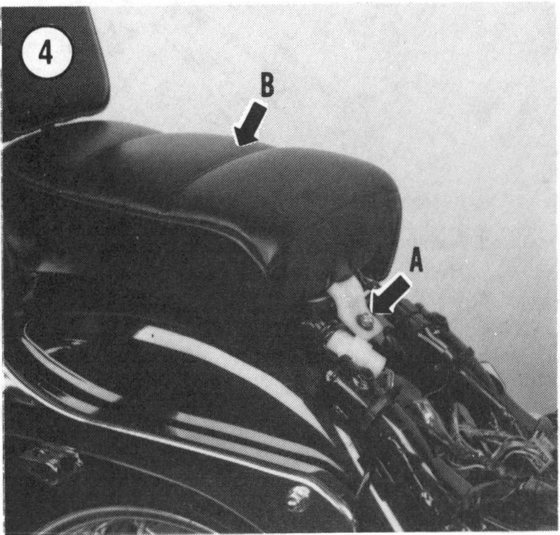

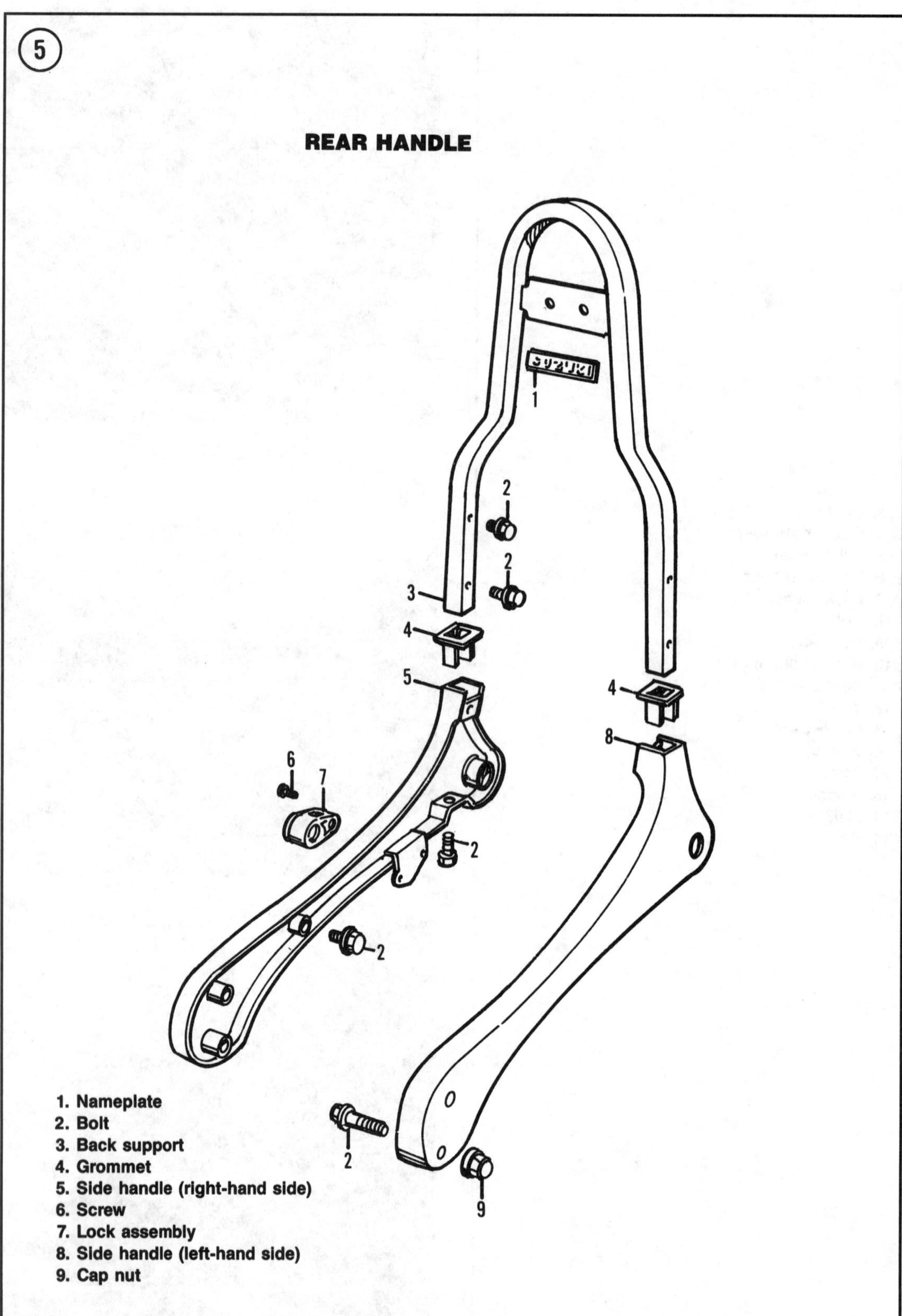
5
REAR HANDLE
SUZUKI
1
2
2
3
4
5
4
8
6
7
2
2
2
9
1. Nameplate
2. Bolt
3. Back support
4. Grommet
5. Side handle (right-hand side)
6. Screw
7. Lock assembly
8. Side handle (left-hand side)
9. Cap nut

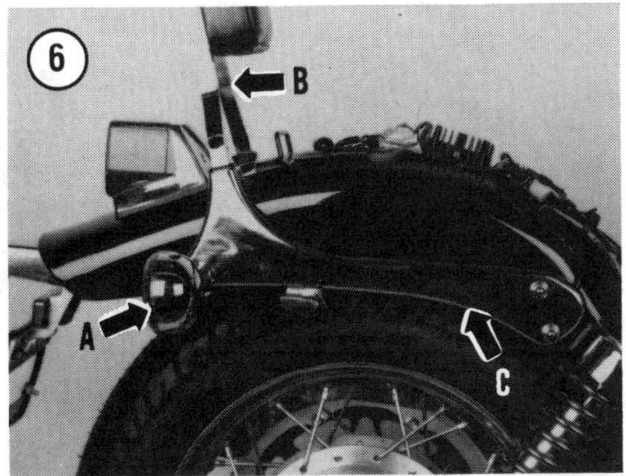


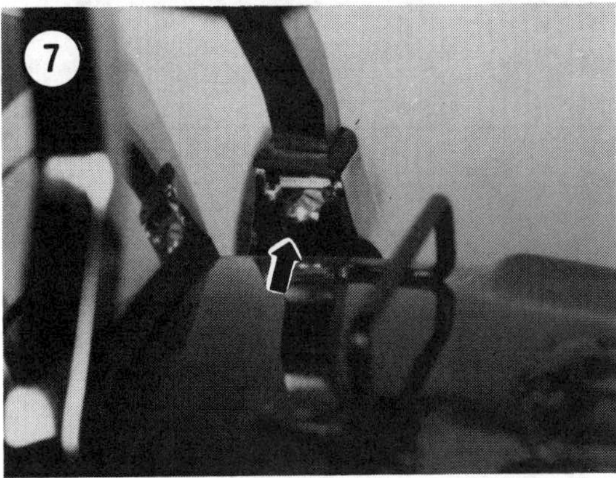


## REAR FENDER

### Removal/Installation

1. Remove the seat and rear handle as described in this chapter.
2. Remove the voltage regulator/rectifier as described in Chapter Eight.
3. Disconnect the electrical connectors for the taillight/brake light assembly and the license plate light. It is not necessary to remove either assembly—they can remain attached to the rear fender.
4. Remove the rear wheel as described in Chapter Ten.
5. Disconnect any electrical wires from clamps above and below the fender.
6. Remove the bolts and lockwashers securing the rear fender to the frame and remove the rear fender.
7. Install by reversing these removal steps.
8. Tighten the bolts securely.

## SIDESTAND

Refer to **Figure 8** for this procedure.

1. Place wood block(s) under the frame and engine to support the bike in an upright position.
2. Place the side stand in the upright position.

8

**SIDESTAND ASSEMBLY**

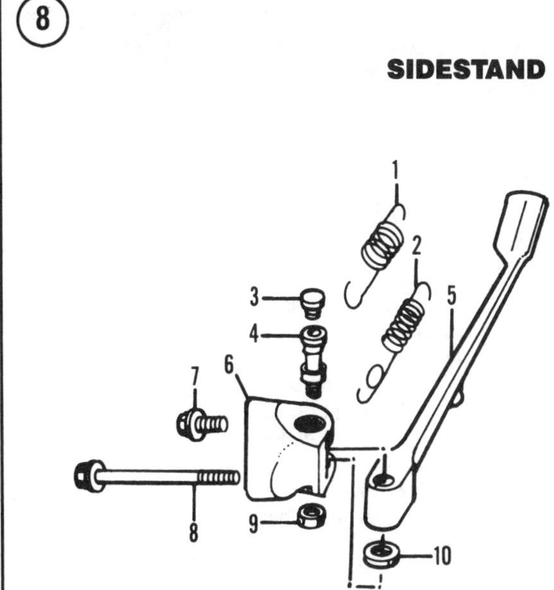


1. Return spring (1987-1988)
2. Return spring (1986)
3. Trim cap
4. Pivot bolt
5. Sidestand
6. Mounting bracket
7. Bolt
8. Bolt
9. Nut
10. Shim

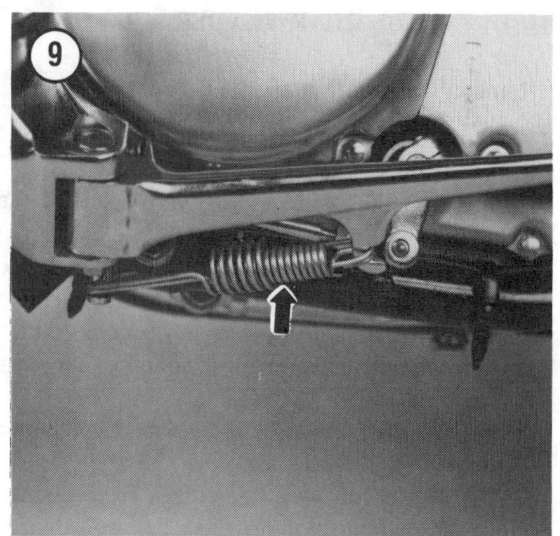

(11)

**FOOTPEG ASSEMBLIES**

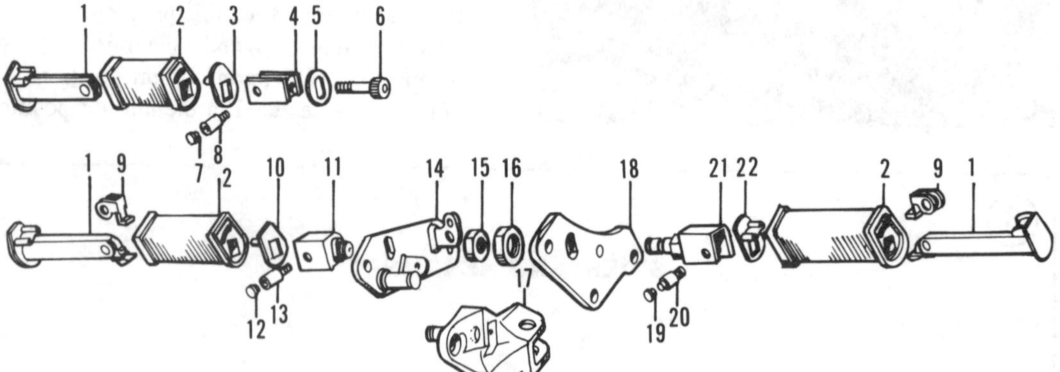

1. Support bar
2. Rubber pad
3. Special washer
4. Holder
5. Washer
6. Allen bolt
7. Trim cap
8. Special Allen bolt
9. Spring
10. Special washer
11. Holder
12. Trim cap
13. Special Allen bolt
14. Mounting bracket (right-hand side)
15. Nut
16. Nut
17. Front left-hand mounting bracket
18. Mounting bracket (left-hand side)
19. Trim cap
20. Special Allen bolt
21. Holder
22. Special washer

3. Using Vise Grips, disconnect the return spring (**Figure 9**) from the pin on the sidestand.
4. Remove the cap (**Figure 10**) from the top of the pivot bolt.
5. Remove the bolt and nut securing the sidestand to the frame mounting bracket.
6. Remove the sidestand from the mounting bracket. Don't lose the shim on the lower portion of the pivot point.
7. Install by reversing these removal steps. Note the following during installation.

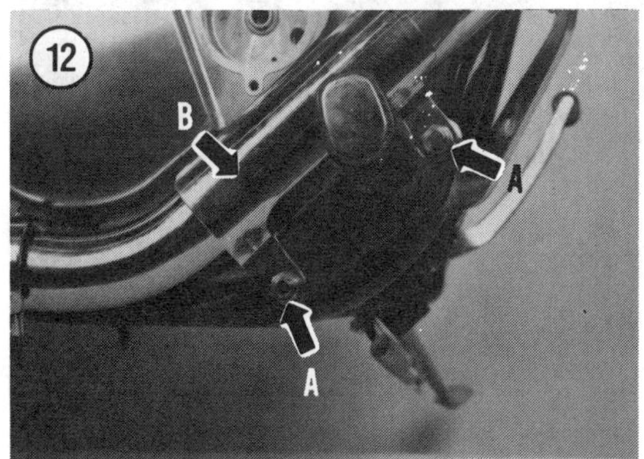


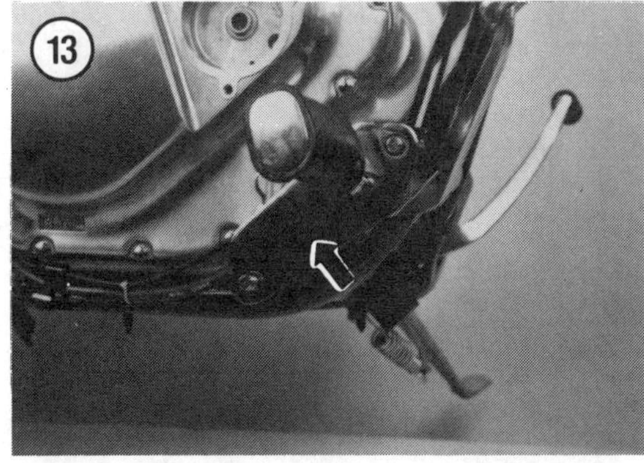

8. Apply a light coat of multipurpose grease to the pivot points on the frame mounting area and the sidestand prior to installation.
9. Tighten the pivot bolt and nut securely.

## FOOTPEGS

Refer to **Figure 11** for this procedure.

### Front Footpeg Removal/Installation

1. Remove the trim cap from the end of the Allen bolt.
2. Remove the Allen bolt securing each footpeg to its footpeg holder and remove the footpeg.

3A. On the right-hand side, if footpeg bracket removal is necessary, perform the following:

a. Remove the cap nuts and washers (A, **Figure 12**) on the engine front mounting through-bolts.
b. Remove the exhaust pipe heat shield (B, **Figure 12**).

*NOTE*

***Figure 13*** *is shown with the exhaust system removed for clarity. It is not necessary to remove the system for this procedure.*

c. Pull the front right-hand footpeg and front brake pedal assembly (**Figure 13**) off the through-bolts.

*NOTE*

*If the footpeg and brake pedal assembly are going to be left off for some time, reinstall the washers and cap nuts onto the through-bolts.*

d. Remove the nut (**Figure 14**) securing the footpeg bracket assembly to the backing plate and remove the footpeg assembly.

3B. On the left-hand side, if footpeg bracket removal is necessary, remove the bolts securing the footpeg bracket to the frame and remove the bracket assembly.

4. Install by reversing these removal steps. Note the following during installation.
5. Tighten the bolt(s) securely and install the cap in the Allen bolt receptacles.

### Rear Footpeg Removal/Installation

1. Remove the trim cap from the end of the Allen bolt.
2. Remove the Allen bolt securing the footpeg to the footpeg holder and remove the footpeg.
3. Remove the rear wheel as described in Chapter Ten.

*NOTE*
***Figure 15** is shown with the swing arm removed for clarity. It is not necessary to remove the swing arm for this procedure.*

4. If necessary, remove the Allen bolt (**Figure 15**) securing the footpeg holder to the swing arm and remove the holder.

5. Install by reversing these removal steps. Note the following during installation.

6. Tighten the bolt(s) securely and install the cap in the Allen bolt receptacles.

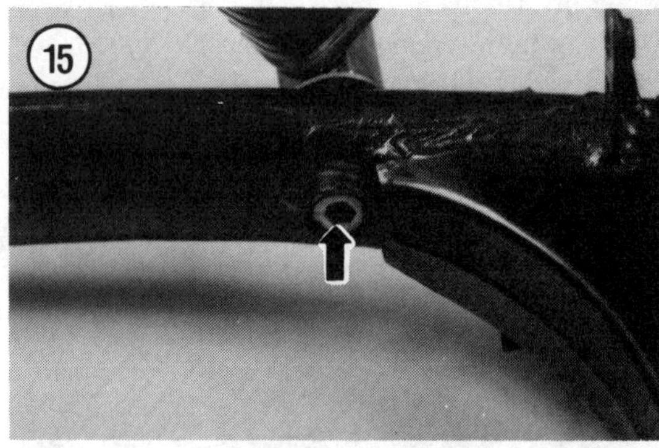

# INDEX

## A



## B



## C



## D



## E



## F



13

## V



## W

# 1986 SUZUKI SAVAGE

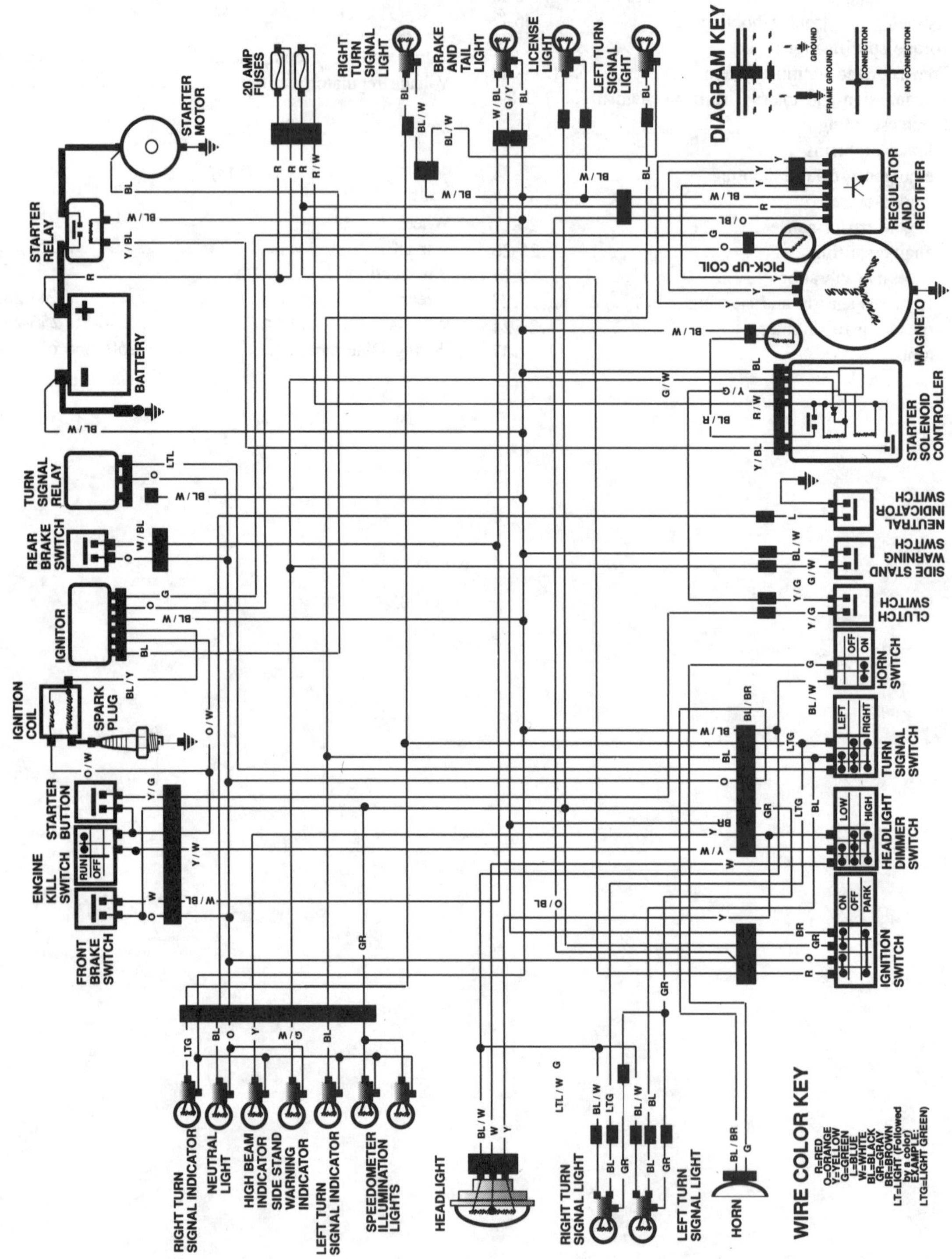

# 1987-1988 SUZUKI SAVAGE

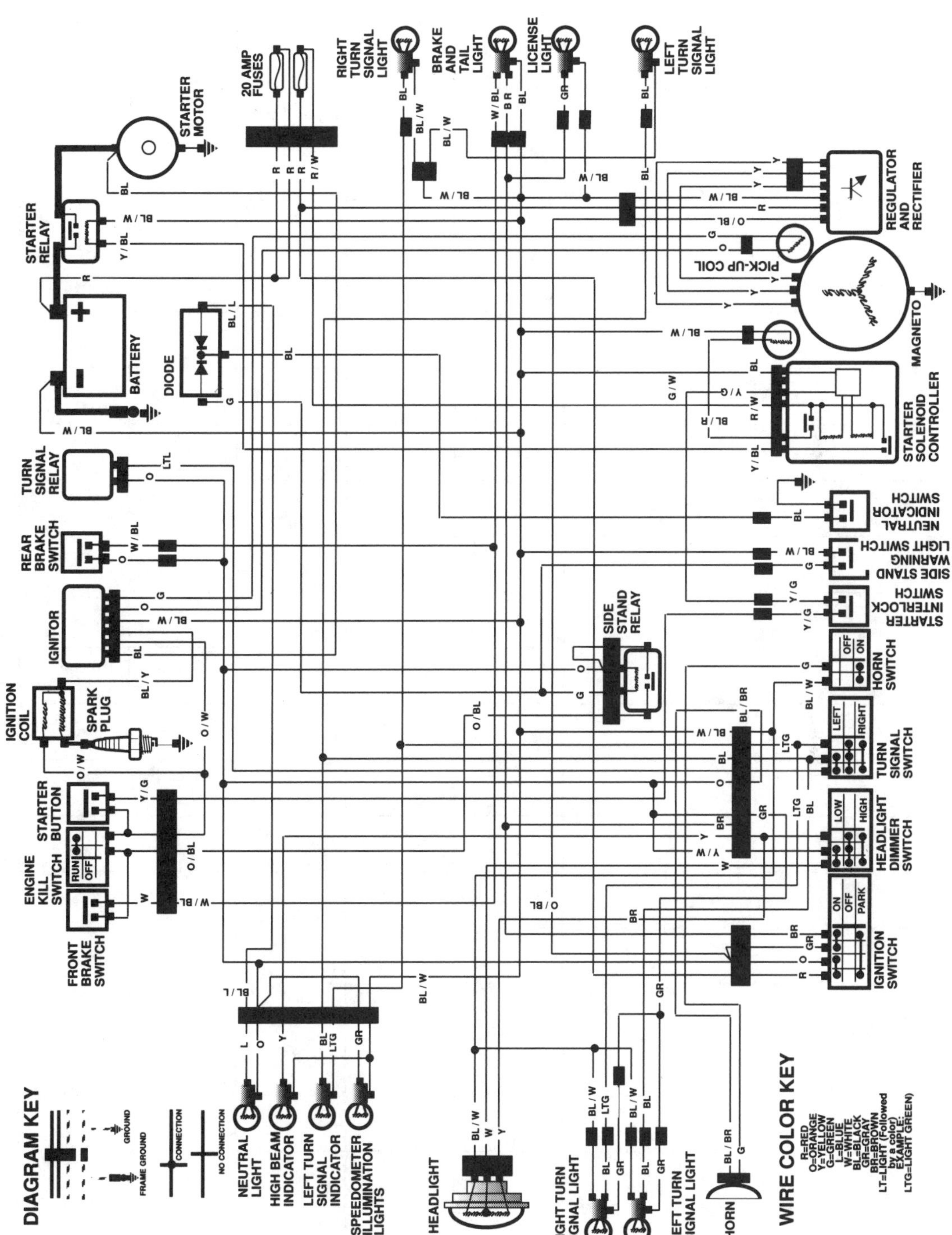

# MAINTENANCE LOG

| Service Performed | Mileage Reading | | | | |
|---|---|---|---|---|---|
| Oil change (example) | 2,836 | 5,782 | 8,601 | | |
| | | | | | |
| | | | | | |
| | | | | | |
| | | | | | |
| | | | | | |
| | | | | | |
| | | | | | |
| | | | | | |
| | | | | | |
| | | | | | |
| | | | | | |
| | | | | | |
| | | | | | |
| | | | | | |
| | | | | | |
| | | | | | |
| | | | | | |
| | | | | | |
| | | | | | |
| | | | | | |
| | | | | | |
| | | | | | |
| | | | | | |
| | | | | | |